SOCIAL RESEARCH METHODS

QUALITATIVE AND QUANTITATIVE APPROACHES

THIRD EDITION

W. LAWRENCE NEUMAN

University of Wisconsin at Whitewater

Allyn and Bacon

Boston   London   Toronto   Sydney   Tokyo   Singapore

To Diane, for service well beyond the call of duty, and to Tina and many other students who have an interest in research methods

Vice President, Editor in Chief, Social Sciences: Karen Hanson
Editorial Assistant: Jennifer Jacobson
Executive Marketing Manager: Joyce Nilsen
Production Administrator: Annette Joseph
Production Coordinator: Susan Freese
Editorial-Production Service: TKM Productions
Composition Buyer: Linda Cox
Manufacturing Buyer: Megan Cochran
Cover Administrator: Linda Knowles

Copyright © 1997, 1994, 1991 by Allyn & Bacon
A Viacom Company
160 Gould Street
Needham Heights, MA 02194

Many of the designations used by manufacturers and sellers to distinguish their products are claimed as trademarks. Where those designations appear in this book, and Allyn and Bacon was aware of a trademark claim, the trademark symbol has been used.

Library of Congress Cataloging-in-Publication Data
Neuman, William Lawrence
    Social research methods: qualitative and quantitative approaches
 / W. Lawrence Neuman.—3rd ed.
    p. cm.
    Includes bibliographical references and indexes.
    ISBN 0-205-19356-0
    1. Sociology—Research—Methodology. 2. Social sciences—
Research—Methodology. I. Title.
HM48.N48   1997
301'.01—dc20
                                       96-1085
                                         CIP

Printed in the United States of America

10 9 8 7 6   01 00 99 98

CONTENTS

PART I
SOCIAL SCIENCE RESEARCH AND METHODOLOGY

PART II
RESEARCH USING QUANTITATIVE DATA

PART III
RESEARCH USING QUALITATIVE DATA

PART IV
FINAL CONSIDERATIONS

APPENDIXES

PREFACE TO THE THIRD EDITION

This third edition of *Social Research Methods: Qualitative and Quantitative Approaches* continues to evolve from the same basic principles found in the first and second editions.

First, I want to reemphasize that I see both qualitative and quantitative techniques of investigation into the social world as valuable. I am equally wary of the qualitative researcher who automatically rejects all quantitative techniques, statistics, and so on and the quantitative researcher who places little value on in-depth qualitative research. Yes, real differences exist. Many differences have ontological and epistemological roots. These differences do not mean that researchers need to "circle the wagons," set up guards, and take a stand to defend the hallowed ground of one's viewpoint. Instead, the differences mean there is an opportunity to engage in an ongoing discussion and learn from one another. Also, I do not think that the boundaries between academic disciplines should be allowed to become impediments. I embrace an ecumenical approach and welcome extensive borrowing of ideas and techniques across such boundaries.

Second, I believe we need to better appreciate that research investigations are undertaken by real people who live in particular times and cultural contexts. Serious mistakes may occur when a researcher in a particular culture or subculture and time period ignores the powerful impact of a social-historical context on his or her patterns of thinking and observations. One subtle change in this edition is an increased recognition of how social-political events shape the direction of the social research community. The research enterprise is not totally insulated from its culture. This has dangers as well as benefits.

Third, a theme found throughout the book is that we will never have all the answers or a complete, finished set of rules and techniques for doing research. Methodology is an ongoing dialogue, a work in progress. This means 10 or 20 years from now, many parts of this book should be obsolete. I see this as healthy, because we will learn new things. There should be improvements, additions, refinements, and new techniques.

Last, this edition contains a heightened sensitivity to the relationship between the researcher and the subjects being studied. The *us* (the researchers) versus *them* (subjects) concern is part of a larger issue: how the researcher relates to others. *Others* include all researchers of the scientific community, those holding power in official institutions, larger audiences for findings, and the people being studied. The relationship involves questions of the topics one chooses to study, the orientation one brings to what is studied, how a study is conducted, and what happens to findings.

ACKNOWLEDGMENTS

I am grateful to the following reviewers for their helpful suggestions and comments: Ray Darville, Stephen P. Austin State University; Anne Eisenberg, University of Iowa; Dorothy Everts, Arizona State University; Jane Hood, University of New Mexico; Miguel Korzeniewicz, University of New Mexico; Marilyn Nouri, State University of New York at Oneonta; Chad Richardson, University of Texas–Pan American; Eugene Rosa, Washington State University; Kerry J. Strand, Hood College; and James J. Teevan, University of Western Ontario.

Preface to the Second Edition

Social Research Methods: Qualitative and Quantitative Approaches, second edition, is written for upper-level undergraduate or beginning graduate students in the social sciences and associated applied areas (e.g., criminal justice, education, communication, human resources, marketing, management, public administration, social work). It is based on the premise that doing social research is exciting and fun. The research process involves discovering and learning new things, which are enjoyable experiences. Research can be enjoyable, yet it is also an essential tool for understanding the events and structures of the social world.

People who say that research is irrelevant or unimportant are ignorant of the great potential of research to inform us. They do not recognize the widespread use of social research throughout modern society. Although much important research occurs in colleges, universities, and research institutes, social research is being conducted in many other places for many purposes. In private industry, people in market research, personnel, public relations, and management conduct social research, as do many government agencies, to help them better plan or deliver services. Social workers, counselors, and teachers conduct social research in their jobs to make them better able to help or educate others. Many journalists, lawyers, and people in the criminal justice and health care systems use and conduct social research. Social research takes many forms, and the principles of research apply to many situations in the real world.

I wrote the first edition of this book out of frustration at my failure to find what I wanted in the many texts I tried during years of teaching research methods courses. This text is designed to remedy three of my major frustrations.

My first frustration arose from the fact that few textbooks manage to convey the excitement of doing research by giving some of the specifics of the real-life research process. I believe that students should see social research as a process of discovery, complete with human drama, uncertainty, and setbacks. It is not a mechanical process that follows a cookbook formula but a creative, conceptual process of asking the right questions, operating with partial information, following leads down blind alleys, and making difficult decisions. When conducting social research, the researchers, real people, decide how to proceed on the basis of general principles; they combine many parts of the research process in relation to a research question they are trying to answer. In this book, we will follow the process of some research projects and read the results of research. The historical background of research techniques is outlined, and specific studies are described to show that research is a real-life activity carried out by real people.

A second frustration arose because although almost all social research textbooks pay lip service to qualitative research, few give it serious attention. Students may get the erroneous idea that social research is limited to survey research and other quantitative methods. Survey research is an important method, and this book treats it seriously, but social researchers also learn a great deal from qualitative research methods. Ethnographic and historical research methods are increasingly recognized as vital approaches to the growth of knowledge in social science. In this book, qualitative research is treated as a legitimate and valuable, yet distinct, kind of social research. My stance is ecumenical; to do good social science and gain knowledge, we must look into the social world from both a qualitative and a quantitative perspective. Often, qualitative research has been ignored because it originated in a different philosophical tradition with different assumptions from those of quantitative research. Few texts discuss the philosophical foundations of social science, yet students need a sense of these philosophical principles so that they can understand why research is conducted in particular ways.

A third frustration came from the fact that many introductory social research textbooks attempt to cover sophisticated statistical analysis and technical details of data analysis, while giving limited attention to the basic principles of sound research methodology. The field of social science research methodology is expanding rapidly; new techniques are being developed and old ones elaborated upon. As a result, the gap between the student who is just beginning to learn about research and the modern professional scholar is growing. This book contains a minimum of technical statistical formulas and discussions. Such discussions, though important, should be engaged in only after one masters the fundamentals of doing research: knowing how to ask questions, how to design and proceed through a research project, how to collect data, and what is important to look for in data. Students should focus on how to think about research design and data collection issues and appreciate the ethics of the scientific community before they learn how to calculate specific statistical formulas. This is not to minimize the importance of statistics and computer-based data analysis. I feel they should be taught in complementary courses that are primarily devoted to statistics.

It seems that other instructors shared my concerns. The success of the first edition signalled that peers have accepted my ideas and that I have reached many more students than I could have in my own classroom. Readers of the first edition of *Social Research Methods* will not find drastic changes, but I have done a lot of fine tuning and made many small changes. In addition to smoothing out the language and correcting a few of the diagrams, I have updated examples and added new ones. I believe it is difficult to learn methodology in a vacuum; it becomes easier when there is substantive content. Therefore, I have included

more examples from the rich research literature to show students what researchers are learning. This gives students a better feel for the excitement of research and the enthusiasm that active researchers have for their craft. I have also added diagrams and boxed material to help students better grasp some of the complex information.

In this second edition, I have given increased attention to the relationship between theory and research. Because many students read this book without having completed a single course in social theory, I have kept the discussion at an elementary level. In addition to upgrading the discussion throughout the book, I have added a new separate chapter on theory, Chapter 3. Ideally, a student would concurrently take coordinated courses in research methodology, social theory, and statistics.

This edition gives more attention to feminist research—a growing part of modern social research that has great vitality. More than a passing fad, feminist research touches on fundamental issues about how one does social research. You will find it sprinkled throughout several chapters. In Chapter 4, "The Meanings of Methodology," I added a box that explains both feminist and postmodern approaches.

I want to emphasize that I do not see a rigid dichotomy between quantitative and qualitative research. Rather, I see them as complementary ways of doing research. The distinction is primarily an organizational device, one that also reflects a difference that exists within the practice of social research. My position remains that we need to judge each type of research on its own merits and embrace the strengths it offers.

In sum, this book has several goals: to enable students to become better consumers of others' research and to gain access to more research findings; to give students an understanding of the type of thinking involved in research; to teach them the concepts and terminology researchers use; to provide them with a foundation for further study and work as professional researchers; and to prepare them so that they can conduct small-scale research projects on their own.

Chapter 1

SCIENCE AND RESEARCH

> *The sociologist, then, is someone concerned with understanding society in a disciplined way. The nature of this discipline is scientific. This means that what the sociologist finds and says about the social phenomena he studies occurs within a certain rather strictly defined frame of reference.*
>
> —Peter Berger, *An Invitation to Sociology*, p. 16

INTRODUCTION

In my daily newspaper, among other items, I recently read that alcohol poses a greater risk to women than to men because women digest differently; the U.S. Federal Bureau of Investigation (FBI) discriminated against African-American employees; a U.S. immigration law had the effect of increasing discrimination by employers against Hispanics, Asians, and legal aliens; and cocaine use contributed to about one-fourth of the fatal automobile accidents in New York State. These items come from the results of research. Some results, such as those of alcohol digestion and

immigration law effects, may have future use. Other results have immediate practical implications. The findings on the FBI resulted in a lawsuit.

This book is about social research. In simple terms, research is a way of going about finding answers to questions. Social research is a type of research conducted by sociologists, social scientists, and others to seek answers to questions about the social world. You probably already have some notion of what social research entails. First, let me end possible misconceptions. When I asked students what they thought research entails, I got the following answers:

1

- Based on facts alone, without theory or judgment
- Read or used only by experts or college professors
- Done only in universities by people with Ph.D. degrees
- Going to the library and finding articles on a topic
- Hanging around some exotic place and observing
- Conducting an experiment in which people are tricked into doing something
- Drawing a sample of people and giving them questionnaires
- Looking up lots of tables from government reports or books
- Using computers, statistics, charts, and graphs

The first three of these are wrong, and the others are only parts of social research. It is unwise to confuse one part with the whole. Just as you would never mistake wearing shoes for being fully dressed, you should not mistake any one of these items for social research.

Social research involves many things. It is how a person finds out something new and original about the social world. To do this, a researcher needs to think logically, follow rules, and repeat steps over and over. A researcher combines theories or ideas with facts in a systematic way and uses his or her imagination and creativity. He or she quickly learns to organize and plan carefully and to select the appropriate technique to address a question. A researcher also must be sensitive to treating the people who are being studied in ethical and moral ways. In addition, a researcher must communicate to others clearly.

Social research is a collection of methods people use systematically to produce knowledge. It is an exciting process of discovery, but it requires persistence, personal integrity, tolerance for ambiguity, interaction with others, and pride in doing quality work. You will learn more about the diversity of social research in Chapter 2.

Do not expect this book to transform you into an expert researcher. It can teach you to be a better consumer of research results, give you an understanding of how the research enterprise works, and prepare you to conduct small research projects yourself. After reading this textbook, you will understand research, its meaning, what it can and cannot do, and its role in the larger society.

ALTERNATIVES TO SOCIAL RESEARCH

You learned most of what you know about the social world by an alternative to social research. A great deal of what you know about the social world is based on what your parents and others have told you. You also have knowledge that you have learned from personal experience. The books and magazines you have read and the movies and television you have watched also gave you information. You may also use common sense to learn about the social world.

In addition to being a collection of methods social research is a process for producing knowledge about the social world. It is a more structured, organized, and systematic process than the alternatives.[1] Knowledge from the alternatives is often correct, but knowledge based on research is more likely to be true and has fewer potential errors. It is important to recognize that research does not always produce perfect knowledge. Nonetheless, compared to the alternatives, it is less likely to be flawed. Let us review the alternatives before examining social research.

Authority

You gain knowledge from parents, teachers, and experts and from books and television and other media. When you accept something as being true just because someone in a position of authority says it is true or because it is in an authoritative publication, you are using authority as a basis of knowledge. Relying on the wisdom of authorities has advantages—it is a quick, simple, and cheap way to learn something. Authorities often spend time and effort to learn something, and you can benefit from their experience and work.

Relying on authorities also has limitations. It is easy to overestimate the expertise of other people. You may assume that they are right when they are not. Authorities may speak on fields they know little about; they can be plain wrong. An expert in one area may try to use his or her authority in an unrelated area. Have you ever seen television commercials where an expert in football uses that expertise to try to convince you to buy a car? In addition, there are the questions: Who is or is not an authority? Whom do you believe when different authorities disagree? For example, there was a time when I saw my high school teacher as being an authority on physics. Now I know that his authority does not stand up to that of a Nobel prize winner in physics.

History is full of past experts whom we now see as being misinformed. For example, some "experts" of the past measured intelligence by counting bumps on the skull; other "experts" used bloodletting to try to cure diseases. Their errors seem obvious now, but can you be certain that today's experts will not become tomorrow's fools? Also, too much reliance on authorities can be dangerous to a democratic society. An overdependence on experts lets them keep others in the dark, and they may promote ideas that strengthen their power and position. When we have no idea of how the experts arrived at their knowledge, we lose some of our ability to make judgments for ourselves.

Tradition

People sometimes rely on tradition for knowledge. Tradition is a special case of authority—the authority of the past. Tradition means you accept something as being true because "it's the way things have always been." For example, my father-in-law said that "drinking a shot of whiskey cures a cold." When I asked about his statement, he said that he had learned it from his father when he was a child, and it had come down from past generations. Tradition was the basis of the knowledge for the cure.

Here is an example more from the social world. Many people believe that children who are raised at home by their mothers grow up to be better adjusted and have fewer personal problems than those raised in other settings. People "know" this, but how did they learn it? Most accept it

because they believe (rightly or wrongly) that it was true in the past or is the way things have always been.

Some traditional social knowledge begins as simple prejudice. A belief such as "people from that side of the tracks will never amount to anything" or "you never can trust anyone of that race" comes down from the past. Even if traditional knowledge was once true, it can become distorted as it is passed on, and soon it is no longer true. People may cling to traditional knowledge without real understanding; they assume that because something may have worked or been true in the past, it must always be true.

Common Sense

You know a lot about the social world from your ordinary reasoning or common sense. You rely on what everyone knows and what "just makes sense." For example, it "just makes sense" that murder rates are higher in nations that do not have a death penalty, because people are less likely to kill if they face execution for doing so. This and other widely held "common sense" beliefs, such as that poor youth are more likely to commit deviant acts than those from the middle class or that most Catholics do not use birth control, are false.

Common sense is valuable in daily living, but it can allow logical fallacies to slip into your thinking. For example, the "gambler's fallacy" says: "If I have a long string of losses playing a lottery, the next time I play, my chances of winning will be better." In terms of probability and the facts, this is false. Also, common sense contains contradictory ideas that go unnoticed because people use the ideas at different times—for example, "opposites attract" and "birds of a feather flock together." Common sense can originate in tradition. It is useful and sometimes correct, but it also contains errors, misinformation, contradiction, and prejudice.

Media Myths

Television shows, movies, and newspaper and magazine articles are important sources of information about social life. For example, most people who have no contact with criminals learn about crime by watching television shows and movies and by reading newspapers. However, the portrayals of crime and of many other things on television do not accurately reflect social reality. Instead, the writers who invent or "adapt" real life for television shows and movie scripts distort reality either out of ignorance or because they rely on authority, tradition, and common sense. Their primary goal is to entertain, not to present reality accurately. Although journalists who write for newspapers and newsmagazines try to present a realistic picture of the world, they must write stories in short time periods with limited information and within editorial guidelines.

Unfortunately, the media tend to perpetuate the myths of a culture. For example, the media show that most people who receive welfare are black (most are actually white), that most people who are mentally ill are violent and dangerous (only a small percentage actually are), and that most people who are elderly are senile and in nursing homes (a tiny minority are). Also, a selective emphasis on an issue by the media can change public thinking about it (see Box 1.1). For example, television repeatedly shows low-income, inner-city, African-American youth using illegal drugs. Eventually, most people "know" that urban blacks use illegal drugs at a much higher rate than other groups in the United States, even though this notion is false.

Personal Experience

If something happens to you, if you personally see it or experience it, you accept it as true. Personal experience, or "seeing is believing," has a strong impact and is a forceful source of knowledge. Unfortunately, personal experience can lead you astray. Something similar to an optical illusion or mirage can occur. What appears true may actually be due to a slight error or distortion in judgment. The power of immediacy and direct personal contact is very strong. Even knowing that, people sometimes make mistakes or fall for illusions. Sometimes people believe what they see or experience rather than what is revealed by careful research designed to avoid such errors.

The four errors of personal experience reinforce each other and can occur in other areas, as well. They are a basis for misleading people through propaganda, cons or fraud, magic, stereo-

---

Box 1.1 _____

Cyberporn Myths versus Research

In the competition for sales and advertising revenue, the media sometimes sensationalize an idea or finding based on scanty evidence. Yet widespread publicity may cause many people to accept the finding as true or to falsely believe that it is backed by a solid scientific study. In the summer of 1995, *Time* magazine, the leading U.S. news weekly, ran a front-page story on Cyberporn. The term refers to electronically sending and receiving pornography by way of computers on the Internet. The magazine's attention-grabbing cover showed a bewildered-looking child in front of a computer. The frightening story, citing a Carnegie Mellon University study, suggested that computer networks were being flooded with lurid pornography that any child with a computer could access. Major television news programs quickly amplified the alarm, and soon thereafter politicians in Washington demanded tough new laws.

Upon closer inspection, it was learned that the hysteria was based on a single unpublished study conducted by an undergraduate and riddled with serious methodological flaws. In the rush to get the story out, the magazine failed to have proper research professionals evaluate it. Besides circumventing the scientific community's review process and depending on a single, shoddy study by someone who was unqualified, the article had a misleading tone. It failed to emphasize that less than one-half of 1 percent of Internet messages involve pornography. Whatever the moral offense of Cyberporn, the media's message lacked solid evidence and careful research.

typing, and some advertising. The first problem, which is the most frequent, is *overgeneralization*. It occurs when you have some evidence that you believe and then assume that it applies to many other situations, too. Limited generalization may be appropriate; under certain conditions, a small amount of evidence can explain a larger situation. The problem is that people often generalize well beyond limited evidence. There are many individuals, areas, and situations about which people know little or nothing, so generalizing from the little they do know might seem reasonable. For example, over the years, I have known five blind people. All of them were very friendly. Can I conclude that all blind people are friendly? Do the five people with whom I had personal experience fully represent all blind people?

A second common error is *selective observation*. It occurs when you take special notice of some people or events and generalize from them. People often focus on or observe particular cases or situations, especially when they fit preconceived ideas. We often seek out evidence that confirms what we already know or believe and ignore the range of cases and contradictory information. We are sensitive to features that confirm our ideas—features that might otherwise go unnoticed. For example, I believe overweight people are friendly. This belief may be based on stereotypes, what my mother told me, or whatever. I observe overweight people and, without awareness, pay particular attention to their smiling, laughing, and so on. Without realizing it, I notice and remember people and situations that reinforce my preconceived ideas. Some psychologists have studied people's tendencies to "seek out" and distort their memories to make them more consistent with what they already think. I "overinterpret" gestures or smiles, pay less attention to contradictory evidence, and do not look for unfriendly behavior among overweight people.

A third error is *premature closure*. It often operates with and reinforces the first two errors. Premature closure occurs when you feel you have all the answers and do not need to listen, seek information, or raise questions any longer. Unfortunately, most people are a little lazy or get

a little sloppy in everyday experiences. We take a few pieces of evidence or look at events for a short while and then think we have it figured out. We look for evidence to confirm or reject an idea and stop when a small amount of evidence is present. In a word, we jump to conclusions. I know three people who smoked six packs of cigarettes a day and lived to be 80 years old; therefore, people who smoke lots of cigarettes will live to age 80.

The last error is the *halo effect*. It comes in many forms, but basically, it says people overgeneralize from what we interpret to be highly positive or prestigious. We give things or people we respect a halo, or a strong reputation. We let the prestige "rub off" on other things or people about which we know little. Thus, I pick up a report by a person from a prestigious university, say Harvard or Cambridge University. I assume that the author is smart and talented and that the report will be excellent. I do not make this assumption about a report by someone from Unknown University. I begin to form an opinion and prejudge the report and do not approach it by considering its own merits alone.

HOW SCIENCE WORKS

The critical factor that separates social research from other ways of knowing about the social world is that it uses a scientific approach. *Social research* is more than a collection of methods and a process for creating knowledge; it is a process for producing new knowledge about the social world that uses a *scientific* approach. Let us take a brief look at "science," a subject to which we will return in Chapter 4.

Science

When most people hear the word *science*, the first image that comes to mind is one of test tubes, computers, rocket ships, and people in white lab coats. These outward trappings are a part of science. Some sciences, such as the natural sciences—biology, chemistry, physics, and zoology—deal with the physical and material world (e.g., rocks, plants, chemicals, stars, blood, electricity, etc.). The natural sciences are the basis of new technology and receive a lot of publicity. Most people first think of them when they hear the word *science*.

The social sciences, such as anthropology, psychology, political science, and sociology, involve the study of people—their beliefs, behavior, interaction, institutions, and so forth. Fewer people associate these disciplines with the word *science*. They are sometimes called *soft sciences*. This is not because their work is sloppy or lacks rigor but because their subject matter, human social life, is fluid, formidable to observe, and hard to measure precisely with laboratory instruments. The subject matter of a science (e.g., human attitudes, protoplasm, or galaxies) determines the techniques and instruments (e.g., surveys, microscopes, or telescopes) used by it.

Science is a social institution and a way to produce knowledge. It has not always been around; it is a human invention. What people now call science grew from a major shift in thinking that began with the Age of Reason or Enlightenment period in western European history, which occurred between the 1600s and the early 1800s. The Enlightenment ushered in a wave of new thinking. It included a faith in logical reasoning, an emphasis on experiences in the material world, a belief in human progress, and a questioning of traditional religious authority. It began with the study of the natural world and spread to the study of social life. The importance of science in modern society and as a basis for seeking knowledge is associated with the societal transformation called the Industrial Revolution. The advancement of science or of fields within science, such as sociology, does not just happen. It is punctuated by the triumphs and struggles of individual researchers. It is also influenced by significant social events such as war, depression, government policy, or shifts in public support.[2]

At one time, all people created new knowledge using prescientific or nonscientific methods. These included the alternatives discussed previously and other methods that are less widely accepted in modern society (e.g., oracles, mysticism, magic, astrology, or spirits). Before science became fully entrenched, such prescientific systems were generally accepted. They were an unquestioned way to produce knowledge that people took to be true. Such prescientific methods still exist but are secondary to science. Some people use nonscientific methods to study topics beyond the scope of science (e.g., religion, art, philosophy). People in advanced modern society believe that most aspects of the social and natural world are within the scope of science. Today, few people seriously question science as a legitimate way to produce knowledge about modern society.

Science refers to both a system for producing knowledge and the knowledge produced from that system. The system evolved over many years and is slowly but constantly changing. It combines assumptions about the nature of the world and knowledge; an orientation toward knowledge; and sets of procedures, techniques, and instruments for gaining knowledge. It is visible in a social institution called the scientific community.

The knowledge of science is organized in terms of theories. For now, *social theory* can be defined as a system of interconnected abstractions or ideas that condense and organize knowledge

"I'm a social scientist, Michael. That means I can't explain electricity or anything like that, but if you ever want to know about people I'm your man."

Source: Drawing by Handelsman; © 1986 The New Yorker Magazine, Inc.

about the social world. Several types of social theory are discussed in Chapter 3. Social theory is like a map of the social world; it helps people visualize the complexity in the world and explains why things happen.

Scientists gather data using specialized techniques and use the data to support or reject theories. *Data* are the empirical evidence or information that one gathers carefully according to rules or procedures. The data can be *quantitative* (i.e., expressed as numbers) or *qualitative* (i.e., expressed as words, pictures, objects). *Empirical* evidence refers to observations that people experience through the senses—touch, sight, hearing, smell, and taste. This confuses people, because researchers cannot use their senses to directly observe many aspects of the social world about which they seek answers (e.g., intelligence, attitudes, opinions, feelings, emotions, power, authority, etc.). Researchers have many specialized techniques to observe and indirectly measure such aspects of the social world.

The Scientific Community

Science is given life through the operation of the scientific community, which sustains the assumptions, attitudes, and techniques of science. The *scientific community* is a collection of people and a set of norms, behaviors, and attitudes that bind them together to sustain the scientific ethos. It is a community because it is a group of interacting people who share ethical principles, beliefs and values, techniques and training, and career paths. It is not a geographic community. Rather, it is a professional community whose members share an outlook on and a commitment to scientific research. For the most part, the scientific community includes both the natural and social sciences.[3]

Many people outside the core scientific community use scientific research techniques. A range of practitioners and technicians apply research techniques that have been developed and refined by the scientific community. They apply the knowledge and procedures originated within the scientific community. For example, many people use a research technique created by the scientific community (e.g., a survey) without pos-

sessing a deep knowledge of research, without inventing new methods of research, and without advancing science itself. Yet, those who use the techniques or results of science will be able to do so better if they also understand the principles and processes of the scientific community.

The boundaries of this community and its membership are defined loosely. There is no membership card or master roster. Many people treat a Ph.D. degree in a scientific field as an informal "entry ticket" to membership in the scientific community. The Ph.D., which stands for doctorate of philosophy, is an advanced graduate degree beyond the master's that prepares one to conduct independent research. Some researchers do not have Ph.D.s and not all those who receive Ph.D.s enter occupations in which they conduct research. They enter many occupations and may have other responsibilities (e.g., teaching, administration, consulting, clinical practice, advising, etc.). In fact, about one-half of the people who receive scientific Ph.D.s do not follow careers as active researchers.

At the core of the scientific community are researchers who conduct studies on a full-time or half-time basis, usually with the help of assistants. Many research assistants are graduate students, and some are undergraduates. Working as a research assistant is the way that most scientists gain a real grasp on the details of doing research.

Colleges and universities employ most members of the scientific community's core. Some scientists work for the government or private industry in organizations such as Bell Labs, the National Opinion Research Center, or the Rand Corporation. Most are found at the approximately 200 research universities and institutes located in half a dozen advanced industrialized countries. Thus, the scientific community may be scattered geographically, but its members tend to work together in small clusters.

How big is the scientific community? This is not an easy question to answer. Using the broadest definition (including all scientists and those in science-related professions, such as engineers), about 15 percent of the labor force in advanced industrialized countries are members of the scientific community. A better way to look at the scientific community is to look at the basic unit of the larger community: the discipline (e.g., sociology, biology, psychology, etc.). Scientists are most familiar with a particular discipline because knowledge is specialized. In the United States, there are about 17,000 professional sociologists, 132,000 architects, 650,000 lawyers, and 1,257,000 accountants. Each year, about 500 people receive Ph.D.s in sociology, 16,000 receive medical degrees, and 38,000 receive law degrees.

About one-half of the Ph.D. degree holders do not conduct research for a living. A discipline such as sociology may have about 8,000 active members of the scientific community. Many researchers complete only one or two studies in their careers. A minority conduct dozens of studies. These numbers drop down to as few as 100 people for topic areas or specialties within disciplines (e.g., study of divorce or the death penalty).[4] The outcomes of the scientific community affect the lives of millions of people, yet most ongoing research and new knowledge on a topic may depend on the efforts of a few hundred people.

The Norms of the Scientific Community

Behavior in any human community is regulated by social norms. The scientific community is governed by a set of professional norms and values that researchers learn and internalize during many years of schooling. The norms are mutually reinforcing and contribute to the unique role of the scientist.[5] The settings in which active researchers work and the very operation of the system of science reinforces the norms.[6] Like other social norms, professional norms are ideals of proper conduct. Because researchers are real people, their prejudices, egos, ambitions, personal lives, and the like may affect their professional behavior. The norms of science do not always work perfectly in practice and are occasionally violated.[7] Likewise, it is important to remember that the operation of science does not occur in a vacuum isolated from the real world. Diverse social, political, and economic forces affect its development and influence how it operates.

The five basic norms of science are listed in Box 1.2. They differ from those in other social

---

Box 1.2

Norms of the Scientific Community

1. *Universalism*. Irrespective of who conducts research (e.g., old or young, male or female) and regardless of where it was conducted (e.g., United States or France, Harvard or Unknown University), the research is to be judged only on the basis of scientific merit.
2. *Organized skepticism*. Scientists should not accept new ideas or evidence in a carefree, uncritical manner. Instead, all evidence should be challenged and questioned. Each research study is subjected to intense criticism and scrutiny. The purpose of the criticism is not to attack the individual; rather, it is to ensure that the research can stand up to close examination.
3. *Disinterestedness*. Scientists must be neutral, impartial, receptive, and open to unexpected observations or new ideas. Scientists should not be rigidly wedded to a particular idea or point of view. They should accept, even look for, evidence that runs against their positions and should honestly accept all findings based on high-quality research.
4. *Communalism*. Scientific knowledge must be shared with others; it belongs to everyone. Creating scientific knowledge is a public act, and the findings are public property, available for all to use. The way in which the research is conducted must be described in detail. New knowledge is not formally accepted until other researchers have reviewed it and it has been made publicly available in a special form and style.
5. *Honesty*. This is a general cultural norm, but it is especially strong in scientific research. Scientists demand honesty in all research; dishonesty or cheating in scientific research is a major taboo.

---

institutions (e.g., business, government) and set scientists apart. Scientists largely check on each other to see that the norms are followed. For example, consistent with the norm of *universalism*, scientists will admire a brilliant, creative researcher even if he or she has strange personal habits or a disheveled appearance. Scientists may argue intensely with one another and "tear apart" a research report as part of the norm of *organized skepticism*. They usually listen to new ideas, no matter how strange. Following *disinterestedness*, scientists take results as being tentative, to be accepted only until something better comes along. They love to have other scientists read and react to their research, and some have led fights against censorship. This is consistent with the norm of *communalism*. Scientists expect *honesty* in the conduct and reporting of research and are aghast when anyone cheats at research.

The Scientific Method and Attitude

You have probably heard of the scientific method, and you may be wondering how it fits into all this. The *scientific method* is not one single thing. It refers to the ideas, rules, techniques, and approaches that the scientific community uses. The method arises from a loose consensus within the community of scientists. A discussion of the fundamental methods of social research is found in Chapter 4.

It is better to focus on the *scientific attitude*, or a way of looking at the world. It is an attitude that values craftsmanship, with pride in creativity, high-quality standards, and hard work. As Grinnell (1987:125) stated:

> Most people learn about the "scientific method" rather than about the scientific attitude. While the "scientific method" is an ideal construct, the scientific attitude is the way people have of looking at the world. Doing science includes many methods; what makes them scientific is their acceptance by the scientific collective.

Journal Articles in Science

You may have read an article in a sociology scholarly journal or a specialized magazine. When the scientific community creates new knowledge, it appears in academic books or scholarly journal articles. A more detailed discussion of scholarly journals is in Chapter 5. The primary forms in which research findings or new scientific knowledge appear are *scholarly journal articles*. They are how scientists formally communicate with one another and disseminate the results of scientific research. They are also part of the much discussed explosion of knowledge. Each discipline or field has over 100 journals, each of which publishes many articles every year. For example, a leader among the nearly 200 sociology journals, the *American Sociological Review*, publishes about 65 articles each year. The journal article is a crucial part of the research process and the scientific community, but it is not always well understood.[8]

Consider what happens once a researcher completes a study. First, he or she writes a description of the study and the results as a research report or a paper in a special format. Often, he or she gives an oral presentation of the paper at a meeting of a professional association, such as the American Sociological Association, and sends a copy of it to a few scientists for their comments and suggestions. Next, the researcher sends copies to the editor of a scholarly journal such as the *Sociological Quarterly* or the *Social Science Quarterly*. Each editor, a respected researcher who has been chosen by other scientists to oversee the journal, removes the title page, which is the only place the author's name appears, and sends the paper to several referees for a *blind review*. The referees are scientists who have conducted research in the same specialty area or topic. The review is "blind" because the referees do not know who conducted the research and the author does not know the referees. This reinforces the norm of universalism, because referees judge the paper on its merits alone. They evaluate the research on the basis of its clarity, originality, standards of good research, and contribution to knowledge. Journals want to publish research that is well done and that significantly advances knowledge. The referees return their evaluations to the editor, who decides to reject the paper, to ask the author for revisions, or to accept it for publication.

Some scholarly journals are widely read and highly respected. They receive many more papers than they can publish. This means that most of the papers are rejected, and only a very select few are accepted. For example, a few leading sociology journals reject over 90 percent of the papers sent to them. Even less highly esteemed journals may reject half of the research papers submitted for consideration. Thus, before an article is published in a scholarly journal, it has been screened. In this way, its publication represents tentative acceptance by the scientific community. Once published, the article becomes a piece of knowledge added to that which is already considered science.

Unlike the authors of articles for the popular magazines found at newsstands, who are paid for writing, scientists are not paid for publishing in scholarly journals. In fact, they may have to pay a small fee to help defray costs just to have their papers considered. Researchers are happy to make their research available to their peers (i.e., other scientists and researchers) through scholarly journals. Likewise, the referees are not paid for reviewing papers. They consider it an honor to be asked to conduct the reviews and a responsibility of membership in the scientific community. The scientific community imparts great respect to researchers who publish many articles in the foremost scholarly journals because the articles confirm that these researchers are leaders in advancing the primary goal of the scientific community—to contribute to the accumulation of scientific knowledge.

A researcher gains prestige and honor within the scientific community, respect from peers, and a reputation as an accomplished researcher through such publications. Researchers want to earn the respect of their peers—other highly trained scientists who are most knowledgeable about the research issues. In addition, an impressive record of respected publications helps a researcher obtain awards, prizes, job offers, a following of students, improved working conditions, and increases in salary.[9]

You may never publish an article in a scholarly journal, but you will probably read such articles. They are a vital component of the system of scientific research. The results of most research (i.e., most new scientific knowledge) first appear in scholarly journals. Researchers read the journals to learn about the research others conducted, the methods they used, and the results they obtained. You can participate in the process by which new knowledge is communicated.

Science as a Transformative Process

You can think of research as the use of scientific methods to transform ideas, hunches, and questions, sometimes called *hypotheses*, into scientific knowledge. This book reveals the transformative process of social science research. *Transformation* means altering something, converting it from one thing into another. In the research process, a researcher starts with guesses or questions and applies specialized methods and techniques to this raw material. At the end of the process, a finished product of value appears: scientific knowledge. A highly productive researcher is one who creates a great deal of new knowledge that greatly improves people's understanding of the world.

You may be starting to feel that the research process is beyond you. After all, it involves complex technical skills and the high-powered scientific community. Yet, the fundamentals of conducting research are accessible to most people. With education and practice, you can learn to do scientific research. In addition to assimilating the scientific attitude or culture, you will need to master how and when to apply research techniques. After reading this book, you should grasp them. Soon you will be able to conduct small-scale research projects yourself.

STEPS OF THE RESEARCH PROCESS

The Steps

The research process requires a sequence of steps. The different types of research are covered in Chapters 2 and 4. Various approaches suggest somewhat different steps, but most seem to follow the seven steps discussed here.

The process begins with a researcher selecting a *topic*—a general area of study or issue such as divorce, crime, homelessness, or powerful elites. A topic is too broad for conducting research. This is why the next step is crucial. The researcher narrows down, or *focuses*, the topic into a specific research question that he or she can address in the study (e.g., "Do people who marry younger have a higher divorce rate?"). When learning about a topic and narrowing the focus, the researcher usually reviews past research, or the *literature*, on a topic or question. Chapter 5 discusses how to do a literature review. The researcher also develops a possible answer, or hypothesis. As Chapter 3 will show, theory can be important at this stage.

After specifying a research question, the researcher plans how he or she will carry out the specific study or research project. The third step involves making decisions about the many practical details of doing the research (e.g., whether to use a survey or observe in the field, how many subjects to use, which questions to ask). Now the researcher is ready to gather the data or evidence (e.g., ask people the questions, record answers).

Once the researcher has collected the data, his or her next step is to manipulate or analyze the data to see any patterns that emerge. The patterns in the data or evidence help the researcher interpret or give meaning to the data (e.g., "People who marry young in cities have higher divorce rates, but those in rural areas do not"). Finally, the researcher writes a report that describes the background to the study, how he or she conducted it, and what he or she discovered.

The neat seven-step process shown in Figure 1.1 is oversimplified. In practice, researchers rarely complete step 1, then leave it to move to step 2, and so on. Research is more of an interactive process in which steps blend into each other. A later step may stimulate reconsideration of a previous one. The process is not strictly linear; it may flow in several directions before reaching an end. Research does not abruptly end at step 7. It is an ongoing process, and the end of one study often stimulates new thinking and fresh research questions.

The seven steps are followed for one research project. A researcher applies one cycle of the steps in a single research project or a research study on a specific topic. Each project

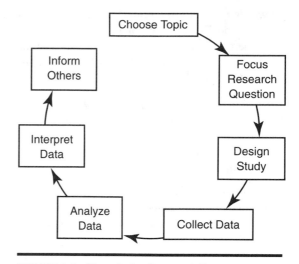

FIGURE 1.1   Steps in the Research Process

builds on prior research and contributes to a larger body of knowledge. The larger process of scientific discovery and accumulating new knowledge requires the involvement of many researchers in numerous research projects all at the same time. A single researcher may be working on multiple research projects at once, or several researchers may collaborate on one project. Likewise, one project may result in one scholarly article or several, and sometimes several smaller projects are reported in a single article. It may help to look at Figure 1.1 for a summary of the steps after reading the following examples.

Examples

The parts of the research process can be seen in two published articles on very different topics. I will identify the parts in each. In the first example, the authors conducted a survey of students at one college in five different years to explore trends in religious attitudes. The second example is more complex. The author examined historical documents and statistical information to explain why the number of inmates in U.S. mental hospitals increased about 800 percent early in the twentieth century.

Example 1. In 1986, Philip Hastings of Williams College and Dean Hodge of Catholic University published an article in the journal *Social Forces* called "Religious and Moral Attitude Trends among College Students, 1948–84."

Choose a Topic. The topic of the study was the moral attitudes of college students. The authors asked how student attitudes had changed from 1948 to 1984. They saw students as the pacesetters of cultural change, who modify their attitudes more than older adults.

Focus the Project. Media reports and past studies of student attitudes suggested that attitudes of the 1980s were a return to the conservatism of the 1950s. The authors asked whether religious and moral beliefs also shifted. They noted that studies on college students from the 1920s through the 1970s found shifts in the strength of student religious beliefs. These shifts paralleled periods of conservatism and liberalism on general social and political issues. The authors hypothesized that religious and moral beliefs would become more conservative in the 1980s than the 1970s. This followed the shift to more conservative attitudes on nonreligious issues found in other studies of students. The authors also wanted to see whether any changes had occurred since their publication of a similar study on student religious attitudes five years earlier.

Design the Study. In 1948, Philip Hastings used questionnaires to ask a sample of 205 students at Williams College about their religious attitudes. Students were given approximately 20 questions regarding their religious beliefs. For example, one question asked whether students believed that science and religion were irreconcilable. The students were also asked about religious upbringing, family income, and other background factors. The design was to ask students at the same college the same questions in later years so that trends in attitudes could be detected.

Gather the Data. The 1948 questionnaire was distributed to random samples of Williams College students in 1967, 1974, 1979, and 1984. Questions on moral issues were added in 1974.

An example moral question is "Should laws against homosexual acts between consenting adults be repealed?"

Analyze the Data. The authors wanted to be sure that they were comparing similar students over time. Until 1970, Williams College admitted only men, so female students were excluded from the 1974, 1979, and 1984 data. In addition, almost half of the 1948 students were veterans, but few students in later years were veterans. To make comparisons, the responses of veterans were removed. The authors constructed percentage tables to show how students answered the religion questions in each of the five years. They also made percentage tables for moral attitude questions for 1974 to 1984.

Interpret the Findings. The authors found that the percentage of students who retained their parents' religion was high before 1967, dropped between 1967 and 1974, and rose in 1979 and 1984. On most religious questions, there was a decline in conservative attitudes between 1948 and 1974, but there was a reversal from 1974 to 1984. On moral questions, the questionnaire answers also showed increases in conservative attitudes toward sex and drugs. The responses also suggested that students felt less of a moral obligation to society between 1974 and 1984. For example, in 1974, 83 percent of students agreed that Americans had a moral obligation to conserve resources; this dropped to 72 percent in 1984. The authors concluded that the religious attitudes of Williams College students became increasingly liberal between the 1940s and early 1970s but became more traditional after the mid-1970s. They concluded that the religious and moral attitudes of college students follow the overall political climate of the country.

Inform Others. The report of the research was written and submitted to *Social Forces* for publication.

Example 2. In 1991, John Sutton of the University of California, Santa Barbara, published an article in the *American Sociological*

Review called "The Political Economy of Madness: The Expansion of the Asylum in Progressive America."

Choose a Topic. The topic of the study was a large growth in the number of people in insane asylums and its relationship to public policy.

Focus the Project. The study focused on a dramatic increase in the number of people in U.S. insane asylums between the 1880s and the 1920s. It built on two books on the history of mental illness in the United States written by another researcher, Gerald Grob. The books documented that many criminologists, charity experts, and physicians criticized prisons, mental hospitals, almshouses, and reformatories as inhumane and called for reforms in the 1880s and 1890s. Despite some reforms in the penal system and almshouses, the number of people in asylums grew from 40,000 to over 260,000 between 1880 and 1923, and people feared an "epidemic of madness." Grob had argued that the almshouses for poor people were harshly criticized and most were closed. Yet, no system of welfare was created in their place, especially for the thousands of impoverished elderly in the poorhouses. In this era, prior to social welfare programs, the asylum was one of the only institutions open to them. Without alternatives, thousands of poverty-stricken people were classified as insane as a way to get food, shelter, and care.

Sutton built on Grob's work and focused his study using a theory that says that governments try to expand, responding to public crises in ways that will protect or expand the power of government officials. Sutton noted that most government resources before the 1930s were located in state governments, in which the political party in power provided patronage and construction jobs in order to expand its power. He hypothesized that the growth rate in asylum inmates would vary across different states, depending on the need to expand political power and the availability of economic resources in each state.

Design the Study. Sutton studied the details of the historical context and how mental hospitals operated in the period. He also identified statistics to measure the economic and political characteristics of each state.

Gather the Data. Sutton examined historical studies on psychiatry, mental hospitals, and government policy in the period. He also gathered quantitative data on the size of insane populations, political competition, wealth available to states, and other state characteristics.

Analyze the Data. Sutton was able to predict the size of the increase in numbers of asylum inmates in a state largely on the basis of its political and economic characteristics. The insane population grew fastest in states that had more resources, more intense competition between political parties, more older people, and more people in cities. At the time, many people in some states received federal government assistance because they or a relative had fought on the Union side in the U.S. Civil War. Sutton found that asylums grew much less rapidly in states where more people were getting such federal assistance.

Interpret the Findings. Sutton argued that asylum expansion occurred because there was no federal government solution to the poverty problem. He agreed with Grob that many impoverished older people were classified as insane by the loose methods of early psychiatry. But he went beyond Grob to show that this did not happen equally across the country. The insane populations grew most where there was little help for impoverished people from federal government assistance, where sufficient state-level resources existed to build and staff the asylums, and where greater competition between political parties formed a need to create patronage jobs. At this time, most of the jobs in asylums and the funds to build the asylums were given out by state-level political party officials. Thus, the state government response to the crisis of thousands of impoverished elderly people, who had no place to go when the old almshouses were shut down, was to build and staff many new asylums where there was little federal assistance. This was done when political parties sought to expand their power and stay in office by using tax revenue to swell the ranks of those who depended on the party for their jobs. Asylum expansion was a method to deal with the poor people while providing jobs controlled by the political party in power in the state government.

Inform Others.   Prior to its publication in the *American Sociological Review*, this study was reported at a meeting of the American Sociological Association and at Stanford University.

QUALITATIVE AND QUANTITATIVE SOCIAL RESEARCH

You will learn about both qualitative and quantitative styles of doing social research in this book. After the first several chapters, the two styles will be used to help organize most remaining chapters. Chapters 6 through 12 focus on quantitative research, and Chapters 13 through 16 focus on qualitative research. Each category uses several specific research techniques (e.g., survey, interview, historical analysis), yet there is much overlap between the type of data and the style of research. Most qualitative-style researchers examine qualitative-type data, and vice versa. However, sometimes qualitative researchers examine quantitative data, and vice versa. Both styles are widely used in social research, but each is rooted on a distinct logic or approach to social science (discussed in Chapter 4).

Unfortunately, there is a lot of ill will between the followers of each style of research, as some find it difficult to understand or appreciate the other style. Thus, Joel Levine (1993:xii) wrote, "Quantitative social science," which he called "real social science," faced opposition but it "won the battle." Denzin and Lincoln (1994) argued that qualitative research has expanded greatly in the recent decades and is rapidly displacing outdated quantitative-style research.

Although both styles of research share basic principles of science, the two approaches differ in significant ways (see Table 1.1). Each has its strengths and limitations, topics or issues where it glitters, and classic studies that provide remarkable insights into social life. I agree with King, Keohane, and Verba (1994:5), who stated that the best research "often combines the features of each."

No matter what style they adopt, researchers try to avoid the errors discussed earlier in this chapter, to be systematic in gathering data, and to use the idea of comparison extensively. By understanding both styles, you will know about a broader range of research and can use both in complementary ways. Charles Ragin (1994:92) has explained one way the styles complement each other:

The key features common to all qualitative methods can be seen when they are contrasted with quantitative methods. Most quantitative data techniques are data condensers. They condense data

TABLE 1.1   Quantitative Style versus Qualitative Style

QUANTITATIVE STYLE	QUALITATIVE STYLE
Measure objective facts	Construct social reality, cultural meaning
Focus on variables	Focus on interactive processes, events
Reliability is key	Authenticity is key
Value free	Values are present and explicit
Independent of context	Situationally constrained
Many cases, subjects	Few cases, subjects
Statistical analysis	Thematic analysis
Researcher is detached	Researcher is involved

Sources: Cresswell (1994), Denzin and Lincoln (1994), Guba and Lincoln (1994), and Mostyn (1985).

in order to see the big picture. . . . Qualitative methods, by contrast, are best understood as data enhancers. When data are enhanced, it is possible to see key aspects of cases more clearly.

WHY CONDUCT SOCIAL RESEARCH?

Where can you find people conducting social research? Students, professors, professional researchers, and scientists in universities, research centers, and the government, with an army of assistants and technicians, conduct much social research. This research is not visible to the average person. Although the results may appear only in specialized publications or textbooks, the basic knowledge and research methods that professional researchers develop become the basis for all other social research.

In addition to those in universities, people who work for newspapers, television networks, market research firms, schools, hospitals, social service agencies, political parties, consulting firms, government agencies, personnel departments, public interest organizations, insurance companies, or law firms may conduct research as part of their jobs. Numerous people make use of social research techniques. The findings from this social research usually yield better informed, less biased decisions than the guessing, hunches, intu-

ition, and personal experience that were previously used (see Box 1.3). Unfortunately, those being studied may feel overstudied or overloaded by the research. For example, the many exit poll studies by the mass media during elections have prompted a backlash of people refusing to vote and debates over legal restrictions on such polling. Also, some people misuse or abuse social research—use sloppy research techniques, misinterpret findings, rig studies to find previously decided results, and so on. But the hostile reactions to such misuse may be directed at research in general instead of at the people who misuse it.

People conduct social research for many reasons. Some want to answer practical questions (e.g., "Will a reduction in average class size from 25 to 20 increase student writing skills?"). Others want to make informed decisions (e.g., "Should our company introduce flextime to reduce employee turnover?"). Still others want to change society (e.g., "What can be done to reduce rape?"). Finally, those in the scientific community seek to build basic knowledge about society (e.g., "Why is the divorce rate higher for blacks than for whites?").

CONCLUSION

In this chapter, you learned what social research is, how the research process operates, and who

Box 1.3

The Practitioner and Social Science

Science does not, and cannot, provide people with fixed, absolute Truth. This is because science is a slow, incomplete process of reducing untruth. It is a quest for the best possible answers carried out by a collection of devoted people who labor strenuously in a careful, systematic, and open-minded manner. Many people are uneasy with the painstaking pace, hesitating progress, and incertitude of science. They demand immediate, absolute answers. Many turn to religious fanatics or political demagogues who offer final, conclusive truths in abundance.

What does this mean for diligent practitioners (e.g., human service workers, health care professionals, criminal justice officers, journalists, or policy ana-

lysts) who have to make prompt decisions in their daily work? Must they abandon scientific thinking and rely only on common sense, personal conviction, or political doctrine? No. They, too, can use social scientific thinking. Their task is difficult but possible. They must conscientiously try to locate the best knowledge currently available; use careful, independent reasoning; avoid known errors or fallacies; and be wary of any doctrine offering complete, final answers. Practitioners must always be open to new ideas, use multiple information sources, and constantly question the evidence offered to support a course of action.

conducts research. You also learned about alternatives to research—ways to get fast, easy, and practical knowledge that, nonetheless, often contains error, misinformation, and false reasoning. You saw how the scientific community works, how social research fits into the scientific enterprise, and how the norms of science and journal articles are crucial to the scientific community. You also learned the steps of research.

Social research is for, about, and conducted by *people*. Despite the attention to the principles, rules, or procedures, remember that social research is a human activity. Researchers are people, not unlike yourself, who became absorbed in a desire to create and discover knowledge. Many find social research to be fun and exciting. They conduct it to discover new knowledge and to gain a richer understanding of the social world. Whether you become a professional social researcher, someone who applies a few research techniques as part of a job, or just someone who uses the results of research, you will benefit from learning about the research process. You will be enriched if you can begin to create a personal link between yourself and the research process.

C. Wright Mills offered the following valuable advice in his *Sociological Imagination* (1959:196):

> *You must learn to use your life experiences in your intellectual work: continually to examine and interpret it. In this sense craftsmanship is the center of yourself and you are personally involved in every intellectual product upon which you may work.*

KEY TERMS

blind review	overgeneralization	scientific method
communalism	premature closure	selective observation
data	qualitative data	social research
disinterestedness	quantitative data	social theory
empirical	scholarly journal article	universalism
halo effect	scientific attitude	
organized skepticism	scientific community	

REVIEW QUESTIONS

1. What sources of knowledge are alternatives to social research?
2. Why is social research usually better than the alternatives?
3. Is social research always right? Can it answer any question? Explain.
4. How did science and oracles serve similar purposes in different eras?
5. What is the scientific community? What is its role?
6. What are the norms of the scientific community? What are their effects?
7. How does a study get published in a scholarly social science journal?
8. What steps are involved in conducting a research project?
9. What does it mean to say that research steps are not rigidly fixed?
10. What types of people do social research? For what reasons?

NOTES

1. For more on fallacies, see Babbie (1995:23–25), Kaplan (1964), and Wallace (1971).

2. The rise of science is discussed in Camic (1980), Lemert (1979), Merton (1970). Wuthnow (1979), and

Ziman (1976). For more on the historical development of the social sciences, see Eastrope (1974), Laslett (1992), Ross (1991), and Turner and Turner (1991).

3. For more on the scientific community, see Cole (1983), Cole, Cole, and Simon (1981), Collins (1983), Collins and Restivo (1983), Greenberg (1967), Hagstrom (1965), Merton (1973), Stoner (1966), and Ziman (1968).

4. See Cappell and Guterbock (1992) and Ennis (1992) for recent studies of sociological specialties.

5. For more on the social role of the scientist, see Ben-David (1971), Camic (1980), and Tuma and Grimes (1981).

6. Norms are discussed in Hagstrom (1965), Merton (1973), and Stoner (1966).

7. Violations of norms are discussed in Blume (1974) and Mitroff (1974).

8. The communication and publication system is described in Bakanic et al. (1987), Blau (1978), Cole (1983), Crane (1967), Gusfield (1976), Hargens (1988), Mullins (1973), Singer (1989), and Ziman (1968).

9. For more on the system of reward and stratification in science, see Cole and Cole (1973). Cole (1978), Fuchs and Turner (1986), Gaston (1978), Gustin (1973), Long (1978), Meadows (1974), and Reskin (1977).

RECOMMENDED READINGS

Agnew, Neil McK., and Sandra W. Pyke. (1991). *The science game: An introduction to research in the social sciences*, 5th ed. Englewood Cliffs, NJ: Prentice Hall. This short book provides an overview of social research with whimsical examples and creative diagrams. The authors discuss the general system of science and experimental research.

Berger, Bennett M., ed. (1990). *Authors of their own lives: Intellectual autobiographies of twenty American sociologists*. Berkeley: University of California Press. This collection of essays shows that leading social researchers are real people with personal lives. The autobiographical essays trace the personal and professional events that shaped the careers of a diverse set of sociologists who have made significant contributions.

Frost, Peter, and Ralph Stablein, eds. (1992). *Doing exemplary research*. Newbury Park, CA: Sage. This is a look at the human side of research. It scrutinizes seven articles in organizational analysis, detailing the author's personal autobiographic adventure to create and publish the article. It provides commentary on the nuts and bolts of research and lots of practical tips.

Hunt, Morton. (1985). *Profiles of social research: The scientific study of human interactions*. New York: Russell Sage Foundation. Hunt provides an overview of different methods of doing social research and stories of how five research studies were conducted. He reveals the drama and excitement of discovery in social research in descriptions of the social lives of researchers and the evolution of ideas during the research process.

Mills, C. Wright. (1959). *The sociological imagination*. New York: Oxford University Press. In this classic on sociological thinking and research, Mills comments on developing an overall orientation to social science and discusses several important issues of social research. His appendix on intellectual craftsmanship gives valuable practical advice to the beginning social researcher.

Ziman, John. (1976). *The force of knowledge: The scientific dimension of society*. New York: Cambridge University Press. Ziman provides a broad outline of the growth of science and technology over the past 200 years. He argues that science is fundamentally a social activity in which the public communication of how research was done and of findings is central.

CHAPTER 2

DIMENSIONS OF RESEARCH

> *The objective of academic research, whether by sociologists, political scientists, or anthropologists, is to try to find answers to theoretical questions within their respective fields. In contrast, the objective of applied social research is to use data so that decisions can be made.*
>
> —Herbert J. Rubin, *Applied Social Research*, pp. 6–7

INTRODUCTION

Three years after they graduated from college. Tim and Sharon met for lunch. Tim asked Sharon, "So, how is your new job as a researcher for Social Data, Inc.? What are you doing?" Sharon answered. "Right now I'm working on an applied research project on day care in which we're doing a cross-sectional survey to get descriptive data for an evaluation study." Sharon's description of her research project on the topic of day care touches on four dimensions of social research. This chapter discusses those dimensions.

The picture of social research I presented in Chapter 1 was a simplified one. Research comes in several shapes and sizes. Before a researcher begins to conduct a study, he or she must decide on a specific type of research. Good researchers understand the advantages and disadvantages of each type, although most end up specializing in one.

In this chapter, you will learn about the four dimensions of social research: (1) the purpose of doing it, (2) its intended use, (3) how it treats time, and (4) the research techniques used in it. The four dimensions reinforce one another; that is, a purpose tends to go with certain techniques and particular uses. Few studies are pure types, but the dimensions simplify the complexity of conducting research.

Before conducting a research project, a researcher makes several decisions. By understanding the dimensions of research, you will be better prepared to make such decisions. In addition, an awareness of the types of research and how they fit into the research process will make it easier for you to read and understand published studies.

DIMENSIONS OF RESEARCH

The Purpose of a Study

If you ask someone why he or she is conducting a study, you might get a range of responses: "My boss told me to"; "It was a class assignment"; "I was curious"; "My roommate thought it would be a good idea." There are almost as many reasons to do research as there are researchers. Yet, the purposes of social research may be organized into three groups based on what the researcher is trying to accomplish—explore a new topic, describe a social phenomenon, or explain why something occurs.[1] Studies may have multiple purposes (e.g., both to explore and to describe), but one purpose is usually dominant.

Exploration.   Perhaps you have explored a new topic or issue in order to learn about it. If the issue was new or researchers had written little on it, you began at the beginning. This is called *exploratory research*. The researcher's goal is to formulate more precise questions that future research can answer. Exploratory research may be the first stage in a sequence of studies. A researcher may need to conduct an exploratory study in order to know enough to design and execute a second, more systematic and extensive study.

Research on AIDS (acquired immune deficiency syndrome) illustrates exploratory research. When AIDS first appeared, around 1980, no one knew what type of disease it was, or even if it was a disease. No one knew what caused it, how it spread, or why it appeared. Officials knew only that people were entering hospitals with symptoms that no one had seen before, that they failed to respond to any treatment, and that they died quickly. It took many exploratory medical and social science studies before researchers knew enough to design precise studies about the disease.

Exploratory studies often go unpublished. Instead, researchers incorporate them into more systematic research that they publish later. An example of a published exploratory study is Gaither Loewenstein's 1985 article in *Sociological Quarterly*, "The New Underclass: A Contemporary Sociological Dilemma." The purpose of the research was to explore the idea "that a new underclass is emerging in America, comprised of the previously mobile working class citizens." Because the "new" underclass in which

the author was interested emerged during the 1980s, little was known about it when he began. Loewenstein wanted to learn whether a new underclass was developing. He read other studies and theories of social class, examined labor market statistics, interviewed 50 public assistance (welfare) applicants aged 18 to 30, and spent 16 months with a social group of working-class young people. The author's initial fuzzy idea, which arose from his informal social interaction with friends, became clearer and more developed during the research process.

Exploratory research rarely yields definitive answers. It addresses the "what" question: "What is this social activity really about?" It is difficult to conduct because there are few guidelines to follow. Everything about a topic is potentially important. The steps are not well defined and the direction of inquiry changes frequently. This can be frustrating for researchers, who may feel adrift or that they are "spinning their wheels."

Exploratory researchers are creative, open minded, and flexible; adopt an investigative stance; and explore all sources of information. Researchers ask creative questions and take advantage of *serendipity*, those unexpected or chance factors that have larger implications. For example, researchers expected to find that the younger a child was at immigration to a new nation, the less the negative impact on that child when going on to college. Instead, they unexpectedly discovered that children who immigrated in a specific age group (between ages 6 and 11) were especially vulnerable to the disruption of immigration, more so than either older or younger children.[2]

Exploratory researchers frequently use qualitative data. The techniques for gathering qualitative data are less wedded to a specific theory or research question. Qualitative research tends to be more open to using a range of evidence and discovering new issues (see Box 2.1).

Description.   You may have a more highly developed idea about a social phenomenon and want to describe it. *Descriptive research* presents a picture of the specific details of a situation,

Box 2.1

Goals of Exploratory Research

- Become familiar with the basic facts, people, and concerns involved.
- Develop a well–grounded mental picture of what is occurring.
- Generate many ideas and develop tentative theories and conjectures.
- Determine the feasibility of doing additional research.
- Formulate questions and refine issues for more systematic inquiry.
- Develop techniques and a sense of direction for future research.

social setting, or relationship. Much of the social research found in scholarly journals or used for making policy decisions is descriptive.

Descriptive and exploratory research have many similarities. They blur together in practice. In descriptive research, the researcher begins with a well-defined subject and conducts research to describe it accurately. The outcome of a descriptive study is a detailed picture of the subject. For example, results may indicate the percentage of people who hold a particular view or engage in specific behaviors—for example, that 10 percent of parents physically or sexually abuse their children.

A descriptive study presents a picture of types of people or of social activities. For example, Donald McCabe (1992) studied cheating among U.S. college students. He was interested in how people rationalize deviance. He thought that they developed justifications that neutralized or turned back moral disapproval, in order to protect their self-images and deflect self-blame. He conducted a survey of over 6,000 students and found that two-thirds admitted to cheating on a major test or assignment at least once. Six major types of cheating appeared to be common. When McCabe asked the students why they cheated, he discovered that they justified their behavior using four major *neutralization strategies*. The most common strategy,

cited by over half of the cheaters, was a denial of responsibility. In this strategy, people claim that forces beyond their control, such as a heavy workload or peer behavior, justifies the deviance. Other rationalizations given by cheating students included a denial that anyone is hurt, condemnation of the teacher, or an appeal to higher loyalties such as friendship. The example article on students' religious attitudes summarized in Chapter 1 was a descriptive study, which described how student attitudes changed over time.

Descriptive research focuses on "how" and "who" questions ("How did it happen?" "Who is involved?"). Exploring new issues or explaining why something happens (e.g., why students neutralize cheating or why students hold specific religious beliefs) is less of a concern for descriptive researchers than describing how things are.

A great deal of social research is descriptive. Descriptive researchers use most data-gathering techniques—surveys, field research, content analysis, historical-comparative research. Only experimental research is less ineffective (see Box 2.2).

Explanation.   When you encounter an issue that is already known and have a description of it, you may begin to wonder *why* things are the way they are. The desire to know "why," to explain, is the purpose of *explanatory research*. It builds on

Box 2.2

Goals of Descriptive Research

- Provide an accurate profile of a group.
- Describe a process, mechanism, or relationship.
- Give a verbal or numerical picture (e.g., percentages).
- Find information to stimulate new explanations.
- Present basic background information or a context.
- Create a set of categories or classify types.
- Clarify a sequence, set of stages, or steps.
- Document information that contradicts prior beliefs about a subject.

exploratory and descriptive research and goes on to identify the reason something occurs. Going beyond focusing a topic or providing a picture of it, explanatory research looks for causes and reasons. For example, a descriptive researcher may discover that 10 percent of parents abuse their children, whereas the explanatory researcher is more interested in learning *why* parents abuse their children (see Box 2.3).

Scott South and Kim Lloyd (1995) conducted an explanatory study to explain divorce rates. They tested a theory that says the chance of a divorce increases when there is an ample supply of potential alternative partners with whom a married person comes into contact. In other words, a demographic factor (i.e., the availability of alternative spouses) has a negative impact on marriage stability. Evidence suggested that a large percent of recently divorced persons had prior involvement with someone other than their spouses. Among other results, South and Lloyd discovered that divorce rates were higher in areas where there was an imbalance in the sex ratio and where many unmarried women worked full time. The authors explained a higher divorce rate in these areas by a greater opportunity for social interaction between married men and unmarried women in the workplace. Such interaction takes place in a general social climate that emphasizes personal fulfillment and individual choice and permits divorce to end unsatisfactory marriages.

The Use of Research

For over a century, sociology has had two wings. Researchers in one adopt a more detached, scientific, and academic orientation; those in the other are more activist, pragmatic, and reform oriented. This is not a rigid separation. Researchers in the two wings cooperate and maintain friendly relations. Some move from one wing to another at different stages in their careers. The difference in orientation revolves around how to use social research. In simple terms, some focus on using research to advance general knowledge, whereas others use it to solve specific problems. Those who seek an understanding of the fundamental nature of social reality are engaged in *basic research* (also called academic research or pure research). Applied researchers, by contrast, primarily want to apply and tailor knowledge to address a specific practical issue. They want to answer a policy question or solve a pressing social problem.

Basic Research. Basic research advances fundamental knowledge about the social world. It focuses on refuting or supporting theories that explain how the social world operates, what makes things happen, why social relations are a certain way, and why society changes. Basic research is the source of most new scientific ideas and ways of thinking about the world. It can be exploratory, descriptive, or explanatory; however, explanatory research is the most common.

Many nonscientists criticize basic research and ask, "What good is it?" They consider basic research to be a waste of time and money because it does not have a direct use or help resolve an immediate problem. It is true that knowledge produced by basic research often lacks practical applications in the short term. Yet, basic research provides a foundation for knowledge and understanding that are generalizable to many policy areas, problems, or areas of study. Basic research

---

Box 2.3

Goals of Explanatory Research

- Determine the accuracy of a principle or theory.
- Find out which competing explanation is better.
- Advance knowledge about an underlying process.
- Link different issues or topics under a common general statement.
- Build and elaborate a theory so it becomes more complete.
- Extend a theory or principle into new areas or issues.
- Provide evidence to support or refute an explanation or prediction.

is the source of most of the tools—methods, theories, and ideas—that applied researchers use. Really big breakthroughs in understanding and significant advances in knowledge usually come from basic research. In contrast to applied researchers, who want quick answers to questions for use within the next month or year, basic researchers painstakingly seek answers to questions that could have an impact on thinking for over a century.

The questions asked by basic researchers seem impractical. For example, research on an unrelated topic—the causes of cancer in chickens—conducted over a decade before AIDS was discovered now provides the most promising source for advances in research on the AIDS virus. Basic research by the 1975 Nobel Prize winner Howard Temin laid the foundation for understanding how viruses work and has had major implications for questions that did not even exist when he conducted his path-breaking research years ago. Today's computers could not exist without the pure research in mathematics conducted over a century ago, for which there was no known practical application at the time.

Police officers, officials trying to prevent delinquency, or counselors of youthful offenders may see little direct relevance to basic research on the question, "Why does deviant behavior occur?" Basic research rarely helps practitioners directly with their everyday concerns. Nevertheless, it stimulates new ways of thinking about deviance that have the potential to revolutionize and dramatically improve how practitioners deal with the problem. Although policymakers and service providers often feel that basic research is of little relevance, public policies and social services will be ineffective and misguided unless they are based on an understanding of actual causes.

A new idea or fundamental knowledge is not generated only by basic research. Applied research, too, can build new knowledge. Nonetheless, basic research is essential for nourishing the expansion of knowledge. Researchers at the center of the scientific community conduct most of the basic research.

Applied Research.   Applied researchers try to solve specific policy problems or help practitioners accomplish tasks.[3] Theory is less central to them than seeking a solution to a specific problem for a limited setting—for example, "Will the number of auto accidents involving drunk students decline if student governments sponsor alcohol-free parties?" *Applied research* is frequently descriptive research, and its main strength is its immediate practical use.

People employed by businesses, government agencies, social service agencies, health organizations, and educational institutions conduct applied research. It often affects our daily lives. Decisions to market a new product, to choose one policy over another, or to continue or end a public program may be based on applied research.

The scientific community is the primary consumer of basic research. The consumers of applied research findings are practitioners such as teachers, counselors, and case workers, or decision makers such as managers, committees, and officials. Often, someone other than the researcher who conducted the study uses the results of applied research. The use of the results may be beyond the researcher's control. This means that applied researchers have an obligation to translate findings from scientific technical language into the language of decision makers or practitioners.

The results of applied research are less likely to enter the public domain in publications. Results may be available only to a small number of decision makers or practitioners, who decide whether or how to put the research results into practice and who may or may not use the results wisely. For example, Neuberg (1988) found that the results of the famous Seattle–Denver "negative income tax" experiment of the 1960s and 1970s was seriously misinterpreted and distorted in newspaper accounts. Despite serious problems with the study and cautions from researchers, politicians used its results to justify cuts in government programs they disliked.

Because applied research has immediate implications or involves controversial issues, it often generates conflict. This is not new. For example, in 1903, Charles Ellwood conducted an applied study of the jails and poorhouses in Missouri and documented serious deficiencies. His research report generated great public indignation, and he was accused of slandering the state that gave him employment (Turner and Turner, 1991:181).

William Foote Whyte (1984) encountered conflict over findings in his applied research on a factory in Oklahoma and on restaurants in Chicago. In the first case, the management was more interested in defeating a union than in learning about employment relations; in the other, restaurant owners sought to make the industry look good rather than have findings made public on the nitty-gritty of its operations.

Robert Merton (1973) warned that some calls for applied research on major policy issues are merely a delaying tactic by officials who want to deflect criticism for inaction or postpone a decision until after the political heat dies down.

Applied and basic researchers adopt different orientations toward research methodology (see Table 2.1). Basic researchers emphasize high scientific standards and try to conduct near-perfect research. Applied researchers make more trade-

offs. They may compromise scientific rigor to get quick, usable results. But compromise is no excuse for sloppy research. Applied researchers squeeze research into the constraints of an applied setting and balance rigor against practical needs. Such balancing requires an in-depth knowledge of research and an awareness of the consequences of compromising standards.

Types of Applied Research.   Practitioners use several types of applied research. Some of the major ones are discussed here.

Action research is applied research that treats knowledge as a form of power and abolishes the line between research and social action. There are several types of action research, but most share common characteristics: those who are being studied participate in the research process; research incorporates ordinary or popular knowledge; research focuses on power with a goal of empowerment; research seeks to raise conscious or increase awareness; and research is tied directly to political action.

Action researchers try to equalize power relations between themselves and research subjects,

TABLE 2.1   Basic and Applied Social Research Compared

BASIC	APPLIED
1. Research is intrinsically satisfying and judgments are by other sociologists.	1. Research is part of a job and is judged by sponsors who are outside the discipline of sociology.
2. Research problems and subjects are selected with a great deal of freedom.	2. Research problems are "narrowly constrained" to the demands of employers or sponsors.
3. Research is judged by absolute norms of scientific rigor, and the highest standards of scholarship are sought.	3. The rigor and standards of scholarship depend on the uses of results. Research can be "quick and dirty" or may match high scientific standards.
4. The primary concern is with the internal logic and rigor of research design.	4. The primary concern is with the ability to generalize findings to areas of interest to sponsors.
5. The driving goal is to contribute to basic, theoretical knowledge.	5. The driving goal is to have practical payoffs or uses for results.
6. Success comes when results appear in a scholarly journal and have an impact on others in the scientific community.	6. Success comes when results are used by sponsors in decision making.

Source: Adapted from Freeman and Rossi (1984:572–573).

and they oppose having more control, status, and authority than those they study. These researchers try to advance a cause or improve conditions by expanding public awareness. They are explicitly political, not value neutral. Because the goal is to improve the conditions and lives of research participants, formal reports, articles, or books become secondary. Action researchers assume that knowledge develops from experience, particularly the experience of social-political action. They also assume that ordinary people can become aware of conditions and learn to take actions that can bring about improvement.

Action research is associated with the critical social science approach discussed in Chapter 4. It attracts researchers who hold specific perspectives (e.g., environmental, radical, African American, feminist, etc.). For example, most feminist research has a dual mission: to create social change by transforming gender relations and to contribute to the advancement of knowledge (Reinharz, 1992:252). A feminist researcher who studies sexual harassment might both recommend policy changes to reduce it as well as inform potential victims so they can protect themselves and defend their rights. An action researcher who studies homeless shelters might link research to mobilizing homeless people for marches and lobbying for improved conditions. In one situation, action research involved working to preserve a town that was to be destroyed by a dam project. An action researcher worked together with union officials and management to redesign work to prevent layoffs. In developing nations, action researchers work among illiterate, impoverished peasants to teach literacy, study local conditions, and spread an awareness of conditions, and to attempt to improve them.[4] William Gamson (1992:xviii) described a seminar on action research at Boston College that drew students from the Social Economy and Social Justice graduate program:

> The participants in this seminar . . . are activist-scholars oriented to the concrete problems involved in mobilizing people for collective action. Participants are or have been involved in the Central American solidarity movement, the nuclear freeze movement, the movements for more equitable health care and decent housing, the labor movement. . . . Members of the seminar write papers, run workshops, and consult on media strategy for various movement organizations, as well as conduct research.

A second type of applied research is *social impact assessment*.[5] It may be part of a larger environmental impact statement required by government agencies. Its purpose is to estimate the likely consequences of a planned change. Such an assessment can be used for planning and making choices among alternative policies—for example, to estimate the ability of a local hospital to respond to an earthquake; to determine changes in housing if a major new highway is built; or to assess the impact on college admissions and long-term debt if all college students received interest-free loans to be paid back over 20 years, with payments based on the size of their incomes. Researchers conducting social impact assessment examine many outcomes and often work in an interdisciplinary research team. The impact on several areas can be measured or assessed (see Box 2.4).

Box 2.4

Areas Assessed in Social Impact Studies

- Community service (e.g., school enrollments, speed of police responses)
- Social conditions (e.g., the races of friends that children are likely to make based on play areas; crime rates; the ability of elderly people to feel that they can care for themselves)
- Economic impact (e.g., changes in income levels, business failure rate)
- Demographic consequences (e.g., changes in the mix of old and young people, population movement into or out of an area)
- Environment (e.g., changes in air quality or noise levels)
- Health outcomes (e.g., changes in occurrence of diseases or presence of harmful substances)
- Psychological well-being (e.g., changes in stress, fear, or self-esteem)

Evaluation research is a widely used type of applied research[6] that addresses the question, "Did it work?" Smith and Glass (1987:31) defined *evaluation* as "the process of establishing value judgments based on evidence." Example evaluation research questions are: Does a Socratic teaching technique improve learning over lecturing? Does a law enforcement program of mandatory arrest reduce spouse abuse? Does a flex-time program increase employee productivity? Evaluation research measures the effectiveness of a program, policy, or way of doing something. It is frequently descriptive but can be exploratory or explanatory. Evaluation researchers use several different research techniques (e.g., survey, field). If it can be used, the experimental technique is usually most effective.

Practitioners involved with a policy or program may conduct evaluation research for their own information or at the request of outside decision makers, who sometimes place limits on researchers by setting boundaries on what can be studied and determining the outcome of interest. For example, suppose the Department of Justice asks a researcher to evaluate whether a policy of mandatory arrests reduces spouse abuse. The department asks a researcher to evaluate one police department over one year and defines the outcome of interest as the number of spouse abuse calls to the police and the number of cases at a local hospital emergency room. The Department of Justice may not be concerned about other outcomes, such as the policy's effect on alcohol use, job loss by abusers, or divorce. It may be interested only in its own policy and not in making comparisons with an alternative program offered by a human service agency.

Ethical and political conflicts often arise in evaluation research because people have opposing interests in the findings about a program. Research results can affect getting a job, building political popularity, or promoting an alternative program. People who are personally displeased with the finding often try to attack the researcher or his or her methods as being sloppy, biased, or inadequate. In addition to creating controversy and being attacked, evaluation researchers are sometimes subjected to pressures to rig a study before they begin. For example, a researcher might be told to find results showing that a school's program to curb drug abuse works. The school officials who hired the evaluation researcher are publicly associated with the program and have spent a great deal of time and money on it. If the researcher finds that the program was a total failure, the officials will be embarrassed, will be criticized for wasting public funds, and may even lose their jobs. Such ethical issues are aggravated by limits on the cost of the research, time limits on completing a study, the degree of cooperation of those involved, and the accessibility of information. (You can read more about ethical issues in Chapter 17.)

For example, Toni Makkai and John Braithwaite (1993) conducted a study to evaluate whether businesses better comply with government regulations if inspecting officials give praise. In 1987, the Australian government established 31 quality standards for nursing homes, and inspection teams randomly visited nursing homes to check compliance with the standards. The researchers mailed questionnaires to inspectors to learn whether they gave praise to nursing home staff for meeting at least some standards, and, if so, the type and degree of praise. They next checked records on the subsequent quality of the homes. They learned that where inspectors gave praise, the nursing homes improved their overall compliance on the 31 standards.

Two types of evaluation research are formative and summative. *Formative evaluation* is built-in monitoring or continuous feedback on a program used for program management. *Summative evaluation* looks at final program outcomes. Both are usually necessary. In the foregoing example on the use of praise, summative evaluation was used because it occurred one time after the praise was given. The researchers could add formative evaluation by checking the ongoing inspections by officials to ensure that standards are being met and by continuously monitoring the quality of the nursing homes.

Evaluation research is a part of the administration of many organizations (e.g., schools, government agencies, businesses). One example is the *Planning, Programming, and Budgeting System (PPBS)*, first used by the U.S. Department of Defense in the 1960s. PPBS is based on the idea that researchers can evaluate a program by measuring its accomplishments on the basis of its stated goals and objectives. An evaluator divides a program into components and analyzes each component with regard to its costs (staff, supplies, etc.) and accomplishments in achieving program objectives. For example, a women's health center offers pregnancy education. The program components are outreach, education, counseling, and referrals. The program objectives are to reach out to women who believe they are pregnant, provide education about pregnancy, counsel women about their health risks and concerns, and refer pregnant women to health care providers or family planning agencies. An evaluation researcher will examine the cost of each part of the program and measure how well the program meets its objectives. The researcher may ask how much staff time and how many supplies are used for outreach, how many calls or inquiries have resulted from those efforts, and whether the efforts increased the number of women from targeted groups coming to the center.[7]

Applied researchers use two tools, needs assessment and cost-benefit analysis, in social impact assessment and evaluation research. In a *needs assessment*, a researcher collects data to determine major needs and their severity. It is often a preliminary step before a government agency or charity decides on a strategy to help people. Yet, it often becomes tangled in the complex relations within a community. A researcher may confront dilemmas or difficult issues.

One issue is to decide on the group to target for the assessment. Should the researcher focus on the needs of homeless people sleeping in a park, working people who lose large amounts of money betting at a race track, or executives who drink too much at the country club? The most visible need may not be the most serious one. Whom does the researcher ask or observe? Should he or she ask the executives about the needs of the homeless?

A second issue is that people may not express a need in a way that links it directly to policies or long-term solutions. A researcher may find that homeless people say they need housing. After examining the situation, however, he or she may determine that housing would be available if the homeless had jobs. The housing need is caused by a need for jobs. The need for jobs, in turn, may be caused by a need for skills and for certain types of businesses. Thus, to address the housing need, it may be necessary to attract specific types of businesses and provide training in job skills. The apparent surface need may be linked to a deeper problem or condition. People may not be aware of the causes of a need. For example, a need for health care may be caused by drinking polluted water, poor diet, and a lack of exercise. Is this a need for more health care or is it a need for better water treatment and a public health education program?

A third issue is that people often have multiple needs. If a researcher finds that people need to reduce pollution, to eliminate gangs, and to improve transport services, which is most important? A good needs assessment identifies both the expressed and the less visible needs of a target group, as well as the more serious or widespread needs. A researcher must trace links among related needs to identify those of highest priority.

Another issue is that a needs assessment may generate political controversy or suggest solutions beyond local control. Powerful groups may not want some needs documented or publicized. The researcher who finds that a city has a lot of unreported crime may tarnish the image of a safe, well-run city promoted by the Chamber of Commerce and the city government. A needs assessment that documents racial discrimination may embarrass civic leaders who prefer to present themselves in public as unprejudiced. The needs of one group, such as people who bet too much at the race track, may be linked to the actions of another group that benefits by creating that need, such as the race track's owners and employees. Once a researcher documents needs and offers a resolution to them, he or she may be caught between opposing groups. What would the reaction be if a needs assessment concluded that the needs of factory workers for better conditions would be best met if they joined a union and went on strike? If it said that the needs of students would be best served by firing a school principal? Powerful groups may attempt to squash the continuation of a needs assessment or try to censor its results. If locally felt needs are caused by major international relations, decisions made in distant corporate headquarters, or changes in the global economy, a needs assessment may be only a timid "Band-Aid solution."

Social impact studies often include a *cost-benefit analysis*. Economists developed cost-benefit analysis, in which the researcher estimates the future costs and benefits of one or several proposed actions and gives them monetary values. In brief, it works like this: A researcher identifies all the consequences of a proposed action. Next, he or she assigns each consequence a monetary value. The consequences may include intangibles such as clean air, low crime rates, political freedom, scenic beauty, low stress levels, and even human life itself. Often, the researcher assigns a probability or likelihood to the occurrence of various consequences. Next, policymakers or others identify negative consequences (costs) and positive ones (benefits). Finally, costs are compared to benefits, and policymakers decide whether they balance.

Cost-benefit analysis appears to be a neutral, rational, and technical decision-making strategy, but it can be controversial. People do not necessarily agree on what are positive and negative consequences. For example, I may see widening a nearby road as a benefit because it will let me travel to work much more rapidly. But the homeowner who lives along the road may see the same action as a cost because it will remove some of his or her lot and he or she will then experience more noise, pollution, and congestion.

There are two ways to assign monetary values to costs and benefits. *Contingency evaluation* asks people how much something is worth to them. For example, I may want to estimate the cost of air pollution that has health consequences for the average person. I might ask people: How

much is it worth to you not to cough a lot and miss work two days a year due to asthma? If the average value assigned by people is $150 in a town of 20,000, then the contingency evaluation or subjective benefit of health would be $150 × 20,000 per year = $3 million. I might balance this against higher profits for a company or more jobs created by allowing the pollution. A problem with this estimation is that people rarely give accurate estimates and different people may assign very different values. To an impoverished person, coughing and missing work may be worth $500, but for a wealthy person, it may be $10,000. In this example, polluting companies would tend to move to towns with low-income people, worsening their living conditions.

Using the same example, *actual cost evaluation* estimates the actual medical and job loss costs. I would estimate the health impact and then add up medical bills and costs for employers to get replacement workers. For example, if medical treatment averages $100 per person and a replacement worker costs an extra $150, the cost of treating 10,000 people each year and hiring 5,000 replacement workers for two days would be $100 × 10,000 people = $100,000 plus $300 × 5,000 workers = $1,500,000, for a total of $1.6 million. This method ignores pain and suffering, inconvenience and indirect costs (e.g., a parent stays home with a sick child, a child is unable to play sports because of asthma). To balance the costs with benefits by this method, the polluting factory would need to earn an extra $1.6 million in profits.

A significant issue for cost-benefit analysis is the assumption that everything has a price (learning, health, love, happiness, human dignity, chastity) and that people assign similar valuations. It also raises serious moral and political concerns. Cost-benefit calculations usually favor upper-income people over low-income or poor people. This occurs because the relative value of a cost or benefit depends on one's wealth and income. Saving 15 minutes in a commute to work is assigned a greater value or benefit for high-income people than for the same 15-minute time savings for low-income people; 15 minutes of a high-income person's time is worth more. Likewise, cutting a road through an impoverished neighborhood has a lower cost, because of lower property values, than putting the road through an area of high-cost homes.

Cost-benefit analysis tends to conceal the moral-political aspect of questions. For instance, the balance between the human cost of "pulling the plug" on a life-support machine for a very ill person and the benefit of saving large expenses to keep the machines operating has both moral and economic aspects. The moral aspect stands out in decisions that involve a single identifiable person with whom the decision maker has an emotional attachment. Few of us solely look at this issue in terms of economic costs and benefits. The moral aspect can get lost in a decision that involves people who are not easily identified as individuals among a large group and for whom decision makers lack direct, personal contact. A moral aspect remains, even if the focus is on the economic costs and benefits.

The Time Dimension in Research

Another dimension of social research is the treatment of time. An awareness of the time dimension will help you read or conduct research because different research questions or issues incorporate time in different ways.

Some studies give you a snapshot of what is going on at a single, fixed-time point and allow you to analyze it in detail. Other studies provide a moving picture that lets you follow events, people, or social relations over periods of time. Quantitative research is divided into two groups: a single point in time (cross-sectional research) versus multiple time points (longitudinal research). Quantitative research looks at a large group of cases, people, or units and measures a limited number of features. A case study is more distinct. It usually involves qualitative methods and focuses on one or a few cases during a limited time period.

Cross-Sectional.   Most sociological research takes a snapshot approach to the social world. In *cross-sectional research*, researchers observe at one point in time. Cross-sectional research is usually the simplest and least costly alternative. Its disadvantage is that it cannot capture social processes or change. Cross-sectional research can be exploratory, descriptive, or explanatory but it is most consistent with a descriptive approach to research. An example of cross-sectional research is the descriptive study by McCabe (1992) on cheating by college students.

Longitudinal Research.   Researchers using *longitudinal research* examine features of people or other units at more than one time. It is usually more complex and costly than cross-sectional research but it is also more powerful, especially when researchers seek answers to questions about social change. Descriptive and explanatory researchers use longitudinal approaches. We will now consider three types of longitudinal research: time series, panel, and cohort.

Time-series research is a longitudinal study in which the same type of information is collected on a group of people or other units across multiple time periods. Researchers can observe stability or change in the features of the units or can track conditions over time. The study by Hastings and Hodge (1986) in Chapter 1 was a form of time-series research. Tom Marvell and Carlisle Moody's (1995) also used time series in their study on the impact of enhanced prison terms for felonies committed with guns. Their study is also a type of evaluation research, although few legislators base their actions on research, so the findings may not affect future laws or policy. The researchers examined the impact on firearm sentence-enhancement laws in the United States. The laws impose extra prison time or a minimum prison term for felonies committed with a gun. Such laws have been enacted in 49 states in the past 25 years. For 44 states that had strong sentence-enhancement laws, Marvell and Moody examined data on various features (e.g., prison population, crime rates, prison admissions, whether guns were used in specific crimes) for the years 1971 to 1993. They concluded, "We found little evidence to support the intended purposes of firearm sentencing enhancement, reducing crime rates and gun use" (1995:269).

The *panel study* is a powerful type of longitudinal research. It is more difficult to conduct than time-series research. In a panel study, the researcher observes exactly the same people, group, or organization across time periods. Panel research is formidable to conduct and very costly. Tracking people over time is often difficult because some people die or cannot be located. Nevertheless, the results of a well-designed panel study are very valuable. Even short-term panel studies can clearly show the impact of a particular life event. For example, Debra Umberson and Meichu Chen (1994) studied 2,867 people who were interviewed twice, in 1986 and 1989. During the intervening three years, 207 experienced the death of a biological parent. Umberson and Chen found that this life event contributed to more psychological distress, increased alcohol consumption, and decreased physical health.

Another panel study by Daniel Nagin, David Farrington and Terrie Moffitt (1995) looked at the impact of deviance in youth on long-term criminal activity and problems in adulthood. They examined data on 411 males from a working-class section of London who were first studied when they were about 8 years old, in 1961–62. The same men were followed until they were 32 years old, except for 8 who died. The men were interviewed at two-year intervals. Data were collected throughout the years on many personality, background, and deviant behavior measures. The men's families, teachers, and friends were also interviewed. The researchers classified the men into four groups based on self-reported delinquency, ranging from nondelinquent to high-level chronic. The main finding was that those who were deviant only in adolescence appeared to be very similar to nonoffenders by the age of 32, except they were more likely to drink alcohol to excess and use illegal drugs.

A *cohort analysis* is similar to the panel study, but rather than observing the exact same people, a category of people who share a similar life experience in a specified time period is studied. Cohort analysis is "explicitly macroanalytic,"

which means researchers examine the category as a whole for important features (Ryder, 1992:230). The focus is on the cohort, or category, not on specific-individuals. Commonly used cohorts include all people born in the same year (called *birth cohorts*), all people hired at the same time, all people who retire in a one- or two-year time frame, and all people who graduate in a given year. Unlike panel studies, researchers do not have to locate the exact same people for cohort studies. They only need to identify those who experienced a common life event. For example, my wife and I both graduated from high school in 1968 and came of age in the late 1960s. We belong to a late-1960s cohort who shared many life experiences at a stage in the life cycle. Howard Schuman and Cheryl Rieger (1992) examined cohort effects in a study of Americans' attitudes toward the 1991 Persian Gulf War. They found that people who grew up in the time of the World War II era saw Saddam Hussein as being like Hitler and Iraq as being like Germany in the 1930s. People who grew up in the 1960s, however, were more likely to see the situation as similar to the Vietnam War.

Case Studies.   In cross-sectional and longitudinal research, a researcher examines features on many people or units, either at one time period or across time periods. In both, a researcher precisely measures a common set of features on many cases, usually expressed in numbers. In *case-study research*, he or she examines very many features of a very few cases in-depth over a duration of time. Cases can be individuals, groups, organizations, movements, events, or geographic units. The data are usually more detailed, varied, and extensive. Most involve qualitative data about a few cases. Qualitative and case-study research are not identical, but "almost all qualitative research seeks to construct representations based on in-depth, detailed knowledge of cases" (Ragin, 1994:92).[8]

In a case study, a researcher may intensively investigate one or two cases or compare a limited set of cases, focusing on a several factors. Case study uses the logic of analytic instead of enumerative induction. In it, the researcher carefully selects one or a few key cases to illustrate an issue and study it (or them) in detail analytically. He or she considers the specific context of the case and examines how its parts are configured. This contrasts with longitudinal studies in which the researcher collects data on many units or cases then looks for patterns in the mass of numbers. The researcher looks more for averages or patterns across many units or cases.[9]

Case studies help researchers connect the micro level, or the actions of individual people, to the macro level, or large-scale social structures and processes (Vaughan, 1992). "The logic of the case study is to demonstrate a causal argument about how general social forces shape and produce results in particular settings" (Walton 1992b: 122). Case-study research raises questions about the boundaries and defining characteristics of a case. Such questions help in the generation of new thinking and theory. "Case studies are likely to produce the best theory" (Walton, 1992b: 129).

Researchers gather case-study data for a period of time. Data may be collected over months, years, or across many decades. Sutton's (1991) study of asylums in Chapter 1 is a case study that combined time-series research with qualitative data to study the case of asylum growth. John Walton's (1992a) *Western Times and Water Wars* is a case study of one community, Owens Valley, California. Walton stated, "I have tried . . . to tell a big story through the lens of a small case" (xviii). The community engaged in social protest as it attempted to control its key resource (water) and destiny. The protest took different forms, on and off, for over 100 years. Walton used diverse forms of data, including direct observation, formal and informal interviews, census statistics, maps, old photos and newspapers, various historical documents, and official records.

A case study with a more narrow scope is Christopher Smith's (1995) study of Asian immigration into Flushing, New York, during the 1980s. The Asian population living in Flushing (a community in the borough of Queens of New York City) grew from 2,571 (5.6 percent of the total) in 1970 to 19,508 (35.8 percent) in 1990. Smith examined the causes of this change and described the process and its consequences. His data included census and official statistical records, maps, historical accounts, and field work.

A last example case study is Randy Stoeker's (1993) study of a neighborhood movement in Minneapolis. He used participant observation, including participatory action research, which he supplemented with interviews, oral history, city documents, and written histories. In his conclusion, Stoeker warns, "As with any case study, while we can accurately specify the causal process within the case, generalizing is more difficult" (1993:181).

DATA COLLECTION TECHNIQUES USED

Every researcher collects data using one or more techniques. This section is a brief overview of the main techniques. In later chapters, you will read about these techniques in detail and learn how to use them. The techniques may be grouped into two categories: *quantitative*, collecting data in the form of numbers, and *qualitative*, collecting data in the form of words or pictures. Some techniques are more effective when addressing specific kinds of questions or topics. It takes skill, practice, and creativity to match a research question to an appropriate data collection technique.

Quantitative Data

Experiments. *Experimental research* uses the logic and principles found in natural science research. Experiments can be conducted in laboratories or in real life. They usually involve a relatively small number of people and address a well-focused question. Experiments are most effective for explanatory research. They are often limited to topics for which a researcher can manipulate the situation in which people find themselves.

In most experiments, the researcher divides the people being studied into two or more groups. He or she then treats both groups identically, except that one group but not the other is given a condition he or she is interested in: the "treatment." The researcher measures the reactions of both groups precisely. By controlling the setting for both groups and giving only one the treatment, the researcher can conclude that any differences in the reactions of the groups are due to the treatment alone.

Robert Bohm (1990) conducted an experiment to learn whether making a public commitment to an opinion prevents attitude change. In a previous experiment, he gave one group of students extensive information about the death penalty issue and gave none to another group. He measured support for the death penalty with a questionnaire that students completed in private. Both groups initially showed strong support for the death penalty. After several months, however, the group receiving extensive information on the death penalty greatly lowered their support for it. The other group did not change. In a second experiment, Bohm again divided students into two groups. Subjects in the experimental group enrolled in a special class on the death penalty, whereas the control group students enrolled in other courses. This time, he measured death penalty opinions by having students publicly state their opinions in each class session. In contrast to the large opinion change in the experimental group that he found in the earlier experiment, Bohm found no change during the semester and no difference between the experimental and control groups. He concluded that making their opinion public inhibits people from changing it, even when they are confronted with overwhelming factual information in support of making a change.

Surveys.   A survey researcher asks people questions in a written questionnaire (mailed or handed to people) or during an interview, then records answers. The researcher manipulates no situation or condition; people simply answer questions. In *survey research*, the researcher ask many people numerous questions in a short time period. He or she typically summarizes answers to questions in percentages, tables, or graphs. Surveys give the researcher a picture of what many people think or report doing. A survey researcher often uses a sample, or a smaller group of selected people (e.g., 150 students), but generalizes results to a larger group (e.g., 5,000 students) from which the smaller group was chosen. Survey techniques are often used in descriptive or explanatory research.

Dana Britton (1990) used survey research to study homophobia, the irrational condemnation of homosexuals. Previous research found that males, less well educated people, and socially and religiously conservative people are more likely to be homophobic. Britton thought that people who support traditional gender roles, are more religious, and show a preference for the company of the same sex would be more homophobic. For example, fear of homosexuality would be stronger in all-male settings than in mixed-sex settings. He randomly selected 322 adults in a southwestern U.S. city and interviewed them with six questions about homophobia. Other questionnaire items asked about sex-appropriate behavior for males and females, religiosity, a preference for members of one's own gender, and a preference for the maintenance of single-sex institutions. For example, did a person agree with the statement, "In general, I feel most comfortable with members of my own sex?" Britton found the strongest homophobia among supporters of traditional gender roles, the more religious, and those preferring same-sex relations.

Content Analysis.   *Content analysis* is a technique for examining information, or content, in written or symbolic material (e.g., pictures, movies, song lyrics). In content analysis, a researcher first identifies a body of material to analyze (e.g., books, newspapers, films) and then creates a system for recording specific aspects of it. The system might include counting how often certain words or themes occur. Finally, the researcher records what was found in the material. He or she often measures information in the content as numbers and presents it as tables or graphs. This technique lets a researcher discover features in the content of large amounts of material that might otherwise go unnoticed. Content analysis is used for exploratory and explanatory research but is most often used in descriptive research.

Lynn Lovdal (1989) used content analysis to find out whether television commercials reinforce traditional sex-role stereotypes. Previous research had demonstrated that this was the case in the 1970s. Her research question was whether this had changed after a decade of publicity about changing sex roles. Lovdal video-recorded all television commercials on two major U.S. television networks between 8:00 P.M. and 10:00 P.M. during a two-week period in 1988. Next, she created a coding system to classify the product and the sex of the product representative, the setting as either home or other, and the sex of voice-overs. She classified products as either domestic (e.g., shampoo, food, make-up, or cleaning products) or nondomestic (e.g., cars, cameras, travel). She and another coder coded 353 commercials.

Lovdal learned that 91 percent used voice-overs, with 90 percent of the voices being male. When a woman's voice was used, she usually spoke to a cat, dog, or baby. Compared to research during the 1970s, voice-overs had increased from 69 percent, but the proportion of male voices remained the same. In a home setting, 64 percent showed a woman as product representative, down from 78 percent in the 1970s. Lovdal found comparable percentages for men in out-of-home settings. Men were product representatives for most nondomestic products and women for most domestic products. Lovdal concluded that commercials had changed relatively little. She noted that past research had found that children who watched more television developed more sexist attitudes than those who watched little. Past research also showed that women who watched commercials portraying sex-role stereotypes tended to deemphasize personal achievement.

Existing Statistics.   In *existing statistics research*, a researcher locates a source of previously collected information, often in the form of government reports or previously conducted surveys. He or she then reorganizes or combines the information in new ways to address a research question. Locating sources can be time consuming, so the researcher needs to consider carefully the meaning of what he or she finds. Frequently, a researcher does not know whether the information of interest is available when he or she begins a study. Sometimes, the existing quantitative information consists of stored survey or other data that a researcher reexamines using various statistical procedures. This is called *secondary analysis research*. Existing statistics research can be used for exploratory, descriptive, or explanatory purposes but is most frequently used for descriptive research.

Steven Stack (1990) used existing statistics to study the effect of divorce on suicide in Denmark between 1951 and 1980. He noted that most research on suicide was based on data from the United States, where a link was found between marital dissolution and suicide. Because unemployment was also linked to suicide, he considered it at the same time. Stack noted that Denmark differs from the United States in many ways. It has a smaller, more homogeneous population, a lower divorce rate, and a more extensive system of social welfare services. Stack's data came from the United Nations World Health Organization, the United Nations *Statistical Yearbook*, and the *Yearbook of International Labor Statistics* by the International Labor Office. After analysis, he found evidence that the pattern seen in the United States—that additional suicides result from divorce—also occurs in Denmark.

Qualitative Data

Field Research.   Most field researchers conduct case studies on a small group of people for some length of time. *Field research* begins with a loosely formulated idea or topic. Next, researchers select a social group or site for study. Once they gain access to the group or site, they adopt a social role in the setting and begin observing. The researchers observe and interact in the field setting for a period from a few months to several years. They get to know personally the people being studied and may conduct informal interviews. They take detailed notes on a daily basis. During the observation, they consider what they observe and refine or focus ideas about its significance. Finally, they leave the field site.

They reread their notes and prepare written reports. Field research is usually used for exploratory and descriptive studies; it is rarely used for explanatory research.

Janet Fitchen used field research in *Endangered Spaces, Enduring Places* (1991). She was interested in understanding the U.S. farm crisis of the 1980s. Her study was based on several rural counties in upstate New York and on 400 interviews or periods of observation that occurred between 1985 and 1990. On many days, she left home at 6:00 A.M. and spent the next 16 hours driving to or visiting people in the rural communities. Her interviews and observations took place at village cafés, feed mills, elementary schools, cow barns, town meetings, parades, social service agencies, county fairs, farm homes, and workshops for local teachers. In addition to reading research reports on the farm crisis and changes in agriculture, Fitcher read the local newspapers, statistical profiles, reports of local agencies, records of local governments, and brochures put out by local groups. She interviewed local editors and reporters, farmers, public officials, teachers, storekeepers, veterinarians, retired people, and others. She interviewed some of them several times during the five-year study. She interviewed some alone and others in small groups in many settings—over kitchen tables, on the street, in barns, in fields, in offices. Fitchen scheduled some of the interviews, but others began by chance when she stopped to ask directions or was stuck in a small café on a rainy afternoon. The interviews were informal, tailored to the interviewee, and open ended (i.e., without a fixed set of questions or answer categories). She did not use a tape recorder but took extensive field notes during or immediately after her field visits. Fitchen discussed many themes—how rural people see themselves, rural poverty, the impact of large corporations locating plants in small towns, local results of social service cuts, and so forth. The book is peppered with lengthy quotes from Fitchen's field notes that show her complete immersion and personal involvement in the research. She reported (p. 285),

> *conducting this research has been exciting and fun, and I have genuinely enjoyed listening and probing. Many of my informants have enjoyed the interaction as well: Many commented that they were pleased to have the opportunity to tell their side of the story.*

Historical-Comparative Research. *Historical-comparative research* examines aspects of social life in a past historical era or across different cultures. The study on asylums by John Sutton, described in Chapter 1, is an example of this type of research. Researchers who use this technique may focus on one historical period or several, compare one or more cultures, or mix historical periods and cultures. This kind of research combines theory with data collection. As with field research, a researcher begins with a loosely formulated question. He refines and elaborates it during the research process. Researchers often use a mix of evidence including existing statistics,

TABLE 2.2 Dimensions of Social Research

PURPOSE FOR STUDY	USE OF STUDY	TIME IN STUDY	DATA COLLECTION TECHNIQUE
Exploratory	Basic	Cross-sectional	Quantitative data:
Descriptive	Applied:	Longitudinal:	▬ Experiment
Explanatory	▬ Action	▬ Panel	▬ Survey
	▬ Impact	▬ Time series	▬ Content analysis
	▬ Evaluation	▬ Cohort analysis	▬ Existing statistics
		Case study	Qualitative data:
			▬ Field research
			▬ Comparative historical

documents (books, newspapers, diaries, photographs, and maps), observations, and interviews. Historical-comparative research an be exploratory, descriptive, or explanatory and can blend types, but it is usually descriptive.

Gordon Laxer's (1989) *Open for Business: The Roots of Foreign Ownership in Canada* uses historical-comparative research. Laxer asked why most business in Canada, the world's eighth largest manufacturing country, is under foreign control. He compared the Canadian experience since the late nineteenth century to that of the United States and European nations. Laxer studied numerous historical accounts of industrialization in several major countries. He concluded that foreign ownership in Canada is due to internal divisions that weakened a coherent national culture, failure to restrict foreign investment, slow development of markets, and a rigid system of banking. This combination of factors encouraged a reliance on large-scale foreign investment during critical periods of industrialization.

CONCLUSION

This chapter gave you an overview of the dimensions of social research. You saw that research can be classified in a number of different ways (e.g., by its purpose, by its research technique, etc.) and that the dimensions of research loosely overlap with each other (see Table 2.2). The dimensions of research provide a "road map" through the terrain that is social research.

In the next chapter, we turn to social theory. You read about theory in Chapter 1 and it was mentioned again in this chapter. In Chapter 3, you will learn how theory and research methods work together and about several types of theory.

KEY TERMS

action-oriented research
applied research
basic research
case-study research
cohort analysis
content analysis
cost-benefit analysis
cross-sectional research
descriptive research
evaluation research

existing statistics research
experimental research
explanatory research
exploratory research
field research
formative evaluation research
historical-comparative research
longitudinal research
needs assessment
panel study

Planning, Programming, and
     Budgeting System
secondary analysis research
serendipity
social impact assessment
summative evaluation research
survey research
time-series research

REVIEW QUESTIONS

1. When is exploratory research used, and what can it accomplish?
2. What types of results are produced by a descriptive research study?
3. What is explanatory research? What is its primary purpose?
4. What are the major differences between basic and applied research?
5. Who is likely to conduct basic research, and where are results likely to appear?
6. Explain the differences among the three types of applied research.
7. How do time-series, panel, and cohort studies differ?
8. What are some potential problems with cost-benefit analysis?

9. What is a needs assessment? What complications can occur when conducting one?

10. Explain the difference between qualitative and quantitative research.

NOTES

1. Explanatory, exploratory, and descriptive research are also discussed in Babbie (1995:84–86), Bailey (1987:38–39), and Churchill (1983:56–77).

2. See Guy, Edgley, Arafat, and Allan (1987:54–55) for discussion.

3. Finsterbusch and Motz (1980), Freeman (1983), Lazarsfeld and Reitz (1975), Olsen and Micklin (1981), and Rubin (1983) discuss applied research. Also see Whyte's (1986) critique of social research that is not applied and instances in which social research affects public issues. McGrath, Martin, and Kulka (1982) discuss judgment calls that are relevant in applied research.

4. See Cancian and Armstead (1992), Reason (1994), and Whyte (1989).

5. Social impact research is discussed in Chadwick, Bahr, and Albrecht (1984:313–342), Finsterbusch and Motz (1980:75–118), and Finsterbush and Wolf (1981). Also see Rossi, Wright, and Weber-Burdin (1982) and Wright and Rossi (1981) on "natural hazards" and social science.

6. For a brief introduction to evaluation research, see Adams and Schvaneveldt (1985:315–328), Finsterbusch and Motz (1980:119–158), and Smith and Glass (1987). A more complete discussion can be found in Burnstein, Freeman, and Rossi (1985) Freeman (1992), and Rossi (1982), Rossi and Freeman (1985), Saxe and Fine (1981), and Weiss (1972).

7. PPBS and related evaluation research are discussed in Smith and Glass (1987:41–49).

8. For discussions of case-study research, see Miller (1992), Mitchell (1984), Ragin (1992a, 1992b), Stake (1994), Vaughan (1992), Walton (1992b), and Yin (1988).

9. See Mitchell (1984) and Stake (1994).

RECOMMENDED READINGS

Burnstein, Leigh, Howard E. Freeman, and Peter H. Rossi, eds. (1985). *Collecting evaluation data: Problems and solutions*. Beverly Hills, CA: Sage. This collection of 13 essays covers program evaluation in the areas of health, crime, education, and employment and training. The essays underscore the types of conditions and constraints faced by evaluation researchers. Difficulties in conducting experiments in field settings, in training nonresearchers, and in using administrative records are discussed. In addition to identifying data collection problems, the authors suggest possible solutions.

Finsterbusch, Kurt, and Annabelle Bender Motz. (1980). *Social research for policy decisions*. Belmont, CA: Wadsworth. Finsterbusch and Motz introduce applied social research. They discuss the role of applied research for policymaking within a societal context and provide separate chapters on social impact assessment and evaluation research.

Hakim, Catherine. (1987). *Research design: Strategies and choices in the design of social research*. Boston: Allen and Unwin. Hakim provides an overview of various research techniques. She discusses strategies and trade-offs to consider in selecting one technique over the other, as well as applied and basic research.

House, Ernest R. (1980). *Evaluating with validity*. Beverly Hills, CA: Sage. House gives an overview of the different types of evaluation research and discusses some strengths and weaknesses of each. He also describes principles to use in judging the quality of evaluation research. There is a discussion of moral principles involved in conducting evaluation research and a critique of some types of evaluation studies.

Yin, Robert K. (1988). *Case study research*, rev. ed. Beverly Hills, CA: Sage. This is a useful introduction to the case-study method. Yin describes the strengths of the method and important strategies for using it.

CHAPTER 3

THEORY AND RESEARCH

> *One of the major functions of theory is to order experience with the help of concepts. It also selects relevant aspects and data among the enormous multitude of "facts" that confront the investigator of social phenomena.*
> —Lewis Coser, "The Uses of Classical Sociological Theory," p. 170

INTRODUCTION

Suppose you want to make sense of the hostility between people of different races. Trying to understand it, you ask a teacher, who responds:

> *Most racially prejudiced people learn negative stereotypes about another racial group from their families, friends, and others in their immediate surroundings. If they lack sufficient intimate social contact with members of the group or intense information that contradicts those stereotypes, they remain prejudiced.*

This makes sense to you because it is consistent with what you know about how the social world works. This is an example of a small-scale social theory, a type that researchers use when conducting a study.

What do you think of when you hear the word *theory*? Theory is one of the least well understood terms for students learning social science. My students' eyelids droop if I begin a class by saying, "Today we are going to examine the theory of . . ." The mental picture many students have of theory is something that floats high among the clouds. My students have called it "a tangled maze of jargon" and "abstractions that are irrelevant to the real world." The beginning of one textbook on social theory (Craib, 1984:3) echoes this perspective:

> *The very word "theory" sometimes seems to scare people, and not without good reason. Much modern social theory is either unintelligible, or banal, or pointless. . . . Few people feel at home with theory or use it in a productive way.*

Contrary to these views, theory plays an important role in research and is an essential ally for the researcher. Researchers use theory differently in various types of research, but some type of theory is present in most social research. It is less evident in applied or descriptive than in basic or explanatory research. In simple terms, researchers interweave a story about the operation of the social world (the theory) with what they observe when they examine it systematically (the data).

WHAT IS THEORY?

In Chapter 1, I defined *social theory* as a system of interconnected abstractions or ideas that condenses and organizes knowledge about the social world. It is a compact way to think of the social world. People are always creating new theories about how the world works. Theory encounters data in research.

Many people confuse the history of social thought, or what great thinkers said, with social theory. The classical social theorists (e.g., Durkheim, Weber, Marx, Tonnies) played an important role in generating innovative ideas. They developed original theories that laid the foundation for subsequent generations of social thinkers. People study the classical theorists because they provided many creative and interrelated ideas at once. They radically changed the way people understood and saw the social world. We still study them because it is rare to have such geniuses who generated many original, insightful ideas and fundamentally shifted how people saw the social world.

People often use theories without making them explicit or labeling them as such. For example, newspaper articles or television reports on social issues usually have unstated social theories embedded within them. A news report on the difficulty of implementing a school desegregation plan will contain an implicit theory about race relations. Likewise, political leaders frequently express social theories when they discuss public issues. Politicians who claim that inadequate education causes poverty or that a decline in traditional moral values causes higher crime rates are expressing theories. Compared to the theories of social scientists, such laypersons' theories tend to be less systematic, less well formulated, and harder to test with empirical evidence.

Social science theory seems complicated compared to laypersons' theories. Luckily, a principle of good theory called *parsimony* helps. Parsimony means simpler is better. A parsimonious theory has minimal complexity, with no redundant or excess elements. Parsimony says a more powerful theory does more with less, and the less complex of two equally convincing theories is better.

Almost all research involves some theory, so the question is less *whether* you should use theory than *how* you should use it. Being explicit about the theory makes it easier to read someone else's research or to conduct your own. An awareness of how theory fits into the research process helps to clarify murky issues. Better designed, easier to understand, and better conducted studies result. Most researchers disparage atheoretical or "crude empiricist" research.

Theories come in many shapes and sizes. In this chapter, I provide an elementary introduction to social theory. You will encounter theory in later chapters as well.

SOCIAL THEORY VERSUS IDEOLOGY

Many people find the relationship between a social scientific theory and a social-political ideology controversial and confusing. Few people outside the scientific community examine social scientific theories, but most people encounter diverse ideologies in the mass media or from the champions of particular points of view. Controversy arises because the scientific community recognizes theory as essential for clarifying and building scientific knowledge, while it condemns ideology as illegitimate obfuscation that is antithetical to science. Confusion also arises because each has multiple definitions, both explain similar events in the world, and they can overlap in places.

There are similarities between theory and ideology (see Box 3.1). Both theory and ideology explain many events in the world: why crime occurs, why some people are poor, why divorce rates are high in some places, and so on. Social scientific theory and an ideology both contain assumptions about the nature of the social world. They both focus on what is or is not important in it, contain a system of ideas or concepts, and specify relations among the concepts. Both provide explanations of why things are the way they are and what needs to be changed to alter conditions.

An *ideology* is a type of theory or explanation of events in the social world. It is a quasi-theory that lacks critical features required of a scientific theory. Many ideologies look a lot like legitimate scientific theories. One feature of ideologies is that they have fixed, strong, and unquestioned assumptions. They are full of unquestioned absolutes and normative categories (what is right/wrong, moral/immoral, good/bad). The assumptions may be founded on faith or rooted in particular social circumstances. Many ideologies

advance or protect the interests of a particular group or sector of society.

Ideologies are closed belief and value systems that change very little. They are closed to contradictory evidence and use circular reasoning. Ideologies are logically "slippery" and prevent falsification. This makes them immune to significant change. Their capacity to develop or change is extremely limited, because they already have all the answers. In ideology, lines between assertions about what *is* the case (ideals or values) and beliefs about what *should be* the case blur together.

Ideologies selectively present and interpret empirical evidence. They often use techniques of personal experience or conviction (e.g., overgeneralization, selective observation, premature closure) that fall short of a scientific approach. It is difficult to test ideological principles or confront them with opposing evidence. In a way, ideology is "blind"; it cannot acknowledge contradictory evidence. Even if overwhelming evidence is amassed, the ideology will not bend or change. A true, hard-core believer in an ideology will reject

---

Box 3.1 _____

Social Theory and Ideology

SIMILARITIES

- Contains a set of assumptions or a starting point
- Explains what the social world is like, how/why it changes
- Offers a system of concepts/ideas
- Specifies relationships among concepts, tells what causes what
- Provides an interconnected system of ideas

DIFFERENCES

Ideology	**Social Theory**
- Offers absolute certainty	- Conditional, negotiated understandings
- Has all the answers	- Incomplete, recognizes uncertainty
- Fixed, closed, finished	- Growing, open, unfolding, expanding
- Avoids tests, discrepant findings	- Welcomes tests, positive and negative evidence
- Blind to opposing evidence	- Changes based on evidence
- Locked into specific moral beliefs	- Detached, disconnected, strong moral stand
- Highly partial	- Neutral considers all sides
- Has contradictions, inconsistencies	- Strongly seeks logical consistency, congruity
- Rooted in specific position	- Transcends/crosses social positions

or refuse to recognize evidence. He or she will refuse to abandon core value premises and rigidly adhere to principles. It is a "don't confuse me with facts, I know I'm right" attitude. Supporters often react with fear and hostility to those who disagree or present carefully gathered contradictory information.

The distinction between ideology and theory has implications for how a person conducts research. A researcher can never test and show an ideology to be true or false. By contrast, a researcher can test a scientific theory or parts of it and show them to be false. Social scientific theories alone are empirically testable, and they are constantly evolving. Researchers try to directly confront a theory with evidence. They look at all relevant evidence, both that supporting and that opposing a theory, in a disinterested way. They do not know for sure whether the evidence will support a theory. If the evidence repeatedly fails to support a theory, it is changed or replaced.

Theories are logically consistent. If a contradiction occurs, researchers try to resolve it. Theories are also open ended, always growing or developing to higher levels. If theories fail to develop, they often get replaced by competing theories. Rarely do theories claim to have all the answers. Instead, they often contain areas of uncertainty or incomplete knowledge and only offer partial or tentative answers. Researchers constantly test theories and are skeptical toward them. The theory itself is often disinterested or detached from the position of any specific social group or sector of society. Most theories stand apart from specific social relationships. This makes them perplexing to people who are only self-interested or who operate from a particular social position.

THE PARTS OF THEORY

Concepts

Concepts are the building blocks of theory.[1] A *concept* is an idea expressed as a symbol or in words. Natural science concepts are often expressed in symbolic forms, such as Greek let-

ters (e.g., π) or formulas (e.g., $s = d/t$; $s =$ speed, $d =$ distance, $t =$ time). Most social science concepts are expressed as words. The exotic symbols of natural science theory make many people nervous, but the use of everyday words in specialized ways in social science theory can also create confusion.

I do not want to exaggerate the distinction between concepts expressed as words and concepts expressed as symbols. Words, after all, are symbols too; they are symbols we learn with language. Height is an example of a concept with which you are already familiar. For example, I can say the word *height* or write it down; the spoken sounds and written words are part of the English language. The combination of letters in the sound symbolizes, or stands for, the idea of a *height*. Chinese or Arabic characters, the French word *hauteur*, the German word *Höhe*, the Spanish word *altura*—all symbolize the same idea. In a sense, a language is merely an agreement to represent ideas by sounds or written characters that people learned at some point in their lives. Learning concepts and theory is like learning a language.[2]

Concepts are everywhere, and you use them all the time. Height is a simple concept from everyday experience. What does it mean? It is easy to use the concept of *height*, but describing the concept itself is difficult. It represents an abstract idea about physical relations. How would you describe it to a very young child or a creature from a distant planet who was totally unfamiliar with it? A new concept from a social theory may seem just as alien to you when you encounter it for the first time. Height is a characteristic of a physical object, the distance from top to bottom. All people, buildings, trees, mountains, books, and so forth have a height. We can measure height or compare it. A height of zero is possible, and height can increase or decrease over time. As with many words, we use the word in several ways. You may have heard such expressions as the height of the battle, the storm, the summer, auto sales, or fashion.

The word *height* refers to an abstract idea. We associate its sounds and its written form with that idea. There is nothing inherent in the sounds that make up the word and the idea it represents. The connection is arbitrary, but it is still useful. People can express the abstract idea to one another using the symbol alone.

Concepts have two parts: a *symbol* (word or term) and a *definition.* We learn definitions in many ways. I learned the word *height* and its definition from my parents. I learned it as I learned to speak and was socialized to the culture. My parents never gave me a dictionary definition. I learned it through a diffuse, nonverbal, informal process. My parents showed me many examples; I observed and listened to others use the word; I used the word incorrectly and was corrected; and I used it correctly and was understood. Eventually I mastered the concept.

This example shows how people learn concepts in everyday language and how we share concepts. Suppose my parents had isolated me from television and other people, then taught me that the word for the idea *height* was *zdged.* I would have had difficulty communicating with others. People must share the terms for concepts and their definitions if they are to be of value.

Everyday culture is filled with concepts, but many of them have vague and unclear definitions. Likewise, the values and experiences of people in a culture may limit everyday concepts. Everyday concepts are often rooted in misconceptions or myth. Social scientists borrow some concepts from everyday culture, but they refine these concepts and add new ones. Many concepts social scientists first developed have diffused into the larger culture and become less precise. Concepts such as sexism, life-style, peer group, urban sprawl, and social class began as precise, technical concepts in social theory.

We create concepts from personal experience, creative thought, or observation. The classical theorists originated many concepts. Researchers created some by subdividing or combining other concepts. The example studies in Chapters 1 and 2 contained social science concepts. Other example concepts include family system, gender role, socialization, self-worth, frustration, and displaced aggression.

Social science concepts form a specialized language, or *jargon.* Specialists use jargon as a shorthand way to communicate with one another. Most fields have their own jargon. Physicians, lawyers, engineers, accountants, plumbers, and auto mechanics all have specialized languages. They use their jargon to refer to the ideas and objects with which they work. I read a book with the terms used by publishers and printers in order to understand their jargon—terms such as *idiot tape, fonts, cropping, halftone, galley proof, kiss impression, hickeys, widows*, and *kerning.* For people on the inside, jargon is a speedy, effective, and efficient way to communicate. But jargon also has negative connotations. Some people misuse it to confuse, exclude, or denigrate others. Using jargon among nonspecialists fails to communicate; it is like speaking English to people who know only Korean.

Some concepts, especially simple, concrete concepts such as *book* or *height*, can be defined through a simple nonverbal process. Most social science concepts are more complex and abstract. They are defined by formal, dictionary-type definitions that build on other concepts. It may seem odd to use concepts to define other concepts, but we do this all the time. For example, I defined *height* as a distance between top and bottom. *Top, bottom*, and *distance* are all concepts. We often combine simple, concrete concepts from ordinary experience to create more abstract concepts. *Height* is more abstract than *top* or *bottom.* The more abstract concepts refer to aspects of the world we do not directly experience. They organize our thinking and extend our understanding of reality.

Concepts vary in their *level of abstraction.* They are on a continuum from most concrete to most abstract. Very concrete ones refer to straightforward physical objects or familiar experiences (e.g., *height, school, age, family income, housing*). More abstract concepts refer to ideas that have a diffuse, indirect expression (e.g., *family dissolution, racism, social control, political power, deviance, intelligence*, or *cognitive dissonance*). Social researchers created many of these in theory as a way of better grasping the social world.

Researchers define scientific concepts more precisely than those we use in daily discourse. Social theory requires well-defined concepts. The definition of a concept helps to link theory with research. A valuable goal of exploratory research, and of most good research, is to clarify and refine concepts. Weak, contradictory, or unclear definitions of concepts restrict the advance of knowledge. After noting that there are many definitions of a *gang* with little consensus, Ball and Curry (1995:239) argued that

> few if any gang researchers and theorists have been sufficiently conscious of their own definition strategies, with the result that their definitions carry too many latent connotations, treated correlations or consequences as properties or causes, or contributed to similar errors of logic.

Concept Clusters. We rarely use concepts in isolation. Rather, they form interconnected groups, or *concept clusters*. This is true for concepts in everyday language as well as for those in social theory. Theories contain collections of associated concepts that are consistent and mutually reinforcing. Together, they form a web of meaning. For example, if I want to discuss a concept such as *urban decay*, I will need a set of associated concepts (e.g., *urban expansion, economic growth, urbanization, suburbs, center city, revitalization, mass transit, racial minorities*).

Some concepts take on a range of values, quantities, or amounts. Examples of this kind of concept are *amount of income, temperature, density of population, years of schooling,* and *degree of violence*. We call them *variables,* and you will read about them in Chapter 6. Other concepts express types of nonvariable phenomena (e.g., *bureaucracy, family, revolution, homeless,* and *cold*). Theories use both kinds of concepts.

Assumptions. Concepts contain built-in *assumptions*, statements about the nature of things that are not observable or testable. We accept them as a necessary starting point. Concepts and theories build on assumptions about the nature of human beings, social reality, or a particular phenomenon. Assumptions often remain hidden or unstated. One way for a researcher to deepen his or her understanding of a concept is to identify the assumptions on which it is based.

For example, the concept *book* assumes a system of writing, people who can read, and the existence of paper. Without such assumptions, the idea of a *book* makes little sense. A social science concept, such as *racial prejudice*, rests on several assumptions. These include people who make distinctions among individuals based on their racial heritage, attach specific motivations and characteristics to membership in a racial group, and make judgments about the goodness of specific motivations and characteristics. If race became irrelevant, people would cease to distinguish among individuals on the basis of race, to attach specific characteristics to a racial group, and to make judgments about characteristics. If that occurred, the concept of *racial prejudice* would cease to be useful for research. Almost all concepts contain assumptions about social relations or how people behave.

Classifications. Some concepts are simple; they have only one dimension and vary along a single continuum. Others are complex; they have multiple dimensions or many subparts. You can break complex concepts into a set of simple, or single-dimension, concepts. For example, Rueschemeyer, Stephens, and Stephens (1992: 43–44) stated that democracy has three dimensions. *Democracy* means (1) regular, free elections with universal suffrage; (2) an elected legislative body that controls government; and (3) freedom of expression and association. The authors recognized that each dimension varies by degree. They classified the dimensions to create a set of types of regimes. Regimes very low on all three dimensions are totalitarian, those high on all three are democracies, and ones with other mixes are either authoritarian or liberal oligarchies.

Classifications are important in many theories. They are partway between a single, simple concept and a theory.[3] They help to organize abstract, complex concepts. To create a new classification, a researcher logically specifies and combines the characteristics of simpler concepts. You can best grasp this idea by looking at some examples.

The *ideal type* is a well-known classification. Ideal types are pure, abstract models that define the essence of the phenomenon in question. They are mental pictures that define the central aspects of a concept. Ideal types are not explanations because they do not tell why or how something occurs. They are smaller than theories, and researchers use them to build a theory. They are broader, more abstract concepts that bring together several narrower, more concrete concepts. Qualitative researchers often use ideal types to see how well observable phenomena match up to the ideal model. For example, Max Weber developed an ideal type of the concept *bureaucracy*. Many people use Weber's ideal type (see Box 3.2). It distinguishes a bureaucracy from other organizational forms (e.g., social movements, kingdoms). It also clarifies critical features of a kind of organization that people once found nebulous and hard to think about. No real-life organization perfectly matches the ideal type, but the model helps us think about and study bureaucracy.

Another type of classification is the *typology*, or taxonomy,[4] in which a researcher combines two or more unidimensional, simple concepts, such that the intersection of simple concepts forms new concepts. The new concepts or types express the complex interrelation between the simple concepts.

> *One of the chief merits of a typology is parsimony. . . . A well constructed typology can work miracles in bringing order out of chaos. It can transform the overwhelming complexity of an apparent eclectic congeries of numerous apparently diverse cases into a well-ordered set of a few rather homogenous types. (Bailey, 1992:2193)*

Robert Merton's anomie theory of deviance argues that people can understand nondeviance, or conformity, and deviance by considering two key concepts: the goals a culture defines as worth pursuing and the means to achieve those goals that a society defines as legitimate. Merton's typology rests on two concepts: (1) whether people accept or reject the goals and (2) whether the means people use to reach the goals are legitimate or not. His typology identifies types of deviance and conformity based on the two concepts (see Table 3.1).

Conformity, or nondeviance, occurs when people accept cultural goals (e.g., obtaining a high income) and use a socially legitimate means

---

Box 3.2 _____

Max Weber's Ideal Type of Bureaucracy

- It is a continuous organization governed by a system of rules.
- Conduct is governed by detached, impersonal rules.
- There is division of labor, in which different offices are assigned different spheres of competence.
- Hierarchical authority relations prevail; that is, lower offices are under control of higher ones.
- Administrative actions, rules, and so on are in writing and maintained in files.
- Individuals do not own and cannot buy or sell their offices.
- Officials receive salaries rather than receiving direct payment from clients in order to ensure loyalty to the organization.
- Property of the organization is separate from personal property of officeholders.

Source: Adapted from Chafetz (1978:72).

TABLE 3.1 Robert Merton's Modes of Individual Adaptation

MODE OF ADAPTATION	SOCIETAL GOALS	INSTITUTIONAL MEANS
I. Conformity	Accept	Accept
II. Innovation	Accept	Reject
III. Ritualism	Reject	Accept
IV. Retreatism	Reject	Reject
V. Revolution	Substitute new	Substitute new

to reach them (e.g., getting a good job and working hard). Deviance occurs when this is not the case (e.g., when someone robs a bank instead of working hard). Merton's classification of how individuals adapt to cultural goals and means to reach them summarizes his complex concept and labels each subpart. For example, *retreatism* describes a person who rejects both cultural goals and the socially legitimate means to achieve them—such as a chronic alcohol user or a religious hermit. This type of deviant rejects the cultural goal of appearing respectable and acquiring material possessions (e.g., house, car). He or she also rejects the legitimate means of reaching the goal (e.g., being honest, working at a job).

A second example of a typology comes from social stratification. Erik O. Wright updated and summarized Karl Marx's theory of social classes in capitalism. He noted that, for Marx, inequality and exploitation are based on control over three types of resources: investments (i.e., profit-making property or capital), the organization of production, and labor power (i.e., the work of other people). Wright said that the organization of a society defines social classes. The organization of a class society creates positions that confer control over the three types of resources to those occupying the positions (see Table 3.2). People in positions that control all three resources constitute the most powerful or dominant class. In market economies, this is the capitalist class. Its members include the major investors, owners, and presidents of banks or corporations.

Capitalists make investment decisions (e.g., whether and where to build a new factory), determine how to organize production (e.g., use robots or low-wage workers), and give orders to others. The class near the bottom consists of workers. They occupy positions in which they have no say over investments or how to organize production. They lack authority over others and must follow orders to keep their jobs. Managers and supervisors, who assist the capitalists, are between the two major classes. They are a quasi-class that had not yet fully appeared in the 1800s when Marx developed his theory. They control some but not all of the major resources of society.

Wright's classification also points out the position of another class about which Marx wrote, the petit (small) bourgeoisie, consisting of small-scale self-employed proprietors or farmers. Members of this class own and operate their own businesses but employ no one except family members. Marx thought this class would shrink and disappear, but it is still with us today. Like Merton's classification, Wright's scheme shows how to combine a set of simpler concepts (i.e., types of resources owned or not owned) into a more powerful idea (i.e., the structure of social classes in capitalist society).

Relationships

Theories contain many concepts, their definitions, and assumptions. More significantly, theories specify how concepts relate to one

TABLE 3.2 Erik Wright's System of Social Classes

	CONTROL OVER SOCIETAL RESOURCE		
SOCIAL CLASS	*Investments*	*Production*	*Labor*
Capitalists	+	+	+
Managers	−	+	+
Supervisors	−	−	+
Workers	−	−	−
Petty bourgeoisie	+	+	−

+ means has control, − means no or little control

another. Theories tell us whether or not concepts are related and, if they are, how they relate to each other. In addition, theories state why the relationship does or does not exist.

E. M. Beck and Stewart Tolnay (1990) presented a theory about lynching, the killing of African Americans by hanging carried out by mobs of white people in the southern United States from the late 1800s to the 1930s. They said that lynching was related to economic distress (i.e., lower prices received by whites for the cotton grown in the area) but not to blacks committing crimes (i.e., an increasing incidence of crimes committed by African Americans). Their theory stated connections among the three concepts—lynching, economic distress, and black victimization.

Many theories make a causal statement, or a *proposition*, about the relation among variables. "A proposition is a theoretical statement that specifies the connection between two or more variables, informing us how variation in one concept is accounted for by variation in another" (Turner, 1985:25). It is a relationship expressed in a theory, such as: Economic distress among the white population caused an increase in mob violence against African Americans. When a researcher empirically tests or evaluates a relationship, it is called a *hypothesis*. You will learn more about hypotheses in Chapter 6. After many careful tests of a hypothesis confirm the proposition, the scientific community begins to develop confidence that the proposition is true.

A social theory contains concepts, a relationship among concepts, and a causal mechanism, or reason, for the relationship. A *causal mechanism* is a statement of how things work, such as: When people fear a loss, they strike out at those they believe to be their direct competitors and who have less social or political power. Reasons for a relationship are other logically connected assumptions and propositions. It could be an assumption, such as: After the Civil War, whites in southern United States held a deep resentment over the loss of their racially based social status. This might be combined with a proposition: The absence of strong, legitimate,

and formal social control over perceived deviants or outgroup members, combined with a high level of frustration about deviant or outgroup actions, causes an ingroup to adopt nonlegal but traditional means of asserting social control. Propositions do not exist in isolation; they are part of a web of interconnected concepts, relations, and assumptions.

Scope

Some concepts are highly abstract, some are at a middle level of abstraction, and some are at a concrete level. Theories with many abstract concepts apply to a wider range of social phenomena than those with concrete concepts. An example of an abstract theoretical relationship is: Increased size creates centralization, which in turn creates greater formalization. *Size, centralization*, and *formalization* are abstract ideas. They can refer to features of a group, organization, or society. We can translate this to say that as an organization or group gets bigger, authority and power relations within it become centralized and concentrated in a small elite. The elite will tend to rely more on written policies, rules, or laws to control and organize others in the group or organization.

By contrast, the least abstract, simplest, or lowest level relationship is an *empirical generalization*. It is a simple relationship that is concrete and uncomplicated. A researcher creates one when he or she generalizes about a regularity he or she observes. A theory on a topic often implies many generalizations, which can be elementary hypotheses. Here is an example of an empirical generalization: Most people I know who drive small Japanese-made automobiles are under 30 years of age. The generalization contains two concepts: type of car and age of driver. It states a relationship: that a type of car, defined by size and country of origin, is associated with or related to an age group. To become a full theory, it needs additional elaboration and greater breadth to explain why this occurs.

When building or extending a theory and specifying its relationships, a researcher needs to think clearly about the types of units, cases, or situations to which the theory applies.

Most theoretical ideas are formulated in general terms and thus applicable to some universe of cases. Sometimes these general claims are explicit (e.g., a theory of ethnic relations applies to all ethnic relations), and sometimes the claims are taken to be general because a theory's scope conditions have been left unspecified. (Ragin, 1992b:219)

Thinking explicitly about a theory's scope will make it stronger and allow the researcher to communicate it more clearly to others.

In a study of skin tone and social stratification among African Americans, Verna Keith and Cedric Herring (1991) linked an empirical generalization to theory. They tested the empirical generalization that African Americans with lighter skin tones have more education and higher incomes than do those with darker tones. They found support for this generalization, but why? Their theory filled in the picture. It said that whites were more willing to extend privileges and advantages to slaves with lighter skin tones because this indicated partial white ancestry. For 200 years under slavery, whites' prevailing racial ideology attributed superior talents to slaves with white ancestry. Also, for aesthetic reasons, the white aristocracy preferred light-skinned slaves for personal service and sexual relationships. These relations make it easier for lighter-skinned slaves to purchase their freedom. Thus, over many years, African Americans with lighter skin tones had opportunities to obtain skills, education, and advantages that were denied their darker-skinned brethren. After slavery ended, lighter skin was still common in the social elite within the African-American community. Subsequent intermarriage among people with similar amounts of education and income perpetuated the link of skin tone to economic advantage. The larger theory makes the empirical generalization richer by connecting it to other ideas about social relations under slavery, differential opportunities to obtain education, and patterns of selecting marriage partners.

FACT VERSUS THEORY

A long-standing issue in discussions of testing scientific theory is the line between fact and theory. There are two extreme positions. At one extreme is the unrefined *empiricist* position. It says that facts and theories are totally different. Theories belong to the world of soft, indistinct mental images, values, and ideas. Facts are part of the empirical world of hard, settled, observable things that are uncontaminated by theories or ideas. Ideas or theories belong to the world of thought that also contains illusions, dreams, imagination, speculation, and misconceptions. Theories can slide into speculation, illusion, or fiction. To avoid this, theory must be tested against the hard, empirical facts of "real" material reality. The extreme empiricist says that what we see is what there is. This position urges the researcher to improve measures until he or she approaches the position of a person with crystal clear, perfect vision and who is not fooled by optical illusions or visual tricks.

The opposite is the extreme *relativist* position. It says that reality is what we think it is. More precisely, what we take to be reality is very strongly shaped by our cultural beliefs, thoughts, or mental images of it. We can never fully escape the powerful influence of our thoughts. We cannot test theories against hard, objective facts, because all facts are shaped by formal or informal theories. An extreme relativist says that our desires, ideas, and beliefs so strongly distort our vision that the social world we see contains mirages that our minds create. We are unable to see things that our ideas and beliefs do not allow us to see.

Some researchers adopt one or the other extreme, but most fall somewhere in the middle. Those in the middle say that theories and our categories of thought influence what we take to be facts or observations of the world. Nevertheless, there is a separate reality "out there" independent of our ideas. The difficulty is that we can never get a pure, simple, direct, and unmodified measure of that reality. Our attempts to get at facts are forever clouded or tainted by our cultural beliefs, theories, and ideas. We only see a distorted image of what is really there. Our vision of reality is blurred, as if we are looking through a warped or cloudy glass. Facts we observe are always an imperfect, indirect, and distorted representation of what actually exists.

Deeper philosophical issues in the debate are further explored in Chapter 4. This debate affects how we do social research in two ways. First, it means we make allowances for the distortion. Everyone, except the most extreme empiricist, warns that our views of data might involve some distortion due to our ideas and beliefs. The issue becomes how to control for such distortion and the degree to which such control is possible or desirable. Second, the process of research by many different people over time is likely to reduce or control distortion. Except for some postmodernists (see Chapter 4), most scholars believe that many well-conducted studies by diverse, independent, open-minded, and freely communicating researchers will get closer to the reality "out there" in the long run.

THEORIES

Theory can be baffling to students and professionals because it comes in so many forms. We can categorize a theory by (1) the direction of reasoning, (2) the level of social reality that it explains, (3) whether it is formal or substantive (4) the forms of explanation it employs, and (5) the overall framework of assumptions and concepts in which it is embedded. Fortunately, all logically possible combinations of direction, level, explanation, and framework are not equally viable. There are only about a half-dozen serious contenders.

Direction

Researchers approach the building and testing of theory from two directions. Some begin with abstract thinking. They logically connect the ideas in theory to concrete evidence, then test the ideas against the evidence. Others begin with spe-

cific observations of empirical evidence. On the basis of the evidence, they generalize and build toward increasingly abstract ideas. In practice, most researchers are flexible and use both approaches at various points in a study.

Deductive. In a *deductive approach*, you begin with an abstract, logical relationship among concepts, then move toward concrete empirical evidence. You may have ideas about how the world operates and want to test these ideas against "hard data." Beck and Tolnay's (1990) study on lynching, referred to earlier, used deductive logic. They began with a theory about lynching and economic distress. The theory suggested the evidence they should gather. After they had gathered and analyzed the data, they learned that the findings supported their theory.

Inductive. If you use an *inductive approach*, you begin with detailed observations of the world and move toward more abstract generalizations and ideas. When you begin, you may have only a topic and a few vague concepts. As you observe, you refine the concepts, develop empirical generalizations, and identify preliminary relationships. You build the theory from the ground up. Jane Fitchen (1991) used inductive reasoning in her study of the rural crisis, described in Chapter 2. She began with a few general ideas about the farm crisis. Gradually, as she interviewed and observed, she expanded her research focus from farm issues to broader issues of rural communities. She refined concepts and generated empirical generalizations. Eventually, she developed a theory of how people adopt a self-identity as a rural community.

Another example is Josepha Schiffman's (1991) study of two antinuclear groups in the San Francisco area. Her main finding was that different groups within the same broader political movement adopt very different strategies and actions based on how they define power in society. This finding only arose during her detailed observations. It differed from her initial goal: to learn how a single movement organization resolved internal conflicts. As she said, "My data forced me to redefine the project." Theoretical generalization generated by an inductive approach is called *grounded theory* (see Figure 3.1).

Level of Theory

We can divide social theories into three broad groupings by the level of social reality with which they deal. Most of us devote the majority of our time to thinking about the micro level of reality, the individuals we see and interact with on a day-by-day basis. *Micro-level theory* deals with small slices of time, space, or numbers of people. The concepts are usually not very abstract.

Erving Goffman's theory of "face work" is a micro-level theory. Goffman stated that people engage in rituals during face-to-face interaction. An individual adopts a "line" in interaction that defines the type of situation and the type of person he or she is in the situation. For example, in a classroom setting, I present a line of being a friendly teacher. Others in the interaction—students—accommodate the face I present and con-

form to it in an unwritten code of appropriate behavior. I present the face by engaging in certain behaviors (e.g., I turn on the lights, walk to the front of the room, speak to everyone in the room). I also adopt a particular manner (e.g., I stand and smile, make eye contact, inquire about personal events). Others in the classroom cooperate in the ritual. This sustains the social construction of my face. Students avoid certain topics, show deference, and overlook minor errors in my presentation. This is "face work" in Goffman's theory.

Macro-level theory concerns the operation of larger aggregates such as social institutions, entire cultural systems, and whole societies. It uses more concepts that are abstract.

Gerhard Lenski (1966) presented a macro-level theory of social stratification that explains overall societal inequality across thousands of years of human societies. Lenski argued that the amount of surplus a society produces (i.e., the amount beyond what people need for bare subsistence) increases with the development of human society. He argued that the surplus grew as human society developed from a simple hunting and

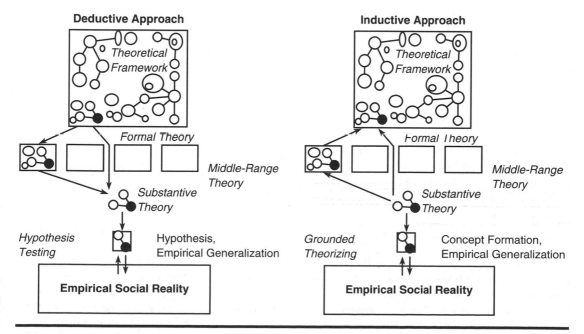

FIGURE 3.1 Deductive and Inductive Theorizing

gathering form to an agrarian form and then to a modern industrial form. Inequality increased as a small group in society took control of the surplus. Inequality peaked historically in agrarian societies and declined in industrial society because the size and complexity of modern society diffused power across more social groups. As they gained some power, the various groups were able to get some of the surplus. Dividing the surplus among more groups reduced inequality.

Meso-level theory is relatively rare. It attempts to link macro and micro levels or to operate at an intermediate level. Theories of organizations, social movements, or communities are often at this level.

Collins (1988:451–466) offered a meso-level theory of control in organizations. This theory identifies three basic methods to control people in a large organization: coerce them (e.g., threaten them with a beating), offer them material rewards (e.g., pay increases), or use internal controls (e.g., socialization, promotion possibilities, creation of a subculture of commitment). Likewise, organizations have five administrative devices for controlling people: (1) using surveillance (e.g., watching over people), (2) inspecting outcomes (e.g., the number of products produced), (3) providing rules and written instructions, (4) controlling information, and (5) constricting the environment (e.g., enforcing when and where work is done). Each method of control and administrative device has negative side effects. For example, people who feel watched will behave in a ritual manner and put on the appearance of working whenever they believe they are being watched. The controls are effective with different work tasks. The best controls for tasks requiring a high degree of initiative and judgment and involving a lot of uncertainty (e.g., those of a teacher or a surgeon) are internal controls (e.g., professional socialization) and information control (e.g., the idea that experts are the only ones who know costs). By contrast, people doing predictable tasks with standardized products (e.g., punch-press operators) respond better to material rewards (e.g., piece rate pay) and monitoring of output (e.g., counting production units).

Formal and Substantive Theories

We can distinguish substantive from formal theory (Layder, 1993:42–43). *Substantive theory* is developed for a specific area of social concern, such as delinquent gangs, secondary classrooms, or race relations. *Formal theory* is developed for a broad conceptual area in general theory, such as deviance, socialization, or power. If you want to test, generate, or extend a substantive theory, then you should think of cases within the same substantive area. For example, you might compare several delinquent gangs, but you do not have to theorize about deviance in general. If you want to test, generate, or extend formal theory, then you should compare cases within the same formal area. For example, you might examine various forms of deviance (medical, legal, folkways). You can do this without reference to the details of substantive areas (e.g., unsual medical treatment, traffic law violation, unusual behavior on a bus). Eventually, substative and formal theory can be connected. There is no need to force all thinking into a single theory; in fact, "the cumulative progress of theory is enhanced by the encouragement of multiple substantive and formal theories" (Layder, 1993:44).

Forms of Explanation

Prediction and Explanation. A theory's primary purpose is to explain. Many people confuse prediction with explanation. Some researchers even argue that the prediction is a major goal of research, but most acknowledge that explanation is essential. There are two meanings or uses of the term *explanation.* Researchers focus on *theoretical explanation*, a logical argument that tells why something occurs. It refers to a general rule or principle. These are a researcher's theoretical argument or connections among concepts. The second type of explanation, *ordinary explanation*, makes something clear or describes something in a way that illustrates it and makes it intelligible. For example, a good teacher "explains" in the ordinary sense. The two types of explanation can blend together. This occurs when a researcher explains (i.e., makes intelligible) his or her explanation (i.e., a logical argument involving theory).

Prediction is a statement that something will occur. It is easier to predict than to explain, and an explanation has more logical power than prediction because good explanations also predict. An explanation rarely predicts more than one outcome, but the same outcome may be predicted by opposing explanations. Although it is less powerful than explanation, many people are entranced by the dramatic visibility of a prediction.

A gambling example illustrates the difference between explanation and prediction. If I enter a casino and consistently and accurately predict the next card to appear or the next number on a roulette wheel, it will be sensational. I may win a lot of money, at least until the casino officials realize I am always winning and expel me. Yet, my method of making the predictions is more interesting than the fact that I can do so. Telling you what I do to predict the next card is more fascinating than being able to predict by itself.

Here is another example. You know that the sun "rises" each morning. You can predict that at some time, every morning, whether or not clouds obscure it, the sun will rise. But why is this so? One explanation is that the Great Turtle carries the sun across the sky on its back. Another explanation is that a god sets his arrow ablaze, which appears to us as the sun, and shoots it across the sky. Few people today believe these ancient explanations. The explanation you probably accept involves a theory about the rotation of the earth and the position of the sun, the star of our solar system. In this explanation, the sun only appears to rise. The sun does not move; its apparent movement depends on the earth's rotation. We are on a planet that both spins on its axis and orbits around a star millions of miles away in space. All three explanations make the same prediction: The sun rises each morning. As you can see, a weak explanation can produce an accurate prediction. A good explanation depends on a well-developed theory and is confirmed in research by empirical observations.

Now that you have an idea of what *explanation* means, we can turn to the three ways researchers explain—causal, structural, and interpretive. The forms of explanation refer to the way in which a researcher tells others why social events occur or why social relations assume a particular pattern.

Causal Explanation.   *Causal explanation* the most common type, is used when the relationship is one of cause and effect. We use it all the time in everyday language, but everyday language tends to be sloppy and ambiguous. What do we mean when we say *cause*? For example, you may say that poverty causes crime or that looseness in morals causes an increase in divorce. This does not tell how or why the causal process works. Researchers try to be more precise and exact when discussing causal relations.

Philosophers have long debated the idea of cause. It has been a controversial idea since the writings of the eighteenth-century Scottish philosopher David Hume (1711–1776). Some people argue that causality occurs in the empirical world, but it cannot be proved. Causality is "out there" in objective reality, and researchers can only try to find evidence for it. Others argue that causality is only an idea that exists in the human mind, a mental construction, not something "real" in the world. This second position holds that causality is only a convenient way of thinking about the world. Without entering into the philosophical debate, many researchers pursue causal relationships.

You need three things to establish causality: temporal order, association, and the elimination of plausible alternatives. An implicit fourth condition is an assumption that a causal relationship makes sense or fits with broader assumptions or a theoretical framework. Let us examine the three basic conditions.

The *temporal order* condition means that a cause must come before an effect. This common-sense assumption establishes the direction of causality: from the cause toward the effect. You may ask: How can the cause come after what it is to affect? It cannot, but temporal order is only one of the conditions needed for causality. Temporal order is necessary but not sufficient to infer causality. Sometimes people make the mistake of talking about "cause" on the basis of temporal order alone. For example, a professional baseball player pitches no-hit games when he kisses his wife just before a game. The kissing occurred before the no-hit games. Does that mean the kissing is the cause of the pitching performance? It is very unlikely. As another example, race riots occurred in four separate cities in 1968, one day after an intense wave of sunspots. The temporal ordering does not establish a causal link between sunspots and race riots. After all, all prior human history occurred before some specific event. The researcher wants to learn whether a specific previous event causes an event or pattern. The temporal order condition simply eliminates from consideration potential causes that occurred later in time.

It is not always easy to establish temporal order. With cross-sectional research, temporal order is tricky. For example, a researcher finds that people who have a lot of education are also less prejudiced than others. Does more education cause a reduction in prejudice? Or do highly prejudiced people avoid education or lack the motivation, self-discipline, and intelligence needed to succeed in school? Here is another example. The students who get high grades in my class say I am an excellent teacher. Does getting high grades make them happy, so they return the favor by saying that I am an excellent teacher—that is, high grades cause a positive evaluation? Or am I doing a great job, so students study hard and learn a lot, which the grades reflect—that is, their learning causes them to get high grades? It is a chicken-and-egg problem. To resolve it, a researcher needs to bring in other information or design research that specifically tests for the temporal order.

Simple causal relations are unidirectional, operating in a single direction from the cause to the effect. Most studies examine unidirectional relations. More complex theories specify reciprocal-effect causal relations—that is, a mutual causal relationship or simultaneous causality. For example, studying a lot causes a student to get good grades, but getting good grades also motivates the student to continue to study. Theories often have reciprocal or feedback relationships, but these are difficult to test. Some researchers call unidirectional relations nonrecursive and reciprocal-effect relations recursive.

A researcher also needs an *association* for causality. Two phenomena are associated if they occur together in a patterned way or appear to act together. People sometimes confuse correlation with association. Correlation has a specific technical meaning, whereas association is a more general idea. A correlation coefficient is a statistical measure that indicates the amount of association, but there are many ways to measure association. Sometimes, researchers call association *concomitant variation* because two variables vary together. Figure 3.2 shows 38 people from a lower-income neighborhood and 35 people from an upper-income neighborhood. Can you see an association between race and income level?

More people mistake association for causality than confuse it with temporal order. For example, when I was in college, I got high grades on the exams I took on Fridays but low grades on those I took on Mondays. There was an association between the day of the week and the exam grade, but it did not mean that the day of the week caused the exam grade. Instead, the reason was that I worked 20 hours each weekend and was very tired on Mondays. As another example, the number of children born in India increased until the late 1960s, then slowed in the 1970s. The number of U.S.-made cars driven in the United States increased until the late 1960s, then slowed in the 1970s. The number of Indian children born and the number of U.S. cars driven are associated: they vary together or increase and decrease at the same time. Yet there is no causal connection. By coincidence, the Indian government instituted a birth control program that slowed the number of births at the same time that Americans were buying more imported cars.

A researcher needs to show association to demonstrate causality. If he or she cannot find an association, a causal relationship is unlikely. This

Lower Income   **Upper Income**

FIGURE 3.2   Association of Income and Race

is why researchers attempt to find correlations and other measures of association. Yet, a researcher can find an association without causality. The association eliminates potential causes that are not associated. It cannot definitely identify a cause. It is a necessary but not a sufficient condition. In other words, you need it for causality, but it is not enough alone.

An association does not have to be perfect (i.e., every time one variable is present, the other also is) to show causality. In the example involving exam grades and days of the week, there is an association if on 10 Fridays I got 7 A's, 2 B's, and 1 C, whereas my exam grades on 10 Mondays were 6 D's, 2 C's, and 2 B's. An association exists, but the days of the week and the exam grades are not perfectly associated. The race and income-level association shown in Figure 3.2 is also an imperfect association.

Eliminating alternatives means that a researcher interested in causality needs to show that the effect is due to the causal variable and not to something else. It is also called *no spuriousness* because an apparent causal relationship that is actually due to an alternative but unrecognized cause is called a spurious relationship. You will read about spurious relationships in Chapter 6.

Researchers can observe temporal order and associations. They cannot observe the elimination of alternatives. They can only demonstrate it indirectly. Eliminating alternatives is an ideal because eliminating all possible alternatives is impossible. A researcher tries to eliminate major alternative explanations in two ways: through built-in design controls and by measuring potential hidden causes. Experimental researchers build controls into the study design itself to eliminate alternative causes. They isolate an experimental situation from the influence of all variables except the main causal variable.

Researchers also try to eliminate alternatives by measuring possible alternative causes. This is common in survey research and is called *controlling for* another variable. Researchers use statistical techniques to learn whether the causal variable or something else operates on the effect variable.

Causal explanations are usually in a linear form or state cause and effect in a straight line: *A* causes *B, B* causes *C, C* causes *D*. The foregoing explanations from the studies on skin tone and on lynching illustrate linear causal explanations. The main concepts in both theories were variables; that is, they took on a range of values. Both used one variable (e.g., amount of economic distress or darkness of skin tone) to explain a second variable (e.g., amount of lynching or differences in income and educational level). We can restate them as simple causal propositions: The higher the level of economic distress, the more lynching; or the lighter the skin tone, the greater the income and education level. They were also deductive because they developed the proposition before testing it with data. We can restate the logic of each study in a deductive causal form: If the proposition is true, then we observe certain things in the empirical evidence. Good causal explanations identify a causal relationship and specify a causal mechanism. A simple causal explanation is: X causes Y, Y occurs because of X, where X and Y are concepts (e.g., early marriage and divorce). Some researchers state causality in a predictive form: If X occurs, then Y follows. Causality can be stated in many ways: X leads to Y, X produces Y, X influences Y, X is related to Y, the greater X the higher Y.

Here is a simple causal theory: A rise in unemployment causes an increase in child abuse. The subject to be explained is an increase in the occurrence of child abuse. What explains it is a rise in unemployment. We "explain" the increase in child abuse by identifying its cause. A complete explanation also requires elaborating the causal mechanism. My theory says that when people lose their jobs, they feel a loss of self-worth. Once they lose self-worth, they become easily frustrated, upset, and angry. Frustrated people often express their anger by directing violence toward those with whom they have close personal contact (e.g., friends, spouse, children). This is especially true if they do not understand the source of the anger or cannot direct it toward its true cause (e.g., an employer, government policy, or "economic forces").

The unemployment and child abuse example illustrates a chain of causes and a causal mechanism. Researchers can test different parts of the chain. They might test whether unemployment rates and child abuse occur together, or whether frustrated people become violent toward the people close to them. A typical research strategy is to divide a larger theory into parts and test various relationships against the data.

Diagrams of Causal Relations among Variables. At minimum, you need a cause and an effect for a causal relationship. Consider this hypothesis: "The more often married people of the same religion attend religious services together, the less likely they are to be divorced." This hypothesis links "attendance at religious services" and "likelihood of divorce." It has three other elements: the group or universe it refers to (married people of the same religion), the direction of causality (from religious attendance to divorce), and the sign of the relationship (the higher or more frequent religious attendance, the less the chance of a divorce). Researchers express theories in words, pictures, or both. They often draw diagrams of the causal relations to present a simplified picture of a relationship and see it at a glance. Such symbolic representations supplement verbal descriptions of causal relations and convey complex information. They are a shorthand way to show theoretical relations.

The simplest diagram is a two-variable model, as in Figure 3.3(a). Researchers represent variables using letters, circles, or boxes. The convention is to represent a cause by an X and the effect by a Y. The arrow shows the direction of causality (e.g., from independent to dependent variable). Sometimes, researchers use subscripts when there is more than one cause (e.g., X_1, X_2), as in Figure 3.3(b). Relationships among variables are symbolized by lines with arrows. Causal relations are represented by straight lines. Associations that do not imply a causal relationship are represented by curved lines with arrows on each end. A single arrow on a line represents a unidirectional relationship. Arrows on both ends of a straight line represent reciprocal relationships.

Relationships between variables can be positive or negative. Researchers imply a positive relationship if they say nothing. A *positive relationship* means that a higher value on the causal variable goes with a higher value on the effect variable. For example, the more education a person has, the longer his or her life expectancy is. A *negative relationship* means that a higher value on the causal variable goes with a lower value on

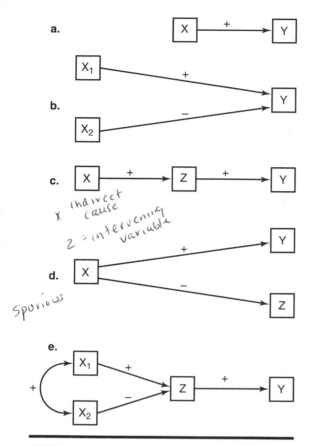

FIGURE 3.3 Causal Diagrams

the number of hours a child fights with peers (X_2) has a negative effect on well-being (Y). Diagrams (c) and (d) also show three-variable relationships. The theoretical causal pattern is different in each. Diagram (c) shows a simple linear causal chain. It says X effects Z, which in turn affects Y. For example, X represents knowledge of political events, Z is attendance at political rallies, and Y stands for making a donation to a candidate. The theory expressed by diagram (c) says that one's knowledge of politics causes one to attend political rallies, which, in turn, causes a political donation. In (d), the theory says that X has effects Y and Z, but that Y and Z are distinct. The theory expressed in (d) would say that political knowledge increases attendance at rallies and donations, but that those who attend rallies do not necessarily donate money. In other words, donations and attendance at rallies are two distinct outcomes, both caused by political knowledge.

Diagram (e) illustrates a model of a four-variable theory. In it, two causal variables are associated, but the theory states that neither is the cause of the other (e.g., they may occur at the same time). Here is an example of the relationships in diagram (e)—anxiety about grades (X_1) causes more hours of studying (Z); at the same time, spending many hours at parties (X_2) causes fewer hours of studying (Z). Grade anxiety (X_1) and hours at parties (X_2) are associated; those who party a lot begin to worry about their grades, and those who are worried party to suppress their anxiety. Many hours of studying (Z) causes higher grades (Y). The relationship between anxiety and partying is descriptive and noncausal. Diagramming relationships also helps us translate complex abstract theories into a compact picture. We will return to causal diagrams in Chapter 6.

Structural Explanation. A *structural explanation* is used with functional and pattern theories. Unlike a causal effect chain, which is similar to a string of balls lined up that hit one another in sequence, it is more similar to a wheel with spokes from a central idea or a spider web in which each strand forms part of the whole. A

the effect variable. For example, the more frequently a couple attends religious services, the lower the chances of their divorcing each other. In diagrams, a plus sign (+) signifies a positive relationship and a negative sign (–) signifies a negative relationship.

Figure 3.3 presents some samples of relationships that can be diagrammed. Researchers would not use a diagram for a very simple two-variable relationship like the one in Figure 3.3(a). As researchers add variables and increase the complexity of relationships, they find diagrams more helpful. Diagram (b) shows a slightly more complex relationship with two causal variables. It might state that the number of hours parents spend talking with a child (X_1) affects the child's sense of well-being (Y), and

researcher making a structural explanation uses a set of interconnected assumptions, concepts, and relationships. Instead of causal statements, he or she uses metaphors or analogies so that relationships "make sense." The concepts and relations within a theory form a mutually reinforcing system. In structural explanations, a researcher specifies a sequence of phases or identifies essential parts that form an interlocked whole.

There are several types of structural explanation. One type is *network theory*.[5] A network theorist says that a behavior or social relationship occurs when certain patterns of interaction take place, when aspects of social relations overlap in time or space, or when relationships follow a developmental sequence.

A network theorist explains something by referring to a broader pattern, a set of syntax rules, or structures. His or her explanation shows how a specific event is just one part of a larger pattern, is one building block in a bigger structure, or is a one link within a much larger system of linkages. It is a form of reasoning like that used to explain why people use language in specific ways; that is, there are syntax rules that state that *X* goes with *Y* or that sentences need a noun and a verb. The researcher explains an event by identifying the syntax rule that covers the event.

Roger Gould's (1991) theory of the social mobilization in the Paris Commune of 1871 is an example of a structural explanation. The Paris Commune was a famous rebellion and takeover of the city of Paris—and very nearly of the government of France—by masses of poor and working people who were led by socialists, Marxists, and radicals. It was a two-month experiment in democratic socialism with free education, worker cooperatives, and radical social reforms. The Commune ended with a brutal battle in which 25,000 Parisians died, most of them shot after surrendering to the national army.

Gould said that people came from different social networks, which shaped their involvement in collective action. Thus, prior to their recruitment into the Paris Commune rebellion, people had social ties to one another. By knowing these ties, Gould predicted who was likely to join. His theory said that isolated people are unlikely to join. People join when those with whom they have intimate social relations join. In addition, a person's location within a web of social ties is important. People at the center of a dense web of ties (i.e., those who have multiple strong ties) are pulled more strongly than those on the periphery (i.e., those with only one or a few weak ties). Gould found that people from the same Paris neighborhood were recruited into a single battalion in the revolutionary defense guard. The new organization, the guard, was built on previous informal ties from the neighborhood—ties of family, neighbor, co-worker, or friend. This created intense intrabattalion loyalty. At the same time, a few people from the neighborhood, some whom were central in it, went to other battalions. This created loyalty across guard battalions. Gould predicted the pattern of battalion behavior from the positions people held in the overlapping social networks of the neighborhood and the guard battalion. He explained the actions of battalions and their responses to events by referring to a broader pattern of social ties among people.

Structural explanation is also used in *functional theory*.[6] Functional theorists explain an event by locating it within a larger, ongoing, balanced social system. They often use biological metaphors. These researchers explain something by identifying its function within a larger system or the need it fulfills for the system. Functional explanations are in this form: "*L* occurs because it serves needs in the system *M*." Theorists assume that a system will operate to stay in equilibrium and to continue over time.

A functional theory of social change says that, over time, a social system, or society, moves through developmental stages, becoming increasingly differentiated and more complex. It evolves a specialized division of labor and develops greater individualism. These developments create greater efficiency for the system as a whole. Specialization and individualism create temporary disruptions. The traditional ways of doing things weaken, but new social relations emerge. The system generates new ways to fulfill functions or satisfy its needs.

Matthijus Kalmijn (1991) used a functional explanation to explain a shift in how Americans select marriage partners. He relied on secularization theory, which holds that ongoing historical processes of industrialization and urbanization shape the development of society. During these modernization processes, people rely less on traditional ways of doing things. Religious beliefs and local community ties weaken, as does the family's control over young adults. People no longer live their entire lives in small, homogeneous communities. Young adults become more independent from their parents and from the religious organizations that formerly played a critical role in selecting marriage partners.

Society has a basic need to organize the way people select marriage partners and find partners with whom they share fundamental values. In modern society, people spend time away from small local settings in school settings. In these school settings, especially in college, they meet other unmarried people. Education is a major socialization agent in modern society. Increasingly, it affects a person's future earnings, moral beliefs and values, and ways of spending leisure time. This explains why there has been a trend in the United States for people to marry less within the same religion and increasingly to marry persons with a similar level of education. In traditional societies, the family and religious organization served the function of socializing people to moral values and linking them to potential marriage partners who held similar values. In modern society, educational institutions largely fulfill this function for the social system.

Interpretive Explanation. The purpose of *interpretive explanation* is to foster understanding. The interpretive theorist attempts to discover the meaning of an event or practice by placing it within a specific social context. He or she tries to comprehend or mentally grasp the operation of the social world, as well as get a feel for something or to see the world as another person does. Because each person's subjective world view shapes how he or she acts, the researcher attempts to discern others' reasoning and view of things.

The process is similar to decoding a text or work of literature. Meaning comes from the context of a cultural symbol system.

Richard Lachmann (1988) used an interpretive explanation in his study of graffiti in New York City. Graffiti is an illegal art form. Lachman noted that the career of a deviant is shaped by how nondeviants label and respond to deviants. He explored how graffiti mentors recruit new artists and teach the young artists that there is an audience for graffiti. He described the career of graffiti artists by placing it in the social context of low-income, inner-city neighborhoods. For example, escaping from police is part of the excitement of the career, and many artists are arrested for other crimes. Skilled artists create murals covering 60-foot subway cars and develop an independent style. Lachmann explained the search for fame and advancement in a career by referring to the culture, constraints, and values of ghetto neighborhoods. Nondeviant artists who appreciate the talent displayed by graffiti artists also shape their career paths.

Theoretical Frameworks

So far, you have learned about theory and empirical generalization. Many researchers use middle-range theory. Middle-range theories are slightly more abstract than empirical generalizations or specific hypotheses. As Robert Merton (1967:39) stated, "Middle-range theory is principally used in sociology to guide empirical inquiry."

Middle-range theories can be formal or substantive. We can organize the terms about theory by the degree of abstraction suggested. From the most concrete to the most abstract are empirical generalizations, middle-range theories, and frameworks. A *theoretical framework* (also called a paradigm or theoretical system) is more abstract than a formal or substantive theory. Figure 3.1 shows the levels and how they are used in inductive and deductive approaches to theorizing.

Researchers do not make precise distinctions among the degrees of abstraction. When they conduct a study, they primarily use middle-range theory and empirical generalization. They rarely use a theoretical framework directly in empirical research. A researcher may test parts of a theory on a topic and occasionally contrast parts of the theories from different frameworks. Box 3.3 illustrates the various degrees of abstraction with Matthijus Kalmijn's study of changing marriage partner selection.

Sociology has several major theoretical frameworks.[7] The frameworks are orientations or sweeping ways of looking at the social world. They provide collections of assumptions, concepts, and forms of explanation. Frameworks include many formal or substantive theories (e.g., theories of crime, theories of the family). Thus, there can be a structural functional theory, an exchange theory, and a conflict theory of the family. Theories within the same framework share assumptions and major concepts. Some frameworks are oriented more to the micro level, others focus on more macro-level phenomena. As you will see in Chapter 4, each is associated with an approach to research methodology. Box 3.4 shows four major frameworks in sociology and briefly describes the key concepts and assumptions of each.

THEORY AND RESEARCH: THE DYNAMIC DUO

You have seen that theory and research are interrelated. Only the naive, new researcher mistakenly believes that theory is irrelevant to research or that a researcher just collects the data. Researchers who attempt to proceed without theory or fail to make it explicit may waste time collecting useless data. They easily fall into the trap of hazy and vague thinking, faulty logic, and imprecise concepts. They may find it difficult to converge onto a crisp research issue or to generate a lucid account of their study's purpose. They often find themselves adrift as they attempt to design or conduct empirical research.

The reason is simple. Theory frames how we look at and think about a topic. It gives us concepts, provides basic assumptions, directs us to the important questions, and suggests ways for us to make sense of data. Theory enables us to con-

---

Box 3.3 _____

Levels of Theory in "Shifting Boundaries" by Matthijus Kalmijn (1991)

Theoretical Framework: Structural functionalism holds that the processes of industrialization and urbanization change human society from a traditional to a modern form. In this process of modernization, social institutions and practices evolve. This evolution includes those that fill the social system's basic needs, socialize people to cultural values, and regulate social behavior. Institutions that filled needs and maintained the social system in a traditional society are superseded by modern ones.

Formal Theory: Secularization theory says that during modernization, people shift away from a reliance on traditional religious beliefs and local community ties. In traditional society, institutions that conferred ascribed social status (family, church, and community) also controlled socialization and regulated social life. In modern society, they are superseded by secular institutions (e.g., education, government, and media) that confer achievement-oriented status.

Middle-Range Substantive Theory: A theory of intermarriage patterns notes that young adults in modern society spend less time in small, local settings, where family, religion, and community all have a strong influence. Instead, young adults spend increasing amounts of time in school settings. In these settings, especially in college, they have opportunities to meet other unmarried people. In modern society, education has become a major socialization agent. It affects future earnings, moral beliefs and values, and leisure interests. Thus, young adults select marriage partners less on the basis of shared religious or local ties and more on the basis of common educational levels.

Empirical Generalization: Americans once married others with similar religious beliefs and affiliation. This practice is being replaced by marriage to others with similar levels of education.

---

nect a single study to the immense base of knowledge to which other researchers contribute. To use an analogy, theory helps a researcher see the forest instead of just a single tree. Theory

Box 3.4 _____

Major Theoretical Frameworks in Sociology

Structural Functionalism

Major Concepts: system, equilibrium, dysfunction, division of labor

Key Assumptions: Society is a system of interdependent parts that is in equilibrium or balance. Over time, society has evolved from a simple to a complex type, which has highly specialized parts. The parts of society fulfill different needs or functions of the social system. A basic consensus on values or a value system holds society together.

Exchange Theory

Major Concepts: opportunities, rewards, approval, balance, credit

Key Assumptions: Human interactions are similar to economic transactions. People give and receive resources (symbolic, social approval, or material) and try to maximize their rewards while avoiding pain, expense, and embarrassment. Exchange relations tend to be balanced. If they are unbalanced, persons with credit can dominate others.

Symbolic Interactionism

Major Concepts: self, reference group, role-playing, perception

Key Assumptions: People transmit and receive symbolic communication when they socially interact. People create perceptions of each other and social settings. People largely act on their perceptions. How people think about themselves and others is based on their interactions.

Conflict Theory

Major Concepts: power, exploitation, struggle, inequality, alienation

Key Assumptions: Society is made up of groups that have opposing interests. Coercion and attempts to gain power are ever-present aspects of human relations. Those in power attempt to hold onto their power by spreading myths or by using violence if necessary.

---

increases a researcher's awareness of interconnections and of the broader significance of data.

Theory has a place in virtually all research, but its prominence varies. It is generally less central in applied-descriptive research than in basic-explanatory research. Its role in applied and descriptive research may be indirect. The concepts are often more concrete, and the goal is not to create general knowledge. Nevertheless, researchers use theory in descriptive research to refine concepts, evaluate assumptions of a theory, and indirectly test hypotheses.

Theory does not remain fixed over time; it is provisional and open to revision. Theories grow into more accurate and comprehensive explanations about the make up and operation of the social world in two ways. They advance as theorists toil to think clearly and logically, but this effort has limits. The way a theory makes significant progress is by interacting with research findings.

The scientific community expands and alters theories based on empirical results. Researchers who adopt a more deductive approach use theory to guide the design of a study and the interpretation of results. They refute, extend, or modify the theory on the basis of results. As researchers continue to conduct empirical research testing a theory, they develop confidence that some parts of it are true. Researchers may modify some propositions of a theory or reject them if several well-conducted studies have negative findings. A theory's core propositions and central tenets are more difficult to test and are refuted less often. In a slow process, researchers may decide to abandon or change a theory as the evidence against it mounts over time and cannot be logically reconciled (see Table 3.3).

Researchers adopting an inductive approach follow a slightly different process. Inductive theorizing begins with a few assumptions and broad

TABLE 3.3 Aspects of Social Theory

DIRECTION OF APPROACH	LEVEL OF REALITY	FORMAL OR SUBSTANTIVE	FORM OF EXPLANATION	DEGREE OF ABSTRACT	THEORETICAL FRAMEWORK
Inductive	Micro	Substantive	Interpretative	Empirical generalization	Symbolic interaction
			Causal	Middle range	Exchange
Deductive	Macro	Formal			
					Structural functional
			Structural	Framework	
					Conflict

orienting concepts. Theory develops from the ground up as the researchers gather and analyze the data. Theory emerges slowly, concept by concept and proposition by proposition in a specific area. The process is similar to a long pregnancy. Over time, the concepts and empirical generalizations emerge and mature. Soon, relationships become visible, and researchers weave together knowledge from different studies into more abstract theory.

CONCLUSION

In this chapter, you learned about social theory—its parts, purposes, and types. The dichotomy between theory and research is an artificial one. The value of theory and its necessity for conducting good research should be clear. Researchers who proceed without theory rarely conduct top-quality research and frequently find themselves in a quandary. Likewise, theorists who proceed without linking theory to research or anchoring it to empirical reality are in jeopardy of floating off into incomprehensible speculation and conjecture. You are now familiar with the scientific community, the dimensions of research, and social theory. In the next chapter, you will examine the competing approaches researchers adopt when they do social science.

KEY TERMS

association
assumption
causal explanation
classification
concept cluster
deductive approach
empirical generalization
functional theory

grounded theory
ideal type
inductive approach
jargon
level of abstraction
macro-level theory
meso-level theory
micro-level theory

negative relationship
network theory
parsimony
positive relationship
prediction
proposition
temporal order
typology

REVIEW QUESTIONS

1. How do concrete and abstract concepts differ? Give examples.
2. How do researchers use ideal types and classifications to elaborate concepts?
3. How do concepts contain built-in assumptions? Give examples.

4. What is the difference between inductive and deductive approaches to theorizing?

5. Describe how the micro, meso, and macro levels of social reality differ.

6. Discuss the differences between prediction and theoretical explanation.

7. What are the three conditions for causality? Which one is never completely demonstrated? Why?

8. Why do researchers use diagrams to show causal relationships?

9. How do structural and interpretive explanations differ from one another?

10. What is the role of the major theoretical frameworks in research?

NOTES

1. For more detailed discussions of concepts, see Chafetz (1978:45–61), Hage (1972:9–85), Kaplan (1964:34–80), Mullins (1971:7–18), Reynolds (1971), and Stinchcombe (1973a).

2. Turner (1980) provides an interesting discussion of how sociological explanation and theorizing can be conceptualized as translation.

3. Classifications are discussed in Chafetz (1978: 63–73) and Hage (1972).

4. For more on typologies and taxonomies, see Blalock (1969:30–35), Chafetz (1978:63–73), Reynolds (1971: 4–5), and Stinchcombe (1968:41–47).

5. Network theory is discussed in Collins (1988: 412–428) and Galaskiewicz and Wasserman (1993).

6. An introduction to functional explanation can be found in Chafetz (1978:22–25).

7. Introductions to alternative theoretical frameworks and social theories are provided in Craib (1984), Phillips (1985:44–59), and Skidmore (1979). An elementary introduction is given in Chapter 1 of Bart and Frankel (1986).

RECOMMENDED READINGS

Collins, Randall. (1988). *Theoretical sociology.* New York: Harcourt Brace Jovanovich. This introduction to social theory uses the macro, micro, and meso distinction to organize many theories. It provides an overview of many classical and contemporary theories.

Craib, Ian. (1984). *Modern social theory: From Parsons to Habermas.* New York: St. Martins. Craib's introduction to contemporary theory is strongest in its presentation of two theoretical frameworks, structural-functionalism and critical theory, a modern form of conflict theory.

Giddens, Anthony. (1971). *Capitalism and modern social theory: An analysis of the writings of Marx,* *Durkheim and Max Weber.* New York: Cambridge University Press. This is a respected summary and discussion of the three major classical theories—those of Marx, Weber, and Durkheim.

Little, Daniel. (1991). *Varieties of social explanation: An introduction to the philosophy of social science.* Boulder, CO: Westview. Little emphasizes the major forms of explanation used in social science. He provides examples from specific studies and evaluates recent developments in social theory. He discusses causal, interpretive, and functional theories.

CHAPTER 4

THE MEANINGS OF METHODOLOGY

The confusion in the social sciences—it should now be obvious—is wrapped up with the long-continuing controversy about the nature of Science.

—C. Wright Mills, *The Sociological Imagination*, p. 119

INTRODUCTION

Many people, including professionals outside the social sciences, ask: Are sociology and related social sciences real science? They think only of the natural sciences (physics, chemistry, biology). In this chapter, we examine the meaning of *science* in the social sciences. We build on the ideas about the scientific community and the varieties of social research and theory discussed in the previous three chapters. This chapter is concerned more with the method of inquiry—how we know—than with specific techniques for gathering and examining data. It looks at the questions: What are researchers trying to do when they conduct research? How do researchers conduct research?

The question "Where is science in social science?" is relevant to anyone wishing to learn social research methods, because the answer is found in the methods used by researchers. Research methodology is what makes social science scientific. The question is an important one, with a long history of debate. It has been asked repeatedly since the social sciences originated. Classical social theorists such as Auguste Comte, Emile Durkheim, Karl Marx, John Stuart Mill, and Max Weber pondered this question. Despite two centuries of discussion and debate, the question remains with us today. Obviously, it does not have a simple answer.

A question for which there are multiple answers does not mean that anything goes; it means that social researchers choose from *alternative approaches* to science. Each approach has its own set of philosophical assumptions and principles and its own stance on how to do research. The approaches are rarely declared explicitly in research reports, and many researchers have only

60

a vague awareness of them. Yet, the approaches play an important role and are found across the social sciences and their related applied fields.[1]

Randall Collins (1989:134) argued that the debate over whether the social sciences are scientific comes from an overly rigid definition of *science*. He remarked, "Modern philosophy of science does not destroy sociological science; it does not say that science is impossible, but gives us a more flexible picture of what science is." The approaches in this chapter help link abstract issues in philosophy to concrete research techniques. They proscribe what good social research involves, justify why one should do research, relate values to research, and guide ethical behavior. They are broad frameworks within which researchers conduct studies. Carl Couch (1987:106) summarized it as follows:

> The ontological and epistemological positions of these . . . research traditions provide the foundation of one of the more bitter quarrels in contemporary sociology. . . . Each side claims that the frame of thought they promote provides a means for acquiring knowledge about social phenomena, and each regards the efforts of the other as at best misguided. . . . They differ on what phenomena should be attended to, how one is to approach phenomena, and how the phenomena are to be analyzed.

By the end of this chapter, you should have three answers to the question: What is scientific about social scientific research? One answer will be for each of the three approaches to be discussed. You may find the pluralism of approaches confusing at first, but once you learn them, you will find that other aspects of research become clearer. Specific research techniques are based on the general approaches discussed in this chapter. The techniques (e.g., experiments, participant observation) will make more sense to you and will be learned faster if you are aware of the logic and assumptions on which they are based. In addition, the approaches presented here will help you understand the diversity you may encounter as you read social research studies. Also, the three approaches give you an opportunity to make an informed choice among alternatives for the type of research you may want to pursue. You might feel more comfortable with one approach or another.

THE THREE APPROACHES

We need to begin by recognizing that the meaning of science was not written in stone or handed down as a sacred text; it has been an evolving human creation. Until the early 1800s, only philosophers and religious scholars who engaged in armchair speculation studied or wrote about human behavior. The classical theorists made a major contribution to modern civilization when they argued that the social world could be studied using science. They contended that rigorous, systematic observation of the social world, combined with careful, logical thinking, could provide a new and valuable type of knowledge about human relations. In modern times, science has become the accepted way to gain knowledge. So when people accepted the claim that society could be studied by using science, it was a revolutionary idea with important ramifications.

Once the idea of a science of the social world gained acceptance, the issue became: What does such a science look like, and how is it conducted? Some people went to the already accepted natural sciences (physics, biology, chemistry) and copied their methods. Their argument was simple: The legitimacy of the natural sciences rests on the scientific method, so social scientists should adopt the same method.

Many researchers accepted this answer, but it poses certain difficulties. First, there is a debate over what *science* means, even in the natural sciences. The scientific method is only a loose set of abstract, vague principles that provide little guidance. Scholars who specialize in the history and philosophy of science have explored multiple ways to do scientific research and have found that scientists use several methods. Second, some scholars say that human beings are qualitatively different from the objects of study in the natural sciences (stars, rocks, plants, chemical compounds). Humans think and learn, have an awareness of themselves and their past, and possess motives and reasons. These unique human characteristics mean that a special science is needed to study the social life of people.

Social researchers did not stop while the philosophers debated. Practicing researchers developed ways to do research based on their informal notions of science. This added to the confusion. Leading researchers used techniques to conduct social research that sometimes deviated from the philosopher's ideal model of good science.

The three approaches in this chapter are based on a major reevaluation of social science that began in the 1960s.[2] The three alternatives to social science are the core ideas distilled from many specific arguments. They are ideal types or idealized, simplified models of more complex arguments. In practice, few social researchers agree with all parts of an approach. Often, they mix elements from each. Yet, these approaches represent fundamental differences in outlook and alternative assumptions about social science research.[3] The approaches are different ways of looking at the world—ways to observe, measure, and understand social reality. They begin from very different positions, even when all end up looking at the same thing or saying the same thing.

"Basically, we're all trying to say the same thing."

Source: Drawing by Gahan Wilson: © 1992 The New Yorker Magazine, Inc.

To simplify the discussion, I have organized the assumptions and ideas of the approaches into answers to the following eight questions:

1. Why should one conduct social scientific research?
2. What is the fundamental nature of social reality? (the ontological question)
3. What is the basic nature of human beings?
4. What is the relationship between science and common sense?
5. What constitutes an explanation or theory of social reality?
6. How does one determine whether an explanation is true or false?
7. What does good evidence or factual information look like?
8. Where do social/political values enter into science?

The three approaches are *positivism, interpretive social science,* and *critical social science.* Most ongoing social research is based on the first two. Positivism is the oldest and the most widely used approach. As philosopher of science Richard Miller (1987:4) observed, "Positivism is the most common philosophical outlook on science. Yet there are current alternatives to it with extremely broad appeal." The interpretative approach has held a strong minority position in debates for over a century. Critical social science is less commonly seen in scholarly journals. It is included to give you the full range of debate over the meaning of social science, and because it criticizes the other approaches and tries to move beyond them.

Each approach is associated with different traditions in social theory and diverse research techniques. The linkage among the broad approaches to science, social theories, and research techniques is not strict. The approaches are similar to a research program, research tradition, or scientific paradigm. A *paradigm*, an idea made famous by the philosopher of science Thomas Kuhn (1970), means a basic orientation to theory and research. There are many definitions of *paradigm*. In general, a scientific paradigm is a whole system of thinking. It includes basic assumptions, the important questions to be answered or puzzles to be solved, the research techniques to be used, and examples of what good scientific research looks like. For example, sociology is called a multiparadigm science because no single paradigm is all-powerful; instead, several compete with each other.[4]

POSITIVIST SOCIAL SCIENCE

Positivist social science is used widely, and *positivism*, broadly defined, is the approach of the natural sciences. In fact, most people never hear of alternative approaches. They assume that the positivist approach *is* science. There are many versions of positivism, and it has a long history within the philosophy of science and among researchers.[5] Yet, for many researchers, it has come to be a pejorative label to be avoided. Jonathan Turner (1992:1511) observed, "*Positivism* no longer has a clear referent, but it is evident that, for many, being a positivist is not a good thing." The answers to the eight questions give you a picture of what a positivist approach sees as constituting social science. Varieties of positivism go by names such as logical empiricism, the accepted or conventional view, postpositivism, naturalism, the covering law model, and behaviorism.

Positivism arose from a nineteenth-century school of thought by the Frenchman who founded sociology—Auguste Comte (1798–1857). Comte's major work in six volumes, *Cours de Philosophie Positivistic* (*The Course of Positive Philosophy*) (1830–1842), outlined many principles of positivism still used today. British philosopher John Stuart Mill (1806–1873) elaborated and modified the principles in his *A System of Logic* (1843). Classical French sociologist Emile Durkheim (1858–1917) outlined a version of positivism in his *Rules of the Sociological Method* (1895), which became a key textbook for positivist social researchers.

Positivism is associated with many specific social theories. Best known is its linkage to the structural-functional, rational choice, and exchange-theory frameworks. Positivist researchers prefer precise quantitative data and often use experiments, surveys, and statistics. They

seek rigorous, exact measures and "objective" research, and they test hypotheses by carefully analyzing numbers from the measures. Many applied researchers (administrators, criminologists, market researchers, policy analysts, program evaluators, and planners) embrace positivism. Critics charge that positivism reduces people to numbers and that its concerns with abstract laws or formulas are not relevant to the actual lives of real people.

Positivism says that "there is only *one* logic of science, to which any intellectual activity aspiring to the title of 'science' must conform" (Keat and Urry, 1975:25, emphasis in original). Thus, the social sciences and the natural sciences must use the same method. In this view, differences between the natural and social sciences are due to the immaturity or youth of the social sciences and their subject matter. Eventually, all science, including the social sciences, will be like the most advanced science, physics. Differences among the sciences may exist as to their subject matter (e.g., geology requires different techniques than does astrophysics or microbiology because of the objects being studied), but all sciences share a common set of principles and logic.

Positivism sees social science as an *organized method for combining deductive logic with precise empirical observations of individual behavior in order to discover and confirm a set of probabilistic causal laws that can be used to predict general patterns of human activity.*

The Questions

1. *Why should one conduct social scientific research?*

The ultimate purpose of research is scientific explanation—to discover and document universal laws of human behavior. Another important reason is to learn about how the world works so that people can control or predict events. This latter idea is sometimes called an *instrumental orientation*. It is a technical interest that assumes knowledge can be used as a tool or instrument to satisfy human wants and to control the physical and social environment. Once people discover the laws that govern human life, we can use them to alter social relations, to improve how things are done, and to predict what will happen. For example, a positivist uses a theory of how we learn to identify key factors of an educational system (e.g., class size, student body habits, teacher education) that predict increased student learning. He or she conducts a study and precisely measures factors to verify causal laws in the theory. The positivist then builds knowledge that is used by an education official to change a school environment in ways that will improve learning by students. This view is summarized by a defender of the positivist approach, Jonathan Turner (1985:39), who stated that the "social universe is amenable to the development of abstract laws that can be tested through the careful collection of data" and that researchers need to "develop abstract principles and models about invariant and timeless properties of the social universe."

Positivists say that scientists are engaged in a never-ending quest for knowledge. As more is learned, new complexities are discovered and there is still more to learn. Early versions of positivism maintained that humans can never know everything because only God possesses such knowledge; however, as creatures placed on this planet with great capacity for knowledge, humans have a duty to discover as much as they can.

2. *What is the fundamental nature of social reality?*

Modern positivists hold that social and physical reality is real. It exists "out there" and is waiting to be discovered. This idea notes that human perception and intellect may be flawed, and reality may be difficult to pin down, but it does exist. Moreover, social reality is not random; it is patterned and has order. Without this assumption (i.e., if the world were chaotic and without regularity), logic and prediction would be impossible. Science lets humans discover this order and the laws of nature. "The basic, observational laws of science are considered to be true, primary and certain, because they are built into the fabric of the natural world. Discovering a law is like discovering America, in the sense that both are already

waiting to be revealed" (Mulkay, 1979:21).

Two other assumptions are that basic patterns of social reality are stable and knowledge of them is additive. The regularity in social reality does not change over time, and laws discovered today will hold in the future. We can study many parts of reality one at a time, then add the fragments together to get a picture of the whole. Some early versions of this assumption said that the order in nature was created by and is evidence of the existence of God or a supreme being.

3. *What is the basic nature of human beings?*

In positivism, humans are assumed to be self-interested, pleasure-seeking, rational individuals. People operate on the basis of external causes, with the same cause having the same effect on everyone. We can learn about people by observing their behavior, what we see in external reality. This is more important than what happens in internal, subjective reality. Sometimes, this is called a *mechanical model of man* or a behaviorist approach. It means people respond to external forces that are as real as physical pressures on objects. Emile Durkheim (1938:27) stated, "Social phenomena are things and ought to be studied as things." External reality suggests that researchers do not have to examine unseen, internal motivations of an individual's behavior.

Positivists say that human behavior or social institutions do not just happen because of what a person wants. Human events can be explained with reference to *causal laws*, which describe causes and effects. They identify forces that operate in a manner similar to natural laws in the hard sciences. This suggests that the idea of free will is largely fiction and describes only aspects of human behavior that science has not yet conquered.

Few positivists believe in absolute determinism, wherein people are mere robots or puppets who must always respond exactly the same. Rather, the causal laws are probabilistic. Laws hold for large groups of people or occur in many situations. Researchers can estimate the odds of a predicted behavior. In other words, the laws permit us to make accurate predictions of how often a social behavior will occur within a large group.

The causal laws cannot predict the specific behavior of a specific person in each situation. However, they can say that under conditions *X, Y,* and *Z*, there is a 95 percent probability that one-half of the people will engage in a specified behavior. For example, researchers cannot predict how John Smith will vote in the next election. However, after learning dozens of facts about John Smith and using laws of political behavior, researchers can accurately state that there is an 85 percent chance that he (and people like him) will vote for candidate C. This does not mean that Mr. Smith cannot vote for whomever he wants. Rather, his voting behavior is patterned and shaped by outside social forces.

4. What is the relationship between science and common sense?

Positivists see a clear separation between science and nonscience. Of the many ways to seek truth, science is special—the "best" way. Scientific knowledge is better than and will eventually replace the inferior ways of gaining knowledge (e.g., magic, religion, astrology, personal experience, tradition). Science borrows some ideas from common sense, but it replaces the parts of common sense that are sloppy, logically inconsistent, unsystematic, and full of bias. The scientific community—with its special norms, scientific attitudes, and techniques—can regularly produce "Truth," whereas common sense does so only rarely and inconsistently.

A researcher working in a positivist tradition often creates a whole new vocabulary—a set of scientific ideas and associated terms. He or she wants to use ideas that are more logically consistent and carefully thought out and refined than the ideas found in everyday common sense. The positivist researcher "should formulate new concepts at the outset and not rely on lay notions, . . . There is a preference for the precision which is believed possible in a discipline-based language rather than the vague and imprecise language of everyday life" (Blaikie, 1993: 206). In his *Rules of the Sociological Method*, Emile Durkheim warned the researcher to "resolutely deny himself the use of those concepts formed outside of science" and

to "free himself from those fallacious notions which hold sway over the mind of the ordinary person" (quoted in Gilbert, 1992:4).

5. What constitutes an explanation or theory of social reality?

Positivist scientific explanation is *nomothetic* (*nomos* means law in Greek); it is based on a system of general laws. Science explains why social life is the way it is by discovering causal laws. Explanation takes the form; *Y* is caused by *X* because *Y* and *X* are specific instances of a causal law. In other words, a positivist explanation states the general causal law that applies to or covers specific observations about social life. This is why positivism is said to use a *covering law model* of explanation.

Positivism assumes that the laws operate according to strict, logical reasoning. Researchers connect causal laws and the specific facts observed about social life with deductive logic. Positivists believe that eventually laws and theories of social science will be expressed in formal symbolic systems, with axioms, corollaries, postulates, and theorems. Someday, social science theories will look similar to those in mathematics and the natural sciences.

The laws of human behavior should be universally valid, holding in all historical eras and in all cultures. As noted before, the laws are stated in a probabilistic form for aggregates of people. For example, a positivist explanation of a rise in the crime rate in Toronto in the 1990s refers to factors (e.g., rising divorce rate, declining commitment to traditional moral values) that could be found anywhere at any time: in Bombay in the 1890s, Chicago in the 1940s, or Singapore in the 2010s. The factors logically follow from a general law (e.g., the breakdown of a traditional moral order causes an increase in the rate of criminal behavior).

6. How does one determine whether an explanation is true or false?

Positivism developed during the Enlightenment (post–Middle Ages) period of Western thinking (see Bernard, 1988:12–21). It includes an important Enlightenment idea: People can recognize truth and distinguish it from falsehood by applying reason, and, in the long run, over centuries, the human condition can improve through the use of reason and the pursuit of truth. As knowledge grows and ignorance declines, conditions will improve. This optimistic belief that knowledge accumulates over time plays a role in how positivists sort out true from false explanations.

In positivism, to be seriously considered, explanations must meet two conditions: they must (1) have no logical contradictions and (2) be consistent with observed facts. Yet, this is not sufficient. *Replication* is also needed (see Hegtvedt, 1992). Any researcher can replicate or reproduce the results of others. This puts a check on the whole system for creating knowledge. It ensures honesty because it repeatedly tests explanations against the hard, objective facts. An open competition exists among opposing explanations, impartial rules are used, neutral facts are accurately observed, and logic is rigorously followed. Over time, scientific knowledge accumulates as different researchers conduct independent tests of a theory and add up the findings. For example, a researcher finds that rising unemployment is associated with increased child abuse in San Diego, California. A causal relationship between unemployment and child abuse is not demonstrated with just one study, however. Confirming a causal law depends on finding the same relationship in other cities with other researchers conducting independent tests using careful measures of unemployment and child abuse.

7. *What does good evidence or factual information look like?*

Positivism is dualist; it assumes that the cold, observable facts are fundamentally distinct from ideas, values, or theories. Empirical facts exist apart from personal ideas or thoughts. We can observe them by using our sense organs (eyesight, smell, hearing, touch) or special instruments that extend the senses (e.g., telescopes, microscopes, Geiger counters). Some researchers express this idea as a language of empirical fact and a language of abstract theory. If people disagree over

facts, it must be due to the improper use of measurement instruments or to sloppy or inadequate observation. "Scientific explanation involves the accurate and precise measurement of phenomena" (Derksen and Gartrell, 1992:1714). Knowledge of observable reality obtained using our senses is superior to other knowledge (e.g., intuition, emotional feelings); it allows us to separate true from false ideas about social life.

Positivists combine this idea of the privileged status of empirical observation with the assumption that subjective understanding of the empirical world is shared. Factual knowledge is not based on just one person's observations and reasoning. It must be capable of being communicated and shared by others. Rational people who independently observe facts will agree on them. This is called *intersubjectivity*, or the shared subjective acknowledgment of the facts. Many positivists accept a version of falsification doctrine outlined by the Anglo-Austrian philosopher Sir Karl Popper (1902–1991) in the *Logic of Scientific Discovery* (1931). Popper argued that claims to knowledge "can never be proven or fully justified, they can only be refused" (Phillips, 1987:3). Good evidence for a causal law involves more than piling up supporting facts; it involves looking for evidence that contradicts the causal law. In a classic example, if I want to test the claim that all swans are white, and I find 1,000 white swans, I have not totally confirmed a causal law or pattern. All it takes is locating one black swan to refute my claim—one piece of negative evidence. This means that researchers search for disconfirming evidence, and even then, the best they can say is, "Thus far, I have not been able to locate any, so the claim might be right."

8. *Where do social/political values enter into science?*

Positivists argue for a *value-free science* that is objective. There are two meanings of the term *objective*: that observers agree on what they see and that science is not based on values, opinions, attitudes, or beliefs (Derksen and Gartrell, 1992:1715). Positivists see science as a special, distinctive part of society that is free of personal, political, or religious values. It operates independently of the social and cultural forces affecting other human activity. It involves applying strict rational thinking and systematic observation in a manner that transcends personal prejudices, biases, and values. The norms and operation of the scientific community keep science objective. Scientists are socialized to unique professional norms and values. Researchers accept and internalize the norms as part of their membership in the scientific community. The scientific community has created an elaborate system of checks and balances to guard against value bias. A researcher's proper role is to be a "disinterested scientist."[6] The positivist view on values has had a immense impact on how people see ethical issues and knowledge.

> To the degree that a positivist theory of scientific knowledge has become the criterion for all knowledge, moral insights and political commitments have been delegitimized as irrational or reduced to mere subjective inclination. Ethical judgments are now thought of as personal opinion. (Brown, 1989:37)

Summary

You probably find many positivist assumptions familiar because the positivist approach is widely taught as being the same as science. Few people are aware of the origins of positivist assumptions. An early religious aspect exists in some assumptions because the scholars who developed them in western Europe during the eighteenth and nineteenth centuries had religious training and lived in a cultural-historical setting that assumed specific religious beliefs. Many positivist assumptions will reappear when you read about quantitative research techniques and measurement in later chapters. A positivist approach implies that a researcher begins with a general cause-effect relationship that he or she logically derives from a possible causal law in general theory. He or she logically links the abstract ideas of the relationship to precise measurements of the social world. The researcher remains detached, neutral, and objective as he or she measures aspects of social life, examines evidence, and replicates the research of others. These processes lead to an empirical test of and confirmation for the laws of social life as outlined in a theory.

When and why did positivist social science become dominant? The story is long and complicated. Many present it as a natural advance or the inevitable progress of pure knowledge. Positivist social science expanded largely due to changes in the larger political-social context. Positivism gained dominance in the United States and became the model for social research in many nations after World War II, once the United States became the leading world power. A thrust toward objectivism—a strong version of positivism—developed in U.S. sociology during the 1920s. Objectivism grew as researchers shifted away from social reform-oriented studies with less formal or precise quantitative techniques toward rigorous techniques in a "value-free" manner modeled on the natural sciences. They created careful measures of the external behavior of individuals to produce quantitative data that could be subjected to statistical analysis. Objectivism displaced locally based studies that were action oriented and largely qualitative. It grew because competition among researchers for prestige and status combined with other pressures, including funds from private foundations (e.g., Ford Foundation, Rockefeller Foundation), university administrators who wanted to avoid unconventional politics, a desire by researchers for a public image of serious professionalism, and the information needs of expanding government and corporate bureaucracies. These pressures combined to redefine social research. The less technical, applied local studies conducted by social reformers (often women) were often overshadowed by apolitical, precise quantitative research by male professors in university departments.[7]

INTERPRETIVE SOCIAL SCIENCE

Interpretive social science can be traced to German sociologist Max Weber (1864–1920) and German philosopher Wilhem Dilthey (1833–1911). In his major work, *Einleitung in die Geisteswissenschaften* (*Introduction to the Human Sciences*) (1883), Dilthey argued that there were two fundamentally different types of science: *Naturwissenschaft* and *Geisteswissenschaft*. The former is based on *Erklärung*, or abstract explanation. The latter is rooted in an empathetic understanding, or *Verstehen*, of the everyday lived experience of people in specific historical settings. Weber argued that social science needed to study *meaningful social action*, or social action with a purpose. He embraced *Verstehen* and felt that we must learn the personal reasons or motives that shape a person's internal feelings and guide decisions to act in particular ways.

> We shall speak of "social action" wherever human action is subjectively related in meaning to the behavior of others. An unintended collision of two cyclists, for example, shall not be called social action. But we will define as such their possible prior attempts to dodge one another. . . . Social action is not the only kind of action significant for sociological causal explanation, but it is the primary object of an "interpretive sociology." (Weber, 1981:159)

Interpretive social science is related to *hermeneutics*, a theory of meaning that originated in the nineteenth century. The term comes from a god in Greek mythology, Hermes, who had the job of communicating the desires of the gods to mortals. It "literally means making the obscure plain" (Blaikie, 1993:28). Hermeneutics is largely found in the humanities (philosophy, art history, religious studies, linguistics, and literary criticism). It emphasizes a detailed reading or examination of *text*, which could refer to a conversation, written words, or pictures. A researcher conducts "a reading" to discover meaning embedded within text. Each reader brings his or her subjective experience to a text. When studying the text, the researcher/reader tries to absorb or get inside the viewpoint it presents as a whole, and then develop a deep understanding of how its parts relate to the whole. In other words, true meaning is rarely simple or obvious on the surface; one

reaches it only through a detailed study of the text, contemplating its many messages and seeking the connections among its parts.

There are several varieties of interpretive social science (ISS): hermeneutics, constructionism, ethnomethodology, cognitive, idealist, phenomenological, subjectivist, and qualitative sociology.[8] An interpretive approach is associated with the symbolic interactionist, or the 1920s–1930s Chicago School in sociology. It is often called a qualitative method of research.

Interpretive researchers often use participant observation and field research. These techniques require that researchers spend many hours in direct personal contact with those being studied. Other ISS researchers analyze transcripts of conversations or study videotapes of behavior in extraordinary detail, looking for subtle nonverbal communication, to understand details of interactions in their context. A positivist researcher will precisely measure selected quantitative details about thousands of people and use statistics, whereas an interpretive researcher may live a year with a dozen people and use careful methods to gather large quantities of detailed qualitative data to acquire an in-depth understanding of how they create meaning in everyday life.

In contrast to positivism's instrumental orientation, the interpretive approach adopts a *practical orientation*. It is concerned with how ordinary people manage their practical affairs in everyday life, or how they get things done. ISS is concerned with how people interact and get along with each other. In general, the interpretive approach is *the systematic analysis of socially meaningful action through the direct detailed observation of people in natural settings in order to arrive at understandings and interpretations of how people create and maintain their social worlds.*

The Questions

1. *Why should one conduct social scientific research?*

For interpretive researchers, the goal of social research is to develop an understanding of social life and discover how people construct meaning in natural settings. An interpretive researcher wants to learn what is meaningful or relevant to the people being studied, or how individuals experience daily life. The researcher does this by getting to know a particular social setting and seeing it from the point of view of those in it. The researcher shares the feelings and interpretations of the people he or she studies and sees things through their eyes. Summarizing the goal of his 10-year study of Willie, a repair shop owner in a rural area, the interpretive researcher Douglas Harper (1987:12) said, "The goal of the research was to share Willie's perspective."

Interpretive researchers study *meaningful social action*, not just the external or observable behavior of people. Social action is the action to which people attach subjective meaning: it is activity with a purpose or intent. Nonhuman species lack culture and the reasoning to plan out things and attach purpose to their behavior; therefore, social scientists should study what is unique to human social behavior. The researcher must take into account the social actor's reasons and the social context of action. For example, a physical reflex such as eye blinking is human behavior that is rarely an intentional social action (i.e., done for a reason or with human motivation), but in some situations, it can be such a social action (i.e., a wink). The activities of social actors need more than simply to have a purpose; they must also be social and "for action to be regarded as social and to be of interest to the social scientist, the actor must attach subjective meaning to it and it must be directed towards the activities of other people" (Blaikie, 1993:37).

The interpretive approach notes that human action has little inherent meaning. It acquires meaning among people who share a meaning system that permits them to interpret it as a socially relevant sign or action. For example, raising one finger in a situation with other people can express social meaning; the specific meaning it expresses (e.g., a direction, an expression of friendship, a vulgar sign) depends on the cultural meaning system that the social actors share.

2. *What is the basic nature of social reality?*

The interpretive approach sees human social life as an accomplishment. It is intentionally created out of the purposeful actions of interacting social beings. In contrast to the realist idea (shared by positivist and critical social science) that social life is "out there," independent of human consciousness, ISS says social reality is not waiting to be discovered. Instead, the social world is largely what people perceive it to be. Social life exists as people experience it and give it meaning. It is fluid and fragile. People maintain it by interacting with others in ongoing processes of communication and negotiation. They operate on the basis of untested assumptions and taken-for-granted knowledge about people and events around them.

The interpretive approach holds that social life is based on social interactions and socially constructed meaning systems. People possess an internally experienced sense of reality. This subjective sense of reality is crucial to grasp human social life. External human behavior is an indirect and often obscure indicator of true social meaning. ISS says that "access to other human beings is possible, however, only by indirect means: what we experience initially are gestures, sound, and actions and only in the process of understanding do we take the step from external signs to the underlying inner life" (Bleicher, 1980:9).

For interpretive researchers, social reality is based on people's definitions of it. A person's definition of a situation tells him or her how to assign meaning in constantly shifting conditions. For example, my social reality includes ways to act toward a female called *mother*. I hug her, give her gifts on her birthday, and confide in her. I learned to do this through cultural role expectations and years of experience in a close social relationship. Yet, the social reality of the relationship is not fixed. The definition of the situation can change dramatically. The social reality would be shattered, for example, if the same woman became demented, no longer recognized me, and was institutionalized as insane.

Positivists assume that everyone shares the same meaning system and that we all experience the world in the same way. The interpretive approach says that people may or may not experience social or physical reality in the same way. Key questions for an interpretive researcher are: How do people experience the world? Do they create and share meaning? ISS points to numerous examples in which several people have seen, heard, or even touched the same physical object, yet come away with different meanings or interpretations of it. The interpretive researcher argues that positivists avoid important questions and impose one way of experiencing the world on others. By contrast, ISS assumes that multiple interpretations of human experience, or realities, are possible. In sum, the ISS approach sees social reality as consisting of people who construct meaning and create interpretations through their daily social interaction.

3. *What is the basic nature of human beings?*

Ordinary people are engaged in a process of creating flexible systems of meaning through social interaction. They then use such meanings to interpret their social world and make sense of their lives. Human behavior may be patterned and regular, but this is not due to preexisting laws waiting to be discovered. The patterns are created out of evolving meaning systems or social conventions that people generate as they socially interact. Important questions for the interpretive researcher are: What do people believe to be true? What do they hold to be relevant? How do they define what they are doing?

Interpretive researchers want to discover what actions mean to the people who engage in them. It makes little sense to try to deduce social life from abstract, logical theories that may not relate to the feelings and experiences of ordinary people. People have their own reasons for their actions, and researchers need to learn the reasons people use. Individual motives are crucial to consider even if they are irrational, carry deep emotions, and contain false facts and prejudices.

Some interpretive researchers say that the laws sought by positivists may be found only after the scientific community understands how people create and use meaning systems, how common sense develops, and how people apply their common sense to situations. Other interpretive researchers say there are no such laws of human social life, so the search is futile. Schwandt (1994:130) noted, "Contemporary interpretativists and constructivists are not likely to hold that there are any unquestioned *foundations* for any interpretation" (emphasis in original). In other words, the creation of meaning and the sense of reality is only what people think it is, and no set of meanings are better or superior to others. For example, an interpretive researcher sees the desire to discover laws of human behavior in which unemployment causes child abuse as premature at best and dangerous at worst. Instead, he or she wants to understand how people subjectively experience unemployment and what the loss of a job means in their everyday lives. Likewise, the interpretive researcher wants to learn how child abusers account for their actions, what reasons they give for abuse, and how they feel about abusing a child. He or she explores the meaning of being unemployed and the reasons for abusing a child in order to understand what is happening to the people who are directly involved.

4. *What is the relationship between science and common sense?*

Positivists see common sense as inferior to science. By contrast, interpretive researchers argue that ordinary people use common sense to guide them in daily living; therefore, one must first grasp common sense. People use common sense all the time. It is a stockpile of everyday theories people use to organize and explain events in the world. It is critical to understand common sense because it contains the meanings that people use when they engage in routine social interactions.

An interpretive approach says that common sense and the positivist's laws are alternative ways to interpret the world; that is, they are distinct meaning systems. Neither common sense nor scientific law has all the answers. Neither is inferior or superior to the other. Instead, interpretive researchers see each as important in its own domain; each is created in a different way for a different purpose.

Ordinary people could not function in daily life if they based their actions on science alone. For example, in order to boil an egg, people use unsystematic experiences, habits, and guesswork. A strict application of natural science would require one to know the laws of physics that determine heating the water and the chemical laws that govern the changes in the egg's internal composition. Even natural scientists use common sense when they are not "doing science" in their area of expertise.

The interpretive approach says that common sense is a vital source of information for understanding people. A person's common sense and sense of reality emerge from a pragmatic orientation and set of assumptions about the world. People do not know that common sense is true with absolute certainty, but they must assume that it is true in order to get anything accomplished. The interpretive philosopher, Alfred Schutz (1899–1959), called this the *natural attitude*. It is the assumption that the world existed before you arrived and it will continue to exist after you depart. People develop ways to maintain or reproduce a sense of reality based on systems of meaning that they create in the course of social interactions with others.

5. *What constitutes an explanation or theory of social reality?*

Positivists believe that social theory should be similar to natural science theory with deductive axioms, theorems, and interconnected causal laws. Instead of a maze of interconnected laws and propositions, theory for ISS tells a story. ISS theory describes and interprets how people conduct their daily lives. It contains concepts and limited generalizations, but it does not dramatically depart from the experience and inner reality of the people being studied.

The interpretive approach is ideographic and inductive. *Ideographic* means the approach provides a symbolic representation or "thick" description of something else. An interpretive research report may read more like a novel or a biography than like a mathematical proof. It is rich in detailed description and limited in abstraction. An interpretive analysis of a social setting, like the interpretation of a literary work, has internal coherence and is rooted in the text, which here refers to the meaningful everyday experiences of the people being studied.

Interpretive theory gives the reader a feel for another's social reality. The theory does this by revealing the meanings, values, interpretive schemes, and rules of living used by people in their daily lives. For example, it may describe major typifications people use in a setting to recognize and interpret their experiences. A *typification* is an informal model, scheme, or set of beliefs that people use to categorize and organize the flow of the daily events they experience.

Thus, interpretive theory resembles a map that outlines a social world or a tourist guidebook that describes local customs and informal norms. For example, an interpretive report on professional gamblers tells the reader about the careers and daily concerns of such people. It describes the specific individuals studied, the locations and activities observed, and the strategies used to gamble. The reader learns how professional gamblers speak, how they view others, and what their fears or ambitions are. The researcher gives a few generalizations and organizing concepts. The bulk of the report is a detailed description of the gambling world. The theory and evidence are interwoven to create a unified whole; the concepts and generalizations are wedded to their context.

6. *How does one determine whether an explanation is true or false?*

Positivists evaluate a theory by using set procedures to test hypotheses. They logically deduce from theory, collect data, and analyze facts in ways that other scientists can replicate. An explanation is considered to be true when it stands up to replication. For ISS, a theory is true if it makes sense to those being studied and if it allows others to understand deeply or enter the reality of those being studied. The theory or description is accurate if the researcher conveys a deep understanding of the way others reason, feel, and see things. Prediction may be possible, but it is a type of prediction that occurs when two people are very close, as when they have been married for a long time. An interpretive explanation documents the actor's point of view and translates it into a form that is intelligible to readers. Smart (1976:100) calls this the *postulate of adequacy*:

> The postulate of adequacy asserts that if a scientific account of human action were to be presented to an individual actor as a script it must be understandable to that actor, translatable into action by the actor and furthermore comprehensible to his fellow actors in terms of a common sense interpretation of everyday life.

An interpretive researcher's description of another person's meaning system is a *secondary account*. Like a traveler telling about a foreign land, the researcher is not a native. Such an outside view never equals a primary account given by those being studied, but the closer it is to the native's primary account, the better. For example, one way to test the truthfulness of an interpretive study of professional gambling is to have professional gamblers read it and verify its accuracy. A good report tells a reader enough about the world of professional gambling so that if the reader absorbed it and then met a professional gambler, the understanding of gambling jargon, outlook, and life-style might lead the gambler to ask whether the reader was also a professional gambler.

7. *What does good evidence or factual information look like?*

Good evidence in positivism is observable, precise, and independent of theory and values. By contrast, ISS sees the unique features of specific contexts and meanings as essential to understand social meaning. Evidence about social action cannot be isolated from the context in which it occurs or the meanings assigned to it by the social actors involved. As Max Weber (1978:5) said, "Empathic or appreciative accuracy is attained when, through sympathetic participation, we can adequately grasp the emotional context in which the action took place."

ISS sees facts as fluid and embedded within a meaning system in the interpretive approach; they are not impartial, objective, and neutral. Facts are context-specific actions that depend on the interpretations of particular people in a social setting. What the positivist assumes—that neutral outsiders observe behavior and see unambiguous, objective facts—an ISS researcher takes as a question to be addressed: How do people observe ambiguities in social life and assign meaning? Interpretive researchers say that social situations contain a great deal of ambiguity. This makes it almost impossible to discover straightforward, objective facts. Most behaviors or statements can have several meanings and can be interpreted in multiple ways. In the flow of ambiguous social life, people are constantly "making sense" by reassessing clues in the situation and assigning meanings until they "know what's going on." For example, I see a woman holding her hand out, palm forward. Even this simple act carries multiple potential meanings; I do not know its meaning without knowing the social situation. It could mean that she is warding off a potential mugger, drying her nail polish, hailing a taxi, admiring a new ring, telling oncoming traffic to stop for her, or requesting five bagels at a deli counter (see Brown, 1989:34). People are able to assign appropriate meaning to an act or statement only if they take the social context in which it occurs into account.

Interpretive researchers rarely ask objective survey questions, aggregate the answers of many people, and claim to have something meaningful. Each person's interpretation of the survey question must be placed in a context (e.g., the individual's previous experiences or the survey interview situation), and the true meaning of a person's answer will vary according to the interview or questioning context. Moreover, because each person assigns a somewhat different meaning to the question and answer, combining answers only produces nonsense.

When studying a setting or data, interpretive researchers of the ethnomethodological school often use bracketing. *Bracketing* is a mental exercise in which the researcher identifies then sets aside taken-for-granted assumptions used in a social scene. The researcher questions and reexamines ordinary events that have an "obvious" meaning to those involved. For example, at an office work setting, one male co-worker in his late 20s says to the male researcher, "We're getting together for softball after work tonight. Do you want to join us?" What is *not said* is that the researcher should know the rules of softball, own a softball glove, and change from a business suit into other clothing before the game. It is "obvious" that another co-worker down the hall in a wheelchair will not be asked to play, nor will the 60-year-old nonathletic female supervisor standing nearby. Bracketing reveals what "everyone knows"—what people assume but rarely say. It helps a researcher reveal key features of the social scene that make other events possible. It makes visible the underlying scaffolding of understandings on which actions are based.

8. *When do social/political values enter into science?*

The positivist researcher calls for eliminating values and operating within an apolitical environment. The interpretive researcher, by contrast, argues that researchers should reflect on, reexamine, and analyze personal points of view and feelings as a part of the process of studying others. The interpretive researcher needs, at least temporarily, to empathize with and share in the social and political commitments or values of those he or she studies.

Interpretive research does not try to be value free. Indeed, ISS questions the possibility of achieving it. This is because interpretive research sees values and meaning infused everywhere in everything. What the positivist calls value freedom is just another meaning system and value—the value of positivist science. The interpretive researcher urges making values explicit and does not assume that any one set of values is better or worse. The researcher's proper role is to be a "passionate participant" (Guba and Lincoln 1994:115), involved with those being studied.

Summary

The interpretive approach existed for many years as the loyal opposition to positivism. Although some positivist social researchers accept the interpretive approach as useful in exploratory research (see Chapter 2), few positivists consider it to be scientific. You will read again about the interpretive outlook when you examine field research and, to a lesser degree, historical-comparative research in later chapters. The interpretive approach is the foundation of social research techniques that are sensitive to context, that use various methods to get inside the ways others see the world, and that are more concerned with achieving an empathic understanding of feelings and world views than with testing laws of human behavior.

CRITICAL SOCIAL SCIENCE

Critical social science (CSS) offers a third alternative to the meaning of methodology. Versions of this approach are called dialectical materialism, class analysis, and structuralism.[9] CSS mixes nomothetic and ideographic approaches. It agrees with many of the criticisms the interpretive approach directs at positivism, but it adds some of its own and disagrees with ISS on some points. This approach is traced to Karl Marx (1818–1883), Sigmund Freud (1856–1939), and was elaborated on by Theodor Adorno (1903–1969), Erich Fromm (1900–1980), and Herbert Marcuse (1898–1979). CSS is often associated with conflict theory, feminist analysis, and radical psychotherapy. It is also tied to critical theory, first developed by the Frankfurt School in Germany in the 1930s.[10] CSS criticized positivist science as being narrow, antidemocratic and nonhumanist in its use of reason. This was outlined in Adorno's essays, "Sociology and Empirical Research" (1976a) and "The Logic of the Social Sciences" (1976b). The well-known living representative of the school, Jurgen Habermas (1929–   ), advanced critical social science in his *Knowledge and Human Interests* (1971). In the field of education, Paulo Freire's *Pedagogy of the Oppressed* (1970) also falls within the CSS approach. Recently, a philosophical approach called *realism* has been integrated into CSS.[11]

ISS criticizes positivism for failing to deal with the meanings of real people and their capacity to feel and think. It also believes positivism ignores the social context and is antihumanist. CSS agrees with these criticisms of positivism. CSS also believes that positivism defends the status quo because it assumes an unchanging social order instead of seeing current society as a particular stage in an ongoing process.

Critical researchers criticize the interpretive approach for being too subjective and relativist. The critical researcher says that ISS sees all points of view as equal. The interpretive approach treats people's ideas as more important than actual conditions and focuses on localized, micro-level, short-term settings while ignoring the broader and long-term context. ISS is overly concerned with subjective reality. To critical researchers, ISS is amoral and passive. It does not take a strong value position or actively help people to see false illusions around them so that they can improve their lives. In general, CSS defines social science as a *critical process of inquiry that goes beyond surface illusions to uncover the real structures in the material world in order to help people change conditions and build a better world for themselves.*

The Questions

1. *Why should one conduct social scientific research?*

Critical researchers conduct research to critique and transform social relations. They do this by revealing the underlying sources of social relations and empowering people, especially less powerful people. The purpose of critical research is to change the world. More specifically, social research should uncover myths, reveal hidden truths, and help people to change the world for themselves. In CSS, the purpose is "to explain a social order in such a way that it becomes itself the catalyst which leads to the transformation of this social order" (Fay, 1987:27).

The critical social researcher is action oriented. He or she is dissatisfied with the way things are and seeks dramatic improvements. A positivist researcher usually tries to solve problems as they are defined by government or corporate elites, without "rocking the boat." By contrast, the critical researcher may create problems by "intentionally raising and identifying more problems than the ruling elites in politics and administration are able to accommodate, much less to 'solve'" (Offe, 1981:34–35). The critical researcher asks embarrassing questions, exposes hypocrisy, and investigates conditions in order to encourage dramatic grass-roots action. "The point of all science, indeed all learning, is to change and develop out of our understandings and reduce illusion. . . . Learning is the reducing of illusion and ignorance; it can help free us from domination by hitherto unacknowledged constraints, dogmas and falsehoods" (Sayer, 1992:252).

For example, a critical researcher conducts a study showing that there is racial discrimination in rental housing in a city. White landlords refuse to rent to minority tenants. A critical researcher would not just publish a report and then wait for the fair housing office of the city government to act. The researcher gives the report to newspapers and meets with grass-roots organizations to discuss the results of the study. He or she works with activists to mobilize political action in the name of social justice. When grass-roots people picket the landlords' offices, flood the landlords with racial minority applicants for apartments, or organize a march on city hall demanding action, the critical researcher predicts that the landlords will be forced to rent to minorities. The goal of research is to empower.

> *Critical research can be best understood in the context of the empowerment of individuals. Inquiry that aspires to the name critical must be connected to an attempt to confront the injustice of a particular society or sphere within the society. Research thus becomes a transformative endeavor unembarrassed by the label "political" and unafraid to consummate a relationship with an emancipatory consciousness. (Kincheloe and McLaren, 1994:140)*

2. *What is the fundamental nature of social reality?*

Like positivism, CSS adopts a realist position (i.e., social reality is "out there" to be discovered). It differs from positivism in that it is historical realism in which reality is seen as constantly shaped by social, political, cultural, and similar factors. Social reality evolves over time. It may be misleading on the surface and have unobservable enduring real structures of power underneath. CSS assumes that social reality always changes and the change is rooted in the tensions, conflicts, or contradictions of social relations or institutions. CSS focuses on change and conflict, especially paradoxes or conflicts that are inherent in the very way social relations are organized. Such paradoxes or inner conflicts reveal much about the true nature of social reality.

A biological analogy illustrates such paradoxes. Death and birth appear to be opposites, yet death begins with birth. We begin to die the day we are born. This sounds strange at first, but our bodies begin to age and decay as we live. There is an inner contradiction. Birth necessarily brings about its negation, death. Thus, the inner tension between living and aging goes on all the time. In order to live, our bodies must age, or move toward death. Death and birth are less the opposites they appear to be than the interlocked parts of a single larger process of change. Sometimes, this idea of a paradoxical inner conflict or contradiction that brings about change is called the *dialectic*.

Change can be uneven—extremely slow for long periods of time, then suddenly speed up. The critical researcher studies the past or different societies in order to better see change or to discover alternative ways to organize social life. CSS is interested in the development of new social relations, the evolution of social institutions or societies, and the causes of major social change.

A critical approach notes that social change and conflict are not always apparent or observable. The social world is full of illusion, myth, and distortion. Initial observations of the world are only partial and often misleading because the human senses are limited and so is our knowl-edge. Illusion and myth are how social reality operates. The appearances in surface reality do not have to be based on conscious deception. The immediately perceived characteristics of objects, events, or social relations rarely reveal everything. These illusions allow some groups in society to hold power and exploit others. Karl Marx, German sociologist and political thinker, stated this forcefully (Marx and Engels 1947:39): "The ideas of the ruling class are in every epoch the ruling ideas; . . . The class which has the means of material production at its disposal, has control at the same time over the means of mental production, so that . . . the ideas of those who lack the means of mental production are subject to it."

The critical science approach argues that social reality has multiple layers. Behind the immediately observable surface reality lie deep structures or unobservable mechanisms. The events and relations of superficial social reality are based on deep structures beneath the surface of casual observation. We can uncover or expose such structures with effort. Intense and directed questioning, a good theory about where to look, a clear value position, and a historical orientation help the critical researcher probe below the surface reality and discover the deep structures.

ISS and CSS both see social reality as changing and subject to socially created meanings. The critical science approach disagrees with the ISS emphasis on micro-level interpersonal interactions and its acceptance of any meaning system. CSS says that although subjective meaning is important, there are real, objective relations that shape social relations. The critical researcher questions social situations and places them in a larger, macro-level historical context.

For example, an interpretive researcher studies the interactions of a boss and his secretary and provides a colorful account of their rules of behavior, interpretive mechanisms, and systems of meaning. By contrast, the critical researcher begins with a point of view (e.g., feminist) and notes issues ignored in an interpretive description: Why are bosses male and secretaries female? Why do the roles of boss and secretary have unequal power? Why are such roles created in large organizations throughout our society? How did the unequal power come about historically, and were secretaries always female? How do sex roles in society affect the relationship? Why can the boss make off-color jokes among friends about sleeping with the secretary, while the secretary is humiliated? How are the roles of boss and secretary in conflict based on the everyday conditions of life faced by the boss (large salary, country club membership, new car, large home, retirement plan, stock investments) and those of the secretary (low hourly pay, children to care for, concerns about how to pay bills, television as her only recreation)? Can the secretary join with others to challenge the power of her boss and similar bosses?

3. *What is the basic nature of human beings?*

Positivism views social forces almost as if they had a life of their own and operated regardless of people's personal wishes. Such social forces have power over and operate on people. The critical science approach rejects this idea as reification. *Reification* is giving the creations of your own activity a separate, alien existence. It is separating or removing yourself from what you have created, until you no longer recognize it as part of you or as something you helped to bring about. Once you no longer see your contributions and treat what you have helped to create as an outside force, you lose control over your destiny.

For example, two people meet, fall in love, marry, and set up a household. Within two years, the male feels helpless and trapped by unseen forces. He fights with his wife over child care and household chores. The man's social values say that it is wrong for him to change diapers or wash dishes. His agreement to marry and adopt a particular life-style are creations of his socialization and personal decisions. Thus, the unseen forces acting on him that make him feel trapped and helpless are his own social creations, although he forgets this. If he becomes aware of the forces that trap him (i.e., societal values, social roles, and his own decisions) and takes action to change them (i.e., modifies his life-style), he may be able to find a solution and to feel less trapped.

The critical researcher says that people have a great deal of unrealized potential. People are creative, changeable, and adaptive. Despite their creativity and potential for change, however, people can also be misled, mistreated, and exploited by others. They become trapped in a web of social meanings, obligations, and relationships. They fail to see how change is possible and thus lose their independence, freedom, and control over their lives. This happens when people allow themselves to become isolated and detached from others in similar situations. The potential of people can be realized if they dispel their illusions and join collectively to change society. People can change the social world, but delusion, isolation, and oppressive conditions in everyday life often prevent them from realizing their dreams.

For example, for generations, most Americans believed the myth that women were inferior to men, that men had an inherent right to make major decisions, and that women were incapable of professional responsibilities. Before the 1960s, most people believed that women were less capable than men. By the 1980s, only a minority continued to hold such a belief. The dramatic change in belief and social relations resulted from a new consciousness and organized political action to destroy a myth that existed in laws, customs, and official policies, as well as—most importantly—in the everyday beliefs of most people.

4. *What is the relationship between science and common sense?*

The CSS position on common sense is based on the idea of *false consciousness*—that people are mistaken and act against their own true best interests as defined in objective reality. Objective reality lies behind myth and illusion. False consciousness is meaningless for ISS because it implies that a social actor uses a meaning system that is false or out of touch with objective reality. The interpretive approach says that people create and use such systems and that researchers can only describe such systems, not judge their value. The critical science approach says that social researchers should study subjective ideas and

What it does as research —

common sense because these shape human behavior. Yet, they are full of myth and illusion. CSS assumes that there is an objective world in which there is unequal control over resources and power on which common sense is based.

The structures that critical researchers talk about are not easy to see. In order to see structures, researchers must first demystify them and pull back the veil of their surface appearances. Careful observation is not enough. It does not tell what to observe, and observing an illusion does not dispel it. A researcher must use theory to dig beneath surface relations, to observe periods of crisis and intense conflict, to probe interconnections, to look at the past, and to consider future possibilities. Uncovering the deeper level of reality is difficult, but it is essential because surface reality is full of ideology, myth, distortion, and false appearances. "Common sense tends to naturalize social phenomena and to assume that what is, must be. A social science which builds uncritically on common sense . . . reproduces these errors" (Sayer, 1992:43).

5. *What constitutes an explanation or theory of social reality?*

Positivism is based on the idea of *determinism*: Human behavior is determined by causal laws over which humans have little control. ISS assumes *voluntarism*: People have a large amount of free will to create social meanings. The critical science approach falls between the other two. It is partially deterministic and partially voluntaristic. CSS says that people are constrained by the material conditions, cultural context, and historical conditions in which they find themselves. The world people live in limits their options and shapes their beliefs and behavior. Yet, people are not locked into an inevitable set of social structures, relationships, or laws. People can develop new understandings or ways of seeing that enable them to change these structures, relationships, and laws. They need first to develop a vision of the future and work together for change, then they can overcome those who oppose them. In a nutshell, people do shape their destiny, but not under conditions of their own choosing.

A complete critical science explanation does several things: It demystifies illusion, describes the underlying structure of conditions, explains how change can be achieved, and provides a vision of a possible future. Critical theory does more than describe the unseen mechanisms that account for observable reality; it also critiques conditions and implies a plan of change.

The critical science approach focuses less on fixed laws of human behavior because the laws are seen as changing. Human behavior is only partially governed by laws or constraints imposed by underlying social structures. People can change most of the apparent laws of society, although this is difficult and involves a long struggle. By identifying the causal mechanisms, the trigger or the levers of social relations, CSS explains how and why certain actions will bring about change.

6. *How does one determine whether an explanation is true or false?*

Positivists test theories by deducing hypotheses, testing hypotheses with replicated observations, and then combining results to support laws. Interpretive researchers collect support for theories by seeing whether the meaning system and rules of behavior make sense to those being studied. Critical theory seeks to provide people with a resource that will help them understand and change their world. A researcher tests critical theory by describing accurately conditions generated by underlying structures then by applying that knowledge to change social relations. A good critical theory teaches people about their own experiences, helps them to understand their historical role, and can be used by ordinary people to improve conditions.

Critical theory informs practical action or suggests what to do, but theory is also modified on the basis of its use. A critical theory grows and interacts with the world it seeks to explain. Because a critical approach tries to explain and change the world by penetrating hidden structures that are in constant change, the test of an explanation is not static. Testing theory is a dynamic, ongoing process of applying theory and modifying it. Knowledge grows by an ongoing process of eroding ignorance and enlarging insights through action.

The critical approach uses *praxis* to separate good from bad theory. It puts the theory into practice and uses the outcome of practical applications to reformulate theory. *Praxis* means that explanations are valued when they help people really understand the world and to take action that changes it. As Andrew Sayer (1992:13) argued, "Knowledge is primarily gained through activity both in attempting to change our environment (through labor or work) and through interaction with other people."

Critical research tries to eliminate the division between the researcher and those being researched, the distinction between science and everyday life. For example, a critical researcher develops an explanation for housing discrimination. He or she tests the explanation by acting on it and using it to try to change conditions. If the explanation says that underlying economic relations cause discrimination and that landlords refuse to rent to minorities because it is profitable to rent only to whites, then political actions that make it profitable to rent to minorities should change the landlords' behavior. By contrast, if the explanation says that an underlying racial hatred and not the profit motive causes landlords to discriminate, then actions based on profit will be unsuccessful. The critical researcher would then examine race hatred as the basis of landlord behavior through new studies combined with new political action.

7. *What does good evidence or factual information look like?*

Positivism assumes that there are incontestable neutral facts on which all rational people agree. Its dualist doctrine says that social facts are like objects. They exist separate from values or theories. The interpretive approach sees the social world as made up of created meaning, with people creating and negotiating meanings. It rejects positivism's dualism, but it substitutes an emphasis on the subject. Evidence is whatever resides in the subjective understandings of

those involved. The critical approach tries to bridge the object-subject gap. It says that the facts of material conditions exist independent of subjective perceptions, but that facts are not theory neutral, Instead, facts require an interpretation from within a framework of values, theory, and meaning.

For example, it is a "fact" that the United States spends a much greater percentage of its gross national product (GNP) on health care than any other advanced industrial nation, and yet it has the 14th lowest infant death rate. A critical researcher interprets the fact by noting that the United States has many people without health care and no system to cover everyone. The fact includes the way the health care is delivered to some through a complex system of for-profit insurance companies, pharmaceutical firms, hospitals, and others who benefit greatly from the current arrangement. Some powerful groups are getting rich while weaker or poor sectors of society are getting low quality or no health care. Critical researchers look at the facts and ask who benefits and who loses?

Theory helps a critical researcher find new facts and to separate the important from the trivial ones. The theory is a type of map telling researchers where to look for facts and how to interpret them once they are uncovered. The critical approach says that theory does this in the natural sciences as well. For example, a biologist looks into a microscope and sees red blood cells—a "fact" based on a theory about blood and cells and a biologist's education about microscopic phenomena. Without this theory and education, a biologist sees only meaningless spots. Clearly, then, facts and theories are interrelated.

For example, in *Inequality in Africa*, Wayne Nafziger (1988) used a critical perspective. He criticized "facts" on income inequality because they measured only money income in societies where money is not widely used. He also criticized interpretations of "facts" on issues such as land distribution and infant mortality rates. Such facts ignored the number of people living on a farm and ignored those outside one group in a nation (South African whites) that has drastically lower infant mortality rates than others in the same nation. Instead, Nafziger looked for a wide variety of facts (e.g., birth rates, urban-rural gaps, ethnic divisions, international trade, political power) and went behind the surface facts to connect them to one another. He asked: Why is Africa the only region in the world to become more impoverished since World War II? His theory helped him identify a number of major social groups (e.g., government leaders) and classes (e.g., peasants). Nafziger also asked whether various trends or policies served the interests of each group.

All theories are not equally useful for finding and understanding key facts. Theories are based on beliefs and assumptions about what the world is like and on a set of moral-political values. CSS says that some values are better than others.[12] Thus, in order to interpret facts, one must understand history, adopt a set of values, and know where to look for underlying structures. Different versions of critical science offer different value positions (e.g., Marxism versus feminism).

8. *When do social/political values enter into science?*

The critical approach has an activist orientation. Social research is a moral-political activity that requires the researcher to commit to a value position. CSS rejects positivist value freedom as a myth. It also attacks the interpretive approach for its *relativism* (the idea that everything is relative and nothing is absolute). In the interpretive approach, the reality of the genius and the reality of the idiot are equally valid and important. There is little, if any, basis for judging between alternative realities or conflicting viewpoints. For example, the interpretive researcher does not call a racist viewpoint wrong, because any viewpoint is true for those who believe in it. The critical approach says that there is only one, or a very few, correct points of view. Other viewpoints are plain wrong or misleading. All social research *necessarily* begins with a value or a moral point of view. For CSS, being objective is not being value free. Objectivity means a nondistorted, true picture of reality; "it challenges the belief that science must be protected from politics. It argues that some politics—the politics for emancipatory social change—can increase the objectivity of science" (Harding, 1986:162).

Critical social science says that to deny that a researcher has a point of view is itself a point of view. It is a technician's point of view: Conduct research and ignore the moral questions; satisfy a sponsor and follow orders. Such a view says that science is a tool or instrument anyone can use. This view was strongly criticized when Nazi scientists committed inhumane experiments and then claimed that they were blameless because they "just followed orders" and were "just scientists." Positivism adopts such an approach and produces technocratic knowledge—a form of knowledge best suited for use by the people in power to dominate or control other people.[13] For CSS, "the political use of behavioral science has made positivism into a legitimating ideology of dominant groups . . . value-freedom itself has come to provide an ethic for calculated bureaucratic control" (Brown, 1989:39).

The critical approach rejects positivism and ISS as being detached and concerned with studying the world instead of acting on it. CSS holds that knowledge is a type of power. Social science knowledge can be used to control people, it can be hidden in ivory towers for intellectuals to play games with, or it can be given to people to help them take charge of and improve their lives. What a researcher studies, how he or she studies it, and what happens to the results involve values and morality, because knowledge can have tangible effects on people's lives. The researcher who studies trivial behavior, who fails to probe beneath the surface, or who buries the results in a university library is making a moral choice. The choice is to take information from the people being studied without involving them or liberating them. Critical science questions the morality of such a choice, even if it is not a conscious one. The researcher's proper role is to be the "transformative intellectual" (Guba and Lincoln, 1994:115).

Summary

Although few full-time researchers adopt the critical science approach, it is often adopted by community action groups, political organizations, and social movements. It only rarely appears in scholarly journals. Critical researchers may use any research technique, but they tend to favor the historical-comparative method. This is because of its emphasis on change and because it helps researchers uncover underlying structures. Critical researchers differ from the others less in the research techniques they use than in how they approach a research problem, the kinds of questions they ask, and their purposes for doing research.

FEMINIST AND POSTMODERN RESEARCH

You may hear about two additional approaches that are still in a formative stage and are less well known than the three major ones. They are feminist and postmodern social research. Both criticize positivism and offer alternatives that build on interpretive and critical social science. They are still embryonic, having gained visibility only in the late 1980s.

Feminist research is conducted by people, almost all of them women, who hold a feminist self-identity and consciously use a feminist perspective. They use multiple research techniques. Feminist methodology attempts to give a voice to women and to correct the male-oriented perspective that has predominated in the development of social science. It is inspired by works such as *Women's Ways of Knowing* (Belenky, Clinchy, Goldberger, and Tarule, 1986) that argue that women learn and express themselves differently than men.

Feminist research is based on a heightened awareness that the subjective experience of women differs from an ordinary interpretative perspective (Olsen, 1994). Many feminist researchers see positivism as being consistent with a male point of view; it is objective, logical, task oriented, and instrumental. It reflects a male emphasis on individual competition, on dominat-

ing and controlling the environment, and on the hard facts and forces that act on the world. In contrast, women emphasize accommodation and gradually developing human bonds. They see the social world as a web of interconnected human relations, full of people linked together by feelings of trust and mutual obligation. Women tend to emphasize the subjective, empathetic, process-oriented, and inclusive sides of social life. Feminist research is also action oriented and seeks to advance feminist values (see Box 4.1).

Feminist researchers argue that much non-feminist research is sexist, largely as a result of broader cultural beliefs and a preponderance of male researchers. The research overgeneralizes from the experience of men to all people, ignores gender as a fundamental social division, focuses on men's problems, uses male as points of reference, and assumes traditional gender roles. For example, a traditional researcher would say that a family has a problem of unemployment when the adult male in it cannot find stable work. When a woman in the same family cannot find stable work outside the home, it is not considered an equal family problem. Likewise, the concept

Box 4.1 _____

Characteristics of Feminist Social Research

— Advocacy of a feminist value position and perspective
— Rejection of sexism in assumptions, concepts, and research questions
— Creation of empathic connections between the researcher and those he or she studies
— Sensitivity to how relations of gender and power permeate all spheres of social life
— Incorporation of the researcher's personal feelings and experiences into the research process
— Flexibility in choosing research techniques and crossing boundaries between academic fields
— Recognition of the emotional and mutual-dependence dimensions in human experience
— Action-oriented research that seeks to facilitate personal and societal change

unwed mother is widely used by traditional researchers, but is not a parallel of _unwed father_.

The feminist approach sees researchers as fundamentally gendered beings. Researchers necessarily have a gender that will shape how they experience reality, and therefore it affects their research (Cook and Fonow, 1990). In addition to gender's impact on individual researchers, basic theoretical assumptions and the scientific community appear as gendered cultural contexts. Gender has a pervasive influence in culture and shapes basic beliefs and values that cannot be simply isolated and insulated in the social processes of scientific inquiry (Longino, 1990).

Feminist researchers are not objective or detached; they interact and collaborate with the people they study. They fuse their personal and professional lives. For example, feminist researchers will attempt to comprehend an interviewee's experiences while sharing their own feelings and experiences. This process may give birth to a personal relationship between researcher and interviewee that might mature over time. Shulamit Reinharz (1992:263) argued, "This blurring of the disconnection between formal and personal relations, just as the removal of the distinction . . . between the research project and the researcher's life, is a characteristic of much, if not all, feminist research."

The impact of a woman's perspective and her desire to seek and gain an intimate, profound relationship with what she studies occurs even in the biological sciences.[14] Feminist researchers tend to avoid quantitative analysis and experiments. They are rarely rigidly attached to one method; rather, they use multiple methods, often qualitative research and case studies. Sherry Gorelick (1991) criticized the affinity of many feminist researchers for interpretive social science. She feels that ISS becomes limited to the consciousness of those being studied and fails to reveal hidden structures. Gorelick wants feminist researchers to adopt a more critical approach and to advocate social change more assertively.

Postmodern research is part of the larger postmodern movement or evolving understanding of the contemporary world that includes art,

music, literature, and cultural criticism. It began in the humanities and has roots in the philosophies of existentialism, nihilism, and anarchism and in the ideas of Heidegger, Nietzsche, Sartre, and Wittgenstein. Postmodernism is a rejection of modernism. _Modernism_ refers to basic assumptions, beliefs, and values that arose in the Enlightenment era. Modernism relies on logical reasoning; it is optimistic about the future and believes in progress, it has confidence in technology and science, and it embraces humanist values (i.e., judging ideas based on their effect on human welfare). Modernism holds that there are standards of beauty, truth, and morality about which most people can agree (Brannigan, 1992).

Postmodern research sees no separation between the arts or humanities and social sciences. It shares the critical social science goal of demystifying the social world. It seeks to deconstruct or tear apart surface appearances to reveal the internal hidden structure. Like extreme forms of ISS, postmodernism distrusts abstract explanation and holds that research can never do more than describe, with all descriptions equally valid. A researcher's description is neither superior nor inferior to anyone else's and only describes the researcher's personal experiences. Going beyond interpretive and critical social science, it attempts to radically transform or dismantle social science. Extreme postmodernists reject the possibility of a science of the social world. Postmodernists distrust all systematic empirical observation and doubt that knowledge is generalizable or accumulates over time. They see knowledge as taking numerous forms and as unique to particular people or specific locales. Pauline Rosenau (1992:77) argued, "Almost all postmodernists reject truth as even a goal or ideal because it is the very epitome of modernity. . . . Truth makes reference to order, rules, and values; depends on logic, rationality and reason, all of which the postmodernists question."

Postmodernists object to presenting research results in a detached and neutral way. The researcher or author of a report should never be hidden when someone reads it; his or her presence needs to be unambiguously evident in the report. Thus, a postmodern research report is similar to a work of art. Its purpose is to stimulate others, to give pleasure, to evoke a response, or to arouse curiosity. Postmodern reports often have a theatrical, expressive, or dramatic style of presentation. They may be in the form of a work of fiction, a movie, or a play. The postmodernist argues that the knowledge about social life created by a researcher may be better communicated through a skit or musical piece than by a scholarly journal article. Its value lies in telling a story that may stimulate experiences within the people who read or encounter it. Postmodernism is antielitist and rejects the use of science to predict and to make policy decisions. Postmodernists oppose those who use positivist science to reinforce power relations and bureaucratic forms of control over people (see Box 4.2).

CONCLUSION

You have learned two basic things in this chapter. First, there are competing approaches to social research based on different philosophical assumptions about the purpose of science and the nature of social reality. Second, the three ideal-type approaches to social science answer basic questions about research differently (see Table 4.1). Most researchers operate primarily within one approach, but many also combine elements from the others.

Remember that you can study the same topic from any of these approaches, but each approach implies going about it differently. This can be illustrated with the topic of discrimination and job competition between minority and majority groups in four countries: aborigines in the Australian outback, Asians in western Canada, African Americans in the midwestern United States, and Pakistanis in London.

A researcher who adopts a positivist approach first deduces hypotheses from a general theory about majority-minority relations. The theory is probably in the form of causal statements or predictions. For example, Stone (1985:56) cited one theory that "seeks to explain complex patterns in terms of a few key variables. This can be useful in attempts to predict the possible development of race and ethnic relations." The researcher

---

Box 4.2 _____

Characteristics of Postmodern Social Research

- Rejection of all ideologies and organized belief systems, including all social theory
- Strong reliance on intuition, imagination, personal experience, and emotion
- Sense of meaninglessness and pessimism, belief that the world will never improve
- Extreme subjectivity in which there is no distinction between the mental and the external world
- Ardent relativism in which there are infinite interpretations, none superior to another
- Espousal of diversity, chaos, and complexity that is constantly changing
- Rejection of studying the past or different places since only the here and now is relevant
- Belief that causality cannot be studied because life is too complex and rapidly changing
- Assertion that research can never truly represent what occurs in the social world

---

next gathers data from existing government statistics or conducts a survey to precisely measure the factors that the theory identifies, such as the form of initial contact, the ratio of numbers in majority versus minority groups, or the visibility of racial differences. Finally, the researcher uses statistics to formally test the theory's predictions about the degree of discrimination and the intensity of job competition.

An interpretive researcher personally talks with and observes specific people from both the minority groups and the majority groups in each of the four countries. His or her conversations and observations are used to learn what each group feels to be its major problem and whether group members feel that discrimination or job competition are everyday concerns. The researcher puts what people say into the context of their daily affairs (e.g., paying rent, getting involved in family disputes, having run-ins with the law, getting sick). After he or she sees what the minority or

TABLE 4.1 A Summary of Differences among the Three Approaches to Research

	POSITIVISM	INTERPRETIVE SOCIAL SCIENCE	CRITICAL SOCIAL SCIENCE
1. Reason for research	To discover natural laws so people can predict and control events	To understand and describe meaningful social action	To smash myths and empower people to change society radically
2. Nature of social reality	Stable preexisting patterns or order that can be discovered	Fluid definitions of a situation created by human interaction	Conflict filled and governed by hidden underlying structures
3. Nature of human beings	Self-interested and rational individuals who are shaped by external forces	Social beings who create meaning and who constantly make sense of their worlds	Creative, adaptive people with unrealized potential, trapped by illusion and exploitation
4. Role of common sense	Clearly distinct from and less valid than science	Powerful everyday theories used by ordinary people	False beliefs that hide power and objective conditions
5. Theory looks like	A logical, deductive system of interconnected definitions, axioms, and laws	A description of how a group's meaning system is generated and sustained	A critique that reveals true conditions and helps people see the way to a better world
6. An explanation that is true	Is logically connected to laws and based on facts	Resonates or feels right to those who are being studied	Supplies people with tools needed to change the world
7. Good evidence	Is based on precise observations that others can repeat	Is embedded in the context of fluid social interactions	Is informed by a theory that unveils illusions
8. Place for values	Science is value free, and values have no place except when choosing a topic	Values are an integral part of social life: no group's values are wrong, only different	All science must begin with a value position; some positions are right, some are wrong

majority people thinks about discrimination, how they get jobs, how people in the other group get jobs, and what they actually do to get or keep jobs, he or she describes findings in terms that others can understand.

A critical researcher begins by looking at the larger social and historical context. This includes factors such as the invasion of Australia by British colonists and the nation's history as a prison colony, the economic conditions in Asia that caused people to migrate to Canada, the legacy of slavery and civil rights struggles in the United States, and the rise and fall of Britain's colonial empire and the migration of people from its ex-colonies. He or she inquires from a moral/critical standpoint: Does the majority group discriminate against and economically exploit the minority? The researcher looks at many sources to document the underlying pattern of exploitation and to measure the amount of discrimination in each nation. He or she may examine statistical information on income dif- ferences between groups, personally examine living situations and go with people to job inter- views, or conduct surveys to find out what peo- ple now think. Once the researcher finds out how discrimination keeps a minority group from get- ting jobs, he or she gives results to minority group organizations, gives public lectures on the findings, and publishes results in newspapers read by minority group members in order to expose the true conditions and to encourage political-social action.

What does all this about three approaches mean to you in a course on social research? First, it means that there is no single, absolutely correct approach to social science research. This does not mean that anything goes, nor that there is no ground for tentative agreement (see Box 4.3). Rather, means that the basis for doing social research is not settled. In other words, more than one approach is currently "in the running." Perhaps this will always be the case. An aware- ness of the approaches will help you when you

---

Box 4.3

Common Features of the Three Approaches to Social Science

1. *All are empirical.* Each is rooted in the observable reality of the sights, sounds, behaviors, situa- tions, discussions, and actions of people. Research is never based on fabrication and imagination alone.
2. *All are systematic.* Each emphasizes meticulous and careful work. All reject haphazard, shoddy, or sloppy thinking and observation.
3. *All are theoretical.* The nature of theory varies, but all emphasize using ideas and seeing patterns. None holds that social life is chaos and disorder; all hold that explanation or understanding is pos- sible.
4. *All are public.* All say a researcher's work must be candidly expressed to other researchers; it should be made explicit and shared. All oppose keeping the research processes hidden, private, or secret.
5. *All are self-reflective.* Each approach says

researchers need to think about what they do and be self-conscious. Research is never done in a blind or unthinking manner. It involves serious contemplation and requires self-awareness.
6. *All are open-end processes.* All see research as constantly moving, evolving, changing, asking new questions, and pursuing leads. None see it as static, fixed, or closed. Current knowledge or research procedures are not "set in stone" and settled. They involve continuous change and an openness to new ways of thinking and doing things.

Thus, despite their differences, all the ap- proaches say that the social sciences strive to cre- ate systematically gathered, empirically based theo- retical knowledge through public processes that are self-reflective and open ended.

read research reports. Often, researchers will rely on one of these approaches, but rarely will they tell you which one they are using.

Second, it means that what you try to accomplish when you do research (i.e., discover laws, identify underlying structures, describe meaning systems) will vary with the approach you choose. The fit between the three approaches and types of research discussed in Chapter 2 is loose. For example, positivists are likely to conduct cost-benefit analysis, interpretive researchers are likely to do exploratory research, and critical researchers favor action-oriented research. By being aware of the approaches when you do social research, you can make an informed decision about the type of study to conduct.

Third, the various techniques used in social research (sampling, interviewing, participant observation, etc.) are ultimately based on the assumptions of the different approaches. Often, you will see a research technique presented without the background reasoning on which it was originally based. By knowing about the approaches, you can better understand the principles on which the specific research techniques are based. For example, the precise measures and logic of experimental research flows directly from positivism, whereas field research is based on an interpretive approach or a more qualitative method to social inquiry.

So far, we have looked at the overall operation of the research process, different types of studies and theory, and the three fundamental approaches to social research. By now, you should have a grasp of the basic contours of social research. In the next chapter, you will see how to locate reports of specific research projects.

KEY TERMS

causal laws	interpretive social science	postmodern research
critical social science	intersubjectivity	postulate of adequacy
dialectic	meaningful social action	practical orientation
feminist research	mechanical model of man	praxis
hermeneutics	nomothetic	relativism
ideographic	paradigm	value-free science
instrumental orientation	positivist social science	*Verstehen*

REVIEW QUESTIONS

1. What is the purpose of social research according to each approach?
2. How does each approach define social reality?
3. What is the nature of human beings according to each approach?
4. How are science and common sense different in each approach?
5. What is social theory according to each approach?
6. How does each approach test a social theory?
7. What does each approach say about facts and how to collect them?
8. How is value-free science possible in each approach? Explain.
9. How are the criticisms of positivism by the interpretive and critical science approaches similar?
10. How does the model of science and the scientific community presented in Chapter 1 relate to each of the three approaches?

NOTES

1. For educational research, see Bredo and Feinberg (1982) and Guba and Lincoln (1994); for psychology, see Harre and Secord (1979) and Rosnow (1981); for political science, see Sabia and Wallulis (1983); and for economics, see Hollis (1977) and Ward (1972). A general discussion of alternatives can be found in Nowotny and Rose (1979).

2. See especially Friedrichs (1970), Giddens (1976), Gouldner (1970), and Phillips (1971). General introductions are provided by Harre (1972), Suppe (1977), and Toulmin (1953).

3. Divisions of the philosophies of social science similar to the approaches discussed in this chapter can be found in Benton (1977), Blaikie (1993), Bredo and Feinberg (1982), Fay (1975), Fletcher (1974), Guba and Lincoln (1994), Keat and Urry (1975), Lloyd (1986), Mulkay (1979), Sabia and Wallulis (1983), Smart (1976), and Wilson (1970).

4. For discussions of paradigms, see Eckberg and Hill (1979), Kuhn (1970, 1979), Masterman (1970), Ritzer (1975), and Rosnow (1981).

5. In addition to the works listed in note 3, Halfpenny (1982) and Turner (1984) provide overviews of positivism in sociology. Also see Giddens (1978). Lenzer (1975) is an excellent introduction to Auguste Comte.

6. See Couch (1987). Also see Longino (1990:62–82) for an excellent analysis of objectivity in positivism and more broadly.

7. For a discussion, see Bannister (1987), Blumer (1991a, 1991b, 1992), Deegan (1988), Geiger (1986), Gillespie (1991), Lagemann (1989), Ross (1991), Schwendinger and Schwendinger (1974), and Silva and Slaughter (1980).

8. In addition to the works in note 3, interpretive science approaches are discussed in Berger and Luckman (1967), Bleicher (1980), Cicourel (1973), Garfinkel (1967, 1974b), Geertz (1979), Glaser and Strauss (1967), Holstein and Gubrium (1994), Leiter (1980), Mehan and Wood (1975), Silverman (1972), and Weber (1974, 1981).

9. In addition to the works in note 3, critical science approaches are discussed in Burawoy (1990), Fay (1987), Glucksmann (1974), Harding (1986), Harvey (1990), Keat (1981), Lane (1970), Lemert (1981), Mayhew (1980, 1981), Sohn-Rethel (1978), Veltmeyer (1978), Wardell (1979), Warner (1971), and Wilson (1982). Also see Dickson (1984).

10. For a discussion of the Frankfurt School, see Bottomore (1984), Held (1980), Martin (1973), and Slater (1977). For more on the works of Habermas, see Holub (1991), McCarthy (1978), Pusey (1987), and Roderick (1986).

11. For discussions of realism, see Bhaskar (1975), Miller (1987), and Sayer (1992).

12. See Sprague and Zimmerman (1989) on feminists' privileged perspectives of women and see Rule (1978a, 1978b) on constituencies that researchers favor.

13. See Habermas (1971, 1973, 1979) for a critical science critique of positivism as being technocratic and used for domination. He suggests an emancipatory alternative. Also see note 10.

14. See Evelyn Fox Keller's (1983) biography of Barbara McClintock and her other essays on gender and science (1985, 1990). Also see Longino (1990), Chapters 6 and 7.

RECOMMENDED READINGS

Berger, Peter, and Thomas Luckman. (1967). *The social construction of reality: A treatise in the sociology of knowledge.* Garden City, NY: Anchor. This is a classic work within the interpretive approach to social science. It gives a forceful statement of how what we consider to be real is based on social meanings that are constructed and reconstructed by people during social interactions with each other.

Blaikie, Norman. (1993). *Approaches to social inquiry*, Cambridge, MA: Polity Press. Blaikie offers a clear overview of a wide variety of approaches and issues in how social science is to be conducted. He gives special attention to the contrast between a critical-realist and an interpretive or constructivist approach.

Fay, Brian. (1987). *Critical social science: Liberation and its limits.* Ithaca, NY: Cornell University Press. This is Fay's second book on the different approaches to social science. Here, he has presented a clear statement of what a critical social science should involve, its major parts, and its weaknesses.

Guba, Egon G., and Yvonna S. Lincoln. (1994). Competing paradigms in qualitative research. In *Handbook of qualitative research*, edited by

Norman K. Denzin and Yvonna S. Lincoln, pp. 105–117. Thousand Oaks, CA: Sage. This is an up-to-date overview of the three major approaches written from an interpretive point of view.

Halfpenny, Peter. (1982). *Positivism and sociology: Explaining social life.* London: George Allen and Unwin. This short book traces the origin of positivism to Comte, summarizes some of the varieties of positivism within sociology, and discusses how positivism is related to the use of social statistics and explanation.

Reinharz, Shulamit. (1992). *Feminist methods in social research.* New York: Oxford University Press. Reinharz discusses how a feminist approach to research differs from other approaches and identifies its common features. In addition, she explains how feminist researchers use many specific research techniques, case studies, content analysis, oral history, cross-cultural research, experimental, survey, field research, and survey research. She cites hundreds of example studies taken from social science fields.

Rosenau, Pauline Marie. (1992). *Post-modernism and the social sciences.* Princeton, NJ: Princeton University Press. This is a relatively accessible and even-handed introduction to postmodernism in the social sciences. Rosenau traces its origins and outlines its implications for methodology. She also identifies two major tendencies in contemporary postmodern thinking and evaluates its potential.

Sayer, Andrew. (1992). *Method in social science: A realist approach,* 2nd ed. New York: Routledge. This is a well-written introduction to the realist philosophy of science and its implications for the social sciences.

CHAPTER 5

READING OTHER PEOPLE'S RESEARCH

Typically, the scientific paper or monograph presents an immaculate appearance which reproduces little or nothing of the intuitive leaps, false starts, mistakes, loose ends, and happy accidents that actually cluttered up the inquiry. The public record of science therefore fails to provide many of the source materials needed to reconstruct the actual course of scientific developments.

—Robert Merton, *On Theoretical Sociology*, p. 4

INTRODUCTION

In the previous chapters, you learned about the general process and approaches to research. I referred to examples from published reports of research. It is now time to locate and read research reports.

Reviewing the accumulated knowledge about a question is an essential early step in the research process, no matter which approach to social science you adopt. As in other areas of life, it is best to find out what is already known about a question before trying to answer it yourself. The

cliché about wasting time reinventing the wheel is a reminder to do your homework before beginning an endeavor that requires an investment of time and effort. This is true for the consumer of research and for the professional researcher beginning a study.

This chapter examines the literature review as part of the research process. After reading it, you should understand the role of the literature review and its purpose in a specific study. You should know how to conduct a review. You will have another reason for learning about your college library, although this chapter cannot substitute for a visit to the library and assistance from a professional librarian. Finally, you will learn about six types of reviews, and you will see differences between good and bad reviews. The skills you use to conduct a high-quality literature review will improve your understanding of the research process.

We begin by looking at the various purposes the review can serve. We will also discuss what the *literature* is, where to find it, and what it contains. Next, we will explore techniques for systematically conducting a review. Finally, we will look at how to write a review and its place in a research report.

WHY CONDUCT A LITERATURE REVIEW?

A literature review is based on the assumption that knowledge accumulates and that we learn from and build on what others have done. Scientific research is not an activity of isolated hermits who ignore others' findings. Rather, it is a collective effort of many researchers who share their results with one another and who pursue knowledge as a community. Although some studies may be especially important and individual researchers may become famous, a specific research project is just a tiny part of the overall process of creating knowledge. Today's studies build on those of yesterday. Researchers read studies to compare, replicate, or criticize them for weaknesses.

Reviews vary in scope and depth. Different kinds of reviews are stronger at fulfilling one or another of four goals (see Box 5.1). It may take a researcher over a year to complete an extensive professional summary review of all the literature on a broad question. The same researcher might complete a highly focused review in a very specialized area in a few weeks. When beginning a review, a researcher decides on a topic or field of knowledge to examine, how much depth to go into, and the kind of review to conduct. The six kinds are ideal types (see Box 5.2). A specific review often combines features of several kinds.

All reviews follow the first goal—to show familiarity and establish credibility—to some degree. It is one reason teachers ask students to

---

Box 5.1 _____

Goals of a Literature Review

1. *To demonstrate a familiarity with a body of knowledge* and establish credibility. A review tells a reader that the researcher knows the research in an area and knows the major issues. A good review increases a reader's confidence in the researcher's professional competence, ability, and background.
2. *To show the path of prior research* and how a current project is linked to it. A review outlines the direction of research on a question and shows the development of knowledge. A good review places a research project in a context and demonstrates its relevance by making connections to a body of knowledge.
3. *To integrate and summarize what is known* in an area. A review pulls together and synthesizes different results. A good review points out areas where prior studies agree, where they disagree, and where major questions remain. It collects what is known up to a point in time and indicates the direction for future research.
4. *To learn from others and stimulate new ideas.* A review tells what others have found so that a researcher can benefit from the efforts of others. A good review identifies blind alleys and suggests hypotheses for replication. It divulges procedures, techniques, and research designs worth copying so that a researcher can better focus hypotheses and gain new insights.

---

write library research term papers. A review that only demonstrates familiarity with an area is rarely published, but it often is part of an educational program. When this goal is combined with the fourth goal, it is a *self-study review*. In addition to giving others confidence in a reviewer's command of a field, it has the side benefit of building the reviewer's self-confidence.

The most common reason for writing a literature review is the second goal: creating links to a developing body of knowledge. This is a background or *context review*. It usually appears at the beginning of a report or article. It introduces the

Box 5.2 _____

Six Types of Reviews

1. Self-study reviews increase the reader's confidence.
2. Context reviews place a specific project in the big picture.
3. Historical reviews trace the development of an issue over time.
4. Theoretical reviews compare how different theories address an issue.
5. Methodological reviews point out how methodology varies by study.
6. Integrative reviews summarize what is known at a point in time.

rest of a research report and establishes the significance and relevance of a research question. It tells the reader how a project fits into the big picture and its implications for a field of knowledge. The review can emphasize how the current research continues a developing line of thought, or it can point to a question or unresolved conflict in prior research to be addressed.

Another kind of review combines the second and third goals. The *historical review* traces the development of an idea or shows how a particular issue or theory has evolved over time. Researchers conduct historical reviews only on the most important ideas in a field. These reviews are also used in studies of the history of thought. Sometimes they are helpful, when students are introduced to an area, to show how we got to where we are today. They may show how, during the advance of knowledge, a single past idea split into different parts or separate ideas combined into broad thought.

The *theoretical review* primarily follows the third goal. It presents different theories that purport to explain the same thing, then evaluates how well each accounts for findings. In addition to examining the consistency of predictions with findings, a theoretical review may compare theories for the soundness of their assumptions, logical consistency, and scope of explanation. Researchers also use it to integrate two theories or

extend a theory to new issues. It sometimes forms a hybrid—the historical-theoretical review.

The *integrative review* presents the current state of knowledge and pulls together disparate research reports in a fast-growing area of knowledge. Researchers may publish such valuable reviews as an article to provide a service to other researchers.

The *methodological review* is a specialized type of the integrative review. In it, a researcher evaluates the methodological strength of past studies. It describes conflicting results and shows how different research designs, samples, measures, and so on account for different results. For example, a researcher may discover that all experiments that relied on males yielded different results than those that used both sexes.

A *meta-analysis* is a special technique researchers use in an integrative review, or more often, in a methodological review.[1] The researcher gathers the details about a large number of research projects (e.g., sample size, when published, size of the effects of variables) and then statistically analyzes this information. For example, Armstrong and Lusk (1987) conducted a meta-analysis on return postage in mail surveys. They searched the literature extensively and found 34 studies that examined the effects of including postage, of first-class versus business-reply postage, and of commemorative versus standard stamps. They examined the type of postage that is most likely to get respondents to return a questionnaire. For each study, they looked at the number of questionnaires mailed out, the percentage returned, and the types of postage used. The researchers found that when first-class postage was used instead of business reply, the questionnaire return rate was consistently higher by about 9 percent.

Stephen Cox and William Davidson (1995) used meta-analysis to examine findings on whether alternative education programs help juvenile delinquents. These nontraditional programs are designed specifically for troubled youths, using low student/teacher ratios, an unstructured environment, and individualized learning. The authors first conducted a computerized search of three sources: ERIC (Educational Resources

Information Circuit), PSYCHLIT, and NCJRS (National Criminal Justice Reference Service) for the years 1966 to 1993. They looked for all citations that mentioned alternative education programs for youth and found 241 citations. They next read each to see whether the article met three criteria: (1) mentioned a separate curriculum, (2) was held in a separate location or building, (3) included quantitative measures of program outcomes. Of the 241 studies, only 87 met all three criteria. The researchers then checked whether the studies used specific statistical measures or tests; they found that 57 studies had the statistics. After statistically analyzing the results of the 57 studies, the authors learned that such programs slightly improve school performance and self-esteem but do not directly reduce delinquent behavior.

WHERE DO I FIND THE RESEARCH LITERATURE?

Researchers present reports of their research projects in several written forms. For the most part, you can find them only in a college or university library. Researchers publish studies as books, scholarly journal articles, dissertations, government documents, or policy reports. They also present them as papers at the meetings of professional societies. This section briefly discusses each type and gives you a simple road map on how to access them.

You can find the results of research in textbooks, newspapers, popular magazines (e.g., *Time, New Statesman, Economist*), and radio or television news, but these are not true reports of scientific research. Rather, they are condensed summaries of true reports. Authors or journalists selected them for their popular appeal or teaching usefulness and rewrote them for a general audience. Such popularizations lack essential details that the scientific community requires for a serious evaluation of the research and for use in building the knowledge base.

Scholarly Journals

A researcher who conducts a complete literature review will examine all research outlets.

Different types of reports require different search strategies. We begin with scholarly journals because they are the place in which most reports appear and are the most crucial outlet. As you saw in Chapter 1, they are central to the communication system of science.

Sociology is criticized in the popular press for its severe proliferation of journals. Critics charge that numerous journals have sprung up that permit any study, no matter how flawed or trivial, to be published, and that no one reads the articles. The evidence does not support this view. One study (Hargens, 1988) found that rejection rates were higher in the social than in the natural sciences, and that rejection rates are higher now than 20 years ago. Another study (Hargens, 1991) found that a little over 200 journals publish sociological research. This number has been stable since the 1970s, and the number of journals and articles has remained roughly parallel to the number of Ph.D. sociologists. As for the claim that no one reads the articles, for a sample of 379 articles, 43 percent were referred to in other studies in the first year and 83 percent within six years of publication.

Your college library has a section for scholarly journals and magazines, or, in some cases, they may be mixed with books. Look at a map of library facilities or ask a librarian to find this section. The most recent issues, which look like thin paperbacks or thick magazines, are often physically separate in a "current periodicals" section. This is done to store them temporarily and make them available until the library receives all the issues of a volume. Most often, libraries bind all issues of a volume together as a book before adding it to their permanent collection.

Scholarly journals from many different fields are placed together with popular magazines. All are periodicals, or *serials* in the jargon of librarians. Thus, you will find popular magazines (*Time, Road and Track, Cosmopolitan, Atlantic Monthly*) next to journals for astronomy, chemistry, mathematics, literature, and philosophy as well as sociology, psychology, social work, and education. Some fields have more scholarly journals than others. The "pure" academic fields usually have more than the "applied" or practical fields such as marketing or social work. The journals are listed by title in a card catalog or a computerized catalog system. Libraries can provide you with a list of the periodicals to which they subscribe.

Many libraries do not retain physical, paper copies of older journals. To save space and costs, they retain only microfilm versions. There are hundreds of scholarly journals in most academic fields, with each costing $50 to $1,500 per year. Only the large research libraries subscribe to all of them. You may have to borrow a journal or photocopy of an article from a distant library through an *interlibrary loan service*, a system by which libraries lend books or materials to other libraries. Few libraries allow people to check out recent issues of scholarly journals. You should plan to use these in the library. A few experimental scholarly journals are available in an electronic form, to be read using computers and a service called Internet.

Once you find the periodicals section, wander down the aisles and skim what is on the shelves. You will see volumes containing many research reports. Each title of a scholarly journal has a call number like that of a regular library book. Libraries often arrange them alphabetically by title. Because journals change titles, it may create confusion if the journal is shelved under its original title.

Scholarly journals differ by field and by type. Most contain articles that report on research in an academic field. Thus, most mathematics journals contain reports on new mathematical studies or proofs, literature journals contain commentary and literary criticism on works of literature, and sociology journals contain reports of sociological research. Some journals cover a broad field (e.g., sociology, psychology, education, political science) and contain reports from the entire field. Others specialize in a subfield (e.g., the family, criminology, early childhood education, comparative politics). There are also a few hybrids or "crossover" publications that try to bridge the gap between academic scholarly journals and popular magazines (e.g., *Psychology Today, Society*). Another hybrid focuses on how to teach or use knowledge in an area (e.g., *Teaching Sociology, Teaching Psychology*). Some journals contain a mix of research reports, book reviews, and so on, whereas others contain only research reports. A few journals specialize in book review articles, literature reviews, policy analysis, and theoretical essays.

Scholarly journals are published as rarely as once a year or as frequently as weekly. Most appear four to six times a year. For example, *Sociological Quarterly* appears four times a year. To assist in locating articles, librarians and scholars have developed a system for tracking scholarly journals and the articles in them. Each issue is assigned a date, volume number, and issue number. This information makes it easier to locate an article. Such information—along with details such as author, title, and page number—is called an article's *citation* and is used in bibliographies. When a journal is first published, it begins with volume 1, number 1, and continues increasing the numbers thereafter. Although most journals follow a similar system, there are enough exceptions that you have to pay close attention to citation information. For most journals, each volume is one year. If you see a journal issue with volume 52, it probably means that the journal has been in existence for 52 years. Most, but not all, journals begin their publishing cycle in January.

Most journals number pages by volume, not by issue. The first issue of a volume usually begins with page 1, and page numbering continues throughout the entire volume. For example, the first page of volume 52, issue 4, may be page 547. Most journals have an index for each volume and a table of contents for each issue that lists the title, the author's or authors' names, and the page on which the article begins. Issues contain as few as 1 or 2 articles or as many as 50. Most have 8 to 18 articles, which may be 5 to 50 pages long. The articles often have *abstracts*, short summaries on the first page of the article or grouped together at the beginning of the issue.

An article's citation is the key to locating it. Suppose you want to read the study on skin tone and stratification among African Americans. If you go to the bibliography of this textbook, you will read its citation as follows:

> Keith, Verna M., and Cedric Herring. (1991). Skin tone and stratification in the black community. *American Journal of Sociology*, 97:760–778.

This tells you that you can find the article in an issue of *American Journal of Sociology* published in 1991. The citation does not give you the month or the issue, but it provides the volume number, 97, and the page numbers, 760–778.

There are many ways to cite the literature. Formats for citing literature in the text itself vary, with the internal citation format of using an author's last name and date of publication in parentheses being very popular. The full citation appears in a separate bibliography or reference section. There are many styles for full citations of journal articles, with books and other types of works each having a separate style. When citing articles, it is best to check with an instructor, journal, or other outlet for the desired format. Almost all include the names of authors, article title, journal name, and volume and page numbers. Beyond these basic elements, there is great variety. Some include the authors' first names, others use initials only. Some include all authors, others give only the first one. Some include information on the issue or month of publication, others do not (see Table 5.1).

Citation formats can get complex. Two major reference tools on the topic in social science are the *Chicago Manual of Style*, which has nearly 80 pages on bibliographies and reference formats, and the *American Psychological Association Publication Manual*, which devotes about 60 pages to the topic. In sociology, the *American Sociological Review* style, with 2 pages of style instructions, is widely followed.

Books

Books communicate many types of information, provoke thought, and entertain. There are many types of books: picture books, textbooks, short story books, novels, popular fiction or nonfiction, religious books, children's books, and others. Our concern here is with those books containing reports of original research or collections of research articles. Libraries shelve these books and assign call numbers to them, as they do with other types of books. You can find citation information on them (e.g., title, author, publisher) in the library's catalog system.

Hargens (1991) noted that sociological researchers cite books about as often as articles. He sees the literature in sociology as being between that of the natural sciences and that of the humanities. The natural sciences rely more on articles and the humanities more on books.

It is not easy to distinguish a book that reports on a piece of research from other books. You are more likely to find such books in a college or university library. Some publishers, such as university presses, specialize in publishing them. Nevertheless, there is no guaranteed method for identifying one without reading it.

Some types of social research are more likely to appear in book form than others. For example, studies by anthropologists and historians are more likely to appear in book-length reports than are those of economists or psychologists. Yet, some anthropological and historical studies are articles, and some economic and psychological studies appear as books. In education, social work, sociology, and political science, the results of long, complex studies may appear both in two or three articles and in book form. Studies that involve detailed clinical or ethnographic descriptions and complex theoretical or philosophical discussions usually appear as books. Finally, an author who wants to communicate to scholarly peers and to the educated public may write a book that bridges the scholarly, academic style and a popular nonfiction style, such as James Hunter's *Culture Wars* (1991).

Locating original research articles in books can be difficult because there is no single source listing them. Three types of books contain collections of articles or research reports. The first is designed for teaching purposes. Such books, called *readers*, may include original research reports. Usually, they gather together articles on a

TABLE 5.1   Different Reference Citations for a Journal Article

The oldest journal of sociology in the United States, *American Journal of Sociology*, reports a study on homeless youth in Toronto by Bill McCarthy and John Hagan. It appeared on pages 597–627 of the November 1992 issue (number 3) of the journal, which begins counting issues in March. It was in volume 98, its 98th year. Here are ways to cite the article. Two very popular styles are those of the *American Sociological Review (ASR)* and American Psychological Association (APA).

ASR STYLE

McCarthy, Bill and John Hagan. 1992. "Mean streets: The theoretical significance of situational delinquency among homeless youths." *American Journal of Sociology* 98:597–627.

APA STYLE

McCarthy, B., & Hagan, J. (1992). Mean streets: The theoretical significance of situational delinquency among homeless youths. *American Journal of Sociology, 98,* 597–627.

OTHER STYLES

McCarthy, B., and J. Hagan. "Mean Streets: The Theoretical Significance of Situational Delinquency among Homeless Youths," *American Journal of Sociology* 98 (1992), 597–627.

McCarthy, Bill and John Hagan, 1992.
   "Mean streets: The theoretical significance of situational delinquency among homeless youths." *Am. J. of Sociol.* 98:597–627.

McCarthy, B. and Hagan, J. (1992). "Mean streets: The theoretical significance of situational delinquency among homeless youths." *American Journal of Sociology* 98 (November): 597–627.

McCarthy, Bill and John Hagan. 1992.
   "Mean streets: The theoretical significance of situational delinquency among homeless youths." *American Journal of Sociology* 98(3):597–627.

McCarthy, B. & J. Hagan. (1992). Mean streets: The theoretical significance of situational delinquency among homeless youths. *American Journal of Sociology* 98, 597–627.

Bill McCarthy and John Hagan, "Mean Streets: the Theoretical Significance of Situational Delinquency among Homeless Youths," *American Journal of Sociology* 98, no. 3 (1980): 597–627.

topic from scholarly journals and are edited to be easier for nonspecialists to read and understand.

The second type of collection is designed for scholars and may gather together journal articles or may contain original research or theoretical essays on a specific topic. Some collections contain articles from journals that are difficult to locate. They may include original research reports organized around a specialized topic. The table of contents lists the titles and authors. Libraries shelve these collections with other books, and some library catalog systems include them.

Finally, there are annual research books that contain reports on studies that are not found elsewhere. These are hybrids between scholarly journals and collections of articles: they appear year after year, with volume numbers for each year, but they are not journals. These volumes, such as the *Review of Research in Political Sociology* and *Comparative Social Research*, are shelved with books. Some annual books specialize in literature reviews (e.g., *Annual Review of Sociology, Annual Review of Anthropology*). There is no comprehensive list of these books as there is for scholarly journals. The only way someone new to an area can find out about them is by spending a lot of time in the library or asking a researcher who is already familiar with a topic area.

Citations or references to books are easier than article citations. They include the author's name, book title, year and place of publication, and publisher's name.

Dissertations

All graduate students who receive the Ph.D. degree are required to complete a work of original research, which they write up as a dissertation thesis. The dissertation is bound and shelved in the library of the university that granted the Ph.D. About half of all dissertations are eventually published as books or articles. Because dissertations report on original research, they can be valuable sources of information. Some students who receive the master's degree conduct original research and write a master's thesis, but fewer master's theses involve serious research, and they are much more difficult to locate than unpublished dissertations.

Specialized indexes list dissertations completed by students at accredited universities. For example, *Dissertation Abstracts International* lists dissertations with their authors, titles, and universities. This index is organized by topic and contains an abstract of each dissertation. You can borrow most dissertations via interlibrary loan from the degree-granting university if the university permits this. An alternative is to purchase a copy from a national dissertation microfilm/photocopy center like the one at the University of Michigan, Ann Arbor, for U.S. universities. Some large research libraries contain copies of dissertations from other libraries if others have previously requested them.

Government Documents

The federal government of the United States, the governments of other nations, state or provincial-level governments, the United Nations, and other international agencies such as the World Bank, all sponsor studies and publish reports of the research. Many college and university libraries have these documents in their holdings, usually in a special "government documents" section. These reports are rarely found in the catalog system. You must use specialized lists of publications and indexes, usually with the help of a librarian, to locate these reports. Most college and university libraries hold only the most frequently requested documents and reports.

Policy Reports and Presented Papers

A researcher conducting a thorough review of the literature will examine these two sources, which are difficult for all but the trained specialist to obtain. Research institutes and policy centers (e.g., Brookings Institute, Institute for Research on Poverty, Rand Corporation) publish papers and reports. Some major research libraries purchase these and shelve them with books. The only way to be sure of what has been published is to write directly to the institute or center and request a list of reports.

Each year, the professional associations in academic fields (e.g., sociology, political science, psychology) hold annual meetings. Hundreds of researchers assemble to give, listen to, or discuss oral reports of recent research. Most of these oral reports are available as written papers to those attending the meeting. People who do not attend the meetings but who are members of the association receive a program of the meeting, listing each paper to be presented with its title, author, and author's place of employment. They can write directly to the author and request a copy of the paper. Many, but not all, of the papers are later published as articles. The papers may be listed in indexes or abstract services (to be discussed).

HOW TO CONDUCT A SYSTEMATIC REVIEW

Define and Refine a Topic

Just as a researcher must plan and clearly define a topic and research question when beginning a research project, you need to begin a literature review with a clearly defined, well-focused research question and a plan. A good review topic should be as focused as a research question. (You can read more about focusing research questions in the next chapter.) For example, "divorce" or "crime" is much too broad. A more appropriate review topic might be "the stability of families with stepchildren" or "economic inequality and crime rates across nations." If you conduct a context review for a research project, it should be slightly broader than the specific research question being tested. Often, a researcher will not finalize a specific research question for a study until he or she has reviewed the literature. The review helps bring greater focus to the research question.

Design a Search

After choosing a focused research question for the review, the next step is to plan a search strategy. The reviewer needs to decide on the type of review, its extensiveness, and the types of materials to include. The key is to be careful, systematic, and organized. Set parameters on your search: how much time you will devote to it, how far back in time you will look, the minimum number of research reports you will examine, how many libraries you will visit, and so forth.

Also, decide how to record the bibliographic citation for each reference you find and how to take notes (e.g., in a notebook, on 3×5 cards, in a computer file). Develop a schedule, because several visits are usually necessary. You should begin a file folder or computer file in which you can place possible sources and ideas for new sources. As the review proceeds, it should become more focused.

Locate Research Reports

Locating research reports depends on the type of report or "outlet" of research being searched. As a general rule, use multiple search strategies in order to counteract the limitations of a single search method.

Articles in Scholarly Journals.   As discussed earlier, most social research is published in scholarly journals. These journals are the vehicles of communication in science. Before beginning a search, pick up a journal in an area with which you are somewhat familiar and skim its contents. There are dozens of journals, many going back decades, each containing many articles. The task of searching for articles can be formidable. Luckily, specialized publications make the task easier.

You may have used an index for general publications such as the *Reader's Guide to Periodical*

Literature. Many academic fields have "abstracts" or "indexes" for the scholarly literature (e.g., *Psychological Abstracts, Social Sciences Index, Sociological Abstracts, Gerontological Abstracts*). For education-related topics, the Educational Resources Information Center (ERIC) system is especially valuable. There are over 100 such publications. You can usually find them in the reference section of a library. Many abstracts or index services as well as ERIC are available via computer access, which speeds the search process (see Appendix D).

Abstracts or indexes are published on a regular basis (monthly, six times a year, etc.) and allow a reader to look up articles by author name or subject. The journals covered by the abstract or index are listed in it, often in the front. An index, such as the *Social Sciences Index*, lists only the citation, whereas an abstract such as *Sociological Abstracts* lists the citation and has a copy of the article's abstract. Abstracts do not give you all the findings and details of a research project. Researchers use abstracts to screen articles for relevance, then locate the more relevant articles. Abstracts may also include papers presented at professional meetings. Table 5.2 has an example of what an article from *Social Theory and Practice* looks like in *Sociological Abstracts* and the *Social Sciences Index*. A related weekly publication, *Current Contents*, has copies of the table of contents pages of many scholarly journals and books that contain articles. It also has indexes by keywords in a title and by author.

It may sound as if all you have to do is to go find the index in the reference section of the library and look up a topic. Unfortunately, things are more complicated than that. In order to cover the studies across many years, you may have to look through many issues of the abstracts or indexes. Also, the subjects or topics listed in the abstracts or indexes are broad. The specific research question that interests you may fit into several subject areas. You should check each one. For example, for the topic of illegal drugs in high schools, you might look up these subjects: drug addiction, drug abuse, substance abuse, drug laws, illegal drugs, high schools, secondary

TABLE 5.2 Excerpt from *Sociological Abstracts* and *Social Sciences Index*

If you were interested in articles on pornography and looked it up in the subject index of *Sociological Abstracts*, you would find the following (from *Sociological Abstracts*, 1986, Volume 13. Subject Index, page 1316).[a]

Populism
  new political cultures, U.S. cities: post-1960s; Q7952

Pornography
  antipornography activism, Canada, eroticization of violence vs. power, political economy perspective:
    Q9033
  children's sexual victimization, commercial pornography; Q8577
  feminist antipornography arguments, defamation vs. degradation endorsement; Q7916
  obscenity/pornography laws, sexual power issue; Q9139
  sexual/aggressive content, mainstream vs. "triple-X" adult videos; content analysis; Vancouver, British
    Columbia; Q7911

Positivism
  social sciences, new realist philosophy, positivist limitations; Q7220

If you noticed the "feminist antipornography arguments" article and looked it up using the abstract reference Q7916, you would find the following:

86Q7916
  Soble, Alan (Saint John's U. Collegeville, MN 56321), Pornography: Defamation and the Endorsement of
    Degradation, UM *Social Theory and Practice*, 1985, 11, 1, spring, 61–87
Two recent feminist antipornography arguments, both of which are appealed to in academic writings & political activity, are examined & found defective. The first argument, that pornography defames women, fails because it assumes that pornographic items make claims about women, which is unsupportable given pornography's nature as fantasy. The second argument, that pornography endorses the degradation of women, fails because its proponents have not shown what pornography endorses or how. It is concluded that an item of pornography does not reliably endorse any specific action.

If you looked up the same topic and article in the *Social Sciences Index*, you would find this (from *Social Sciences Index*, April 1985–March 1986, Volume 12, page 1182).[b]

Porket, J. L.
  Unemployment in the midst of labour waste. Survey 29:19–18 Spr '85
Pornography
  See also Obscenity (Law)
  Aesthetics East and West; the bare facts of life [Hong Kong's adult magazines] I. Buruma. Far East Econ
    Rev 126:51–3 O 4 '84
  Minneapolis veto: "cherished, protected speech." D. M. Fraser. Hum Rights 12:27 Spr '85
  Outlawing pornography: what we gain, what we lose. E. Chemerinsky; P. J. McGeady. Hum Rights 12:24–6
    + Spr '85
  Pornography: defamation and the endorsement of degradation. A. Soble. Soc Theory Pract 11:61–87 Spr '85
  War declared on obscene materials. [China] Beijing Rev 28:8–9 Ag 5 '85
Pornstein, Marc H. and Krinksy, Sharon J.
  Perception of symmetry in infancy: the salience of vertical symmetry and the perception of pattern wholes.
    bibl J Exp Child Psychol 39:1–19 F '85

---

[a]Copyright Sociological Abstracts, Inc. All rights reserved. Used with permission.

[b]*Social Sciences Index*, April 1985–March 1986, Volume 12, p. 1182. Copyright © 1986 by the H. W. Wilson Company. Material reproduced by permission of the publisher.

schools. Many of the articles under a subject area will not be relevant for your literature review. Also, there is a 3- to 12-month time lag between the publication of an article and its appearance in the abstracts or indexes. Unless you are at a major research library, the most useful article may not be available in your library. You can obtain it only by using an interlibrary loan service, or it may be in a foreign language that you do not read.

Most research-oriented libraries subscribe to the *Social Science Citation Index (SSCI)* of the Institute for Scientific Information. This is a valuable resource with information on over 1,400 journals. It is similar to other indexes and abstracts, but it takes time to learn how to use it. The SSCI comes in four books. One is a source index, which provides complete citation information on journal articles. The other three books refer to articles in the source book. They are organized by subject, by the university or research center for which the researcher works, or by authors who are cited in the reference sections of other articles.

You can begin a SSCI search in one of three ways: (1) with a subject (e.g., alcohol use among children), (2) with a known research center (e.g., the Center for Alcohol Studies at Rutgers, the State University of New Jersey), or (3) with an earlier article (e.g., Kandel's "Drug and Drinking Behavior among Youth" in the 1980 *Annual Review of Sociology*). The first search directs you to the authors of current research reports. The second search identifies all authors from the same research center who published articles. The third search directs you to all citations included in earlier article's reference section. This last type of search is important when a researcher wants to trace research that influenced other research. For example, you find a 1980 article relevant. The SSCI tells you all articles published since 1980 that listed it in their reference section. Even if your library does not have the *Social Science Citation Index*, a good search principle is to examine the bibliography of articles to find additional articles or books on a topic.

Another resource for locating articles is the computerized literature search, which works on the same principle as an abstract or an index. Researchers organize computerized searches in several ways—by author, by article title, by subject, or by keyword. A *keyword* is an important term for a topic that is likely to be found in a title. You will want to use six to eight keywords in most computer-based searches and consider several synonyms. The computer's searching method can vary and most only look for a keyword in a title or abstract. If you choose too few words or very narrow terms, you will miss a lot of relevant articles. If you choose too many words or very broad terms, you will get a huge number of irrelevant articles. The best way to learn the appropriate breadth and number of keywords is by trial and error.

In a study I conducted on how college students define *sexual harassment* (Neuman, 1992), I used the following keywords: *sexual harassment, sexual assault, harassment, gender equity, gender fairness*, and *sex discrimination*. I later discovered a few important studies that lacked any of these keywords in their titles. I also tried the keywords *college student* and *rape*, but got huge numbers of unrelated articles that I could not even skim.

There are numerous computer-assisted search databases or systems. Some may be "on line" at your library, some are on CD-ROM (Compact Disk, Read Only Memory) in a local computer, others are available through the Internet or another long-distance connection. (The Internet is explained more in Appendix D.) For now, it is sufficient to say that it is a system that connects millions of computers around the world to each other. A person with a computer and an Internet hook-up can search some article index collections, the catalogs of libraries, and other information sources around the globe if they are available on the Internet.

All computerized searching methods share a similar logic, but each has its own method of operation to learn. In my study, I looked for sources in the previous seven years and used five computerized databases of scholarly literature: the *Social Science Index, CARL (Colorado Area Research Library), Sociofile, the Social Science Citation Index*, and *PsychLit*.

Often, the same articles will appear in multiple scholarly literature databases, but each database may identify a few new articles not found in the others. This points to a critical lesson: "Do not rely exclusively on computerized literature searches, on abstracting services, [or] on the literature in a single discipline, or on an arbitrarily defined time period" (Bausell, 1994: 24). For example, I discovered several excellent sources not listed in any of the computerized databases that had been published in earlier years by studying the bibliographies of the relevant articles.

The process in my study was fairly typical. Based on my keyword search, I quickly skimmed or scanned the titles or abstracts of over 200 sources. From these, I selected about 80 articles, reports, and books to read. I found about 49 of the 80 sources valuable, and they appear in the bibliography of the published article.

Scholarly Books. Finding scholarly books on a subject can be difficult. The subject topics of library catalog systems are usually incomplete and too broad to be useful. Moreover, they list only books that are in a particular library system, although you may be able to search other libraries for interlibrary loan books. Libraries organize books by call numbers based on subject matter. Again, the subject matter classifications may not reflect the subjects of interest to you or all the subjects discussed in a book. Once you learn the system for your library, you will find that most books on a topic will share the main parts of the call number. In addition, librarians can help you locate books that may be in other libraries. For example, the *Library of Congress National Union Catalog* lists all books in the U.S. Library of Congress. Librarians have access to sources that list books at other libraries, or you can use Internet. There is no sure-fire way to locate relevant books. Use multiple search methods, including a look at journals that have book reviews and the bibliographies of articles.

Dissertations. A publication called *Dissertation Abstracts International* lists most dissertations. Like the indexes and abstracts for journal articles,

it organizes dissertations by broad subject category, author, and date. Researchers look up all titles in the subject areas that include a topic. Unfortunately, after you have located the dissertation title and abstract, you may find that obtaining a copy of it takes time and involves added costs.

Government Documents. The "government documents" sections of libraries contain specialized lists of government documents. A useful index for documents issued by the U.S. federal government is the *Monthly Catalog of Government Documents*, which is often available on computer. It has been issued since 1885, but other supplemental sources should be used for research into documents more than a decade old. The catalog has an annual index, and monthly issues have subject, title, and author indexes. *Indexes to Congressional Hearings*, another useful source, lists committees and subjects going back to the late 1930s. The *Congressional Record* contains debate of the U.S. Congress with synopses of bills, voting records, and changes in bills. *United States Statutes* lists each individual U.S. federal law by year and subject. The *Federal Register*, a daily publication of the U.S. government, contains all rules, regulations, and announcements of federal agencies. It has both monthly and annual indexes. There are other indexes that cover treaties, technical announcements, and so forth. Other governments have similar lists. For example, the British government's *Government Publications Index* lists government publications issued during a year. *Parliamentary Papers* lists official social and economic studies going back 200 years. It is usually best to rely on the expertise of librarians for assistance in using these specialized indexes. The topics used by index makers may not be the best ones for your specific research question.

Policy Reports and Presented Papers. These are the most difficult sources to locate. They are listed in some bibliographies of published studies; some are listed in the abstracts or indexes. To locate these studies, try several methods: Write to research centers and ask for lists of publications, obtain lists of papers presented at professional meetings, and so forth. Once you locate a research report, try writing to the relevant author or institute.

What to Record

After you locate a source, you should write down all details of the reference (full names of authors, titles, volume, issue, pages, etc.). It is usually best to record more than the minimum needed to form a citation Most researchers create one set of cards or a computer file with the full references and another with notes on the research report. Create a code or indicator to link unambiguously the reference or source of the notes to each note card or file. For example, put the last name of the first author and the year of the book or article on each note card or record. You can quickly look up the complete reference in a set of reference cards or file organized by author's last name and date. You will find it much easier to take all notes on the same type and size of paper or card, rather than having some notes on sheets of papers, others on cards, and so on. Researchers have to decide what to record about an article, book, or other source. It is better to err in the direction of recording too much rather than too little. In general, record the hypotheses tested, how major concepts were measured, the main findings, the basic design of the research, the group or sample used, and ideas for future study (see Box 5.3). It is wise to examine the report's bibliography and note sources that you can add to your search.

Photocopying all relevant articles or reports will save you time recording notes and will ensure that you will have an entire report. You can make notes on the photocopy. There are several warnings about this practice. First, photocopying can be expensive for a large literature search. Second, be aware of and obey copyright laws. U.S. copyright laws permit photocopying for personal research use. Third, remember to record or photocopy the entire article, including all citation information. Fourth, organizing entire articles can be cumbersome, especially if several different parts of a single article are being used. Finally, unless you highlight carefully or take good notes, you may have to reread the entire article later.

Box 5.3

How to Read Journal Articles

1. Read with a clear purpose or goal in mind. Are you reading for basic knowledge or to apply it to a specific question?
2. Skim the article before reading it all. What can you learn from the title, abstract, summary and conclusions, and headings? What are the topic, major findings, method, and main conclusion?
3. Consider your own orientation. What is your bias toward the topic, the method, the publication source, and so on, that may color your reading?
4. Marshal external knowledge. What do you already know about the topic and the methods used? How credible is the publication source?
5. Evaluate as you read the article. What errors are present? Do findings follow the data? Is the article consistent with assumptions of the approach it takes?
6. Summarize information as an abstract with the topic, the methods used, and the findings. Assess the factual accuracy of findings and cite questions about the article.

Source: Adapted from Katzer, Cook, and Crouch (1991: 199–207).

Organize Notes

After gathering a large number of references and notes, you need an organizing scheme. One approach is to group studies or specific findings by skimming notes and creating a mental map of how they fit together. Try several organizing schemes before settling on a final one. Organizing is a skill that improves with practice. For example, place notes into piles representing common themes, or draw charts comparing what different reports state about the same question, noting agreements and disagreements.

In the process of organizing notes, you will find that some references and notes do not fit and should be discarded as irrelevant. Also, you may discover gaps or areas and topics that are relevant but that you did not examine. This necessitates return visits to the library.

There are many organizing schemes. The best one depends on the purpose of the review. A context review implies organizing recent reports around a specific research question. A historical review implies organizing studies by major theme and by the date of publication. An integrative review implies organizing studies around core common findings of a field and the main hypotheses tested. A methodological review implies organizing studies by the topic and, within topic, by the design or method used. A theoretical review implies organizing studies by the theories and major thinkers being examined.

Write the Review

A literature review requires planning and good, clear writing, which requires a lot of rewriting. This step is often merged with organizing notes. All the rules of good writing (e.g., clear organizational structure, an introduction and conclusion, transitions between sections, etc.) apply to writing a literature review. Keep your purposes in mind when you write, and communicate clearly and effectively.

To prepare a good review, read articles and other literature critically. Recall that skepticism is a norm of science. It means that you should not accept what is written simply on the basis of the authority of its having been published. Question what you read, and evaluate it. The first hurdle to overcome is thinking something must be perfect just because it has been published.

Critically reading research reports requires skills that take time and practice to develop. Despite a peer review procedure and high rejection rates, errors and sloppy logic slip in. When reading an article, read carefully to see whether the introduction and title really fit with the rest of the article. Sometimes, titles, abstracts, or the introduction are misleading. They may not fully explain the research project's method and results. An article should be logically tight, and all the parts should fit together. Strong logical links should exist between parts of the argument. Weak articles make leaps in logic or omit transitional steps. Likewise, articles do not always make their theory or approach to research explicit. Be pre-

pared to read the article more than once to determine its underlying theory or approach. (See Box 5.4 on taking notes on an article.)

The most critical areas of an article to read are the methods and results sections. Few studies are perfect. Researchers do not always describe the methods they used as fully as they should. Sometimes, the results presented in tables or charts do not match what the researcher says. For example, an author might overlook an important result in a table, while giving minor results too much attention. The careful reader evaluates how the research project was done and reads the data that are presented. Too frequently, authors give one interpretation and ignore equally possible interpretations. Also be careful when reading conclusions. Do not assume that they are entirely consistent with all the data; check the data for yourself.

WHAT DOES A GOOD REVIEW LOOK LIKE ONCE IT IS WRITTEN?

An author should communicate a review's purpose to the reader by its organization. The *wrong* way to write a review is to list a series of research reports with a summary of the findings of each. This fails to communicate a sense of purpose. It reads as a set of notes strung together. Perhaps the reviewer got sloppy and skipped over the important organizing step in writing the review. The *right* way to write a review is to organize common findings or arguments together. A well-accepted approach is to address the most important ideas first, to logically link statements or findings, and to note discrepancies or weaknesses in the research (see Box 5.5 for an example). You should paraphrase a few critical quotes and summarize the key findings (also see Appendix C).

CONCLUSION

Literature reviews allow consumers of social science access to the information in research reports. They show the reviewer's familiarity with a body of knowledge; they show the path prior research has taken and how a current project is linked to it;

Box 5.4 _____

Example of Notes on an Article

FULL CITATION ON BIBLIOGRAPHY CARD

Pierce, John C., M. A. E. Steger, N. P. Lovrich, B. S. Steel, 1988. "Public Information on Acid Rain in Canada and the United States." _Social Science Quarterly_ 69:193–202.

NOTE CARD

Pierce et al. 1988	TOPICS: Factors that shape people's knowledge about public issues. Acid Rain. Self-interest. U.S. and Canada

Based on a prior study, the researchers note that education alone does not lead to knowledge about a public policy issue. Knowledge can be based on characteristics of the individual (e.g., gender, income, education), which works in general regardless of a specific policy, or on motivation due to the relevance of a policy for individual self-interest. They are interested in how knowledge on a public issue results from a person's motivation to acquire information. They looked at one policy, acid rain, and asked: Does motivation affect knowledge in different settings—Canadian culture, which is more collectivistic and where people are the victims of U.S. policy and the individualistic U.S. culture?

Hypotheses   People acquire knowledge about a public issue when they perceive it affecting their self-interest.

Method   The authors mailed questionnaires to samples of 1,000 people living in Michigan and 1,000 in Ontario. A little over half were completed and returned. They measured knowledge about the issue in four ways. They also looked at motivational variables, including general characteristics and the personal sensitivity or relevance of the issue.

Findings   Using statistics and percentaged tables, they found that motivational factors (e.g., personal sensitivity and relevance) led to greater knowledge of the acid rain issue than general characteristics, although both had some effect. Motivation or personal relevance was stronger in Canada, where the national context heightened sensitivity.

they can integrate and summarize the current knowledge in a topic area; they are a way for researchers to learn from others; and they often stimulate new ideas and insights.

In this chapter, you learned about six types of literature reviews. You also learned the many outlets for research studies. Most are found only in college or university libraries. The most important outlets are scholarly journals and books. Other outlets include Ph.D. dissertations, government documents and policy reports, and papers presented at professional meetings.

Box 5.5 _____

Examples of Good and Bad Reviews

EXAMPLE OF BAD REVIEW

Sexual harassment has many consequences. Adams, Kottke, and Padgitt (1983) found that some women students said they avoided taking a class or working with certain professors because of the risk of harassment. They also found that men and women students reacted differently. Their research was a survey of 1,000 men and women graduate and undergraduate students. Benson and Thomson's study in *Social Problems* (1982) lists many problems created by sexual harassment. In their excellent book, *The Lecherous Professor*, Dziech and Weiner (1990) give a long list of difficulties that victims have suffered.

Researchers study the topic in different ways. Hunter and McClelland (1991) conducted a study of undergraduates at a small liberal arts college. They had a sample of 300 students and students were given multiple vignettes that varied by the reaction of the victim and the situation. Jaschik and Fretz (1991) showed 90 women students at a mideastern university a videotape with a classic example of sexual harassment by a teaching assistant. Before it was labeled as *sexual harassment* few women called it that. When asked whether it was sexual harassment, 98 percent agreed. Weber-Burdin and Rossi (1982) replicated a previous study on sexual harassment, only they used students at the University of Massachusetts. They had 59 students rate 40 hypothetical situations. Reilley, Carpenter, Dull, and Bartlett (1982) conducted a study of 250 female and 150 male undergraduates at the University of California at Santa Barbara. They also had a sample of 52 faculty. Both samples completed a questionnaire in which respondents were presented vignettes of sexual-harassing situations that they were to rate. Popovich et al. (1986) created a nine-item scale of sexual harassment. They studied 209 undergraduates at a medium-sized university in groups of 15 to 25. They found disagreement and confusion among students.

EXAMPLE OF BETTER REVIEW

The victims of sexual harassment suffer a range of consequences, from lowered self-esteem and loss of self-confidence to withdrawal from social interaction, changed career goals, and depression (Adams, Kottke, and Padgitt, 1983; Benson and Thomson, 1982; Dziech and Weiner, 1990). For example, Adams, Kottke, and Padgitt (1983) noted that 13 percent of women students said they avoided taking a class or working with certain professors because of the risk of harassment.

Research into campus sexual harassment has taken several approaches. In addition to survey research, many have experimented with vignettes or presented hypothetical scenarios (Hunter and McClelland, 1991; Jaschik and Fretz, 1991; Popovich et al., 1987; Reilley, Carpenter, Dull, and Barlett, 1982; Rossi and Anderson, 1982; Valentine-French and Radtke, 1989; Weber-Burdin and Rossi, 1982). Victim verbal responses and situational factors appear to affect whether observers label a behavior as harassment. There is confusion over the application of a sexual harassment label for inappropriate behavior. For example, Jaschik and Fretz (1991) found that only 3 percent of the women students shown a videotape with a classic example of sexual harassment by a teaching assistant initially labeled it as *sexual harassment*. Instead, they called it "sexist," "rude," "unprofessional," or "demeaning." When asked whether it was sexual harassment, 98 percent agreed. Roscoe et al. (1987) reported similar labeling difficulties.

A literature review requires a plan and a clear idea of the topic. When conducting a literature search, researchers use multiple search strategies because each single way of conducting a search has weaknesses. It is often necessary to consult with a reference librarian and use specialized publications called abstracts or indexes. Computerized searches can also be helpful, although they have limitations. Once you have located studies, take good notes and record and file details about the citation. A good review communicates with the reader and is organized around themes.

KEY TERMS _____

abstract   integrative review   methodological review
citation   interlibrary loan service   self-study review
context review   keyword   theoretical review
historical review   meta-analysis

REVIEW QUESTIONS _____

1. What are the four major goals of a review of the literature?

2. What type of review is likely to organize studies in chronological order?

3. What is the major purpose of a theoretical review?

4. Which outlet of reports on research studies is easiest to locate?

5. How would you go about locating a dissertation?

6. What is the page-numbering system used in most scholarly journals?

7. What are the three types of books that contain collections of research articles, and which of the three contains all original research studies?

8. List the first several steps in conducting a systematic review.

9. How does one go about doing a computerized literature search? What are its advantages and disadvantages?

10. What distinguishes a strong from a weak literature review?

NOTE _____

1. See Hunter, Schmidt, and Jackson (1982).

RECOMMENDED READINGS _____

American Psychological Association. (1994). *Publication manual of the American Psychological Association, 4th ed.*. Washington, DC: American Psychological Association. This large manual is written specifically for psychologists, but it has a lot of detailed information that other social scientists and practitioners will find useful. In addition to describing citation formats, it includes information on proper writing style and grammar, the organization and layout of research reports, and the process of submitting a manuscript for publication in a scholarly journal.

Bart, Pauline, and Linda Frankel. (1986). *The student sociologist's handbook*, 4th ed. New York: Random House. This is an introduction to using the research literature for the sociology student. It has excellent discussion of the mechanics of library research, and it describes a variety of soci-ology journals and indexes. There is even an overview of government documents.

Beasley, David. (1988). *How to use a research library*. New York: Oxford University Press. As the title suggests, this book describes how to use a major research library. Many of the procedures described in the book apply to any research library. The examples in the book are taken from the New York Public Library, which is one of the few city public research libraries. Most research libraries are located at major universities. There are also specialized research libraries (e.g., the Newberry Library in Chicago) and the major U.S. government research library, the Library of Congress.

Light, Richard J., and David B. Pillemer. (1984). *Summing up: The science of reviewing research*. Cambridge, MA: Harvard University Press. The authors provide an innovative approach to conducting a comprehensive review of research literature and synthesizing it. The book is organized around four themes: A review needs a precise research question to guide it; disagreements among findings are valuable; quantitative and qualitative studies both have important roles to play; and, despite their usefulness, statistical techniques are not a substitute for conceptual clarity in determining what a body of literature says.

Rose, Gerry. (1982). *Deciphering sociological research*. Beverly Hills, CA: Sage. This book is divided into two parts. Part I explains how to read and figure out what is said in a research report; Part II presents 12 articles published between 1953 and 1976. The author emphasizes the importance of identifying the type of study and its link to theory (as Chapter 3 in this book discussed) and the approach to research used (as discussed in Chapter 4) in order to decipher an article.

CHAPTER 6

QUANTITATIVE RESEARCH DESIGNS

> *How people counted and measured reveals underlying assumptions about the subject under study, assumptions ranging from plain old bias . . . to ideas about the structure of society and of knowledge. In some cases, the activity of counting and measuring itself altered the way people thought about what they were quantifying.*
>
> —Patricia Cline Cohen, *A Calculating People*, p. 206

INTRODUCTION TO POSITIVIST RESEARCH

In previous chapters, you saw how the research process works in general terms, encountered approaches to social science, and learned about literature reviews. We now turn to designing a quantitative research project. Quantitative research relies primarily on assumptions from the positivist approach to science.

In this chapter, you will learn the language of quantitative research—a language of variables, hypotheses, units of analysis, and causal explanation. The logical errors that may arise when developing a causal explanation illustrate why it is essential to understand the components of research design.

After you learn the language and ideas of quantitative research design, you will also learn how to refine a general topic into a research question. The task of refining a diffuse topic into a well-focused research problem or question is a critical step in the research process. You will find that designing a high-quality quantitative research project is much easier if you begin with a well-focused research question to answer.

LEARNING THE LANGUAGE OF VARIABLES AND HYPOTHESES

What Is a Variable?

Variation and Variables. The *variable* is a central idea in quantitative research. Simply defined, a variable is a concept that varies. The language of quantitative research is a language of variables and relationships among variables.

In Chapter 3, you learned about two types of concepts: those that refer to a fixed phenomenon (e.g., the ideal type of bureaucracy) and those that vary in quantity, intensity, or amount (e.g., amount of education). The second type of concept and measures of the concepts are variables. Variables take on two or more values. Once you begin to look for them, you will see variables all over. For example, gender is a variable; it can take on two values: male or female. Marital status is a variable; it can take on the values of never married single, married, divorced, or widowed. Type of crime committed is a variable; it can take on values of robbery, burglary, theft, murder, and so forth. Family income is a variable; it can take on values from zero to billions of dollars. A person's attitude toward abortion is a variable; it can range from strongly favoring legal abortion to strongly believing in antiabortion.

The values or the categories of a variable are its *attributes*. It is easy to confuse variables with attributes. Variables and attributes are related, but they have distinct purposes. The confusion arises because the attribute of one variable can itself become a separate variable with a slight change in definition. The distinction is between concepts themselves that vary and conditions within concepts that vary. For example, "male" is not a variable; it describes a category of gender and is an attribute of the variable "gender." Yet, a related idea, "degree of masculinity," is a variable. It describes the intensity or strength of attachment to attitudes, beliefs, and behaviors associated with the concept of *masculine* within a culture. "Married" is not a variable; it is an attribute of the variable "marital status." Related ideas such as "number of years married" or "depth of commitment to a marriage" are variables. Likewise, "rob-

bery" is not a variable; it is an attribute of the variable "type of crime." "Number of robberies," "robbery rate," "amount taken during a robbery," and "type of robbery" are all variables because they vary or take on a range of values.

You need to redefine concepts of interest in a quantitative research project into the language of variables. As the examples of variables and attributes illustrate, slight changes in definition change a nonvariable into a variable concept. As you saw in Chapter 3, concepts are the building blocks of theory; they organize thinking about the social world. Clear concepts with careful definitions are essential in theory.

Types of Variables. Researchers who focus on causal relations usually begin with an effect, then search for its causes. Variables are classified into three basic types, depending on their location in a causal relationship. The cause variable, or the one that identifies forces or conditions that act on something else, is the *independent variable*. The variable that is the effect or is the result or outcome of another variable is the *dependent variable*. The independent variable is "independent of" prior causes that act on it, whereas the dependent variable "depends on" the cause.

It is not always easy to determine whether a variable is independent or dependent. Two questions help you identify the independent variable. First, does it come before other variables in time? Independent variables come before any other type. Second, if the variables occur at the same time, does the author suggest that one variable has an impact on another variable? Independent variables affect or have an impact on other variables. Research topics are often phrased in terms of the dependent variables because dependent variables are the phenomenon to be explained. For example, suppose a researcher examines the reasons for an increase in the crime rate in Dallas, Texas; the dependent variable is the crime rate.

A basic causal relationship requires only an independent and a dependent variable. A third type of variable, the *intervening variable*, appears in more complex causal relations. It comes between the independent and dependent variables and shows the link or mechanism between them. Advances in knowledge depend not only on documenting cause-and-effect relationships but also on specifying the mechanisms that account for the causal relation. In a sense, the intervening variable acts as a dependent variable with respect to the independent variable and acts as an independent variable toward the dependent variable.

For example, the French sociologist Emile Durkheim developed a theory of suicide that specified a causal relationship between marital status and suicide rates. Durkheim found evidence that married people are less likely to commit suicide than single people. He believed that married people have greater social integration (i.e., feelings of belonging to a group or family) and thought that a major cause of one type of suicide was that people lacked a sense of belonging to a group. Thus, his theory can be restated as a three-variable relationship: marital status (independent variable) causes the degree of social integration (intervening variable), which affects suicide (dependent variable). Specifying the chain of causality makes the linkages in a theory clearer and helps a researcher test complex explanations.[1]

Simple theories have one dependent and one independent variable, whereas complex theories can contain dozens of variables with multiple independent, intervening, and dependent variables. For example, a theory of criminal behavior (dependent variable) identifies four independent variables: an individual's economic hardship, opportunities to commit crime easily, membership in a deviant subgroup of society that does not disapprove of crime, and lack of punishment for criminal acts. A multicause explanation usually specifies the independent variable that has the greatest causal effect.

A complex theoretical explanation contains a string of multiple intervening variables that are linked together. For example, family disruption causes lower self-esteem among children, which causes depression, which causes poor grades in school, which causes reduced prospects for a good job, which causes a lower adult income. The chain of variables is: family disruption (independent), childhood self-esteem (intervening), depression (intervening), grades in school (intervening), job prospects (intervening), adult income (dependent).

Two theories on the same topic may have different independent variables or predict different independent variables to be important. In addition, theories may agree about the independent and dependent variables but differ on the intervening variable or causal mechanism. For example, two theories say that family disruption causes lower adult income, but for different reasons. One theory holds that disruption encourages children to join deviant peer groups that are not socialized to norms of work and thrift. Another emphasizes the impact of the disruption on childhood depression and poor academic performance, which directly affect job performance.

A single research project usually tests only a small part of a full causal chain. For example, a research project examining six variables may take the six from a large, complex theory with two dozen variables. Explicit links to a larger theory strengthen and clarify a research project. This applies to most research and is especially true for explanatory, basic research, which is the model for most quantitative research.

Causal Relationships and Hypotheses

The Hypothesis and Causality.   A *hypothesis* is a proposition to be tested or a tentative statement of a relationship between two variables. Hypotheses are guesses about how the social world works; they are stated in a value-neutral form. Kerlinger (1979:35) noted.

> *hypotheses are much more important in scientific research than they would appear to be just by knowing what they are and how they are constructed. They have a deep and highly significant purpose of taking man out of himself, so to speak. . . . Hypotheses are powerful tools for the advancement of knowledge, because, although formulated by man, they can be tested and shown to be correct or incorrect apart from man's values and beliefs.*

A causal hypothesis has five characteristics (see Box 6.1). The first two characteristics define the minimum elements of a hypothesis. The third restates the hypothesis. For example, the hypothesis that attending religious services reduces the probability of divorce can be restated as a prediction: Couples who attend religious services frequently have a lower divorce rate than do couples who rarely attend religious services. The prediction can be tested against empirical evidence. The fourth characteristic states that the hypothesis should not be viewed in isolation. It should be logically tied to a research question and to a theory. Researchers test hypotheses to answer the research question or to find empirical support for a theory. The last characteristic requires that a researcher use empirical data to test the hypothesis. Statements that are necessarily true as a result of logic, or questions that are impossible to answer through scientific observation (What is the "good life"? Is there a God?) cannot be scientific hypotheses.

Causal hypotheses can be stated in several ways. Sometimes the word *cause* is used, but this is not necessary. For example, a causal hypothesis between religious attendance and a reduced likelihood of divorce can be stated in 10 different ways (see Box 6.2).

Researchers avoid using the term *proved* when testing hypotheses. You might hear the

---

Box 6.2 _____

Ways to State Causal Relations

- Religious attendance *causes* reduced divorce.
- Religious attendance *leads* to reduced divorce.
- Religious attendance *is related* to reduced divorce.
- Religious attendance *influences* the reduction of divorce.
- Religious attendance *is associated with* reduced divorce.
- Religious attendance *produces* reduced divorce.
- Religious attendance *results* in reduced divorce.
- If people attend religious services, *then* the likelihood of divorce will be reduced.
- *The higher* religious attendance, *the lower* the likelihood of divorce.
- Religious attendance *reduces* the likelihood of divorce.

---

word *proof* used in journalism, courts of law, or advertisements, but you will rarely hear research scientists use it. A jury says that the evidence "proves" someone guilty, or a television commercial states, "Studies prove that our aspirin cures headaches the fastest." This is not the language of scientific research. In the language of science, knowledge is tentative, and creating knowledge is an ongoing process that avoids premature closure.

Scientists do not say they have proved a hypothesis or the causal relationship it represents. Proof implies finality, absolute certainty, or something that does not need further investigation. *Proof* is too strong a term for the cautious world of science. Evidence supports or confirms, but does not prove, the hypothesis. Even after hundreds of studies show the same results, as with the link between cigarette smoking and lung cancer, scientists do not say that they have absolute proof.

The best science can say is that overwhelming evidence, or all studies to date, support or are consistent with the hypothesis. Scientists do not

---

Box 6.1 _____

Five Characteristics of Causal Hypotheses

1. It has at least two variables.
2. It expresses a causal or cause-effect relationship between the variables.
3. It can be expressed as a prediction or an expected future outcome.
4. It is logically linked to a research question and a theory.
5. It is falsifiable; that is, it is capable of being tested against empirical evidence and shown to be true or false.

want to close off the possibility of discovering new evidence that might contradict past findings. They do not want to cut off future inquiry or stop exploring intervening mechanisms. History contains many examples of relationships that were once thought to be proved but were later found to be in error. *Proof* is used when referring to logical or mathematical relations, as in a mathematical proof, but not in discussing empirical research.

Testing and Refining Hypothesis. Knowledge rarely advances on the basis of one test of a single hypothesis, although a researcher may test one hypothesis in a research project. In fact, it is easy to get a distorted picture of the research process by focusing on a single research project that tests one hypothesis. Knowledge develops over time as researchers throughout the scientific community test many hypotheses. It grows from shifting and winnowing through many hypotheses. Each hypothesis represents an explanation of a dependent variable. If the evidence fails to support some hypotheses, they are gradually eliminated from consideration. Those that receive support remain in contention. Theorists and researchers are constantly creating new hypotheses to challenge those that have received support.

Figure 6.1 represents an example of the process of shifting through hypotheses over time. At a given starting point (1960), there are eight contending hypotheses. Over the years, different researchers test the hypotheses until, by 2000, two hypotheses remain as possibilities. Neither had been developed in the beginning; the others were created as researchers sorted out existing evidence and developed new theories. The process continues into the future as the hypotheses are tested against empirical evidence.

Scientists are a skeptical group. Support for a hypothesis in one research project is not sufficient for them to accept it. The principle of replication says that a hypothesis needs several tests with consistent and repeated support to gain broad acceptance. Another way to strengthen confidence in a hypothesis is to test related causal linkages in the theory from which it comes.

The strongest contender or the hypothesis with the greatest empirical support is accepted as the best explanation at the time. The logic suggests that the more alternatives we test a hypothesis against, the greater our confidence in it. Some tests of hypotheses are called *crucial experiments* or crucial studies. This is a type of study where

> *two or more alternative explanations for some phenomenon are available, each being compatible with the empirically given data; the crucial experiment is designed to yield results that can be accounted for by only one of the alternatives, which is thereby shown to be "the correct explanation." (Kaplan, 1964:151–152)*

Thus, the infrequent crucial experiment or research project is an important test of theory. Hypotheses from two different theories confront each other in crucial experiments, and one is knocked out of the competition. It is rare, but significant, when it occurs.

Types of Hypotheses. Hypotheses are links in a theoretical causal chain and can take several forms. Researchers use them to test the direction and strength of a relationship between variables. When a hypothesis defeats its competitors, or offers alternative explanations for a causal relation, it indirectly lends support to the researcher's explanation. A curious aspect of hypothesis testing is that researchers treat evidence that supports a hypothesis differently from evidence that opposes it. They give negative evidence more importance. The idea that negative evidence is critical when evaluating a hypothesis comes from the *logic of disconfirming hypotheses.*[2] It is associated with Karl Popper's idea of falsification (see Chapter 4) and with the use of null hypotheses (see later in this section).

Recall the preceding discussion of proof. A hypothesis is never completely proved, but it can be disproved. A researcher with supporting evidence can say only that the hypothesis remains a possibility or that it is still in the running. Negative evidence is more significant because the hypothesis becomes "tarnished" or "soiled" if the evidence fails to support it. This is because a hypothesis

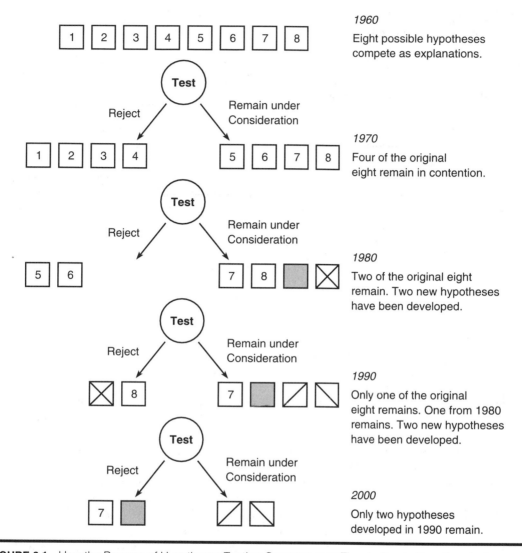

FIGURE 6.1   How the Process of Hypotheses Testing Operates over Time to Create New Knowledge and Contending Hypotheses

makes predictions. Negative and disconfirming evidence shows that the predictions are wrong. Positive or confirming evidence for a hypothesis is less critical because alternative hypotheses may make the same prediction. A researcher who finds confirming evidence for a prediction may not elevate one explanation over its alternatives.

For example, a man stands on a street corner with an umbrella and claims that his umbrella protects him from falling elephants. His hypothesis that the umbrella provides protection has supporting evidence. He has not had a single elephant fall on him in all the time he has had his umbrella open. Yet, such supportive evidence is weak; it also is consistent with an alternative hypothesis— that elephants do not fall from the sky. Both predict that the man will be safe from falling elephants. Negative evidence for the hypothesis—the one elephant that falls on him and his umbrella, crushing both—would destroy the hypothesis for good.

Researchers test hypotheses in two ways: a straightforward way and a null hypothesis way. Many quantitative researchers, especially experimenters, frame hypotheses in terms of a *null hypothesis* based on the logic of the disconfirming hypotheses. They test hypotheses by looking for evidence that will allow them to accept or reject the null hypothesis. Most people talk about a hypothesis as a way to predict a relationship. The null hypothesis does the opposite. It predicts no relationship. For example, Sarah believes that students who live on campus in dormitories get higher grades than students who live off campus and commute to college. Her null hypothesis is that there is no relationship between residence and grades. Researchers use the null hypothesis with a corresponding *alternative hypothesis* or experimental hypothesis. The alternative hypothesis says that a relationship exists. Sarah's alternative hypothesis is that students' on-campus residence has a positive effect on grades.

For most people, the null hypothesis approach is a backward way of hypothesis testing. Null hypothesis thinking rests on the assumption that researchers try to discover a relationship, so hypothesis testing should be designed to make finding a relationship more demanding. A researcher who uses the null hypothesis approach only directly tests the null hypothesis. If evidence supports or leads the researcher to accept the null hypothesis, he or she concludes that the tested relationship does not exist. This implies that the alternative hypothesis is false. On the other hand, if the researcher can find evidence to reject the null hypothesis, then the alternative hypothesis remains a possibility. The researcher cannot prove the alternative; rather, by testing the null hypothesis, he or she keeps the alternative hypothesis in contention. When null hypothesis testing is added to confirming evidence, the argument for an alterative hypothesis can grow stronger over time.

Many people find the null hypothesis to be confusing. Another way to think of it is that the scientific community is extremely cautious. It prefers to consider a causal relationship to be false until mountains of evidence show it to be true. This is similar to the Anglo-American legal idea of innocent until proved guilty. A researcher assumes, or acts as if, the null hypothesis is correct until *reasonable doubt* suggests otherwise. Researchers who use null hypotheses generally use it with specific statistical tests (e.g., *t*-test or *F*-test). Thus, a researcher may claim there is reasonable doubt in a null hypothesis if a statistical test suggests that the odds of it being false are 99 in 100. This is what a researcher means when he or she says that statistical tests allow him or her to "reject the null hypothesis at the .01 level of significance" (inferential statistics are briefly discussed in Chapters 9 and 12).

Another type of hypothesis is the *double-barreled hypothesis*.[3] Researchers should avoid using it; it shows unclear thinking and creates confusion. A double-barreled hypothesis puts two distinct relationships in one hypothesis. For example, a researcher states a hypothesis: Poverty and a high concentration of teenagers in an area cause property crime to increase. This is double barreled. It could mean either of two things: that poverty *or* a high concentration of teenagers causes property crime, or that *only* the combination of poverty with a high concentration of teenagers causes property crime. If the "either one" hypothesis is intended, and only one independent variable has an effect, the results of hypothesis testing are unclear. For example, if evidence shows that poverty causes crime but a concentration of teenagers does not, is the hypothesis supported? If the combination hypothesis is intended, then a researcher really means that the joint occurrence of poverty with a high concentration of teenagers only, and neither alone, causes property crime. If a researcher intends the combination meaning, it is not double barreled. Researchers should be clear and state the combination hypothesis so that the particular form in which the variables go together or are combined is made explicit. This is often called an *interaction effect* (interaction effects are discussed later).

Other Aspects of Explanation

Clarity about Units and Levels of Analysis. It is easy to become confused at first about the ideas of units and levels of analysis. Nevertheless, they are important ideas for clearly thinking through and planning a research project. All studies have both units and levels of analysis, but few researchers explicitly identify them as such. The levels and units of analysis are restricted by the topic and the research question. In other words, there is a rough match between the topic or research question and the units or levels of analysis that one can use.

A *level of analysis* is the level of social reality to which theoretical explanations refer. The level of social reality varies on a continuum from micro level (e.g., small groups or individual processes) to macro level (e.g., civilizations or structural aspects of society). The level includes a mix of the number of people, the amount of space, the scope of the activity, and the length of time. For example, very micro-level analysis can involve a few seconds of interaction between two people in the same small room. Very macro-level analysis can involve billions of people on several continents across centuries. Most social research uses a level of analysis that lies between these extremes.

The level of analysis delimits the kinds of assumptions, concepts, and theories that a researcher uses. For example, I want to study the topic of dating among college students. I use a micro-level analysis and develop an explanation that uses concepts such as interpersonal contact, mutual friendships, and common interests. My hypothesis is that students are likely to date someone with whom they have had personal contact in a class, share friends in common, and share common interests. The topic and focus fit with a micro-level explanation because they are targeted at the level of face-to-face interaction among individuals. Another example topic is how inequality affects the forms of violent behavior in a society. Here, I chose a more macro-level explanation because of the topic and the level of social reality at which it operates. I am interested in the degree of inequality (e.g., the distribution of wealth, property, income, and other resources) throughout a society and in patterns of societal violence (e.g., aggression against other societies, sexual assault, feuds between families). The topic and research question suggest macro-level concepts and theories.

The *unit of analysis* refers to the type of unit a researcher uses when measuring variables. Common units in sociology are the individual, the group (e.g., family, friendship group), the organization (e.g., corporation, university), the social category (e.g., social class, gender, race), the social institution (e.g., religion, education, the family), and the society (e.g., a nation, a tribe). Although the individual is the most commonly used unit of analysis, it is by no means the only one. Different theories emphasize one or another unit of analysis, and different research techniques are associated with specific units of analysis. For example, the individual is usually the unit of analysis in survey and experimental research.

As an example, the individual is the unit of analysis in a survey in which 150 students are asked to rate their favorite football player. The individual is the unit because each individual student's response is recorded. On the other hand, a study that compares the amounts different colleges spend on their football programs would use the organization (the college) as the unit of analysis because the spending by colleges is being compared and each college's spending is recorded.

Researchers use units of analysis other than individuals, groups, organizations, social categories, institutions, and societies. For example, a researcher wants to determine whether the speeches of two candidates for president of the United States contain specific themes. The researcher uses content analysis and measures the themes in each speech of the candidates. Here, the speech is the unit of analysis. Geographic units of analysis are also used. A researcher interested in determining whether cities that have a high number of teenagers also have a high rate of vandalism would use the city as the unit of analysis. This is because the researcher measures the percentage of teenagers in each city and the amount of vandalism for each city.

The units of analysis determine how a researcher measures variables. They also correspond loosely to the level of analysis in an explanation. Thus, social-psychological or micro levels of analysis fit with the individual as a unit of analysis, whereas macro levels of analysis fit with the social category or institution as a unit. Theories and explanations at the micro level generally refer to features of individuals or interactions among individuals. Those at the macro level refer to social forces operating across a society or relations among major parts of a society as a whole.

Researchers use levels and units of analysis to design research projects, and being aware of them helps researchers avoid logical errors in causality (see the next section). For example, a study that examines whether colleges in the North spend more on their football programs than do colleges in the South implies that information is gathered on spending by college and the location of each college. The unit of analysis—the organization or, specifically, the college—flows from the research problem and tells the researcher to collect data from each college.

Researchers choose among different units or levels of analysis for similar topics or research questions. The choices are based on the theory examined and on the researcher's concerns. For example, a researcher could conduct a project on the topic of patriarchy and violence with society as the unit of analysis for the research question, "Are patriarchal societies more violent?" He or she would collect data on societies and classify each society by its degree of patriarchy and its level of violence. On the other hand, if the research question was, "Is the degree of patriarchy within a family associated with violence against a spouse?" the unit of analysis could be the group or the family, and a more micro level of analysis would be appropriate. The researcher could collect data on families by measuring the degree of patriarchy within different families and the level of violence between spouses in these families. The same topic can be addressed with different levels and units of analysis because patriarchy can be a variable that describes an entire society, or it can describe social relations within one family. Likewise, violence

can be defined as general behavior across a society, or as the interpersonal actions of one spouse toward the other.

Potential Errors in Causal Explanation. Developing good explanations requires that researchers watch for statements that appear to be causal hypotheses on the surface but are not. Five fallacies or misleading statements are discussed next.

Ecological Fallacy. The *ecological fallacy* arises from a mismatch of units of analysis. It refers to a poor fit between the units for which a researcher has empirical evidence and the units for which he or she wants to make statements. It is due to imprecise reasoning and generalizing beyond what the evidence warrants. It occurs when a researcher gathers data at a *higher* or an *aggregated* unit of analysis but wants to make a statement about a *lower* or *disaggregated* unit. It is a fallacy because what happens in one unit of analysis does not always hold for a different unit of analysis.[4] Thus, if a researcher gathers data for large aggregates (e.g., organizations, entire countries) and then draws conclusions about the behavior of individuals from those data, he or she is committing the ecological fallacy. You can avoid this error by ensuring that the unit of analysis you use in an explanation is the same as or very close to the unit on which you collect data (see Box 6.3).

Example. Tomsville and Joansville each have about 45,000 people living in them. Tomsville has a high percentage of upper-income people. Over half of the households in the town have family incomes of over $160,000. The town also has more motorcycles registered in it than any other town of its size. The town of Joansville has many poor people. Half its households live below the poverty line. It also has fewer motorcycles registered in it than any other town its size. But it is a *fallacy* to say, on the basis of this information alone, that rich people are more likely to own motorcycles or that the evidence shows a relationship between family income and motorcycle ownership. The reason is that we do not know which families in Tomsville or Joansville own motorccles. We only know about

Box 6.3

Example of Ecological Fallacy

Hightop University has five sections of a course entitled Western History, each with 50 students. Last year, the dean discovered cheating in the sections and looked at the following data that included the gender composition of each section. The dean calculated a very high correlation between cheating and gender. It is plotted in the Graph A.

Section	a	b	c	d	e
# Cheaters	2	4	6	8	10
% Women	80	60	40	30	20

Unfamiliar with the *ecological fallacy*, the dean concluded that men tend to be cheaters and instituted a policy to monitor male students.

You studied the *ecological fallacy* and recognize that the dean's data on characteristics on entire sections of students do not provide evidence on individual cheating behavior. You asked for data on the gender breakdown of the individual cheating students, which is shown in the following:

Section	a	b	c	d	e
Male Cheaters	1	2	3	4	5
Female Cheaters	1	2	3	4	5
Total Cheaters	2	5	6	8	10

You immediately notice that half of the cheaters are female in all sections, and there is no association between the percent of women in a section and the percent of male cheaters. Your plot of the data looks like Graph B. You then explain to the dean that men and women are equally likely to cheat and there is no gender difference in cheating.

The dean's chart is correct, in that it shows the data. The problem is that it is *not* evidence for a statement about gender differences in individual student behavior. Perhaps another unmeasured factor accounts for the pattern (i.e., it is a *spurious relationship*), or maybe a section with fewer women creates a social atmosphere in the classroom that supports a norm to cheat among both men and women equally. These are issues for additional study.

Despite a clear pattern of observations in Graph A, it is not the type of evidence to support a conclusion that men are more likely to cheat than women. One must have the right type of evidence (on individuals) to draw conclusions about individual cheating behavior.

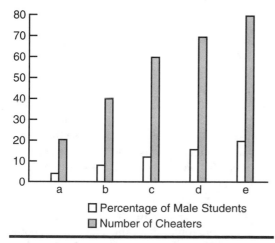

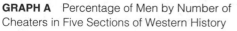

☐ Percentage of Male Students
▨ Number of Cheaters

GRAPH A Percentage of Men by Number of Cheaters in Five Sections of Western History

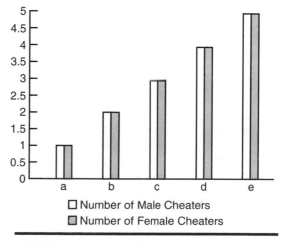

☐ Number of Male Cheaters
▨ Number of Female Cheaters

GRAPH B Number of Cheaters by Gender in Five Sections of Western History

the two variables—average income and number of motorcycles—for the towns as a whole. The unit of analysis for observing variables is the town as a whole. Perhaps all of the low- and middle-income families in Tomsville belong to a motorcycle club, and not a single upper-income family belongs. Or perhaps one rich family and five poor ones in Joansville each own motorcycles. In order to make a statement about the relationship between family ownership of motorcycles and family income, we have to collect information on families, not on towns as a whole.

Reductionism.   Another problem involving mismatched units of analysis and imprecise reasoning about evidence is *reductionism*, also called the fallacy of nonequivalence (see Box 6.4). This error occurs when a researcher explains macro-level events but has evidence only about specific individuals. It occurs when a researcher observes a *lower* or *disaggregated* unit of analysis but makes statements about the operations of *higher* or *aggregated* units. It is a mirror image of the mismatch error in the ecological fallacy. A researcher who has data on how individuals behave but makes statements about the dynamics of macro-level units is committing the error of reductionism. It occurs because it is often easier to get data on concrete individuals. Also, the operation of macro-level units is more abstract and nebulous. Stanley Lieberson has argued that this error, which he says is common in social research, leads to inconsistencies, contradictions, and confusion. He (1985:108, 113–114) forcefully stated,

> *associations on the lower level are irrelevant for determining the validity of a proposition about processes operating on the higher level. As a matter of fact, no useful understanding of the higher-level structure can be obtained from lower-level analysis. . . . If we are interested in the higher-level processes and events, it is because we operate with the understanding that they have distinct qualities that are not simply derived by summing up the subunits.*

As with the ecological fallacy, you can avoid this error by ensuring that the unit of analysis in your

explanation is very close to the one for which you have evidence.

Researchers who fail to think precisely about the units of analysis and those who do not couple data with the theory are likely to commit the ecological fallacy or reductionism. They make a mistake about the data appropriate for a research question, or they may seriously overgeneralize from the data.

You can make assumptions about units of analysis other than the ones you study empirically. Thus, research on individuals rests on assumptions that individuals act within a set of social institutions. Research on social institutions is based on assumptions about individual behavior. We know that many micro-level units form macro-level units. The danger is that it is easy to slide into using the causes or behavior of micro units, such as individuals, to explain the actions of macro units, such as social institutions. What happens among units at one level does not necessarily hold for different units of analysis. Sociology is a discipline that rests on the fundamental belief that a distinct level of social reality exists beyond the individual. Explanations of this level require data and theory that go beyond the individual alone. The causes, forces, structures, or processes that exist among macro units cannot be reduced to individual behavior.

Example.   Why did World War I occur? You may have heard that it was because a Serbian shot an archduke in the AustroHungarian Empire in 1914. This is reductionism. Yes, the assassination was a factor, but the macro-political event between nations—war—cannot be reduced to a specific act of one individual. If it could, we could also say that the war occurred because the assassin's alarm clock worked and woke him up that morning. If it had not worked, there would have been no assassination, so the alarm clock caused the war! The event, World War I, was much more complex and was due to many social, political, and economic forces that came together at a point in history. The actions of specific individuals had a role, but only a minor one compared to these macro forces. Individuals affect events, which

Box 6.4

Error of Reductionism

Suppose you pick up a book and read the following:

> *American race relations changed dramatically during the Civil Rights Era of the 1960s. Attitudes among the majority, white population shifted to greater tolerance as laws and court rulings changed across the nation. Opportunities that had been legally and officially closed to all but the white population—in the areas of housing, jobs, schooling, voting rights, and so on—were opened to people of all races. From the* Brown *vs.* Board of Education *decision in 1955, to the Civil Rights Act of 1964, to the War on Poverty from 1966 to 1968, a new, dramatic outlook swept the country. This was the result of the vision, dedication, and actions of America's foremost civil rights leader, Dr. Martin Luther King, Jr.*

This says: *dependent variable* = major change in U.S. race relations over a 10- to 13-year period; *independent variable* = King's vision and actions.

If you know much about the civil rights era, you see a problem. The entire civil rights movement and its successes are attributed to a single individual. Yes, one individual does make a difference and helps build and guide a movement, but the *movement* is missing. The idea of a social-political movement as a causal force is reduced to its major leader. The distinct social phenomenon—a movement—is obscured. Lost are the actions of hundreds of thousands of people (marches, court cases, speeches, prayer meetings, sit-ins, rioting, petitions, beatings, etc.) involved in advancing a shared goal and the responses to them. The movement's ideology, popular mobilization, politics, organization, and strategy

are absent. Related macro-level historical events and trends that may have influenced the movement (e.g., Vietnam War protest, mood shift with the killing of John F. Kennedy, black separatist politics, black migration to urban North) are also ignored.

This error is not unique to historical explanations. Many people think only in terms of individual actions and have an individualist bias, sometimes called *methodological individualism*. This is especially true in the extremely individualistic U.S. culture. The error is that it disregards units of analysis or forces beyond the individual. The *error of reductionism* shifts explanation to a much lower unit of analysis. One could continue to reduce from an individual's behavior to biological processes in a person, to micro-level neurochemical activities, to the subatomic level.

Most people live in "social worlds" focused on local, immediate settings and their interactions with a small set of others, so their everyday sense of reality encourages seeing social trends or events as individual actions or psychological processes. Often, they become blind to more abstract, macro-level entities—social forces, processes, organizations, institutions, movements, or structures. The idea that all social actions cannot be reduced to individuals alone is the core of sociology. In his classic work *Suicide*, Emile Durkheim fought methodological individualism and demonstrated that larger, unrecognized social forces explain even highly individual, private actions.

---

eventually, in combination with larger-scale social forces and organizations, affect others and move nations, but individual actions alone are not the cause. Thus, it is likely that a war would have broken out at about that time even if the assassination had not occurred.

Tautology. The *tautology* is circular reasoning—when something is "true by definition." A tautology looks like a causal relationship but is not one. It occurs through a slip in language, a

confusion between a definition and a causal relationship. A scientific hypothesis must be capable of being shown to be false with empirical evidence. Tautologies cannot be empirically tested or shown to be false because they state a logical or semantic relationship, not an empirical, causal one. You can avoid this error by considering whether a hypothesis can be restated as a definition. If you can substitute an equal sign for the causal arrow between the independent and dependent variables, you probably have a tautology.

Example. A conservative is a person with certain attitudes, beliefs, and values (desires less government regulation, no taxes on upper-income people, a strong military, religion in public schools, an end to antidiscrimination laws). It is a tautology to say that wanting less regulation, a strong military, and so on *causes* conservatism. In sloppy everyday usage, we can say, "Sally is conservative *because* she believes that there should be less regulation." This looks like a causal statement, but it is not a causal explanation. The set of attitudes is a *reason* to label Sally as a conservative, but those attitudes cannot be the *cause* of Sally's conservatism. Her attitudes *are* conservatism, so the statement is true by definition. It would be impossible ever to come up with evidence showing that those attitudes were not associated with conservatism.

Teleology. This is another case in which something looks like a causal relationship but is not one because it cannot be tested empirically. It is due to a slip in language. A *teleology* arises when a vague future condition or an abstract, diffuse idea about the "nature of the world" is used to explain something specific. It is untestable and violates temporal order in causal explanations. You can avoid this error by carefully examining the independent variable or cause in an explanation.

Example. The statement, "The nuclear family is the dominant family form in Western industrial societies *because* it is functional for the survival of the society," is an untestable teleological statement from structural functional theory. It is saying "society's survival" *causes* "development of family form." Yet, the only way we can observe whether or not a society survives is after the fact, or as a consequence of its having had a form of the family. Here is another example of a teleological statement: "Because it was the destiny of the United States to become a major world power, we find thousands of immigrants entering the Western frontier during the early nineteenth century." This says that "becoming a major world power," which occurred from 1920 to 1945, caused "westward migration," which took place between 1850 and 1890. It uses the obscure term *destiny*, which, like

other similar terms (e.g., "in God's plan"), cannot be observed in causal relationships.

Spuriousness. To call a relationship between variables spurious means that it is false, a mirage. Researchers get excited if they think they have found a spurious relationship because they can show the world to be more complex than it appears on the surface. Because any association between two variables might be spurious, researchers are cautious when they discover that two variables are associated; upon further investigation, it may not be the basis for a causal relationship. It may be an illusion, just like the mirage that resembles a pool of water on a road during a hot day.

Spuriousness occurs when two variables are associated but are not causally related because there is actually an unseen third factor that is the real cause (see Box 6.5). The third variable causes both the apparent independent and the dependent variable. It accounts for the observed association. In terms of conditions for causality, the unseen third factor represents a more powerful alternative explanation.

You may say, "O.K., I should be wary of correlations or associations, but how can I tell whether a relationship is spurious, and how do I find out what the mysterious third factor is?" You will need to use statistical techniques (discussed later in this book) to test whether an association is spurious. To use them, you need a theory or at least a guess about possible third factors, based on how you think the world operates. Actually, spuriousness is based on some commonsense logic that you already use. For example, you already know that there is an association between the use of air conditioners and ice cream cone consumption. If you measured the number of air conditioners in use and the number of ice cream cones sold for each day, you would find a strong correlation, with more cones sold on the days when more air conditioners are in use. But you know that eating ice cream cones does not cause people to turn on air conditioners. Instead, both variables are caused by a third factor: hot days. The third factor is unseen until you figure it out logically. You could verify the same thing through statistics by

Box 6.5

Spuriousness Example

In their study of the news media, Neuman, Jusr and Crigler (1992) found a correlation between type of news source and knowledge. People who prefer to get their news from television are less knowledgeable than those who get it from print sources. This correlation is often interpreted as "dumbing down" of information. In other words, television news causes people to know little.

The authors found that the relationship was spurious, however, "We were able to show that the entire relationship between television news preference and lower knowledge scores is spurious" (p. 113). They found that a third variable, initially unseen, explained both to a preference for television news and a level of knowledge about current events. They said, "We find that what is really causing the television-is-the-

problem effect is the preference for people with lower cognitive skill to get their news from television" (p. 98). The missing or hidden variable was "cognitive skill." The authors defined cognitive skill as a person's ability to use reason and manipulate abstract ideas. In other words, people who find it difficult to process abstract, complex information turn to television news. Others may also use the high-impact, entertaining television news sources, but they use it less and heavily supplement it with other more demanding, information-rich print sources. People who have weak information skills also tend to be less knowledgeable about current events and about other topics that require abstract thought or dealing with complex information.

---

measuring the daily temperature as well as ice cream consumption and air conditioner use. In social research, opposing theories help people figure out which third factors are relevant for many topics (e.g., the causes of crime or the reasons for war or child abuse).

Example.   Tall 15-year-olds seem to enjoy football and sports more than they enjoy shopping for clothes. Moreover, there is a strong correlation between height and preference for football. This does not mean that height *causes* a pro-football preference; the relationship is spurious because a third factor, gender, is operating. Fifteen-year-old boys are taller than 15-year-old girls, and boys prefer football. Thus, height itself may have nothing to do with liking football. Rather, a person's gender produces the height differences and is also associated with socialization to enjoy football and other sports. In fact, it could be that, among boys, the taller ones actually prefer basketball or track over football. If rescarchers observe height and football preference alone and ignore gender, they will be misled.

Figure 6.2 shows in graphic form the five errors discussed in this section.

SELECTING AND REFINING RESEARCH TOPICS

Selecting a Topic

Your first step when beginning a research project is to select a topic.[5] There is no formula for selecting a topic. Whether you are an experienced researcher or just beginning, the best guide is to conduct research on something that interests you. There are many sources of topics. Box 6.6 suggests ways to choose topics. The techniques for choosing topics are not limited to quantitative research but apply to all types of research.

From a Topic to a Specific Research Question

Social researchers do not conduct research on a topic, although a topic is an essential starting point. A topic is just that—a starting point. Researchers refine and narrow down a topic into a problem or question. A common mistake of new researchers is to fail to narrow a topic sufficiently, or to try to jump from a broad topic directly into a research project without first creating a research question. In quantitative research, you need a nar-

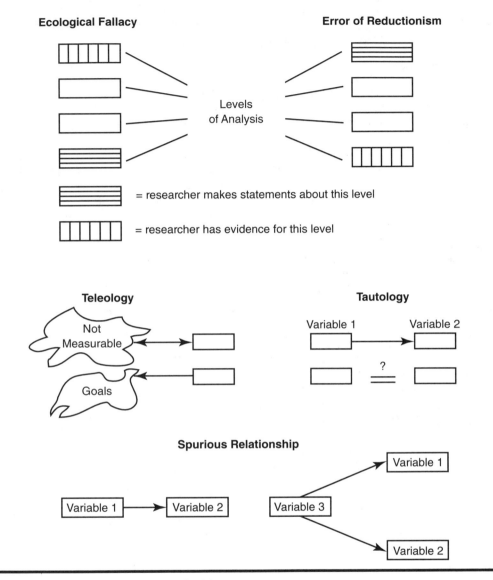

FIGURE 6.2 Five Errors in Explanation to Avoid

rowly focused research question before you design a research project.

Research projects are designed around research problems or questions. It is possible to phrase many potential research questions for most topics. Before designing a project, focus on a specific research problem within a broad topic. For example, the personal experience

example in Box 6.6 suggests labor unions as a topic. "Labor unions" is a topic, not a research question or a problem. In any large library, you will find hundreds of books and thousands of articles written by sociologists, historians, economists, management officials, political scientists, and others on unions. The books and articles focus on different aspects of the topic

Box 6.6

Ways to Select Topics

1. *Personal experience*: You can choose a topic based on something that happens to you or those you know. For example, while you work a summer job at a factory, the local union calls a strike. You do not have strong feelings either way, but you are forced to choose sides. You notice that tensions rise. Both management and labor become hostile toward each other. This experience suggests unions or organized labor as a topic.

2. *Curiosity based on something in the media*: Sometimes you read a newspaper or magazine article or see a television program and leave with questions. What you read raises questions or suggests replicating what others' research found. For example, you read a *Newsweek* article on the homeless, but you do not really know much about who they are, why they are homeless, whether this has always been a problem, and so forth. This suggests the homeless as a topic.

3. *The state of knowledge in a field*: Basic research is driven by new research findings and theories that push at the frontiers of knowledge. As theoretical explanations are elaborated and expanded, certain issues or questions need to be answered for the field to move forward. As such issues are identified and studied, knowledge advances. For example, you read about attitudes toward capital punishment and realize that most research points to an underlying belief in the innate wickedness of criminals among capital punishment supporters. You notice that no one has yet examined whether people who belong to certain religious groups that teach such a belief in wickedness support capital punishment, nor

has anyone mapped the geographic location of these religious groups. Your knowledge of the field suggests a topic for a research project, beliefs about capital punishment, and religion in different regions.

4. *Solving a problem*: Applied research topics often begin with a problem that needs a solution. For example, as part of your job as a dorm counselor, you want to help college freshmen establish friendships with each other. Your problem suggests friendship formation among new college students as a topic.

5. *Social premiums*: This is a term suggested by Singleton and colleague (1988:68). It means that some topics are "hot" or offer an opportunity. For example, you read that there is a lot of money available to conduct research on nursing homes, but few people are interested in doing so. Your need of a job suggests nursing homes as a topic.

6. *Personal values*: Some people are highly committed to a set of religious, political, or social values. For example, you are strongly committed to racial equality and become morally outraged whenever you hear about racial discrimination. Your strong personal belief suggests racial discrimination as a topic.

7. *Everyday life*: Potential topics can be found throughout everyday life in old sayings, novels, songs, statistics, and what others say (especially those who disagree with you). For example, you hear that the home court advantage is very important in basketball. This statement suggests "home court advantage" as a topic for research.

---

and adopt many perspectives on it. Before proceeding to design a research project, you must narrow and focus the topic. An example research question is "How much did U.S. labor unions contribute to racial inequality by creating barriers to skilled jobs for African Americans in the post–World War II period?"

When starting research on a topic, ask yourself: What is it about the topic that is of greatest interest? For a topic about which you know little, first get background knowledge by reading about it. Research questions refer to the relationships among a small number of variables. Identify a limited number of variables and specify the relationships among them.

A research question has one or a small number of causal relationships. Box 6.7 lists some ways to focus a topic into a research question. For

Box 6.7 _____

Techniques for Narrowing a Topic into a Research Question

1. *Examine the literature:* Published articles are an excellent source of ideas for research questions. They are usually at an appropriate level of specificity and suggest research questions that focus on the following:
   a. Replicate a previous research project exactly or with slight variations.
   b. Explore unexpected findings discovered in previous research.
   c. Follow suggestions an author gives for future research at the end of an article.
   d. Extend an existing explanation or theory to a new topic or setting.
   e. Challenge findings or attempt to refute a relationship.
   f. Specify the intervening process and consider linking relations.
2. *Talk over ideas with others:*
   a. Ask people who are knowledgeable about the topic for questions about it that they have thought of.
   b. Seek out those who hold opinions that differ from yours on the topic and discuss possible research questions with them.
3. *Apply to a specific context:*
   a. Focus the topic onto a specific historical period or time period.
   b. Narrow the topic to a specific society or geographic unit.
   c. Consider which subgroups or categories of people/units are involved and whether there are differences among them.
4. *Define the aim or desired outcome of the study:*
   a. Will the research question be for an exploratory, explanatory, or descriptive study?
   b. Will the study involve applied or basic research?

Another technique for focusing a research question is to specify the *universe* to which the answer to the question can be generalized. All research questions, hypotheses, and studies apply to some group or category of people, organizations, or other units. The universe is the set of units that the researcher wishes to explain. For example, your research question is about the effects of a new attendance policy on learning by high school students. The universe is all high school students. We will discuss this idea again in Chapter 9.

When refining a topic into a research question, when designing a research project, and when formulating hypotheses, you also need to consider practical limitations. Designing a perfect research project is an interesting academic exercise, but if you expect to carry out a research project, practical limitations will have an impact on its design.

Major limitations include time, costs, access to resources, approval by authorities, ethical concerns, and expertise. If you have 10 hours a week for five weeks to conduct a research project, but the answer to a research question will take five years to uncover, reformulate the research question more narrowly. Estimating the amount of time required to answer a research question is difficult. The hypotheses specified, the research technique used, and the type of data collected all play significant roles. Experienced researchers are the best source of good estimates.

Cost is another limitation. As with time, there are inventive ways to answer a question within limitations, but it may be impossible to answer some questions because of the expense involved. For example, a research question about the attitudes of all sports fans toward their team mascot can be answered only with a great investment of time and money. Narrowing the research question to how students at two different colleges feel about their mascots might make it more manageable.

Access to resources is a common limitation. Resources can include the expertise of others, special equipment, or information. For example, a research question about burglary rates and family income in many different nations is almost impossible to answer because information on burglary

example, the question, "What causes divorce?" is not a good research question. A better research question is, "Is age at marriage associated with divorce?" The second question suggests two variables: age of marriage and divorce.

and income is not collected or available for most countries. Some questions require the approval of authorities (e.g., to see medical records) or involve violating basic ethical principles (e.g., causing serious physical harm to a person to see the person's reaction). The expertise or background of the researcher is also a limitation. Answering some research questions involves the use of data collection techniques, statistical methods, knowledge of a foreign language, or skills that the researcher may not have. Unless the researcher can acquire the necessary training or can pay for another person's services, the research question may not be practical.

From the Research Question to Hypotheses

It is difficult to move smoothly from a broad topic to a hypothesis, but the leap from a well-formulated research question to hypotheses is a short one. Hints about hypotheses are embedded within a good research question. In addition, hypotheses are tentative answers to research questions (see Box 6.8).

Consider an example research question: "Is age at marriage associated with divorce?" The question contains two variables: "age at marriage" and "divorce." To develop a hypothesis, a researcher asks, "Which is the independent variable?" The independent variable is "age at marriage" because marriage must logically precede divorce. The researcher also asks, "What is the direction of the relationship?" The hypothesis could be: "The lower the age at time of marriage, the greater the chances that the marriage will end in divorce." This hypothesis answers the research question and makes a prediction. Notice that the research question can be reformulated and better focused now: "Are couples who marry younger more likely to divorce?"

Several hypotheses can be developed for one research question. Another hypothesis from the same research question is: "The smaller the difference between the ages of the marriage partners at the time of marriage, the less likely that the marriage will end in divorce." In this case, the variable "age at marriage" is specified differently.

Hypotheses can specify that a relationship holds under some conditions but not others. As Lieberson (1985:198) remarked, "In order to evaluate the utility of a given causal proposition, it is important that there be a clear-cut statement of the conditions under which it will operate." For example, a hypothesis states: "The lower the age of the partners at time of marriage, the greater the chances that the marriage will end in divorce, unless it is a marriage between members of a tight-knit traditional religious community in which early marriage is the norm."

Formulating a research question and developing a hypothesis do not have to proceed in fixed stages. A researcher can formulate a tentative research question, then develop possible hypotheses. The process of developing hypotheses helps a researcher state the research question more precisely. The process is interactive and involves creativity.

Where Is the Theory?

You may be wondering: Where does theory fit into the process of moving from a topic to a hypothesis I can test? Recall from Chapter 3 that theory takes many forms. Researchers use general theoretical issues and puzzles as a source of topics. Theories and theoretical frameworks provide researchers with concepts and ideas that they turn into variables. Theory provides the reasoning or mechanism that helps researchers connect variables into a research question. A hypothesis can be both an answer to a research question and an untested proposition from a theory. Researchers can express a hypothesis at an abstract, conceptual level. They can also restate it in a more concrete, measurable form, as you will see in the next chapter.

You first saw the steps of a research project in Chapter 1. Figure 6.3 gives a slightly different picture of the steps. It shows intermediate steps and the processes used to narrow a topic into a hypothesis. It also shows how the abstract theoretical level blends into the concrete empirical level as a researcher moves toward the data collection stage.

Box 6.8 _____

Examples of Good and Bad Research Questions

BAD RESEARCH QUESTIONS

Not Empirically Testable, Nonscientific Questions
- Should abortion be legal?
- Is it right to have capital punishment?

General Topics, Not Research Questions
- Treatment of alcohol and drug abuse
- Sexuality and aging

Set of Variables, Not Questions
- Capital punishment and racial discrimination
- Urban decay and gangs

Too Vague, Ambiguous
- Do police affect delinquency?
- What can be done to prevent child abuse?

Need to Be Still More Specific
- Has the incidence of child abuse risen?
- How does poverty affect children?
- What problems do children who grow up in poverty experience that others do not?

GOOD QUESTIONS

Exploratory Questions
- Has the actual incidence of child abuse changed in Wisconsin in the past 10 years?

Descriptive Questions
- Is child abuse, violent or sexual, more common in families that have experienced a divorce than in intact, never-divorced families?
- Are the children raised in poverty households more likely to have medical, learning, and social-emotional adjustment difficulties than nonpoverty children?

Explanatory Questions
- Does the emotional instability created by experiencing a divorce increase the chances that divorced parents will physically abuse their children?
- Is a lack of sufficent funds for preventive treatment a major cause of more serious medical problems among children raised in families in poverty?

EXAMPLE STUDIES

Before looking at how to conduct a study, you should see how the ideas in this chapter—topic, research question, hypotheses, independent and dependent variables, universe, and unit of analysis—are used in real studies.

Experiment

The *topic* of Neapolitan's (1988) "The Effects of Different Types of Praise and Criticism on Performance" is suggested in the title, the use of positive or negative feedback (praise or criticism) to affect performance. The author reveals the theoretical tradition he uses by applying the concepts *reinforcement* and *attribution*. These concepts come from attribution and behavior modification theories in social psychology.

The *research question* is: Which of four types of praise/criticism has the largest impact on improving how well people perform? Four types of praise or criticism are considered: specific product praise (i.e., your paper is good), general actor praise (i.e., you are a good student), specific product criticism, and general actor criticism. These are taken from a typology developed by another researcher. The author does not specify the type of performance and uses the term in a general way.

The main *hypothesis* is that specific product praise (SPP) has a positive effect on performance. The research project described in the method section involved 240 sociology college students enrolled in one of seven Introduction to Sociology classes. Students were asked to write a paragraph summarizing the ideas in a written passage during

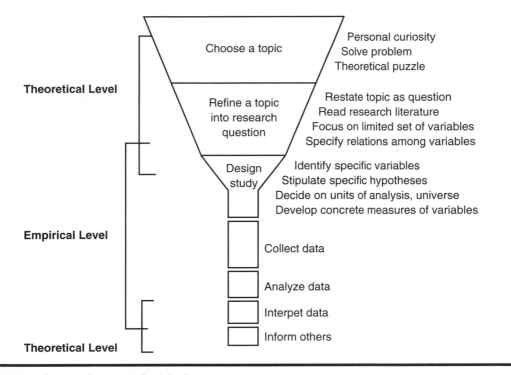

FIGURE 6.3 Steps in Research Revisited

class time. The students were randomly given one of four evaluations of their paragraph one week later. An equal number of students (60) received each evaluation. The four evaluations (supposedly from an English professor) corresponded to the four types of praise/criticism (e.g., the paragraph is well structured, you are a fine writer, the paragraph is poorly structured, you are a poor writer).

The *independent variable* is the type of praise or criticism in the evaluation. The researcher gave the students an evaluation of their writing and falsely told them that the evaluations came from an English professor. Students were then asked to write a second paragraph. The improvement in the second paragraph over the first represented the *dependent variable*, or performance. The improvement was measured by having the paragraphs graded by two evaluators who assigned scores from 1 (very poor) to 10 (very good) and by looking at differences between the first and second score.

The Results section of Neapolitan's study shows the percentage of students in each of the four groups whose scores declined, did not change, or improved. The author found that 70 percent of students who received SPP improved. This was higher than for the other three types of praise or criticism. There was little improvement for students who received the general actor praise or the specific product criticism. Unexpectedly, a little over half of the students who received the general actor criticism improved.

In a Discussion section, the author summarizes the findings. He is unsure why the result for general actor criticism was found and speculates that the students attributed the criticism to the evaluators instead of seeing it as a true reflection of their performance.

The *universe* to which the results apply includes all people. Most experimental research generalizes to everyone when no particular group is specified. The *unit of analysis* is the individual, or student, because the variables and measures are characteristics of individuals. This is an explanatory study that attempts to advance basic knowledge but also has applied implications.

Survey Research

The *topic* of Bankston and Thompson's (1989) article, "Carrying Firearms for Protection," is evident in the title. The researchers discussed the research on firearms in the United States, which has largely examined the ownership of guns. They developed a focused *research question*: "To what degree do people who carry firearms when away from home do so out of a fear of crime?"

The authors mailed questionnaires to over 4,000 people in Louisiana, asking about their attitudes and background characteristics in addition to whether they carried a firearm. Eventually, the authors limited the study to whites and had full data on a little over 1,000 people. The main *hypothesis* they tested was whether people who fear crime the most and who believe that a gun will protect them are most likely to carry a firearm. The authors' main *independent variable* was fear of crime, and they specified an *intervening variable*: a belief that guns provide effective protection. The *dependent variable* was how often a person carried a gun when away from home. The authors found that about one-third of the respondents carried a firearm on at least some occasions.

In the Results section, the authors examined the effects of variables on how often a person carried a firearm. They found that a fear of crime did not directly affect how often a person carried a weapon, but a belief in the effectiveness of having a gun for protection had a large effect. People who thought that carrying a gun offered personal protection tended to be younger, less well educated rural males who thought crime was a serious problem and who feared crime.

The authors noted that Louisiana is a southern state with some of the least restrictive laws on purchasing or carrying firearms. The *universe* for the results may be limited to whites in other areas of the southern United States. The *unit of analysis* of the study was the individual.

Content Analysis

The article by Barlow, Barlow, and Chiricos (1995), "Economic Conditions and Ideologies of Crime in the Media," uses content analysis. The *topic* of the study is how the media portrays crime and criminals. The *hypothesis* was that the media give a distorted picture of crime, and the distortion is linked to changes in economic conditions. In particular, the authors predicted that more negative images of crime and criminals occur when unemployment is high or the economy is in a recession. Thus, the *independent variable* was the unemployment rate and the *dependent variable* was how negative the offender was presented. The authors also looked at overall distortion in terms of a mismatch between crime statistics and crime that gets media attention. The *research question* is, "Does the news media give a distorted picture of crime, with the distortion based on a value and belief system that condemns offenders most harshly when economic conditions are bad?"

The data for the study came from *Time* magazine. The authors sampled various years (1953, 1958, 1975, 1982) that had different economic conditions and looked at all articles during the year that dealt with crime, criminal justice, or criminals. They found 175 articles. The *unit of analysis* is the article. The *universe* for the study is all crime-related articles that appeared in major U.S. mass circulation news magazines from the 1950s to the 1980s.

The authors also looked at the crime rate, change in the crime rate, characteristics of offenders, and types of crime as violent or nonviolent during the selected years. They rated the image of the offender in each article as to how positive or negative it appeared. A negative image showed the offender as being without remorse, as lacking a reason for the crime, as unprincipled or lying, or as unlikely to be rehabilitated. A more positive image showed the offender as confused and willing to make changes, as trying to make the best of a bad situation, as forced into crime as a result of circumstances, or as caught up in the criminal justice system.

The authors found that negative images were more common in high unemployment periods. Specifically, 62 percent of the images in high unemployment periods were negative versus 32 percent in low unemployment periods. Other patterns of distortion were also found. For example, the authors discovered that 73 percent of the articles focused on violent crime, which made up about 10 percent of crimes known to police in the selected years. Some 74 percent of the articles that included a reference to the offender's race stated that the offender was nonwhite, whereas the percent of arrests involving nonwhites in the selected years was 28 percent. Last, despite the strong connection between employment conditions and crime, only 3 percent of the articles included information on whether the offender had a job or was unemployed.

Existing Statistics

Stack's (1987) "Celebrities and Suicide: A Taxonomy and Analysis, 1948–1983" used existing statistical information. As the title implies, the *topic* involves celebrities and suicide. In the introduction, the author noted that most of the 2,500 research reports on the impact of the media on violence are experiments. He said that his research project looks at "the effects of newspaper accounts of suicides in the real world" (p. 401). He developed a theory of imitative suicide and focused on celebrities. Thus, on the first page, the author narrowed the topic, criticized prior research, and stated the goals of developing and testing a theory.

Stack noted that three theories explain the link between suicide stories and imitative suicides. He cited the writings of the French sociologist Gabriel Tardé (1843–1904) as a source of insight into imitation and outlined the differential identification theory, which says that people imitate the actions of people who they feel are superior to them. In modern times, the mass media shape public opinion. In addition, people identify with elites and celebrities because they represent the realm of the superior. The *research question* is, "Which types of celebrity-elite members are most apt to trigger imitative suicides?" (p. 403).

Stack identified several types of elite celebrities: political, entertainment, artistic, villain (e.g., famous terrorists), and economic elites. He gave a rationale for why the suicide of a member of each group increases the suicide rate.

Stack reported that information on the number of suicide deaths in the United States for the years 1948 to 1983 came from U.S. Public Health Service sources. The number of suicides is turned into a suicide rate, the *dependent variable*, by dividing it by the number of people in the United States.

The key *independent variable* was identified as "a nationally publicized suicide story of a celebrity." Suicides were identified by looking in a publication called *Facts on File*. A celebrity is anyone whose name appeared in the *New York Times* annual indexes "in at least two of the five years before his/her death" (p. 404). The author assumed that the impact of a suicide story is greatest within two weeks of its publication. Each month was noted as being one in which a celebrity suicide story did or did not occur. Stories appearing after the 23rd of a month counted as part of the following month.

Two other measures of the independent variable captured the "degree of publicity": the number of column-inches in the newspaper devoted to the story and the number of national newspapers in which the story appeared on page one. Examples of celebrities in several of the categories and a list of 38 celebrity suicides that occurred between 1948 and 1983 appear in an appendix to the article.

The author said that the *unit of analysis* is the month, because the suicide rate is computed for each month, 1948 to 1983. The other variables were measured by month as well. Thus, the data included information for 432 months (12 months for 36 years).

The Analysis section of Stack's study describes the statistical techniques used and presents the results in a table showing each type of celebrity in association with the monthly suicide rate. Only entertainment celebrity suicide stories had a large association with the overall suicide rate.

Stack examined two refined measures of the independent variable: multiple coverage on page one and column-inches. He asked, "Within celebrity categories, can we expect that the greater the media attention paid to a story, the greater the increase in the suicide rate?" (p. 407). Again, the results showed a positive relationship between the amount of front-page and overall newspaper space given to a celebrity suicide and the size of the increase in general suicide rates.

A weakness of the study is that the author did not demonstrate that the individuals who committed suicide actually read the suicide reports (e.g., that they subscribed to the newspapers). To do this would have made the research project much more difficult and expensive to complete.

There are three potential *universes* to which results might be generalized. The first can be other nations, because the research involved only the United States. Second, it can be years beyond the 1948–1983 period examined. Third, it can be other reports of suicide by a famous person. The results can be generalized beyond the impact of national newspaper reports of widely known celebrities on national suicide rates to the impact of any media report of the suicide of any locally well-known person on regional or local suicide rates. This is an example of basic research: Its goal is to expand knowledge by explaining changes in the suicide rate by identifying a causal factor that acts on it.

CONCLUSION

In this chapter, you learned about the components of quantitative research that are based on a positivist approach to research. Quantitative research techniques share a language and logic from positivism that separates them from research techniques based on other approaches.

You learned that the language of quantitative research is one of variables, causal relations, and hypotheses. Quantitative research design uses a deductive logic. When using it, you begin with a general topic, narrow it down to research questions and hypotheses, and, finally, test hypotheses against empirical evidence.

You saw that theoretical explanations and concepts are a critical part of research design. Explanations and concepts are the basis of variables and their interrelationships.

You also learned about dangers in constructing causal explanations. Several types of logical errors (ecological fallacy, reductionism, tautology, teleology, and spuriousness) can plague causal explanations. As we saw in Chapter 4, positivist science emphasizes the importance of logical rigor, consistency, and an absence of contradiction in theoretical explanation. Efforts to avoid the logical errors in causal explanation are consistent with this emphasis.

Once you have narrowed topics, explanations, and research into hypotheses and variables, the next step is to measure the variables to test hypotheses with empirical evidence. Positivist approaches give special importance to precise measurement. They demand careful, objective measurement of the empirical world.

Precise quantitative measures of variables should be used whenever possible. In the next two chapters, we will examine measurement in quantitative research. They extend the discussion of variables and use a similar logic. It is important to address general issues of measurement before we examine how the four quantitative research techniques measure variables and collect data so you can test hypotheses.

KEY TERMS

alternative hypothesis	hypothesis	reductionism
attributes	independent variable	spuriousness
crucial experiment	intervening variable	tautology
dependent variable	level of analysis	teleology
double-barreled hypothesis	logic of disconfirming hypotheses	unit of analysis universe
ecological fallacy	null hypothesis	variable

REVIEW QUESTIONS

1. Describe the differences between independent, dependent, and intervening variables.

2. Why don't we *prove* results in social research?

3. How are units of analysis and levels of analysis related to each other?

4. What two hypotheses are used if a researcher uses the logic of disconfirming hypotheses? Why is negative evidence stronger?

5. Restate the following in terms of a hypothesis with independent and dependent variables: "The number of miles a person drives in a year affects the number of visits a person makes to filling stations, and there is a positive unidirectional relationship between the variables."

6. What is the unit of analysis for the hypothesis in question 5?

7. What would a diagram of the variables for a spurious relationship look like?

8. How can you determine whether an explanation is a tautology?

9. In what ways do ecological fallacy and reductionism involve problems with the units of analysis?

10. What is the relationship between a topic, a research question, and a hypothesis?

NOTES

1. See Lieberson (1985:185–187) for a discussion of basic and superficial variables in a set of causal linkages. Davis (1985) and Stinchcombe (1968) provide good general introductions to making linkages among variables in social theory.

2. The logic of disconfirming hypothesis is discussed in Singleton, Straits, and McAllister (1988:56–60).

3. See Bailey (1987:43) for a discussion of this term.

4. The general problem of aggregating observation and making causal inferences is discussed in somewhat technical terms in Blalock (1982:-237–264) and in Hannan (1985). O'Brien (1992) argues that the ecological fallacy is one of a whole group of logical fallacies in which levels and units of analysis are confused and overgeneralized.

5. Problem choice and topic selection are discussed in Campbell, Daft, and Hulin (1982) and in Zuckerman (1978).

RECOMMENDED READINGS

Blalock, Hubert M., Jr. (1969). *Theory construction: From verbal to mathematical formulations*. Englewood Cliffs, NJ: Prentice-Hall. As the subtitle suggests, this book explains how to take verbal sociological theories and convert them into a mathematical form. The mathematics required is fairly low level (an appendix reviews elementary calculus). The book is very helpful for seeing how complex explanations of social relations can be turned into precise, logical, quantifiable statements.

Campbell, John P., Richard L. Daft, and Charles L. Hulin. (1982). *What to study: Generating and developing research questions*. Beverly Hills, CA: Sage. This is an unusual book. It is primarily about how to look for and ask research questions. The main topic area with which the authors are concerned is organizations, but their suggestions have applicability to most topic areas.

Davis, James A. (1985). *The logic of causal order*. Beverly Hills, CA: Sage. This very short (66 pages) book elaborates on the system for diagraming causal relationships among variables. In addition to providing many examples and rules for the logic of causal diagrams, the author gives an introduction to using various statistics to examine the meaning of different patterns of causal relationships.

Lieberson, Stanley, (1985). *Making it count: The improvement of social research and theory*. Berkeley: University of California Press. This is an enjoyable and informative book on the basics of a sophisticated positivist approach to social research. The author is critical of many practices used by social researchers for their lack of sufficient logic and rigor. The book contains few formulas or statistics; instead, the author uses logical argument and systematic thinking to make his points. The discussions of causality, levels of analysis, control variables, and research questions are very good.

CHAPTER 7

QUANTITATIVE SOCIAL SCIENCE MEASUREMENT

Measurement, in short, is not an end in itself. Its scientific worth can be appreciated only in an instrumentalist perspective, in which we ask what ends measurement is intended to serve, what role it is called upon to play in the scientific situation, what functions it performs in inquiry.

—Abraham Kaplan, *The Conduct of Inquiry*, p. 171

INTRODUCTION

Many people look surprised when social researchers claim to measure strange, invisible things such as affection, self-esteem, ideology, political power, or alienation. In this chapter, you will learn about how social researchers measure. Measurement is critical in quantitative social science. We will examine the key principles of quantitative measurement, review the ideas of reliability and validity, examine the fundamentals of measurement theory, and explore measurement techniques. The previous chapter gave you a background for quantitative measurement. This chapter extends the discussion on research design in two ways. First, research design and measurement share common positivist assumptions and principles. Second, the process of designing, arranging, and planning a research project prior to collecting data extends into the measurement process. Clear thinking about the variables is needed before a researcher can use measures to collect data.

In quantitative research, the process of measurement begins after a researcher has formulated a research question and determined the variables and units of analysis that he or she will use in a research project. When developing measures, the researcher is not primarily concerned with whether a variable is the independent or dependent in a hypothesis; rather, the main concern is to develop clear definitions and to create measures that will yield precise, accurate findings.

Quantitative measurement is a deductive process. It involves taking a concept, *construct*,[1] or idea, then developing a measure (a device, procedure, or instrument) to observe it empirically. The process begins with concepts and ends with specific, concrete indicators. A researcher then uses the measures to produce data in the form of numbers. Actually, the process is interactive, because concepts become clearer and better defined as a researcher develops measures for them.

WHY MEASURE?

We use many measures in our daily lives. For example, this morning I woke up and hopped onto a bathroom scale to see how well my diet is working. I glanced at a thermometer to find out whether or not to wear a coat. Next, I got into my car and checked the gas gauge to be sure I could make it to campus. As I drove, I watched the speedometer so I would not get a speeding ticket. By 8:00 A.M., I had measured weight, temperature, gasoline volume, and speed—all measures about the physical world. Such precise, well-developed measures, which we use in daily life, are fundamental in the natural sciences.

We also measure the nonphysical world in everyday life, but usually in less exact terms. We are measuring when we say that a restaurant is excellent, that Pablo is really smart, that Karen has a negative attitude toward life, that Johnson is really prejudiced, or that the movie last night had a lot of violence in it. However, such everyday judgments as "really prejudiced" or "a lot of violence" are imprecise, vague, or intuitive measures. This does not have to be the case. Social measurement can be systematic and yield precise results, which can be replicated. Precision means expression in fine degrees or exact terms. For example, in measuring height, it is less precise to say, "I am about 6 feet tall" than to say "I am 2 meters, 4 centimeters, and 2 millimeters tall in my bare feet."

Measures Extend Our Senses

Measurement extends our senses. For example, the astronomer or biologist uses the telescope or the microscope to extend natural vision. In contrast to our senses, scientific measurement is more sensitive, varies less with the specific observer, and yields more exact quantitative information. You recognize that a thermometer gives more specific, precise information about temperature than touch can. Likewise, a good bathroom scale gives you more specific, constant, and precise information about the weight of a 5-year-old girl than you get by lifting her and calling her "heavy" or "light." Social measures provide precise information about social reality.

In addition to adding precision and objectivity, scientific measurement helps people observe what is otherwise invisible. Measurement extends human senses. It lets us observe things that were once unseen and unknown but were predicted by theory.

Before you can measure, you need a clear idea about what you are interested in. For example, you cannot see or feel magnetism with your natural senses. Magnetism comes from a theory about the physical world. You observe its effects indirectly; for example, metal flecks move near a magnet. The magnet allows you to "see" or measure the magnetic fields that theory tells you exist. Natural scientists have invented thousands of measures to "see" very tiny things (molecules or insect organs) or very large things (huge geological land masses or planets) that are not observable through ordinary senses. In addition, researchers are constantly creating new measures.[2]

Some of the things a social researcher is interested in measuring are easy to see (e.g., age, sex, skin color), but most cannot be directly observed (e.g., attitudes, ideology, divorce rates, deviance, sex roles). Like the natural scientist who invents indirect measures of the "invisible" objects and forces of the physical world, the social researcher devises measures for difficult-to-observe aspects of the social world. For example, suppose you heard a principal complain about teacher morale in a school. You can create a measure for the morale of teachers. The measure of morale should be systematic and produce precise, quantitative data that others can replicate.

Parts of the Measurement Process

Before you can measure, you need to begin with a concept. You also need to distinguish what you are interested in from other things. The idea that you first need a construct or concept of what is to be measured simply makes sense. How can you observe or measure something unless you know what you are looking for? For example, a biologist cannot observe a cell unless he or she first knows what a cell is, has a microscope, and has learned to distinguish it from noncell "stuff" or "junk" under the microscope. The process of measurement involves more than just having a measurement instrument (e.g., a microscope). In order to mea-

sure, the researcher needs three things: a construct, a measurement instrument, and an ability to recognize what one is looking for.[3]

For example, I want to measure teacher morale. I first define *teacher morale*. What does the construct of *morale* mean? As a variable construct, it takes on different values—high versus low or good versus bad morale. Next, I create a measure of my construct. This could take the form of survey questions, an examination of school records, or observations of teachers. Finally, I distinguish morale from other things in the answers to survey questions, school records, or observations.

A social researcher's job is more difficult than that of the natural scientist because social measurement involves talking with people or observing their behavior. Unlike the planets, cells, or chemicals that the natural scientist measures, the answers people give and their actions can be ambiguous. People can react to the very fact that they are being asked questions or observed. Thus, the social researcher has a double burden. First, he or she must have a clear construct, a good measure, and an ability to recognize what is being looked for. Second, he or she tries to measure aspects of fluid and confusing social life—aspects that may change just because of an awareness that a researcher is trying to measure them.

MEASUREMENT AND RESEARCH DESIGN

Researchers need measures to test hypotheses and gather data. The researcher chooses a general topic and refines it into a focused research problem or question. He or she further refines it into testable hypotheses or statements about causal relationships with at least two variables. After the variables are identified in hypotheses, the researcher is ready to begin the task of measurement, and measurement begins with conceptualization.

Conceptualization

At the beginning of the measurement process, a researcher conceptualizes and operationalizes each variable in a hypothesis. *Conceptualization* is the process of taking a construct or concept and refining it by giving it a conceptual or theoretical definition. A *conceptual definition* is a definition in abstract, theoretical terms. In the example, this step came when I asked, "What does *morale* mean?" It refers to other ideas or constructs. There is no magical way to turn a construct into a precise conceptual definition. It involves thinking carefully, observing directly, consulting with others, reading what others have said, and trying possible definitions.

A good definition has one clear, explicit, and specific meaning. There is no ambiguity or vagueness. Some scholarly articles have been devoted to conceptualizing key concepts. Melbin (1978) conceptualized *night* as a frontier, Jack Gibbs (1989) analyzed the meaning of the concept of *terrorism*, and Ball and Curry (1995) discussed ways to conceptualize what a *street gang* means. In addition to being a precondition for creating high-quality measures, as you read in Chapter 3 on theory, researchers need clear, unambiguous definitions of concepts to develop sound explanations.

A single construct can have several definitions, and people may disagree over definitions. Conceptual definitions are linked to theoretical frameworks and to value positions. For example, a conflict theorist may define *social class* as the power and property a group of people in society has or lacks. A structural functionalist defines it in terms of individuals who share a social status, life-style, or subjective identification. Although people disagree over definitions, it is always important to state explicitly which definition is being used.

Some constructs are more abstract than others. For example, some constructs (e.g., alienation) are highly abstract and complex. They contain lower-level concepts within them (e.g., powerlessness), which can be made even more specific (e.g., a feeling of little power over where one can live). Other constructs are concrete and simple (e.g., age). When developing definitions, you need to be aware of how complex and abstract a construct is. For example, a concrete construct such as *age* is easier to define (e.g., number of years that have passed since birth) than is a complex, abstract concept such as *morale*.

How can I develop a conceptual definition of *teacher morale*, or at least a tentative working definition to get started? I begin with my everyday understanding of the idea of morale—something vague like "how people feel about things." I ask some of my friends how they define it. I also look at an unabridged dictionary and a thesaurus. They give definitions such as "confidence, spirit, zeal, cheerfulness, esprit de corps, mental condition towards something." I go to the library and search the research literature on morale or teacher morale to see how others have defined it. If someone else has already given an excellent definition, I might borrow it (citing the source, of course). If I do not find a definition that fits my purposes, I turn to theories of group behavior, individual mental states, and the like for ideas. As I collect various definitions, parts of definitions, and related ideas, I begin to see the boundaries of the core idea.

By now, I have a lot of definitions and need to sort them out. Most say that morale is a spirit, feeling, or mental condition toward something, or a group feeling. I separate the two extremes of my construct. This helps me turn the concept into a variable. High morale involves confidence, optimism, cheerfulness, feelings of togetherness, and willingness to endure hardship for the common good. Low morale is the opposite; it is a lack of confidence, pessimism, depression, isolation, selfishness, and an unwillingness to put forth effort for others.

I am interested in *teacher* morale, I learn about teachers to specify the construct to them. One strategy is make a list of examples of high or low teacher morale. High teacher morale includes saying positive things about the school, not complaining about extra work, or enjoying being with students. Low morale includes complaining a lot, not attending school events unless required to, or looking for other jobs.

Morale involves a feeling toward something else; a person has morale with regard to something. I list the various "somethings" toward which teachers have feelings (e.g., students, parents, pay, the school administration, other teachers, the profession of teaching). This raises an issue that frequently occurs when developing a definition. Are there several kinds of teacher morale or are all these "somethings" aspects of one construct? There is no perfect answer. I have to decide whether morale means a single, general feeling with different parts or dimensions, or several distinct feelings.

What unit of analysis does my construct apply to: a group or an individual? Is morale a characteristic of an individual, of a group (e.g., a school), or of both? I decide that for my purposes morale applies to groups of people only. This tells me that the unit of analysis in my research project will be a group: all teachers in a school.

A researcher wants to distinguish the construct of interest from related ones. How is my construct of teacher morale similar to or different from related concepts? For example, does *morale* differ from *mood*? I decide that mood is more individual and temporary than morale. Likewise, morale differs from optimism and pessimism, which are outlooks about the future held by individuals. Morale is a group feeling that includes positive or negative feelings about the future as well as other beliefs and feelings.

As you can see, conceptualization is a process of thinking through the meanings of a construct. By now, I know that teacher morale is a mental state or feeling that ranges from high (optimistic, cheerful) to low (pessimistic, depressed); it has several dimensions (morale regarding students, morale regarding other teachers); it is a characteristic of a group; and it persists for a period of months. I have a much more specific mental picture of what I want to measure than when I began. If I had not conceptualized, I would have tried to measure what I started with— "how people feel about things."

Once you develop a definition, test it mentally by thinking of circumstances related to your construct and whether they are included in or excluded from the definition. This requires familiarity with situations in the social world in which the construct exists. It is difficult to develop good definitions for constructs from areas of social life about which the researcher knows nothing.

Because few of you are familiar with the details of teacher morale, let me switch to an example with which you probably have personal experience: family unity. I define *family unity* as the feeling of closeness and sharing many daily living and leisure time activities within a family. It combines three ideas: shared feelings, shared activities, and family. One critical part of my definition is the family. What is a family? A *family* is traditionally defined as two adults who are legally married to each other and who have natural or adopted children. This seems simple, but this definition creates problems. For example, I know two people who are legally married, but who have not lived together for five years and will probably never get a legal divorce. Are they a family? What about the following relationships, none of which fits a standard definition of a family:

- A married couple who are raising children who are not biologically their own and whom they have not legally adopted
- A married couple who do not have any children
- A divorced woman who lives with her two young children
- A couple who have lived together for six years without getting legally married and who have three children
- A stable homosexual couple who have lived together as marital partners for 10 years
- Two elderly neighbors who have moved in together to look after and care for each other, and who share their pension money and all living arrangements

Most official or legal definitions of a family for purposes of insurance, inheritance, and the like define the foregoing relationships as nonfamilies, although some are now being contested. Yet, if you talked to the people in these relationships, saw how they lived, and probed into their feelings about each other, you would find few differences from the social relations in a traditional family.

The point is that conceptual definitions need to be consistent with your meaning of the construct. My construct of *family* includes all the relationships listed here many of which others do not call a family. Thus, my definition includes the relationships from my construct. If it did not, I would not be measuring the construct in which I am really interested.

Operationalization

After you have a working definition ("working" because it can be modified), you are ready for *operationalization*—the process of developing an operational definition for the construct. An *operational definition* is a definition in terms of specific operations, measurement instruments, or procedures. It is sometimes referred to as the *indicator* or measure of a construct.

There are usually multiple ways to measure a construct. Some are better or worse and more or less practical than others. The key is to fit your measure to your specific conceptual definition, to the practical constraints within which you must operate (e.g., time, money, available subjects), and to the research techniques you know or can learn. You can develop a new measure from scratch, or it can be a measure that is already being used by other researchers (see Box 7.1). Operationalization links the language of theory with the language of empirical measures. Theory is full of abstract concepts, assumptions, relationships, definitions, and causality. Empirical measures describe how people concretely measure specific variables. They refer to specific operations or things people use to indicate the presence of a construct that exists in observable reality.

The link between indicators and constructs is a central issue for quantitative measurement. During operationalization, a researcher links the world of ideas to observable reality. Rules of correspondence or auxiliary theory link the conceptual definitions of constructs to concrete measures or operations for measuring constructs.[4] *Rules of correspondence* are logical statements of how an indicator corresponds to an abstract construct. For example, a rule of correspondence states that a person's verbal agreement with a set of 10 specific statements is evidence that the person holds strongly antifeminist beliefs and values. Likewise, an *auxiliary theory* explains how and why

Box 7.1 _____

Five Suggestions for Coming Up with a Measure

1. *Remember the conceptual definition.* The underlying principle for any measure is to match it to the specific conceptual definition of the construct that will be used in the study.
2. *Keep an open mind.* Do not get locked into a single measure or type of measure. Be creative and constantly look for better measures. Avoid what Kaplan (1964:28) called the "law of the instrument," which means being locked into using one measurement instrument for all problems.
3. *Borrow from others.* Do not be afraid to borrow from other researchers, as long as credit is given. Good ideas for measures can be found in other studies or modified from other measures.
4. *Anticipate difficulties.* Logical and practical problems often arise when trying to measure variables of interest. Sometimes a problem can be anticipated and avoided with careful forethought and planning.
5. *Do not forget your units of analysis.* Your measure should fit with the units of analysis of the study and permit you to generalize to the universe of interest.

indicators and constructs connect. Such theories play a crucial role in research. Carmines and Zeller (1979:11) noted, "The auxiliary theory specifying the relationship between concepts and indicators is equally important to social research as the substantive theory linking concepts to one another." For example, a researcher wants to measure alienation. An auxiliary theory suggests that the construct has four parts, each in a different sphere of life: family relations, work relations, relations with community, and relations with friends. The theory further specifies that certain behaviors or feelings in each sphere of life express alienation. For instance, in the sphere of work, an indicator of alienation is that a person feels a total lack of control over when, where, and with whom he or she works, what he or she does when working, or how fast he or she must work.

Figure 7.1 illustrates the measurement process for two variables that are linked together in a theory and a hypothesis. There are three levels to consider: conceptual, operational, and empirical.[5] At the most abstract level, the researcher is interested in the causal relationship between two constructs, or a *conceptual hypothesis*. At the level of operational definitions, the researcher is interested in testing an *empirical hypothesis* to determine the degree of association between indicators. This is the level at which correlations, statistics, questionnaires, and the like are used. The third level is the concrete empirical world. If the operational indicators of variables (e.g., questionnaires) are logically linked to a construct (e.g., racial discrimination), they will capture what actually happens in the empirical social world and relate it to the conceptual level.

The measurement process links together the three levels, moving deductively from the abstract to the concrete. A researcher first conceptualizes a variable, giving it a clear conceptual definition. Next, he or she operationalizes it by developing an operational definition or set of indicators for it. Last, he or she uses the indicators by applying them in the empirical world. The links from abstract constructs to empirical reality allows the researcher to test empirical hypotheses. Those empirical tests are logically linked back to a conceptual hypothesis and causal relations in the world of theory.

How do I give my teacher morale construct an operational definition? First, I read the research reports of others and see whether a good indicator already exists. If there are no existing indicators, I invent one from scratch. Morale is a mental state or feeling, so I measure it indirectly through people's words and actions. I might develop a questionnaire for the teachers and ask them about their feelings toward the dimensions of morale in my definition. I might go to the school and observe the teachers in the teachers' lounge, interacting with students, and at school activities. I might use school personnel records on teacher behaviors for statements that indicate morale (e.g., absences, requests for letters of recommendation for other jobs, performance reports). I might survey students, school administrators, and others to find out what they think about teacher morale. Whichever indicator I choose, I further refine my conceptual definition as I develop it (e.g., write specific questionnaire questions).

A hypothesis has at least two variables, and

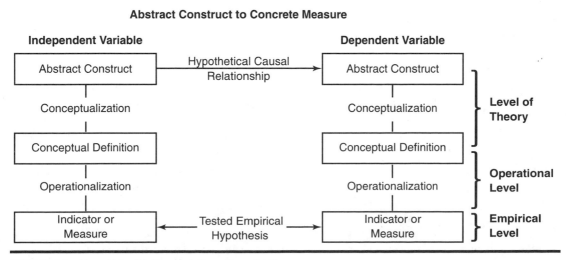

Abstract Construct to Concrete Measure

FIGURE 7.1 Conceptualization and Operationalization

the processes of conceptualization and operationalization are necessary for each variable. In the preceding example, morale is not a hypothesis. It is one variable. It could be a dependent variable caused by something else, or it could be an independent variable causing something else. It depends on my theoretical explanation and hypothesis.

Here is another example of measuring concepts. Seeman and Anderson (1983) tested the hypotheses that alienated people drink more alcohol. They measured alcohol drinking by a series of questions that tapped different aspects of the construct "drinking behavior." They defined the construct as having three subdimensions: frequency of drinking, quantity consumed per drinking occasion, and behavioral impairment due to drinking. They operationalized each dimension as several survey questions and combined the answers to questions to form an overall drinking measure. For example, the researchers measured the behavioral impairment subdimension by asking six questions about how often the respondent missed work because of drinking, was worried about drinking, drank on the job, drank before noon, drank alone, or had family quarrels as a result of drinking. In this way, the authors created a concrete quantitative indicator of drinking behavior.

RELIABILITY AND VALIDITY

Reliability and validity are central issues in all scientific measurement. Both concern how concrete measures, or indicators, are developed for constructs. Reliability and validity are salient in social research because constructs in social theory are often ambiguous, diffuse, and not directly observable. Perfect reliability and validity are virtually impossible to achieve. Rather, they are ideals researchers strive for. Researchers want to maximize the reliability and validity of indicators. *Reliability* tells us about an indicator's dependability and consistency. *Validity* tells us whether an indicator actually captures the meaning of the construct in which we are interested. If indicators

have a low degree of reliability or validity, then the final results will be questionable.

Reliability

Definition. Reliability deals with an indicator's dependability. If you have a reliable indicator or measure, it gives you the same result each time the same thing is measured (as long as what you are measuring is not changing). *Reliability* means that the information provided by indicators (e.g., a questionnaire) does not vary as a result of characteristics of the indicator, instrument, or measurement device itself. For example, I get on my bathroom scale and read my weight. I get off and get on again and again. I have a reliable scale if it gives me the same weight each time—assuming, of course, that I am not eating, drinking, changing clothing, and so forth. An unreliable scale is one that registers different weights each time even though my "true" weight does not change. Another example is my car speedometer. If I am driving at a constant slow speed on a level surface, but the speedometer needle jumps from one end to the other, my speedometer is not a reliable indicator of how fast I am traveling. Actually, there are three types of reliability.[6]

Three Types of Reliability
Stability Reliability. Stability reliability is reliability across time. It addresses the question: Does the measure or indicator deliver the same answer when applied in different time periods? The weight-scale example just given is of this type of reliability. You can examine an indicator's degree of stability reliability by using the *test-retest method,* with which you retest or readminister the indicator to the same group of people. If what you are measuring is stable and the indicator has stability reliability, then you will get the same results each time. A variation of the test-retest method is to give an alternative form of the test, but the alternative form has to be very similar. For example, I have a hypothesis about gender and seating patterns in a college cafeteria. I measure my dependent variable (seating patterns) by observing and recording the number of

male and female students at tables, and noting who sits down first, second, third, and so on for a three-hour period. If, as I am observing, I get tired or distracted, or I forget to record and miss more people toward the end of the three hours, then my indicator does not have a high degree of stability reliability.

Representative Reliability. *Representative reliability* is reliability across subpopulations or groups of people. It addresses the question: Does the indicator deliver the same answer when applied to different groups? An indicator has high representative reliability if it yields the same result for a construct when applied to different subpopulations (e.g., different classes, races, sexes, age groups). For example, I ask a question about a person's age. If people in their twenties answered my question by overstating their true age, whereas people in their fifties understated their true age, then the indicator has a low degree of representative reliability. To have representative reliability, the measure needs to give accurate information for every age group.

A *subpopulation analysis* determines whether an indicator has this type of reliability. The analysis involves comparing the indicator across different subpopulations or subgroups and uses independent knowledge about subpopulations. For example, I want to test the representative reliability of a questionnaire item that asks about a person's education. I conduct a subpopulation analysis to see whether the question works equally well for men and women. I ask both men and women the question. I then obtain independent information (e.g., check school records) and check to see whether the errors in answering the question are equal for men and women. The item has representative reliability if there are no differences in the error rate for men and women.

Equivalence Reliability. *Equivalence reliability* applies when researchers use *multiple indicators*—that is, when multiple specific measures are used in the operationalization of a construct (e.g., several items in a questionnaire all measure the same construct). It addresses the question: Does the measure yield consistent results across different indicators? If several different indicators measure the same construct, then a reliable measure gives the same result with all indicators.

Researchers examine equivalence reliability on examinations and long questionnaires with the *split-half method*. This involves dividing the indicators of the same construct into two groups, usually by a random process, and determining whether both halves give the same results. For example, I have 14 items on a questionnaire. All measure political conservatism among college students. If my indicators (i.e., questionnaire items) have equivalence reliability, then I can randomly divide them into two groups of 7 and get the same results. For example, I use the first 7 questions and find that a class of 50 business majors is twice as conservative as a class of 50 education majors. I get the same results using the second 7 questions. There are also special statistical measures (e.g., Cronbach's alpha) to determine this type of reliability.

A special type of equivalence reliability is interrater or *intercoder reliability*. It arises when there are several observers, raters, or coders of information. In a sense, each person who is observing is an indicator. A measure is reliable if the observers, raters, or coders agree with each other. It is a common type of reliability reported in content analysis studies, but it can be used whenever multiple raters or coders are involved. For example, I hire six students to observe student seating patterns in a cafeteria. If all six are equally skilled at observing and recording, I can combine the information from all six into a single reliable measure. But if one or two students are lazy, inattentive, or sloppy, then my measure will have lower reliability. Intercoder reliability can be tested by having several coders measure the exact same thing, then comparing the measures. For instance, I have three coders independently code the seating patterns during the same hour on three different days. I compare the recorded observations. If they agree, I can be confident of my measure's intercoder reliability. Special statistical techniques measure the degree of intercoder reliability.

How to Improve Reliability. It is rare to have perfect reliability. There are four principles to follow to increase the reliability of measures: (1) clearly conceptualize constructs, (2) use a precise level of measurement, (3) use multiple indicators, and (4) use pilot tests.

Clearly Conceptualize All Constructs. Reliability increases when a single construct or subdimension of a construct is measured. This means developing unambiguous, clear theoretical definitions. Constructs should be specified to eliminate "noise" (i.e., distracting or interfering information) from other constructs. Each measure should indicate one and only one concept. Otherwise, it is impossible to determine which concept is being "indicated." For example, the indicator of a pure chemical compound is more reliable than one in which the chemical is mixed with other material or dirt. In the latter case, it is difficult to separate the "noise" of other material from the pure chemical.

Let us return to teacher morale. I should be sure to separate morale from related concepts (e.g., mood, personality, spirit, job attitude). If I did not do this, I could not be sure what I was really measuring. I might develop an indicator for morale that also indicates personality; that is, the construct of personality contaminates that of morale and produces a less reliable indicator. Bad measurement occurs when one indicator is used to operationalize different constructs (e.g., using the same questionnaire item to indicate morale and personality).

Increase the Level of Measurement. Levels of measurement are discussed in greater detail later. Indicators at higher or more precise levels of measurement are more likely to be reliable than less precise measures because the latter pick up less detailed information. If more specific information is measured, then it is less likely that anything other than the construct will be captured. The general principle is: Try to measure constructs at the most precise level possible. However, it is more difficult to measure at higher levels of measurement. For example, if I have a choice of measuring morale as either high or low, or in 10 categories from extremely low to extremely high, it would be better to measure it in 10 refined categories.

Use Multiple Indicators of a Variable. A third way to increase reliability is to use *multiple indicators*, because two (or more) indicators of the same construct are better than one.[7] Figure 7.2 illustrates the use of multiple indicators in hypothesis testing. Three indicators of the one independent variable construct are combined into an overall measure, *A*, and two indicators of a dependent variable are combined into a single measure, *B*. For example, I have three specific measures of

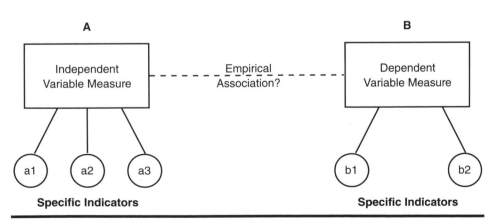

FIGURE 7.2 Measurement Using Multiple Indicators

A, which is teacher morale: answers to a survey question on attitudes about school, number of absences for reasons other than illness and requests for transfers, and number of complaints others heard a teacher voice. I also have two measures of my dependent variable *B*, giving students extra attention: number of hours teacher spent staying after school hours to meet individually with students and whether the teacher inquires frequently about a student's progress in other classes.

Multiple indicators do two things. First, they let a researcher take measurements from a wider range of the content of a conceptual definition. Some writers call this *sampling from the conceptual domain*. Different aspects of the construct can be measured, each with its own indicator. Second, one indicator (e.g., one question on a questionnaire) may be imperfect, but several measures are less likely to have the same (systematic) error. Multiple indicator measures tend to be more stable than measures with one item.

Use Pretests, Pilot Studies, and Replication. A fourth principle for improving reliability is to use a pretest or pilot version of a measure first. Develop one or more draft or preliminary versions of a measure and try them before applying the final version in a hypothesis-testing situation. This takes more time and effort, but it is likely to produce reliable measures. For example, in my survey of teacher morale, I go through many drafts of a question before the final version. I test early versions by asking people the question and checking to see whether it is clear.

The principle of using pilot tests extends to replicating the measures other researchers have used. For example, I search the literature and find measures of morale that have been used in past research. I may want to build on and use a previous measure if it is a good one, citing the source, of course, and giving proper credit. In addition, I may want to add new indicators and compare them to the previous measure. In this way, the quality of the measure can improve over time, as long as the same definition is used. See Table 7.1 for a summary of reliability types.

Validity

Definition. *Validity* is an overused term and is often confused with related ideas. Sometimes, it is used to mean "true" or "correct." There are several general types of validity. Here, we are concerned with *measurement validity*. There are also several types of measurement validity. Nonmeasurement types of validity are briefly mentioned in the section on other uses of the terms *reliability* and *validity*.

When a researcher says that an indicator is valid, it is valid for a particular purpose and definition. The same indicator can be valid for one purpose (i.e., a research question with units of analysis and universe) but less valid or invalid for others. For example, the measure of morale discussed here (e.g., questions about feelings toward school) might be valid for measuring morale among teachers but invalid for measuring the morale of police officers.[8]

At its core, measurement validity is the degree of fit between a construct and indicators of it. It refers to how well the conceptual and operational definitions mesh with each other. The better the fit, the greater the measurement validity. Validity is more difficult to achieve than reliability. We cannot have absolute confidence about validity, but some measures are *more valid* than others. The reason we can never achieve absolute validity is that constructs are abstract ideas, whereas indicators refer to concrete observation. This is the gap between our mental pictures about the world and the specific things we do at particular times and places. Bohrnstedt (1992b:2217) has argued that validity is a matter of degree; it cannot be determined directly. Validity is part of a dynamic process that grows by accumulating evidence over time, and without it, all measurement becomes meaningless.

Some researchers use rules of correspondence to reduce the gap between abstract ideas and specific indicators. (Rules of correspondence were discussed earlier.) They are logical statements about the fit between indicators and definitions. For example, a rule of correspondence is: If a teacher agrees with statements that "things have

TABLE 7.1   Summary of Measurement Reliability and Validity Types

RELIABILITY	VALIDITY
It is a dependable measure	*It is a true measure*
Stability—over time	Face—in the judgment of others
Representative—across subgroups	Content—captures the entire meaning
Equivalence—across indicators	Criterion—agrees with an external source
	■ Concurrent—agrees with a preexisting measure
	■ Predictive—agrees with future behavior
	Construct—multiple indicators are consistent
	■ Convergent—alike ones are similar
	■ Discriminant—different ones differ

gotten worse at this school in the past five years" and that "there is little hope for improvement," this indicates low morale on the part of the teacher. Another way of talking about measurement validity is the *epistemic correlation*. This refers to a make-believe or hypothetical correlation between a specific indicator and the essence of the construct that the indicator measures. We cannot measure such correlations directly because correlations between a measure and an abstraction are impossible, but they can be estimated with advanced statistical techniques.[9]

Four Types of Measurement Validity

Face Validity.   The easiest type of validity to achieve and the most basic kind of validity is *face validity*. It is a judgment by the scientific community that the indicator really measures the construct. In other words, it addresses the question: On the face of it, do people believe that the definition and method of measurement fit? It is a consensus method of measurement validity. For example, few people would accept a measure of college student math ability using a question that asked students: $2 + 2 = ?$ This is not a valid measure of college-level math ability on the face of it. Recall that the principle of organized skepticism in the scientific community means that aspects of research are scrutinized by others.[10] See Table 7.1

for a summary of types of measurement validity. Figure 7.3 presents the types in pictoral form.

Content Validity.   Content validity is actually a special type of face validity. *Content validity* addresses the question: Is the full content of a definition represented in a measure? A conceptual definition holds ideas; it is a "space" containing ideas and concepts. Measures should sample or represent all ideas or areas in the conceptual space. Content validity involves three steps. First, specify the content in a construct's definition. Next, sample from all areas of the definition. Finally, develop an indicator that taps all of the various parts of the definition.

An example of content validity is my definition of *feminism* as a person's commitment to a set of beliefs creating full equality between men and women in areas of the arts, intellectual pursuits, family, work, politics, and authority relations. I create a measure of feminism in which I ask two survey questions: (1) Should men and women get equal pay for equal work and (2) should men and women share household tasks? My measure has low content validity because the two questions ask only about pay and household tasks. They ignore the other areas (intellectual pursuits, politics, authority relations, and other aspects of work and family). For a content-valid measure, I must either expand the measure or narrow the definition.[11]

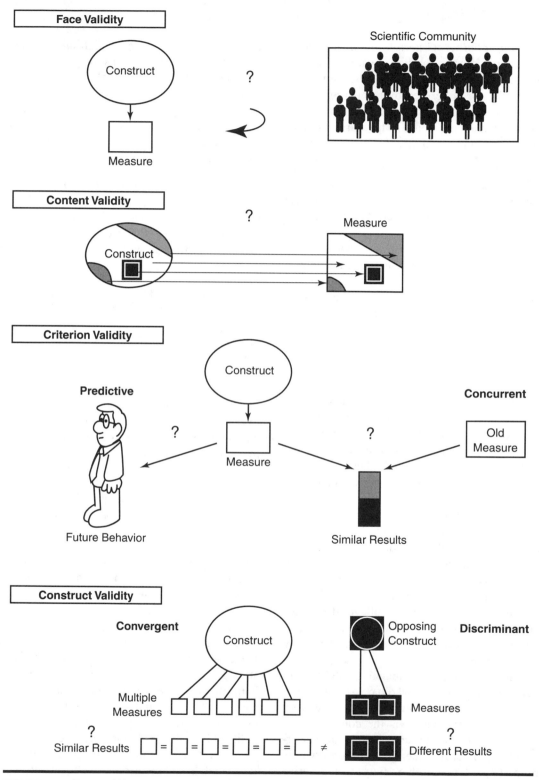

FIGURE 7.3 Types of Validity

Criterion Validity.   *Criterion validity* uses some standard or criterion that is known to indicate a construct accurately. In other words, the validity of an indicator is verified by comparing it with another measure of the same construct in which a researcher has confidence. There are two subtypes of this kind of validity.[12]

Concurrent.   To have *concurrent validity*, an indicator must be associated with a preexisting indicator that is judged to be valid (i.e., it has face validity). For example, you create a new test to measure intelligence. For it to be concurrently valid, it should be highly associated with existing IQ tests (assuming the same definition of intelligence is used). This means that most people who score high on the old measure should also score high on the new one, and vice versa. The two measures may not be perfectly associated, but if they measure the same or a similar construct, it is logical for them to yield similar results.

Predictive.   Criterion validity whereby an indicator predicts future events that are logically related to a construct is called *predictive validity*. It cannot be used for all measures. The measure and the action predicted must be distinct from but indicate the same construct. Predictive measurement validity should not be confused with prediction in hypothesis testing, where one variable predicts a different variable in the future. For example, the Scholastic Aptitude Test (SAT) that many U.S. high school students take measures scholastic aptitude—the ability of a student to perform in college. If the SAT has high predictive validity, then students who get high SAT scores will subsequently do well in college. If students with high scores perform the same as students with average or low scores, then the SAT has low predictive validity.

Another way to test predictive validity is to select a group of people who have specific characteristics and predict how they will score (very high or very low) vis-à-vis the construct. For example, I have a measure of political conservatism. I predict that members of conservative groups (e.g., John Birch Society, Conservative Caucus, Daughters of the American Revolution, Moral Majority) will score high on it, whereas members of liberal groups (e.g., Democratic Socialists, People for the American Way, Americans for Democratic Action) will score low. I "validate" the measure with the groups—that is, I pilot test it by using it on members of the groups. It can then be used as a measure of political conservatism for the general public.

Construct Validity.   *Construct validity* is for measures with multiple indicators. It addresses the question: If the measure is valid, do the various indicators operate in a consistent manner? It requires a definition with clearly specified conceptual boundaries.

Convergent.   This kind of validity applies when multiple indicators converge or are associated with one another. *Convergent validity* means that multiple measures of the same construct hang together or operate in similar ways. For example, I measure the construct "education" by asking people how much education they have completed, looking up school records, and asking the people to complete a test of school knowledge. If the measures do not converge (i.e., people who claim to have a college degree have no records of attending college, or those with college degrees perform no better than high school dropouts on my tests), then my measure has weak convergent validity and I should not combine all three indicators into one measure.

Discriminant.   Also called divergent validity, *discriminant validity* is the opposite of convergent validity. It means that the indicators of one construct hang together or converge, but also diverge or are negatively associated with opposing constructs. It says that if two constructs A and B are very different, then measures of A and B should not be associated. For example, I have 10 items that measure political conservatism. People answer all 10 in similar ways. But I also put 5 questions on the same questionnaire that measure political liberalism. My measure of conservatism has discriminant validity if the 10 conservatism items both hang together and are negatively associated with the 5 liberalism ones.

Other Uses of the Terms *Reliable* and *Valid*

Many words have multiple definitions, including *reliability* and *validity*. This creates confusion unless we distinguish among alternative uses of the same word.

Reliability. We use *reliability* in everyday language. A reliable person is one who is dependable, stable, and responsible; a reliable car is dependable and trustworthy. This means the person responds in similar, predictable ways in different times and conditions; the same can be said for the car. In addition to measurement reliability, researchers sometimes say a study or its results are reliable (e.g., Yin, 1988). By this, they mean that the method of conducting a study or the results from it can be reproduced or replicated by other researchers.

Internal Validity. *Internal validity* means there are no errors internal to the design of the research project.[13] It is used primarily in experimental research to talk about possible errors or alternative explanations of results that arise despite attempts to institute controls. High *internal validity* means there are few such errors. Low internal validity means that such errors are likely.

External Validity. *External validity* is used primarily in experimental research. It is the ability to generalize findings from a specific setting and small group to a broad range of settings and people. It addresses the question: If something happens in a laboratory or among a particular group of subjects (e.g., college students), can the findings be generalized to the "real" (nonlaboratory) world or to the general public (nonstudents)? High external validity means that the results can be generalized to many situations and many groups of people. Low external validity means that the results apply only to a very specific setting.

Statistical Validity. *Statistical validity* means that the correct statistical procedure is chosen and its assumptions are fully met. Different statistical tests or procedures are appropriate for different conditions, which are discussed in textbooks that describe the statistical procedures.

All statistics are based on assumptions about the mathematical properties of the numbers being used. A statistic will be invalid and its results nonsense if the major assumptions are violated. For example, to compute an average (actually the mean, which is discussed in a later chapter), one cannot use information at the nominal level of measurement (to be discussed). For example, suppose I measure the race of a class of students. I give each race a number: whites = 1, blacks = 2, Asian = 3, others = 4. It makes no sense to say that the "mean" race of a class of students is 1.9 (almost black?). This is a misuse of the statistical procedure, and the results are invalid even if the computation is correct. The degree to which statistical assumptions can be violated or bent (the technical term is *robustness*) is a topic in which professional statisticians take great interest.

RELATIONSHIP BETWEEN RELIABILITY AND VALIDITY

Reliability is necessary for validity and is easier to achieve than validity. Although reliability is necessary in order to have a valid measure of a concept, it does not guarantee that a measure will be valid. It is not a sufficient condition for validity. A measure can produce the same result over and over (i.e., it has reliability), but what it measures may not match the definition of the construct (i.e., validity).

A measure can be reliable but invalid. For example, I get on a scale and get weighed. The weight registered by the scale is the same each time I get on and off. But then I go to another scale—an "official" one that measures true weight—and it says that my weight is twice as great. The first scale yielded reliable (i.e., dependable and consistent) results, but it did not give a valid measure of my weight.

A diagram might help you see the relationship between reliability and validity. Figure 7.4 illustrates the relationship between the concepts by using the analogy of a target. The bull's-eye represents a fit between a measure and the definition of the construct.

A Bull's Eye = A Perfect Measure

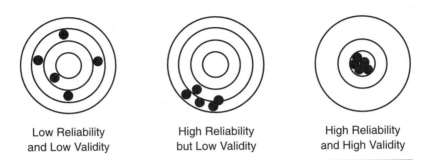

| Low Reliability and Low Validity | High Reliability but Low Validity | High Reliability and High Validity |

FIGURE 7.4   Illustration of Relationship between Reliability and Validity
Source: Adapted from Babbie (1995:128).

Validity and *reliability* are usually complementary concepts, but in some special situations they conflict with each other. Sometimes, as validity increases, reliability is more difficult to attain, and vice versa. This occurs when the construct has a highly abstract and not easily observable definition. Reliability is easiest to achieve when the measure is precise and observable. Thus, there is a strain between the true essence of the highly abstract construct and measuring it in a concrete manner. For example, "alienation" is a very abstract, highly subjective construct, often defined as a deep inner sense of loss of one's humanity that diffuses across many aspects of one's life (e.g., social relations, sense of self, orientation toward nature). Highly precise questions in a questionnaire give reliable measures, but there is a danger of losing the subjective essence of the concept.

Some strongly positivist researchers argue that this means that alienation and constructs based on personal feelings and experiences are bad concepts and should be avoided. Others, who accept a more interpretive or critical approach to science, argue that these concepts should be retained. They say that measurement must be more flexible and less precise, using qualitative methods. Measurement issues ultimately return to assumptions about how to conduct research and how the concepts are defined.

LEVELS OF MEASUREMENT

Levels of measurement is an abstract but important and widely used idea. Basically, it says that some ways a researcher measures a construct are at a higher or more refined level, and others are crude or less precisely specified. The level of measurement depends on the way in which a construct is conceptualized—that is, assumptions about whether it has particular characteristics. The level of measurement affects the kinds of indicators chosen and is tied to basic assumptions in a construct's definition. The way in which a researcher conceptualizes a variable limits the levels of measurement that he or she can use and has implications for how measurement and statistical analysis can proceed.

Continuous and Discrete Variables

Variables can be thought of as being either continuous or discrete. *Continuous variables* have an infinite number of values or attributes that flow along a continuum. The values can be divided into many smaller increments; in mathematical theory, there is an infinite number of increments. Examples of continuous variables include temperature, age, income, crime rate, and amount of schooling. *Discrete variables* have a relatively fixed set of separate values or variable attributes.

Instead of a smooth continuum of values, discrete variables contain distinct categories. Examples of discrete variables include gender (male or female), religion (Protestant, Catholic, Jew, Muslim, atheist), and marital status (never married single, married, divorced or separated, widowed). Whether a variable is continuous or discrete affects its level of measurement.

Four Levels

Precision and Levels. The idea of levels of measurement expands on the difference between continuous and discrete variables and organizes types of variables for their use in statistics. The four *levels of measurement* categorize the degree of precision of measurement.[14]

Deciding on the appropriate level of measurement for a construct often creates confusion. The appropriate level of measurement for a variable depends on two things: (1) how a construct is conceptualized and (2) the type of indicator or measurement that a researcher uses.

The construct itself limits the level of precision. The way a researcher conceptualizes a construct can limit how precisely it can be measured. For example, some of the variables listed earlier as continuous can be reconceptualized as discrete. Temperature can be a continuous variable (e.g., degrees, fractions of degrees) or it can be crudely measured with discrete categories (e.g., hot or cold). Likewise, age can be continuous (how old a person is in years, months, days, hours, and minutes) or treated as discrete categories (infancy, childhood, adolescence, young adulthood, middle age, old age). Yet, most discrete variables cannot

be conceptualized as continuous variables. For example, sex, religion, and marital status cannot be conceptualized as continuous; however, related constructs *can* be conceptualized as continuous (e.g., femininity, degree of religiousness, commitment to a marital relationship).

The level of measurement limits the statistical measures that can be used. A wide range of powerful statistical procedures are available for the higher levels of measurement, but the types of statistics that can be used with the lowest levels are very limited.

There is a practical reason to conceptualize and measure variables at higher levels of measurement. You can collapse higher levels of measurement to lower levels, but the reverse is not true. In other words, it is possible to measure a construct very precisely, gather very specific information, and then ignore some of the precision. But it is not possible to measure a construct with less precision or with less specific information and then make it more precise later.

Distinguishing among the Four Levels. The four levels from lowest to greatest or highest precision are nominal, ordinal, interval, and ratio. Each level gives a different type of information (see Table 7.2). *Nominal* measures indicate only that there is a difference among categories (e.g., religion: Protestant, Catholic, Jew, Muslim: racial heritage: African, Asian, Caucasian, Hispanic, other). *Ordinal* measures indicate a difference, *plus* the categories can be ordered or ranked (e.g., letter grades: A, B, C, D, F; opinion measures: Strongly Agree, Agree, Disagree, Strongly Disagree). *Interval* measures everything the first

TABLE 7.2 Characteristics of the Four Levels of Measurement

LEVEL	DIFFERENT CATEGORIES	RANKED	DISTANCE BETWEEN CATEGORIES MEASURED	TRUE ZERO
Nominal	Yes			
Ordinal	Yes	Yes		
Interval	Yes	Yes	Yes	
Ratio	Yes	Yes	Yes	Yes

two do, *plus* it can specify the amount of distance between categories (e.g., Fahrenheit or Celsius temperature: 5°, 45°, 90°; IQ scores: 95, 110, 125). Arbitrary zeros may be used in interval measures; they are just there to help keep score. *Ratio* measures do everything all the other levels do, *plus* there is a true zero, which makes it possible to state relations in terms of proportion or ratios (e.g., money income: $10, $100, $500; years of formal schooling: 1 year, 10 years, 13 years). In most practical situations, the distinction between interval and ratio levels makes little difference. The arbitrary zeros of some interval measures can be confusing. For example, a rise in temperature from 30 to 60 degrees is not really a doubling of the temperature, although the numbers double, because zero degrees is not the absence of all heat.

Discrete variables are nominal and ordinal, whereas continuous variables can be measured at the interval or ratio level. A ratio-level measure can be turned into an interval, ordinal, or nominal level. The interval level can always be turned into an ordinal or nominal level. But the process does not work the other way!

In general, if it is necessary to use ordinal measurement, use at least five ordinal categories and obtain many observations, because the distortion created by collapsing a continuous construct into a smaller number of ordered categories is minimized as the number of categories and the number of observations increase.[15]

The ratio level of measurement is rarely used in the social sciences. For most purposes, it is indistinguishable from interval measurement. The only difference is that ratio measurement has a "true zero." This can be confusing because some measures, like temperature, have zeros that are not true zeros. The temperature can be zero, or below zero, but zero is an arbitrary number when it is assigned to temperature. This can be illustrated by comparing zero degrees Celsius with zero degrees Fahrenheit—they are different temperatures. In addition, doubling the degrees in one system does not double the degrees in the other. Likewise, it does not make sense to say that it is "twice as warm," as is possible with ratio mea-

surement, if the temperature rises from 2 to 4 degrees, from 15 to 30 degrees, or from 40 to 80 degrees. Another common example of arbitrary—not true—zeros occurs when measuring attitudes where numbers are assigned to statements (-1 = disagree, 0 = no opinion, $+1$ = agree). True zeros exist for variables such as income, age, or years of education. Examples of the four levels of measurement are shown in Table 7.3.

INTRODUCTION TO MEASUREMENT THEORY

Measurement theory is the name for a body of mathematical and methodological theory on reliability, validity, and related topics.[16] Measurement theory gets quite technical, but a general introductory summary of its core assumption can help you understand the principles of good measurement. Measurement theory is based on the idea that an empirical measure of a concept reflects three components: (1) the true construct or an absolutely perfect measure of it, (2) systematic error, and (3) random error. People can see only the empirical measure; the three components are unobserved, hypothetical ideas about what measurement involves. The parts of measurement can be symbolically expressed as follows:

X *Observation:* The empirical indicator or observation
T *True measure:* Ideal, pure construct
S *Systematic error:* Bias; any error that is not random
R *Random error:* Nonsystematic, unavoidable, chance errors

Thus, measurement theory assumes that a specific observation is made up of the construct and of two components that are called errors because they represent deviations from the true construct. If this is put in the form of an equation, it becomes:

$$X = T + S + R$$

This equation is the core of measurement theory. In plain English, it says that an empirical observation by a researcher actually comprises three unseen sources: the construct plus two kinds

TABLE 7.3 Example of Levels of Measurement

VARIABLE (Level of Measurement)	HOW VARIABLE MEASURED
Religion (nominal)	Different religious denominations (Jewish, Catholic, Lutheran, Baptist) are not ranked, just different (unless one belief is conceptualized as closer to heaven).
Attendance (ordinal)	"How often do you attend religious services? (O) Never, (1) less than once a year, (3) several times a year, (4) about once a month, (5) two or three times a week, or (8) several times a week?" This might have been measured at a ratio level if the exact number of times a person attended was asked instead.
IQ Score (interval)	Most intelligence tests are organized with 100 as average, middle, or normal. Scores higher or lower indicate distance from the average. Someone with a score of 115 has somewhat above average measured intelligence for people who took the test, while 90 is slightly below. Scores of below 65 or above 140 are rare.
Age (ratio)	Age is measured by years of age. There is a true zero (birth). Note that a 40-year-old has lived twice as long as a 20-year-old.

of potential errors or possible sources of deviation from the true construct.

In the preceding section, you saw that perfect measurement validity is a perfect match between an empirical indicator and the construct it indicates (or its theoretical definition). The measurement theory equation says that an empirical observation and the construct are equal when there are no measurement errors—that is, when the two components that represent potential errors equal zero. Thus, using the equation and measurement theory, we can restate the definition of perfect measurement validity as $X = T$. Researchers use the equation to think about and improve validity by focusing their attention on the two possible types of errors, S and R, and how to get them to equal zero.

Let us focus on the R, or random error, part of the equation first. Probability theory from mathe-matics says that in the long run, over enough cases, the R becomes zero and drops out of the equation. In the language of statistical theory, the random error has an *expected value* of zero. Without getting into complex probability theory, this happens because errors that are truly random cancel each other out in the long run. Various mathematical proofs and empirical tests show that over a very large number of separate events (e.g., several million), truly random processes stabilize around a true value and errors become zero. For example, I flip a perfectly balanced coin in a truly random way for 10 million times. The "errors"—or in this situation, getting more heads than tails or vice versa—will disappear. I can be extremely certain that my flipping will result in 50 percent heads and 50 percent tails. Another example is that of driving a car at a constant speed. Assume that I have a valid and reliable speedometer and I try to drive exactly 50 kilometers per hour, no more and no less. I will be slightly above this speed at some times and slightly below it at other times. If my errors are truly random, the speeds over and under 50 kilometers per hour will cancel each other, or the expected value of the deviations above and below the speed will be zero and my speed will be 50 kilometers per hour. Researchers do not worry a lot about random error. They assume that there is always some random error, but that, over enough replications or cases, it can be safely ignored.

Once we ignore random error, an observation (X) equals the true construct (T) and systematic or nonrandom error (S). Systematic error is a potentially avoidable error that distorts results in a systematic manner. An example of a systematic error can be a poorly worded question that causes most respondents to answer in a particular way, or an interviewer's attempts to get respondents to answer in a particular way. Systematic error is at the heart of validity and reliability. It prevents indicators from measuring what they claim to measure (i.e., the true construct). Thus, another way to think about improving measurement is to eliminate systematic error or *bias*.[17]

Systematic error shows how causal inferences from empirical data can be in error. What was said earlier about measurement validity can be restated as validity when the observed measure (X) equals the true measure (T). $X = T$ when the systematic error (S) is zero.

There are many possible sources of systematic errors. For example, a lack of stability reliability is a type of systematic error. My bathroom scale lacks stability reliability because the spring in it is getting weaker, so I appear to be getting lighter with each successive measurement of my weight. This error in measuring my weight is a type of systematic error that undermines validity. In the example of driving 50 kilometers per hour, my random errors may cancel each other out, but if my speedometer was systematically showing a lower speed, my observation would not be a valid measure. The measurement theory equation is a way to show that any measurement bias or deviation (i.e., nonzero value for systematic error) reduces measurement validity.

THE PRINCIPLE OF HETEROGENEOUS OBSERVATION

Another principle of good quantitative measurement is that of *heterogeneous observation*. This principle simply says that, all things being equal, many diverse or heterogeneous observations provide stronger evidence than one or very similar observations. Two applications illustrate the principle: replication and triangulation.

Replication

You are familiar with the principle of *replication*. It simply means redoing the same thing with an expectation of the same result. Ideally, the replication is conducted independently by a different researcher. The way a construct is measured, a specific finding or an entire study can be replicated. Replicating the measurement of a construct reinforces its validity, and replicating a finding increases confidence in the initial findings.

The logic of replication implies that different researchers are unlikely to make the same errors. If the same findings are reproduced, then systematic error is less likely. If the same findings cannot be reproduced, then questions are raised about the initial findings.

Although replication is a basic principle of positivist science, it is infrequent in practice. Many studies are not replicated, or the replications are not published.

The reason for replication can be illustrated with an example from daily life. I want to keep rabbits out of my vegetable garden. I ask my neighbor for advice, and he says that he kept rabbits out of his garden by planting marigolds along the border. I try the same thing. I replicate what he did by planting marigolds around the border of my garden. If it works, I have confidence in his advice or in the causal relationship between marigolds and rabbits. If it does not work, I question whether it is really an effective method of rabbit control. I wonder why I could not replicate it; this becomes the basis for further research.

Whether you are dealing with rabbits in a garden or with a social research question, the fail-

ure to replicate is usually due to one of four reasons or some combination of them (see Box 7.2).

Triangulation

Surveyors measure the distances between objects
and survey the landscape by viewing points from
different angles—a process called triangulation.
They look at something from different angles or
viewpoints to get a fix on its true position (see
Figure 7.5). In social research, *triangulation*

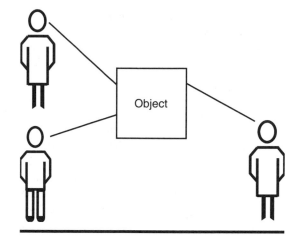

FIGURE 7.5 Triangulation: Observing from
Different Viewpoints

Box 7.2 _____

Reasons That Replication Fails

1. The original causal relationship is true, but the
   conditions of the replication differ. The original
   relation holds only under specific, but unstated,
   conditions. It is then necessary to find the
   conditions under which the original relationship
   holds. For example, a different type of rabbit is
   interested in my garden, or I plant vegetables that
   rabbits like to eat but my neighbor does not.
2. The original causal relationship is true, but it was
   not a true replication because the second test
   was conducted differently. This occurs when the
   description of the original research procedure is
   not specific enough or the researcher doing the
   replication was not careful enough. For example,
   I was cheap and did not plant enough marigolds,
   or my neighbor forgot to tell me when to plant the
   marigolds, or I planted the marigolds late, after
   the rabbits had discovered the delights of my
   garden.
3. The original causal relationship is spurious. It was
   actually due to a different independent variable in
   the original situation—one that was not apparent
   at first. For example, my neighbor has a dog and
   I do not, and it was his dog's barking and not the
   marigolds that kept the rabbits away.
4. The original causal relationship is false. It was not
   reported correctly or is due to random chance.
   For example, my neighbor lied. He has rabbits in
   his garden too, or the rabbits just accidentally
   missed my neighbor's garden the year he planted
   marigolds.

means using different types of measures, or data
collection techniques, in order to examine the
same variable. It is a special use of multiple indicators.[18] An example of triangulation in measuring someone's mental health is to have an expert
interview the person, interview friends and family
members about the person's behavior, have the
person complete a personality multiple-choice
test, and have five observers watch the person's
behavior for many hours.

The basic idea is that measurement improves
when diverse indicators are used. As the diversity
of indicators gets greater, our confidence in measurement grows, because getting identical measurements from highly diverse methods implies
greater validity than if a single or similar methods
had been used.

Think of the mental health example just discussed. You take a 10-question multiple-choice
test on your mental health and are told that you
are "mentally ill." Would you not prefer to have
your behavior observed by two trained independent observers for a week and have a four-hour
interview with a psychiatrist before you are sent
to a mental hospital? If the test results, independent observers, and psychiatrists all agreed,
would you be more likely to accept their assessment? Would the three different types of assess-

ment give you greater confidence in the diagnosis than taking two more multiple-choice tests?

SPECIALIZED MEASURES: SCALES AND INDEXES

In this last section of this chapter, we will look at a number of specialized measures, including scales and indexes. Researchers have created thousands of different scales and indexes to measure social variables.[19] For example, scales and indexes have been developed to measure the degree of formalization in bureaucratic organizations, the prestige of occupations, the adjustment of people to a marriage, the intensity of group interaction, the level of social activity in a community, the degree to which a state's sexual assault laws reflect feminist values, and the level of socioeconomic development of a nation. I cannot discuss the thousands of scales and indexes. Instead, I will focus on principles of scale and index construction and explore some major types.

Keep two things in mind. First, virtually every social phenomenon can be measured. Some constructs can be measured directly and produce precise numerical values (e.g., family income). Other constructs require the use of surrogates or proxies that indirectly measure a variable and may not be as precise (e.g., predisposition to commit a crime). Second, a lot can be learned from measures used by other researchers. You are fortunate to have the work of thousands of researchers to draw on. It is not always necessary to start from scratch. You can use a past scale or index, or you can modify it for your own purposes. Grosof and Sardy (1985:163) have warned that creating rating scales and attitude measures "is a particularly difficult and delicate enterprise and requires a great deal of careful thought." Like the general process of knowledge creation, the process of creating measures for a construct evolves over time. Measurement is an ongoing process with constant change; new concepts are developed, theoretical definitions are refined, and scales or indexes that measure old or new constructs are improved.

Indexes and Scales

You may find the terms *index* and *scale* confusing because they are often used interchangeably. One researcher's scale is another's index. Both produce ordinal- or interval-level measures of a variable. To add to the confusion, scale and index techniques can be combined in one measure. Scales and indexes give a researcher more information about variables and make it possible to assess the quality of measurement. Scales and indexes increase reliability and validity, and they aid in data reduction; that is, they condense and simplify the information that is collected (see Box 7.3).

Mutually Exclusive and Exhaustive Attributes

Before discussing scales and indexes, it is important to review features of good measurement. The

---

Box 7.3 _____

Scales and Indexes: Are They Different?

For most purposes, you can treat scales and indexes as interchangeable. Social researchers do not use a consistent nomenclature to distinguish between them.

A *scale* is a measure in which a researcher captures the intensity, direction, level, or potency of a variable construct. It arranges responses or observations on a continuum. A scale can use a single indicator or multiple indicators. Most are at the ordinal level of measurement.

An *index* is a measure in which a researcher adds or combines several distinct indicators of a construct into a single score. This composite score is often a simple sum of the multiple indicators. It is used for content and convergent validity. Indexes are often measured at the interval or ratio level.

Researchers sometimes combine the features of scales and indexes in a single measure. This is common when a researcher has several indicators that are scales (i.e., that measure intensity or direction). He or she then adds these indicators together to yield a single score, thereby creating an index.

_____

attributes of all measures, including nominal-level measures, should be mutually exclusive and exhaustive.

Mutually exclusive attributes means that an individual or unit of analysis needs to fit into one and only one attribute of a variable. For example, a variable measuring type of religion, with the attributes Christian, non-Christian, and Jewish, is not mutually exclusive. Judaism is both a non-Christian religion and Jewish, so a Jewish person fits into both the non-Christian and the Jewish category. Likewise, a variable measuring type of city, with the attributes river port city, state capital, and interstate exit, lacks mutually exclusive attributes. One city could be all three (a river port state capital with an interstate exit), any one of the three, or none of the three.

Exhaustive attributes means that all cases fit into one of the attributes of a variable. When measuring religion, a measure with the attributes Catholic, Protestant, and Jewish is not exclusive. The individual who is a Buddhist, a Moslem, or an agnostic does not fit anywhere. The attributes should be developed so that every possible situation is covered. For example, Catholic, Protestant, Jewish, or other is an exclusive and mutually exclusive set of attributes.

Unidimensionality

In addition to being mutually exclusive and exhaustive, scales and indexes should also be unidimensional or one dimensional. *Unidimensionality* means that all the items in a scale or index should fit together, or measure a single construct. Unidimensionality was hinted at in the previous discussions of construct and content validity. Unidimensionality says: If you are going to combine several specific pieces of information into a single score or measure, all the pieces should be measuring the same thing. One of the more advanced techniques—factor analysis (to be discussed later in this chapter)—is often used to test for the unidimensionality of data.

There is an apparent contradiction between using a scale or index to combine parts or subparts of a construct into one measure and the criteria of unidimensionality. It is only an apparent contradiction, however, because constructs are theoretically defined at different levels of abstraction. General, higher-level or more abstract constructs can be defined as containing several subparts. Each subdimension is a part of the construct's overall content.

For example, I define the construct "feminist ideology" as a general ideology about gender in society. Feminist ideology is a highly abstract and general construct. It includes specific beliefs and attitudes towards social, economic, political, family, and sexual relations. The ideology's five belief areas are subparts of the single general construct. The subparts are mutually reinforcing and together form a system of beliefs about the dignity, strength, and power of women.

If feminist ideology is unidimensional, then there is a unified belief system that varies from very antifeminist to very profeminist. We can check whether the parts are a single construct by testing the convergence validity of a measure that includes multiple indicators. The multiple indicators tap the construct's subparts. If one belief area (e.g., sexual relations) is consistently distinct from the other areas in empirical tests, then we question the construct validity of the measure and its unidimensionality.

It is easy to become confused: a specific measure can be an indicator of a unidimensional construct in one situation and indicate a subpart of a different construct in another situation. This is possible because constructs can be used at different levels of abstraction.

For example, a person's attitude toward gender equality with regard to pay is more specific and less abstract than feminist ideology (i.e., beliefs about gender relations throughout society). An attitude toward equal pay can be both a unidimensional construct in its own right and a subpart of the more general and abstract unidimensional construct, *ideology toward gender relations*.

INDEX CONSTRUCTION

The Purpose

You hear about indexes all the time. For example, U.S. newspapers report the Federal Bureau of Investigation (FBI) crime index and the consumer price index (CPI). The FBI index is the sum of police reports on seven so-called index crimes (criminal homicide, aggravated assault, forcible rape, robbery, burglary, larceny of $50 or more, and auto theft). It began with the Uniform Crime Report in 1930 (see Rosen 1995). The CPI, which is a measure of inflation, is created by totaling the cost of buying a list of goods and services (e.g., food, rent, utilities) and comparing the total to the cost of buying the same list in the previous year. The consumer price index has been used by the U.S. Bureau of Labor Statistics since 1919; wage increases, union contracts, and social security payments are based on it. An *index* is a combination of items into a single numerical score. Various components or subparts of a construct are each measured, then combined into one measure.

There are many types of indexes. For example, if you take an exam with 25 questions on different parts of a course, the total number of questions correct is a kind of index. It is a composite measure in which each question measures a small piece of knowledge, and all the questions scored correct or incorrect are totaled to produce a single measure.

Indexes measure the most desirable place to live (based on unemployment, commuting time, crime rate, recreation opportunities, weather, and so on), the degree of crime (based on combining the occurrence of different specific crimes), the mental health of a person (based on the person's adjustment in various areas of life), and the like.

One way to demonstrate that indexes are not very complicated is to use one. Answer yes or no to the seven questions that follow on the characteristics of an occupation. Base your answers on your thoughts regarding the following four occupations: long-distance truck driver, medical doctor, accountant, telephone operator. Score each answer 1 for yes and 0 for no.

1. Does it pay a good salary?
2. Is the job secure from layoffs or unemployment?
3. Is the work interesting and challenging?
4. Are its working conditions (e.g., hours, safety, time on the road) good?
5. Are there opportunities for career advancement and promotion?
6. Is it prestigious or looked up to by others?
7. Does it permit self-direction and the freedom to make decisions?

Total the seven answers for each of the four occupations. Which had the highest and which had the lowest score? The seven questions are my operational definition of the construct *good occupation*. Each question represents a subpart of my theoretical definition. A different theoretical definition would result in different questions, perhaps more than seven.

Creating indexes is so easy that it is important to be careful that every item in the index has face validity. Items without face validity should be excluded. Each part of the construct should be measured with at least one indicator. Of course, it is better to measure the parts of a construct with multiple indicators.

Another example of an index is a college quality index (see Box 7.4). My theoretical definition says that a high-quality college has six distinguishing characteristics: (1) fewer students per faculty member, (2) a highly educated faculty, (3) more books available in the library, (4) fewer students dropping out of college, (5) more students who go on to advanced degrees, and (6) faculty members who publish books or scholarly articles. I score 100 colleges on each item, then add the scores for each to create an index score of college quality that can be used to compare colleges.

Indexes can be combined with one another. For example, in order to strengthen my college quality index, I add a subindex on teaching quality. The index contains eight items: (1) average size of classes, (2) percentage of class time de-

Box 7.4 _____

Example of Index

A quality-of-college index is based on the following six items:

1. Number of students per faculty member
2. Percentage of faculty members with Ph.D. degrees
3. Number of books in the library per student
4. Percentage of entering freshmen who fail ever to receive a degree
5. Percentage of students who go on to receive an advanced degree
6. Number of books and scholarly articles published by faculty members

In symbolic form, where:

Q = overall college quality
R = number of students per faculty member
F = percentage of faculty with Ph.D.s
B = number of books in library per student
D = percentage of freshmen who drop out or do not finish
A = percentage of graduates who go for an advanced degree
P = number of publications per faculty member

Unweighted formula: $(-1) R + (1) F + (1) B + (-1) D + (1) A + (1) P = Q$
Weighted formula: $(-2) R + (2) F + (1) B + (-3) D + (1) A + (3) P = Q$

Old Ivy College

Unweighted: $(-1) 13 + (1) 80 + (1) 334 + (-1) 14 + (1) 28 + (1) 4 = 419$
Weighted: $(-2) 13 + (2) 80 + (1) 334 + (-3) 14 + (1) 28 + (3) 4 = 466$

Local College

Unweighted: $(-1) 20 + (1) 82 + (1) 365 + (-1) 25 + (1) 15 + (1) 2 = 419$
Weighted: $(-2) 20 + (2) 82 + (1) 365 + (-3) 25 + (1) 15 + (3) 2 = 435$

Big University

Unweighted: $(-1) 38 + (1) 95 + (1) 380 + (-1) 48 + (1) 24 + (1) 6 = 419$
Weighted: $(-2) 38 + (2) 95 + (1) 380 + (-3) 48 + (1) 24 + (3) 6 = 392$

voted to discussion, (3) number of different classes each faculty member teaches, (4) availability of faculty to students outside the classroom, (5) currency and amount of reading assigned, (6) degree to which assignments promote learning, (7) degree to which faculty get to know each student, and (8) student ratings of instruction. Similar subindex measures can be created for other parts of the college quality index. They can be combined into a more global measure of college quality. This further elaborates the definition of the construct "quality of college."

Weighting

An important issue in index construction is whether to weight items. Unless it is otherwise stated, assume that an index is unweighted. Likewise, unless you have a good theoretical reason for assigning different weights, use equal weights. An *unweighted index* is an index in which each item has equal weight. It involves adding up the items without modification, as if each were multiplied by 1 (or –1 for items that are negative).

In a weighted index, a researcher values or weights some items more than others. The size of weights can come from theoretical assumptions, the theoretical definition, or a statistical technique such as factor analysis (to be discussed). Weighting changes the theoretical definition of the construct.

For example, I decide to elaborate the theoretical definition of the college quality index. I decide that the student/faculty ratio and number of faculty with Ph.D.s are twice as important as the number of books in the library per student or the percentage of students pursuing advanced degrees. Also, the percentage of freshmen who drop out and the number of publications per faculty member are three times more important than books in the library or percentage pursuing an advanced degree. This is easier to see when it is expressed as a formula.

The number of students per faculty member and the percentage who drop out have negative signs because, as they get larger, the quality of the college gets lower. The weighted and unweighted indexes can produce different results. Consider Old Ivy College, Local College, and Big University. All have identical unweighted index scores, but the colleges have different quality scores after weighting.

Weighting produces different index scores, but in most cases, weighted and unweighted indexes yield similar results. Researchers are concerned with the relationship between variables, and weighted and unweighted indexes usually give similar results for the relationships between variables.[20]

Missing Data

Missing data can be a serious problem when constructing an index. Validity and reliability are threatened whenever data for some cases are missing. There are four ways to attempt to resolve the problem (see Box 7.5), but none fully solve it.

For example, I construct an index of the

Box 7.5 _____

Ways to Deal with Missing Data

1. *Eliminate all cases for which any information is missing.* If Finland is removed from the study, the index will be reliable for the nations on which information is available. This is a problem if other nations have missing information. A study of 50 nations may become a study of 20 nations. Also, the cases with missing information may be similar in some respect (e.g., all are in eastern Europe or in the Third World), which limits the generalizability of findings.

2. *Substitute the average score for cases where data are present.* The average literacy score from the other nations is substituted. This "solution" keeps Finland in the study but gives it an incorrect value. For an index with few items or for a case that is not "average," this creates serious validity problems.

3. *Insert data based on nonquantitative information about the case.* Other information about Finland (e.g., percentage of 13- to 18-year-olds in high school) is used to make an informed guess about the literacy rate. This "solution" is marginally acceptable in this situation. It is not as good as measuring Finland's literacy, and it relies on an untested assumption—that one can predict the literacy rate from other countries' high school attendance rate.

4. *Insert a random value.* This is unwise for the development index example. It might be acceptable if the index had a very large number of items and the number of cases was very large. If that were the situation, however, then eliminating the case is probably a better "solution" that produces a more reliable measure.

---

degree of societal development in 1975 for 50 nations. The index contains four items: life expectancy, percentage of homes with indoor plumbing, percentage of population that is literate, and number of telephones per 100 people. I locate a source of United Nations statistics for my information. The values for Belgium are 68 + 87 + 97 + 28; for Turkey, the scores are 55 + 36 + 49 + 3; for Finland, however, I discover that literacy data are unavailable. I check other sources of information, but none has the data because they were not collected.

Rates and Standardization

You have heard of crime rates, rates of population growth, or the unemployment rate. Some indexes and single-indicator measures are expressed as rates. Rates involve standardizing the value of an item to make comparisons possible. The items in an index frequently need to be standardized before they can be combined.

Standardization involves selecting a base and dividing a raw measure by the base. For example, City A had 10 murders and City B had 30 murders in the same year. In order to compare murders in the two cities, the raw number of murders needs to be standardized by the city population. If the cities are the same size, City B is more dangerous. But City B may be safer if it is much larger. For example, if City A has 100,000 people and City B has 600,000, then the murder rate per 100,000 is 10 for City A and 5 for City B.

Standardization makes it possible to compare different units on a common base. The process of standardization, also called *norming*, removes the effect of relevant but different characteristics in order to make the differences on important variables visible. For example, there are two classes of students. An art class has 12 smokers and a biology class has 22 smokers. A researcher can compare the rate or incidence of smokers by standardizing the number of smokers by the size of the classes. The art class has 32 students and the biology class has 143 students. One method of standardization that you already know is the use of percentages, whereby measures are standardized to a common base of 100. In terms of percentages, it is easy to see that the art class has more than twice the rate of smokers (37.5 percent) than the biology class (15.4 percent).

A critical question in standardization is deciding what base to use. In the examples given, how did I know to use city size or class size as the base? The choice is not always obvious; it depends on the theoretical definition of a construct.

Different bases can produce different rates.

For example, the unemployment rate can be defined as the number of people in the work force who are out of work. The overall unemployment rate is:

$$\text{Unemployment rate} = \frac{\text{Number of unemployed people}}{\text{Total number of people working}}$$

We can divide the total population into subgroups to get rates for subgroups in the population such as white males, black females, black males between the ages of 18 and 28, or people with college degrees. Rates for these subgroups may be more relevant to the theoretical definition or research problem. For example, a researcher believes that unemployment is an experience that affects an entire household or family and that the base should be households, not individuals. The rate will look like this:

$$\text{New unemployment rate} = \frac{\text{Number of households with at least one unemployed person}}{\text{Total number of households}}$$

Different conceptualizations suggest different bases and different ways to standardize. When combining several items into an index, it is best to standardize items on a common base (see Box 7.6).

SCALES

The Purpose

Scaling, like index construction, creates an ordinal, interval, or ratio measure of a variable expressed as a numerical score. Scales are common in situations where a researcher wants to measure how an individual feels or thinks about something. Some call this the hardness or potency of feelings.

Scales are used for two related purposes. First, scales help in the conceptualization and operationalization processes. Scales show the fit between a set of indicators and a single construct.

Box 7.6

Standardization

MEDALS GAINED AT THE OLYMPIC GAMES IN SEOUL, SOUTH KOREA, FOR A SET OF 15 NATIONS, 1988

MEDALS WON

RANK	COUNTRY	Gold	Silver	Bronze	Total	Weighted Total*
1	USSR	55	31	46	132	82
2	East Germany	37	35	30	102	62
3	USA	36	31	27	94	59
4	West Germany	11	14	15	40	22
5	South Korea	12	10	11	33	20
6	Hungary	11	6	6	23	15
7	France	6	4	6	16	9
8	Japan	4	3	7	14	8
9	New Zealand	3	2	8	13	6
10	Sweden	0	4	7	11	4
11	Canada	3	2	5	10	5
12	Kenya	5	2	2	9	6.5
13	Brazil	1	2	3	6	3
14	Norway	2	3	0	5	3.5
15	Finland	1	1	2	4	2

The nations are ranked by total medals won. Notice how the ranking of nations changes slightly as each medal is given a weight.

RANK	COUNTRY	TOTAL MEDALS PER 100 MILLION POPULATION	
1	East Germany	600	Once we standardize the total number of medals by the population size of each nation, the ranking changes a great deal. For example, Norway jumps from 14 to 4, and the USA falls from 3 to 12. Is it fair to rank nations as if they were the same, ignoring the fact that some have over 50 times more people from whom to draw? For example, there are about as many Norwegians in Norway as there are Americans in the state of Wisconsin. Which better informs you about the relative athletic talent and training of the people of a nation—unstandardized or standardized ranks?
2	New Zealand	405	
3	Hungary	210	
4	Norway	165	
5	Sweden	140	
6	South Korea	85	
7	Finland	80	
8	West Germany	65	
9	Kenya	55	
10	USSR	50	
12	USA	40	
13	Canada	40	
14	Brazil	25	
15	Japan	12	

*Weighted total: Gold = 1, Silver = .5, Bronze = .25.

Source: Adapted from Horn (1993:45).

For example, a researcher believes that there is a single ideological dimension that underlies people's judgments about specific policies (e.g., housing, education, foreign affairs). Scaling can help determine whether a single construct—"conservative/liberal ideology"—underlies the positions people take on specific policies.

Second, scaling produces quantitative measures and can be used with other variables to test hypotheses. This second purpose of scaling is our primary focus because it involves scales as a technique for measuring a variable.

Logic of Scaling

As stated before, scaling is based on the idea of measuring the intensity, hardness, or potency of a variable.

Graphic rating scales are an elementary form of scaling. People indicate a rating by checking a point on a line that runs from one extreme to another. This type of scale is easy to construct and use. It conveys the idea of a continuum, and assigning numbers helps people think about quantities. Scales assume that people with the same subjective feeling mark the graphic scale at the same place.

Figure 7.6 is an example of a "feeling thermometer" scale that is used to find out how people feel about various groups in society (e.g., the National Organization of Women, the Ku Klux Klan, labor unions, physicians). This type of measure has been used by political scientists in the National Election Study since 1964 to measure attitudes toward candidates, social groups, and issues.[21]

Commonly Used Scales

Likert Scale. You have probably used *Likert scales*; they are widely used and very common in survey research. They were developed in the 1930s by Rensis Likert to provide an ordinal-level measure of a person's attitude.[22] Likert scales are called summated-rating or additive scales because a person's score on the scale is computed by summing the number of responses the person gives. Likert scales usually ask people to indicate whether they agree or disagree with a statement. Other modifica-

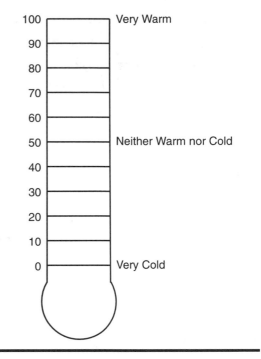

FIGURE 7.6 "Feeling Thermometer" Graphic Rating Scale

tions are possible; people might be asked whether they approve or disapprove, or whether they believe something is "almost always true." Box 7.7 presents several examples of Likert scales.

Likert scales need a minimum of two categories, such as "agree" and "disagree." Using only two choices creates a crude measure and forces distinctions into only two categories. It is usually better to use four to eight categories. A researcher can combine or collapse categories after the data are collected, but data collected with crude categories cannot be made more precise later.

You can increase the number of categories at the end of a scale by adding "strongly agree," "somewhat agree," "very strongly agree," and so forth. Keep the number of choices to eight or nine at most. More distinctions than that are probably not meaningful, and people will become confused. The choices should be evenly balanced (e.g., "strongly agree," "agree" with "strongly disagree," "disagree"). Nunnally (1978:521) stated,

Box 7.7 _____

Examples of Types of Likert Scales

THE ROSENBERG SELF-ESTEEM SCALE

All in all, I am inclined to feel that I am a failure:

(1) Almost always true	(4) Seldom true
(2) Often true	(5) Never true
(3) Sometimes true	

A STUDENT EVALUATION OF INSTRUCTION SCALE

Overall, I rate the quality of instruction in this course as:

Excellent   Good   Average   Fair   Poor

A MARKET RESEARCH MOUTHWASH RATING SCALE

Brand	Dislike Completely	Dislike Somewhat	Dislike a Little	Like a Little	Like Somewhat	Like Completely
X	_____	_____	_____	_____	_____	_____
Y	_____	_____	_____	_____	_____	_____

WORK GROUP SUPERVISOR SCALE

My supervisor:

	Never	Seldom	Sometimes	Often	Always
Lets members know what is expected of them	1	2	3	4	5
Is friendly and approachable	1	2	3	4	5
Treats all unit members as equals	1	2	3	4	5

As the number of scale steps is increased from 2 up through 20, the increase in reliability is very rapid at first. It tends to level off at about 7, and after about 11 steps, there is little gain in reliability from increasing the number of steps.

Researchers have debated about whether to offer a neutral category (e.g., "don't know," "undecided," "no opinion") in addition to the directional categories (e.g., "disagree," "agree"). A neutral category implies an odd number of categories. I will discuss this topic in Chapter 10.

A researcher can combine the items in a series of Likert scale questions into a composite index if all items measure a single construct. Consider the Likert scale example in Box 7.8. Tony is for big business and against unions. He answers the ten

Likert scale questions: SD, SD, SA, A, D, SA, D, SA, SA, A. Barbara is opposed to big business and supports unions. She answers A, SA, D, D, SA, SD, A, SD, A, SD. In the example, 1 to 4 is assigned to each Likert scale answer so that a pro-union index can be formed. Questions 1, 2, 5, and 7 indicate a pro-union position and are scored SA = 4, A = 3, D = 2, SD = 1, whereas questions 3, 4, 6, 8, 9, and 10 are scored the opposite: SA = 1, A = 2, D = 3, SD = 4. Tony gets a score of $1 + 1 + 1 + 2 + 2 + 1 + 2 + 1 + 1 + 2 = 14$, whereas Barbara scores $3 + 4 + 3 + 3 + 4 + 4 + 3 + 4 + 3 + 4 = 35$.

Notice that agreement suggests a probusiness opinion for some questions, whereas agreeing with other questions indicates an antibusiness opinion. The reason for switching directions in

Box 7.8 _____

Example of a Likert Scale Used to Create Index

Below are ten statements about business and unions. Indicate your opinion by circling whether you strongly agree, agree, disagree, or strongly disagree.

	Strongly Agree	Agree	Strongly Disagree	Disagree
1. Big business has too much power today.	SA (4)	A (3)	D (2)	SD (1)
2. The gains workers have made are chiefly due to labor unions.	SA (4)	A (3)	D (2)	SD (1)
3. The profits of large companies help everyone.	SA (1)	A (2)	D (3)	SD (4)
4. Large companies are essential for a strong nation.	SA (1)	A (2)	D (3)	SD (4)
5. Labor unions are needed to protect working people.	SA (4)	A (3)	D (2)	SD (1)
6. The gains labor unions make are at the expense of other people.	SA (1)	A (2)	D (3)	SD (4)
7. Our country would be better if large companies were broken up into smaller ones.	SA (4)	A (3)	D (2)	SD (1)
8. Labor unions are too big and powerful for the good of the country.	SA (1)	A (2)	D (3)	SD (4)
9. Government regulation slows economic growth and business initiative.	SA (1)	A (2)	D (3)	SD (4)
10. Most unions are run by a tiny group of corrupt bosses and thugs.	SA (1)	A (2)	D (3)	SD (4)

Note: Values in parentheses () would not be presented to a respondent answering the questionnaire but would be added later by a researcher.

_____

this way is to avoid the problem of the *response set*. The response set, also called response style and response bias, is the tendency of some people to answer a large number of items in the same way (usually agreeing) out of laziness or a psychological predisposition. For example, if items are worded so that saying "strongly agree" always indicates a pro-union stance, we would not know whether a person who always strongly agreed had a strong pro-union attitude or simply had a tendency to agree with questions. The person might be answering "strongly agree" out of habit or a tendency to agree. Researchers word statements in alternative directions, so that anyone who

agrees all the time appears to answer inconsistently or to have a contradictory opinion.

Researchers often combine many Likert-scaled attitude indicators into an index. The scale and indexes have properties that are associated with improving reliability and validity. An index uses multiple indicators, which improves reliability. The use of multiple indicators that measure several aspects of a construct or opinion improves content validity. Finally, the index scores give a more precise quantitative measure of a person's opinion. For example, each person's opinion can be measured with a number from 10 to 40, instead of in four categories:

"strongly agree," "agree," "disagree," "strongly disagree."

Instead of scoring Likert items from 1 to 4, as in the previous example, the scores –2, –1, +1, +2 could be used. This scoring has an advantage in that a zero implies neutrality or complete ambiguity, whereas a high negative number means an attitude that opposes the opinion represented by a high positive number.

The numbers assigned to the response categories are arbitrary. Remember that the use of a zero does not give the scale or index a ratio level of measurement. Likert scale measures are at the ordinal level of measurement because responses indicate a ranking only. Instead of 1 to 4 or –2 to +2, the numbers 100, 70, 50, and 5 would have worked. Also, do not be fooled into thinking that the distances between the ordinal categories are intervals just because numbers are assigned. Although the number system has nice mathematical properties, the numbers are used for convenience only. The fundamental measurement is only ordinal.[23]

The simplicity and ease of use of the Likert scale is its real strength. When several items are combined, more comprehensive multiple indicator measurement is possible. The scale has two limitations: Different combinations of several scale items can result in the same overall score or result, and the response set is a potential danger.

Thurstone Scaling. Researchers sometimes want a measure with one numerical continuum, but the attitude variable in which they are interested has several characteristics or aspects. For example, a dry-cleaning business, Quick and Clean, wants to find out its image in Greentown compared to that of its major competitor, Friendly Cleaners. The researcher working for Quick and Clean conceptualizes a person's attitude toward the business as having four subparts or aspects: attitude toward location, hours, service, and cost. Quick and Clean is seen as having more convenient hours and locations, but higher costs and discourteous service, whereas Friendly Cleaners is seen as having low cost and friendly service, but inconvenient hours and locations. Unless the researcher knows how the four aspects relate to

the core attitude—image of the dry cleaner—he or she cannot say which business is generally viewed more favorably. During the late 1920s, Louis Thurstone developed scaling methods for assigning numerical values in such situations. These are now called Thurstone scaling or the method of equal-appearing intervals.[24]

Thurstone scaling is based on the *law of comparative judgment*. The law addresses the issue of measuring or comparing attitudes when each person makes a unique judgment. In other words, it anchors or fixes the position of one person's attitude relative to that of others as each makes an individual subjective judgment.

The law of comparative judgment states that it is possible to identify a single "most common response" for each object or concept being judged. Although different people arrive at somewhat different judgments, the individual judgments cluster around a single most common response. The dispersion of individual judgments around the common response follows a general statistical pattern called the normal distribution. From the law, it follows that, if many people agree that two objects differ, the most common responses for the two objects will be distant from each other. By contrast, if many people are confused or disagree about the differences between two objects, the common responses of the two objects will be closer to each other.

In Thurstone scaling, a researcher develops many statements (e.g., more than 100) regarding the object of interest, then uses many judges (e.g., 100) to reduce the number to a smaller set (e.g., 20) by eliminating ambiguous statements. Each judge rates the statements on an underlying continuum (e.g., favorable to unfavorable). The researcher examines the ratings and keeps those statements based on two factors: (1) agreement among the judges and (2) the statement's location on a range of possible values. The final set of statements is used to form a measurement scale that spans a range of values.

Thurstone scaling begins with a large number of evaluative statements that should be exhaustive and cover all shades of opinion. Each should be clear and precise, and should express a single opinion. Good statements refer to the present and are not capable of being interpreted as facts. They are unlikely to be endorsed by everyone, are stated as simple sentences, and avoid words such as *always* and *never*. Researchers get ideas for writing the statements from reviewing the literature, from the mass media, from personal experience, and from asking others. For example, statements about the dry-cleaning business might include the four aspects listed before, plus the following:

— I think X Cleaners dry cleans clothing in a prompt and timely manner.
— In my opinion, X Cleaners keeps its stores looking neat and attractive.
— I do not think that X Cleaners does a good job removing stains.
— I believe that X Cleaners charges reasonable prices for cleaning coats.
— I believe that X Cleaners returns clothing clean and neatly pressed.
— I think that X Cleaners has poor delivery service.

A researcher next locates 50 to 300 judges. The judges do not have to be experts on the topic, but they should be familiar with the object or concept in the statements. Each judge receives a set of statement cards and instructions. Each card has one statement on it, and the judges place each card in one of several piles. The number of piles is usually 7, 9, 11, or 13. The piles represent a range of values (e.g., favorable to neutral to unfavorable) with regard to the object or concept being evaluated. Each judge places cards in rating piles independently of the other judges.

After the judges place all cards in piles, the researcher creates a chart cross-classifying the piles and the statements. For example, 100 statements and 11 piles results in an 11×100 chart, or a chart with $11 \times 100 = 1,100$ boxes. The number of judges who assigned a rating to a given statement is written into each box of the chart. Statistical measures (beyond the present discussion) are used to compute the average rating of each statement and the degree to which the judges agree or disagree.

The researcher keeps the statements with the greatest between-judge agreement, or interrater reliability, as well as statements that represent the entire range of values. For example, suppose 100 statements were rated. The researcher computes the agreement score of each statement. Next, the location of the high-agreement scores across the continuum of 11 values (highly unfavorable, neutral, highly favorable) is examined. The researcher collapses the categories used by the judges into fewer categories and selects the four statements with the greatest agreement among judges for each of five categories to identify 20 statements.

The researcher has 20 statements, 4 for each range of the value scale. The statements are randomly mixed. The 20 statements are next presented to people who are asked whether they agree or disagree with the statement (see Box 7.9 for another example).

With Thurstone scaling, a researcher can construct an attitude scale or select statements from a larger collection of attitude statements. The method is seldom used today because of its limitations:

1. It measures only agreement or disagreement with statements, not the intensity of agreement or disagreement.
2. It assumes that judges and others agree on where statements appear in a rating system.
3. It is time consuming and costly.
4. It is possible to get the same overall score in several ways because agreement or disagreement with different combinations of statements can produce the same average.

Nevertheless, Thurstone scaling selects attitude items that are relatively unambiguous. It can be combined with Likert or other methods to create ordinal-level measures.

Bogardus Social Distance Scale. The *Bogardus social distance scale* measures the social distance separating ethnic or other groups from each other. It is used with one group to determine how much distance it feels toward a target or "outgroup." It was developed in the 1920s by Emory Bogardus to measure the willingness of members of different ethnic groups to associate with each other. It can

Box 7.9

Example of Thurstone Scaling

Variable Measured: Opinion with regard to the death penalty.

Step 1: Develop 120 statements about the death penalty using personal experience, the popular and professional literature, and listening to others.

EXAMPLE STATEMENTS

1. I think that the death penalty is cruel and unnecessary punishment.
2. Without the death penalty, there would be many more violent crimes.
3. I believe that the death penalty should be used only for a few extremely violent crimes.
4. I do not think that anyone was ever prevented from committing a murder because of fear of the death penalty.
5. I do not think that people should be exempt from the death penalty if they committed a murder even if they are insane.
6. I believe that the Bible justifies the use of the death penalty.
7. The death penalty itself is not the problem for me, but I believe that electrocuting people is a cruel way to put them to death.

Step 2: Place each statement on a separate card or sheet of paper and make 100 sets of the 120 statements.

Step 3: Locate 100 persons who agree to serve as judges. Give each judge a set of the statement and instructions to place them in one of 11 piles, from 1 = highly unfavorable statement through 11 = highly favorable statement.

Step 4: The judges place each statement into one of the 11 piles (e.g., Judge #1 puts statement 1 into pile #2; Judge #2 puts the same statement into pile #1; Judge #3 also puts it into pile #2, Judge #4 puts it in pile #3, and so on).

Step 5: Collect piles from judges and create a chart summarizing their responses. See the example chart that follows.

CHART OF NUMBER OF JUDGES RATING EACH STATEMENT
RATING PILE

| | Unfavorable | | | | Neutral | | | | | Favorable | | |
Statement	1	2	3	4	5	6	7	8	9	10	11	Total
1	23	60	12	5	0	0	0	0	0	0	0	100
2	0	0	0	0	2	12	18	41	19	8	0	100
3	2	8	7	13	31	19	12	6	2	0	0	100
4	9	11	62	10	4	4	0	0	0	0	0	100

Step 6: Compute the average rating and degree of agreement by judges. For example, the average for question 1 is about 2, so there is high agreement; the average for question 3 is closer to 5, and there is much less agreement.

Step 7: Choose the final 20 statements to include in the death penalty opinion scale. Choose statements if the judges showed agreement (most placed an item in the same or a nearby pile) and ones that reflect the entire range of opinion, from favorable to neutral to unfavorable.

Step 8: Prepare a 20-statement questionnaire, and ask people in a study whether they agree or disagree with the statements.

be used to see how close or distant people feel toward some other group (e.g., a religious minority or a deviant group).[25]

The scale has a simple logic. People respond to a series of ordered statements; those that are most threatening or most socially distant are at one end, and those that might be least threatening or socially intimate are at the other end. The logic of the scale assumes that a person who refuses contact or is uncomfortable with the socially distant items will refuse the socially closer items.

Researchers use the scale in several ways. For example, people are given a series of statements: People from Group X are entering your country, are in your town, work at your place of employment, live in your neighborhood, become your personal friends, marry your brother or sister. People are asked whether they feel comfortable with the statement or if the contact is acceptable. It is also possible to ask whether they feel uncomfortable with the relationship. People may be asked to respond to all statements, or they may keep reading statements until they are not comfortable with a relationship. There is no set number of statements required; the number usually ranges from five to nine.

A researcher can use the Bogardus scale to see how distant people feel from one "outgroup" versus another (see Box 7.10). The measure of social distance can be used as either an independent or a dependent variable. For example, a researcher believes that social distance from a group is greatest for people who have some other characteristic. A hypothesis might be that feelings of social distance by whites from Vietnamese boat people is negatively associated with education; that is, the least well educated feel the most distant. Social distance from boat people is the dependent variable, and amount of education is the independent variable.

The social distance scale is a convenient way to determine how close a respondent feels toward a social group. It has two potential limitations. First, a researcher needs to tailor the categories to a specific outgroup and social setting. Second, it is not easy for a researcher to compare how a respondent feels toward several different groups unless the respondent completes a similar social distance scale for all outgroups at the same time. Of course, how a respondent completes the scale and the respondent's actual behavior in specific social situations may differ.

Semantic Differential. Osgood's *Semantic Differential* was developed in the 1950s to provide an indirect measure of how a person feels about a concept, object, or other person. The technique measures subjective feelings toward something by using adjectives. This is because people communicate evaluations through adjectives in spoken and written language. Because most adjectives have polar opposites (e.g., *light/dark, hard/soft, slow/fast*), it uses polar opposite adjectives to create a rating measure or scale. The Semantic Differential captures the connotations associated with whatever is being evaluated and provides an indirect measure of it.

The Semantic Differential has been used for many purposes. In marketing research, it tells how consumers feel about a product; political advisers use it to discover what voters think about a candidate or issue; and therapists use it to determine how a client perceives himself or herself.

To use the Semantic Differential, a researcher presents subjects with a list of paired opposite adjectives with a continuum of 7 to 11 points between them. The subjects mark the spot on the continuum between the adjectives that expresses their feelings. The adjectives can be very diverse and should be well mixed (e.g., positive items should not be located mostly on either the right or the left side). Studies of a wide variety of adjectives in English found that they fall into three major classes of meaning: evaluation (*good–bad*), potency (*strong–weak*), and activity (*active–passive*). Of the three classes of meaning, evaluation is usually the most significant. The analysis of results is difficult, and a researcher needs to use statistical procedures to analyze a subject's feelings toward the concept.

Results from a Semantic Differential tell a researcher how one person perceives different concepts or how different people view the same concept. For example, political analysts might discover that young voters perceive their candidate as traditional, weak, and slow, and as halfway between good and bad. Elderly voters perceive the

Box 7.10

Example of Bogardus Social Distance Scale

A researcher wants to find out how socially distant freshmen college students feel from exchange students from two different countries, Nigeria and Germany. She wants to see whether students feel more distant from students coming from black Africa or from Europe. She uses the following series of questions in an interview:

Please give me your first reaction, yes or no, whether you personally would feel comfortable having an exchange student from (name of country):

_____ As a visitor to your college for a week

_____ As a full-time student enrolled at your college

_____ Taking several of the same classes you are taking

_____ Sitting next to you in class and studying with you for exams

_____ Living a few doors down the hall on the same floor in your dormitory

_____ As a same-sex roommate sharing your dorm room

_____ As someone of the opposite sex who has asked you to go out on a date

HYPOTHETICAL RESULTS
Percentage of Freshmen Who Report Feeling Comfortable

	Nigeria	Germany
Visitor	100%	100%
Enrolled	98%	100%
Same class	95%	98%
Study together	82%	88%
Same dorm	71%	83%
Roommate	50%	76%
Go on date	42%	64%

The results suggest that freshmen feel more distant from Nigerian students than from German students. Almost all feel comfortable having the international students as visitors, enrolled in the college, and taking classes. Feelings of distance increase as interpersonal contact increases, especially if the contact involves personal living settings or activities not directly related to the classroom.

---

candidate as leaning toward strong, fast, and good, and as halfway between traditional and modern. In the example in Box 7.11, a person rated two concepts. The pattern of responses for each concept illustrates how this individual feels about the concepts. This person views the two concepts differently and appears to feel rather negatively about the idea of divorce.

There are techniques for creating three-dimen-

sional diagrams of results.[26] The three aspects are diagrammed in three-dimensional "semantic space." In the diagram, "good" is up and "bad" is down, "active" is left and "passive" is right, "strong" is away from the viewer and "weak" is close.

Guttman Scaling. *Guttman scaling*, or cumulative scaling, differs from the previous scales or indexes in that researchers use it to evaluate data

Box 7.11

Example of Semantic Differential

Please read each pair of adjectives below, then place a mark on the blank space that comes closest to your first impression feeling. There are no right or wrong answers.

How do you feel about the idea of divorce?

Left	1	2	3	4	5	6	7	8	9	Right
Bad		x								Good
Deep								x		Shallow
Weak			x							Strong
Fair								x		Unfair
Quiet									x	Loud
Modern	x									Traditional
Simple						x				Complex
Fast		x								Slow
Dirty		x								Clean

How do you feel about the idea of marriage?

Left	1	2	3	4	5	6	7	8	9	Right
Bad									x	Good
Deep		x								Shallow
Weak								x		Strong
Fair		x								Unfair
Quiet			x							Loud
Modern									x	Traditional
Simple						x				Complex
Fast								x		Slow
Dirty							x			Clean

after they are collected. This means that researchers must design a study with the Guttman scaling technique in mind. Louis Guttman developed the scale in the 1940s to determine whether a relationship existed among a set of indicators or measurement items. He used multiple indicators to document an underlying single dimension or cumulative intensity of a construct.[27]

Guttman scaling begins with measuring a set of indicators or items. These can be questionnaire items, votes, or observed characteristics. Guttman scaling measures many different phenomena (e.g., patterns of crime or drug use, characteristics of societies or organizations, voting or political participation, psychological disorders). The indicators are usually measured in a simple yes/no or present/absent fashion. From 3 to 20 indicators can be used. The researcher selects items on the belief that there is a logical relationship among them. He or she then places the results into a Guttman scale and determines whether the items form a pattern that corresponds to the relationship.

Once a set of items is measured, the researcher considers all possible combinations of responses for the items. For example, three items are measured: whether a child knows her age, her telephone number, and three local elected political officials. The little girl may know her age but no other answer, or all three, or only her age and telephone number. In fact, for three items there are eight possible combinations of answers or patterns of responses, from not knowing any through knowing all three. There is a mathematical way to compute the number of combinations (e.g., 2^3), but you can write down all the combinations of yes or no for three questions and see the eight possibilities.

The logical relationship among items in Guttman scaling is hierarchical. Most people or cases have or agree to lower order items. The smaller number of cases that have the higher order items also have the lower order ones, but not vice versa. In other words, the higher order items build on the lower ones. The lower order items are necessary for the appearance of the higher order items.

An application of Guttman scaling, known as *scalogram analysis*, lets a researcher test whether a hierarchical relationship exists among the items. For example, it is easier for a child to know her age than her telephone number, and to know her telephone number than the names of political leaders. The items are called *scalable*, or capable of forming a Guttman scale, if a hierarchical pattern exists.

The patterns of responses can be divided into two groups: scaled and errors (or nonscalable). The scaled patterns for the child's knowledge example would be: not knowing any item, knowing only age, knowing only age plus phone number, knowing all three. Other combinations of answers (e.g., knowing the political leaders but not her age) are possible but are nonscalable. If a hierarchical relationship exists among the items, then most answers fit into the scalable patterns.

The strength or degree to which items can be scaled is measured with statistics that measure whether the responses can be reproduced based on a hierarchical pattern. Most range from zero to 100 percent. A score of zero indicates a random pattern, or no hierarchical pattern. A score of 100 percent indicates that all responses to the answer fit the hierarchical or scaled pattern. Alternative statistics to measure scalability have also been suggested.[28]

See Box 7.12 for an example of a study of drug use among high school students using Guttman scaling. The results suggest that the items are Guttman scalable; that is, there is a hierarchical pattern of drug use among the high school students. Students who use "hard" or illegal drugs are likely also to use "soft" or legal drugs. Few students who use illegal drugs fail to use legal drugs, but some students use only legal drugs but not illegal drugs.

Clogg and Sawyer (1981) studied American attitudes toward abortion using Guttman scaling by looking at different conditions under which people thought abortion was acceptable (e.g., mother's health in danger, pregnancy resulting from rape). They discovered that 84.2 percent of responses fit into a scaled response pattern. Another example of the use of Guttman scaling is presented in McIver and Carmines (1981:55–58), who studied roll call votes of U.S. senators on a 1975 law to create a federal consumer protection agency. They examined votes on 12 substantive amendments to the law and discovered that the senators voted in a Guttman scalable pattern 92 percent of the time.

SOCIAL INDICATORS

During the 1960s, some social scientists, dissatisfied with the information available to decision makers, spawned the "social indicators' movement." Its purpose was to develop indicators of social well-being. Many hoped that information about social well-being could be combined with widely used indicators of economic performance (e.g., gross national product) to better inform government and other policymaking officials. Thus, social indicator researchers wanted to measure the quality of social life so that such information could influence public policy.[29]

Today, there are many books, articles, and reports on social indicators, and even a scholarly journal, *Social Indicators Research,* devoted to the creation and evaluation of social indicators. The U.S. Census Bureau produced a report, *Social Indicators*, and the United Nations has many measures of social well-being in different nations.

A *social indicator* is any measure of social well-being used in policy. There are many specific indicators that are operationalizations of well-being. For example, social indicators have been developed for the following areas: population, family, housing, social security and welfare, health and nutrition, public safety, education and training, work, income, culture and leisure, social mobility, and participation.

A more specific example of a social indicator is the FBI's uniform crime index. It indicates the amount of crime in U.S. society. Social indicators can measure negative aspects of social life, such as the infant mortality rate (the death rate of infants

Box 7.12 _____

Example of Use of Guttman Scaling

A researcher wants to determine the pattern of drug use among a group of 80 high school students. You are interested in four major drug types: cigarette smoking, alcohol use, marijuana use, and cocaine use. The students were asked four separate questions (among others in a questionnaire), and the pattern of their answers could be organized into four categories:

DRUG USED

Answer Pattern	Cigarettes	Alcohol	Marijuana	Cocaine	Number of Students
1	No	No	No	No	8
2	Yes	No	No	No	15
3	Yes	Yes	No	No	25
4	Yes	Yes	Yes	No	13
5	Yes	Yes	Yes	Yes	7
6	No	Yes	Yes	Yes	1
7	No	No	Yes	Yes	2
8	No	No	No	Yes	1
9	No	No	Yes	No	2
10	No	Yes	No	No	5
11	No	Yes	No	Yes	0
12	No	Yes	Yes	No	0
13	Yes	No	Yes	No	0
14	Yes	No	Yes	Yes	0
15	Yes	Yes	No	Yes	1
16	Yes	No	No	Yes	0
				Total	80

Answer patterns 1 to 5 are "scaled," but 6 to 16 are not.

(Note that frequently "yes" and "no" are symbolized by + and 0, respectively.)

---

during the first year of life) or alcoholism, or they can indicate positive aspects, such as job satisfaction or the percentage of housing units with indoor plumbing. Social indicators often involve implicit value judgments (e.g., which crimes are serious or what constitutes a good quality of life).

Researchers developed quality-of-life indexes from measures of pollution, overcrowding, food, and material standards of living. For example, a researcher might rank 65 large metropolitan areas on the basis of a weighted index of 150 indicators of the quality of life. Indicators could include newspaper circulation per 1,000 population (indicating information), percentage of households with one or more automobiles (indicating mobility), and percentage of population over 25 years of age who had completed four years of high school. Environmental, economic, political, health, and social conditions could also be measured. In the past, cities such as Portland, Oregon, were rated the highest, whereas Jersey City, New Jersey, was the lowest.

SPECIALIZED TECHNIQUES FOR INDEX AND SCALE CONSTRUCTION

Three sophisticated statistical techniques that social researchers use to construct or evaluate scales or indexes are presented here. The three are not an exhaustive set. There are dozens of similar techniques. They are presented here as examples of the powerful techniques professional researchers often use. You will need to acquire a background in statistics and learn to use computer programs before you will be able to use these techniques.

The purpose of introducing you to the techniques is twofold. First, you may encounter them in the methods, analysis, or results sections of scholarly journal articles. This introduction will help you understand why they are being used. Second, the logic of the techniques reinforces the basic principles of measurement and index or scale construction that you have already learned. The logic illustrates how the principles are extended to complex, sophisticated applications. Although the three techniques use advanced statistics, their logic is consistent with basic measurement principles.

Factor Analysis

Factor analysis is a group of sophisticated statistical techniques that require a computer to conduct.[30] Statistical training is necessary to use factor analysis properly. Improperly used, it creates nonsense. Factor analysis helps researchers construct indexes, test the unidimensionality of scales, assign weights to items in an index, and statistically reduce a large number of indicators to a smaller set. The statistical theory and algebra on which factor analysis is based is beyond the level of this book, but its conceptual principles are not difficult to grasp. The fundamental logic of factor analysis is based on the idea that it is possible to manipulate statistically the empirical relationships among several indicators to reveal a common unobserved factor or hypothetical construct.

When conducting factor analysis, a researcher begins with a number of items he or she believes to measure a single construct. At least five indicators are recommended. The indicators should be measured at the ordinal, interval, or ratio level. The interval or ratio level is preferred, and extra caution is necessary for ordinal-level measurement.

The researcher gives the factor analysis computer program characteristics of the variables and technical information. The factor analysis results tell a researcher how well the items or indicators relate to an underlying factor or hypothetical construct. For example, factor analysis results tell the researcher whether the items all load, or are associated with, one or more than one factor.

Factor analysis also produces factor scores, which can be used as weights in creating an index. These scores represent how strongly each indicator is associated with the unobserved factor. For example, I conduct an Australian survey in which there were 16 Likert scale items that measure attitudes toward Japan. I use factor analysis to tell me whether the 16 items are explained by two factors. For example, 5 attitude items load on a factor that indicates a fear of military conflict construct. The other 11 items load on a factor that indicates antagonism toward a different racial group. The meaning of a factor comes from looking at the items that load on it. I can combine each set of items into two separate indexes of attitudes toward Japan.

Q-Sort Analysis

Q-sort analysis is a close relative of factor analysis.[31] Like factor analysis, the technique requires statistical background beyond the scope of this book. It illustrates an interesting scaling logic as well.

Q-sort methodology uses *ipsative scoring*, as opposed to *normative scoring*, which is used in most scaling or index techniques. With normative scoring, a person rates each item in an index or scale independently. With ipsative scoring, a person is forced to decide between the items, so a decision on one item affects other items.

For example, I rank movie stars. When I choose an actor as number one, it means that no other actor can be number one. The decision about one item (i.e., the number-one actor) affects or limits my decision about other items. This is ipsative scoring. By contrast, with normative scoring, I rate a list of actors from "highly like" to "highly dislike," as with a Likert scale. I could rate several actors "highly like." My decision to rate one actor does not limit my decisions about rating others.

Q-sort analysis begins with people ranking statements about a concept or object. In a manner somewhat like Thurstone scaling, people are given a large number of statements (e.g., 30 to 50) and asked to sort them. The statements are taken from popular writings on a topic, everyday conversations, television programs, and the like, and should represent diverse ways people think about a topic.

Instead of piles along one continuum, the Q-sort technique has people place statements into boxes in a grid that varies along two continua. There are as many boxes in the grid as there are statements. Each statement goes into one box. One continuum (e.g., right to left) indicates how positive or negative a person feels about the statement. The other continuum (e.g., up and down) indicates the strength of commitment to the positive or negative feelings about statements. The decision to place a statement in a box excludes placing any other statements in the same location. The raw data for Q-sort are the statements as they are organized in the grid.

In factor analysis, the researcher enters the data from many indicators, and the computer program produces a small number of factors. In Q-sort analysis, the researcher enters the grid location of statements, and the computer program identifies clusters or sets of people. Thus, Q-sort analysis shows which people organize statements in similar ways.

Q-sort analysis identifies how people organize their thinking on a topic on the basis of how they organized statements in the grid. It gives a researcher a map of major positions on an issue held by people. For example, 20 people place 45 statements about Arab-Israeli relations into a grid. The results of Q-sort analysis shows a researcher that the 20 people think about Arab-Israeli relations in one of three main ways: (1) a concern for Israeli security and fear of Arabs, (2) frustration with U.S. support for Israel and resentment toward Israel, or (3) a feeling that the world balance of power depends on what happens with Israel and its neighbors.

Cluster Analysis

As with factor and Q-sort analysis, cluster analysis is a sophisticated statistical technique that will be described only briefly and in general terms.[32]

Cluster analysis is a technique for organizing information or items measuring a variable. It statistically organizes relationships among a large number of items and places them into groups. The grouping or classification procedure uses statistical techniques like those in factor analysis and Q-sort analysis. The technique groups items by similarity and difference.

Factor analysis results tell a researcher how each item relates to one or more unobserved factors. Results look like a list of items with a number next to each; the number is the association between an item and a factor. Results from Q-sort analysis tell a researcher how people organize statements and show that people organize statements in a small number of ways. Results consist of the list of people with a number next to each person representing the degree to which a person followed one of a few patterns for organizing statements.

Cluster analysis results, by contrast, are in the form of a graph or picture, which resembles a tree diagram because it looks like the branches of a tree. Lines extend from a trunk, to large branches, to smaller branches, and so forth to tiny twigs. There are several levels of branching. The branching diagram shows a researcher which items are similar to each other and which are different. Each item in the cluster analysis represents a tiny twig, and the pattern of connections illustrates similarity and differences. Two items that share connections to a common nearby branch are more similar than two items that share no common branch until they reach the trunk.

For example, a researcher asks mental patients 556 true/false statements in a personality test. Cluster analysis organizes the 566 items into "twigs" of a tree diagram. There are four major levels of branching: twigs to small branches, small branches to medium branches, medium branches to large branches, and large branches to the trunk. At each level, the branching shows groups of items that represent psychological disorders, or shows how sets of psychological disorders form common psychotic types. A researcher examines the pattern of branching to see how the answers to items form groups and how the groups in turn can be grouped.

CONCLUSION

In this chapter, you learned about the process of quantitative, deductive measurement. You followed from a construct in theory through the processes of conceptualizing and operationalizing a variable to specific, concrete indicators. You also learned about two key ideas in measurement: reliability and validity. In addition, you saw how researchers apply the principles of measurement when they create indexes and scales, and you read about some major scales they use.

Beyond the core ideas of reliability and validity, you now know principles of good measurement: Create clear definitions for concepts, use multiple indicators, employ heterogeneous observation, and, as appropriate, weigh and standardize the data. These principles hold across all fields of study (e.g., family, criminology, inequality, race relations) and across the many quantitative research techniques (e.g., experiments, surveys).

Now that you understand how variables are measured or turned into numbers, you are ready to obtain people or units on which the variables will be measured. The next chapter explores experimental research. Experimental design illustrates how to use principles of causality and measurement.

As you are probably beginning to realize, a sound research project involves doing a good job in each phase of research. Serious mistakes or sloppiness in any one phase can do irreparable damage to the results, even if the other phases of the research project were conducted in a flawless manner.

KEY TERMS

auxiliary theory
bias
Bogardus Social Distance
   Scale
cluster analysis
conceptual definition
conceptual hypothesis
conceptualization
concurrent validity
construct validity
content validity
continuous variables
convergent validity
criterion validity
discrete variables
discriminant validity
empirical hypothesis
epistemic correlation
equivalence reliability
exhaustive attributes

external validity
face validity
factor analysis
Guttman scaling
heterogeneous observation
indicator
index
intercoder reliability
internal validity
interval-level measurement
law of comparative judgment
levels of measurement
Likert scale
measurement validity
multiple indicators
mutually exclusive attributes
nominal-level measurement
ordinal-level measurement
operational definition
operationalization

predictive validity
Q-sort analysis
ratio-level measurement
reliability
representative reliability
rules of correspondence
Semantic Differential
social indicator
split-half method
stability reliability
standardization
statistical validity
subpopulation analysis
test-retest method
Thurstone scaling
triangulation
unidimensionality
validity

REVIEW QUESTIONS

1. What are the three basic parts of measurement, and how do they fit together?
2. What is the difference between reliability and validity, and how do they complement each other?
3. What are ways to improve the reliability of a measure?
4. How do the levels of measurement differ from each other?
5. What are the differences between convergent, content, and concurrent validity? Can you have all three at once? Explain your answer.
6. Why are multiple indicators usually better than one indicator?
7. What is the difference between the logic of a scale and that of an index?
8. Why is unidimensionality an important characteristic of a scale?
9. What are advantages and disadvantages of weighting indexes?
10. How does standardization make comparisons easier?

NOTES

1. The terms *concept, construct*, and *idea* are used more or less interchangeably, but there are differences in meaning between them. An *idea* is any mental image, belief plan, or impression. It refers to any vague impression, opinion, or thought. A *concept* is a thought, a general notion, or a generalized idea about a class of objects. A *construct* is a thought that is systematically put together, an orderly arrangement of ideas, facts, and impressions. The term *construct* is used here because its emphasis is on taking vague concepts and turning them into systematically organized ideas.

2. Duncan (1984:220–239) presented some worthwhile cautions from a positivist approach on the issue of measuring anything.

3. See Grinnell (1987:5–18) for further discussion.

4. See Blalock (1982:25–27) and Costner (1985) on rules of correspondence or the auxiliary theories that connect abstract concept with empirical indicators. Also see Zeller and Carmines (1980:5) for a diagram that illustrates the place of the rules in the process of measurement. In his presidential address to the American Sociological Association in 1979, Hubert Blalock said, "I believe that the most serious and important problems that require our immediate and concerted attention are those of conceptualization and measurement" (Blalock, 1979a:882).

5. See Bailey (1984:1986) for a discussion of the three levels.

6. See Bohrnstedt (1992a) and Carmines and Zeller

(1979) for discussions of reliability and various types of reliability.

7. See Sullivan and Feldman (1979) on multiple indicators. A more technical discussion can be found in Herting (1985), Herting and Costner (1985), and Scott (1968).

8. See Carmines and Zeller (1979:17). For a discussion of the many types of validity, see Brinberg and McGrath (1982).

9. The epistemic correlation is discussed in Costner (1985) and in Zeller and Carmines (1980:50–51, 137–139).

10. Kidder (1982) discussed the issue of disagreements over face validity, such as acceptance of a measure's meaning by the scientific community, but not the subjects being studied.

11. This was adapted from Carmines and Zeller (1979:20–21).

12. For a discussion of types of criterion validity, see Carmines and Zeller (1979:17–19) and Fiske (1982) for construct validity.

13. See Cook and Campbell (1979) for elaboration.

14. See Borgatta and Bohrnstedt (1980) and Duncan (1984:119–155) for a discussion and critique of the topic of levels of measurement.

15. Johnson and Creech (1983) examined the measurement errors that occur when variables that are conceptualized as continuous are operationalized in a series of ordinal categories. They argued that errors

caused by using categories (compared to a precise continuous measure) are not serious if more than four categories and large samples are used.

16. See Blalock (1982) and Zeller and Carmines (1980) for more in-depth discussions of measurement theory in the social sciences.

17. See Carmines and Zeller (1979:13–15) and Nunally (1978).

18. For additional discussions of multiple indicators, see Blalock (1982:76–85, 265–272) and Sullivan and Feldman (1979).

19. For compilations of indexes and scales used in social research, see Brodsky and Smitherman (1983), Miller (1991), Robinson, Rusk, and Head (1972), Robinson and Shaver (1969), and Schuessler (1982).

20. For a discussion of weighted and unweighted index scores, see Nunnally (1967:534).

21. Feeling thermometers are discussed in Wilcox, Sigelman, and Cook (1989).

22. For more information on Likert scales, see Anderson, Basilevsky, and Hum (1983:252–255), Converse (1987:72–75), McIver and Carmines (1981:22–38), and Spector (1992).

23. Some researchers treat Likert scales as interval-level measures, but there is disagreement on this issue. Statistically, it makes little difference if the Likert scale has at least five response categories and an approximately even proportion of people answer in each category.

24. McIver and Carmines (1981:16–21) have an excellent discussion of Thurstone scaling. Also see discussions in Anderson et al. (1983:248–252), Converse (1987:66–77), and Edwards (1957). The example used here is partially borrowed from Churchill (1983: 249–254), who described the formula for scoring Thurstone scaling.

25. The social distance scale is described in Converse (1987:62–69). The most complete discussion can be found in Bogardus (1959).

26. The Semantic Differential is discussed in Nunnally (1978:535–543). Also see Heise (1965, 1970) on the analysis of scaled data.

27. See Guttman (1950).

28. See Bailey (1987:349–351) for a discussion of an improved method for determining scalability called Minimal Marginal Reproducibility (from Edwards 1957), which gives accurate measures of scalability. He also cited McConaghy (1975), who discusses techniques that improve upon the Minimal Marginal Reproducibility measure. Guttman scaling can involve more than yes/no choices and a large number of items, but the complexity increases quickly and computers are needed for Guttman scalogram analysis. A more elaborate and sophisticated discussion of Guttman scaling can be found in Anderson et al. (1983:256–260), Converse (1987:189–195), McIver and Carmines (1981:40–71), and Nunnally (1978:63–66). Clogg and Sawyer (1981) presented alternatives to Guttman scaling.

29. A discussion of social indicators can be found in Carley (1981). Also see Duncan (1984:233–235), Bauer (1966), Juster and Land (1981), Land (1992), Rossi and Gilmartin (1980), and Taylor (1980). Also see Ferriss (1988) on the using of social indicators for planning and social forecasting.

30. Factor analysis is discussed in Kim and Mueller (1978). For more technical discussions, see Bohrnstedt and Borgatta (1981) and Jackson and Borgatta (1981). Duncan (1984:209–216) offered a critique of factor analysis.

31. Q-sort analysis is discussed in Brown (1980, 1986), Nunnally (1967:544–558), and McKeown (1988).

32. Cluster analysis is introduced in Aldenderfer and Blashfield (1984). Also see Bailey (1975, 1983) and Lorr (1983) for social science applications.

RECOMMENDED READINGS

Blalock, Hubert M., Jr. (1979). Measurement and conceptualization problems: The major obstacle to integrating theory and research. *American Sociological Review*, 44:881–894. Though a bit technical at times, this is a comprehensive statement about measurement from a positivist approach. It addresses the question of how theory relates to measurement. It was Blalock's presidential address to the American Sociological Association. His 1982 book (see bib-

liography) expands on the ideas presented in this article.

Carley, Michael. (1981). *Social measurement and social indicators: Issues of policy and theory*. Boston: Allen and Unwin. This is a good introduction to the history, theory, and application of social indicators. The author confronts many of the difficult issues in social indicator research. The book includes discussion of quality-of-life and national social reporting indicators. Its comparison of British and U.S. research involving social movements adds a nice comparative perspective.

Carmines, Edward G., and Richard A. Zeller. (1979). *Reliability and validity assessment.* Beverly Hills, CA: Sage. This short (70-page) book condenses an influential book by Zeller and Carmines on measurement (see bibliography). It is a lucid introduction to measurement theory and includes excellent discussions of reliability and validity. The types and methods for measuring reliability are especially valuable.

Miller, Delbert C. (1991). *Handbook of research design and social measurement*, 5th ed. Newbury Park, CA: Sage. In addition to a short introduction to research design. Miller presents an extensive listing of scales and indexes that have been used in research. The listing includes references to where the scale or index was published and information on tests of its reliability and/or validity.

Schuessler, Karl. (1985). *Measuring social life feelings.* San Francisco: Jossey-Bass. The author surveyed the multiplicity of scales and measuring instruments for concepts such as morale, alienation, life satisfaction, anomie, and social isolation. He found many instances of the use of the same items in very different constructs. Schuessler reduced the number of different questions to 237 and used factor analysis to identify 17 factors that appear to summarize major dimensions of life satisfaction.

CHAPTER 8

EXPERIMENTAL RESEARCH

Experimentation, the principal scientific method to be emphasized here, involves at a simple level the comparison of groups or individuals who have been differentially exposed to changes in their environment.
—Leonard Saxe and Michelle Fine, *Social Experiments*, p. 45

INTRODUCTION AND SHORT HISTORY

In the previous chapters, you learned about the foundations of quantitative social research. In this chapter, you will learn how to conduct a particular type of quantitative research. We begin with experimental research. It is the easiest to grasp and is used across many other fields of science.

Experimental research builds on the principles of a positivist approach more directly than do the other research techniques.[1] Researchers in the natural sciences (e.g., chemistry and physics), related applied fields (e.g., agriculture, engineering, medicine), and the social sciences conduct experiments. The logic that guides an experiment on plant growth in biology or testing a metal in engineering is applied in experiments on human social behavior. Although it is most widely used in psychology, the experiment is found in education, criminal justice, journalism, marketing, nursing, political science, social work, and sociology. This chapter focuses first on the experiment conducted in a laboratory under controlled conditions, then looks at experiments conducted in the field.

The experiment's basic logic extends common-sense thinking. Common-sense experiments are less careful or systematic than scientifically based experiments. In commonsense language, *an experiment* means modifying something in a situation, then comparing an outcome to what existed without the modification. For example, I try to start my car. To my surprise, it does not start. I "experiment" by cleaning off the battery connections, then try to start it again. I modified something (cleaned the connections) and compared the outcome (whether the car started) to the previous situation (it did not start). I began with an implicit "hypothesis"—a buildup of crud on the connections is the reason the car is not starting, and once the crud is cleaned off, the car will start. This illustrates three things researchers do in experiments: (1) begin with a hypothesis, (2) modify something in a situation, and (3) compare outcomes with and without the modification.

Compared to the other social research techniques, experimental research is the strongest for testing causal relationships because the three conditions for causality (temporal order, association, no alternative explanations) are clearly met in experimental designs.

Research Questions Appropriate for an Experiment

The Issue of an Appropriate Technique.   Social researchers use different research techniques (e.g., experiments, surveys) because some research questions can be addressed with certain techniques but not with others. New researchers often ask which research technique best fits which problem. This is difficult to answer because there is no fixed match between problem and technique. The answer is: Make an informed judgment.

General guidelines exist for fitting techniques to problems. Beyond guidelines, you can develop judgment from reading research reports, understanding the strengths and weaknesses of different techniques, assisting more experienced researchers with their research, and gaining practical experience.

Research Questions for Experimental Research.
The logic of experimental design guides the types of research problems best addressed by experi-

ments. A crucial factor is that in experimental design, a researcher changes a situation and has control over the setting in which the change is introduced. Only those research problems that let a researcher manipulate conditions are appropriate for experimental research. For example, experimental research cannot answer problems such as: Do people who complete a college education increase their average annual income? Researchers cannot randomly assign thousands of people across the country to a college or noncollege group. Even when a whole nation is not involved, many situations cannot be controlled. For example, do people who have younger siblings (brothers and sisters) have better leadership skills than only children? Researchers cannot assign couples to groups and then force them to produce or not produce children so that they can examine leadership skills.

Social scientists are more limited than natural scientists in the degree to which they can intervene for research purposes. Social researchers are very creative in inventing treatments for independent variables (e.g., pressure to conform, anxiety, cooperation, high self-esteem), but they cannot manipulate or create many independent variables (e.g., sex, marital status, age, religious belief, level of income, parents' political affiliation, or size of community where raised). Researchers must decide which is most effective for answering the specific question, within practical and ethical limitations. For example, a research question is: Does fear of crime affect the behaviors of elderly people by motivating them to seek self-protection and security? An experimental researcher creates different levels of fear of crime among groups of elderly subjects. To create a fear of crime, he or she has subjects read about crimes, shows them films about crime, or places them in fear-inducing situations (e.g., in a locked room with a dangerous looking person who makes threatening statements). Next, the researcher measures whether the subjects act in self-protective ways (e.g., push a button to create a physical barrier between themselves and the dangerous person) or answer questions about hypothetical situations involving security in certain ways (e.g., plan to buy new locks).

Other techniques (e.g., survey research) can address the same issue. A survey researcher asks elderly people questions about how much they fear crime and what they have done for self-protection and security. The researcher measures fear by asking subjects to tell how much they already fear crime on the basis of their previous experiences.

A source of confusion is that researchers can use a prior fixed condition (e.g., age or sex) as a variable in experiments. For example, Spillers (1982) asked whether age affected a child's decision to play with a child who is disabled. Her subjects were 32 preschool and 32 third-grade children. She showed each subject four pairs of photos, each pair showing one child in a wheelchair and the other standing. The children in the photographs were mixed for physical attractiveness, age, and sex. Each subject was asked, "Which child would you like to play with?" Spillers found that more third-graders than preschool children accepted the child with disabilities. Spillers did not modify the independent variable—age—to find its effect on the dependent variable—playmate choice—but she manipulated the decision process and controlled the setting in which it occurred.

A Short History of the Experiment in Social Research

The experimental method was borrowed by the social sciences from the natural sciences, and began in psychology. It was not widely accepted in psychology until after 1900.[2]

Wilhelm M. Wundt (1832–1920), a German psychologist and physiologist, introduced the experimental method into psychology. During the late 1800s, Germany was the center of graduate education, and leading social scientists from around the world went to Germany to study. Wundt established a laboratory for experimentation in psychology that became a model for many other social researchers. By 1900, researchers at many U.S. and other universities established psychology laboratories to conduct experimental social research. The experiment replaced a more

philosophical, introspective, integrative approach that was closer to interpretive social science. For example, William James (1842–1910), the foremost U.S. philosopher and psychologist of the 1890s, did not use or embrace the experimental method.

From the turn of the century to the time of World War II, the experimental method was elaborated and became entrenched in social research. The method's widespread appeal was that it offered an objective, unbiased, scientific way to study human mental and social life at a time when the scientific study of social life was just gaining acceptance.

Four trends speeded the expansion of the experimental method in this period: the rise of behaviorism, the spread of quantification, various changes in research subjects, and practical applications.

Behaviorism is a school of psychology founded in the 1920s by the American John B. Watson (1878–1958) and extended by B. F. Skinner (1904–1990). It emphasized measuring observable behavior or outcomes of mental life and advocated the experimental method for conducting rigorous empirical tests of hypotheses. It became an influential, if not the dominant, school in American psychology.

Quantification, or measuring social phenomena with numbers, also grew between 1900 and 1940. Researchers reconceptualized social constructs so that they could be quantified, and other constructs (e.g., spirit, consciousness, will) were jettisoned from empirical research. An example is measuring mental ability by the IQ test. Originally developed by Alfred Binet (1857–1911), a Frenchman, the intelligence test was translated into English and revised by 1916. It was widely used, and the ability to express something as subjective as mental ability in a single score had public appeal as an objective way to rank and sort people. In fact, between the years of 1921 and 1936, over 5,000 articles were published on intelligence tests.[3] Many scaling and index techniques were developed in this period, and social researchers began to use applied statistics.

Early reports of empirical social research gave the names of the people who participated in research, and most early subjects were professional researchers. During the first half of the twentieth century, reports treated subjects anonymously and only reported the results of their actions. Subjects were increasingly college students or school children. These changes reflected an increasingly objective and distant relationship between the researcher and the people studied.

People increasingly used experimental methods for applied purposes. For example, intelligence testing was adopted by the U.S. Army during World War I to sort thousands of men into different positions. The leader of the "scientific management" movement, Frederick W. Taylor (1856–1915), advocated the use of the experimental method in factories and worked with management to modify factory conditions to increase worker productivity.

Through the 1950s and 1960s, researchers continued to use the experimental method. They became concerned with artifacts, or sources of alternative explanations that could slip into experimental design. They discovered new artifacts and created ways to reduce these possible sources of systematic error in experiments with new research designs and statistical procedures. Experiments became more logically rigorous, and by the 1970s, methodological criteria were increasingly used to evaluate research. A related trend that began in the 1960s was the increased use of deception and a concern with ethical issues. For example, a now common practice of debriefing did not come into use until the mid-1960s.[4] The experiment is still widely used because of its logical rigor and simplicity, consistency with positivist assumptions, and relatively low cost.

RANDOM ASSIGNMENT

Social researchers frequently want to compare. For example, a researcher has two groups of 15 students and wants to compare the groups on the basis of a key difference between them (e.g., a course that one group completed). Or a researcher has five groups of customers and wants to compare the groups on the basis of one characteristic (e.g., geographic location). The cliché, "compare apples to apples, don't compare apples to oranges," is not about fruit: it is about comparisons, and it means that a valid comparison depends on comparing things that are fundamentally alike. Random assignment facilitates comparison in experiments by creating similar groups.

When making comparisons, researchers want to compare cases that do not differ with regard to variables that offer alternative explanations. For example, a researcher compares two groups of students to determine the impact of completing a course. In order to be compared, the two groups must be similar in most respects except for taking the course. If the group that completed the course is also older than the group that did not, for example, the researcher cannot determine whether completing the course or being older accounts for differences between the groups.

Why Randomly Assign?

Random assignment is a method for assigning cases (e.g., individuals, organizations) to groups for the purpose of making comparisons. It is a way to divide or sort a collection of cases into two or more groups in order to increase one's confidence that the groups do not differ in a systematic way. It is a mechanical method; the assignment is automatic, and the researcher cannot make assignments on the basis of personal preference or the features of specific cases.

Random assignment is random in a statistical or mathematical sense, not in an everyday sense. In everyday speech, *random* means unplanned, haphazard, or accidental, but it has a specialized meaning in mathematics. In probability theory, *random* describes a process in which each case has a known chance of being selected. Random selection lets a researcher calculate the odds that a specific case will be sorted into one group over another. Thus, the selection process obeys mathematical laws, which makes precise calculations possible. For example, a random process is one in which all cases have an exactly equal chance of ending up in one or the other group.

The wonderful thing about a random process is that over many separate random occurrences, predictable things happen. Although the process is entirely due to chance and it is impossible to predict a specific outcome at a specific time, very accurate predictions are possible over many situations.

Random assignment or randomization is unbiased because a researcher's desire to confirm a hypothesis or a research subject's personal interests do not enter into the selection process. *Unbiased* does not mean that groups with identical characteristics are selected in each specific situation of random assignment. Instead, it says something close to that: The probability of selecting a case can be mathematically determined; and in the long run, the groups will be identical.

How to Randomly Assign

Random assignment is very simple in practice. A researcher begins with a collection of cases (individuals, organizations, or whatever the unit of analysis is), then divides it into two or more groups by a random process, such as asking people to count off, tossing a coin, or throwing dice. For example, a researcher wants to divide 32 people into two groups of 16. A random method is writing each person's name on a slip of paper, putting the slips in a hat, mixing the slips with eyes closed, then drawing the first 16 names for group 1 and the second 16 for group 2.

Because random assignment for a specific situation only gives probabilities, a specific situation can be unusual and the groups can differ. For example, it is possible, though extremely unlikely, that all cases with one characteristic will end up in one group (see the example in Box 8.1).

Matching versus Random Assignment

If the purpose of random assignment is to get two (or more) equivalent groups, would it not be simpler to match the characteristics of cases in each group? Some researchers match cases in groups on certain characteristics, such as age and sex. Matching is an alternative to random assignment, but it is an infrequently used one.

Matching presents a problem: What are the relevant characteristics to match on, and can one locate exact matches? Individual cases differ in thousands of ways, and the researcher cannot know which might be relevant. For example, a researcher compares two groups of 15 students. There are 8 males in one group, which means there should be 8 males in the other group. Two males in the first group are only children; one is from a divorced family, one from an intact family. One is tall, slender, and Jewish; the other is short, heavy, and Methodist. In order to match groups, does the researcher have to find a tall Jewish male only child from a divorced home and a short Methodist male only child from an intact home? The tall, slender, Jewish male only child is 22 years old and is studying to become a physician. The short, heavy Methodist male is 20 years old and wants to be an accountant. Does the researcher also need to match the age and career aspirations of the two males? True matching soon becomes an impossible task.

EXPERIMENTAL DESIGN LOGIC

The Language of Experiments

Experimental research has its own language or set of terms and concepts. You already encountered the basic ideas: random assignment, independent and dependent variables. In experimental research, the cases or people used in research projects and on whom variables are measured are called the *subjects*.

Parts of the Experiment. We can divide the experiment into seven parts. Not all experiments have all these parts, and some have all seven parts plus others. The following seven, to be discussed here, make up a true experiment:

1. Treatment or independent variable
2. Dependent variable
3. Pretest
4. Posttest
5. Experimental group
6. Control group
7. Random assignment

Box 8.1 _____

Example of Three Methods of Random Assignment to Two Groups

Step 1:   Begin with a collection of cases with various characteristics:

Here are 30 cases in a random order with characteristics A, B, or C (A, B, and C represent any characteristic (e.g., eye color, religion, race):

A B B C A C A B C A C B A C A B C A B C A C A A B B C A B C

Step 2:   Devise a mechanical procedure to select an equal number of cases into each group via a random process.

Random Selection Method #1:   Assign every other name to a group:

A B B C A C A B C A C B A C A B C A B C A C A A B B C A B C
1 2 1 2 1 2 1 2 1 2 1 2 1 2 1 2 1 2 1 2 1 2 1 2 1 2 1 2 1 2

OUTCOME OF METHOD 1

Group 1	Group 2
As 7	4
Bs 3	6
Cs 5	5

Random Selection Method #2:   Assign the first half to one group, the other half to a second group:

A B B C A C A B C A C B A C A B C A B C A C A A B B C A B C
1 1 1 1 1 1 1 1 1 1 1 1 1 1 1 2 2 2 2 2 2 2 2 2 2 2 2 2 2 2

OUTCOME OF METHOD 2

Group 1	Group 2
As 6	5
Bs 4	5
Cs 5	5

Random Selection Method #3:   Flip a fair coin. Heads goes to Group 1, tails goes to Group 2:

A B B C A C A B C A C B A C A B C A B C A C A A B B C A B C
H H T H T T H H T H T T T H T T H T H H H H T H T T H T T H

OUTCOME OF METHOD 3

Group 1	Group 2
As 5	6
Bs 3	6
Cs 7	3

Note: Group 1 and Group 2 were arbitrarily assigned, and one could reverse the order of 1 and 2 and get equivalent results.

_____

In most experiments, a researcher creates a situation or enters into an ongoing situation, then modifies it. The *treatment* (or the stimulus or manipulation) is what the researcher modifies. The term comes from medicine, in which a physician administers a treatment to patients; the physician intervenes in a physical or psychological condition to change it. It is the independent variable or a combination of independent variables. In earlier examples of measurement, a researcher developed a measurement instrument or indicator (e.g., a survey question), then applied it to a person or case. In experiments, researchers "measure" independent variables by creating a condition or situation. For example, the independent variable is "degree of fear or anxiety"; the levels are high fear and low fear. Instead of asking subjects whether they are fearful, experimenters put subjects into either a high-fear or a low-fear situation. They measure the independent variable by manipulating conditions so that some subjects feel a lot of fear and others feel little.

Researchers go to great lengths to create treatments. Some are as minor as giving different groups of subjects different instructions. Others can be as complex as putting subjects into situations with elaborate equipment, staged physical settings, or contrived social situations to manipulate what the subjects see or feel. Researchers want the treatment to have an impact and produce specific reactions, feelings, or behaviors.

For example, a mock jury decision is one type of a treatment. Johnson (1985) asked subjects to watch a videotape of a child-abuse trial about a man who brought his 2-year-old son to an emergency room with a skull fracture. The videotapes were the same, except that in one, the man's attorney argued that the father was a highly religious person who followed the word of God in the Bible in all family affairs. In the other videotape, no such statement was made. The dependent variable was a decision of guilty or innocent and a recommended sentence for guilty decisions. Contrary to common sense, Johnson found that subjects were more likely to find the religious defendant guilty and to recommend longer sentences.

Dependent variables or outcomes in experimental research are the physical conditions, social behaviors, attitudes, feelings, or beliefs of subjects that change in response to a treatment. Dependent variables can be measured by paper-and-pencil indicators, observation, interviews, or physiological responses (e.g., heartbeat, sweating palms). An example is a study by Stephens, Cooper, and Kinney (1985) on helping people who are disabled. In the experiment, subjects were 40 males and 40 females walking across a university campus, who encountered either a woman who was severely physically disabled in a wheelchair or a woman with no disabilities. The woman asked for help in finding a lost earring in a hallway. The dependent variable was the number of minutes the subject spent helping find the earring, as measured by an observer a short distance away who appeared to be reading a book.

Frequently, a researcher measures the dependent variable more than once during an experiment. The *pretest* is the measurement of the dependent variable prior to introduction of the treatment. The *posttest* is the measurement of the dependent variable after the treatment has been introduced into the experimental situation.

Experimental researchers often divide subjects into two or more groups for purposes of comparison. A simple experiment has two groups, only one of which receives the treatment. The *experimental group* is the group that receives the treatment or in which the treatment is present. The group that does not receive the treatment is called the *control group*. When the independent variable takes on many different values, more than one experimental group is used.

Steps in Conducting an Experiment. Following the basic steps of the research process, experimenters decide on a topic, narrow it into a testable research problem or question, then develop a hypothesis with variables. Once a researcher has the hypothesis, the steps of experimental research are clear.

A crucial early step is to plan a specific experimental design (to be discussed). The researcher decides the number of groups to use, how and when to create treatment conditions, the number of times to measure the dependent variable, and what the groups of subjects will experience from beginning to end. He or she also develops measures of the dependent variable and pilot tests the experiment (see Box 8.2).

The experiment itself begins after a researcher locates subjects and randomly assigns them to groups. Subjects are given precise, preplanned instructions. Next, the researcher measures the dependent variable in a pretest before the treatment. One group is then exposed to the treatment. Finally, the researcher measures the dependent variable in a posttest. He or she also interviews subjects about the experiment before they leave. The researcher records measures of the dependent variable and examines the results for each group to see whether the hypothesis receives support.

Control in Experiments. Control is crucial in experimental research.[5] A researcher wants to control all aspects of the experimental situation to isolate the effects of the treatment and eliminate alternative explanations. Aspects of an experimental situation that are not controlled by the researcher are alternatives to the treatment for change in the dependent variable and undermine his or her attempt to establish causality.

Experimental researchers use deception to control the experimental setting. *Deception* occurs when the researcher intentionally misleads subjects through written or verbal instructions, the actions of others, or aspects of the setting. It may involve the use of *confederates* or stooges—people who pretend to be other subjects or bystanders but who actually work for the researcher and deliberately mislead subjects. Through deception, the researcher tries to control what the subjects see and hear and what they believe is occurring. For example, a researcher's instructions falsely lead subjects to believe that they are participating in a study about group cooperation. In fact, the experiment is about male/female verbal interaction, and what subjects say is being secretly tape recorded. Deception lets the researcher control the subjects' definition of the situation. It prevents them from altering their cross-sex verbal behavior because they are unaware of the true research topic. By focusing their attention on a false topic, the researcher induces the unaware subjects to act "naturally." For realistic deception, researchers may invent false treatments and dependent variable measures to keep subjects unaware of the true ones. The use of deception in experiments raises ethical issues (to be discussed).

Box 8.2 _____

Steps in Conducting an Experiment

1. Begin with a straightforward hypothesis that is appropriate for experimental research.
2. Decide on an experimental design that will test the hypothesis within practical limitations.
3. Decide how to introduce the treatment or create a situation that induces the independent variable.
4. Develop a valid and reliable measure of the dependent variable.
5. Set up an experimental setting and conduct a pilot test of the treatment and dependent variable measures.
6. Locate appropriate subjects or cases.
7. Randomly assign subjects to groups (if random assignment is used in the chosen research design) and give careful instructions.
8. Gather data for the pretest measure of the dependent variable for all groups (if a pretest is used in the chosen design).
9. Introduce the treatment to the experimental group only (or to relevant groups if there are multiple experimental groups) and monitor all groups.
10. Gather data for posttest measure of the dependent variable.
11. *Debrief* the subjects by informing them of the true purpose and reasons for the experiment. Ask subjects what they thought was occurring. Debriefing is crucial when subjects have been deceived about some aspect of the experiment.
12. Examine data collected and make comparisons between different groups. Where appropriate, use statistics and graphs to determine whether or not the hypothesis is supported.

Design Notation

Experiments can be designed in many ways. *Design notation* is a shorthand system for symbolizing the parts of experimental design.[6] Once you learn design notation, you will find it easier to think about and compare designs. For example, design notation expresses a complex, paragraph-long description of the parts of an experiment in five or six symbols arranged in two lines. It uses the following symbols: O = observation of dependent variable; X = treatment, independent variable; R = random assignment. The Os are numbered with subscripts from left to right based on time order. Pretests are O_1, posttests O_2. When the independent variable has more than two levels, the Xs are numbered with subscripts to distinguish among them. Symbols are in time order from left to right. The R is first, followed by the pretest, the treatment, and then the posttest. Symbols are arranged in rows, with each row representing a group of subjects. For example, an experiment with three groups has an R (if random assignment is used), followed by three rows of Os and Xs. The rows are on top of each other because the pretests, treatment, and posttest occur in each group at about the same time. Table 8.1 gives the notation for many standard experimental designs.

TABLE 8.1   Summary of Experimental Designs with Notation

NAME OF DESIGN	DESIGN NOTATION
Classical experimental design	R $\quad$ O X O $\quad\quad$ O $\quad\quad$ O
Preexperimental Designs	
One-shot case study	X O
One-group pretest-posttest	O X O
Static group comparison	X O X O
Quasi-Experimental Designs	
Two-group posttest only	R $\quad$ X $\quad\quad$ O $\quad\quad\quad\quad$ O
Interrupted time series	O O $\quad$ O O X O O O
Equivalent time series	O X $\quad$ O X $\quad$ O X O X O
Latin square designs	R $\quad$ O X_a O X_b O X_c O O X_b O X_a O X_c O O X_c O X_b O X_a O O X_a O X_c O X_b O O X_b O X_c O X_a O O X_c O X_a O X_b O
Solomon four-group design	R $\quad$ O $\quad\quad$ X $\quad\quad$ O $\quad\quad$ O $\quad\quad\quad\quad$ O $\quad\quad\quad\quad\quad$ X $\quad\quad$ O $\quad\quad\quad\quad\quad\quad\quad\quad$ O
Factorial designs	R $\quad$ X_1 Z_1 O X_1 Z_2 O X_2 Z_1 O X_2 Z_2 O

Types of Design

Researchers combine parts of an experiment (e.g., pretests, control groups) together into an *experimental design*. For example, some designs lack pretests, some do not have control groups, and others have many experimental groups. Certain widely used standard designs have names.

You should learn the standard designs for two reasons. First, in research reports, researchers give the name of a standard design instead of describing it. When reading reports, you will be able to understand the design of the experiment if you know the standard designs. Second, the standard designs illustrate common ways to combine design parts. You can use them for experiments you conduct or create your own variations.

The designs are illustrated with two examples. In the first, a researcher wants to find out whether learning is faster if accompanied by quiet classical music or by silence. The experiment involves having rats run a maze. The treatment is classical music, and the dependent variable is the speed of completing the maze. In the second example, the researcher wants to find out whether students are more accepting of violence after viewing a horror film. The treatment is a film with violence and gore, and the dependent variable is the subjects' attitudes toward violence.

Classical Experimental Design. All designs are variations of the *classical experimental design*, the type of design discussed so far, which has random assignment, a pretest and a posttest, an experimental group, and a control group. In example 1, the researcher randomly divides rats into two groups and measures their speed. Rats run the maze and the researcher records speeds; one group hears music and the other does not. In example 2, the researcher randomly divides students into two groups and measures their attitudes with a questionnaire. One group watches a violent horror film, the other a nonhorror film; the researcher then measures attitudes again.

Preexperimental Designs. Some designs lack random assignment and are compromises or shortcuts. These *preexperimental designs* are used in situations where it is difficult to use the classical design. They have weaknesses that make inferring a causal relationship more difficult.

One-Shot Case Study Design. Also called the one-group posttest-only design, the *one-shot case study design* has only one group, a treatment, and a posttest. Because there is only one group, there is no random assignment. In example 1, the researcher puts a group of rats in a maze with classical music playing and records their speed. In example 2, the researcher shows a group of students a horror film, then measures their attitudes with a questionnaire. A weakness of this design is that it is difficult to say for sure that the treatment caused the dependent variable. If subjects were the same before and after the treatment, the researcher would not know it.

One-Group Pretest-Posttest Design. This design has one group, a pretest, a treatment, and a posttest. It lacks a control group and random assignment. In example 1, the researcher measures the speed of a group of rats, has them run a maze while he or she plays music, and measures their speed again. In example 2, the researcher gives a group of students an attitude questionnaire to complete, shows a horror film, then has them complete another questionnaire. This is an improvement over the one-shot case study because the researcher measures the dependent variable both before and after the treatment. But it lacks a control group. The researcher cannot know whether something other than the treatment occurred between the pretest and the posttest to cause the outcome.

Static Group Comparison. Also called the posttest-only nonequivalent group design, *static group comparison* has two groups, a posttest, and treatment. It lacks random assignment and a pretest. In example 1, the researcher has two groups of rats. One group runs a maze with music, the other without music. He or she measures each group's speed. In example 2, the researcher lets students form two groups themselves. He or she shows one group a horror film and the other a nonhorror film. Both groups then complete the questionnaire. A weakness is that any posttest outcome difference between the groups could be due to group differences prior to the experiment instead of to the treatment.

A static group comparison experiment is Shively's (1992) study on perceptions of Western films among Native Americans and Anglos. Her hypothesis was that a person's ethnically based cultural background influences what that person sees or enjoys in a film with relevant themes. Shively created matched samples of 20 Native American males and 20 Anglo males (European ancestry). The subjects lived in a town of about 1,200 on an Indian reservation in the western United States. The groups were matched on income, education, employment status, occupation, and age. They ranged in age from 36 to 64 years. Both groups watched *The Searchers*, a 1956 western film starring John Wayne that was a top-grossing film in the 1950s. It shows the standard "cowboy and Indian" conflict. The film was watched in private homes with a group of five ethnically similar male friends.

Shively measured views on the film (the dependent variable) with a written questionnaire and group interview. She found that both groups liked the film, enjoyed its "action," and most identified with one of the lead "cowboy" characters. No one favored the Native Americans, who were portrayed in the film with negative stereotypes as violent savages. The Native American subjects identified with cowboys in the film and saw them as similar to contemporary Native Americans. A difference was that the Native American subjects enjoyed the landscape scenery and the portrayal of an idealized cowboy way of life, which they saw as a myth or fantasy. By contrast, the Anglos saw the film as authentic history; they took it to be reality. Another difference was that the Native American subjects rated bravery and toughness as making a good hero in a Western. Anglos did not rate these high, but rated honesty and intelligence as top characteristics. Shively indirectly manipulated the independent variable, which was the subject's ethnicity combined with viewing the film. She used two groups, but no pretest, and substituted matching for randomization.

Quasi-Experimental and Special Designs. These designs, like the classical design, make identifying a causal relationship more certain than do preexperimental designs. *Quasi-experimental designs* help researchers test for causal relationships in a variety of situations where the classical design is difficult or inappropriate. They are called *quasi* because they are variations of the classical experimental design. Some have randomization but lack a pretest, some use more than two groups, others substitute many observations of one group over time for a control group. In general, the researcher has less control over the independent variable than in the classical design.

Two-Group Posttest-Only Design. This is identical to the static group comparison, with one exception: the groups are randomly assigned. It has all the parts of the classical design except a pretest. The random assignment reduces the chance that the groups differed before the treatment, but without a pretest, a researcher cannot be as certain that the groups began the same on the dependent variable. For example, Johnson and Johnson (1985) used a two-group posttest-only design. In the experiment, sixth-grade students were randomly assigned to one of two conditions: work groups in which points were awarded for how well the entire class learned material, or groups in which each group competed against others for points. All groups were mixed by race, sex, and ability level. Several dependent variables were measured, including academic achievement, cooperation across racial groups, and attitude toward others. The dependent variables were only measured after working in groups on an instruction unit for 10 days. The main result was that cooperative groups were more likely to promote cooperation and friendship across racial lines.

Interrupted Time Series. In an *interrupted time series* design, a researcher uses one group and makes multiple pretest measures before and after the treatment. For example, after remaining level for many years, in 1979, cigarette taxes jumped 35 percent. Taxes remained relatively constant for the next 10 years. The hypothesis is that increases in taxes lower cigarette consumption. A researcher plots the rate of cigarette consumption for 1970 through 1990. The researcher notes that cigarette consumption was level during the nine years prior to the new taxes, then dropped in 1979 and stayed about the same for the next 10 years.

Equivalent Time Series. An *equivalent time series* is another one-group design that extends over a time period. Instead of one treatment, it has a pretest, then a treatment and posttest, then treatment and posttest, then treatment and posttest, and so on. For example, people who drive motorcycles were not required to wear helmets before 1975, when a law was passed requiring helmets. In 1981, the law was repealed because of pressure from motorcycle clubs. The helmet law was reinstated in 1989. The researcher's hypothesis is that wearing protective helmets results in a lower number of head injury deaths in accidents. The researcher plots head injury death rates in motorcycle accidents over time. He or she finds the rate was very high prior to 1975, dropped sharply between 1975 and 1981, then rose to pre-1975 levels between 1981 and 1989, then dropped again from 1989 to the present.

Latin Square Designs. Researchers interested in how several treatments given in different sequences or time orders affect a dependent variable can use a *Latin square design*. For example, a geography instructor has three units to teach students: map reading, using a compass, and the longitude/latitude (LL) system. The units can be taught in any order, but the teacher wants to know which order most helps students learn. In one class, students first learn to read maps, then how to use a compass, then the LL system. In another class, using a compass comes first, then map reading, then the LL system. In a third class, the instructor first teaches the LL system, then compass usage, and ends with map reading. The teacher gives tests after each unit, and students take a comprehensive exam at the end of the term. The students were randomly assigned to classes, so the instructor can see whether presenting units in one sequence or another resulted in improved learning.

Solomon Four-Group Design. A researcher may believe that the pretest measure has an influence on the treatment or dependent variable. A pretest can sometimes sensitize subjects to the treatment or improve their performance on the posttest (see the discussion of testing effect to come). Richard L. Solomon developed the *Solomon four-group design* to address the issue of pretest effects. It combines the classical experimental design with the two-group posttest-only design and randomly assigns subjects to one of four groups. For example, a mental health worker wants to determine whether a new training method improves clients' coping skills. The worker measures coping skills with a 20-minute test of reactions to stressful events. Because the clients might learn coping skills from taking the test itself, a Solomon four-group design is used. The mental health worker randomly divides clients into four groups. Two groups receive the pretest; one of them gets the new training method and the other gets the old method. Another two groups receive no pretest; one of them gets the new method and the other the old method. All four groups are given the same posttest and the posttest results are compared. If the two treatment (new method) groups have similar results, and the two control (old method) groups have similar results, then the mental health worker knows pretest learning is not a problem. If the two groups with a pretest (one treatment, one control) differ from the two groups without a pretest, then the worker concludes that the pretest itself may have an effect on the dependent variable.

Factorial Designs. Sometimes, a research question suggests looking at the simultaneous effects of more than one independent variable. A *factorial design* uses two or more independent variables in combination. Every combination of the categories in variables (sometimes called *factors*) is examined. When each variable contains several categories, the number of combinations grows very quickly. The treatment or manipulation is not each independent variable; rather, it is each combination of the categories. For example, a researcher examines the productivity of work groups. The research question is: Does productivity vary under different combinations of group cooperation and stress? The independent variables are "level of cooperation" and "degree of stress," and the dependent variable is "productivity." The level of cooperation has two categories, cooperative and noncooperative; the degree of stress has three categories, high, medium, and low. There are six combinations of categories for the two variables (see Box 8.3).

The treatments in a factorial design can have two kinds of effects on the dependent variable: main effects and interaction effects. Only *main effects* are present in one-factor or single-treatment designs. In a factorial design, specific combinations of independent variable categories can also have an effect. They are called *interaction effects* because the categories in a combination interact to produce an effect beyond that of each variable alone. For example, Bardack and McAndrew (1985) wanted to determine the effects of physical attractiveness and appropriate dress on the decision to hire someone. They had six photographs of females with either high, average, or low attractiveness and appropriate or inappropriate clothing. Subjects saw one of the six photographs with identical resumés and were asked to decide whether to hire the person for an entry-level managerial position in a major corporation. Both variables affected the decision to hire; that is, subjects were more likely to hire attractive and appropriately dressed people. In addition to these main effects, the experimenters found interaction effects; attractive and well-dressed women were much more likely to be hired than would be expected as a result of either dress or appearance alone. Combined, the two factors gave an extra boost to the hiring decision, with physical attractiveness having a stronger effect.

The effects can be shown in the example of the impact of cooperation and stress on the productivity of five-person work groups. A researcher measures productivity by the percentage of a complicated jigsaw puzzle completed in two hours. There is a separate group for each combination, so the researcher computes the number of groups by multiplying the number of levels or categories in each variable. The stress variable has three levels and the cooperation variable two levels, so the re-

searcher uses six groups, one for each combination (see Box 8.3).

The researcher pays subjects in the cooperative groups equally by dividing the reward by five. The subjects in competitive groups are paid a percentage of the group reward based on the number of pieces each one correctly places. In the low-stress situation, the researcher gives the group one dollar for each one percent of the puzzle completed in two hours, up to $100. In the medium-stress situation, he or she uses the same pay system but adds a $50 bonus if the puzzle is completed in one hour. In the high-stress condition, he or she pays the group $100 for a completed puzzle and nothing if it is incomplete, and he or she also doubles the reward to $200 if the group completes the puzzle in one hour.

The main effect for the cooperation factor is that cooperative groups (no matter what the stress level) have higher productivity than the competitive groups. The main effect for the stress factor is that productivity rises as stress increases, whether or not the groups are cooperative. The left-hand graph in Box 8.3 shows main effects. It suggests that for each level of stress, cooperative groups outperform competitive groups, and for both groups, productivity is higher as the level of stress goes up.

The researcher hypothesizes interaction effects—that is, that specific combinations of the two factors produce specific effects on the dependent variable. For example, he or she finds that cooperative groups work best in high-stress situations, competitive groups best in low-stress situations, and both types of groups equally under medium levels of stress (see the right-hand graph in Box 8.3).

Researchers discuss factorial design in a shorthand way. A "two by three factorial design" is written 2×3. It means that there are two treatments, with two categories in one and three categories in the other. A $2 \times 3 \times 3$ design means that there are three independent variables, one with two categories and two with three categories each.

Valentine-French and Radtke (1989) used a $2 \times 2 \times 3$ factorial design to study the effect of victim reaction to sexual harassment blame. The subjects were 120 male and 120 female undergraduate volunteers from the University of Calgary. The researchers operationalized the

Box 8.3 _____

Example of Factorial Design with Two Variables

LEVEL OF COOPERATION		DEGREE OF STRESS		
		Low	Medium	High
Competitive		Group 1	Group 2	Group 3
Cooperative		Group 4	Group 5	Group 6

Group Number			Design Notation		
1			X_1	Z_1	O
2			X_1	Z_2	O
3		R	X_1	Z_3	O
4			X_2	Z_1	O
5			X_2	Z_2	O
6			X_2	Z_3	O

Where:
X_1 = noncooperative group, X_2 = cooperative group
Z_1 = low stress, Z_2 = medium stress, Z_3 = high stress

GRAPHS PLOTTING HYPOTHETICAL RESULTS

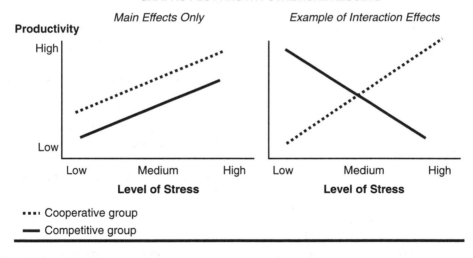

Main Effects Only

Example of Interaction Effects

Productivity (High–Low) vs. Level of Stress (Low, Medium, High)

•••• Cooperative group
▬ Competitive group

independent variable as an audiotaped vignette in which a professor guaranteed a good grade to a student if she or he was willing to cooperate, permitted caressing of the student's shoulder, and let the professor kiss her or him on the cheek. The experimenters varied the situation by having the student victim be male or female and by using one of three endings: the victim blamed his or her own behavior for the incident, blamed the professor, or gave no reaction. Thus, there were six combinations of victim gender and endings.

The subjects did not know the purpose of the study and listened to the vignette alone. The experimenters measured various background characteristics of the subjects with a questionnaire, as well as the main dependent variable—attribution of blame, or who was at fault. They operationalized the variable as an eight-item index measured with a 7-point Likert scale. Valentine-French and Radtke found that women were more likely to label the incident as sexual harassment and blame the professor. Both genders were more likely to blame a female victim. Male subjects, more than females, blamed the victim when the victim made a statement of self-blame. This was a $2 \times 2 \times 3$ factorial design because three independent variables were examined: the subject's gender, the victim's gender, and the victim's reactions.

INTERNAL AND EXTERNAL VALIDITY

The Logic of Internal Validity

Internal validity means the ability to eliminate alternative explanations of the dependent variable. Variables, other than the treatment, that affect the dependent variable are threats to internal validity. They threaten the researcher's ability to say that the treatment was the true causal factor producing change in the dependent variable. Thus, the logic of internal validity is to rule out variables other than the treatment by controlling experimental conditions and through experimental designs. Next, we examine major threats to internal validity.

Threats to Internal Validity

The following are 10 common threats to internal validity.[7]

Selection Bias.   *Selection bias* is the threat that subjects will not form equivalent groups. It is a problem in designs without random assignment. It occurs when subjects in one experimental group have a characteristic that affects the dependent variable. For example, in an experiment on physical aggressiveness, the treatment group unintentionally contains subjects who are football, rugby, and hockey players, whereas the control group is made up of musicians, chess players, and painters. Another example is an experiment on the ability of people to dodge heavy traffic. All subjects assigned to one group come from rural areas, and all subjects in the other grew up in large cities. An examination

of pretest scores helps a researcher detect this threat, because no group differences are expected.

History.   This is the threat that an event unrelated to the treatment will occur during the experiment and influence the dependent variable. *History effects* are more likely in experiments that continue over a long time period. For example, halfway through a two-week experiment to evaluate subject attitudes toward space travel, a spacecraft explodes on the launch pad, killing the astronauts. The history effect can occur in the cigarette tax example discussed earlier (see the discussion of interrupted time series design). If a public antismoking campaign or reduced cigarette advertising also began in 1979, it would be hard to say that higher taxes caused less smoking.

Maturation.   This is the threat that some biological, psychological, or emotional process within the subjects and separate from the treatment will change over time. *Maturation* is more common in experiments over long time periods. For example, during an experiment on reasoning ability, subjects become bored and sleepy and, as a result, score lower. Another example is an experiment on the styles of children's play between grades 1 and 6. Play styles are affected by physical, emotional, and maturation changes that occur as the children grow older, instead of or in addition to the effects of a treatment. Designs with a pretest and control group help researchers determine whether maturation or history effects are present, because both experimental and control groups will show similar changes over time.

Testing.   Sometimes, the pretest measure itself affects an experiment. This *testing effect* threatens internal validity because more than the treatment alone affects the dependent variable. The Solomon four-group design helps a researcher detect testing effects. For example, a researcher gives students an examination on the first day of class. The course is the treatment. He or she tests learning by giving the same exam on the last day of class. If subjects remember the pretest questions and this affects what they learned (i.e., paid attention to) or how they answered questions on the posttest, a testing effect is present. If testing effects occur, a researcher cannot say that the treatment alone has affected the dependent variable.

Instrumentation. This threat is related to stability reliability. It occurs when the *instrument* or dependent variable measure changes during the experiment. For example, in a weight-loss experiment, the springs on the scale weaken during the experiment, giving lower readings in the posttest. Another example might have occurred in an experiment by Bond and Anderson (1987) on the reluctance to transmit bad news. The experimenters asked subjects to tell another person the results of an intelligence test and varied the test results to be either well above or well below average. The dependent variable was the length of time it took to tell the test taker the results. Some subjects were told that the session was being videotaped. During the experiment, the video equipment failed to work for one subject. If it had failed to work for more than one subject or had worked for only part of the session, the experiment would have had instrumentation problems. (By the way, subjects took longer to deliver bad news only if they thought they were doing so publicly—that is, being videotaped.)

Mortality. *Mortality*, or attrition, arises when some subjects do not continue throughout the experiment. Although the word *mortality* means death, it does not necessarily mean that subjects have died. If a subset of subjects leaves partway through an experiment, a researcher cannot know whether the results would have been different if they had stayed. For example, a researcher begins a weight-loss program with 50 subjects. At the end of the program, 30 remain, each of whom lost 5 pounds with no side effects. The 20 who left could have differed from the 30 who stayed, changing the results. Maybe the program was effective for those who left, and they withdrew after losing 25 pounds. Or perhaps the program made subjects sick and forced them to quit. Researchers should notice and report the number of subjects in each group during pretests and posttests to detect this threat to internal validity.

Statistical Regression. *Statistical regression* is not easy to grasp intuitively. It is a problem of extreme values or a tendency for random errors to move group results toward the average. It can occur in two ways.

One situation arises when subjects are unusual with regard to the dependent variable. Because they begin as unusual or extreme, subjects are unlikely to respond further in the same direction. For example, a researcher wants to see whether violent films make people act violently. He or she chooses a group of violent criminals from a high-security prison, gives them a pretest, shows violent films, then administers a posttest. To the researcher's shock, the criminals are slightly less violent after the film, whereas a control group of nonprisoners who did not see the film are slightly more violent than before. Because the violent criminals began at an extreme, it is unlikely that a treatment could make them more violent; by random chance alone, they appear less extreme when measured a second time.[8]

A second situation involves a problem with the measurement instrument. If many subjects score very high (at the ceiling) or very low (at the floor) on a variable, random chance alone will produce a change between the pretest and the posttest. For example, a researcher gives 80 subjects a test, and 75 get perfect scores. He or she then gives a treatment to raise scores. Because so many subjects already had perfect scores, random errors will reduce the group average because those who got perfect scores can randomly move in only one direction—to get some answers wrong. An examination of scores on pretests will help researchers detect this threat to internal validity.

Diffusion of Treatment or Contamination. *Diffusion of treatment* is the threat that subjects in different groups will communicate with each other and learn about the other's treatment. Researchers avoid it by isolating groups or having subjects promise not to reveal anything to others who will become subjects. For example, subjects participate in a day-long experiment on a new way to memorize words. During a break, treatment group subjects tell those in the control group about the new way to memorize, which control group subjects then use. A researcher needs outside information such as postexperiment interviews with subjects to detect this threat.

Compensatory Behavior. Some experiments provide something of value to one group of subjects but not to another, and the difference becomes known. The inequality may produce pressure to reduce differences, competitive rivalry between groups, or resentful demoralization. All these types of *compensatory behavior* can affect the dependent variable in addition to the treatment. For example, one school system receives a treatment (longer lunch breaks) to produce gains in learning. Once the inequality is known, subjects in the control group demand equal treatment and work extra hard to learn and overcome the inequality. Smith and Glass (1987:136) called this the *John Henry effect*. Another group becomes demoralized by the unequal treatment and withdraws from learning. It is difficult to detect this threat unless outside information is used (see the earlier discussion of diffusion of treatment).

Experimenter Expectancy. Although it is not always considered a traditional internal validity problem, the experimenter's behavior, too, can threaten causal logic.[9] A researcher may threaten internal validity, not by purposefully unethical behavior but by indirectly communicating *experimenter expectancy* to subjects. Researchers may be highly committed to the hypothesis and indirectly communicate the hypothesis or desired findings to subjects. For example, a researcher studying reactions toward the disabled deeply believes that females are more sensitive toward the disabled than males are. Through eye contact, tone of voice, pauses, and other nonverbal communication, the researcher unconsciously encourages female subjects to report positive feelings toward the disabled; the researcher's nonverbal behavior is the opposite for male subjects.

Here is a way to detect experimenter expectancy. A researcher hires assistants and teaches them experimental techniques. The assistants train subjects and test their learning ability. The researcher gives the assistants fake transcripts and records showing that subjects in one group are honor students and the others are failing, although in fact the subjects are identical. Experimenter expectancy is present if the fake honor students, as a group, do much better than the fake failing students.

The *double-blind experiment* is designed to control researcher expectancy. In it, people who have direct contact with subjects do not know the details of the hypothesis or the treatment. It is *double* blind because both the subjects and those in contact with them are blind to details of the experiment (see Figure 8.1). For example, a researcher wants to see if a new drug is effective. Using pills of three colors—green, yellow, and pink—the researcher puts the new drug in the yellow pill, puts an old drug in the pink one, and makes the green pill a *placebo*—a false treatment that appears to be real (e.g., a sugar pill without any physical effects). Assistants who give the pills and record the effects do not know which color contains the new drug. Only another person who does not deal with subjects directly knows which colored pill contains the drug and examines the results.

External Validity and Field Experiments

Even if an experimenter eliminates all concerns about internal validity, external validity remains a potential problem. *External validity* is the ability to generalize experimental findings to events and settings outside the experiment itself. If a study lacks external validity, its findings hold true only in experiments, making them useless to both basic and applied science. In this section, we look at types of external validity and factors that influence it.

Realism. Are experiments realistic? There are two types of realism to consider.[10] *Experimental realism* is the impact of an experimental treatment or setting on subjects; it occurs when subjects are caught up in the experiment and are truly influ-

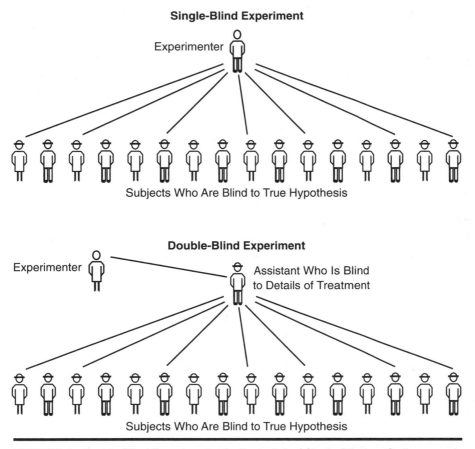

FIGURE 8.1   Double-Blind Experiments: An Illustration of Single-Blind, or Ordinary, and Double-Blind Experiments

enced by it. It is weak if subjects remain unaffected by the treatment, which is why researchers go to great lengths to create realistic conditions. As Aronson and Carlsmith (1968:25) noted,

> *All experimental procedures are "contrived" in the sense that they are invented. Indeed, it can be said that the art of experimentation rests primarily on the skill of the investigator to judge the procedure which is the more accurate realization of his conceptual variable and has the greatest impact and the more credibility for the subject.*

Mundane realism asks: Is the experiment like the real world? For example, a researcher studying learning has subjects memorize four-letter non-

sense syllables. Mundane realism would be stronger if he or she had subjects learn factual information used in real life instead of something invented for an experiment alone.

Mundane realism most directly affects external validity—the ability to generalize from experiments to the real world.[11] Two aspects of experiments can be generalized. One is from the subjects to other people. If the subjects are college students, can the researcher generalize results to the entire population, most of whom are not college students? Another aspect is generalizing from an artificial treatment to everyday life. For example, can one generalize from subjects watching a two-hour horror movie in a classroom to the impact of watching violent television programs over many years?

Reactivity.   Subjects may react differently in an experiment than they would in real life because they know they are part of a study; this is called *reactivity.* The *Hawthorne effect* is a specific kind of reactivity.[12] The name comes from a series of experiments by Elton Mayo at the Hawthorne, Illinois, plant of Westinghouse Electric during the 1920s and 1930s. Researchers modified many aspects of working conditions (e.g., lighting, time for breaks) and measured productivity. They discovered that productivity rose after each modification, no matter what it was. This curious result occurred because the workers did not respond to the treatment, but to the additional attention they received from being part of the experiment and knowing that they were being watched. Later research questioned whether this occurred, but the name is still used for an effect from the attention of researchers. A related effect is the effect of something new, which may wear off over time. Smith and Glass (1987:148) have called this the *novelty effect.*

Demand characteristics are another type of reactivity. Subjects may pick up clues about the hypothesis or goal of an experiment, and they may change their behavior to what they think is demanded of them (i.e., support the hypothesis) in order to please the researcher. For example, Chebat and Picard (1988) wanted to see whether people are more persuaded by one-sided (showing only positive features) versus two-sided (showing both positive features and limitations) advertisements. They created professional advertisements for a new soap and a car, with a one-sided and a two-sided advertisement for each. They presented the advertisements to 434 undergraduates at the University of Québec at Montréal who were asked to complete questionnaires with eight Likert-type questions on the acceptance of the advertising message. They stated (1988:356), "To avoid any potential bias or experimental 'demand' that the presence of the researchers might introduce. . . , the questionnaires were administered by graduate research assistants."

A last type of reactivity is the *placebo effect,* observed when subjects are given the placebo but respond as if they had received the real treatment. For example, in an experiment on stopping smoking, subjects are given either a drug to reduce their dependence on nicotine or a placebo. If subjects who received the placebo also stop smoking, then participating in an experiment and taking something that subjects believed would help them quit smoking had an effect. The subjects' belief in the placebo alone affected the dependent variable.

Field Experiments.   This chapter has focused on experiments conducted under the highly controlled conditions of a laboratory. Experiments are also conducted in real-life or field settings. In field settings, a researcher has less control over the experimental conditions. The amount of control varies on a continuum. At one end is the highly controlled *laboratory experiment,* which takes place in a specialized setting or laboratory; at the opposite end is the *field experiment,* which takes place in the "field"—in natural settings such as a subway car, a liquor store, or a public sidewalk. Subjects in field experiments are usually unaware that they are involved in an experiment and react in a natural way. For example, researchers have had a confederate fake a heart attack on a subway car to see how the bystanders react.[13]

A dramatic example is a field experiment by Harari, Harari, and White (1985) on whether a male passerby will attempt to stop an attempted rape. In this experiment, conducted at San Diego State University, an attempted rape was staged on a somewhat isolated campus path in the evening. The staged attack was clearly visible to unsuspecting male subjects who approached alone or in groups of two or three. In the attack, a female student was grabbed by a large man hiding in the bushes. As the man pulled her away and tried to cover her mouth, the woman dropped her books. She struggled and screamed. "No, no! Help, help, please help me!" and "Rape!" Hidden observers told the actors when to begin to stage the attack and noted the actions of subjects. Assistance was measured as movement toward the attack site or movement toward a police officer visible across a nearby parking lot. The study found that 85 percent of men in groups and 65 percent of men walking alone made a detectable move to assist the woman.

The amount of experimenter control is related to internal and external validity. Laboratory experiments tend to have greater internal validity but lower external validity; that is, they are logically tighter and better controlled, but less generalizable. Field experiments tend to have greater external validity but lower internal validity; that is, they are more generalizable but less controlled. Quasi-experimental designs are more common. For example, in the experiment involving the staged attempted rape, the experimenters recreated a very realistic situation with high external validity. It had more external validity than putting people in a laboratory setting and asking them what they would do hypothetically. Yet, subjects were not randomly assigned. Any man who happened to walk by became a subject. The experimenters could not precisely control what the subject heard or saw. The measurement of subject response was based on hidden observers who may have missed some subject responses.

PRACTICAL CONSIDERATIONS

Every research technique has informal tricks of the trade. They are pragmatic and based on common sense but account for the difference between the successful research projects of an experienced researcher and the difficulties a novice researcher faces. Three are discussed here.

Planning and Pilot Tests

All social research requires planning, and most quantitative researchers use pilot tests. During the planning phase of experimental research, a researcher thinks of alternative explanations or threats to internal validity and how to avoid them. The researcher also develops a neat and well-organized system for recording data. In addition,

he or she should devote serious effort to pilot testing any apparatus (e.g., computers, video cameras, tape recorders) that will be used in the treatment situation, and he or she must train and pilot test confederates. After the pilot tests, the researcher should interview the pilot subjects to uncover aspects of the experiment that need refinement.

Instructions to Subjects

Most experiments involve giving instructions to subjects to set the stage. A researcher should word instructions carefully and follow a prepared script so that all subjects hear the same thing. This ensures reliability. The instructions are also important in creating a realistic cover story when deception is used. Aronson and Carlsmith (1968:46) noted, "One of the most common mistakes the novice experimenter makes is to present his instructions too briefly."

Postexperiment Interview

At the end of an experiment, the researcher should interview subjects, for three reasons. First, if deception was used, the researcher needs to *debrief* the subjects, telling them the true purpose of the experiment and answering questions. Second, he or she can learn what the subjects thought and how their definitions of the situation affected their behavior. Finally, he or she can explain the importance of not revealing the true nature of the experiment to other potential subjects.

RESULTS OF EXPERIMENTAL RESEARCH: MAKING COMPARISONS

Comparison is the key to all research. By carefully examining the results of experimental research, a researcher can learn a great deal about threats to internal validity, and whether the treatment has an impact on the dependent variable. For example, in the Bond and Anderson (1987) experiment on delivering bad news, discussed earlier, it took an average of 89.6 and 73.1 seconds to deliver favorable versus 72.5 or 147.2 seconds to deliver unfavorable test scores in private or public settings, respectively. A comparison shows that delivering bad news in public takes the longest, whereas good news takes a bit longer in private.

A more complex illustration of such comparisons is shown in Table 8.2 on the results of a series of five weight-loss experiments using the classical experimental design. In the example, the 30 subjects in the experimental group at Enrique's Slim Clinic lost an average of 50 pounds, whereas the 30 in the control group did not lose a single pound. Only one person dropped out during the experiment. Susan's Scientific Diet Plan had equally dramatic results, but 11 people in her experimental group dropped out. This suggests a problem with experimental mortality. People in the experimental group at Fred's Fat Farm lost 11 pounds compared to 2 pounds for the control group, but the control group and the experimental group began with an average of 31 pounds difference in weight. This suggests a problem with selection bias. Bob's Blubber Watchers had no experimental mortality or selection bias problems, but those in the experimental group lost no more weight than those in the control group. It appears that the treatment was not effective. Pauline's Pounds Off also avoided selection bias and experimental mortality problems. People in her experimental group lost 32 pounds, but so did those in the control group. This suggests that the maturation, history, or diffusion of treatment effects may have occurred. Thus, the treatment at Enrique's Slim Clinic appears to be the most effective one.

A WORD ON ETHICS

Ethical considerations are a significant issue in experimental research because experimental research is intrusive (i.e., it interferes). Treatments may involve placing people in contrived social settings and manipulating their feelings or behaviors. Dependent variables may be what subjects say or do. The amount and type of intrusion is lim-ited by ethical standards. Researchers must be very careful if they place subjects in physical danger or in embarrassing or anxiety-inducing situations. They must painstakingly monitor events and control what occurs.

Second, deception is common in social experiments, but it involves misleading or lying to subjects. Such dishonesty is not condoned as acceptable in itself and is acceptable only as the means to achieve a goal that cannot be achieved otherwise. Even for a worthy goal, deception can be used only with restrictions. The amount and type of deception should not go beyond what is minimally necessary, however. Subjects should be debriefed and informed of the true purpose of the research.

Ethics is discussed in detail in the last chapter. The important thing to remember is that the major responsibility for what happens to subjects directly or indirectly as a consequence of their involvement in research rests with the researcher. Social researchers should always treat subjects with respect and dignity. They should not lose their sensitivity to other people and should never treat subjects as inanimate objects or mere guinea pigs who exist only for the researcher's needs.

CONCLUSION

In this chapter, you learned about random assignment and the methods of experimental research. Random assignment is an effective way to create two (or more) groups, which can be treated as equivalent and hence compared. In general, experimental research provides precise and relatively unambiguous evidence for a causal relationship. It follows the positivist approach and produces quantitative results that can be analyzed with statistics.

This chapter also examined the parts of an experiment and how they can be combined to produce different experimental designs. In addition to the classical experimental design, you learned about preexperimental and quasi-experimental designs. You also learned how to express them using design notation.

TABLE 8.2 Comparisons of Results, Classical Experimental Design, Weight-Loss Experiments

	ENRIQUE'S SLIM CLINIC			BOB'S BLUBBER WATCHERS	
	Pretest	*Posttest*		*Pretest*	*Posttest*
Experimental	190 (30)	140 (29)	Experimental	190 (30)	188 (29)
Control group	189 (30)	189 (30)	Control group	192 (29)	189 (28)

	SUSAN'S SCIENTIFIC DIET PLAN			PAULINE'S POUNDS OFF	
	Pretest	*Posttest*		*Pretest*	*Posttest*
Experimental	190 (30)	141 (19)	Experimental	190 (30)	158 (30)
Control group	189 (30)	189 (28)	Control group	191 (29)	159 (28)

	FRED'S FAT FARM			SYMBOLS FOR COMPARISON PURPOSES	
	Pretest	*Posttest*		*Pretest*	*Posttest*
Experimental	160 (30)	152 (29)	Experimental	A (A)	C (C)
Control group	191 (29)	189 (29)	Control group	B (B)	D (D)

COMPARISONS

	A–B	C–D	A–C	B–D	(A)–(C)	(B)–(D)
Enrique's	1	49	−50	0	−1	0
Susan's	1	48	−49	0	−11	0
Fred's	31	37	−8	−2	−1	0
Bob's	2	1	−2	−3	−1	−1
Pauline's	1	1	−32	−32	0	−1

A–B   Do the two groups begin the same? If not, selection bias may be possibly occurring.

C–D   Do the two groups end the same? If not, the treatment may be ineffective, or there may be strong history, maturation, or diffusion or treatment effects.

A–C   Did the experimental group change? If not, treatment may be ineffective.

(A)–(C) and (B)–(D)   Did the number of subjects in the experimental group or control group change? If a large drop occurs, experimental mortality may be a threat to internal validity.

INTERPRETATION

Enrique's: No internal validity threats evidont, treatment effects

Susan's: Experimental mortality threat likely problem

Fred's: Selection bias likely problem

Bob's: No internal validity threat evident, no treatment effects

Pauline's: History, maturation, diffusion of treatment threats are a likely problem

Note: Numbers are average number of pounds. Numbers in parentheses () are number of subjects per group. Random assignment is made to the experimental or control group.

You learned that internal validity—the internal logical rigor of an experiment—is a key idea in experimental research. Threats to internal validity are possible alternative explanations to the treatment. You also learned about external validity and how field experiments maximize external validity.

The real strength of experimental research is

its control and logical rigor in establishing evidence for causality. In general, experiments tend to be easier to replicate, less expensive, and less time consuming than the other techniques. Experimental research also has limitations. First, some questions cannot be addressed using experimental methods because control and experimental manipulation are impossible. Another limitation is that experiments usually test one or a few hypotheses at a time. This fragments knowledge and makes it necessary to synthesize results across many research reports. External validity is another potential problem because many experiments rely on small nonrandom samples of college students.[14]

You learned how a careful examination and comparison of results can alert you to potential problems in research design. Finally, you saw some practical and ethical considerations in experiments. Deception, in particular, is an issue in experimental research.

In the next chapters, you will examine survey research and other research techniques. The logic of the nonexperimental methods differs from that of the experiment. Experimenters focus narrowly on a few hypotheses. They usually have one or two independent variables, a single dependent variable, a few small groups of subjects, and an independent variable that the researcher induces. By contrast, other social researchers test many hypotheses at once. They measure a large number of independent and dependent variables and use a larger number of randomly sampled subjects. Their independent variables are usually preexisting conditions in subjects.

KEY TERMS

classical experimental design	experimenter expectancy	one-shot case study
compensatory behavior	external validity	placebo
control group	factorial design	placebo effect
debrief	field experiment	posttest
deception	Hawthorne effect	preexperimental designs
demand characteristics	history effects	pretest
dependent variable	internal validity	quasi-experimental designs
design notation	interrupted time series	random assignment
diffusion of treatment	laboratory experiment	reactivity
double-blind experiment	Latin square design	selection bias
equivalent time series	maturation	Solomon four-group design
experimental design	mortality	static group comparison
experimental group	mundane realism	subjects
experimental realism	novelty effect	treatment

REVIEW QUESTIONS

1. What are the seven elements or parts of an experiment?
2. What distinguishes preexperimental designs from the classical design?
3. Which design permits the testing of different sequences of several treatments?
4. A researcher says, "It was a three by two design, with the independent variables level of fear (low, medium, high) and ease of escape (easy/difficult) and the dependent variable anxiety." What does this mean? What is the design notation, assuming that random assignment with posttest only was used?

5. How do the interrupted and the equivalent time series designs differ?

6. What is the logic of internal validity and how does the use of a control group fit into that logic?

7. How does the Solomon four-group design show the testing effect?

8. What is the double-blind experiment and why is it used?

9. Do field or laboratory experiments have greater internal validity? External validity? Explain.

10. What is the difference between experimental and mundane realism?

NOTES

1. Cook and Campbell (1979:9–36, 91–94) argued for a modification of a more rigid positivist approach to causality for experimental research. They suggested a "critical-realist" approach, which shares some features of the critical approach outlined in Chapter 4.

2. For discussions of the history of the experiment, see Danziger (1988), Gillespie (1988), Hornstein (1988), O'Donnell (1985), and Scheibe (1988).

3. See Hornstein (1988:11).

4. For events after World War II, see Harris (1988) and Suls and Rosnow (1988). For a discussion of the increased use of deception, see Reynolds (1979:60).

5. For a discussion of control in experiments, see Cook and Campbell (1979:7–9) and Spector (1981:15–16).

6. The notation for research design is discussed in Cook and Campbell (1979:95–96), Dooley (1984:132–137), and Spector (1981:27–28).

7. For additional discussions of threats to internal validity, see Cook and Campbell (1979:51–68),

Kercher (1992), Spector (1981:24–27), Smith and Glass (1987), and Suls and Rosnow (1988).

8. This example is borrowed from Mitchell and Jolley (1988:97).

9. Experimenter expectancy is discussed in Aronson and Carlsmith (1968:66–70), Dooley (1984:151–153), and Mitchell and Jolley (1988:327–329).

10. Also see Aronson and Carlsmith (1968:22–25).

11. For a discussion of external validity, see Cook and Campbell (1979:70–80).

12. The Hawthorne effect is described in Roethlisberger and Dickenson (1939), Franke and Kaul (1978), and Laig (1992). Also see the discussion in Cook and Campbell (1979:123–125) and Dooley (1984:155–156). Gillespie (1988, 1991) discussed the political context of the experiments and how it shaped them.

13. See Piliavin, Rodin, and Piliavin (1969).

14. See Graham (1992).

RECOMMENDED READINGS

Campbell, Donald T., and Julian C. Stanley. (1963). *Experimental and quasi-experimental designs for research*. Chicago: Rand McNally. This is the classic of experimental design. The basic ideas about threats to internal validity are presented in detail. The discussion of experimental validity (internal and external) and design issues is still valuable.

Cook, Thomas D., and Donald T. Campbell. (1979). *Quasi-experimental design: Design and analysis issues for field settings*. Chicago: Rand McNally. If there were only one book to read on experimental design, this would be it. The authors

cover the basics of experimental logic and causality and advance thinking on experimental design. They explore many potential threats to internal and external validity and present alternative designs.

Huck, Schuyler W., and Howard M. Sandler. (1979). *Rival hypotheses: Alternative interpretations of data based conclusions*. New York: Harper & Row. This is an unusual book, with two sections. The first has short summaries of 100 published research reports on many different topics. The second section is a discussion of internal validity threats or other possible problems that may exist in each report and limit ability of a researcher to draw conclusions about causal relations.

Spector, Paul E. (1981). *Research designs.* Beverly Hills, CA: Sage. This is a short (80-page) introduction to the basic concepts of research design. It includes discussions of threats to internal validity and different experimental designs. The discussion of different types of interaction effects is especially useful.

> *At the beginning of the century statisticians were debating whether*
> *anything less than a complete enumeration of a population would*
> *suffice. . . . Since that time sampling has become widely accepted, and an*
> *impressive array of sampling methods have been devised to enable efficient*
> *and economic samples to be drawn in a variety of practical settings.*
> —Graham Kalton, *Introduction to Survey Sampling*, p. 6

INTRODUCTION

In this chapter, you will learn about sampling. Sampling is based on statistical theories that are not explored in depth here. Instead, my emphasis is on giving you an understanding of sampling concepts and how to apply them in practice. Sampling is a powerful technique with wide applications beyond social research. It is used in such fields as accounting, astronomy, chemistry, manufacturing, and zoology. In social research, it is used primarily in survey research, content analysis, and nonreactive research—the three types of quantitative research techniques we will examine in the upcoming chapters.

TYPES OF SAMPLING

Why Sample?

Sampling, like random assignment, is a process of systematically selecting cases for inclusion in a research project. When a researcher randomly assigns, he or she sorts a collection of cases into two or more groups using a random process. By contrast, in random sampling, he or she selects a smaller subset of cases from a larger pool of cases (see Figure 9.1). A researcher can both sample and randomly assign. He or she can first sample to obtain a smaller set of cases (e.g., 150 people out of 20,000) and then use random assignment to divide the smaller set into groups (e.g., divide the 150 people into three groups of 50).

A researcher gets a set of cases, or a *sample*, from sampling that is more manageable and cost effective to work with than the pool of all cases. For example, it would be much less costly and time consuming to measure variables on 150 than on 20,000 people. The difficulty with using the smaller subset instead of the entire pool is that the researcher is not interested in a small subset of cases alone. Instead, he or she wants to gener-

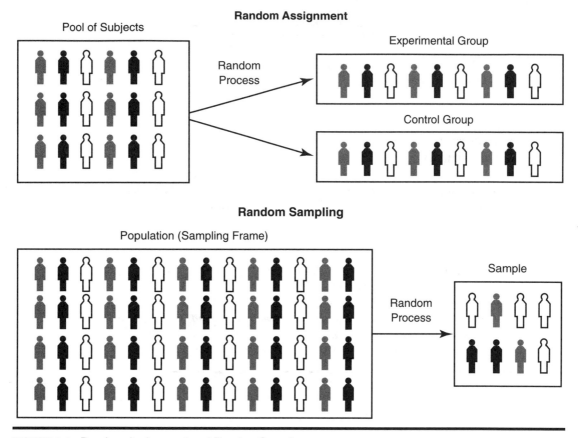

FIGURE 9.1   Random Assignment and Random Sampling

alize to the entire pool. If well done, sampling lets a researcher measure variables on the smaller set of cases but generalize results accurately to all cases.

Your first reaction to the claim that a researcher can use a small subset to generalize accurately to a much larger pool of cases may be one of disbelief. It sounds too good to be true. But sampling is powerful, and it works. With a well-conducted sample, a researcher can measure variables with 2,000 cases, generalize to 200 million, and not be off by more than 2 to 4 percent from the results that would be obtained if all 200 million were used.

How is it possible to use so few cases to generalize accurately to so many? It is not based on trickery or magic but on logical statistical reason-

ing that has been tested repeatedly with empirical evidence. Moreover, a researcher cannot use just any sample to generalize accurately. The sample must be selected according to precise procedures, and statements made about it are subject to limitations.

Populations, Elements, and Sampling Frames

A researcher draws a sample from a larger pool of cases, or *elements*. A *sampling element* is the unit of analysis or case in a population. It can be a person, a group, an organization, a written document or symbolic message, or even a social action (e.g., an arrest, a divorce, a kiss) that is being measured. The large pool is the *population*, which has an important role in sampling. Sometimes, the term *universe* (defined in Chapter 6) is used interchangeably with *population*. To define the population, a researcher specifies the unit being sampled, the geographical location, and the temporal boundaries of populations. Consider the examples of populations in Box 9.1. All the examples include the elements to be sampled (people, businesses, hospital admissions, commercials) and geographical and time boundaries.

A researcher begins with an idea of the population (e.g., all people in a city) but defines it more precisely. The term *target population* refers to the specific pool of cases that he or she wants to study. The ratio of the size of the sample to the size of the target population is the *sampling ratio*. For example, the population has 50,000 people, and a researcher draws a sample of 150 from it. Thus, the sampling ratio is 150/50,000 = 0.003, or 0.3 percent. If the population is 500 and the researcher samples 100, then the sampling ratio is 100/500 = 0.20, or 20 percent.

A population is an abstract concept. How can population be an abstract concept, when there are a given number of people at a certain time? Except for specific small populations, one can never truly freeze a population to measure it. For example, in a city at any given moment, some people are dying, some are boarding or getting off airplanes, and some are in cars driving across city boundaries. The researcher must decide exactly who to count. Should he or she count a city resident who happens to be on vacation when the time is fixed? What about the tourist staying at a hotel in the city when the time is fixed? Should he or she count adults, children, people in jails, those in hospitals? A population, even the population of all people over the age of 18 in the city limits of Milwaukee, Wisconsin, at 12:01 A.M. on March 1, 1996, is an abstract concept. It exists in the mind but is impossible to pinpoint concretely.

Because a population is an abstract concept, except for small specialized populations (e.g., all the students in a classroom), a researcher needs to estimate the population. As an abstract concept, the population needs an operational definition. This process is similar to developing operational definitions for constructs that are measured.

A researcher operationalizes a population by developing a specific list that closely approximates all the elements in the population. This list is a *sampling frame*. He or she can choose from many types of sampling frames: telephone directories, tax records, driver's license records, and so on. Listing the elements in a population sounds simple. It is often difficult because there may be no good list of elements in a population.

A good sampling frame is crucial to good sampling. A mismatch between the sampling frame and the conceptually defined population can be a major source of error. Just as a mismatch between the theoretical and operational definitions of a variable creates invalid measurement, so a mismatch between the sampling frame and the population causes invalid sampling. Researchers try to minimize mismatches. For example, you would like to sample all people in a region of the United States, so you decide to get a list of everyone with a driver's license. But some people do not have driver's licenses, and the lists of those with licenses, even if updated regularly, quickly

Box 9.1 _____

Examples of Populations

1. All persons aged 16 or older living in Australia on December 2, 1989, who were not incarcerated in prison, asylums, and similar institutions
2. All business establishments employing more than 100 persons in Ontario Province, Canada, that operated in the month of July 1991
3. All admissions to public or private hospitals in the state of New Jersey between August 1, 1988, and July 31, 1993
4. All television commercials aired between 7:00 A.M. and 11:00 P.M. Eastern Standard Time on three major U.S. networks between November 1 and November 25, 1996
5. All currently practicing physicians in the United States who received medical degrees between January 1, 1950, and the present
6. All black male heroin addicts in the Vancouver, British Columbia, or Seattle, Washington, metropolitan areas during 1992

go out of date. Next, you try income tax records. But not everyone pays taxes; some people cheat and do not pay, others have no income and do not have to file, others have died or have not begun to pay taxes, and still others have entered or left the area since the last time taxes were due. You try telephone directories, but they are not much better; some people are not listed in a telephone directory, some people have unlisted numbers, and others have recently moved. With a few exceptions (e.g., a list of all students enrolled at a university), sampling frames are almost always inaccurate. A sampling frame can include some of those outside the target population (e.g., a telephone directory that lists people who have moved away) or might omit some of those inside it (e.g., those without telephones).

Any characteristic of a population (e.g., the percentage of city residents who smoke cigarettes, the average height of all women over the age of 21, the belief of people in UFOs) is a population *parameter*. It is the true characteristic of the population. Parameters are determined when all elements in a population are measured. The parameter is never known with absolute accuracy for large populations (e.g., the population of a nation), so researchers must estimate it on the basis of samples. Researchers use information from the sample, called a *statistic*, to estimate population parameters.

A famous case in the history of sampling illustrates the limitations of the technique. The *Literary Digest*, a major U.S. magazine, sent postcards to people before the 1920, 1924, 1928, and 1932 U.S. presidential elections. The magazine took the names for the sample from automobile registrations and telephone directories—the sampling frame. People returned the postcards indicating whom they would vote for. The magazine correctly predicted all four election outcomes. The magazine's success with predictions was well known, and in 1936, it increased the sample to 10 million. The magazine predicted a huge victory for Alf Landon over Franklin D. Roosevelt. But the *Literary Digest* was wrong; Franklin D. Roosevelt won by a landslide. The prediction was wrong for several reasons, but the most important

were mistakes in sampling. Although the magazine sampled a large number of people, its sampling frame did not accurately represent the target population (i.e., all voters). It excluded people without telephones or automobiles, a sizable percentage of the population in 1936, during the worst of the Great Depression of the 1930s. The frame excluded as much as 65 percent of the population and a segment of the voting population (lower income) that tended to favor Roosevelt.[1] The magazine had been accurate in earlier elections because people with higher and lower incomes did not differ in how they voted. Also, during earlier elections, before the Depression, more lower-income people could afford to have telephones and automobiles.

You can learn two important lessons from the *Literary Digest* mistake. First, the sampling frame is crucial. Second, the size of a sample is less important than whether or not it accurately represents the population. A representative sample of 2,500 can give more accurate predications about the U.S. population than a nonrepresentative sample of 10 million or 50 million.

Nonprobability Sampling

Samples can be divided into two groups: those that are based on the principles of randomness from probability theory and those that are not. (See Table 9.1 for a summary.) Sampling based on probability theory lets a researcher say precise things about sampling and use powerful statistics. Samples that are not based on probability theory are more limited. A researcher uses them out of ignorance, because of a lack of time, or in special situations. Except for special situations, quantitative researchers prefer probability samples.

Haphazard, Accidental, or Convenience. *Haphazard sampling* can produce ineffective, highly unrepresentative samples and is not recommended. When a researcher haphazardly selects cases that are convenient, he or she can easily get a sample that seriously misrepresents the population. Such samples are cheap and quick; however, the bias and systematic errors

TABLE 9.1   Types of Samples

NONPROBABILITY	PROBABILITY
Haphazard: Select anyone who is convenient.	*Simple:* Select people based on a true random procedure.
Quota: Select anyone in predetermined groups.	*Systematic:* Select every *k*th person (quasi-random).
Purposive: Select anyone in a hard-to-find target population.	*Stratified:* Randomly select people in predetermined groups.
Snowball: Select people connected to one another.	*Cluster:* Take multistage random samples in each of several levels.

that easily occur make them worse than no sample at all.[2] The person-on-the-street interview conducted by television programs is an example of a haphazard sample. Television interviewers go out on the street with camera and microphone to talk to a few people who are convenient to interview. The people walking past a television studio in the middle of the day do not represent everyone (e.g., homemakers, people in rural areas). Likewise, television interviewers often select people who look "normal" to them and avoid people who are unattractive, poor, very old, or inarticulate.

Another example of a haphazard sample is that of a newspaper that asks readers to clip a questionnaire from the paper and mail it in. Not everyone reads the newspaper, has an interest in the topic, or will take the time to cut out the questionnaire and mail it. Some people will, and the number who do so may seem large (e.g., 5,000), but the sample cannot be used to generalize accurately to the population. Such haphazard samples may have entertainment value, but they can give a distorted view and seriously misrepresent the population.

Quota.   *Quota sampling* is an improvement over haphazard sampling, but it, too, is a weak type of sampling.[3] In quota sampling, a researcher first identifies categories of people (e.g., male and female; or under 30, 30 to 60, over 60), then decides how many to get in each category. Thus, the number of people in various categories of the sample is fixed. For example, a researcher decides

to select 5 males and 5 females under age 30, 10 males and 10 females aged 30 to 60, and 5 males and 5 females over age 60 for a 40-person sample. As with matching in random assignment, it is difficult to represent all population characteristics accurately.

Quota sampling is an improvement because the researcher can ensure that some population differences are in the sample. In haphazard sampling, all those interviewed might be of the same age, sex, or race. But once the quota sampler fixes the categories and number of cases in each category, he or she uses haphazard sampling. For example, the researcher interviews the first 5 males under age 30 he or she encounters, even if all 5 just walked out of the campaign headquarters of a political candidate. Not only is misrepresentation possible because haphazard sampling is used within the categories, but nothing prevents the researcher from selecting people who "act friendly" or who want to be interviewed.

Another case from the history of sampling illustrates the limitations of quota sampling. George Gallup's American Institute of Public Opinion, using quota sampling, successfully predicted the outcomes of the 1936, 1940, and 1944 U.S. presidential elections. But in 1948, Gallup predicted the wrong candidate. The incorrect prediction had several causes (e.g., many voters were undecided, interviewing stopped early), but a major reason was that the quota categories did not accurately represent all geographical areas and all people who actually cast a vote.

Despite its problems, quota sampling is easier, cheaper, and quicker than probability sampling. In probability sampling, a researcher must create a sampling frame, then locate specific individuals in the frame. Specific people may be unavailable, several attempts to contact them are required, and people who are contacted might still refuse.

Purposive or Judgmental.   Serious quantitative researchers avoid the aforementioned nonprobability samples. *Purposive sampling* is an acceptable kind of sampling for special situations. It uses the judgment of an expert in selecting cases or it selects cases with a specific purpose in mind. It is inappropriate if it is used to pick the "average housewife" or the "typical school." With purposive sampling, the researcher never knows whether the cases selected represent the population. It is used in exploratory research or in field research.[4]

Purposive sampling is appropriate in three situations. First, a researcher uses it to select unique cases that are especially informative. For example, a researcher wants to use content analysis to study magazines to find cultural themes. He or she selects a specific popular women's magazine to study because it is trend setting.

Second, a researcher may use purposive sampling to select members of a difficult-to-reach, specialized population. For example, the researcher wants to study prostitutes. It is impossible to list all prostitutes and sample randomly from the list. Instead, he or she uses subjective information (e.g., locations where prostitutes solicit, social groups with whom prostitutes associate) and experts (e.g., police who work on vice units, other prostitutes) to identify a "sample" of prostitutes for inclusion in the research project. The researcher uses many different methods to identify the cases, because his or her goal is to locate as many cases as possible. For example, Harper (1982) formed the sample in his field research study of American tramps and hoboes in the 1970s by befriending "experts" (i.e., tramps) and living with them on trains and in skid row areas. The special populations do not have to

engage in illegal activity. For example, McCall (1980) identified 31 female artists in St. Louis by asking a friend about other artists and by joining a local arts organization.

Another situation for purposive sampling occurs when a researcher wants to identify particular types of cases for in-depth investigation. The purpose is less to generalize to a larger population than it is to gain a deeper understanding of types. For example, Hochschild intensively interviewed 28 people about their beliefs. She selected some because they had low incomes and some because they had high incomes. Some were male and some were female.

> *Obviously, one cannot safely generalize from a sample of this kind to a national population: it would be worthless, for example, for me to point out what percentage of my sample sought more or fewer government services. . . . Intensive interviews are a device for generating insights, anomalies, and paradoxes, which later may be formalized into hypotheses that can be tested by quantitative social science methods. (1981: 23–24)*

In his study of the political influence of corporate elites, Useem (1984) used a type of quota and purposive sampling. He interviewed 72 directors of major British corporations and 57 officials from large U.S. firms. He chose the sample to include both U.S. and British firms and to include some directors who sat on the boards of more than one firm. In addition, he matched firms by industry and size, and limited geographical locations in order to reduce travel costs.

Gamson (1992) used purposive sampling in a focus group study of what working-class people think about politics. (Chapter 10 discusses focus groups.) Gamson wanted a total of 188 working-class people to participate in one of 37 focus groups. He sought respondents who had not completed college but who were diverse in terms of age, ethnicity, religion, interest in politics, and type of occupation. He recuited subjects from 35 neighborhoods in the Boston area by going to festivals, picnics, fairs, and flea markets and posting notices on many public bulletin boards. In addition to explaining the study, respondents were well paid so as to attract people who would not traditionally participate in a study.

Snowball Sampling. Social researchers are often interested in an interconnected network of people or organizations.[5] The network could be scientists around the world investigating the same problem, the elites of a medium-sized city, the members of an organized crime family, persons who sit on the boards of directors of major banks and corporations, or people on a college campus who have had sexual relations with each other. The crucial feature is that each person or unit is connected with another through a direct or indirect linkage. This does not mean that each person directly knows, interacts with, or is influenced by every other person in the network. Rather, it means that, taken as a whole, with direct and indirect links, most are within an interconnected web of linkages.

For example, Sally and Tim do not know each other directly, but each has a good friend, Susan, so they have an indirect connection. All three are part of the same friendship network. Researchers represent such a network by drawing a *sociogram*—a diagram of circles connected with lines. The circles represent each person or case, and the lines represent friendship or other linkages (see Figure 9.2).

Snowball sampling (also called network, chain referral, or reputational sampling) is a method for identifying and sampling (or selecting) the cases in a network. It is based on an analogy to a snowball, which begins small but becomes larger as it is rolled on wet snow and picks up additional snow. Snowball sampling is a multistage technique. It begins with one or a few people or cases and spreads out on the basis of links to the initial cases.

For example, a researcher examines friendship networks among the teenagers in a community. He or she begins with three teenagers who do not know each other. Each teen names four close friends. The researcher then goes to the four friends and asks each to name four close friends, then goes to those four and does the same thing again, and so forth. Before long, a large number

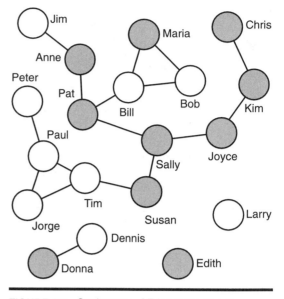

FIGURE 9.2 Sociogram of Friendship Relations

of people are involved. Each person in the sample is directly or indirectly tied to the original teenagers, and several people may have named the same person. The researcher eventually stops, either because no new names are given, indicating a closed network, or because the network is so large that it is at the limit of what he or she can study. The sample includes those named by at least one other person in the network as being a close friend. Ostrander's study of 36 upper-class women used snowball sampling.

> *At the conclusion of each interview, I asked the woman to "suggest another woman of your social group with a background like yours who might be willing to talk with me." This practical way of gaining access to respondents has theoretical as well as methodological advantages. . . . I was referred to women who were considered by their class peers to be representative of the class; thus, I did not speak with women who deviated significantly from the norms of upper class life. But I was most interested in "acceptable" people, since I wanted to learn the established norms and definitions of acceptable. (1984:9, 11)*

The special problems with studying elites is discussed in Chapter 13.

Probability Sampling

Why Random?   The area of applied mathematics called probability theory relies on random processes. The word *random* has a special meaning in mathematics. It refers to a process that generates a mathematically random result; that is, the selection process operates in a truly random method (e.g., no pattern), and a researcher can calculate the probability of outcomes. In a true random process, each element has an equal probability of being selected.

Probability samples that rely on random processes require more work than nonrandom ones. A researcher must identify specific sampling elements (e.g., person) to include in the sample. For example, if conducting a telephone survey, the researcher needs to try to reach the specific sampled person, by calling back four or five times, to get an accurate random sample.[6]

Random samples are most likely to yield a sample that truly represents the population. In addition, random sampling lets a researcher statistically calculate the relationship between the sample and the population—that is, the size of the *sampling error*. A nonstatistical definition of the sampling error is the deviation between sample results and a population parameter due to random processes.

This chapter does not cover the technical and statistical details of random sampling. Instead, it focuses on the fundamentals of how sampling works, the difference between good and bad samples, how to draw a sample, and basic principles of sampling in social research. This does not mean that random sampling is unimportant. Random sampling is crucial, and it is essential to learn the fundamentals. If you plan to pursue a career using quantitative research, you should get more statistical background than space permits here.

Types of Probability Samples
Simple Random.   The *simple random sample* is both the easiest random sample to understand and the one on which other types are modeled. In simple random sampling, a researcher develops an accurate sampling frame, selects elements from the sampling frame according to a mathematically random procedure, then locates the exact element that was selected for inclusion in the sample.

After numbering all elements in a sampling frame, a researcher uses a list of random numbers to decide which elements to select. He or she needs as many random numbers as there are elements to be sampled; for example, for a sample of 100, 100 random numbers are needed. The researcher can get random numbers from a *random-number table*, a table of numbers chosen in a mathematically random way. Random-number tables are available in most statistics and research methods books, including this one (see Appendix

TELL ME AGAIN HOW MANY HUNDRED THOUSAND PEOPLE MY OPINION REPRESENTS!

© 1996 by NEA, Inc.

OPINION POLL

M. THAVES

Source: Used with permission of Bob Thaves.

B). The numbers are generated by a pure random process so that any number has an equal probability of appearing in any position. Computer programs can also produce lists of random numbers.

You may ask, Once I select an element from the sampling frame, do I then return it to the sampling frame or do I keep it separate? The common answer is that it is not returned. Unrestricted random sampling is random sampling with replacement—that is, replacing an element after sampling it so it can be selected again. In simple random sampling without replacement, the researcher ignores elements already selected into the sample.

The logic of simple random sampling can be illustrated with an elementary example—sampling marbles from a jar. I have a large jar with 5,000 red and white marbles in it. The 5,000 marbles are my population, and the parameter I want to estimate is the percentage of red marbles in it. I randomly select 100 marbles (I close my eyes, shake the jar, pick one marble, and repeat the procedure 100 times). I now have a random sample of marbles. I count the number of red marbles in my sample to estimate the percentage of red versus white marbles in the population. This is a lot easier than counting all 5,000 marbles. My sample has 52 white and 48 red marbles.

Does this mean that the population parameter is 48 percent red marbles? Maybe not. Because of random chance, my specific sample might be off. I can check my results by dumping the 100 marbles back in the jar, mixing the marbles, and drawing a second random sample of 100 marbles. On the second try, my sample has 49 white marbles and 51 red ones. Now I have a problem. Which is correct? How good is this random sampling business if different samples from the same population can yield different results? I repeat the procedure over and over until I have drawn 130 different samples of 100 marbles each (see Box 9.2 for results). Most people might empty the jar and count all 5,000, but I want to see what is going on. The results of my 130 different samples reveal a clear pattern. The most common mix of red and white marbles is 50/50. Samples that are close to that split are more frequent than those with more uneven splits. The population parame-

ter appears to be 50 percent white and 50 percent red marbles.

Mathematical proofs and empirical tests demonstrate that the pattern found in Box 9.2 always appears. The set of many different samples is my *sampling distribution*. It is a distribution of different samples that shows the frequency of different sample outcomes from many separate random samples. The pattern will appear if the sample size is 1,000 instead of 100; if there are ten colors of marbles instead of two; if the population has 100 marbles or 10 million marbles instead of 5,000; and if the population is people, automobiles, or colleges instead of marbles. In fact, the pattern will become clearer as more and more independent random samples are drawn from the population.

The pattern in the sampling distribution suggests that over many separate samples, the true population parameter (i.e., the 50/50 split in the preceding example) is more common than any other result. Some samples deviate from the population parameter, but they are less common. When many different random samples are plotted as in the graph in Box 9.2, then the sampling distribution looks like a normal or bell-shaped curve. Such a curve is theoretically important and is used throughout statistics.

The *central limit theorem* from mathematics tells us that as the number of different random samples in a sampling distribution increases toward infinity, the pattern of samples and the population parameter become more predictable. With a huge number of random samples, the sampling distribution forms a normal curve, and the midpoint of the curve approaches the population parameter as the number of samples increases.

Perhaps you want only one sample because you don't have the time or energy to draw many different samples. You are not alone. A researcher rarely draws many samples. He or she usually draws only one random sample, but the central limit theorem lets him or her generalize from one sample to the population. The theorem is about many samples, but lets the researcher calculate the probability of a particular sample being off from the population parameter.

Random sampling does not guarantee that every random sample perfectly represents the

Box 9.2 _____

Example of Sampling Distribution

Red	White	Number of Samples
42	58	1
43	57	1
45	55	2
46	54	4
47	53	8
48	52	12
49	51	21
50	50	31
51	49	20
52	48	13
53	47	9
54	46	5
55	45	2
57	43	1
	Total	130

Number of red and white marbles that were randomly drawn from a jar of 5,000 marbles with 100 drawn each time, repeated 130 times for 130 independent random samples.

Number of Samples

```
31                                         *
30                                         *
29                                         *
28                                         *
27                                         *
26                                         *
25                                         *
24                                         *
23                                         *
22                                         *
21                                     *   *
20                                     *   *   *
19                                     *   *   *
18                                     *   *   *
17                                     *   *   *
16                                     *   *   *
15                                     *   *   *
14                                     *   *   *
13                                     *   *   *   *
12                                 *   *   *   *   *
11                                 *   *   *   *   *
10                                 *   *   *   *   *
 9                                 *   *   *   *   *   *
 8                             *   *   *   *   *   *   *
 7                             *   *   *   *   *   *   *
 6                             *   *   *   *   *   *   *
 5                             *   *   *   *   *   *   *   *
 4                         *   *   *   *   *   *   *   *   *
 3                         *   *   *   *   *   *   *   *   *
 2                     *   *   *   *   *   *   *   *   *   *   *
 1         *   *       *   *   *   *   *   *   *   *   *   *       *
          42  43  44  45  46  47  48  49  50  51  52  53  54  55  56  57
                        Number of Red Marbles in a Sample
```

population. Instead, it means that most random samples will be close to the population most of the time, and that one can calculate the probability of a particular sample being inaccurate. A researcher estimates the chance that a particular sample is off or unrepresentative (i.e., the size of the sampling error) by using information from the sample to estimate the sampling distribution. He or she combines this information with knowledge of the central limit theorem to construct *confidence intervals*.

The confidence interval is a relatively simple but powerful idea. When television or newspaper polls are reported, you may hear about something called the margin of error being plus or minus 2 percentage points. This is a version of confidence intervals. A confidence interval is a range around a specific point. It is used to estimate a population parameter. A range is used because the statistics of random processes do not let a researcher predict an exact point, but they let the researcher say with a high level of confidence (e.g., 95 percent) that the true population parameter lies within a certain range.

The calculations for sampling errors or confidence intervals are beyond the level of this discussion. The sampling distribution is the key idea that lets a researcher calculate the sampling error and confidence interval. Thus, he or she cannot say, "This sample gives a perfect measure of the population parameter," but can say, "I am 95 percent certain that the true population parameter is no more than 2 percent different from what I have found in my sample."

For example, I cannot say, "There are precisely 2,500 red marbles in the jar based on a random sample." I can say, "I am 95 percent certain that the population parameter lies between 2,450 and 2,550." I can combine characteristics of the sample (e.g., its size, the variation in it) with the central limit theorem to predict specific ranges around the parameter with a great deal of confidence.

Systematic Sampling. *Systematic sampling* is simple random sampling with a short cut for random selection. Again, the first step is to number each element in the sampling frame. Instead of

using a list of random numbers, a researcher calculates a *sampling interval*, and the interval becomes his or her quasi-random selection method. The sampling interval (i.e., 1 in k, where k is some number) tells the researcher how to select elements from a sampling frame by skipping elements in the frame before selecting one for the sample.

For instance, I want to sample 300 names from 900. After a random starting point, I select every third name of the 900 to get a sample of 300. My sampling interval is 3. Sampling intervals are easy to compute. I need the sample size and the population size (or sampling frame size as a best estimate). You can think of the sampling interval as the inverse of the sampling ratio. The sampling ratio for 300 names out of 900 is 300/900 = .333 = 33.3 percent. The sampling interval is 900/300 = 3.

In most cases, a simple random sample and a systematic sample yield virtually equivalent results. One important situation in which systematic sampling cannot be substituted for simple random sampling occurs when the elements in a sample are organized in some kind of cycle or pattern. For example, a researcher's sampling frame is organized by married couples with the male first and the female second (see Table 9.2). Such

TABLE 9.2 Problems with Systematic Sampling of Cyclical Data

CASE	
1	Husband
2[d]	Wife
3	Husband
4	Wife
5	Husband
6[a]	Wife
7	Husband
8	Wife
9	Husband
10[a]	Wife
11	Husband
12	Wife

Random start = 2; Sampling interval = 4.
[a]Selected into sample.

a pattern gives the researcher an unrepresentative sample if systematic sampling is used. His or her systematic sample can be nonrepresentative and include only wives because of how the cases are organized. When his or her sample frame is organized as couples, even-numbered sampling intervals result in samples with all husbands or all wives.

Table 9.3 illustrates simple random sampling and systematic sampling. Notice that different names were drawn in each sample. For example, H. Adams appears in both samples, but C. Droullard is only in the simple random sample. This is because it is rare for any two random samples to be identical.

The sampling frame contains 20 males and 20 females (gender is in parenthesis after each name). The simple random sample yielded 3 males and 7 females, and the systematic sample yielded 5 males and 5 females. Does this mean that systematic sampling is more accurate? No. To check this, draw a new sample using different random numbers; try taking the first two digits and beginning at the end (e.g., 82 from 82752, then 23 from 23912). Also draw a new systematic sample with a different random start. The last time the random start was 18. Try a random start of 11 (the last underlined number of the top half of the second column). What did you find? How many of each sex?[7]

Stratified Sampling. In *stratified sampling*, a researcher first divides the population into subpopulations (strata) on the basis of supplementary information.[8] After dividing the population into strata, the researcher draws a random sample from each subpopulation. He or she can sample randomly within strata using simple random or systematic sampling. In stratified sampling, the researcher controls the relative size of each stratum, rather than letting random processes control it. This guarantees representativeness or fixes the proportion of different strata within a sample. Of course, the necessary supplemental information about strata is not always available.

In general, stratified sampling produces samples that are more representative of the population than simple random sampling if the stratum information is accurate. A simple example illustrates why this is so. Imagine a population that is 51 percent female and 49 percent male; the population parameter is a sex ratio of 51 to 49. With stratified sampling, a researcher draws random samples among females and among males so that the sample contains a 51 to 49 percent sex ratio. If the researcher had used simple random sampling, it would be possible for a random sample to be off from the true sex ratio in the population. Thus, he or she makes fewer errors representing the population and has a smaller sampling error with stratified sampling.

Researchers use stratified sampling when a stratum of interest is a small percentage of a population and random processes could miss the stratum by chance. For example, a researcher draws a sample of 200 from 20,000 college students. He or she gets information from the college registrar indicating that 2 percent of the 20,000 students, or 400, are divorced women with children under the age of 5. This group is important to include in the sample. There would be 4 such students (2 percent of 200) in a representative sample, but the researcher could miss them by chance in one simple random sample. With stratified sampling, he or she obtains a list of the 400 such students from the registrar and randomly selects 4 from it. This guarantees that the sample represents the population with regard to the important strata (see Box 9.3).

In special situations, a researcher may want the proportion of a stratum in a sample to differ from its true proportion in the population. For example, the population contains 0.5 percent Eskimos, but the researcher wants to examine Eskimos in particular. He or she oversamples so that Eskimos make up 10 percent of the sample. With this type of disproportionate stratified sample, the researcher cannot generalize directly from the sample to the population without special adjustments.

In some situations, a researcher wants the proportion of a stratum or subgroup to differ from its true proportion in the population. For example, Davis and Smith (1992) reported that the 1987 General Social Survey (explained in

TABLE 9.3   How to Draw Simple Random and Systematic Samples

1. Number each case in the sampling frame in sequence. The list of 40 names is in alphabetical order, numbered from 1 to 40.
2. Decide on a sample size. We will draw two 25 percent (10-name) samples.
3. For a *simple random sample*, locate a random-number table (see excerpt; a fuller table appears in Appendix B). Before using random-number table, count the largest number of digits needed for the sample (e.g., with 40 names, two digits are needed; for 100 to 999, three digits; for 1,000 to 9,999, four digits). Begin anywhere on the random number table (we will begin in the upper left) and take a set of digits (we will take the last two). Mark the number on the sampling frame that corresponds to the chosen random number to indicate that the case is in the sample. If the number is too large (over 40), ignore it. If the number appears more than once (10 and 21 occurred twice in the example), ignore the second occurrence. Continue until the number of cases in the sample (10 in our example) is reached.
4. For a *systematic sample*, begin with a random start. The easiest way to do this is to point blindly at the random number table, then take the closest number that appears on the sampling frame. In the example, 18 was chosen. Start with the random number, then count the sampling interval, or 4 in our example, to come to the first number. Mark it, and then count the sampling interval for the next number. Continue to the end of the list. Continue counting the sampling interval as if the beginning of the list was attached to the end of the list (like a circle). Keep counting until ending close to the start, or on the start if the sampling interval divides evenly into the total of the sampling frame.

No.	Name (Gender)	Simple Random	Systematic	No.	Name (Gender)	Simple Random	Systematic
01	Abrams, J. (M)			18	Green, C. (M)		START,
02	Adams, H. (F)	Yes	Yes (6)				Yes (10)
03	Anderson, H. (M)			19	Goodwanda, T. (F)	Yes	
04	Arminond, L. (M)			20	Harris, B. (M)		
05	Boorstein, A. (M)			21	Hjelmhaug, N. (M)	Yes*	
06	Breitsprecher, P. (M)	Yes	Yes (7)	22	Huang, J. (F)	Yes	Yes (1)
07	Brown, D. (F)			23	Ivono, V. (F)		
08	Cattelino, J. (F)			24	Jaquees, J. (M)		
09	Cidoni, S. (M)			25	Johnson, A. (F)		
10	Davis, L. (F)	Yes*	Yes (8)	26	Kennedy, M. (F)		Yes (2)
11	Droullard, C. (M)	Yes		27	Koschoreck, L. (F)		
12	Durette, R. (F)			28	Koykkar, J. (M)		
13	Elsnau, K. (F)	Yes		29	Kozlowski, C. (F)	Yes	
14	Falconer, T. (M)		Yes (9)	30	Laurent, J. (M)		Yes (3)
15	Fuerstenberg, J. (M)			31	Lee, R. (F)		
16	Fulton, P. (F)			32	Ling, C. (M)		
17	Gnewuch, S. (F)			33	McKinnon, K. (F)		
34	Min, H. (F) Yes	Yes (4)		38	Oh, J. (M)		Yes (5)
35	Moini, A. (F)						
36	Navarre, H. (M)			39	Olson, J. (M)		
37	O'Sullivan, C. (M)			40	Ortiz y Garcia, L. (F)		

EXCERPT FROM A RANDOM-NUMBER TABLE (FOR SIMPLE RANDOM SAMPLE)

150<u>10</u>	18590	001<u>02</u>	94174	22099	42<u>210</u>
901<u>22</u>	382<u>21</u>	215<u>29</u>	047<u>34</u>	60457	000<u>13</u>
67256	13887	941<u>19</u>	01061	27779	11007
13761	23390	12947	445<u>06</u>	36457	21210
81994	666<u>11</u>	16597	076<u>21</u>	51949	44417
79180	25992	46178	62108	43232	23912
07984	47169	88094	15318	01921	82752

*Numbers that appeared twice in random numbers selected.

Box 9.3 _____

Illustration of Stratified Sampling

SAMPLE OF 100 STAFF OF GENERAL HOSPITAL, STRATIFIED BY POSITION

	POPULATION		SIMPLE RANDOM SAMPLE	STRATIFIED SAMPLE	ERRORS COMPARED TO THE POPULATION
POSITION	*N*	*Percent*	*n*	*n*	
Administrators	15	2.88	1	3	−2
Staff physicians	25	4.81	2	5	−3
Intern physicians	25	4.81	6	5	+1
Registered nurses	100	19.23	22	19	+3
Nurse assistants	100	19.23	21	19	+2
Medical technicians	75	14.42	9	14	+5
Orderlies	50	9.62	8	10	−2
Clerks	75	14.42	5	14	+1
Maintenance staff	30	5.77	3	6	−3
Cleaning staff	25	4.81	3	5	−2
Total	520	100.00	100	100	

Randomly select 3 of 15 administrators, 5 of 25 staff physicians, and so on.
Note: Traditionally, *N* symbolizes the number in the population and *n* represents the number in the sample.

The simple random sample overrepresents nurses, nursing assistants, and medical technicians, but underrepresents administrators, staff physicians, and cleaning maintenance staff. The stratified sample gives an accurate representation of each type of position.

Chapter 11) oversampled African Americans. A random sample of the U.S. population yielded 191 blacks. Davis and Smith conducted a separate sample of African Americans to increase the total number of blacks to 544. The 191 black respondents are about 13 percent of the random sample, roughly equal to the percentage of blacks in the U.S. population. The 544 blacks are 30 percent of the disproportionate sample. The researcher who wants to use the entire sample must adjust it to reduce the number of sampled African Americans before generalizing to the U.S. population. Disproportionate sampling helps the researcher who wants to focus on issues most relevant to a subpopulation. In this case, he or she can more accurately generalize to African Americans using the 544 respondents than using a sample of only 191. The larger sample is more likely to reflect the full diversity of the African-American subpopulation.

Cluster Sampling.   Cluster sampling addresses two problems: Researchers lack a good sampling frame for a dispersed population and the cost to reach a sampled element is very high.[9] For example, there is no single list of all automobile mechanics in North America. Even if I got an accurate sampling frame, it would cost much too much to reach many of the sampled mechanics who are geographically spread out. Instead of using a single sampling frame, researchers use a sampling design that involves multiple stages and clusters.

A cluster is a unit that contains final sampling elements but can be treated temporarily as a sampling element itself. A researcher first samples clusters, each of which contains elements, then draws a second sample from within the clusters selected in the first stage of sampling. In other words, the researcher randomly samples clusters, then randomly samples elements from within the selected clusters. This has a big practical advantage. He or she may be able to get a sampling frame of clusters even if a sampling frame of elements is not available. Once clusters are chosen, a sampling frame of elements for the sampled clusters may be created. A second advantage is that the elements within each cluster are close to one another, so there may be savings in reaching the elements.

A researcher draws several samples in stages in cluster sampling. In a three-stage sample, stage 1 is random sampling of big clusters; stage 2 is random sampling of small clusters within each selected big cluster; and the last stage is sampling of elements from within the sampled small clusters. For example, a researcher wants a sample of individuals from Mapleville. First, he or she randomly samples city blocks, then households within blocks, then individuals within households (see Box 9.4). Although there is no accurate list of all residents of Mapleville, there is an accurate list of blocks in the city. After selecting a random sample of blocks, the researcher counts all households on the selected blocks to create a sample frame for each block. He or she then uses the list of households to draw a random sample at the stage of sampling households. Finally, the researcher chooses a specific individual within each sampled household.

Cluster sampling is usually less expensive than simple random sampling, but it is less accurate. Each stage in cluster sampling introduces sampling errors, so a multistage cluster sample has more sampling errors than a one-stage random sample.[10]

A researcher who uses cluster sampling must decide the number of clusters and the number of elements within clusters. For example, in a two-stage cluster sample of 240 people from Mapleville, the researcher could randomly select 120 clusters and select 2 elements from each, or randomly select 2 clusters and select 120 elements in each. Which is best? The general answer is that a design with more clusters is better because elements within clusters (e.g., people living on the same block) tend to be similar to each

other (e.g., people on the same block tend to be more alike than those on different blocks). If few clusters are chosen, many similar elements could be selected, which would be less representative of the total population. For example, the researcher could select two blocks with relatively wealthy people and draw 120 people from each. This would be less representative than a sample with 120 different city blocks and 2 individuals chosen from each.

When a researcher samples from a large geographical area and must travel to each element, cluster sampling significantly reduces travel costs. As usual, there is a trade-off between accuracy and cost.

For example, Alan, Ricardo, and Barbara each plan to visit and personally interview a sample of 1,500 students who represent the population of all college students in North America. Alan obtains an accurate sampling frame of all students and uses simple random sampling. He travels to 1,000 different locations to interview one or two students at each. Ricardo draws a random sample of three colleges from a list of all 3,000 colleges, then visits the three and selects 500 students from each. Barbara draws a random sample of 300 colleges. She visits the 300 and selects 5 students at each. If travel costs average $250 per location, Alan's travel bill is $250,000, Ricardo's is $750, Barbara's is $75,000. Alan's sample is highly accurate, but Barbara's is only slightly less accurate for one-third the cost. Ricardo's sample is the cheapest, but it is not representative at all.

1. *Within-household sampling.*
   Once a researcher samples a household or similar unit (e.g., family or dwelling unit) in cluster sampling, the question arises: Whom should the researcher choose? A potential source of bias is introduced if the first person who answers the telephone, the door, or the mail is used in the sample. The first person who answers should be selected only if his or her answering is the result of a truly random process. This is rarely the case. Certain people are unlikely to be at home, and in

Box 9.4 _____

Illustration of Cluster Sampling

Goal: Draw a random sample of 240 people in Mapleville.

Step 1:   Mapleville has 55 districts. Randomly select 6 districts.

1 2 3* 4 5 6 7 8 9 10 11 12 13 14 15* 16 17 18 19 20 21 22 23 24 25 26
27* 28 29 30 31* 32 33 34 35 36 37 38 39 40* 41 42 43 44 45 46 47 48
49 50 51 52 53 54* 55

* = Randomly selected.

Step 2:   Divide the selected districts into blocks. Each district contains 20 blocks. Randomly select 4 blocks from the district.

Example of District 3 (selected in step 1):

1 2 3 4* 5 6 7 8 9 10* 11 12 13* 14 15 16 17* 18 19 20

* = Randomly selected.

Step 3:   Divide blocks into households. Randomly select households.

Example of Block 4 of District 3 (selected in step 2):

Block 4 contains a mix of single-family homes, duplexes, and four-unit apartment buildings. It is bounded by Oak Street, River Road, South Avenue, and Greenview Drive. There are 45 households on the block. Randomly select 10 households from the 45.

1	#1 Oak Street	16	"	31	"*
2	#3 Oak Street	17*	#154 River Road	32	"*
3*	#5 Oak Street	18	#156 River Road	33	"
4	"	19*	#158 River Road	34	#156 Greenview Drive
5	"	20*	"	35	"*
6	"	21	#13 South Avenue	36	"
7	#7 Oak Street	22	"	37	"
8	"	23	#11 South Avenue	38	"
9*	#150 River Road	24	#9 South Avenue	39	#158 Greenview Drive
10	"*	25	#7 South Avenue	40	"
11	"	26	#5 South Avenue	41	"
12	"	27	#3 South Avenue	42	"
13	#152 River Road	28	#1 South Avenue	43	#160 Greenview Drive
14	"	29*	"	44	"
15	"	30	#152 Greenview Drive	45	"

* = Randomly selected

Step 4:   Select a respondent within each household.

Summary of cluster sampling:
 1 person randomly selected per household
10 households randomly selected per block
 4 blocks randomly selected per district
 6 districts randomly selected in the city
 1 × 10 × 4 × 6 = 240 people in sample

some households one person (e.g., a husband) is more likely than another to answer the telephone or door. Researchers use within-household sampling to ensure that after a random household is chosen, the individual within the household is also selected randomly.

Researchers can randomly select a person within a household in several ways.[11] The most common method is to use a selection table specifying who is to be chosen (e.g., oldest male, youngest female) after the size and composition of the household are known (see Table 9.4). This removes any bias that might arise from choosing the first person to answer the door or telephone, or from the interviewer's selecting the person who appears to be friendliest.

2. *Probability proportionate to size (PPS).*

There are two ways to cluster sample. The method just described is proportionate or unweighted cluster sampling. It is proportionate because the size of each cluster (or number of elements at each stage) is the same. Unfortunately, the more common situation is for the cluster groups to be of different sizes. When this is the case, the researcher must adjust the probability or sampling ratio at various stages in sampling.

The foregoing cluster sampling example with

TABLE 9.4 Within-Household Sampling

Selecting individuals within sampled households. Number selected is the household chosen in Box 9.4.

Number	Last Name	Adults (over Age 18)	Selected Respondent
3	Able	1 male, 1 female	Female
9	Bharadwaj	2 females	Youngest female
10	DiPiazza	1 male, 2 females	Oldest female
17	Wucivic	2 males, 1 female	Youngest male
19	Cseri	2 females	Youngest female
20	Taylor	1 male, 3 females	Second oldest female
29	Velu	2 males, 2 females	Oldest male
31	Wong	1 male, 1 female	Female
32	Gray	1 male	Male
35	Mall-Krinke	1 male, 2 females	Oldest female

EXAMPLE SELECTION TABLE (ONLY ADULTS COUNTED)

Males	Females	Whom to Select	Males	Females	Whom to Select
1	0	Male	2	2	Oldest male
2	0	Oldest male	2	3	Youngest female
3	0	Youngest male	3	2	Second oldest male
4+	0	Second oldest male	3	3	Second oldest female
0	1	Female	3	4	Third oldest female
0	2	Youngest female	4	3	Second oldest male
0	3	Second oldest female	4	4	Third oldest male
0	4+	Oldest female	4	5+	Youngest female
1	1	Female	5+	4	Second oldest male
1	2	Oldest female	5+	5+	Fourth oldest female
1	3	Second oldest female			
2	1	Youngest male			
3	1	Second oldest male			

+ = or more

Alan, Barbara, and Ricardo illustrates the problem with unweighted cluster sampling. Barbara drew a simple random sample of 300 colleges from a list of all 3,000 colleges, but she made a mistake—unless every college has an identical number of students. Her method gave each college an equal chance of being selected—a 300/3,000 or 10 percent chance. But colleges have different numbers of students, so each student does not have an equal chance to end up in her sample.

Barbara listed every college and sampled from the list. A large university with 40,000 students and a small college with 400 students had an equal chance of being selected. But if she chose the large university, the chance of a given student at that college being selected was 5 in 40,000 (5/40,000 = 0.0125 percent), whereas a student at the small college had a 5 in 400 (5/400 = 1.25 percent) chance of being selected. The small-college student was 100 times more likely to be in her sample. The total probability of being selected for a student from the large university was 0.125 percent (10 × 0.0125), while it was 12.5 percent (10 × 1.25) for the small-college student. Barbara violated a principle of random sampling—that each element has an equal chance to be selected into the sample.

If Barbara uses *probability proportionate to size (PPS)* and samples correctly, then each final sampling element or student will have an equal probability of being selected. She does this by adjusting the chances of selecting a college in the first stage of sampling. She must give large colleges with more students a greater chance of being selected and small colleges a smaller chance. She adjusts the probability of selecting a college on the basis of the proportion of all students in the population who attend it. Thus, a college with 40,000 students will be 100 times more likely to be selected than one with 400 students. (See Box 9.5 for another example.)

Random-Digit Dialing.   *Random-digit dialing (RDD)* is a special sampling technique used in research projects in which the general public is interviewed by telephone.[12] It differs from the traditional method of sampling for telephone interviews because a published telephone directory is not the sampling frame.

Three kinds of people are missed when the sampling frame is a telephone directory: people without telephones, people who have recently moved, and people with unlisted numbers. Those without phones (the poor, the uneducated, transients) are missed in any telephone interview study, but the proportion of the general public with a telephone has grown to nearly 95 percent in advanced industrialized nations. As the percentage of the public with telephones has increased, the percentage with unlisted numbers has also grown. Several kinds of people have unlisted numbers: people who want to avoid collection agencies; the very wealthy; and those who want privacy and want to avoid obscene calls, salespeople, and prank calls. In some urban areas, the percentage of unlisted numbers is as high as 40 percent. In addition, people change their residences, so directories that are published annually or less often have numbers for people who have left and do not list those who have recently moved into an area. A researcher using RDD randomly selects telephone numbers, thereby avoiding the problems of telephone directories. The population is telephone numbers, not people with telephones. RDD is not difficult, but it takes time and can frustrate the person doing the calling.

Here is how RDD works in the United States. Telephone numbers have three parts: a three-digit area code, a three-digit exchange number or central office code, and a four-digit number. For example, the area code where I live is 608, and there are many exchanges within the area code (e.g., 221, 993, 767, 455); but not all of the 999 possible three-digit exchanges (from 001 to 999) are active. Likewise, not all of the 9,999 possible four-digit numbers in an exchange (from 0000 to 9999) are being used. Some numbers are reserved for future expansion, are disconnected, or are temporarily withdrawn after someone moves. Thus, a possible U.S. telephone number consists of an active area code, an active exchange number, and a four-digit number in an exchange.

Box 9.5 _____

Example of Probability Proportionate to Size (PPS) Sampling

Dunkirk University has 8,500 students, all of whom live in one of 36 dormitory buildings. Nancy wants to interview students in person but also wants to reduce her travel time. She uses two-stage cluster sampling, sampling dormitories and then students within the dormitories. She draws a 1 in 4 (25 percent) sample of dormitory buildings and a 1 in 10 (10 percent) sample of students in each building. The overall sampling ratio is $0.25 \times 0.10 = 0.025$, or 2.5 percent of the population. The sample size is ($0.025 \times 8,500 = 212.5$), or 212 to 213 students. Each student has a 2.5 in 100 chance of being in the sample. Dormitory buildings include high-rises with 2,000 students, smaller buildings with 250 students, and cottages with 20 students.

BUILDING TYPE	NUMBER OF BUILDINGS	NUMBER OF STUDENTS PER BUILDING	STUDENTS IN BUILDING TYPE
High-rise	3	2,000 each	6,000
Smaller building	8	250 each	2,000
Cottage	25	20 each	500
Total	36		8,500

If Nancy used unweighted cluster sampling, she would sample 1 in 4 of 36 buildings or $36/4 = 9$ buildings. However, this treats a cottage with 20 students as equal to a high-rise with 2,000 students. So Nancy uses PPS and begins by creating equal-sized groups of students within each building—that is, an equal number of sampling elements in the clusters. She decides to make each group equal to the number of elements in the smallest cluster unit (i.e., the 20-person cottage).

High-rises have $2,000/20 = 100$ times the number of students that cottages do.
Smaller buildings have $250/20 = 12.5$ times the number that cottages do.
Number of buildings × number of groups of 20 per building:

$$3 \times 100 = 300$$
$$8 \times 12.5 = 100$$
$$25 \times 1 = 25$$
$$\overline{425 \text{ groups of 20 students}}$$

Nancy's first stage was to draw a 25 percent sample; 25 percent of $425 = 106.25$ (rounding to 106 groups to be sampled).

Nancy randomly samples 106 groups from the list of 425 groups of 20 in dormitory buildings. To do this, she repeats each building by number of groups of 20 in it (e.g., high-rises are repeated 100 times).

1. High-Rise #1	7. High-Rise #1	421. Cottage 21
2. High-Rise #1	8. High-Rise #1	422. Cottage 22
3. High-Rise #1	9. High-Rise #1	423. Cottage 23
4. High-Rise #1	10. High-Rise #1	424. Cottage 24
5. High-Rise #1	11. High-Rise #1	425. Cottage 25
6. High-Rise #1	etc.	

The results of Nancy's sample of 106 groups are as follows:

24 groups from High-Rise #1	24 × 20 =	480 students from High-Rise #1
24 groups from High-Rise #2	24 × 20 =	480 from High-Rise #2
25 groups from High-Rise #3	25 × 20 =	500 from High-Rise #3
0 groups from Small Building #1	0 × 20 =	0 from Small Building #1
6 groups from Small Building #2	6 × 20 =	120 from Small Building #2
3 groups from Small Building #3	3 × 20 =	60 from Small Building #3
4 groups from Small Building #4	4 × 20 =	80 from Small Building #4
3 groups from Small Building #5	3 × 20 =	60 from Small Building #5

(continued)

Box 9.5 (continued)

4 groups from Small Building #6	$4 \times 20 =$	80 from Small Building #6
3 groups from Small Building #7	$3 \times 20 =$	60 from Small Building #7
4 groups from Small Building #8	$4 \times 20 =$	80 from Small Building #8
6 cottages (1, 3, 7, 15, 21, 24)	$6 \times 20 =$	120 from the cottages
106 groups in total		2,120 students in total

Nancy wanted a sample of 212, or 10 percent of the 2,120 chosen in the first stage of sampling. She samples 1 in 10 students from each selected dormitory using simple random sampling techniques and a list of students in each dormitory. For example, 48 students (480/10 = 48) are chosen from High-Rise #1, 8 students (80/10 = 8) are randomly chosen from Small Building #4, and 2 students (20/10 = 2) are chosen from Cottage #1.

In RDD, a researcher identifies active area codes and exchanges, then randomly selects four-digit numbers. A problem is that the researcher can select any number in an exchange. This means that some selected numbers are out of service, disconnected, pay phones, or numbers for businesses; only some numbers are what the researcher wants—working residential phone numbers. Until the researcher calls, it is not possible to know whether the number is a working residential number. This means spending a lot of time getting numbers that are disconnected, for businesses, and so forth. For example, Groves and Kahn (1979:45) found that only about 22 percent of the numbers called were working residential numbers. Research organizations often use computers to select random digits and dial the phone automatically. This speeds the process, but a human must still listen and find out whether the number is a working residential one.

Remember that the sampling element in RDD is the phone number, not the person or the household. Several families or individuals can share the same phone number, and in other situations each person may have a separate phone number or more than one phone number. This means that after a working residential phone is reached, a second stage of sampling is necessary, within household sampling, to select the person to be interviewed.

Box 9.6 presents an example of how the many sampling terms and ideas can be used together in a specific real-life situation.

Consider the sampling problem that Martin and Dean (1993) faced. For a survey on reactions to the AIDs epidemic, they wanted a sample of 700 gay men from New York City. The men had to live in the city, be over age 18, not be diagnosed as having AIDS, and engage in sex with other men. The sample was to represent all areas of the city, diverse lifestyles, and various ethnic backgrounds. The authors began with a purposive sample using five diverse sources to recruit 291 respondents. They first contacted 150 New York City organizations with predominately homosexual or bisexual members. They next screened these to 90 organizations that had eligible men for the study. From the 90, they drew a stratified random sample of 52 organizations by membership size. They randomly selected five members from each of the organizations. Reports of Martin and Dean's study appeared in local news sources. This brought calls from which they got 41 unsolicited volunteers. Another source of 32 men were referrals from respondents who had participated in a small pilot study. In addition, 72 men were identified at an annual New York City Gay Pride Parade. And 15 eligible men were contacted at a New York City clinic and asked to participate.

The researchers next used snowball sampling. They asked each of the 291 respondents to give a recruitment packet to three gay male friends. Each friend who agreed to participate was also asked to give packets to three friends. This continued until it had gone five levels out from the initial 291 men. Eventually, 746 men were recruited into the study. Martin and Dean checked their sample against two random samples of gay

Box 9.6

Example Sample

Sampling has many terms for the different parts of samples or types of samples. A complex sample illustrates how researchers use them. Look at the 1980 sample for the best-known national U.S. survey in sociology, the General Social Survey (discussed in Chapter 11).

The *population* is defined as all resident adults (18 years or older) in the U.S. for the *universe* of all Americans. The *target population* consists of all English-speaking adults who live in households, excluding those living in institutional settings such as college dormitories, nursing homes, or military quarters. The researchers estimated that 97.3 percent of all resident adults lived in households and that 97 percent of the household population spoke sufficient English to be interviewed.

The researchers used a complex multistage probability sample that is both a *cluster sample* and a *stratified sample*. First, they created a national *sampling frame* of all U.S. counties, independent cities, and Standard Metropolitan Statistical Areas (SMSAs), a Census Bureau designation for larger cities and surrounding areas. Each *sampling element* at this first level had about 4,000 households. They divided these elements into strata. The strata were the four major geographic regions as defined by the Census Bureau, divided into metropolitan and nonmetropolitan areas. They then sampled from each strata using *probability proportionate to size (PPS)* random selection, based on the number of

housing units in each county or SMSA. This gave them a sample of 84 counties or SMSAs.

For the second stage, the researchers identified city blocks, census tracts, or the rural equivalent in each county or SMSA. Each *sampling element* (e.g., city block) had a minimum of 50 housing units. In order to get an accurate count of the number of housing units for some counties, a researcher counted addresses in the field. The researchers selected 6 or more blocks within each county or SMSA using PPS to yield 562 blocks.

In the third stage, the researchers used the household as a *sampling element*. They randomly selected households from the addresses in the block. After selecting an address, an interviewer contacted the household and chose an eligible respondent from it. The interviewer looked at a selection table for possible respondents and interviewed a type of respondent (e.g., second oldest) based on the table. In total, 1,934 people were contacted for interviews and 75.9 percent of interviews were completed. This gave a final sample size of 1,468. We can calculate the *sampling ratio* by dividing 1,468 by the total number of adults living in households, which was about 150 million in 1980, which is 0.01 percent. To check the representativeness of their sample, the researchers also compared characteristics of the sample to census results (see Davis and Smith 1992:31–44).

---

men in San Francisco, a random digit dialing sample of 500, and a cluster sample of 823 using San Francisco census tracts. Their sample paralleled those from San Francisco on race, age, and the percent being "out of the closet."

HOW LARGE SHOULD MY SAMPLE BE?

Students and new researchers often ask, "How large does my sample have to be?" The best answer is, "It depends." It depends on the kind of data analysis the researcher plans, on how accurate the sample has to be for the researcher's purposes, and on population characteristics. As you

have seen, a large sample size alone does not guarantee a representative sample. A large sample without random sampling or with a poor sampling frame is less representative than a smaller one with random sampling and an excellent sampling frame.

The question of sample size can be addressed in two ways. One is to make assumptions about the population and use statistical equations about random sampling processes. The calculation of sample size by this method requires a statistical discussion that goes beyond the level of this text.[13] The researcher must make assumptions about the degree of confidence (or number of errors) that is acceptable and the degree of variation in the population.

A second and more frequently used method is a rule of thumb—a conventional or commonly accepted amount. Researchers use it because they rarely have the information required by the statistical method and because it gives sample sizes close to those of the statistical method. Rules of thumb are not arbitrary but are based on past experience with samples that have met the requirements of the statistical method.

One principle of sample sizes is, the smaller the population, the bigger the sampling ratio has to be for an accurate sample (i.e., one with a high probability of yielding the same results as the entire population). Larger populations permit smaller sampling ratios for equally good samples. This is because as the population size grows, the returns in accuracy for sample size shrink.

For small populations (under 1,000), a researcher needs a large sampling ratio (about 30 percent). For example, a sample size of about 300 is required for a high degree of accuracy. For moderately large populations (10,000), a smaller sampling ratio (about 10 percent) is needed to be equally accurate, or a sample size of around 1,000. For large populations (over 150,000), smaller sampling ratios (1 percent) are possible, and samples of about 1,500 can be very accurate. To sample from very large populations (over 10 million), one can achieve accuracy using tiny sampling ratios (0.025 percent) or samples of about 2,500. The size of the population ceases to be relevant once the sampling ratio is very small, and samples of about 2,500 are as accurate for populations of 200 million as for 10 million. These are approximate sizes, and practical limitations (e.g., cost) also play a role in a researcher's decision.

A related principle is that for small samples, small increases in sample size produce big gains in accuracy. Equal increases in sample size produce more of an increase in accuracy for small than for large samples. For example, an increase in sample size from 50 to 100 reduces errors from 7.1 percent to 2.1 percent, but an increase from 1,000 to 2,000 only decreases errors from 1.6 percent to 1.1 percent (Sudman, 1976a:99).

A researcher's decision about the best sample size depends on three things: (1) the degree of accuracy required, (2) the degree of variability or diversity in the population, and (3) the number of different variables examined simultaneously in data analysis. Everything else being equal, larger samples are needed if the population has a great deal of variability or heterogeneity, or if one wants to examine many variables in the data analysis simultaneously. Smaller samples are sufficient when less accuracy is acceptable, when the population is homogeneous, or when only a few variables are examined at a time.

The analysis of data on subgroups also affects a researcher's decision about sample size. If the researcher wants to analyze subgroups in the population, he or she needs a larger sample. For example, I want to analyze four variables for males between the ages of 30 and 40 years old. If this sample is of the general public, then only a small proportion (e.g., 10 percent) of sample cases will be males in that age group. A rule of thumb is to have about 50 cases for each subgroup to be analyzed. Thus, if I want to analyze a group that is only 10 percent of the population, then I should have 10×50 or 500 cases in the sample to be sure I get enough for the subgroup analysis.

DRAWING INFERENCES

A researcher samples so he or she can draw inferences from the sample to the population. In fact, a subfield of statistical data analysis that concerns drawing accurate inferences is called *inferential statistics* (discussed in Chapter 12). The researcher directly observes variables using units in the sample. The sample stands for or represents the population. Researchers are not interested in samples in themselves; they want to infer to the population. Thus, a gap exists between what the researcher concretely has (a sample) and what is of real interest (a population) (see Figure 9.3).

In previous chapters, you saw how the logic of measurement could be stated in terms of a gap between abstract constructs and concrete indicators. Measures of concrete, observable data are approximations for abstract constructs. Researchers use the

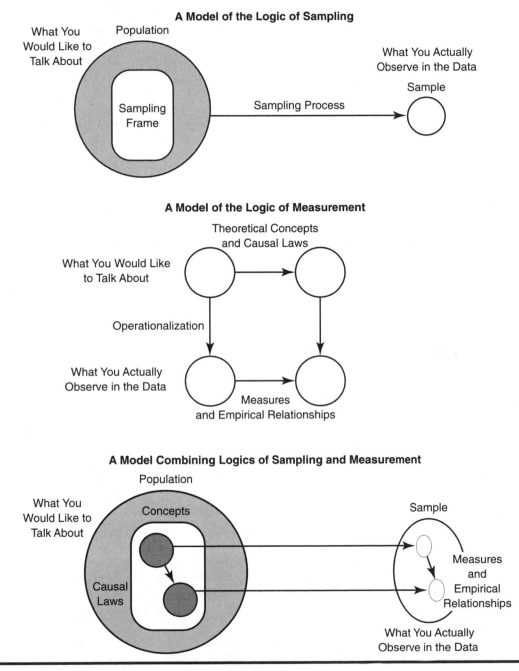

A Model of the Logic of Sampling

What You Would Like to Talk About

Population

Sampling Frame

Sampling Process

What You Actually Observe in the Data

Sample

A Model of the Logic of Measurement

Theoretical Concepts and Causal Laws

What You Would Like to Talk About

Operationalization

What You Actually Observe in the Data

Measures and Empirical Relationships

A Model Combining Logics of Sampling and Measurement

Population

What You Would Like to Talk About

Concepts

Causal Laws

Sample

Measures and Empirical Relationships

What You Actually Observe in the Data

FIGURE 9.3 Model of the Logic of Sampling and of Measurement

approximations to estimate what is of real interest (i.e., constructs and causal laws). Conceptualization and operationalization bridge the gap in measurement just as the use of sampling frames, the sampling process, and inference bridge the gap in sampling.

Researchers put the logic of sampling and the logic of measurement together by directly observing measures of constructs and empirical relationships in samples (see Figure 9.3). They infer or generalize from what they can observe empirically in samples to the abstract causal laws and constructs in the population.

Validity and sampling error have similar functions, as can be illustrated by the analogy between the logic of sampling and the logic of measurement—that is, between what is observed and what is discussed. In measurement, a researcher wants valid indicators of constructs—that is, concrete indicators that accurately represent abstract constructs. In sampling, he or she wants samples that have little sampling error—concrete collections of cases that accurately represent unseen and abstract populations. A valid measure is one that deviates little from the construct it represents. A sample with little sampling error permits estimates that deviate little from population parameters.

Researchers try to reduce sampling errors. The calculation of the sampling error is not presented here, but it is based on two factors: the sample size and the amount of diversity in the sample. Everything else being equal, the larger the sample size, the smaller the sampling error. Likewise, the greater the homogeneity (or the less the diversity) in a sample, the smaller its sampling error.

Sampling error is also related to confidence intervals. If two samples are identical except that one is larger, the one with more cases will have a smaller sampling error and narrower confidence intervals. Likewise, if two samples are identical except that the cases in one are more similar to each other, the one with greater homogeneity will have a smaller sampling error and narrower confidence intervals. A narrow confidence interval means more precise estimates of the population parameter for a given level of confidence. For example, a researcher wants to estimate average annual family income. He or she has two samples. Sample 1 gives a confidence interval of $30,000 to $36,000 around the estimated population parameter of $33,000 for an 80 percent level of confidence. For a 95 percent level of confidence, the range is $23,000 to $43,000. A sample with a smaller sampling error (because it is larger or is more homogeneous) might give a $30,000 to $36,000 range for a 95 percent confidence level.

CONCLUSION

In this chapter, you learned about sampling. Sampling is widely used in social research, especially in survey research and nonreactive research techniques. You learned about four types of sampling that are not based on random processes: haphazard, quota, snowball, and purposive. Only the last two are acceptable, and even then their use depends on special circumstances.[14] In general, probability sampling is preferred because it produces a sample that represents the population and enables the researcher to use powerful statistical techniques. In addition to simple random sampling, you learned about systematic, stratified, and cluster sampling. Although this book does not cover the statistical theory used in random sampling, from the discussion of sampling error, the central limit theorem, and sample size, it should be clear that random sampling produces more accurate and precise sampling.

Before moving on to the next chapter, it may be useful to restate a fundamental principle of social research: Do not compartmentalize the steps of the research process; rather, learn to see the interconnections between the steps. Research design, measurement, sampling, and specific research techniques are interdependent. Unfortunately, the constraints of presenting information in a course or textbook necessitate presenting the parts separately, in sequence. In practice, researchers think about data collection when they design research and develop measures for variables. Likewise, sampling issues influence research design, measurement of variables, and data collection strategies. As you will see in future chapters, good social research depends on simultaneously controlling quality at several different steps—research design, conceptualization, measurement, sampling, and data collection and handling. The researcher who makes major errors at any one stage may make an entire research project worthless.[15]

KEY TERMS

central limit theorem
cluster sampling
confidence intervals
haphazard sampling
inferential statistics
parameter
population
probability proportionate to size (PPS)

purposive sampling
quota sampling
random-digit dialing (RDD)
random-number table
sample
sampling distribution
sampling element
sampling error
sampling frame

sampling interval
sampling ratio
simple random sampling
snowball sampling
sociogram
statistic
stratified sampling
systematic sampling
target population

REVIEW QUESTIONS

1. When is purposive sampling used?

2. When is the snowball sampling technique appropriate?

3. What is a sampling frame and why is it important?

4. Which sampling method is best when the population has several groups and a researcher wants to ensure that each group is in the sample?

5. How can you get a sampling interval from a sampling ratio?

6. When should a researcher consider using probability proportionate to size?

7. What is the population in random-digit dialing? Are sampling frame problems avoided? Explain.

8. How do researchers decide how large a sample to use?

9. How are the logic of sampling and the logic of measurement related?

10. When is random-digit dialing used, and what are its advantages and disadvantages?

NOTES

1. For a discussion of the *Literary Digest* sampling mistake, see Babbie (1995:188–190), Dillman (1978:9–10), Frey (1983:18–19), and Singleton et al. (1988:132–133).
2. See Stern (1979:77–81) on biased samples. He also discusses ways to identify problems with samples in published reports.
3. Quota sampling is discussed in Kalton (1983:91–93) and Sudman (1976a:191–200).
4. For further discussion on purposive sampling, see Grosof and Sardy (1985:172–173) and Singleton et al.

(1988:153–154; 306). Bailey (1987:94–95) described "dimensional" sampling, which is a variation of purposive sampling.
5. For additional discussion of snowball sampling, see Babbie (1995:287), Bailey (1987:97), and Sudman (1976a:210–211). Also see Bailey (1987:366–367), Dooley (1984:86–87), Kidder and Judd (1986:240–241), Lindzey and Byrne (1968:452–525), and Singleton et al. (1988:372–373) for discussions of sociometry and sociograms. Network sampling issues are discussed

in Galaskiewicz (1985), Granovetter (1976), and Hoffmann-Lange (1987).

6. See Traugott (1987) on the importance of persistence in reaching sampled respondents for a representative sample. Also see Kalton (1983:63–69) on the importance of nonresponse.

7. Only one name appears in both. The stratified sample has 6 males and 4 females; the simple random sample has 5 males and 5 females (complete the lower block of numbers, then begin at the far right of the top block).

8. Stratified sampling techniques are discussed in more detail in Frankel (1983:37–46), Kalton (1983:19–28), Mendenhall, Ott, and Scheaffer (1971:53–88), Sudman (1976a:107–130), and Williams (1978:162–175).

9. Cluster sampling is discussed in Frankel (1983:47–57), Kalton (1983:28–38), Kish (1965), Mendenhall, Ott, and Scheaffer (1971:121–141), (171–183), Sudman (1976a:69–84), and Williams (1978:144–161).

10. For a discussion, see Frankel (1983:57–62), Kalton (1983:38–47), Sudman (1976a:131–170), and Williams (1978:239–241).

11. Within-household sampling is discussed in Czaja, Blair, and Sebestik (1982) and in Groves and Kahn (1979:32–36).

12. For more on random-digit dialing issues, see Dillman (1978:238–242), Frey (1983:69–77), Glasser and Metzger (1972), Groves and Kahn (1979:20–21, 45–63), Kalton (1983:86–90), and Waksberg (1978). Kviz (1984) reported that telephone directories can produce relatively accurate sampling frames in rural areas, at least for mail questionnaire surveys. Also see Keeter (1995).

13. See Kraemer and Thiemann (1987) for a technical discussion of selecting a sample size.

14. Berk (1983) argued that sampling that is nonrandom or a sampling process that excludes a nonrandom subset of cases can create seriously inaccurate estimates of causal relations.

15. For a further discussion of sample size calculation, see Grosof and Sardy (1985:181–185), Kalton (1983:82–90), Sudman (1976a:85–105), and Williams (1978:211–227).

RECOMMENDED READINGS

Henry, Gary T. (1990) *Practical sampling.* Newbury Park, CA: Sage. This is a relatively nontechnical introduction to sampling. Henry focuses on practical, applied issues in carrying out a sample. He also discusses different sampling designs, sampling error, and the calculation of sample size. His concept of total error in samples is very useful.

Kalton, Graham. (1983). *Introduction to survey sampling.* Beverly Hills, CA: Sage. This short (96-page) paperback provides a condensed overview of major sampling techniques and issues. Although it is not written for the sampling statistician, the author assumes that readers have a background of one or two courses in elementary statistics. The author includes practical concerns in the discussion.

Mendenhall, William, Lyman Ott, and Richard L. Scheaffer. (1971). *Elementary survey sampling.* Belmont, CA: Duxbury Press. Readers who have had at least one course in statistics and who would like to build on that knowledge to better understand the applied aspects of sampling concepts will find this book useful. Although the authors do not focus on the practical aspects of sampling, they provide a clearly written, step-by-step introduction to statistical issues that arise in different sampling designs.

Sudman, Seymour. (1976). *Applied sampling.* New York: Academic Press. Sudman provides an excellent overview of sampling for the reader who has some statistical background but whose primary interest is in using sampling techniques in the social sciences. The book covers the major sampling issues most researchers will encounter, with practical and elementary statistical discussions of the issues.

Williams, Bill. (1978). *A sampler on sampling.* New York: Wiley. As the title suggests, this book is a sampler, packed with examples and exercises. The examples come from many different fields and show the importance of good sampling. Readers without at least one course in elementary statistics will have difficulty with several of the chapters.

SURVEY RESEARCH

> *Every method of data collection, including the survey, is only an
> approximation to knowledge. Each provides a different glimpse of reality,
> and all have limitations when used alone. Before undertaking a survey the
> researcher would do well to ask if this is the most appropriate and fruitful
> method for the problem at hand. The survey is highly valuable for studying
> some problems, such as public opinion, and worthless for others.*
>
> —Warwick and Lininger, *The Sample Survey*, pp. 5–6

INTRODUCTION

Someone hands you a sheet of paper full of questions. The first reads: "I would like to learn your opinion of the Neuman research methods textbook. Would you say it is (a) well organized, (b) adequately organized, or (c) poorly organized?" You probably would not be shocked by this. It is a kind of survey, and most of us are accustomed to surveys by the time we reach adulthood.

The survey is the most widely used data-gathering technique in sociology, and it is used in many other fields as well. Social researchers and others use surveys for many purposes. In fact, surveys are almost too popular. People sometimes say, "Do a survey" to get information about the social world, when they should be asking, "What is the most appropriate research design?" Despite the popularity of surveys, it is easy to conduct a survey that yields misleading or worthless results. Good surveys require thought and effort. "Surveys, like other scientific and technical tools, can be well made or poorly made and can be used in appropriate or inappropriate ways" (Bradburn and Sudman, 1988:37).

This chapter focuses on surveys in social research because all surveys are based on the professional social research survey. In this chapter, you will learn the main ingredients of good survey research, as well as the limitations of the survey method.

Research Questions Appropriate for a Survey

Survey research developed within the positivist approach to social science.[1] Surveys produce quantitative information about the social world and describe features of people or the social world. They are also used to explain or explore. The survey asks many people (called *respondents*) about their beliefs, opinions, characteristics, and past or present behavior.

Surveys are appropriate for research questions about self-reported beliefs or behaviors. They are strongest when the answers people give to questions measure variables. Researchers usually ask about many things at one time in surveys, measure many variables (often with multiple indicators), and test several hypotheses in a single survey.

Although the categories overlap, the following can be asked in a survey:

1. *Behavior:* How frequently do you brush your teeth? Did you vote in the last city election? When did you last visit a close relative?
2. *Attitudes/beliefs/opinions:* What kind of job do you think the mayor is doing? Do you think other people say many negative things about you when you are not there? What is the biggest problem facing the nation these days?
3. *Characteristics:* Are you married, never married single, divorced, separated, or widowed? Do you belong to a union? What is your age?
4. *Expectations:* Do you plan to buy a new car in the next 12 months? How much schooling do you think your child will get? Do you think the population in this town will grow, shrink, or stay the same?
5. *Self-classification:* Do you consider yourself to be liberal, moderate, or conservative? Into which social class would you put your family? Would you say you are highly religious or not religious?
6. *Knowledge:* Who was elected mayor in the last election? About what percentage of the people in this city are nonwhite? Is it legal to own a personal copy of Karl Marx's *Communist Manifesto* in this country?

A History of Survey Research

The modern survey can be traced back to ancient forms of the census.[2] A *census* includes information on characteristics of the entire population in a territory. It is based on what people tell officials or what officials observe. For example, the *Domesday Book* was a famous census of England conducted in 1085 to 1086 by William the Conqueror. Early censuses assessed the property available for taxation or the young men available for military service. With the development of representative democracy, officials used the census to assign the number of elected representatives based on the population in a district.

The survey has a long and varied history. Its use for social research in the United States and Great Britain began with social reform movements and social service professions documenting the conditions of urban poverty that followed early industrialization. At first, surveys were overviews of an area based on questionnaires and other data. Scientific sampling and statistics were absent. For example, between 1851 and 1864,

Henry Mayhew published the 4-volume *London Labour and the London Poor*, based on conversations with street people and observations of daily life. Charles Booth's 17-volume (1889–1902) *Labour and Life of the People of London* and B. Seebohm Rowntree's *Poverty: A Study of Town Life* (1906) also examined the extent of urban poverty. Similar work appeared in the United States in *Hull House Maps and Papers of 1895* and W. E. B. DuBois's *Philadelphia Negro* (1899).

The *social survey* grew into both the modern quantitative survey research and qualitative field research in a community. From the 1890s to the 1930s, it was the major method of social research practiced by the Social Survey Movement in Canada, Great Britain, and the United States. The Social Survey Movement used systematic empirical inquiry to support social-political reform goals. Today, the social survey would be called an action-oriented community survey. By the mid-1940s, the modern quantitative survey had largely displaced it.

Early social surveys were detailed empirical studies of specific local areas based on many sources of quantitative and qualitative data. Most were exploratory and descriptive. The researchers wanted to inform the public of the problems of industrialism and provide information for democratic decison making by the people of a community. Some leaders of the early social survey—Florence Kelly and Jane Adams of the Hull House and settlement movement, and the African American W. E. B. DuBois—were unable to secure regular work in universities because of race and gender discrimination. Social surveys provide impressive pictures of daily community life. For example, the six-volume *Pittsburgh Survey* published in 1914 was based on face-to-face interviews; existing statistical data on health, crime, and industrial injury; and direct observations.

Four forces greatly reshaped the social survey into modern quantitative survey research in the United States from 1920 to World War II. First, researchers applied statistically based sampling techniques and precise measurement to the survey, especially after the *Literary Digest* debacle (see Chapter 9). Second, researchers created scales and indexes to gather systematic quantitative data on attitudes, opinions, and subjective aspects of social life. Third, many others found uses for the survey and adapted it to a variety of applied areas. Market research emerged as a distinct field and adapted surveys to study consumer behavior. Journalists used surveys to measure public opinion and the impact the radio. Religious organizations and charities used surveys to identify areas of need. Government agencies used surveys to improve services for agricultural and social programs. Also, more social scientists began to use the survey as a source of empirical data for their basic research.

In addition, there was a major reorientation of most empirical social research, especially the survey, away from a mix of methods used by nonacademics to focus on local social problems. The reorientation created respectable, "scientific" methods modeled after the natural sciences. Social research became more professional, objective, and nonpolitical. This reorientation was stimulated by (1) a competition among researchers and universities for status, prestige, and funds; (2) researchers turning away from social reform ideals after the end of the Progressive Era (1895–1915) in U.S. politics; and (3) a program of major private foundations (Carnegie, Rockefeller, Sage) to fund the expansion of quantitative, positivist social research.[3]

Survey research expanded and matured during World War II, especially in the United States. Academic social researchers and practitioners from industry converged in Washington, DC, to work in the war effort. Survey researchers studied morale, consumer demand, production capacity, enemy propaganda, and the effectiveness of bombing. The wartime cooperation helped academic social researchers and applied practitioners learn from each other and gain experience in conducting many large-scale surveys. Academic researchers helped practitioners appreciate precise measurement, sampling, and statistical analysis, while practitioners helped academics learn the practical side of organizing and conducting large-scale surveys.

After World War II, officials dismantled the extensive government survey research establishment. This was, in part, a cost-cutting move. Also, some members of the U.S. Congress feared that others might use survey results to advance social policies, such as helping the unemployed or promoting equal rights for African Americans who lived in racially segregated southern states.

Many researchers returned to universities and created new social research organizations. At first, the universities were hesitant to embrace expanded survey research. Survey research was expensive and involved many people. In addition, traditional social researchers were wary of quantitative research and skeptical of a technique used in private industry. The culture of applied researchers and business-oriented poll takers clashed with that of traditional basic researchers who lacked statistical training. Yet, surveys grew in use. This growth was not limited to the United States. Within three years of the end of World War II, national survey research institutes had been established in France, Norway, Germany, Italy, the Netherlands, Czechoslovakia, and Britain (Scheuch, 1990).

Despite initial uncertainty, survey research grew through the 1970s. For example, about 18 percent of articles published in sociology journals used the survey method in 1939–1940; this rose to 55 percent by 1964–1965. A dramatic expansion of U.S. higher education and of the social science fields during the 1960s also spurred the growth of survey research. More people learned about survey research, and the method gained in popularity. Five factors contributed to the postwar growth of survey research:[4]

1. *Computers:* Computer technology that became available to social scientists by the 1960s made the sophisticated statistical analysis of large-scale survey data sets feasible for the first time. Today, the computer is an indispensable tool for analyzing data from most surveys.

2. *Organizations:* New social research centers with an expertise and interest in quantitative

research were established at U.S. universities. About 50 such centers were created in the years after 1960.

3. *Data storage:* By the 1970s, data archives were created to store and permit the sharing of the large-scale survey data for secondary analysis (discussed in Chapter 11). The collection, storage, and sharing of information on hundreds of variables for thousands of respondents expanded the use of surveys.

4. *Funding:* For about a decade (late 1960s to late 1970s), the U.S. federal government expanded funds for social science research. Total federal spending for research and development in the social sciences increased nearly tenfold from 1960 to the mid-1970s before it declined.

5. *Methodology:* By the 1970s, substantial research was being conducted on ways to improve the validity of surveys. The survey technique advanced as errors were identified and corrected.[5] In addition, researchers created improved statistics for analyzing quantitative data and taught them to a new generation of researchers.

Today, quantitative survey research is a major industry both within and outside universities. Many organizations conduct surveys. The professional survey industry probably employs over 60,000 people in the United States alone. Most of these are part-time workers, assistants, or semiprofessionals. About 6,000 full-time professional survey researchers design and analyze surveys.[8]

Researchers use surveys for basic research in universities and research centers. Researchers in many fields (communication, education, economics, political science, social psychology, and sociology) conduct and analyze surveys. Many U.S. universities have centers for survey research. Major centers include the Survey Research Center at the University of California at Berkeley, the National Opinion Research Center (NORC) at the University of Chicago, and the Institute for Social Research (ISR) at the University of Michigan.

Several applied areas rely heavily on the survey: government, marketing, private policy research, and mass media. Governments around the world at the national and local levels regularly conduct surveys to inform policy decisions. Private-sector survey research can be divided into three types of organizations: opinion polling organizations (e.g., Gallup, Harris, Roper, Yankelovich and Associates), marketing firms (e.g., Nielsen, Market Facts, Market Research Corporation), and nonprofit research organizations (e.g., Mathematica Policy Research, Rand Corporation).[7]

Major television and newspaper organizations regularly conduct surveys. Rossi, Wright, and Anderson, who (1983:14) found 174 polls sponsored by media organizations, stated, "Polling is as much a feature of the media as comics and the horoscope!" In addition, there are many ad hoc or in-house surveys. Businesses, schools, and other organizations conduct small-scale surveys of employees, clients, students, and the like to address specific applied questions.

Survey researchers have formed separate professional organizations. The American Association for Public Opinion Research, founded in 1947, sponsors a scholarly journal devoted to survey research called *Public Opinion Quarterly*. The Council of American Survey Research Organization is an organization for commercial polling firms. There is also an international survey research organization—the World Association of Public Opinion Research.[8]

In the past three decades, the quantitative survey has become a widely used technology for social research both inside and outside universities. Although knowledge about how to conduct a good survey has grown significantly, the explosion of survey applications has outpaced developments in the survey technique as a method to quantitatively measure human social life.

THE LOGIC OF SURVEY RESEARCH

What Is a Survey?

In experiments, researchers place people in small groups and test one or two hypotheses with a few variables. Subjects respond to a treatment created by the researcher. Causality is shown by the timing of the treatment, by observing associations between the treatment and the dependent variable, and by controlling for alternative explanations.

By contrast, survey researchers sample many respondents who answer the same questions. They measure many variables, test multiple hypotheses, and infer temporal order from questions about past behavior, experiences, or characteristics. For example, years of schooling or a respondent's race are prior to current attitudes. An association among variables is measured with statistical techniques.

Experimenters physically control for alternative explanations. Survey researchers measure variables that represent alternative explanations (i.e., control variables), then statistically examine their effects to rule out alternative explanations. They think of alternative explanations when planning a survey and measure the alternatives with control variables.

Survey research is often called correlational. Survey researchers use control variables and correlations in statistical analysis. They approximate the rigorous test for causality that experimenters achieve with their physical control over temporal order and alternative explanations.

Steps in Conducting a Survey

The survey researcher follows a deductive approach. He or she begins with a theoretical or applied research problem and ends with empirical measurement and data analysis. Once a researcher decides that the survey is an appropriate method, two basic steps in a research project—the research design and data collection—can be divided into the substeps outlined in Table 10.1.

In the first phase, the researcher develops an instrument—a survey questionnaire or interview schedule—that he or she uses to measure variables. Respondents read the questions themselves and mark answers on a *questionnaire*. An *interview schedule* is a set of questions read to the respondent by an interviewer, who also records

TABLE 10.1   Details of Two Research Steps in Survey Research

Design and Planning Phase
1. Decide on type of survey (e.g., mail, telephone interview), type of respondent, and the population.
2. Develop the survey instrument/questionnaire:
   a. Write questions to measure variables
   b. Decide on response categories.
   c. Organize question sequence
   d. Design questionnaire layout.
3. Plan a system for recording answers.
4. Pilot test the instrument and train interviewers if necessary.
5. Draw the sample:
   a. Define target population.
   b. Decide on type of sample.
   c. Develop sampling frame.
   d. Decide on sample size.
   e. Select sample.

Data Collection Phase
1. Locate and contact the respondents.
2. Make introductory statements or provide instructions.
3. Ask questions and record answers.
4. Thank respondent and continue to next respondent.
5. End data collection and organize data.

responses. To simplify the discussion. I will use only the term *questionnaires*.

A survey researcher conceptualizes and operationalizes variables as questions. He or she writes and rewrites questions for clarity and completeness, and organizes questions on the questionnaire based on the research question, the respondents, and the type of survey. (The types of surveys are discussed later.)

When preparing a questionnaire, the researcher thinks ahead to how he or she will record and organize data for analysis. He or she pilot tests the questionnaire with a small set of respondents similar to those in the final survey. If interviewers are used, the researcher trains them with the questionnaire. He or she asks respondents in the pilot test whether the questions were clear and explores their interpretations to see whether his or her intended meaning was clear. The researcher also draws the sample during this phase.

After the planning phase, the researcher is ready to collect data. This phase is usually shorter than the planning phase. He or she locates sampled respondents in person, by telephone, or by mail. Respondents are given information and instructions on completing the questionnaire or interview. The questions follow, and there is a simple stimulus/response or question/answer pattern. The researcher accurately records answers or responses immediately after they are given. After all respondents complete the questionnaire and are thanked, he or she organizes the data and prepares them for statistical analysis.

Survey research can be complex and expensive and it can involve coordinating many people and steps. The administration of survey research requires organization and accurate record keeping.[9] The researcher keeps track of each respondent, questionnaire, and interviewer. For example, he or she gives each sampled respondent an identification number, which also appears on the questionnaire. He or she then checks completed questionnaires against a list of sampled respondents. Next, the researcher reviews responses on individual questionnaires, stores original questionnaires, and transfers information from questionnaires to a format for statistical analysis. Meticulous bookkeeping and labeling are essential. Otherwise, the researcher may find that valuable data and effort are lost through sloppiness.

CONSTRUCTING THE QUESTIONNAIRE

Principles of Good Question Writing

A good questionnaire forms an integrated whole. The researcher weaves questions together so they flow smoothly. He or she includes introductory remarks and instructions for clarification and measures each variable with one or more survey questions.

There are two key principles for good survey questions: Avoid confusion and keep the respondent's perspective in mind. Good survey questions give the researcher valid and reliable measures. They also help respondents feel that they understand the question and that their answers are meaningful. Questions that do not mesh with a respondent's viewpoint or that respondents find confusing are not good measures. A survey researcher exercises extra care if the respondents are heterogeneous or come from different life situations than his or her own.

Researchers face a dilemma. They want each respondent to hear exactly the same question, but will the questions be equally clear, relevant, and meaningful to all respondents? If respondents have diverse backgrounds and frames of reference, exactly the same wording may not have the same meaning. Yet, tailoring question wording to each respondent makes comparisons almost impossible. A researcher would not know whether the wording of the question or differences in respondents accounted for different answers.

Question writing is more of an art than a science. It takes skill, practice, patience, and creativity. The principles of question writing are illustrated in the 10 things to avoid when writing survey questions. The list does not include every possible error, only the more frequent problems.[10]

1. *Avoid jargon, slang, and abbreviations.*

Jargon and technical terms come in many forms. Plumbers talk about *snakes*, lawyers about a contract of *uberrima fides*, psychologists about the *Oedipus complex*. Slang is a kind of jargon within a subculture. For example, skid row bums talk about a *snowbird* and skiers about a *hotdog*. Also avoid abbreviations. NATO usually means North Atlantic Treaty Organization, but for a respondent, it might mean something else (National Auto Tourist Organization, Native Alaskan Trade Orbit, North African Tea Office). Avoid slang and jargon unless a specialized population is being surveyed. Target the vocabulary and grammar to the respondents sampled. For the general public, this is the language used on television or in the newspaper (about an eighth-grade reading vocabulary).

2. *Avoid ambiguity, confusion, and vagueness.*

Ambiguity and vagueness plague most question writers. A researcher might make implicit assumptions without thinking of the respodents. For example, the question, "What is your income?" could mean weekly, monthly, or annual; family or personal; before taxes or after taxes; for this year or last year; from salary or from all sources. The confusion causes inconsistencies in how different respondents assign meaning to and answer the question. The researcher who wants before-tax annual family income for last year explicitly asks for it.[11]

Another source of ambiguity is the use of indefinite words or response categories. For example, an answer to the question. "Do you jog regularly? Yes _____ No _____," hinges on the meaning of the word *regularly*. Some respondents may define *regularly* as every day, others as once a week. To reduce respondent confusion and get more information, be specific—ask whether a person jogs "about once a day," "a few times a week." "once a week," and so on. (See Box 10.1 on improving questions.)

Box 10.1

Improving Unclear Questions

Here are three survey questions written by experienced professional researchers. They revised the original wording after a pilot test revealed that 15 percent of respondents asked for clarification or gave inadequate answers (e.g., don't know). As you can see, question wording is an art that may improve with practice, patience and pilot testing.

ORIGINAL QUESTION	PROBLEM	REVISED QUESTION
Do you exercise or play sports regularly?	What counts as exercise?	Do you do any sports or hobbies, physical activities, or exercise, including walking, on a regular basis?
What is the average number of days each week you have butter?	Does margarine count as butter?	The next question is just about butter. Not including margarine. How many days a week do you have butter?
[Following question on eggs] the number of servings in a typical day?	How many eggs is a serving? What is a typical day?	On days when you eat eggs, how many eggs do you usually have?

	RESPONSES TO QUESTION		PERCENTAGE ASKING FOR CLARIFICATION	
	Original	*Revision*	*Original*	*Revision*
Exercise question (% saying "yes")	48%	60%	5%	0%
Butter question (% saying "none")	33%	55%	18%	13%
Egg question (% saying "one")	80%	33%	33%	0%

Source: Adapted from Fowler (1992).

3. *Avoid emotional language and prestige bias.*

Words have implicit connotative as well as explicit denotative meanings. Likewise, titles or positions in society (e.g., president, expert) carry prestige or status. Words with strong emotional connotations and stands on issues linked to people with high social status can color how respondents hear and answer survey questions.

Use neutral language. Avoid words with emotional "baggage" because respondents may react to the emotionally laden words rather than to the issue. For example, the question, "What do you think about a policy to pay murderous terrorists who threaten to steal the freedoms of peace-loving people?" is full of emotional words—such as *murderous, freedoms, steal,* and *peace.*

Also avoid *prestige bias*—associating a statement with a prestigious person or group. Respondents may answer on the basis of their feelings toward the person or group rather than addressing the issue. For example, saying, "Most doctors say that cigarette smoke causes lung disease for those near a smoker. Do you agree?" affects people who want to agree with doctors. Likewise, a question such as, "Do you support the president's policy regarding Zanozui?" will be answered by respondents who have never heard of Zanozui on the basis of their view of the president.

4. *Avoid double-barreled questions.*

Make each question about one and only one topic. A *double-barreled question* consists of two or more questions joined together. It makes a respondent's answer ambiguous. For example, if asked, "Does this company have pension and health insurance benefits?" a respondent at a company with health insurance benefits only might answer either yes or no. The response has an ambiguous meaning, and the researcher cannot be certain of the respondent's intention. Labaw (1980:154) noted "Perhaps the most basic principle of question wording, and one very often ignored or simply unseen, is that only one concept or issue or meaning should be included in a question." A researcher who wants to ask about the joint occurrence of two things—for example, a company with both health insurance and pension benefits—should ask two separate questions.

Also, do not confuse a respondent's belief that a relationship exists between two variables with the empirical measurement of variables in a relationship. For example, a researcher wants to find out whether students rate teachers higher who tell many jokes in class. The two variables are "teacher tells jokes" and "rating the teacher." The *wrong* way to approach the issue is to ask students, "Do you rate a teacher higher if the teacher tells many jokes?" This measures whether or not students *believe* that they rate teachers based on joke telling; it does not measure the relationship. The *correct* way is to ask two separate questions: "How do you rate the teacher?" and "How many jokes does the teacher tell in class?" Then the researcher can examine answers to the two questions to see whether an association exists between them. Beliefs about a relationship are distinct from an actual relationship.

5. *Avoid leading questions.*

Make respondents feel that all responses are legitimate. Do not let them become aware of an answer that the researcher wants. A *leading* (or *loaded*) *question* is one that leads the respondent to choose one response over another by its wording. There are many kinds of leading questions. For example, the question, "You don't smoke, do you?" leads respondents to state that they do not smoke.

Loaded questions can be stated to get either positive or negative answers. For example, "Should the mayor spend even more tax money trying to keep the streets in top shape?" leads respondents to disagree, whereas "Should the mayor fix the pot-holed and dangerous streets in our city?" is loaded for agreement.

6. *Avoid asking questions that are beyond respondents' capabilities.*

Asking something that few respondents know frustrates respondents and produces poor-quality responses. Respondents cannot always recall past details and may not know specific factual information. For example, asking an adult, "How did you feel about your brother when you were 6 years old?" is probably worthless. Asking respondents to make a choice about something they know nothing about (e.g., a technical issue in foreign affairs or an internal policy of an organization) may result in an answer, but one that is unreliable and meaningless. When many respondents are unlikely to know about an issue, use a full-filter question form (to be discussed).

Phrase questions in the terms in which respondents think. For example, few respondents will be able to answer, "How many gallons of gasoline did you buy last year for your car?" Yet, respondents may be able to answer a question about gasoline purchases for a typical week, which the researcher can multiply by 52 to estimate annual purchases.

7. *Avoid false premises.*

Do not begin a question with a premise with which respondents may not agree, then ask about choices regarding it. Respondents who disagree with the premise will be frustrated and not know how to answer. For example, the question, "The post office is open too many hours. Do you want

"Next question: I believe that life is a constant striving for balance, requiring frequent tradeoffs between morality and necessity, within a cyclic pattern of joy and sadness, forging a trail of bittersweet memories until one slips, inevitably, into the jaws of death. Agree or disagree?"

Source: Drawing by Geo. Price; © 1989 The New Yorker Magazine, Inc.

it to open four hours later or close four hours earlier each day?" leaves those who either oppose the premise or oppose both alternatives without a meaningful choice.

A better question explicitly asks the respondent to assume a premise is true, then asks for a preference. For example, "Assuming the post office has to cut back its operating hours, which would you find more convenient, opening four hours later or closing four hours earlier each day?" Answers to a hypothetical situation are not very reliable, but being explicit will reduce frustration.

8. *Avoid asking about future intentions.*

Avoid asking people about what they might do under hypothetical circumstances. Responses are poor predictors of behavior. Questions such as, "Suppose a new grocery store opened down the road. Would you shop at it?" are usually a waste of time. It is better to ask about current or recent attitudes and behavior. In general, respondents answer specific, concrete questions that relate to their experiences more reliably than they do those about abstractions that are beyond their immediate experiences.

9. *Avoid double negatives.*

Double negatives in ordinary language are grammatically incorrect and confusing. For example, "I ain't got no job" logically means that the respondent does have a job, but the second negative is used in this way for emphasis. Such blatant errors are rare, but more subtle forms of the double negative are also confusing. They arise when respondents are asked to agree or disagree with a statement. For example, respondents who *disagree* with the statement, "Students should not be required to take a comprehensive exam to graduate" are logically stating a double negative because they *disagree* with *not* doing something.

10. *Avoid overlapping or unbalanced response categories.*

Make response categories or choices mutually exclusive, exhaustive, and balanced. *Mutually exclusive* means that response categories do not overlap. Overlapping categories that are numerical ranges (e.g., 5–10, 10–20, 20–30) can be easily corrected (e.g., 5–9, 10–19, 20–29). The ambiguous verbal choice is another type of overlapping response category—for example, "Are you satisfied with your job or are there things you don't like about it?" *Exhaustive* means that every respondent has a choice—a place to go. For example, asking respondents, "Are you working or unemployed?" leaves out respondents who are not working but do not consider themselves unemployed (e.g., full-time homemakers, people on vacation, students, the disabled, retired persons). A researcher first thinks about what he or she wants to measure and then considers the circumstances of respondents.

For example, when asking about a respondent's employment, does the researcher want information on the primary job or on all jobs? On full-time work only or both full- and part-time work? On jobs for pay only or on unpaid or volunteer jobs as well?

Keep response categories *balanced*. A case of unbalanced choices is the question, "What kind of job is the mayor doing—outstanding, excellent, very good, or satisfactory?" Another type of unbalanced question omits information—for example, "Which of the five candidates running for mayor do you favor: Eugene Oswego or one of the others?"

Aiding Respondent Recall

Survey researchers have recently examined a respondent's ability to accurately recall past behavior and events when answering survey questions.[12] This always has been a critical issue in oral history and recollections for historical research (see Chapter 15), but it is also an significant issue for survey questions about recent events. Recalling events accurately takes more time and effort than the dozen seconds that respondents have to answer survey questions. Also, one's ability to recall accurately declines over time. Studies in hospitalization and crime victimization show that although most respondents can recall significant events that occurred in the past several weeks, half are inaccurate a year later.

Survey researchers recognize that memory is less trustworthy than once assumed. It is affected by many factors—the topic (threatening or socially desirable), events occurring simultaneously and subsequently, the significance of an event for a person, situational conditions (question wording and interview style), and the respondent's need to have internal consistency. "Evidence now accumulating suggests that the task of recalling if and when events occur is far more difficult than survey researchers typically assumed. Real world events appear to be forgotten rapidly" (Turner and Martin, 1984:296).

The complexity of respondent recall does not mean that survey researchers cannot ask about past events; rather, they need to customize questions and interpret results cautiously. Researchers should provide respondents with special instructions and extra thinking time. They should also provide aids to respondent recall, such as a fixed time frame or location references. Rather than ask, "How often did you attend a sporting event last winter?" they should say, "I want to know how many sporting events you attended last winter. Let's go month by month. Think back to December. Did you attend any sporting events for which you paid admission in December? Now, think back to January. Did you attend any sporting events in January?"

A study by Mooney and Gramling (1991) illustrates the importance of using recall aids. They asked students two types of questions about drinking behavior and found that standard questions, such as, "On the average, how many days a month have you had something to drink (wine, beer, liquor)?" and "On the average, how many drinks do you have each of these times?" yielded much lower results than asking the same question about 12 locations (e.g., bar, relative's home, fraternity/sorority house) and summing the total. Such aided recall reduces omissions and enhances accuracy, but it does not produce over-estimating. Many respondents will *telescope*— compress time when asked about frequency and overreport recent events. Two techniques reduce telescoping: situational framing (e.g., ask the respondent to recall a specific situation and then ask about it) and decomposition (e.g., ask several specifics and add them up—such as how much one drank in a week then total for drinking in a year). Survey researchers who ask about past events or behavior, even within the past year, need to do so with care.

Types of Questions and Response Categories

Threatening versus Nonthreatening Questions. Researchers sometimes ask about sensitive issues or ones that respondents find threatening.[13] Many respondents find questions about sexual behavior, drug or alcohol use, deviant behavior, mental health, illegal activity, or controversial public issues to be threatening. Researchers who ask such questions must do so with extra care.

Threatening questions are part of a broader issue. Respondents may try to present a positive image of themselves to interviewers or researchers instead of giving true answers. Respondents may be ashamed, embarrassed, or afraid to give a truthful answer. Instead, they give what they believe to be the normative or socially desirable answer. This is the *social desirability bias*. This social pressure can cause an overreporting or underreporting of the true situation (see Table 10.2). For example, a virgin adult male may report engaging in sexual intercourse if he believes it is normal to be sexually active, whereas a sexually active teenager in a conservative town may not report sexual activity.

People are likely to overreport being a good citizen (e.g., voting, knowing about issues), being well informed and cultured (e.g., reading, going to cultural events), fulfilling moral responsibilities (e.g., having a job, giving to charity), or having a good family life (e.g., having a happy marriage and good relations with children). For example, Denver respondents were asked whether they gave to a charity. A check of charity records revealed that 34 percent who said they gave in fact did not.[14]

Because most people want to present positive self-images and merge a sense of self with normative expectations, "false claims or exaggerations of socially desirable behavior occur more frequently than untruthful denials, flase claims, minimizations, or exaggerations of socially undesireable behavior" (Wentworth, 1993:180). When a researcher suspects social desirability, he or she may ask several more specific questions and use the techniques for aiding respondent recall.

People are likely to underreport having an illness or disability (e.g., cancer, mental illness, venereal disease), engaging in illegal or deviant behavior (e.g., evading taxes, taking drugs, consuming alcohol, engaging in uncommon sexual practices), or revealing their financial status (e.g., income, savings, debts) (see Table 10.3).

Researchers can increase truthful answers to questions by offering explicit guarantees of confidentiality and by telling respondents that truthful answers are wanted and that any answer is acceptable. They should ask questions on sensitive topics after respondents have developed trust in an interviewer. They can also wait until after asking less threatening warm-up material and providing a meaningful context. They can phrase questions to make it easy for a respondent to admit engaging in the threatening behavior. For example, instead of asking whether a respondent masturbates, they ask, "About how frequently do you masturbate—once a week, once a month, every day, or never?" Another method is to have an introductory statement that states that many people engage in the behavior. Also, by embedding a threatening response within more serious activities, it may be made to seem less deviant. For example, respondents may hesitate to admit shoplifting if it is asked first, but after being asked about armed robbery or burglary, they may admit to shoplifting because it appears less serious.

TABLE 10.2   Threatening Questions and Sensitive Issues

TOPIC	PERCENTAGE VERY UNEASY
Masturbation	56
Sexual intercourse	42
Use of marijuana or hashish	42
Use of stimulants and depressants	31
Getting drunk	29
Petting and kissing	20
Income	12
Gambling with friends	10
Drinking beer, wine, or liquor	10
Happiness and well-being	4
Education	3
Occupation	3
Social activities	2
General leisure	2
Sports activity	1

Source: Adapted from Bradburn and Sudman (1980:68).

TABLE 10.3   Over- and Underreporting Behavior on Surveys

	PERCENTAGE DISTORTED OR ERRONEOUS ANSWERS		
	Face to Face	Phone	Self-Administered
Low-threat/normative:			
Registered to vote	+ 15	+17	+12
Voted in primary	+ 39	+31	+36
Have own library card	+ 19	+21	+18
High-threat:			
Bankruptcy	– 32	– 29	- 32
Drunk driving	– 47	– 46	- 54

Source: Adapted from Bradburn and Sudman, 1980:8).

Survey methods that permit greater anonymity are better for threatening issues. Thus, it may be better to use a mail or self-administered questionnaire. In face-to-face interview situations, respondents can be given a card with responses and just report a letter or number corresponding to their answer.

The techniques to survey sensitive behavior may differ across groups in society. For example, Aquilino and Losciuto (1990) examined the use of legal and illegal drugs among 18- to 34-year-olds using *random digit dialing (RDD)* telephone interviews and self-administered questionnaires with special procedures to protect anonymity (e.g., sealing answers in an unmarked envelope). They found little difference between the two survey methods for white respondents. For black respondents, the self-administered questionnaire was more likely to reveal the use of illegal drugs. (Also see Johnson, Hougland, and Clayton, 1989.)

A complicated invention for asking threatening questions in face-to-face interview situations is the *randomized response technique (RRT)*. The technique uses statistics beyond the level of this book, but the basic idea is to use known probabilities to estimate unknown proportions. Here is how RRT works. An interviewer gives the respondent two questions. One is threatening (e.g., "Do you use heroin?"), the other not threatening (e.g., "Were you born in September?"). A random method (e.g., toss of coin) is used to select the question to answer. The interviewer does not see which question was chosen but records the respondent's answer. The researcher uses knowledge about the probability of the random outcome and the frequency of the nonthreatening behavior to estimate the frequency of the sensitive behavior.

Knowledge Questions. Studies suggest that a large majority of the public cannot correctly answer elementary geography questions or identify important political documents (e.g., the Declaration of Independence). Researchers sometimes want to find out whether respondents know about an issue or topics, but knowledge questions can be threatening because respondents do not want to appear ignorant.[15]

Surveys may measure opinions better if they first ask about factual information, because many people have inaccurate factual knowledge. For example, Nadeau, Miemi, and Levine (1993) found that most Americans seriously overestimate the percent of racial minorities in the population. Only 15 percent of U.S. adults accurately report (plus or minus 6 percent) that 12.1 percent of the U.S. population is African American. Over half believe it is above 30 percent. Similarly, Jews make up about 3 percent of the U.S. population, but a majority (60 percent) of Americans believe the proportion to be 10 percent. Others have found that many Americans oppose foreign aid spending. Their opposition is based on extremely high overestimates of the cost of the programs. When asked what they would prefer to spend on foreign aid, most give an amount much higher than what now is being spent. A researcher might examine which types of people regularly make such overestimates and why many people hold seriously distorted beliefs.

First, a researcher pilot tests questions so that questions are at an appropriate level of difficulty. Little is gained if 99 percent of respondents cannot answer the question. Knowledge questions can be worded so that respondents feel comfortable saying they do not know the answer—for example, "How much, if anything, have you heard about. . . ."

Respondents may overstate their knowledge or recognition of people or events. One way to check this is to use a *sleeper question*—a question or response choice about which a respondent could not possibly know. For example, in a study to determine which U.S. civil rights leaders respondents recognized, the name of a fictitious person was added. The person was "recognized" by 15 percent of the respondents. This implies that actual leaders who were recognized by only 15 percent were probably actually unknown. Another method is to ask respondents to "tell me about the person" after they say they recognize a name in a list.

Skip or Contingency Questions. Researchers avoid asking questions that are irrelevant for a respondent. Yet, some questions apply only to specific respondents. A *contingency question* is a two- (or more) part question.[16] The answer to the first part of the question determines which of two different questions a respondent next receives. Contingency questions select respondents for whom a second question is relevant, Sometimes they are called screen or skip questions. On the basis of the answer to a first question, the respondent or an interviewer is instructed to go to another or to skip certain questions.

The following example is a contingency question, adapted from de Vaus (1986:79).

1. Were you born in Australia?
   [ ] Yes (GO TO QUESTION 2)
   [ ] No _____
      (a) What country were you born in? _____
      (b) How many years have you lived in Australia? _____
      (c) Are you an Australian citizen?
      [ ] Yes   [ ] No
   NOW GO TO QUESTION 2

Open versus Closed Questions

There has been a long debate about open versus closed questions in survey research.[17] An *open-ended* (unstructured, free response) *question* asks a question (e.g., "What is your favorite television program?") to which respondents can give any answer. A *closed-ended* (structured, fixed response) *question* both asks a question and gives the respondent fixed responses from which to choose (e.g., "Is the president doing a very good, good, fair, or poor job, in your opinion?").

Each form has advantages and disadvantages (see Box 10.2). The crucial issue is not which form is best. Rather, it is under what conditions a form is most appropriate. A researcher's choice to use an open- or closed-ended question depends on the purpose and the practical limitations of a research project. The demands of using open-ended questions, with interviewers writing verbatim answers followed by time-consuming coding, may make them impractical for a specific project.

Large-scale surveys have closed-ended questions because they are quicker and easier for both respondents and researchers. Yet something important may be lost when an individual's beliefs and feelings are forced into a few fixed categories that a researcher created. To learn how a respondent thinks, to discover what is really important to him or her, or to get an answer to a question with many possible answers (e.g., age), open questions may be best. In addition, sensitive

Box 10.2 _____

Open versus Closed Questions

ADVANTAGES OF CLOSED

- It is easier and quicker for respondents to answer.
- The answers of different respondents are easier to compare.
- Answers are easier to code and statistically analyze.
- The response choices can clarify question meaning for respondents.
- Respondents are more likely to answer about sensitive topics.
- There are fewer irrelevant or confused answers to questions.
- Less articulate or less literate respondents are not at a disadvantage.
- Replication is easier.

DISADVANTAGES OF CLOSED

- They can suggest ideas that the respondent would not otherwise have.
- Respondents with no opinion or no knowledge can answer anyway.
- Respondents can be frustrated because their desired answer is not a choice.
- It is confusing if many (e.g., 20) response choices are offered.
- Misinterpretation of a question can go unnoticed.
- Distinctions between respondent answers may be blurred.
- Clerical mistakes or marking the wrong response is possible.
- They force respondents to give simplistic responses to complex issues.
- They force people to make choices they would not make in the real world.

ADVANTAGES OF OPEN

- They permit an unlimited number of possible answers.
- Respondents can answer in detail and can qualify and clarify responses.
- Unanticipated findings can be discovered.
- They permit adequate answers to complex issues.
- They permit creativity, self-expression, and richness of detail.
- They reveal a respondent's logic, thinking process, and frame of reference.

DISADVANTAGES OF OPEN

- Different respondents give different degrees of detail in answers.
- Responses may be irrelevant or buried in useless detail.
- Comparisons and statistical analysis become very difficult.
- Coding responses is difficult.
- Articulate and highly literate respondents have an advantage.
- Questions may be too general for respondents who lose direction.
- Responses are written verbatim, which is difficult for interviewers.
- A greater amount of respondent time, thought, and effort is necessary.
- Respondents can be intimidated by questions.
- Answers take up a lot of space in the questionnaire.

_____

topics (e.g., sexual behavior, liquor consumption) may be more accurately measured with closed questions.

The disadvantages of a question form can be reduced by mixing open-ended and closed-ended questions in a questionnaire. Mixing them also offers a change of pace and helps interviewers establish rapport. Periodic probes (i.e., follow-up questions by interviewers) with closed-ended questions can reveal a respondent's reasoning.

Researchers also use *partially open questions* (i.e., a set of fixed choices with a final open choice of "other"), which allows respondents to offer an answer that the researcher did not include.

A total reliance on closed questions can distort results. For example, a study compared open and closed versions of the question, "What is the major problem facing the nation?" Respondents ranked different problems as most important depending on the form of the question. As Schuman and Presser (1979:86) reported, "Almost all respondents work within the substantive framework of the priorities provided by the investigators, *whether or not it fits their own priorities*" (emphasis added). In another study, respondents were asked open and closed questions about what was important in a job. Half of the respondents who answered the open-ended version gave answers that were outside closed-question responses.

Open-ended questions are especially valuable in early or exploratory stages of research. For large-scale surveys, researchers use open questions in pilot tests, then develop closed-question responses from the answers given to the open questions. Glock (1987:50) noted,

> *A major source of data in survey research is the qualitative interview conducted during the planning phases of a project. Such interviews, with a small but roughly representative sample of the population to be surveyed subsequently, afford an indispensable way to learn about the nature of variation and how to go about operationalizing it.*

Researchers writing closed questions have to make many decisions. How many response choices should be given? Should they offer a middle or neutral choice? What should be the order of responses? What types of response choices? How will the direction of a response be measured?

Answers to these questions are not easy. For example, two response choices are too few, but more than five response choices are rarely a benefit. Researchers want to measure meaningful distinctions and not collapse them. More specific responses yield more information, but too many specifics create confusion. For example, rephrasing the question, "Are you satisfied with your dentist?" (which has a yes/no answer) to "How satisfied are you with your dentist—very satisfied, somewhat satisfied, somewhat dissatisfied, or not satisfied at all?" gives the researcher more information and a respondent more choices.

Nonattitudes and the Middle Positions.   Survey researchers debate whether to include choices for neutral, middle, and nonattitudes (e.g., "not sure," "don't know," or "no opinion").[18] Two types of errors can be made: accepting a middle choice or "no attitude" response when respondents hold a nonneutral opinion, or forcing respondents to choose a position on an issue when they have no opinion about it. Researchers also try to avoid both false positives (falsely stating an opinion when one does not know) and false negatives (falsely stating "don't know" when one has an opinion) with more attention given to false positives (Gilljam and Granberg, 1993).

Many fear that respondents will chose nonattitude choices to evade making a choice. Yet, it is usually best to offer a nonattitude choice, because people will express opinions on fictitious issues, objects, and events. By offering a nonattitude (middle or no opinion) choice, researchers identify those holding middle positions or those without opinions.

The issue of nonattitudes can be approached by distinguishing among three kinds of attitude questions: standard-format, quasi-filter, and full-filter questions (see Box 10.3). The *standard-format question* does not offer a "don't know" choice; a respondent must volunteer it. A *quasi-filter question* offers respondents a "don't know" alternative. A *full-filter question* is a special type of contingency question. It first asks if respondents have an opinion, then asks for the opinion of those who state that they do have an opinion.

Many respondents will answer a question if a "no opinion" choice is missing, but they will choose "don't know" when it is offered, or say that they do not have an opinion if asked. Such respondents are called *floaters* because they "float" from giving a response to not knowing.

"We're still debating."

Their responses are affected by minor wording changes, so researchers screen them out using quasi-filter or full-filter questions. Filtered questions do not eliminate all answers to nonexistent issues, but they reduce the problem.

Middle alternative floaters chose a middle position when it is offered, or another alternative if it is not. They have less intense feelings about an issue. There is also a slight *recency effect*; that is, respondents are more likely to choose the last alternative offered. The recency effect suggests that it is best to present responses on a continuum, with the middle or neutral position stated in the middle.

Researchers have two choices: offering a middle position for those who are truly ambiguous or moderate, or omitting the middle choice and forcing respondents to choose a position but following it immediately with a question asking how strongly they feel about the choice. This latter choice is preferred because attitudes have two aspects: direction (for or against) and intensity (strongly held or weakly held). For example, two respondents both oppose abortion, but one holds the opinion fiercely, with a strong commitment, whereas the other holds it weakly.

Agree/Disagree, Rankings or Ratings?   Survey researchers who measure values and attitudes have debated two issues about the responses offered.[19] Should questionnaire items make a statement and ask respondents whether they agree or disagree with it, or should it offer respondents specific alternatives? Should the questionnaire include a set of items and ask respondents to rate them (e.g., approve, disapprove), or should it give them a list of items and force them to rank-order items (e.g., from most favored to least favored)?

It is best to offer respondents explicit alternatives. For example, instead of asking, "Do you agree or disagree with the statement, 'Men are better suited to. . .,' " instead ask, "Do you think men are better suited, women are better suited, or both are equally suited?" Less well educated respondents are more likely to agree with a statement, whereas forced-choice alternatives encourage thought and avoid the *response set* bias—a tendency of some respondents to agree and not really decide.

Researchers create bias if question wording gives respondents a reason for choosing one alternative. For example, respondents were asked whether they supported or opposed a law on energy conservation. The results changed when respondents heard, "Do you support the law or do you oppose it because the law would be difficult to enforce?" instead of simply, "Do you support or oppose the law?"

It is better to ask respondents to choose among alternatives by ranking instead of rating items along an imaginary continuum. Respondents can rate several items equally high, but will place them in a hierarchy if asked to rank them.[20]

Schwartz, Knäuper, Hippler, Noelle-Neumann, and Clark (1991) found that respondents use the numbers assigned to response scales as a clue to how to think about a survey question. They suggest that researchers attach positive and negative numbers to response categories (e.g., −5 to +5) only when they conceptualize a variable in clear bipolar terms and use positive numbers (e.g., 0 to 10) when they conceptualize it along a single continuum. Both positive and negative

Box 10.3 _____

Standard-Format, Quasi-Filter, and Full-Filter Questions

STANDARD FORMAT

Here are some questions about other countries. Do you agree or disagree with this statement? "The Russian leaders are basically trying to get along with America."

QUASI-FILTER

Here is a statement about another country: "The Russian leaders are basically trying to get along with America." Do you agree, disagree, or have no opinion on that?

FULL FILTER

Here is a statement about another country. Not everyone has an opinion on this. If you do not have an opinion, just say so. Here's the statement: "The Russian leaders are basically trying to get along with America." Do you have an opinion on that?
   If yes, do you agree or disagree?

EXAMPLE OF RESULTS FROM DIFFERENT QUESTION FORMS

	Standard Form (%)	Quasi-Filter (%)	Full-Filter (%)
Agree	48.2	27.7	22.9
Disagree	38.2	29.5	20.9
No opinion	13.6*	42.8	56.3

*Volunteered

Source: Adapted from Schuman and Presser (1981:116–125). Standard format is from Fall 1978; quasi- and full-filter are from February 1977.

numbers may be appropriate for a question such as, "How do you feel about defense spending," but positive numbers alone may be better for a question such as, "How successful would you say you are?"

Wording Issues

Survey researchers face two wording issues. The first, discussed earlier, is to use simple vocabulary and grammar to minimize confusion. The second issue involves effects of specific words or phrases. It is trickier because it is not possible to know in advance whether a word or phrase affects responses.[21]

   The well-documented difference between _forbid_ and _not allow_ illustrates the problem of wording differences. Both terms have the same meaning, but many more people are willing to "not allow" something than to "forbid" it. In general, less well educated respondents are most influenced by minor wording differences.

   Certain words seem to trigger an emotional reaction, and researchers are just beginning to learn of them. For example, Smith (1987) found large differences (e.g., twice as much support) in U.S. survey responses depending on whether a question asked about spending "to help the poor" or "for welfare." He suggested that the word _welfare_ has such strong negative connotations for Americans (lazy people, wasteful and expensive programs) that it is best to avoid it.

   Possible _wording effects_ are illustrated by what appears to be a noncontroversial question.

Peterson (1984) examined four ways to ask about age: "How old are you?" "What is your age?" "In what year were you born?" and "Are you . . . 18–24, 25–34, . . . ?" He checked responses against birth certificate records and found that from 98.7 to 95.1 percent of respondents gave correct responses depending on the form of question used. He also found that the form of the question that had the fewest errors had the highest percentage of refusals to answer, and the form with the most errors had the lowest refusal rate. This example suggests that errors in a noncontroversial factual question vary with minor wording changes and that increasing the respondent's willingness to answer may increase errors in responses.

Many respondents are confused by words or their connotations. For example, respondents were asked whether they thought television news was impartial. Researchers later learned that large numbers of respondents had ignored the word *impartial*—a term the middle-class, educated researchers assumed everyone would know. Less than half the respondents had interpreted the word as intended with its proper meaning. Over one-fourth ignored it or had no idea of its meaning. Others gave it unusual meanings, and one-tenth thought it was directly opposite to its true meaning (Foddy, 1993). Presser (1990) found that wording effects in surveys may not change over time. He compared the impact of filter-form questions, wording changes (e.g., *forbid* versus *not allow*), and open versus closed answers in 1976 and 1986. He found that, overall, answers changed during the decade, but the difference between question forms stayed the same. For example, in 1976, 59 percent of Americans said the government is too powerful in a standard-form question and 50 percent in a filter-form question. In 1986, it was 50 percent for the standard form and 40 percent for the filter form.

Questionnaire Design Issues

Length of Survey or Questionnaire. How long should a questionnaire be or an interview last?[22] Researchers prefer long questionnaires or interviews because they are more cost effective. The cost for extra questions—once a respondent has been sampled, has been contacted, and has completed other questions—is small. There is no absolute proper length. The length depends on the survey format (to be discussed) and on the respondent's characteristics. A 10-minute telephone interview is rarely a problem and can usually be extended to 20 minutes. A few researchers stretched this to beyond 30 minutes. Mail questionnaires are more variable. A short (3- or 4-page) questionnaire is appropriate for the general population. Some researchers have had success with questionnaires as long as 10 pages (about 100 items) with the general public, but responses drop significantly for longer questionnaires. For highly educated respondents and a salient topic, using questionnaires of 15 pages may be possible. Face-to-face interviews lasting an hour are not uncommon. In special situations, face-to-face interviews as long as three to five hours have been conducted.

Question Order or Sequence. Survey researchers face two question sequence issues.[23] The first is how to organize items in the overall questionnaire. The second involves context effects of answering specific questions before others.

In general, you should sequence questions to minimize the discomfort and confusion of respondents. A questionnaire has opening, middle, and ending questions. After an introduction explaining the survey, it is best to make opening questions pleasant, interesting, and easy to answer so that they help a respondent to feel comfortable about the questionnaire. Avoid asking many boring background questions or threatening questions first. Organize questions in the middle into common topics. Mixing questions on different topics causes confusion. Orient respondents by placing questions on the same topic together and introduce the section with a short introductory statement (e.g., "Now I would like to ask you questions about housing"). Make question topics flow smoothly and logically, and organize them to assist respondents' memory or comfort levels. Do not end with highly threatening questions, and always end with a "thank you."

Researchers are concerned that the order in which questions are presented may influence respondents' answers. These *order effects* are strongest for respondents who lack strong opinions or who are less well educated. They use previous questions as a context to help them answer later questions (see Box 10.4). You can do two things about specific question order effects: Use a *funnel sequence* of questions—that is, ask more general questions before specific ones (e.g., ask about health in general before asking about specific diseases). Or, divide respondents in half and give one half questions in one order and the other half the alternative order, then examine the results to see whether question order mattered. If question order effects are found, which order tells you what the respondents really think? The answer is that you cannot know for sure.

For example, a few years ago, a class of my students conducted a telephone survey on two topics: concern about crime and attitudes toward a new antidrunk driving law. A random half of the respondents heard questions about the drunk-driving law first: the other half heard about crime first. I examined the results to see whether there was any *context effect*—a difference by topic order. I found that respondents who were asked about the drunk-driving law first expressed less fear about crime than did those who were asked about crime first. Likewise, they were more supportive of the drunk-driving law than were those who first heard about crime. The first topic created a context within which respondents answered questions on the second topic. After they were asked about crime in general and thought about violent crime, drunk driving may have appeared to be a less important issue. By contrast. after they were asked about drunk driving and thought about drunk driving as a crime, they may have expressed less concern about crime in general.

Nonresponse, Refusals, and Response Rates. Have you ever refused to answer a survey? The likelihood that people will agree to a request to complete a questionnaire varies for different types of contact. Charities expect a 1 percent response rate, whereas the census expects a 95 percent rate. Response rates are a big concern in survey research. If a high proportion of the sampled res-

---

Box 10.4 _____

Question Order Effects

QUESTION 1

"Do you think that the United States should let Communist newspaper reporters from other countries come in here and send back to their papers the news as they see it?"

QUESTION 2

"Do you think a Communist country like Russia should let American newspaper reporters come in and send back to America the news as they see it?"

PERCENTAGE SAYING YES

Heard First	Yes to #1 (Communist Reporter)	Yes to #2 (American Reporter)
#1	54%	75%
#2	64%	82%

The context created by answering the first question affects the answer to the second question.

Source: Adapted from Schuman and Presser (1981:29).

pondents do not respond, researchers become cautious about generalizing from the results. If the nonresponders differ from those who respond (e.g., are less educated), low response rates can create bias and weaken validity.

Failure to get a response from a sampled respondent can take several forms: The respondent could not be contacted, he or she was contacted but was unable to complete the survey (e.g., spoke another language, had no time, was ill), he or she refused to complete a questionnaire or refused to be interviewed, or he or she refused to answer some questions.[24]

Public participation in survey research has declined in the United States since the 1950s, especially in urban areas. One report notes that as many as 38 percent of Americans refuse to participate in surveys.[25] This is a disturbing trend for survey researchers. It is due to many factors—a fear of strangers and crime, social isolation, an overload of surveys, and, most important,

> *people who refuse to participate in surveys appear to be more negative about surveys in general, more withdrawn and isolated from their environment and more concerned about maintaining their privacy free of any intrusion by strangers. (Sudman and Bradburn, 1983:11)*

In addition to privacy concerns, an unfavorable past experience with surveys is a major cause of nonresponse. Legitimate survey research is impeded by misused survey techniques, insensitive interviewers, poorly designed or written questionnaires, and inadequate explanations of surveys to respondents.

Survey researchers disagree about what constitutes an adequate response rate. *Adequate* is a judgment call that depends on the population, practical limitations, the topic, and the response with which specific researchers feel comfortable. Most researchers consider anything below 50 percent to be poor and over 90 percent as excellent.

If response rates are below 75 percent, the survey results can differ significantly from what they would be if everyone responded. For example, a survey reports that a majority of respon-

dents favor a product or a new policy, when in fact a majority of the population actually oppose it. This is likely when the response rate is low and those who do not respond have different views from those who do (see Box 10.5).

To complicate matters, researchers calculate response rates in different ways. The same survey can have a 50 to 75 percent rate depending on the formula used. For example, response rates for telephone or face-to-face interviews are usually based on the percentage responding of the number who were located and contacted, not of the number who were sampled.

Response rates for self-administered questionnaires (e.g., those distributed to a class) are close to 100 percent and present little problem. Rates are high for face-to-face interviews (about 90 percent), followed by telephone interviews (about 80 percent). Response rates are a major concern for mail questionnaires. A response rate of 10 to 50 percent is common for a mail survey.

A researcher can increase response rates in several ways. In telephone interview surveys, interviewers can make five callbacks before dropping a respondent. They can keep a record of each call so that they do not always call back at the same time. Ideal times to call vary, but from 6:00 through 9:00 P.M. on Sunday through Thursday is usually a good period of time.

Even with several callbacks, noncontact rates of 20 percent are common. Once interviewers contact a respondent, he or she must be persuaded to cooperate. Refusal rates for telephone interviews are often about 20 percent. Although it is impossible with random digit dialing, cooperation rates on telephone interviews are usually higher if the researcher sends a letter three to five days in advance telling the respondent to expect the interview call. Interviewers give their name, the organization conducting the survey, the general topic of the survey, and the approximate amount of time the interview will take—for example: "My name is Larry Neuman, I am calling for the Survey Research Corporation. I'd like to ask you some questions about your television viewing habits. The interview shouldn't last more than 10 minutes, and your answers will be kept confidential."

Box 10.5 _____

Example of Response Rate Problems

Assuming 70 percent of the respondents respond, how far off could the observed results be from the true population parameter? A series of possible situations is illustrated below:

RESPONSE TO QUESTION	OBSERVED PERCENTAGE OF ANSWERING RESPONDENTS	HYPOTHETICAL RESPONSE OF THOSE NOT RESPONDING	TRUE RESPONSE OF WHOLE POPULATION (PARAMETER)[a]
Favor	50 (35)[b]	60 (18)	53%
Oppose	50 (35)	40 (12)	47%
Favor	50 (35)	90 (27)	62%
Oppose	50 (35)	10 (3)	38%
Favor	20 (14)	60 (18)	32%
Oppose	80 (56)	40 (12)	68%
Favor	20 (14)	90 (27)	41%
Oppose	80 (56)	10 (3)	59%
Favor	45 (31.5)	60 (18)	49.5%
Oppose	55 (38.5)	40 (12)	50.5%
Favor	45 (31.5)	90 (27)	58.5%
Oppose	55 (38.5)	10 (3)	41.5%

[a]This assumes a perfect sampling frame, with no sampling errors or measurement errors. Any such error could increase or decrease the difference between observed survey results and the population parameter.

[b]The number in parentheses is the actual percentage in the population choosing an answer. For example, 50 percent choosing an answer with a 70 percent response rate is 50% × 70% = 35% of the population choosing that answer. The estimate of population parameter is calculated by adding the actual percentage in the population for the observed and the hypothetical nonrespondent answers.

Face-to-face interviewers first have the task of locating a respondent. An advance letter or telephone call to arrange an appointment is wise, but repeat visits may be necessary. Even with an appointment, respondents may hesitate or refuse. Interviewers should have a photo identification card and should explain who is interviewing the respondent and why. Once a respondent is contacted and a well-trained, pleasant interviewer is at the doorstep, most respondents cooperate.

Getting survey responses fom some populations, such as low-income, inner-city minorities, poses a special challenge. Pottick and Lerman (1991) used a journalistic-style letter introducing

the survey and a personal telephone call reminding respondents of an interview. They compared this approach with a standard method using an academic-style letter and a follow-up letter. Their approach produced a more rapid response and more respondents. For example, their technique resulted in 65 pecent participation, compared to 39 percent for the standard method. Their approach also brought in respondents who were more generally pessimistic and those who felt less well understood by government and social service agencies.

There is a large body of literature on ways to increase response rates for mail questionnaires

Box 10.6 _____

Ten Ways to Increase Mail Questionnaire Response

1. Address the questionnaire to specific person, not Occupant, and send it first class.
2. Include a carefully written, dated cover letter on letterhead stationery. In it, request respondent cooperation, guarantee confidentiality, explain the purpose of the survey, and give the researcher's name and phone number.
3. *Always* include a postage-paid, addressed return envelope.
4. The questionnaire should have a neat, attractive layout and reasonable page length.
5. The questionnaire should be professionally printed and easy to read, with clear instructions.
6. Send two follow-up reminder letters to those not responding. The first should arrive about one week after sending the questionnaire, the second a week later. Gently ask for cooperation again and offer to send another questionnaire.
7. Do not send questionnaires during major holiday periods.
8. Do not put questions on the back page. Instead, leave a blank space and ask the respondent for general comments.
9. Sponsors that are local and are seen as legitimate (e.g., government agencies, universities, large firms) get a better response.
10. Include a small monetary inducement ($1) if possible.

(see Box 10.6).[26] Heberlein and Baumgartner (1978) reported 71 factors affecting mail questionnaire response rates.

A meta-analysis of 115 articles on mail survey responses taken from 25 journals published between 1940 and 1988 revealed that cover letters, questionnaires of four pages or less, a return envelope with postage, and a small monetary reward all increase returns (Yammarino, Skiner, and Childers, 1991). Many of the techniques suggested follow the Total Design Method (to be discussed) and help to make the task easy and interesting for respondents.

Format and Layout. There are two format or layout issues: the overall physical layout of the questionnaire and the format of questions and responses.

Questionnaire Layout. Layout is important, whether a questionnaire is for an interviewer or for the respondent.[27] Questionnaires should be clear, neat, and easy to follow. Give each question a number and put identifying information (e.g., name of organization) on questionnaires. Never cramp questions together or create a confusing appearance. A few cents saved in postage or printing will ultimately cost more in terms of lower validity due to a lower response rate or of confusion of interviewers and respondents. Make a *cover sheet* or face sheet for each interview, for administrative use. Put the time and date of interview, the interviewer, the respondent identification number, and the interviewer's comments and observations on it. A professional appearance with high-quality graphics, space between questions, and good layout improves accuracy and completeness and helps the questionnaire flow.

Give interviewers or respondents instructions on the questionnaire. Print instructions in a different style from the questions (e.g., in a different color or font or in all capitals) to distinguish them. This is important for interview surveys so that an interviewer can distinguish between questions for respondents and instructions intended for the interviewer alone.

Layout is crucial for mail questionnaires because there is no friendly interviewer to interact with the respondent. Instead, the questionnaire's appearance persuades the respondent. In mail surveys, include a polite, professional cover letter on letterhead stationery, identifying the researcher and offering a telephone number for questions. Details matter. Respondents will be turned off if they receive a bulky brown envelope with bulk postage addressed to Occupant or if the questionnaire does not fit into the return envelope. Always end with "Thank you for your participation." Interviewers and questionnaires should leave respondents with a positive feeling about the survey and a sense that their participation is appreciated.

Question Format.   Survey researchers decide on a format for questions and responses. Should respondents circle responses, check boxes, fill in dots, or put an × in a blank? The principle is to make responses unambiguous. Boxes or brackets to be checked and numbers to be circled are usually clearest. Also, listing responses down a page rather than across makes them easier to see (see

Box 10.7). As mentioned before, use arrows and instructions for contingency questions. Visual aids are also helpful. For example, hand out thermometer-like drawings to respondents when asking about how warm or cool they feel toward someone. A *matrix question* (or grid question) is a compact way to present a series of questions using the same response categories (see Box 10.7). It saves space and makes it easier for the respondent or interviewer to note answers for the same response categories.

Box 10.7 _____

Question Format Examples

EXAMPLE OF HORIZONTAL VERSUS VERTICAL RESPONSE CHOICES

Do you think it is too easy or too difficult to get a divorce, or is it about right?
[ ] Too Easy   [ ] Too Difficult   [ ] About Right

Do you think it is too easy or too difficult to get a divorce, or is it about right?
[ ] Too easy
[ ] Too difficult
[ ] About right

EXAMPLE OF A MATRIX QUESTION FORMAT

	Strongly Agree	Agree	Disagree	Strongly Disagree	Don't Know
The teacher talks too fast.	[ ]	[ ]	[ ]	[ ]	[ ]
I learned a lot in this class.	[ ]	[ ]	[ ]	[ ]	[ ]
The tests are very easy.	[ ]	[ ]	[ ]	[ ]	[ ]
The teacher tells many jokes.	[ ]	[ ]	[ ]	[ ]	[ ]
The teacher is organized.	[ ]	[ ]	[ ]	[ ]	[ ]

EXAMPLES OF SOME RESPONSE CATEGORY CHOICES

Excellent, Good, Fair, Poor

Approve/Disapprove

Favor/Oppose

Strongly Agree, Agree, Somewhat Agree, Somewhat Disagree, Disagree, Strongly Disagree

Too Much, Too Little, About Right

Better, Worse, About the Same

Regularly, Often, Seldom, Never

Always, Most of Time, Some of Time, Rarely, Never

More likely, Less Likely, No Difference

Very Interested, Interested, Not Interested

Sanchez (1992) examined the effect of two questionnaire layouts on questions about religion asked by experienced interviewers. She found that a clearer layout reduced "not ascertained" responses from 8.8 to 2.04 percent. In addition, when she changed the format for a contingency question to make it clearer, the percentage of interviewers who probed for specific religious denomination increased from about 91 percent to over 99 percent.

Total Design Method. Dillman (1978) developed the *total design method (TDM)* to improve mail and telephone surveys. The method has both theoretical and practical parts. The theory says that a survey is a social interaction in which respondents act on the basis of what they expect to receive in exchange for their cooperation. They cooperate when social costs are low, when the expected benefit exceeds the perceived costs, and when researchers create a feeling of trust. The practical part repeats the advice given here about good question wording and questionnaire design. Thus, a good survey design has pilot tests, minimizes personal costs to respondents, and requires minimal effort and time from respondents. It creates intangible rewards, such as a feeling of doing something of value or being important. It also builds trust between the respondent and the interviewer or survey organization through a professional-looking questionnaire, evidence of a legitimate sponsor, and return postage in advance.

TYPES OF SURVEYS: ADVANTAGES AND DISADVANTAGES

Mail and Self-Administered Questionnaires

Advantages. Researchers can give questionnaires directly to respondents or mail them to respondents who read instructions and questions, then record their answers. This type of survey is by far the cheapest, and it can be conducted by a single researcher. A researcher can send questionnaires to a wide geographical area. The respondent can complete the questionnaire when it is convenient and can check personal records if necessary. Mail questionnaires offer anonymity and avoid interviewer bias. They are very effective, and response rates may be high for a target population that is well educated or has a strong interest in the topic or the survey organization.

Disadvantages. Since people do not always complete and return questionnaires, the biggest problem with mail questionnaires is a low response rate. Most questionnaires are returned within two weeks, but others trickle in up to two months later. Researchers can raise response rates by sending nonrespondents reminder letters, but this adds to the time and cost of data collection.

A researcher cannot control the conditions under which a mail questionnaire is completed. A questionnaire completed during a drinking party by a dozen laughing people may be returned along with one filled out by an earnest respondent. Also, no one is present to clarify questions or to probe for more information when respondents give incomplete answers. Someone other than the sampled respondent (e.g., spouse, new resident) may open the mail and complete the questionnaire without the researcher's knowledge. Different respondents can complete the questionnaire weeks apart or answer questions in a different order than that intended by researchers. Incomplete questionnaires can also be a serious problem.

Researchers cannot visually observe the respondent's reactions to questions, physical characteristics, or the setting. For example, an impoverished 70-year-old white woman living alone on a farm could falsely state that she is a prosperous 40-year-old Asian male doctor living in a nearby town with three children. Such extreme intentional lies are rare, but serious errors can go undetected.

The mail questionnaire format limits the kinds of questions that a researcher can use. Questions requiring visual aids (e.g., look at this picture and tell me what you see), open-ended questions, many contingency questions, and complex questions do poorly in mail questionnaires. Likewise, mail questionnaires are ill suited for the illiterate or near-illiterate in English. Questionnaires mailed to illiterate respondents are not likely to be returned; if they are completed and returned, the questions were probably misunderstood, so the answers are meaningless (see Table 10.4).

Telephone Interviews

Advantages.   The telephone interview is a popular survey method because about 95 percent of the population can be reached by telephone. An interviewer calls a respondent (usually at home), asks questions, and records answers. Researchers sample respondents from lists, telephone directories, or use RDD, and can quickly reach many people across long distances. A staff of interviewers can interview 1,500 respondents across a nation within a few days and, with several callbacks,

response rates can reach 90 percent. Although this method is more expensive than a mail questionnaire, special reduced long distance phone rates help. In general, the telephone interview is a flexible method with most of the strengths of face-to-face interviews but for about half the cost. Interviewers control the sequence of questions and can use some probes. A specific respondent is chosen and is likely to answer all the questions alone. The researcher knows when the questions were answered and can use contingency questions effectively, especially with computer-assisted telephone interviewing (CATI) (to be discussed).

Disadvantages.   Relatively high cost and limited interview length are disadvantages of tele-

TABLE 10.4   Types of Surveys and Their Features

	TYPE OF SURVEY		
FEATURES	*Mail Questionnaire*	*Telephone Interview*	*Face-to-Face Interview*
Administrative issues:			
Cost	Cheapest	Moderate	Expensive
Speed	Slowest	Fastest	Slow to moderate
Length (number of questions)	Moderate	Short	Longest
Response rate	Lowest	Moderate	Highest
Research control:			
Probes possible	No	Yes	Yes
Specific respondent	No	Yes	Yes
Question sequence	No	Yes	Yes
Only one respondent	No	Yes	Yes
Visual observation	No	No	Yes
Success with different questions:			
Visual aids	Limited	None	Yes
Open-ended questions	Limited	Limited	Yes
Contingency questions	Limited	Yes	Yes
Complex questions	Limited	Limited	Yes
Sensitive questions	Some	Some	Some
Sources of bias:			
Social desirability	No	Some	Worse
Interviewer bias	No	Some	Worse
Respondent's reading skill	Yes	No	No

phone interviews. In addition, respondents without telephones are impossible to reach, and the call may come at an inconvenient time. The use of an interviewer reduces anonymity and introduces potential interviewer bias. Open-ended questions are difficult to use, and questions requiring visual aids are impossible. Interviewers can only note serious disruptions (e.g., background noise) and respondent tone of voice (e.g., anger, flippancy) or hesitancy.

Face-to-Face Interviews

Advantages. Face-to-face interviews have the highest response rates and permit the longest questionnaires. They have the advantages of the telephone interview, and interviewers also can observe the surroundings and can use nonverbal communication and visual aids. Well-trained interviewers can ask all types of questions, can ask complex questions, and can use extensive probes.

Disadvantages. High cost is the biggest disadvantage of face-to-face interviews. The training, travel, supervision, and personnel costs for interviews can be high. Interviewer bias is also greatest in face-to-face interviews. The appearance, tone of voice, question wording, and so forth of the interviewer may affect the respondent. In addition, interviewer supervision is less than for telephone interviews, which supervisors monitor by listening in.[28]

Special Situations

There are many kinds of special surveys. One is a survey of organizations (e.g., businesses, schools). Mail questionnaires are usually used, but other methods are possible. A researcher writes questions to ask about the organization. He or she learns who in the organization has the necessary information, because it is essential to contact someone capable of responding. He or she then makes the significance of the survey clear because officials receive many requests for information and do not answer all of them.

Surveying elites requires special techniques.[29] Powerful leaders in business, government, and so on are difficult to reach. Assistants may intercept mail questionnaires, and restricted access can present a formidable obstacle to face-to-face or telephone interviewing. Access is facilitated when a prestigious source calls or sends a letter of introduction. Once the researcher makes an appointment, the researcher, not a hired interviewer, conducts the interviews. Personal interviews with a high percentage of open-ended questions are usually more successful than all closed-ended questions. Confidentiality is a crucial issue and should be guaranteed, since elites often have information that few others do.

The focus group is a special kind of interview situation that is largely nonquantitative.[30] In *focus groups*, a researcher gathers together 6 to 12 people in a room with a moderator to discuss one or more issues for one to two hours. The issue can be a public concern, a product, a television program, a political candidate, or a policy. The moderator introduces issues and ensures that no one person dominates. The moderator is flexible, keeps people on the topic, and encourages discussion. Responses are tape recorded or recorded by a secretary who assists the moderator. The group members should be homogeneous enough to reduce conflict but should not include friends or relatives. Focus groups are useful in exploratory research or to generate new ideas for hypotheses, questionnaire items, and the interpretation of results.

Costs

Professional-quality survey research can be expensive if all costs are considered. The cost varies according to the type of survey used. A simple formula is that for every $1 in cost for mail survey, a telephone interview survey costs about $5 and a face-to-face interview about $15. For example, Dillman (1983) estimated that a 12-page mail survey of 450 respondents costs over $3,000 in 1980 dollars. This estimate is low because the labor to develop and pretest questions and costs associated with data analysis are not included. Groves and Kahn (1979:188–212) estimated the cost of a nationwide, half-hour telephone interview survey of 1,500 respondents at about $40,000 in 1980 dollars. Professional interviewing firms may charge $50 per completed 20-minute interview just for the telephone call and interviewer time. Backstrom and Hursh-Cesar (1981:42) estimated the full costs for a professional survey project at $60,000 in 1980 dollars. Their project has 20-minute face-to-face interviews of 600 respondents in a nearby area. Most of the costs are personnel related. This is not high for professional research, and a comparable project today would exceed $150,000.

On the other hand, a researcher who uses a self-administered questionnaire survey for a narrow applied question can keep costs low. If the researcher works alone and has a small number of respondents, the only costs are the researcher's time, duplication of questionnaires, and data processing. For example, a high school teacher wants to determine how students are using a writing lab. A two-page questionnaire is distributed to a sample of 120 students by other teachers, and the teacher does the data analysis by hand. The total costs, not including the teacher's time, could be under $15.

INTERVIEWING

The Role of the Interviewer

Interviews to gather information occur in many settings. Employers interview prospective employees, medical personnel interview patients, mental health professionals interview clients, social service workers interview the needy, reporters interview politicians and others, police officers interview witnesses and crime victims, and talk-show hosts interview celebrities (see Box 10.8). Survey research interviewing is a specialized kind of interviewing. As with most interviewing, its goal is to obtain accurate information from another person.[31]

The survey interview is a social relationship. Like other social relationships, it involves social roles, norms, and expectations. The interview is a short-term, secondary social interaction between two strangers with the explicit purpose of one person's obtaining specific information from the other. The social roles are those of the interviewer and the interviewee or respondent. Information is obtained in a structured conversation in which the interviewer asks prearranged questions and records answers, and the respondent answers. It differs in several ways from ordinary conversation (see Table 10.5).

An important problem for interviewers is that many respondents are unfamilar with the survey respondents' role and "respondents often do not have a clear conception of what is expected of them" (Turner and Martin, 1984:282). As a result, they substitute another role that may affect their responses. Some believe the interview is an intimate conversation or thearpy session, others see it as a bureaucratic exercise in completing forms, some view it as a citizen referendum on policy choices, others view it as a testing situation, and still others see it as a form of deceit in which interviewers are trying to trick or entrap respondents (Turner and Martin, 1984:262–269). Even in a well-designed, professional survey, follow-up research found that only about half the respondents understand questions exactly as intended by researchers. Respondents reinterpreted questions to make them applicable to their ideosynactic, personal situations or to make them easy to answer (Turner and Martin, 1984:282).

The role of interviewers is difficult. They obtain cooperation and build rapport, yet remain neutral and objective. They encroach on the respondents' time and privacy for information that may not directly benefit the respondents. They try to reduce embarrassment, fear, and suspicion so that respondents feel comfortable revealing information. They may explain the nature of survey research or give hints about social roles in an interview. Good interviewers monitor the pace and direction of the social interaction as well as the content of answers and the behavior of respondents.

Survey interviewers are nonjudgmental and do not reveal their opinions, verbally or nonverbally (e.g., by a look of shock). If a respondent asks for an interviewer's opinion, he or she

Box 10.8

TYPES OF NONRESEARCH INTERVIEWS

1. *Job Interview:* An employer asks open-ended questions to gather information about a candidate for a job and to observe how the candidate presents himself or herself. The candidate (respondent) initiates the contact and attempts to present a positive self-image. The employer (interviewer) tries to discover the candidate's true talents and flaws. A serious, judgmental tone exists, with the employer having the power to accept or reject the candidate. This often creates tension and limited trust. The parties may have conflicting goals and each may use some deception. The results are not confidential.

2. *Assistance Interview:* A helping professional (counselor, lawyer, social worker, medical doctor, etc.) seeks information on a client's problem, including background and current conditions. The helping professional (interviewer) uses the information to understand and translate the client's (respondent's) problem into professional terms for problem resolution. The tone is serious and concerned. There is usually low tension and high mutual trust. The parties share the goal of resolving the client's problem, and deception is rare. The interview results are usually confidential.

3. *Journalistic Interview:* A journalist gathers information from a celebrity, newsmaker, witness, or background person for later use in constructing a newsworthy story. The journalist (interviewer) uses various skills in attempting to get novel information, some which may not be easily revealed, and "quotable quotes" from the news source (respondent). The journalist uses the interview information selectively in combination with other information, usually beyond the respondent's control. The tone and degree of trust and tension vary greatly. The goals of the parties may diverge and each may use deception. The interview results are not confidential and they may get a lot of publicity.

4. *Interrogation or Investigative Interview:* A criminal justice official, auditor, or other person in authority seriously asks questions to obtain information from an accused person or others with information about wrongdoing. The official (interviewer) will use the information as evidence to construct a case against someone (possibly the respondent). The tension is often extreme with mutual distrust. The goals of the parties diverge sharply and each often uses deception. Interview results are rarely confidential and may become part of an official, public record.

5. *Entertainment Interview:* An emcee or show host offers comments and asks open-ended questions to a celebrity or other person who may digress in answers or begin a monologue. The primary goal is to stimulate interest, enjoyment, or gaiety among an audience. Often, the style displayed by each is more central than any information revealed. The host (interviewer) seeks an immediate response or reaction in the audience, while the celebrity (respondent) tries to increase his or her fame or reputation. The tone is light, tension is low, and trust is moderately high. The limited goals of each often converge. They may deceive each other or join in deceiving the audience. The situation is the opposite to one in which confidentially can occur.

People can mix the types of interviews, and people often use several types. For example, the social worker in a social control role instead of a helping role may conduct an investigative interview. Or a police officer helping a crime victim may use an assistance interview instead of an interrogation.

---

politely redirects the respondent and indicates that such questions are inappropriate. For example, if a respondent asks, "What do you think?," the interviewer may answer, "Here, we are interested in what *you* think; what I think doesn't matter." Likewise, if the respondent gives a shocking answer (e.g., "I was arrested three times for beating my infant daughter and burning her with cigarettes"), the interviewer does not show shock, surprise, or disdain but treats the answer in a matter-of-fact manner. He or she helps respondents feel that they can give any truthful answer.

TABLE 10.5   Differences between a Structured Survey Interview and Ordinary Conversation

ORDINARY CONVERSATION	THE SURVEY INTERVIEW
1. Questions and answers from each participant are relatively equally balanced.	1. Interviewer asks and respondent answers most of the time.
2. There is an open exchange of feelings and opinions.	2. Only the respondent reveals feelings and opinions.
3. Judgments are stated and attempts made to persuade the other of a particular points of view.	3. Interviewer is nonjudgmental and does not try to change respondent's opinions or beliefs.
4. A person can reveal deep inner feelings to gain sympathy or as a therapeutic release.	4. Interviewer tries to obtain direct answers to specific questions.
5. Ritual responses are common (e.g., "Uh huh," shaking head, "How are you?" "Fine").	5. Interviewer avoids making ritual responses that influence a respondent and also seeks genuine answers, not ritual responses.
6. The participants exchange information and correct the factual errors that they are aware of.	6. Respondent provides almost all information. Interviewer does not correct a respondent's factual errors.
7. Topics rise and fall and either person can introduce new topics. The focus can shift directions or digress to less relevant issues.	7. Interviewer controls the topic, direction, and pace. He or she keeps the respondent "on task," and irrelevant diversions are contained.
8. The emotional tone can shift from humor, to joy, to affection, to sadness, to anger, and so on.	8. Interviewer attempts to maintain a consistently warm but serious and objective tone throughout.
9. People can evade or ignore questions and give flippant or noncommittal answers.	9. Respondent should not evade questions and should give truthful, thoughtful answers.

Source: Adapted from Gorden (1980:19–25) and Sudman and Bradburn (1983:5–10).

You might ask, "If the survey interviewer must be neutral and objective, why not use a robot or machine?" Machine interviewing has not been very successful because it lacks the human warmth, sense of trust, and rapport that an interviewer creates. An interviewer helps define the situation and ensures that respondents have the information sought, understand what is expected, give relevant answers, are motivated to cooperate, and give serious answers. The interview is a social interaction in which "the behavior of both interviewer and respondent stems from their attitudes, motives, expectations, and perceptions" (Cannell and Kahn, 1968:538).

Interviewers do more than interview respondents. For example, Moser and Kalton (1972: 273) reported that face-to-face interviewers spend only about 35 percent of their time interviewing. About 40 percent is spent in locating the correct respondent, 15 percent in traveling, and 10 percent in studying survey materials and dealing with administrative and recording details.

Stages of an Interview

The interview proceeds through stages, beginning with an introduction and entry. The interviewer gets in the door, shows authorization, and reassures and secures cooperation from the respondent. He or she is prepared for reactions such as, "How did you pick me?" "What good will this do?" "I don't know about this." "What's this about, anyway?" The interviewer can explain why the specific respondent is interviewed and not a substitute.

The main part of the interview consists of asking questions and recording answers. The interviewer uses the exact wording on the questionnaire—no added or omitted words and no rephrasing. He or she asks all applicable questions in order, without returning to or skipping questions unless the directions specify this. He or she goes at a comfortable pace and gives nondirective feedback to maintain interest.

In addition to asking questions, the interviewer accurately records answers. This is easy for closed-ended questions, where interviewers just mark the correct box. For open-ended questions, the interviewer's job is more difficult. He or she listens carefully, must have legible writing, and must record what is said verbatim without correcting grammar or slang. More important, the interviewer never summarizes or paraphrases because this causes a loss of information or distorts answers. For example, the respondent says, "I'm really concerned about my daughter's heart problem. She's only 10 years old and already she has trouble climbing stairs. I don't know what she'll do when she gets older. Heart surgury is too risky for her and it costs so much. She'll have to learn to live with it." If the interviewer writes, "concerned about daughter's health," much is lost.

The interviewer knows how and when to use probes. A *probe* is a neutral request to clarify an ambiguous answer, to complete an incomplete answer, or to obtain a relevant response. Interviewers recognize an irrelevant or inaccurate answer and use probes as needed.[32] There are many types of probes. A three- to five-second pause is often effective. Nonverbal communica-tion (e.g., tilt of head, raised eyebrows, eye contact) also works well. The interviewer can repeat the question or repeat the reply and then pause. She or he can ask a neutral question, such as, "Any other reasons?" "Can you tell me more about that?" "How do you mean?" "Could you explain more for me?" (see Box 10.9).

The last stage is the exit, when the interviewer thanks the respondent and leaves. He or she then goes to a quiet, private place to edit the questionnaire and record other details while they are fresh. Other details include the date, time, and place of the interview; a thumbnail sketch of the respondent and interview situation; the respondent's attitude (e.g., serious, angry, or laughing); and any unusual circumstances (e.g., "Telephone rang at question 27 and respondent talked for four minutes before the interview started again"). He or she notes anything disruptive that happened during the interview (e.g., "Teenage son entered room, sat at opposite end, turned on television with the volume loud, and watched a baseball game"). The interviewer also records personal feelings and anything that was suspected (e.g., "Respondent became nervous and fidgeted when questioned about his marriage"). Converse and Schuman (1974) provided colorful examples of face-to-face interviewing events from such sketches.

Training Interviewers

A large-scale survey requires hiring several interviewers.[33] Few people other than professional survey researchers appreciate the difficulty of the interviewer's job. A professional-quality interview requires the careful selection of interviewers and good training. As with any employment situation, adequate pay and good supervision are important for consistent high-quality performance.

Unfortunately, professional interviewing has not always paid well or provided regular employment. In the past, interviewers were largely drawn from a pool of middle-aged women willing to accept irregular part-time work. Good interviewers are pleasant, honest, accurate, mature, respon-

Box 10.9 _____

Example of Probes and Recording Full Responses
to Closed Questions

Interviewer question: What is your occupation?

Respondent answer: I work at General Motors.
  Probe: What is your job at General Motors? What type of work do you do there?

Interviewer question: How long have you been unemployed?

Respondent answer: A long time.
  Probe: Could you tell me more specifically when your current period of unemployment began?

Interviewer question: Considering the country as a whole, do you think we will have good times during the next year, or bad times, or what?

Respondent answer: Maybe good, maybe bad, it depends, who knows?
  Probe: What do you expect to happen?

RECORD RESPONSE TO A CLOSED QUESTION

Interviewer question: On a scale of 1 to 7, how do you feel about capital punishment or the death penalty, where 1 is strongly in favor of the death penalty, and 7 is strongly opposed to it?
(Favor) 1 _ 2 _ 3 _ 4 _ 5 _ 6 _ 7 _(Oppose)

Respondent's answer: About a 4. I think that all murderers, rapists, and violent criminals should be fired, but I don't favor it for minor crimes like stealing a car.

_____

sible, moderately intelligent, stable, and motivated. They have a nonthreatening appearance, have experience with many types of people, and possess poise and tact. If the survey involves interviewing in high-crime areas, interviewers need extra protection. Researchers may consider interviewers' physical appearance, age, race, sex, languages spoken, and even the interviewer's voice. For example, in a study using trained female telephone interviewers from homogeneous social backgrounds, Oksenberg, Coleman, and Cannell (1986) found fewer refusals for interviewers whose voices had higher pitch and greater pitch variation, and who spoke louder, faster, with clear pronunciation and sounded more pleasant and cheerful.

Researchers train professional interviewers in a one- to two-week training course, which usually includes lectures and reading, observation of expert interviewers, mock interviews in the office and in the field that are recorded and critiqued, many practice interviews, and role playing. The interviewers learn what survey research is about and the role of the interviewer. They become familiar with the questionnaire and the purpose of questions, although not with the answers expected.

Although interviewers largely work alone, researchers use an interviewer supervisor in large-scale surveys with several interviewers. Supervisors are familiar with the area, assist with problems, oversee the interviewers, and ensure that work is completed on time. For telephone interviewing, this includes helping with calls, checking when interviewers arrive and leave, and monitoring interview calls. In face-to-face interviews, supervisors check to find out whether the interview actually took place. This means calling back or sending a confirmation postcard to a sample of respondents. They can also check the response rate and incomplete questionnaires to see whether interviewers are obtaining cooperation, and they may reinterview a small subsample, analyze answers, or observe interviews to see whether interviewers are accurately asking questions and recording answers.

Interviewer Bias

Survey researchers proscribe interviewer behavior to reduce bias. Ideally, the actions of a particular interviewer will not affect how a respondent answers, and responses will not vary from what they would be if asked by any other interviewer. This goes beyond reading each question exactly as worded: "Strictly speaking, interviewer distortion exists whenever there is any deviation from the "true" response (defined in terms of the purpose of the study) in the response elicited and recorded by the interviewer" (Hyman, 1975:226).

Interview bias falls into six categories:

1. Errors by the respondent—forgetting, embarrassment, misunderstanding, or lying because of the presence of others
2. Unintentional errors or interviewer sloppiness—contacting the wrong respondent, misreading a question, omitting questions, reading questions in the wrong order, recording the wrong answer to a question, or misunderstanding the respondent
3. Intentional subversion by the interviewer—purposeful alteration of answers, omission or rewording of questions, or choice of an alternative respondent
4. Influence due to the interviewer's expectations about a respondent's answers based on the respondent's appearance, living situation, or other answers
5. Failure of an interviewer to probe or to probe properly
6. Influence on the answers due to the interviewer's appearance, tone, attitude, reactions to answers, or comments made outside of the interview schedule

Survey researchers are still learning about the factors that influence survey interviews. They know that interviewer expectations can create significant bias. Interviewers who expect difficult interviews have them, and those who expect certain answers are more likely to get them (see Box 10.10). Proper interviewer behavior and exact question reading may be difficult, but the issue is larger.

The social setting in which the interview occurs can affect answers, including the presence of other people. For example, students answer differently depending on whether they are asked questions at home or at school (Zane and Matsoukas, 1979). In general, survey researchers do not want others present because they may affect respondent answers. It may not always make a difference, however, especially if the others are small children.[34] For example, William Aquilino (1993) found that when a spouse is present, respondents are more likely to indicate that a divorce or separation will make them worse off. Also, wives report greater husband contributions to housework when the husband is present. Respondents are also more likely to report fights and premarital cohabitation if the spouse was present.

The interviewer's race or gender may influence the interview. As Bradburn (1983:314) noted,

> The principal conclusion one draws from the available studies of interviewer-respondent characteristics is that interviewer characteristics which are clearly perceivable by respondents, such as sex and race, may make a substantial difference for attitude questions related to these characteristics.

An interviewer's race or ethnic group can affect how respondents answer race or ethnic group questions.[35] For example, African Americans express greater closeness to whites when interviewed by a white as opposed to an African American interviewer. The race of the interviewer may also affect answers to some policy issues, such as support for civil rights leaders and govern-

Box 10.10 _____

Interviewer Characteristics Can Affect Responses

EXAMPLE OF INTERVIEWER EXPECTATION EFFECTS

Asked by Female Interviewer Whose Own	*Female Respondent Reports that Husband Buys Most Furniture*
Husband buys most furniture	89%
Husband does not buy most furniture	15%

Source: Adapted from Hyman (1975:115).

EXAMPLE OF RACE OR ETHNIC APPEARANCE EFFECTS

	PERCENTAGE ANSWERING YES TO:	
Interview	*""Do you think there are too many Jews in government jobs?"*	*""Do you think that Jews have too much power?"*
Looked Jewish with Jewish-sounding	11.7	5.8
Looked Jewish only	15.4	15.6
Non-Jewish appearance	21.2	24.3
Non-Jewish appearance and non-	19.5	21.4

Source: Adapted from Hyman (1975:163).

ment programs. For instance, Hispanic and white-Anglo respondents in Texas answered questions on bilingualism and Hispanic culture differently depending on whether their telephone interviewer was Hispanic or Anglo (Reese et al., 1986).

Race or ethnicity may affect attitudes and self-reports of behavior because of social distance, power differences, or ingroup/outgroup relations. In general, interviewers of the same race or cultural heritage get more accurate responses to sensitive questions. In a multicultural society, researchers should always record the racial-ethnic heritage of both interviewers and respondents.

Gender may also affect interview responses. For example, Kane and MacAulay (1993) found that male respondents were more likely to support work-related gender equality with a woman interviewer. Female respondents were more likely to support gender-related collective action and group policy stands when with a woman inter-

viewer. If the same question asked by the same interviewer is answered differently by men and women, representative reliability is threatened.

Cultural Meanings and Survey Interviews

Research into survey errors and interview bias has advanced thinking about larger issues of how people create social meaning and achieve cultural understanding.[36] Survey researchers are troubled when the same words have different meanings and implications depending on the social situation, who speaks them, how they are spoken, and the social distance between the speaker and listener. Also, respondents do not always understand the social situation of the survey interview, may misinterpret the nature of survey research, and may seek clues for how to answer in the wording of questions or subtle actions of the interviewer. Moreover, "it is important not to lose sight of the fact that the interview setting is itself distinct from other settings in which attitudes are expressed, and hence we should not expect to find complete congruence between attitudes expressed in interviews and in other social contexts" (Turner and Martin, 1984:276).

Initially, survey research was based on a "naive assumption model" (Foddy, 1993:13). Researchers try to improve survey research by reducing the gap between actual experience in conducting surveys and the ideal survey expressed as the model's assumptions. The model's assumptions include the following:

1. Researchers have clearly conceptualized all variables being measured.
2. Questionnaires have no wording, question order, or related effects.
3. Respondents are motivated and willing to answer all the questions asked.
4. Respondents possess complete information and can accurately recall events.
5. Respondents understand each question exactly as the reseacher intends it.
6. Respondents give more truthful answers if they do not know the hypotheses.
7. Respondents give more truthful answers if they receive no hints or suggestions.
8. The interview situation and specific interviewers have no effects on answers.
9. The process of the interview has no impact on the respondents' beliefs or attitudes.
10. Respondents' behaviors match perfectly their verbal responses in an interview.

Some survey researchers are questioning the assumptions of this model. For example, as an interviewer strives to act in a more neutral and uniform way, he or she reduces the type of bias that causes unreliability because of individual interviewer behavior. Yet, such attempts to reduce bias cause other problems according to interpretive or critical social science researchers (see Box 10.11; also see Devault, 1990).[37] Researchers argue that meaning is created in social context; therefore, standard wording will not produce the same meaning for all respondents. For example, some respondents express their values and feelings by telling stories instead of answering straightforward questions with fixed answers. Standard interviewer behavior may actually lower validity, especially for respondents from social groups outside the middle-class world of most survey researchers.

In complex human interaction, people often add interpretative meaning to simple questions. For example, my neighbor asks me the simple question, "How often do you mow your lawn?" I could interpret his question in the following ways:

— How often do I personally mow the lawn (versus having someone else mow it for me)?
— How often do I mow it to cut grass (versus run my lawnmower over it to chop up leaves)?
— How often do I mow the entire lawn (versus cutting the quick-growing parts only)?
— How often do I mow it during an entire season, a month, a week?
— How often to I mow it most seasons (versus last year when my lawnmower was broken several times and it was very dry and the grass grew less tall, so I did not mow it as frequently)?

Within seconds, I make an interpertation and give an answer, but the open-ended, ongoing interaction between myself and the neighbor permits me to ask for clarification and for several follow-up questions that helps us arrive at mutual understanding.

The dilemma is that ordinary conversations contain organizational features that are designed to detect and correct misintepretation and build shared understanding. Many of these very features are controlled in the survey interview situation to ensure that each respondent is treated in a standard way. Standardizing words does not automatically produce standardized meaning. Paradoxically, "the validity of survey data is potentially undermined by the same prohibition against interaction that is intended to ensure reliability" (Suchman and Jordan, 1992:242).

Social meaning does not reside in the words alone. It resides in the social context and interaction among people, and in cultural frames (sometimes divided by gender, race, region, etc.) in

Box 10.11 _____

Interviewing: Positivist and Feminist Approaches

In this chapter you learned the positivist approach to survey research interviewing. In the ideal survey interview, the interviewer withholds her or his own feelings and beliefs. The interviewer should be so objective and neutral that it should be possible to substitute another interviewer and obtain the same responses.

Feminist researchers approach interviewing very differently. Feminist interviewing is similar to qualitative interviewing (to be discussed in Chapter 14). Oakley (1981) criticized positivist survey interviewing as being part of a masculine paradigm. It is a social situation in which the interviewer exercises control and dominance while suppressing the expression of personal feelings. It is manipulative and instrumental. The interviewer and the respondent become merely the vehicles for obtaining the objective data.

The goals of feminist research vary, but two common goals are to give greater visibility to the subjective experience of women and to increase the involvement of the respondent in the research process. Features of feminist interviewing include the following:

- A preference for an unstructured and open-ended format
- A preference for interviewing a person more than once
- Creation of social connections and building a trusting social relationship
- Disclosure of personal experiences by the interviewer
- Drawing on female skills of being open, receptive, and understanding
- Avoiding control and fostering equality by downplaying professional status
- Careful listening, interviewers become emotionally engaged with respondents
- Respondent-oriented direction, not researcher oriented or questionnaire oriented
- Encouragement of respondents to express themselves in ways they are most comfortable—for example, by telling stories or following digressions
- Creation of a sense of empowerment and an esprit de corps among women

---

which people live. For example, men and women think differently about their health, and they will report the same health status differently (Groves, Fultz, and Martin, 1992). Does this mean that far more men are in excellent health than women? Even so-called objective categories in survey research, such as race or ethnicity, can vary greatly in how respondents think subjectively and answer (Smith, 1984). Human responses in interviews are more complex and vary more by situations than outlined by the naive assumption model. For example, "Inaccurate reporting is not a response tendency or a predisposition to be untruthful. Individuals who are truthful on one occasion or in response to particular questions may not be truthful at other times or to other questions" (Wentworth, 1993:130).

Given this complexity and possible distortion, what should the diligent survey researcher

do? The issues of social meaning suggest that a survey researcher should at least supplement closed-ended questionnaires with open-ended questions and probes. This takes more time, requires better-trained interviewers, and produces responses that may be less standardized and more difficult to quantify. Fixed-answer questionnaires based on the naive assumption model imply a more simple and mechanical way of responding than occurs in many situations. The inquiry into interviewer bias, cultural meanings, and the interview as a social situation provides a lesson in how qualitative and quantitative styles of social research complement one another. As quantitative survey researchers strived to eliminate sources of interviewer bias and respondent confusion, they discovered that qualitative researchers offered valuable insights into how people construct meaning in various social settings.

Computer-Assisted Telephone Interviewing

Advances in computer technology and lower computer prices have enabled many professional survey research organizations to install *computer-assisted telephone interviewing (CATI)* systems.[38] With CATI, the interviewer sits in front of a computer terminal (screen with a keyboard) and manually makes calls or has the computer automatically call. Wearing a headset and microphone, the interviewer reads the questions from a computer screen for the specific respondent who is called, then enters the answer via the keyboard. Once he or she enters an answer, the computer shows the next question on the screen.

CATI speeds interviewing and reduces interviewer errors. It also eliminates the separate step of entering information into a computer and speeds data processing. Of course, CATI requires an investment in computer equipment and some knowledge of computers. CATI is valuable for contingency questions because the computer can show the questions appropriate for a specific respondent; interviewers do not have to turn pages looking for the next question. In addition, the computer can check an answer immediately after the interviewer enters it. For example, if an interviewer enters an answer that is impossible or clearly an error (e.g., an *H* instead of an *M* for "Male"), the computer will beep and send a message requesting another answer.

Several companies have developed sofware programs for personal computers that help researchers develop questionnaires and analyze survey data. Four such programs are Survey Pro®, The Survey System®, Survey Analyst®, and Survey Master.® The programs provide guides for writing questions, recording responses, analyzing data, and producing reports. The programs may speed the more mechanical aspects of survey research—such as typing questionnaires, organizing layout, and recording responses—but they cannot substitute for a good understanding of the survey method or an appreciation of its limitations. The researcher must still clearly conceptualize variables, prepare well-worded questions, design the sequence and forms of questions and responses, and pilot test questionnaires. Communicating unambiguously with respondents and eliciting credible responses remain the most important parts of survey research. See Box 10.12 for an example of survey research.

Box 10.12 _____

Example Survey

John Hagan (1990) examined gender discrimination and income inequality among Canadian lawyers. He drew a stratified sample of lawyers in the Toronto area, stratifying by type of employment (large firm, small-to-medium firm, or nonfirm) and gender. In 1985, he mailed 1,609 questionnaires with two follow-up reminders. He received 1,051 back, for a 65.3 percent return rate. The questionnaire asked respondents to put their 1984 before-tax income into one of 26 categories, ranging from under $10,000 to over $500,000. Among those answering the questions, the average income for the 445 female lawyers who responded was $44,210, compared to $86,756 for the 396 male lawyers. The questionnaire also included questions on control variables that were alternative causes to gender for the income gap. These included type of position (e.g., managing partner, solo practitioner), religious background, area of specialization (e.g., tax, family, criminal) years of experience, job history, and prestige of the law school attended. Hagan also conducted follow-up interviews with 50 lawyers in order to understand career patterns. After a detailed statistical analysis that considered the other variables, he concluded that about one-fourth of the gender income gap, $10,636 per year, is caused by gender discrimination. Female lawyers gained income compared to previous years, but the men had larger gains. A man with career advantages, such as an elite education or many years of experience, can better translate the advantages into income than a woman with the same advantages. For example, a man who becomes a managing partner of a medium-to-large firm earns $84,000 more than a man who is a partner in a small firm. By comparison, a woman who is a managing partner in a medium-to-large firm earns $24,000 more than a woman who is a partner in a small firm.

THE ETHICAL SURVEY

Like all social research, people can conduct surveys in ethical or unethical ways. A major ethical issue in survey research is the invasion of privacy.[39] Survey researchers can intrude into a respondent's privacy by asking about intimate actions and personal beliefs. People have a right to privacy. Respondents decide when and to whom to reveal personal information. They are likely to provide such information when it is asked for in a comfortable context with mutual trust, when they believe serious answers are needed for legitimate research purposes, and when they believe answers will remain confidential. Researchers should treat all respondents with dignity and reduce anxiety or discomfort. They are also responsible for protecting the confidentiality of data.

A second issue involves voluntary participation by respondents. Respondents agree to answer questions and can refuse to participate at any time. They give "informed consent" (see Chapter 17) to participate in research. Researchers depend on respondents' voluntary cooperation, so researchers need to ask well-developed questions in a sensitive way, treat respondents with respect, and be very sensitive to confidentiality.

A third ethical issue is the exploition of surveys and pseudosurveys. Because of its popularity, some people use surveys to mislead others. A *pseudosurvey* is when someone uses the survey format in an attempt to persuade someone to do something and has little or no real interest in learning information from a respondent. Charlatans use the guise of conducting a survey to invade privacy, gain entry into homes, or "suggle" (sell in the guise of a survey). An example of a pseudosurvey occurred in the 1994 U.S. election campaign as "suppression polls." In this situation, an unknown survey organization telephoned a potential voter and asked whether the voter supported a given candidate. If the voter supported the candidate, the interviewer asked whether the respondent would still support the candidate if he or she knew that the candidate had an unfavorable characteristic (e.g., had been arrested for drunk driving, used illegal drugs, raised the wages of convicted criminals in prison). The goal of the interview was not to measure candidate support; rather, it was to identify a candidate's supporters then attempt to sway them by giving negative information. I received such a call, as did an unsuccessful candidate for governor who was the object of the suppression poll. No one has been prosecuted for this using campaign tactic.

Another ethical issue is when people misuse survey results or use poorly designed or purposely rigged surveys. People may demand answers from surveys that surveys cannot provide or may not understand a survey's limitations. Those who design and prepare surveys may lack sufficient training to conduct a legitimate survey. Policy decisions made based on careless or poorly designed surveys may result in waste and human hardship. Such misuse makes it important that legitimate researchers conduct methodologically rigorous survey research. Researchers should be aware of and report the limitations of survey results. "It is untenable to confront survey data as if they were error free" (Alwin, 1977:132). Researchers also need to combat unscrupulous politicians, businesspeople, and others who rig surveys to produce deceptive results.

Mass media reporting of survey results and the quality of surveys being reported permits abuse.[40] Few people reading survey results may appreciate it, but researchers should include details about the survey (see Table 10.6) to reduce the misuse of survey research and increase questions about surveys that lack such information. Survey researchers urge the media to include such information, but it is rarely included. Over 88 percent of reports on surveys in the mass media fail to reveal the researcher who conducted the survey, and only 18 percent provide details on how the survey was conducted (Singer, 1988). This occurs while the media report more surveys than other types of social research.

Currently, there are no quality-control standards to regulate the opinion polls or surveys reported in the U.S. media. Researchers have

TABLE 10.6   Ten Items to Include When Reporting Survey Research

1. The sampling frame used (e.g., telephone directories)
2. The dates on which the survey was conducted
3. The population that the sample represents (e.g., U.S. adults, Australian college students)
4. The size of the sample for which information was collected
5. The sampling method (e.g., random)
6. The exact wording of the questions asked
7. The method of the survey (e.g., face to face, telephone)
8. The organizations that sponsored the survey (paid for it and conducted it)
9. The response rate or percentage of those contacted who actually completed the questionnaire
10. Any missing information or "don't know" responses when results on specific questions are reported

made unsuccessful attempts since World War II to require adequate samples, interviewer training and supervision, satisfactory questionnaire design, public availability of results, and controls on the integrity of survey organizations (Turner and Martin, 1984:62). As a result, the mass media report both biased and misleading survey results and rigorous, professional survey results without distinction. The media report "the commonly cited margins of error. . . [that] promote overconfidence in survey estimates. These figures commonly account only for sampling variations and do not take into account other sources of variation in survey estimates" (Turner and Martin, 1984:107). It is not surprising that public confusion and a distrust of all surveys occurs.

CONCLUSION

In this chapter, you learned about survey research. Survey research is the most widely used social research technique. It has a long history, but it has undergone dramatic expansion and maturation in the past three decades. You also learned some principles of writing good survey questions. There are many things to avoid and to include when writing questions. You also learned about the advantages and disadvantages of three types of survey research: mail, telephone interviews, and face-to-face interviews. You saw that interviewing, especially face-to-face interviewing, can be difficult.

Although this chapter focused on survey research, researchers use questionnaires to measure variables in other types of quantitative research (e.g., experiments). The survey, often called the sample survey because random sampling is usually used with it, is a distinct technique. It is a process of asking many people the same questions and examining their answers.

The survey is a process in which researchers translate a research problem into questionnaires, then use these with respondents to create data. Survey researchers involve other people—respondents—who answer to questions. From the answers, the researcher creates quantitative data that he or she analyzes to address the research problem. Survey researchers try to minimize errors, but survey data often contain them. Errors in surveys can compound each other. For example, errors can arise in sampling frames, from nonresponse, from question wording or order, and from interviewer bias. Do not let the existence of errors discourage you from using the survey, however. Instead, learn to be very careful when designing survey research and cautious about generalizing from the results of surveys.

KEY TERMS

census
closed-ended question
computer-assisted telephone
  interviewing (CATI)
context effect
contingency question
cover sheet
double-barreled question
floaters
focus groups
full-filter question
funnel sequence

interview schedule	quasi-filter question	sleeper question
matrix question	questionnaire	social desirability bias
open-ended question	randomized response	standard-format question
order effects	technique (RRT)	telescoping
partially open question	recency effect	threatening questions
prestige bias	respondents	total design method (TDM)
probe	response set	wording effects

REVIEW QUESTIONS _____

1. What are the six types of things surveys often ask about? Give an example of each that is different from the examples in the book.

2. Why are surveys called *correlational*, and how do they differ from experiments?

3. What five changes occurred in the 1960s and 1970s that dramatically affected survey research?

4. Identify 5 of the 10 things to avoid in question writing.

5. What topics are threatening to respondents, and how can a researcher ask about them?

6. What are advantages and disadvantages of open-ended versus closed-ended questions?

7. What are filtered, quasi-filtered, and standard-format questions? How do they relate to floaters?

8. How does ordinary conversation differ from a survey interview?

9. Under what conditions are mail, telephone interviews, or face-to-face interviews best?

10. What is CATI and when might it be useful?

NOTES _____

1. The use of a strict positivist approach within survey research is a source of criticism by those who adopt an interpretative approach. For such criticism, see Biggs (1986), Denzin (1989), Mishler (1986), and Phillips (1971). Also see Carr-Hill (1984b) for a similar criticism from the critical social science approach.

2. The history of survey research is discussed in Converse (1987), Hyman (1991), Rossi et al. (1983), Marsh (1982:9–47), Miller (1983:19–125), Moser and Kalton (1972:6–15), Sudman (1976b), and Sudman and Bradburn (1987).

3. See Blumer (1991a, 1991b), Blumer, Bales, and Sklar (1991), Bannister (1987), Camic and Xie (1994), Cohen (1991), Deegan (1988), Ross (1991), Sklar (1991), Turner (1991), and Yeo (1991).

4. See Converse (1987:383–385), *Statistical Abstract of the United States*, and Rossi et al. (1983:8).

5. As Hyman (1975:4) remarked, "Let it be noted that the demonstration of error marks an advanced stage of a science. All scientific inquiry is subject to error, and it is far better to be aware of what it is, to study the sources in an attempt to reduce it, and to estimate the magnitudes of errors in our findings, than to be ignorant of errors concealed in the data." Examples of research on survey methodology include Bishop, Oldendick, and Tuchfarber (1983, 1984, 1985), Bradburn (1983), Bradburn and Sudman (1980), Cannell, Miller, and Olksenberg (1981), Converse and Presser (1986), Groves and Kahn (1979), Hyman (1991), Schuman and Presser (1981), Smith and Martin (1984), Sudman and Bradburn (1983), and Tanur (1992).

6. See Rossi, Wright, and Anderson (1983:10)

7. See Bayless (1981) on the Research Triangle Institute.

8. For a list of survey organizations, see Bradburn and Sudman (1988).

9. The administration of survey research is discussed in Backstrom and Hursh-Cesar (1981:38–45), Dillman (1978:200–281;1983), Frey (1983:129–169), Groves and Kahn (1979:40–78, 186–212), Prewitt (1983), Tanur (1983), and Warwick and Lininger (1975:20–45, 220–264).

10. Similar lists of prohibitions can be found in Babbie (1990:127–132), Backstrom and Hursh-Cesar (1981: 140–153), Bailey (1987:110–115), Bradburn and Sudman (1988:145–153), Converse and Presser (1986:13–31), deVaus (1986:71–74), Dillman (1978: 95–117), Frey (1983:116–127), Fowler (1984:75–86), Moser and Kalton (1972:318–341), Sheatsley (1983:216–217), Sudman and Bradburn (1983: 132–136), and Warwick and Lininger (1975: 140–148).

11. Sudman and Bradburn (1983:39) suggest that even simple questions (e.g., "What brand of soft drink do you usually buy?") can cause problems. Respondents who are highly loyal to one brand of traditional carbonated sodas can answer the question easily. Other respondents must implicitly address the following questions to answer the question as it was asked: (a) What time period is involved—the past month, the past year, the last 10 years? (b) What conditions count—at home, at restaurants, at sporting events? (c) Buying for oneself alone or for other family members? (d) What is a "soft drink"? Do lemonade, iced tea, mineral water, or fruit juices count? (e) Does "usually" mean a brand purchased as 51 percent or more of all soft drink purchases, or the brand purchased more frequently than any other? Respondents rarely stop and ask for clarification; they make assumptions about what the researcher means.

12. See Abelson et al (1992), Auriat (1993), Bernard et al. (1984), Croyle and Loftus (1992), Krosnick and Abelson (1992), Loftus et al. 1990), Loftus et al. (1992), and Pearson and Dawes (1992).

13. See Bradburn (1983), Bradburn and Sudman (1980), and Sudman and Bradburn (1983) on threatening or sensitive questions. Backstrom and Hursh-Cesar (1981:219) and Warwick and Lininger (1975:150–151) provide useful suggestions as well. Fox and Tracy (1986) discuss the randomized response technique. Also see DeLamater and MacCorquodale (1975) on measuring sexual behavior with survey research and see Herzberger (1993) for general design issues when examining sensitive topics.

14. See DeMario (1984) and Sudman and Bradburn (1983:59).

15. For a discussion of knowledge questions, see Converse and Presser (1986:24–31), Backstrom and Hursh-Cesar (1981:124–126), Sudman and Bradburn (1983:88–118), and Warwick and Lininger (1975:158–160).

16. Contingency questions are discussed in Babbie (1990:136–138), Bailey (1987:135–137), de Vaus (1986:78–80), Dillman (1978:144–146), and Sudman and Bradburn (1983:250–251).

17. For a further discussion of open and closed questions, see Bailey (1987:117–122), Converse (1984), Converse and Presser (1986:33–34), de Vaus (1986:74–75), Geer (1988), Moser and Kalton (1972: 341–345), Sudman and Bradburn (1983:149–155), Schuman and Presser (1979;1981:79–111), and Warwick and Lininger (1975:132–140).

18. For a discussion of the "don't know," "no opinion," and middle positions in response categories, see Backstrom and Hursh-Cesar (1981:148–149), Bishop (1987), Bradburn and Sudman (1988:154), Brody (1986), Converse and Presser (1986:35–37), Duncan and Stenbeck (1988), Poe et al (1988), and Sudman and Bradburn (1983:140–141). The most extensive discussion is found in Schuman and Presser (1981:113–178). For more on filtered questions, see Bishop, Oldendick, and Tuchfarber (1983, 1984) and Bishop, Tuchfarber, and Oldendick (1986).

19. The disagree/agree versus specific alternatives debate is discussed in Bradburn and Sudman (1988:149–151), Converse and Presser (1986:38–39), Schuman and Presser (1981:179–223), and Sudman and Bradburn (1983:119–140). Backstrom and Hursh-Cesar (1981:136–140) discuss forms of asking Likert, agree/disagree questions.

20. The ranking versus ratings issue is discussed in Alwin and Krosnick (1985), Krosnick and Alwin (1988), and Presser (1984). Also see Backstrom and Hursh-Cesar (1981:132–134) and Sudman and Bradburn (1983:156–165) for formats of asking rating and ranking questions.

21. For a discussion of wording effects in questionnaires, see Bradburn and Miles (1979), Peterson (1984), Schuman and Presser (1981:275–296), Sheatsley (1983), and Smith (1987). Hippler and Schwarz (1986) found the same difference between *forbid* and *not allow* in the Federal Republic of Germany, suggesting that the distinction is not unique to the United States or to the English language.

22. The length of questionnaires is discussed in Dillman (1978:51–57; 1983), Frey (1983:48–49),

Herzog and Bachman (1981), and Sudman and Bradburn (1983:226–227).

23. For a discussion of the sequence of questions or question order effects, see Backstrom and Hursh-Cesar (1981:154–176); Bishop, Oldendick, and Tuchfarber (1985); Bradburn (1983:302–304); Bradburn and Sudman (1988:153–154); Converse and Presser (1986:39–40); Dillman (1978:218–220); McFarland (1981); Mckee and O'Brien (1988); Moser and Kalton (1972:346–347); Schuman and Ludwig (1983); Schuman and Presser (1981:23–74); Sudman and Bradburn (1983:207–226); and Schwartz and Hippler (1995).

24. For additional discussion of nonresponse and refusal rates, see Backstrom and Hursh-Cesar (1981:140–141, 274–275); DeMaio (1980); Frey (1983:38–41); Groves and Kahn (1979:218–223); Martin (1985:701–706); Nederhof (1986); Oksenberg et al. (1986); Schuman and Presser (1981:331–336); Sigelman (1982); Steeh (1981); Sudman and Bradburn (1983); and Yu and Cooper (1983). Also see Fowler (1984:46–52) on calculating response rates and bias due to nonresponse. For a discussion of methods for calculating response rates, see Bailey (1987:169), Dillman (1978:49–51), and Frey (1983:38). Bailar and Lanphier (1978:13) noted that improper calculation of response rates is not uncommon, and in a review of surveys found nonresponse rates of 4 to 75 percent.

25. See "Surveys Proliferate, but Answers Dwindle," *New York Times*, October 5, 1990, p. 1, and "Fewer Americans Talking to Research Firms," *Capital Times* (Madison, WI), January 31, 1986, p. 5. Sudman (1976b:114–116) also discusses a growing refusal rate.

26. More extensive discussions of how to increase mail questionnaire return rates can be found in Bailey (1987:153–168), Church (1993), Dillman (1978, 1983), Fox, Crask, and Kim (1988), Goyder (1982), Heberlein and Baumgartner (1978, 1981), Hubbard and Little (1988), Jones (1979), and Willimack et al. (1995). Bailey (1987) has given a useful summary of experiments on return rates. Dillman (1978) has given practical advice on sending out a mailing, including examples of follow-up letters and instructions on folding letters into envelopes with questionnaires.

27. For a discussion of general format and the physical layout of questionnaires, see Babbie (1990), Backstrom and Hursh-Cesar (1981:187–236), Dillman (1978, 1983), Mayer and Piper (1982), Sudman and Bradburn (1983:229–260), and Warwick and Lininger (1975:151–157). Also see Survey Research Center (1976).

28. For additional discussion of comparing types of surveys, see Backstrom and Hursh-Cesar (1981:16–23), Bradburn and Sudman (1988:94–110), Dillman (1978:39–78), Fowler (1984:61–73), and Frey (1983:27–55). For specific details on telephone interviews, see Blankenship (1977), Frey (1983), and Groves and Kahn (1979).

29. Elite interviewing is discussed in Dexter (1970). Also see Useem (1984), Galaskiewicz (1987), Verba and Orren (1985), and Zuckerman (1972). Also see Chapter 13.

30. For additional discussion of focus groups, see Churchill (1983:179–184), Krueger (1988), and Labaw (1980:54–58).

31. For more on survey research interviewing, see Brenner, Brown, and Canter (1985), Cannell and Kahn (1968), Converse and Schuman (1974), Dijkstra and van der Zouwen (1982), Foddy (1993), Gorden (1980), Hyman (1975), Moser and Kalton (1972:270–302), and Survey Research Center (1976). For a discussion of telephone interviewing in particular, see Frey (1983), Groves and Mathiowetz (1984), Jordan, Marcus, and Reeder (1980), and Tucker (1983).

32. The use of probes is discussed in Backstrom and Hursh-Cesar (1981:266–273), Gorden (1980:368–390), and Hyman (1975:236–241).

33. For a discussion of interviewer training and interview expectations, see Backstrom and Hursh-Cesar (1981:237–307), Billiet and Loosveldt (1988), Bradburn and Sudman (1980), Oksenberg, Coleman, and Cannell (1986), Singer and Kohnke-Aguirre (1979), and Tucker (1983). Sudman (1976b:115) noted that middle-class women are less likely nowadays to want to work as interviewers.

34. See Bradburn and Sudman (1980).

35. The race or ethnicity of interviewers is discussed in Anderson, Silver, and Abramson (1988), Cotter et al. (1982), Finkel, Guterbock, and Borg (1991), Gorden (1980:168–172), Reese et al. (1986), Schaffer (1980), Schuman and Converse (1971), and Weeks and Moore (1981).

36. See Bateson (1984), Clark and Schober (1992), Foddy (1993), Lessler (1984), and Turner (1984).

37. See Cicourel (1982), Briggs (1986), and Mishler (1986) for critiques of survey research interviewing.

38. CATI is discussed in Bailey (1987:201–202), Bradburn and Sudman (1988:100–101), Frey (1983: 24–25, 143–149), Groves and Kahn (1979:226), Groves and Mathiowetz (1984), and Karweit and Meyers (1983). Also see Freeman and Merrill (1983).

39. For a discussion of ethical concerns specific to survey research, see Backstrom and Hursh-Cesar (1981:46–50), Fowler (1984:135–144), Frey (1983:177–185), Kelman (1982:79–81), and Reynolds (1982:48–57). Marsh (1982:125–146) and Miller (1983:47–96) provided useful discussions for and against the use of survey research. The use of informed consent is discussed in Singer and Frankel (1982) and in Sobal (1984).

40. On reporting survey results in the media, see Channels (1993) and MacKeun (1984).

RECOMMENDED READINGS

Bradburn, Norman M., and Seymour Sudman. (1988). *Polls and surveys: Understanding what they tell us*. San Francisco: Jossey-Bass. This is an easy-to-read, nontechnical introduction to the variety of polls and surveys. It is less about how to conduct a survey than about what surveys can and cannot tell us. It has an informal style and is written for a lay audience.

Converse, Jean M., and Stanley Presser. (1986). *Survey questions: Handcrafting the standardized questionnaire*. Beverly Hills, CA: Sage. This is a short (74-page) book covering many critical issues in writing questionnaires. It discusses much of the recent research on improving questionnaires in a nontechnical way. It describes the difficult decisions involved in designing questionnaires and has good advice on improving questionnaire writing.

Dillman, Don A. (1978). *Mail and telephone surveys*. New York: Wiley. Although it is now a bit dated, Dillman's book has become a classic in survey research with its discussion of the Total Design Method. It is a comprehensive treatment of mail and telephone surveys. There are many practical hints and suggestions for successful survey research practice.

Fowler, Floyd J., Jr. (1993). *Survey research methods*, 2nd ed. Beverly Hills, CA: Sage. This is a solid, short introduction that summarizes the basics of survey research. It covers the steps in survey research and is a good starting place for the beginning researcher.

Rossi, Peter H., James D. Wright, and Andy B. Anderson (1983). *Handbook of survey research*. New York: Academic. Many of the articles in this book are rather technical for the beginner. Nevertheless, it is a rich source of information on current developments about the full range of survey research methods.

Tanur, Judith M. (Ed.) (1992). *Questions about questions: Inquiries into the cognitive bases of surveys*. New York: Russell Sage Foundation. This excellent collection of 12 articles examines how respondents recall, think, and answer in a survey situation. The articles grapple with the most serious issues in survey interviewing. Theories of how respondents recall and answer, as well as empirical research, are included.

CHAPTER 11

NONREACTIVE RESEARCH AND AVAILABLE DATA

> *There are a number of research conditions in which the sole use of the interview or questionnaire leaves unanswerable rival explanations. The purpose of those less popular measurement classes emphasized here is to bolster these weak spots and provide intelligence to evaluate threats to validity. The payout for using these measures is high, but the approach is more demanding of the investigator.*
>
> —Eugene Webb et al., *Nonreactive Measures in the Social Sciences*, pp. 315–316

INTRODUCTION

Experiments and survey research are both *reactive*; that is, the people being studied are aware of that fact. The techniques in this chapter address a limitation of reactive measures. You will learn about four quantitative research techniques that are *nonreactive*; that is, those being studied are

not aware that they are part of a research project. Nonreactive techniques are largely based on positivist principles but are also used by interpretive and critical researchers.

The first technique you will learn about is not really a distinct technique but a loose collection of inventive nonreactive measures. It is followed by content analysis, which builds on the fundamentals of quantitative research design and is a well-developed research technique in the social sciences. Existing statistics and secondary analysis, the last two techniques, refer to the collection of existing information from government documents or previous surveys. Researchers examine the data in new ways to address new questions. Although the data may have been reactive when first collected, a researcher can address new questions without reactive effects.

NONREACTIVE MEASUREMENT

The Logic of Nonreactive Research

Nonreactive measurement begins when a researcher notices something that indicates a variable of interest. The critical thing about nonreactive or *unobtrusive measures* (i.e., measures that are not obtrusive or intrusive) is that the people being studied are not aware of it but leave evidence of their social behavior or actions "naturally." The observant researcher infers from the evidence to behavior or attitudes without disrupting those being studied. Unnoticed observation is also a type of nonreactive measure. For example, McKelvie and Schamer (1988) unobtrusively observed whether or not drivers stopped at stop signs. They made observations during both daytime and nighttime. Observers noted whether the driver was male or female; whether the driver was alone or with passengers; whether other traffic was present; and whether the car came to a complete stop, a slow stop, or no stop.

Varieties of Nonreactive or Unobtrusive Observation

Nonreactive measures are varied, and researchers have been creative in inventing indirect ways to measure social behavior (see Box 11.1 for examples). Because the measures have little in common except being nonreactive, they are best learned through examples. Some are *erosion measures*, where selective wear is used as a measure, and some are *accretion measures*, where the measures are deposits of something left behind.[1]

Researchers have examined family portraits in different historical eras to see how gender relations within the family are reflected in seating patterns. Urban anthropologists have examined the contents of garbage dumps to learn about lifestyles from what is thrown away (e.g., liquor bottles indicate level of alcohol consumption). Based on garbage, people underreport their liquor consumption by 40 to 60 percent (Rathje and Murphy, 1992:71). Researchers have studied the listening habits of drivers by checking what stations their radios are tuned to when cars are repaired. They have measured interest in different exhibits by noting worn tiles on the floor in different parts of a museum. They have studied differences in graffiti in male versus female high school rest rooms to show gender differences in themes. Some have examined high school yearbooks to compare the high school activities of those who had psychological problems in latter life versus those who did not. Researchers have noted bumper stickers in support of different political candidates to see if one candidate's supporters are more likely than another's to obey traffic laws. Some have even measured television-watching habits by noting changes in water pressure due to the use of toilets during television commercials.[2]

You encountered nonreactive measures in previous chapters of this book. When Lachman (1988) studied graffiti in New York City (discussed in Chapter 3) and when Smith (1995) studied Asian immigration into Flushing, New York (discussed in Chapter 2), each used nonreactive data collection when they walked the streets to observe graffiti or the Asian language signs on stores.

Recording and Documentation

Creating nonreactive measures follows the logic of quantitative measurement, although qualitative researchers also use nonreactive observation. A researcher first conceptualizes a construct, then links the construct to nonreactive empirical evidence, which is its measure. The operational definition of the variable includes how the

Box 11.1

Examples of Nonreactive Measures

PHYSICAL TRACES

Erosion: Wear suggests greater use.
Example: A researcher examines children's toys at a day care that were purchased at the same time. Worn-out toys suggest greater interest by the children.

Accretion: Accumulation of physical evidence suggests behavior.
Example: A researcher examines the brands of aluminum beverage cans in trash or recycling bins in male and female dormitories. This indicates the brands and types of beverages favored by each sex.

ARCHIVES

Running Records: Regularly produced public records may reveal much.
Example: A researcher examines marriage records for the bride and groom's ages. Regional differences suggest that the preference for males marrying younger females is greater in certain areas of the country.

Other Records: Irregular or private records can reveal a lot.
Example: A researcher finds the number of reams of paper purchased by a college dean's office for 10 years when student enrollment was stable. A sizable increase suggests that bureaucratic paperwork has increased.

OBSERVATION

External Appearance: How people appear may indicate social factors.
Example: A researcher watches students to see whether they are more likely to wear their school's colors and symbols after the school team won or lost.

Count Behaviors: Counting how many people do something can be informative.
Example: A researcher counts the number of men and women who come to a full stop and those who come to a rolling stop at a stop sign. This suggests gender difference in driving behavior.

Time Duration: How long people take to do things may indicate their attention.
Example: A researcher measures how long men and women pause in front of the painting of a nude man and in front of a painting of a nude woman. Time may indicate embarrassment or interest in same or cross-sex nudity by each sex.

---

researcher systematically notes and records observations.

Because nonreactive measures indicate a construct indirectly, the researcher needs to rule out reasons for the observation other than the construct of interest. For example, a researcher wants to measure customer walking traffic in a store. The researcher's measure is dirt and wear on floor tiles. He or she first clarifies what the customer traffic means (e.g., Is the floor a path to another department? Does it indicate a good location for a visual display?) Next, he or she systematically measures dirt or wear on the tiles, compares it to that in other locations, and records results on a regular basis (e.g., every month). Finally, the

researcher rules out other reasons for the observations (e.g., the floor tile is of lower quality and wears faster, or the location is near an outside entrance).

CONTENT ANALYSIS

What Is Content Analysis?

Content analysis is a technique for gathering and analyzing the content of text. The *content* refers to words, meanings, pictures, symbols, ideas, themes, or any message that can be communicated. The *text* is anything written, visual, or spoken that serves as a medium for communication. It includes books, newspaper or magazine articles, advertisements, speeches, official documents, films or videotapes, musical lyrics, photographs, articles of clothing, or works of art. For example, Cerulo (1989) studied national anthems.

Content analysis goes back nearly a century and is used in many fields–literature, history, journalism, political science, education, psychology, and so on. At the first meeting of the German Sociological Society, in 1910, Max Weber suggested using it to study newspapers.[3]

You have already read about content analysis studies in this book. The study by Lovdal (1989) on sex-role stereotypes (Chapter 2) and Barlow, Barlow, and Chiricos's (1995) study on crime news (Chapter 6) both used content analysis.

In content analysis, a researcher uses objective and systematic counting and recording procedures to produce a quantitative description of the symbolic content in a text.[4] In fact, Markoff, Shapiro, and Weitman (1974) suggested that "textual coding" might be a better name than content analysis. There are qualitative or interpretive versions of content analysis. The emphasis here is on quantitative data about a text's content.

Qualitative content analysis is not highly respected by most positivist researchers. Nonetheless, feminist researchers and others adopting more critical or interpretative approaches favor it. The criticisms largely reflect the differences among approaches to social science presented in Chapter 4. Quantitative content analysis researchers sometimes include a qualitative evaluation of the content for exploratory purposes, out of sympathy for qualitative approaches, or to give them greater confidence that the quantitative measures are valid.

Content analysis is nonreactive because the process of placing words, messages, or symbols in a text to communicate to a reader or receiver occurs without influence from the researcher who analyzes its content. For example, I, the author of this book, wrote words or drew diagrams to communicate research methods content to you, the student. The way the book was written and the way you read it are without any knowledge or intention of its ever being content analyzed.

Content analysis lets a researcher reveal the content (i.e., messages, meanings, symbols) in a source of communication (i.e., a book, article, movie). It lets him or her probe into and discover content in a different way from the ordinary way of reading a book or watching a television program.

With content analysis, a researcher can compare content across many texts and analyze it with quantitative techniques (e.g., charts, tables). In addition, he or she can reveal aspects of the text's content that are difficult to see. For example, you might watch television commercials and feel that nonwhites rarely appear in commercials for expensive consumer goods (e.g., luxury cars, furs, jewelry, perfume). Content analysis can document—in objective, quantitative terms—whether your vague feelings based on unsystematic observation are true. It yields repeatable, precise results about the text.

Content analysis involves random sampling, precise measurement, and operational definitions for abstract constructs. Coding turns aspects of content that represent variables into numbers. After a content analysis researcher gathers the data, he or she enters them into computers and analyzes them with statistics in the same way that an experimenter or survey researcher would.

Topics Appropriate for Content Analysis

Researchers have used content analysis for many purposes: to study themes in popular songs and religious symbols in hymns, trends in the topics that newspapers cover and the ideological tone of newspaper editorials, sex-role stereotypes in textbooks or feature films, how often people of different races appear in television commercials and programs, answers to open-ended survey questions, enemy propaganda during wartime, the covers of popular magazines, personality characteristics from suicide notes, themes in advertising messages, gender differences in conversations, and so on. Seider (1974) content analyzed the public speeches of U.S. corporate executives. He discovered five ideological themes that executives emphasized more or less depending on the industry of their corporation. Woodrum (1984:1) noted,

> Content analysis remains an underutilized research method with great potential for studying beliefs, organizations, attitudes, and human relations. The limited application and development of content analysis is due more to unfamiliarity with the method and to its historic isolation from mainstream social science than to its inherent limitations.

Generalizations that researchers make on the basis of content analysis are limited to the cultural communication itself. Content analysis cannot determine the truthfulness of an assertion or evaluate the aesthetic qualities of literature. It reveals the content in text but cannot interpret the content's significance. Researchers should examine the text directly. Holsti (1968:602) warned, "Content analysis may be considered as a supplement to, not as a substitute for, subjective examination of documents."

Content analysis is useful for three types of research problems. First, it is helpful for problems involving a large volume of text. A researcher can measure large amounts of text (e.g., years of newspaper articles) with sampling and multiple coders. Second, it is helpful when a topic must be studied "at a distance." For example, content analysis can be used to study historical documents, the writings of someone who has died, or broadcasts in a hostile foreign country. Finally, content analysis can reveal messages in a text that are difficult to see with casual observation. The creator of the text or those who read it may not be aware of all of its themes, biases, or characteristics. For example, authors of preschool picture books may not consciously intend to portray children in traditional stereotyped sex roles, but a high degree of sex stereotyping has been revealed through content analysis.[5] Another example is that of conversations in all-male versus all-female groups. Although people may be unaware of it, in same-sex groups women talk more about inter-

personal matters and social relationships, whereas men talk more about achievement and aggressive themes.[6]

Measurement and Coding

General Issues. Careful measurement is crucial in content analysis because a researcher takes diffuse and murky symbolic communication and turns it into precise, objective, quantitative data. He or she carefully designs and documents procedures for coding to make replication possible. For example, a researcher wants to determine how frequently television dramas portray elderly characters in terms of negative stereotypes. He or she develops a measure of the construct "negative stereotypes of the elderly." The conceptualization may result in a list of stereotypes or negative generalizations about older people (e.g., senile, forgetful, cranky, frail, hard of hearing, slow, ill, in nursing homes, inactive, conservative) that do not accurately reflect the elderly. For example, if 5 percent of people over age 65 are in nursing homes, yet 50 percent of those over age 65 on television are portrayed as being in nursing homes, it is evidence of negative stereotyping.[7]

Constructs in content analysis are operationalized with a *coding system*, a set of instructions or rules on how to systematically observe and record content from text. A researcher tailors it to the type of text or communication medium being studied (e.g., television drama, novels, photos in magazine advertisements). It also depends on the researcher's unit of analysis.

Units. The unit of analysis can vary a great deal in content analysis. It can be a word, a phrase, a theme, a plot, a newspaper article, a character, and so forth. In addition to units of analysis, researchers use other units in content analysis that may or may not be the same as units of analysis: recording units, context units, and enumeration units. There are few differences among them, and they are easily confused, but each has a distinct role. In simple projects, all three are the same.

What Is Measured?　Measurement in content analysis uses *structured observation*: systematic, careful observation based on written rules. The rules explain how to categorize and classify observations. As with other measurement. categories should be mutually exclusive and exhaustive. Written rules make replication possible and improve reliability. Although researchers begin with preliminary coding rules, they often conduct a pilot study and refine coding on the basis of it.

Coding systems identify one or more of four characteristics of text content: frequency, direction, intensity, and space. A researcher measures from one to all four characteristics in a content analysis research project. Each will be briefly explained.

Frequency.　*Frequency* simply means counting whether or not something occurs and, if it occurs, how often. For example, how many elderly people appear on a television program within a given week? What percentage of all characters are they, or in what percentage of programs do they appear?

Direction.　*Direction* is noting the direction of messages in the content along some continuum (e.g., positive or negative, supporting or opposed). For example, a researcher devises a list of ways an elderly television character can act. Some are positive (e.g., friendly, wise, considerate) and some are negative (e.g., nasty, dull, selfish).

Intensity.　*Intensity* is the strength or power of a message in a direction. For example, the characteristic of forgetfulness can be minor (e.g., not remembering to take one's keys when leaving home, taking time to recall the name of someone who has not seen in years) or major (e.g., not remembering one's own name, not recognizing one's children).

Space.　A researcher can record the size of a text message or the amount of space or volume allocated to it. *Space* in written text is measured by counting words, sentences, paragraphs, or space on a page (e.g., square inches). For video or audio text, space can be measured by the amount of time allocated. For example, a character may be present for a few seconds or continuously in every scene of a two-hour program.

Coding, Validity, and Reliability

Manifest Coding.　Coding the visible, surface content in a text is called *manifest coding*. For example, a researcher counts the number of times a phrase or word (e.g., *red*) appears in written text, or whether a specific action (e.g., a kiss) appears in a photograph or video scene. The coding system lists terms or actions which are then located in text. A researcher can use a computer program to search for words or phrases in text and have a computer do the counting work. To do this, he or she learns about the computer program, develops a comprehensive list of relevant words or phrases, and puts the text into a form that computers can read.[8]

Manifest coding is highly reliable because the phrase or word either is or is not present. Unfortunately, manifest coding does not take the connotations of words or phrases into account. The same word can take on different meanings depending on the context. The possibility that there are multiple meanings of a word limits the measurement validity of manifest coding (see Figure 11.1).

For example, I read a book with a *red* cover that is a real *red* herring. Unfortunately, its publisher drowned in *red* ink because the editor couldn't deal with the *red* tape that occurs when a book is *red* hot. The book has a story about a *red* fire truck that stops at *red* lights only after the leaves turn *red*. There is also a group of *Reds* who carry *red* flags to the little *red* schoolhouse. They are opposed by *red*-blooded *red*necks who eat *red* meat and honor the *red*, white, and blue. The main character is a *red*-nosed matador who fights *red* foxes, not bulls, with his *red* cape. *Red*-lipped little *Red* Riding Hood is also in the book. She develops *red* eyes and becomes *red*-faced after eating a lot of *red* peppers in the *red* light district. She is given a *red* backside by her angry mother, a *red*head.

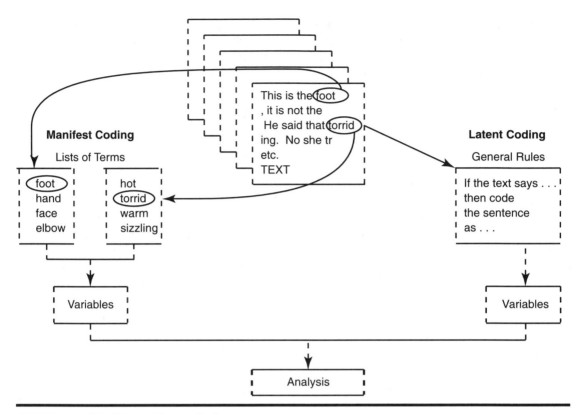

FIGURE 11.1 Manifest and Latent Coding

Latent Coding. A researcher using *latent coding* (also called *semantic analysis*) looks for the underlying, implicit meaning in the content of a text. For example, a researcher reads an entire paragraph and decides whether it contains erotic themes or a romantic mood. His or her coding system has general rules to guide his or her interpretation of the text and for determining whether particular themes or moods are present (see Figure 11.1).

Latent coding tends to be less reliable than manifest coding. It depends on a coder's knowledge of language and social meaning.[9] Training, practice, and written rules improve reliability, but still it is difficult to consistently identify themes, moods, and the like. Yet, the validity of latent coding can exceed that of manifest coding because people communicate meaning in many implicit ways that depend on context, not just in specific words.

A researcher can use both manifest and latent coding. If the two approaches agree, the final result is strengthened; if they disagree, the researcher may want to reexamine the operational and theoretical definitions.

Intercoder Reliability. Content analysis often involves coding information from a very large number of units. A research project might involve observing the content in dozens of books, hundreds of hours of television programming, or thousands of newspaper articles. In addition to coding the information personally, a researcher may hire assistants to help with the coding. He or she teaches coders the coding system and trains them to fill out a recording sheet. Coders should understand the variables, follow the coding system, and ask about ambiguities. A researcher records all decisions he or she makes about how to treat a new specific coding situation after coding begins so that she can be consistent.

A researcher who uses several coders must *always* check for consistency across coders. He or she does this by asking coders to code the same text independently and then checking for consistency across coders. The researcher measures *intercoder reliability*, a type of equivalence reliability, with a statistical coefficient that tells the degree of consistency among coders.[10] The coefficient is *always* reported with the results of content analysis research.

When the coding process stretches over a considerable time period (e.g., more than three months), the researcher also checks stability reliability by having each coder independently code samples of text that were previously coded. He or she then checks to see whether the coding is stable or changing. For example, six hours of television episodes are coded in April and coded again in July without the coders looking at their original coding decisions. Large deviations in coding necessitate retraining and coding the text a second time.

How to Conduct Content Analysis Research

Question Formulation.   As in most research, content analysis researchers begin with a research question. When the question involves variables that are messages or symbols, content analysis may be appropriate. For example. I want to study how newspapers cover a political campaign. My construct "coverage" includes the amount of coverage, the prominence of the coverage, and whether the coverage favors one candidate over another. I could survey people about what they think of the newspaper coverage, but a better strategy is to examine the newspapers directly using content analysis.

Units of Analysis.   A researcher decides on the units of analysis (i.e., the amount of text that is assigned a code). For example, for a political campaign, each issue (or day) of a newspaper is the unit of analysis.

Sampling.   Researchers often use random sampling in content analysis. First, they define the population and the sampling element. For example, the population might be all words, all sentences, all paragraphs, or all articles, in certain types of documents over a specified time period. Likewise, it could include each conversation, situation, scene, episode, or season of certain types of television program over a specified time period. For example, I want to know how women and minorities are portrayed in U.S. weekly newsmagazines. My unit of analysis is the article. My population includes all articles published in *Time, Newsweek*, and *U.S. News and World Report* between 1976 and 1995. I first verify that the three magazines were published in those years and define precisely what is meant by an article. For example, do film reviews count as articles? Is there a minimum size (two sentences) for an article? Is a multipart article counted as one or two articles?

I next examine the three magazines and find that the average issue of each contains 45 articles and that the magazines are published 52 weeks per year. With a 20-year time frame, my population contains over 140,000 articles ($3 \times 45 \times 52 \times 20 = 140,400$). My sampling frame is a list of all the articles. Next, I decide on the sample size and design. After looking at my budget and time, I decide to limit the sample size to 1,400 articles. Thus, the sampling ratio is 1 percent. I also choose a sampling design. I avoid systematic sampling because magazine issues are published cyclically according to the calendar (e.g., an interval of every 52nd issue results in the same week each year). Because issues from each magazine are important, I use stratified sampling. I stratify by magazine, sampling $1,400/3 = 467$ articles from each. I want to ensure that articles represent each of the 20 years, so I also stratify by year. This results in about 23 articles per magazine per year.

Finally, I draw the random sample using a random-number table to select 23 numbers for the 23 sample articles for each magazine for each year. I develop a sampling frame worksheet to keep track of my sampling procedure. See

Table 11.1 for a sampling frame worksheet in which 1,398 sample articles are randomly selected from 140,401 articles.

Variables and Constructing Coding Categories. In my example, I am interested in the construct of an African American or Hispanic woman portrayed in a significant leadership role. I must define "significant leadership role" in operational terms and express it as written rules for classifying people named in an article. For example, if an article discusses the achievements of someone who is now dead, does the dead person have a significant role? What is a significant role—a local Girl Scout leader or a corporate president?

I must also determine the race and sex of people named in the articles. What if the race and sex are not evident in the text or accompanying photographs? How do I decide on the person's race and sex?

Because I am interested in positive leadership roles, my measure indicates whether the role was positive or negative. I can do this with either latent or manifest coding. With manifest coding, I

TABLE 11.1   Excerpt from Sampling Frame Worksheet

Magazine	Issue	Article	Number	ARTICLE In Sample?[a]	SAMPLED Article ID
Time	January 1–7, 1976	pp. 2–3	000001	No	
Time	"	p. 4, bottom	000002	No	
Time	"	p. 4, top	000003	Yes—1	0001
.					
.					
.					
Time	March 1–7, 1995	pp. 2–5	002101	Yes—10	0454
Time	"	p. 6, right column	002102	No	
Time	"	p. 6, left column	002103	No	
Time	"	p. 7	002104	No	
.					
.					
.					
Time	December 24–31, 1995	pp. 4–5	002201	Yes—22	0467
Time	"	p. 5, bottom	002202	No	
Time	"	p. 5, top	002203	Yes—23	0468
Newsweek	January 1–7, 1976	pp. 1–2	010030	No	
Newsweek	"	p. 3	010031	Yes—1	0469
.					
.					
.					
U.S. News	December 25–31, 1995	p, 62	140401	Yes—23	1389

[a]"Yes" means the number was chosen from a random number table. The number after the dash is a count of the number of articles selected for a year.

create a list of adjectives and phrases. If someone in a sampled article is referred to with one of the adjectives, then the direction is decided. For example, the terms *brilliant* or *top performer* are positive, whereas *drug kingpin* or *uninspired* are negative. For latent coding, I create rules to guide judgments. For example, I classify stories about a diplomat resolving a difficult world crisis, a business executive unable to make a firm profitable, or a lawyer winning a case into positive or negative terms (relevant questions for coding each article are in Box 11.2).

In addition to written rules for coding decisions, a content analysis researcher creates a *recording sheet* (also called a coding form or tally sheet) on which to record information (see Box 11.3). Each unit should have a separate recording sheet. The sheets do not have to be pieces of paper; they can be 3×5 or 4×6 file cards, or lines in a computer record or file. When a lot of information is recorded for each recording unit, more than one sheet of paper can be used. When plan-

ning a project, researchers calculate the work required. For example, during my pilot test, I find that it takes an average of 15 minutes to read and code an article. This does not include sampling or locating magazine articles. With approximately 1,400 articles, that is 350 hours of coding, not counting time to verify the accuracy of coding. Because 350 hours is about nine weeks of nonstop work at 40 hours a week, I should consider hiring assistants as coders.

Each recording sheet has a place to record the identification number of the unit and spaces for information about each variable. I also put identifying information about the research project on the sheet in case I misplace it or it looks similar to other sheets I have. Finally, if I use multiple coders, the sheet notes the coder to check intercoder reliability and, if necessary, makes it possible to recode information for inaccurate coders. After completing all recording sheets and checking for accuracy, I can begin data analysis.

Inferences

The inferences a researcher can or cannot make on the basis of results is critical in content analysis. Content analysis describes what is in the text. It cannot reveal the intentions of those who created the text or the effects that messages in the text have on those who receive them. For example, content analysis shows that children's books contain sex stereotypes. That does not necessarily mean that children's beliefs or behaviors are influenced by the stereotypes; such an inference requires a separate research project on children's perceptions.

Here is an example of a content analysis research project. (See Box 11.4 for another example.) Marshall (1986) studied women in a countermovement that opposed granting women the right to vote in the United States of the early twentieth century. A *countermovement* is a conservative movement opposing social change. Some argue that countermovements are based in conflict over status and life-style. Others argue that they are a form of class conflict. Past research has documented that women both supported and opposed the suffrage movement. Marshall's

---

Box 11.2 _____

Example of Latent Coding Questions, Magazine Article Leadership Role Study

1. *Characteristics of the article:* What is the magazine? What is the date of the article? How large is the article? What was its topic area? Where did it appear in the issue? Were photographs used?
2. *People in the article:* How many people are named In the article? Of these, how many are significant in the article? What is the race and sex of each person named?
3. *Leadership roles:* For each significant person in the article, which ones have leadership roles? What is the field of leadership or profession of the person?
4. *Positive or negative roles:* For each leadership or professional role, rate how positively or negatively it is shown. For example, 5 = highly positive, 4 = positive, 3 = neutral, 2 = negative, 1 = highly negative, 0 = ambiguous.

Box 11.3 _____

Example of Blank Coding Sheet

Professor Neuman, Sociology Department   Coder:_____

MINORITY/MAJORITY GROUP REPRESENTATION IN NEWSMAGAZINES PROJECT

ARTICLE #_____   MAGAZINE:_____   DATE:_____   SIZE:_____ col. in.

Total number of people named_____   Number of Photos_____
No. people with significant roles:_____   Article Topic:_____

Person_____:	Race:_____	Gender:_____	Leader?:_____	Field?_____	Rating:_____
Person_____:	Race:_____	Gender:_____	Leader?:_____	Field?_____	Rating:_____
Person_____:	Race:_____	Gender:_____	Leader?:_____	Field?_____	Rating:_____
Person_____:	Race:_____	Gender:_____	Leader?:_____	Field?_____	Rating:_____
Person_____:	Race:_____	Gender:_____	Leader?:_____	Field?_____	Rating:_____
Person_____:	Race:_____	Gender:_____	Leader?:_____	Field?_____	Rating:_____
Person_____:	Race:_____	Gender:_____	Leader?:_____	Field?_____	Rating:_____
Person_____:	Race:_____	Gender:_____	Leader?:_____	Field?_____	Rating:_____

[a]Next to name means person in photograph

EXAMPLE OF COMPLETED RECORDING SHEET FOR ONE ARTICLE

Professor Neuman, Sociology Department   Coder: Susan J.

MINORITY/MAJORITY GROUP REPRESENTATION IN NEWSMAGAZINES PROJECT

ARTICLE # 0454   MAGAZINE: Time   DATE: March 1–7, 1995   SIZE: 14 col. in.

Total number of people named 5   Number of Photos 0
No. people with significant roles: 4   Article Topic: Foreign Affairs

Person 1 :	Race: White	Gender: M	Leader?: Y	Field? Banking	
Rating: 5					
Person 2 :	Race: White	Gender: M	Leader?: N	Field? Government	Rating: NA
Person 3 :	Race: Black	Gender: F	Leader?: Y	Field? Civil Rights	Rating: 2
Person 4 :	Race: White	Gender: F	Leader?: Y	Field? Government	Rating: 0
Person_____:	Race:_____	Gender:_____	Leader?:_____	Field?_____	Rating:_____
Person_____:	Race:_____	Gender:_____	Leader?:_____	Field?_____	Rating:_____
Person_____:	Race:_____	Gender:_____	Leader?:_____	Field?_____	Rating:_____
Person_____:	Race:_____	Gender:_____	Leader?:_____	Field?_____	Rating:_____

research question is: Were antisuffrage arguments based on class or status differences?

Marshall first consulted documents and historical studies on the countermovement. The heyday of the countermovement was between 1911 and 1916, and it was dominated by upper- and middle-class white women. She also content analyzed 68 issues of _The Women's Protest_, a publication of the National Association Opposed to Woman Suffrage published monthly between 1912 and 1918. Each article, letter, or report (recording or "theme unit") was coded. Some 57 percent of all theme units contained a rationale for opposing women's right to vote. In all, Marshall analyzed 2,078 units and found 21 different "rhetorical themes" against woman suffrage. She organized them into four categories: the negative consequences for society, for women, and for

Box 11.4 _____

Social Science in the News

Evans, Krippendorf, Yoon, Posluszny, and Thomas (1990) conducted a content analysis of science results reported in the print media. They examined every issue of the *New York Times*, the *Philadelphia Inquirer*, the *National Enquirer*, and the *Star* for the month of September 1987. The first two of these are prestigious daily urban newspapers, the other two are national weekly tabloid-style "scandal sheets." The authors identified all articles with applied or basic research findings on behavioral, biological, chemical, physical, or social research. They included only articles that had the reporting of findings as a major focus. Thus, a mere mention of a scientist's name was not sufficient. The researchers coded the following items: field of research, type of employment of researcher (e.g., university, government, private firm), researcher's name, original format of research report (e.g., book, article, conference paper), research method used, context of research (i.e., context of prior research, limitations of findings), and length of article. They located 291

scientific research articles. Each article was coded by one member of a team of trained coders. In addition, a random selection of 10 percent of the articles was coded by all coders. Intercoder reliability was 82 percent.

The researchers found that the newspapers published more research (185 articles compared to 106 for the tabloids). Both published more social science research then other types (39 percent to 44 percent). The prestigious newspapers published more research conducted by government agencies, and tabloid weeklies published more university research—90 percent of the newspaper articles compared to 62 percent of those in the tabloids. Both types of media focused on the findings. Only a little over one-third of either publication described or discussed how the research was conducted. Both publication types rarely placed the research in a context of other findings. Almost none told readers about limitations of the findings (e.g., limits on the study's generalizability).

men, and the reasons woman suffrage was unnecessary.

Marshall found that a fear of status loss and class conflict were both evident in antisuffrage arguments, and they were mutually reinforcing. Status loss was evident in themes suggesting that women's voting would destroy the cultured, refined feminine sphere of society located in the home and centered around family and children. The countermovement wanted to keep a female home-based sphere distinct from the nasty, dirty, vulgar male world of politics. Class conflict themes were expressed in attacks on the poor, immigrants, and working-class women who had to work outside the home. Upper- and middle-class women feared that female voters might favor labor legislation, social welfare programs, rights for nonwhites or immigrants, and general equality.

Marshall's research makes the text's meaning accessible for analysis, but she cannot conclude that the articles represent the whole range of

thinking on the issue, or even that those who read the magazine had their opinions shaped by what they read. Her study reveals only the content of published ideas about the issue within a particular politically active group. She can combine it with other data to address larger research questions.

EXISTING STATISTICS/DOCUMENTS AND SECONDARY ANALYSIS

Topics Appropriate for Existing Statistics Research

Many types of information about the social world have been collected and are available to the researcher. Some information is in the form of statistical documents (books, reports, etc.) that contain numerical information. Other information is in the form of published compilations available in a library or on computerized records. In either case, the researcher can search through collections of information with a research question and variables in mind, and then reassemble the information in new ways to address the research question.

It is difficult to specify topics that are appropriate for existing statistics research because they are so varied. Any topic on which information has been collected and is publicly available can be studied. In fact, existing statistics projects may not fit neatly into a deductive model of research design. Rather, researchers creatively reorganize the existing information into the variables for a research question after first finding what data are available.

You learned that experiments are best for topics where the researcher controls a situation and manipulates an independent variable. You saw that survey research is best for topics where the researcher asks questions and learns about reported attitudes or behavior. Earlier, you found that content analysis is for topics that involve the content of messages in cultural communication.

Existing statistics research is best for topics that involve information that has been collected by large bureaucratic organizations. Public or private organizations systematically gather many types of information. Such information is gathered for policy decisions or as a public service. It is rarely collected for purposes directly related to a specific research question. Thus, existing statistics research is appropriate when a researcher wants to test hypotheses involving variables that are also in official reports of social, economic, and political conditions. These include descriptions of organizations or the people in them. Often, such information is collected over long time periods. For example, existing statistics can be used by a researcher who wants to see whether unemployment and crime rates are associated in 150 cities across a 20-year period.

You have read about several existing statistics studies in previous chapters of this book. Existing statistics provided the data for Sutton's (1991) study of asylum growth (Chapter 1), Smith's (1995) study of Asian immigrants (Chapter 2), and Marvell and Moody's (1995) study on sentencing when a weapon was used (Chapter 2). Stack (1987, 1990) used existing statistics in his two studies on suicide (Chapters 2 and 6).

Existing statistics are valuable over time or across nations. Firebaugh and Chen (1995) studied the legacy of the Nineteenth Amendment to the U.S. Constitution, which gave women the right to vote. They wanted to see whether there was a cohort effect (discussed in Chapter 2) of an enduring gender gap in voting. Looking at time-series existing statistics on voting turnout by gender, they found that between 1952 and 1988, the women who grew up in an era before the amendment voted less often. In other words, cohorts from the pre-Nineteenth Amendment era never voted as much as women who grew up later.

Brinton, Lee, and Parish (1995) used cross-national existing government statistics (see Chapter 15) to examine patterns of married women entering the paid labor force in rapidly industrializing nations. Looking at South Korea and Taiwan, they found many similarities. Both had strong patriarchal cultural values and similar education levels for women. Yet, they differed on the percentage of women in the labor force. Korean women were less likely to work outside the home than women in Taiwan. The authors found this was due to different government industrialization policies and differences in how industry grew in each nation.

Locating Data

Locating Existing Statistics. The main sources of existing statistics are government or international agencies and private sources. An enormous volume and variety of information exists. If you plan to conduct existing statistics research, it is wise to discuss your interests with an information professional—in this case, a reference librarian, who can point you in the direction of possible sources.

Many existing documents are "free"—that is, publicly available at libraries—but the time and effort it takes to search for specific information can be substantial. Researchers who conduct existing statistics research spend many hours in libraries. After the information is located, it is recorded on cards, graphs, or recording sheets for later analysis. Often, it is already available in a format for computers to read. For example, instead of recording voting data from books, a researcher could use the national social science data archive at the University of Michigan (to be discussed).

There are so many sources that only a small sample of what is available is discussed here. The single-most valuable source of statistical information about the United States is the *Statistical Abstract of the United States*, which has been published annually (with a few exceptions) since 1878. The *Statistical Abstract* is available in all public libraries and can be purchased from the U.S. Superintendent of Documents. It is a selected compilation of the many official reports and statistical tables produced by U.S. government agencies. It contains the most significant statistical information from hundreds of more detailed government reports. You may want to examine more specific government documents. (The detail of what is available in government documents is mind boggling. For example, you can learn that there were two black females over the age of 75 in Tucumcari City, New Mexico, in 1980.)

The *Statistical Abstract* has 1,400 charts, tables, and statistical lists from over 200 government and private agencies. It is hard to grasp all that it contains (see Table 11.2) until you sit down with the *Abstract* and skim through the tables. A two-volume set summarizes similar information across many years; it is called *Historical Statistics of the U.S.: Colonial Times to 1970*.

Most governments publish similar statistical yearbooks. Australia's Bureau of Statistics produces *Yearbook Australia*, Statistics Canada produces *Canada Yearbook*, New Zealand's Department of Statistics publishes *New Zealand Official Yearbook*, and in the United Kingdom the Central Statistics Office publishes *Annual Abstract of Statistics*.[11] Many nations publish books with historical statistics as well.

Locating government statistical documents is an art in itself. Some publications exist solely to assist the researcher. For example, the *American Statistics Index: A Comprehensive Guide and Index to the Statistical Publications of the U.S.*

Government and Statistics Sources: A Subject Guide to Data on Industrial, Business, Social Education, Financial and Other Topics for the U.S. and Internationally are two helpful guides for the United States.[12] The United Nations and international agencies such as the World Bank have their own publications with statistical information for various countries (e.g., literacy rates, percentage of the labor force working in agriculture, birth rates)—for example, the *Demographic Yearbook. UNESCO Statistical Yearbook*, and *United Nations Statistical Yearbook*.

In addition to government statistical documents, there are dozens of other publications. Many are produced for business purposes and can be obtained only for a high cost. They include information on consumer spending, the location of high-income neighborhoods, trends in the economy, and the like.[13]

Over a dozen publications list characteristics of businesses or their executives. These are found in larger libraries. Three such publications are as follows:

> *Dun and Bradstreet Principal Industrial Businesses* is a guide to approximately 51,000 businesses in 135 countries with information on sales, number of employees, officers, and products.
>
> *Who Owns Whom* comes in volumes for nations or regions (e.g., North America, the United Kingdom, Ireland, Australia). It lists parent companies, subsidiaries, and associated companies.
>
> *Standard and Poor's Register of Corporations, Directors and Executives* lists about 37,000 U.S. and Canadian companies. It has information on corporations, products, officers, industries, and sales figures.

Many biographical sources list famous people and provide background information on them. These are useful when a researcher wants to learn about the social background, career, or other characteristics of famous individuals. The publications are compiled by companies that send out questionnaires to people identified as "important" by some criteria. They are public

TABLE 11.2   A Selected List of the Types of Information in the *Statistical Abstract of the United States* (represents only a tiny percentage of what is available)

Divorce rate by state by year	Death rates by race for different states
Number of burglary arrests resulting in a conviction	Number of public executions by state and race for different years
Deaths from motor vehicle accidents	Millions of dollars in revenue for television networks
State government expenditures for water pollution control	Number of hogs in Arkansas or in any other state
Average monthly temperature for cities of over 50,000 population	Average cost for a dozen eggs in various years
Number of votes for political candidates, by state	Number of submarines France or other nations have
Tons of salt mined, by state	Electricity production of Hungary or other nations
Number of employees in the farm machinery industry	Number of juvenile delinquents per 1,000 population per year
Federal government spending for law enforcement	Average net corporate profit for different sizes of firms
Number of aliens expelled from the country	Percentage of city government revenue coming from liquor store taxes
Number of banks suspended or bankrupt per year	Percentage of all retail sales that tobacco products represent
Average teacher salaries and spending per pupil in each state	Number of square miles of water in each state
Number of handguns legally imported per year	Acres of federally owned land in each state
Housing units without indoor plumbing occupied by different races	Percentage of households with a color television, by family income
Millions of feet of plywood imported and exported per year	Average farm size and farm value by state
Billions of dollars in profits for 170 largest corporations, by year	Average amount spent on newspaper advertising for real estate, by year
Number of new books published in history in a year	Average number of local telephone calls per day in various years
Number of hunting licenses in South Dakota or any other state	Total annual sales of vacuum cleaners per year
Party composition of each state legislature in the United States by year	Average residential rent in selected major metropolitan areas
Average dollars in sales per employee in motor vehicle companies	Number of physicians per 1,000 population in various nations
Number of overnight camping stays in Yosemite National Park	Number of barrels of oil imported to United States from Canada per year
Number of master's degrees granted in sociology in a year by gender	Number of successful and unsuccessful space craft launches by United States and USSR each year since 1957
Military pay for a staff sergeant for various years	

sources of information, but they depend on the cooperation and accuracy of individuals who are selected. See Box 11.5 for examples of biographical sources on Americans.

The publications in Box 11.5 cover only famous Americans, but similar biographical publications exist for many countries. For example, a researcher interested in British banking executives would want to consult *Dictionary of Business Biography* and *Who's Who in British Finance*, whereas information on a famous Canadian would be found in *Canadian Who's Who, Who's Who in Canada*, and the *Dictionary of Canadian Biography*.

Politics has its own specialized publications. There are two basic types. One has biographical information on contemporary politicians. The other type has information on voting, laws

Box 11.5 _____

Public Sources of Biographic Information

Who's Who in America is a popular biographic source that has been published since 1908. It lists the name, birth date, occupation, honors, publications, memberships, education, positions held, spouse, and children's names for those included. Specialized editions are devoted to regions of the United States (e.g., *Who's Who in the East*), to specific occupations (e.g., *Who's Who in Finance and Industry*), and to specific subgroups (e.g., women, Jews, African Americans).

Dictionary of American Biography is a more detailed listing on fewer people than *Who's Who*. It began in

1928 and has supplements to update information. For example, Supplement 7 lists 572 people and devotes about a page to each. It has details about careers, travels, the titles of publications, and relations with other famous people.

Biographical Dictionaries Master Index is an index listing names in the various *Who's Who* publications and many other biographic sources (e.g., *Who's Who in Hockey*). If a researcher knows a name, the index tells where biographic information can be found for the person.

_____

enacted, and the like. Here are three examples of political information publications for the United States:

> *Almanac of American Politics* is a biannual publication that includes photographs and a short biography of U.S. government officials. Committee appointments, voting records, and similar information are provided for members of Congress and leaders in the executive branch.
>
> *America Votes: A Handbook of Contemporary American Election Statistics* contains detailed voting information by county for most statewide and national offices. Primary election results are included down to the county level.
>
> *Vital Statistics on American Politics* provides dozens of tables on political behavior, such as the campaign spending of every candidate for Congress, their primary and final votes, ideological ratings by various political organizations, and a summary of voter registration regulations by state.

Another source of public information consists of lists of organizations (e.g., business, educational) produced for general information

purposes. A researcher can sometimes obtain membership lists of organizations. There are also publications of public speeches given by famous people.

A researcher can combine several sources of existing information in one research project. For example, Freitag (1983) addressed a research question about the backgrounds of officials who served in U.S. regulatory agencies. He went to government documents listing the names of government officials who served in seven agencies from 1887 to 1975, then cross-checked the names with six bibliographical reference sources. By putting the two types of information together, Freitag determined whether individuals with particular careers served in various agencies.

Secondary Survey Data. Secondary analysis is a special case of existing statistics; it is the reanalysis of previously collected survey data or other information. The survey data were originally gathered by others. As opposed to primary research (e.g., experiments, surveys, content analysis), the focus is on analyzing rather than collecting data. Secondary analysis is increasingly used by researchers. It is usually relatively inexpensive; it permits comparisons across groups, nations, or time; it facilitates replication;

and it permits asking about issues not thought of by the original researchers. There are several questions the researcher interested in secondary research should ask (Dale, Arber, and Procter, 1988:27–31; Parcel, 1992): Are the secondary data appropriate for the research question? What theory and hypothesis can a researcher use with the data? Is the researcher already familiar with the substantive area? Does the researcher understand how the data were originally gathered and coded?

In typical stages of research (see Chapter 1), researchers design a project and collect data to address a research question. Yet, large-scale data collection is expensive and difficult. The cost and time required for a major national survey that uses rigorous techniques are prohibitive for most researchers. Fortunately, the organization, preservation, and dissemination of major sur-

vey data sets have improved. Today, there are archives of past surveys that are open to researchers.

The Inter-University Consortium for Political and Social Research (ICPSR) at the University of Michigan is the world's major archive of social science data. Over 17,000 survey research and related sets of information are stored and made available to researchers at modest costs. Other centers hold survey data in the United States and other nations.[14]

A widely used source of survey data for the United States is the *General Social Survey (GSS)*, which has been conducted annually in most years by the National Opinion Research Center at the University of Chicago. In recent years, it has covered other nations as well. The data are made publicly available for secondary analysis at a low cost[15] (see Box 11.6).

Box 11.6 _____

The General Social Survey

The General Social Survey (GSS) is the best-known set of survey data used by social researchers for secondary analysis. The mission of the GSS is "to make timely, high quality, scientifically relevant data available to the social science research community" (Davis and Smith, 1992:1). It is available in many computer-readable formats and is widely accessible for a low cost. Neither datasets nor codebooks are copyrighted. Users may copy or disseminate them without obtaining permission. You can find results using the GSS in over 2,000 research articles and books.

The National Opinion Research Center (NORC) has conducted the GSS almost every year since 1972. A typical year's survey contains a random sample of about 1,500 adult U.S. residents. A team of researchers selects some questions for inclusion, and individual researchers can recommend questions. They repeat some questions and topics each year, include some on a four- to six-year cycle, and add other topics in specific years. For example, in 1988, the special topic was religion, and in 1990, it was intergroup relations.

Interviewers collect the data through face-to-face interviews. The NORC staff carefully selects interviewers and trains them in social science methodology and survey interviewing. About 120 to 140 interviewers work on the GSS each year. About 95 percent are women, and most are middle aged. The NORC recruits bilingual and minority interviewers. Interviewers with respondents are race-matched with respondents. Interviews are typically 90 minutes long and contain approximately 500 questions. The response rate has been 71 to 79 percent. The major reason for nonresponse is a refusal to participate.

The International Social Survey Program conducts similar surveys in other nations. Beginning with the German ALLBUS and British Social Attitudes Survey, participation has grown to include Australia, Austria, Italy, Hungry, Ireland, Israel, the Netherlands, Switzerland, and Poland. The goal is to conduct on a regular basis large-scale national general surveys in which some common questions are asked across cooperating nations.

For example, backlash hypothesis—that white males who work in companies with affirmative action policies are very resentful of programs to aid minorities—was tested with a secondary analysis of GSS data by Taylor (1995). She analyzed already gathered GSS data on white males and looked at their answers to whether affirmative action policies were operating at their workplace and examined their attitudes toward programs to assist racial minorities. Contrary to the backlash hypothesis, Taylor discovered that such men were actually more supportive of programs for minorities than other men.

Reliability and Validity

Existing statistics and secondary data are not trouble free just because a government agency or other source gathered the original data. Researchers must be concerned with validity and reliability, as well as with some problems unique to this research technique. Maier (1991) has an entire book on existing statistics in social research and potential problems with their use.

A common error is the *fallacy of misplaced concreteness*. It occurs when someone gives a false impression of accuracy by quoting statistics in greater detail than warranted by how the statistics are collected and by overloading detail (Horn, 1993:18). For example, in order to impress an audience of one's command of particulars, a politican might say that the population of South Africa is 36,075,861, when he or she should say it is about 36 million.

Units of Analysis and Variable Attributes. A common problem in existing statistics is finding the appropriate units of analysis. Many statistics are published for aggregates, not the individual. For example, a table in a government document has information (e.g., unemployment rate, crime rate) for a state, but the unit of analysis for the research question is the individual (e.g., "Are unemployed people more likely to commit property crimes?"). The potential for committing the ecological fallacy is very real in this situation. It is less of a problem for secondary survey analysis

because researchers can obtain raw information on each respondent from archives.

A related problem involves the categories of variable attributes used in existing documents or survey questions. This is not a problem if the initial data were gathered in many highly refined categories. The problem arises when the original data were collected in broad categories or ones that do not match the needs of a researcher. For example, a researcher is interested in people of Asian heritage. If the racial and ethnic heritage categories in a document are "White," "Black," and "Other," the researcher has a problem. The "Other" category includes people of Asian and other heritages. Sometimes information was collected in refined categories but is published only in broad categories. It takes special effort to discover whether more refined information was collected or is publicly available.

Validity. Validity problems can occur when using existing statistics. One type of problem occurs when the researcher's theoretical definition does not match that of the government agency or organization that collected the information. Official policies and procedures specify definitions for official statistics. For example, a researcher defines a *work injury* as including minor cuts, bruises, and sprains that occur on the job, but the official definition in government reports only includes injuries that require a visit to a physician or hospital. Many work injuries, as defined by the researcher, would not be in official statistics. Another example occurs when a researcher defines people as *unemployed* if they would work if a good job were available, if they have to work part time when they want full-time work, and if they have given up looking for work. The official definition, however, includes only those who are now actively seeking work (full or part time) as unemployed. The official statistics exclude those who stopped looking, who work part time out of necessity, or who do not look because they believe no work is available. In both cases, the researcher's definition differs from that in official statistics (see Box 11.7).

Another validity problem arises when official

Box 11.7 _____

Unemployment Rates versus the Nonemployed

In most countries, the official unemployment rate measures only the unemployed (see below) as a percent of all working people. It would be 50 percent higher if two other categories of nonemployed people were added: involuntary part-time workers and discouraged workers (see below). In some countries (e.g., Sweden, United States), it would be nearly double if it included these people. This does not consider other nonworking people, transitional self-employed, or the underemployed (see below). What a country measures is a theoretical and conceptual definition issue: What construct should art unemployment rate measure and why measure it?

An economic policy or labor market perspective says the rate should measure those ready to enter the labor market immediately. It defines nonworking people as a supply of high-quality labor, an input for use in the economy available to employers. By contrast, a social policy or human resource perspective says the rate should measure those who are not currently working to their fullest potential. The rate should represent people who are not or cannot fully utilize their talents, skills, or time to the fullest. It defines nonworking people as a social problem of individuals unable to realize their capacity to be productive, contributing members of society.

CATEGORIES OF NONEMPLOYED/FULLY UTILIZED

Unemployed people	People who meet three conditions: lack a paying job outside the home, are taking active measures to find work, can begin work immediately if it is offered.
Involuntary part-time workers	People with a job, but work work irregularly or fewer hours than they are able and willing.
Discouraged workers	People able to work and who actively sought it for some time, but being unable to find it, have given up looking.
Other nonworking	Those not working because they are retired, on vacation, temporarily laid off, semidisabled, homemakers, full-time students, or are in the process of moving.
Transitional self-employed	Self-employed who are not working full time because they are just starting a business or are going through bankruptcy.
Underemployed	Persons with a temporary full-time job for which they are seriously overqualified. They seek a permanent job in which they can fully apply their skills and experience.

Source: Adapted from *The Economist*, July 22, 1995, p. 74.

_____

statistics are a surrogate or proxy for a construct in which a researcher is really interested. This is necessary because the researcher cannot collect original data. For example, the researcher wants to know how many people have been robbed, and he or she uses police statistics on robbery arrests as a proxy. But the measure is not entirely valid because many robberies are not reported to the police, and reported robberies do not always result in an arrest.

Another example is a researcher who wants to measure marriages "forced" by a premarital pregnancy. The researcher can use the date of marriage and the date of the birth of a child in official records to estimate whether a marriage was "forced" by a pregnancy. This does not tell him or her that pregnancy was the motivation for the marriage, however. A couple may have planned to marry and the pregnancy was irrelevant, or the pregnancy may have been unknown at the date of marriage. Likewise, some marriages without a recorded birth could be forced by a false belief in pregnancy or a pregnancy that ended in a miscarriage or abortion instead of a birth. In addition, a child might be conceived after the date of marriage, but be born very prematurely. If forced marriages are measured as those where a child was born less than nine months after a marriage date, some will be mislabeled, thereby lowering validity.

A third validity problem arises because the researcher lacks control over how information is collected. All information, even that in official government reports, is originally gathered by people in bureaucracies as part of their jobs. A researcher depends on them for collecting, organizing, reporting, and publishing data accurately. Systematic errors in collecting the initial information (e.g., census people who avoid poor neighborhoods and make up information, or people who put a false age on a driver's license); errors in organizing and reporting information (e.g., a police department that is sloppy about filing crime reports and loses some); and errors in publishing information (e.g., a typographical error in a table) all reduce measurement validity.

Reliability. Problems with reliability can plague existing statistics research. Stability reliability problems develop when official definitions or the method of collecting information changes over time. Official definitions of work injury, disability, unemployment, and the like change periodically. Even if a researcher learns of such changes, consistent measurement over time is impossible. For example, during the early 1980s, the method for calculating the U.S. unemployment rate changed. Previously, the unemployment rate was calculated as the number of unemployed persons divided by the number in the civilian work force. The new method is to divide the number of unemployed by the civilian work force plus the number of people in the military. Likewise, when police departments computerize their records, there is an apparent increase in crimes reported, not because crime increases but due to improved record keeping.

Equivalence reliability can also be a problem. For example, a measure of crime across a nation depends on each police department's providing accurate information. If departments in one region of a country have sloppy bookkeeping, the measure loses equivalence reliability. Likewise, studies of police departments suggest that political pressures to increase arrests are closely related to the number of arrests. For example, political pressure in one city may increase arrests (e.g., a crackdown on crime), whereas pressures in another city may decrease arrests (e.g., to show a drop in crime shortly before an election in order to make officials look better).

Representative reliability is also a problem in official statistics. For example, if the poorly dressed or nonwhite law offender is more likely to be arrested, then crime statistics are not reliable estimates across subpopulations. Other types of statistics can also be affected. Low-income people who dissolve a marriage are less likely to go through expensive divorce proceedings.

Missing Data. One problem that plagues researchers who use existing statistics and documents is that of missing data. Sometimes, the data were collected but have been lost. More frequently, the data were never collected. The decision to collect official information is made within government agencies. The decision to ask questions on a survey whose data are later made publicly available is made by a group of researchers. In both cases, those who decide what to collect may not collect what another researcher needs in order to address a research question. Government agencies start or stop collecting information for political, budgetary, or other reasons. For example, during the early 1980s, cost-cutting measures by the U.S. federal government stopped the collection of information that social researchers found valuable. Missing information is especially a problem when researchers cover long time periods. For example, a researcher interested in the number of work stoppages and strikes in the United States can obtain data from the 1890s to the present, except for a five-year period after 1911 when the federal government did not collect the data.

Example of Existing Statistics/Documents Research

Here is an example that shows how data from existing statistical sources and available documents can be used to address a research question from theories about gender inequality.

Tickamyer (1981) compared two theories of gender inequality that explain sex differences among the wealthy and powerful in the United States. Her research was nonreactive and based on publicly available data. Past research found unequal wealth and property ownership in the United States, with the very wealthy forming a distinct social group with power in society. One theory says that new technology and social organization since the 1920s have eliminated the ways that men gained control over wealth and power. Women's power has grown over time, and social class, not sex, is the primary source of inequality today. Another theory says that sex is an overriding factor. Patriarchal norms and structures take precedence over class inequality. Compared to men, fewer women are wealthy, their patterns of wealth ownership differ, and they are less able to use their wealth to achieve power. Tickamyer's hypotheses are that fewer women are wealthy, their wealth is more likely to be inherited or given as a gift, they have less control over their wealth (more often it is held by banks for them), and they use their wealth differently (more often for arts, civic affairs, and nonbusiness activities).

Tickamyer used two approaches. First, she used a formula to estimate the wealth of the living population from statistics from the U.S. Internal Revenue Service (IRS) on estates larger than $60,000. Second, she collected biographical materials on the wealthy. She found that between the 1920s and the 1970s, over half of all top wealth holders were men. The percentage of women who were top wealth holders increased very slightly over time. Women's wealth was likely to be in the form of trusts and personal property (jewelry, automobiles). Men's wealth was in the form of real estate and mortgages. She concluded that women own "passive" wealth, where few decisions are needed, whereas men own "active" wealth involving business transactions.

Her second approach was to examine business publications (e.g., *Fortune* magazine) to identify people owning at least $100 million. She found 18 women and a sample of 20 men. She then looked up each name in six biographical reference works (e.g., *Who's Who in America*). Six of the 18 women and all 20 of the men were listed in at least one source. Compared to the wealthy men, the women had less education and held fewer positions in government, business, or charity organizations. In addition, Tickamyer checked the membership lists of the boards of directors of the 25 largest U.S. corporations and found that 93 percent of the directors were men.

Tickamyer concluded that although the percentage of women among the wealthy increased slightly over time, men still dominate. Moreover, in contrast to women, men use their wealth to actively influence decisions in government, business, and elsewhere in society.

ISSUES OF INFERENCE AND THEORY TESTING

Inferences from Nonreactive Data

A researcher's ability to infer causality or test a theory on the basis of nonreactive data is limited. It is difficult to use unobtrusive measures to establish temporal order and eliminate alternative explanations. In content analysis, a researcher cannot generalize from the content to its effects on those who read the text, but can only use the correlation logic of survey research to show an association among variables. Unlike the ease of survey research, a researcher does not ask respondents direct questions to measure variables, but relies on the information available in the text.

Ethical Concerns

Ethical concerns are not at the forefront of most nonreactive research because the people being studied are not directly involved. The primary ethical concern is the privacy and confidentiality of using information gathered by someone else. Another ethical issue is that official statistics are social and political products. Implicit theories and value assumptions guide which information is collected and the categories used when gathering it. Measures or statistics that are defined as official and collected on a regular basis are objects of political conflict and guide the direction of policy. By defining one measure as official, public policy is shaped to lead to outcomes that would be different if an alternative, but equally valid, measure had been used. For example, the collection of information on many social conditions (e.g., the number of patients who died while in public mental hospitals) was stimulated by political activity during the Great Depression of the 1930s. Previously, the conditions were not defined as sufficiently important to warrant public attention. Likewise, information on the percentage of nonwhite students enrolled in U.S. schools at various ages is available only since 1953, and for various nonwhite races only since the 1970s. Earlier, such information was not salient for public policy.

The collection of official statistics stimulates new attention to a problem, and public concern about a problem stimulates the collection of new official statistics. For example, drunk driving became an issue once statistics were collected on the number of automobile accidents and on whether alcohol was a factor in an accident.

Political and social values influence decisions about which existing statistics to collect. Most official statistics are designed for top-down bureaucratic or administrative planning purposes. They may not conform to a researcher's purposes or the purposes of those opposed to bureaucratic decision makers. For example, a government agency measures the number of tons of steel produced, miles of highway paved, and average number of people in a household. Information on other conditions such as drinking-water quality, time needed to commute to work, stress related to a job, or number of children needing child care may not be collected because officials say it is unimportant. In many countries, the gross national product (GNP) is treated as a critical measure of societal progress. But GNP ignores noneconomic aspects of social life (e.g., time spent playing with one's children) and types of work (e.g., housework) that are not paid. The information available reflects the outcome of political debate and the values of officials who decide which statistics to collect.[16]

CONCLUSION

In this chapter, you have learned about several types of nonreactive research techniques. They are ways to measure or observe aspects of social life without affecting those who are being studied. They result in objective, numerical information that can be analyzed to address research questions. The techniques can be used in conjunction with other types of quantitative or qualitative social research to address a large number of questions.

As with any form of quantitative data, researchers need to be concerned with measurement issues. It is easy to take available information from a survey or government document, but this does not mean that it measures the construct of interest to the researcher.

You should be aware of two potential problems in nonreactive research. First, the availability of existing information restricts the questions that a researcher can address. Second, the nonreactive variables often have weaker validity because they do not measure the construct of interest. Although existing statistics and secondary data analysis are low-cost research techniques, the researcher lacks control over, and substantial knowledge of, the data collection process. This potential source of errors means that researchers need to be especially vigilant and cautious.

In the next chapter, we move from designing research projects and collecting data to analyzing data. The analysis techniques apply to the quantitative data you learned about in the previous chapters. So far, you have seen how to move from a topic, to a research design and measures, to collecting data. Next, you will learn how to look at data and see what they can tell you about a hypothesis or research question.

KEY TERMS

accretion measures	General Social Survey (GSS)	*Statistical Abstract of the*
coding system	intercoder reliability	*United States*
content	latent coding	structured observation
erosion measures	manifest coding	text
fallacy of misplaced	nonreactive	unobtrusive measures
concreteness	recording sheet	

REVIEW QUESTIONS

1. For what types of research questions is content analysis appropriate?

2. What are the four characteristics of content that are observed and recorded in coding systems?

3. Of what reliability problems should the researcher using existing statistical data be aware?

4. What are the advantages and disadvantages of secondary data analysis?

5. Why do content analysis researchers use multiple coders, and what is the possible problem with doing this?

6. How are inferences limited in content analysis?

7. What units of analysis are used in content analysis?

8. What is the aggregation problem in existing statistics?

9. What are the three validity problems in content analysis?

10. Of what limitations of using existing statistics should researchers be aware?

NOTES

1. See Webb et al. (1981:7–11).
2. For an inventory of nonreactive measures, see Bouchard (1976) and Webb et al. (1981).
3. See Krippendorff (1980:13).
4. For definitions of content analysis, see Holsti (1968:597), Krippendorff (1980:21–24), Markoff et al. (1974:5–6), Stone and Weber (1992), and Weber (1985:81, note 1).
5. Weitzman et al. (1972) is a classic in this type of research.
6. See Aries (1977) for an example.
7. Examples of content analysis studies can be found in Berelson (1952), Carney (1972), McDiarmid (1971), Myers and Margavio (1983), Namenwirth (1970), Sepstrup (1981), Stempel (1971), Stewart (1983), and Stone et al. (1966). Also see Weber (1983) for a discussion of measurement issues in content analysis.
8. Weber (1984, 1985) and Stone and Weber (1992) provided a summary of computerized content analysis techniques.

9. See Andren (1981:58–66) for a discussion of reliability and latent or semantic analysis. Coding categorization in content analysis is discussed in Holsti (1969:94–126).
10. See Krippendorff (1980) for various measures of intercoder reliability. Also see Fiske (1982) for the related issue of convergent validity.
11. Many non-English yearbooks are also produced; for example, *Statistiches Jahrbuch* for the Federal Republic of Germany, *Annuaire Statistique de la France* for France, *Year Book Australia* for Australia, or Denmark's *Statiskisk Ti arsoversigt*. Japan produces an English version of its yearbook called the *Statistical Handbook of Japan*.
12. Guides exist for the publications of various governments—for example, the *Guide to British Government Publications, Australian Official Publications*, or *Irish Official Publications*. Similar publications exist for most nations. For example, *DOD's Par-*

liamentary Companion for the United Kingdom and the *Parliamentary Handbook of the Commonwealth of Australia* are both similar to the *Almanac of American Politics*.

13. See Churchill (1983:140–167) and Stewart (1984) for lists of business information sources.

14. Other major U.S. archives of survey data include the National Opinion Research Center, University of Chicago; the Survey Research Center, University of California–Berkeley; the Behavioral Sciences Laboratory, University of Cincinnati; Data and Program Library Service, University of Wisconsin–Madison; the Roper Center, University of Connecticut–Storrs; and the Institute for Research in Social Science, University of North Carolina–Chapel Hill. Also see Kiecolt and Nathan (1985) and Parcel (1992).

15. The General Social Survey is described in Alwin (1988) and in Davis and Smith (1986).

16. See Block and Burns (1986), Carr-Hill (1984a), Hindess (1973), Horn (1993), Maier (1991), and Van den Berg and Van der Veer (1985). Discussions by Norris (1981) and Starr (1987) are also very helpful.

RECOMMENDED READINGS

Jacob, Herbert. (1984). *Using published data: Errors and remedies*. Beverly Hills, CA: Sage. This short (55-page) book is valuable. As the title suggests, it is about using existing data and focusing on possible errors. The chapters on validity and reliability are very helpful.

Rathje, William, and Cullen Murphy. (1992). *Rubbish: The archaeology of garbage*. New York: Harper. This is a fun but thoughtful look at how researchers have studied garbage to understand human behavior. Written for a lay audience, it reviews many of the studies and techniques used to study what we leave behind.

Stewart, David W. (1984). *Secondary research: Information sources and methods*. Beverly Hills, CA: Sage. Stewart's book is valuable for discovering sources of existing statistics. It contains an introduction to basic issues in secondary research and lists many sources of social science data.

Webb, Eugene J., Donald Campbell, R. Schwartz, L. Sechrest, and J. Grove. (1981). *Nonreactive measures in the social sciences*, 2nd ed. Boston: Houghton Mifflin. This is an update of the social science classic *Unobtrusive Measures* by several of the authors. In addition to a wealth of examples of nonreactive measures, the book includes discussions of ethics in covert measurements, nonreactive observation, the use of archival (existing statistics) data, and limitations on the use of nonreactive measures.

Weber, Robert Philip. (1985). *Basic content analysis*. Beverly Hills, CA: Sage. There are many books on content analysis. Weber provides a moderately sophisticated introduction to the technique, including different content analysis techniques and computer programs to assist the researcher. New as well as experienced researchers who have not used content analysis extensively can learn much from this book.

CHAPTER 12

ANALYZING QUANTITATIVE DATA

> *Statistics may also be regarded as a method of dealing with data. This definition stresses the view that statistics is a tool concerned with the collection, organization, and analysis of numerical facts or observations. . . . The major concern of descriptive statistics is to present information in a convenient, usable, and understandable form.*
> —Richard Runyon and Audry Haber, *Fundamentals of Behavioral Statistics*, p. 6.

INTRODUCTION

If you read a research report or article based on quantitative data, you will probably find it has charts, graphs, and tables full of numbers. Do not be intimidated by them. A researcher provides the charts, graphs, and tables to give you, the reader, a condensed picture of the data. The charts and tables allow you to see the evidence collected by the researcher and learn for yourself what is in it. When you collect your own quantitative data, you will have to use similar techniques to help you to see what is inside the data. You will need to organize and manipulate the quantitative data to get them to reveal things of interest about the social world. In this chapter, you will learn the fundamentals of organizing and analyzing quantitative data. The analysis of quantitative data is a complex field of knowledge. It is as large as the rest of the research methods together. This chapter cannot substitute for a course in social statistics. It covers only the basic statistical concepts and data-handling techniques necessary to understand social research.

Data collected using the techniques in the past chapters are in the form of numbers. The numbers represent values of variables, which measure characteristics of subjects, respondents, or other cases. The numbers are in a raw form, on questionnaires, note pads, recording sheets, or paper.

Researchers do several things to the raw data in order to see what they can say about the research question and hypotheses: Reorganize it into a form suitable for computers, present it in charts or graphs to summarize its features, and interpret or give theoretical meaning to the results.

DEALING WITH DATA

Coding Data

Before a researcher examines quantitative data to test hypotheses, he or she needs to put them in a different form. You encountered the idea of coding data in the last chapter. Here, data *coding* means systematically reorganizing raw data into a format that is machine readable (i.e., easy to analyze using computers). As with coding in content analysis, researchers create and consistently apply rules for transferring information from one form to another.[1]

Coding can be a simple clerical task when the data are recorded as numbers on well-organized recording sheets, but it is very difficult when, for example, a researcher wants to code answers to open-ended survey questions into numbers in a process similar to latent content analysis.

Researchers use a coding procedure and a codebook for data coding. The *coding procedure* is a set of rules stating that certain numbers are assigned to variable attributes. For example, a researcher codes males as 1 and females as 2. Each category of a variable and missing information needs a code. A *codebook* is a document (i.e., one or more pages) describing the coding procedure and the location of data for variables in a format that computers can use.

When you code data, it is very important to create a well-organized, detailed codebook and make multiple copies of it. If you do not write down the details of the coding procedure, or if you misplace the codebook, you have lost the key to the data and will have to recode the raw data all over again.

Researchers begin thinking about a coding procedure and codebook before they collect data. For example, a survey researcher precodes a questionnaire before collecting data. *Precoding* means placing the code categories (e.g., 1 for male, 2 for female) on the questionnaire. Sometimes, to reduce dependence on a codebook, researchers also place the location in the computer format on the questionnaire.

If a researcher does not precode, his or her first step after collecting data is to create a codebook. He or she also gives each case an identification number to keep track of the cases. Next, the researcher transfers the information from each questionnaire into a format that computers can read.

Entering Data

Most computer programs designed for data analysis need the data in a grid format. In the grid, each row represents a respondent, subject, or case. In computer terminology, these are called *data records*. Each is the record of data for a single case. A column or set of columns represents specific variables. It is possible to go from a column and row location (e.g., row 7, column 5) back to the original source of data (e.g., a questionnaire item on marital status for respondent 8). A column or set of columns assigned to a variable is called a data field or just a *field*.

For example, a researcher codes survey data for three respondents in a format for computers like that presented in Table 12.1. People cannot easily read it, and without the codebook, it is worthless. It condenses answers to 50 survey questions for three respondents into three lines or rows. The raw data for many research projects looks like this, except that there may be over 1,000 rows, and the lines may be over 100 columns long. For example, a 15-minute tele-

TABLE 12.1 Coded Data for Three Cases and Codebook

EXCERPT OF CODED DATA

Column
```
00000000011111111112222222222333333333444 ... etc. (tens)
123456789012345678901234567890123456789012 ... etc. (ones)
01 212736302 182738274 10239 18.82 3947461 ... etc.
02 213334821 124988154 21242 18.21 3984123 ... etc.
03 420123982 113727263 12345 17.36 1487645 ... etc.
etc.
```
Raw data for first three cases, columns 1 through 42.

EXCERPT FROM CODEBOOK

Column	Variable Name	Description
1–2	ID	Respondent identification number
3	BLANK	
4	Interviewer	Interviewer who collected the data:
		1 = Susan
		2 = Carlos
		3 = Juan
		4 = Sophia
		5 = Clarence
5	Sex	Interviewer report of respondent's sex
		1 = Male, 2 = Female
6	PresJob	The president of the United States is doing a great job.
		1 = Strongly Agree
		2 = Agree
		3 = No Opinion
		4 = Disagree
		5 = Strongly Disagree
		Blank = missing information

phone survey of 250 students produces a grid of data that is 250 rows by 240 columns.

The codebook in Table 12.1 says that the first two numbers are identification numbers. Thus, the example data are for the first (01), second (02), and third (03) respondents. Notice that researchers use zeros as place holders to reduce confusion between 1 and 01. The 1s are always in column 2; the 10s are in column 1. The codebook says that column 5 contains the variable "sex": Cases 1 and 2 are male and Case 3 is female. Column 4 tells us that Carlos interviewed Cases 1 and 2, and Sophia Case 3.

A researcher transfers information from questionnaires, recording sheets, or similar raw data forms into a format for computers in four ways: code sheets, direct entry, optical scan sheets, and computer-assisted telephone interviewing (CATI). First, he or she can use graph paper or special grid forms for computers (called transfer or *code sheets*) by writing code numbers in squares that correspond to a row and column location, then typing it into a computer. Second, the researcher can sit at a computer and directly type in the data. This *direct-entry method* is easiest if information is already in a similar format, as with content analysis recording sheets. Otherwise, it can be very time consuming and error prone. Third, he or she can put data on an *optical scan sheet*. Special machines—optical scanners—read the information from the sheets into a computer. You may have used optical scan sheets, which are used for scoring multiple-choice tests. They are specially printed forms on which a person fills in boxes or circles using a pencil to indicate a response. The researcher can use the last method if his or her project involved telephone interviewing. CATI (computer-assisted telephone interviewing) was described in Chapter 10. Interviewers wearing telephone headsets sit at a computer keyboard and enter data directly as respondents answer questions during the interview.

Cleaning Data

Accuracy is extremely important when coding data. (See Box 12.1 for an example.) Errors made when coding or entering data into a computer threaten the validity of measures and cause misleading results. A researcher who has a perfect sample, perfect measures, and no errors in gathering data, but who makes errors in the coding process or in entering data into a computer, can ruin a whole research project.

After very careful coding, a researcher checks the accuracy of coding, or "cleans" the data. A researcher may code a 10 to 15 percent random sample of the data a second time. If no coding errors appear, the researcher proceeds; if he or she finds errors, the researcher rechecks all coding.

Researchers verify coding after the data are in a computer in two ways. *Possible code cleaning* (or wild code checking) involves checking the categories of all variables for impossible codes. For example, respondent sex is coded 1 = Male, 2 = Female. Finding a 4 for a case in the field for the sex variable indicates a coding error. A second method, *contingency cleaning* (or consistency checking), involves cross-classifying two variables and looking for logically impossible combinations. For example, education is cross-classified by occupation. If a respondent is recorded as never having passed the eighth grade and also is recorded as being a legitimate medical doctor, the researcher checks for a coding error.

A researcher can modify data after they are in a computer. He or she may not use more refined categories than were used when collecting the original data, but may combine or group information. For example, the researcher may group ratio-level income data into five ordinal categories. Also, he or she can combine information from several indicators to create a new variable or add the responses to several questionnaire items into an index score.

RESULTS WITH ONE VARIABLE

Frequency Distributions

The word *statistics* has several meanings. It can mean a set of collected numbers (e.g., numbers telling how many people live in a city), as well as a branch of applied mathematics used to manipulate and summarize the features of numbers. Social researchers use both types of statistics. Here, we focus on the second type—ways to manipulate and summarize numbers that represent data from a research project.

Descriptive statistics describe numerical data. They can be categorized by the number of variables involved: univariate, bivariate, or multivariate (for one, two, and three or more variables). *Univariate statistics* describe one variable (*uni-* refers to one; *-variate* refers to variable). The easiest way to describe the numerical data of one variable is with a *frequency distribution*. It can be used with nominal-, ordinal-, interval-, or ratio-level data and takes many forms. For example, I have data for 400 respondents. I can summarize the information on the gender of respondents at a glance with a raw count or a percentage frequency distribution (see Figure 12.1). I can present the same information in graphic form. Some common types of graphic representations are the *histogram*, *bar chart*, and *pie chart*. Most people have seen these. The terminology is not exact, but histograms are usually upright bar graphs for interval or ratio data.[2]

For interval- or ratio-level data, a researcher often groups the information into categories. The grouped categories should be mutually exclusive. Interval- or ratio-level data are often plotted in a *frequency polygon*. In it the number of cases or frequency is along the vertical axis, and the values of

Box 12.1 _____

Example of Dealing with Data

There is no good substitute for getting your hands dirty with the data. Here is an example of data preparation from a study I conducted with my students. My university surveyed about one-third of the students to learn their thinking and experience with sexual harassment on campus. A research team drew a random sample, then developed and distributed a self-administered questionnaire. Respondents put answers on optical scan sheets that were similar to the answer sheets used for multiple-choice exams. The story begins with the delivery of over 3,000 optical scan sheets.

After the sheets arrived, we visually scanned each one for obvious errors. Despite instructions to use pencil and fill in each circle neatly and darkly, we found that about 200 respondents used a pen, and another 200 were very sloppy or used very light pencil marks. We cleaned up the sheets and redid them in pencil. We also found about 25 unusable sheets that were defaced or damaged, or were too incomplete (e.g., only the first 2 of 70 questions answered).

Next, we read the usable optical scan sheets into a computer. We had the computer produce the number of occurrences, or frequency, of the attributes for each variable. Looking at them, we discovered several kinds of errors. Some respondents had filled in two responses for a question to which only one answer was requested or possible. Some had filled in impossible response codes (e.g., the numeral 4 for sex, when the only legitimate codes were 1 for male and 2 for female), and some had filled in every answer in the same way, suggesting that they did not take the survey seriously. For each case with an error, we returned to the optical scan sheet to see whether we could recover any information. If we could not recover information, we reclassified the case as a nonresponse or recoded a response as missing information.

The questionnaire had two contingency questions. For each, a respondent who answered "No" to one question was to skip the next five questions. We created a table for each question. We looked to see whether all respondents who answered "No" to the first question skipped or left blank the next five. We found about 35 cases in which the respondent answered "No" but then went on to answer the next five questions. We returned to each sheet and tried to figure out which the respondent really intended. In most cases, it appeared that the respondent meant the "No" but failed to read the instructions to skip questions.

Finally, we examined the frequency of attributes for each variable to see whether they made sense. We were very surprised to learn that about 600 respondents had marked "Native American" for the racial heritage question. In addition, over half of those who had done so were freshmen. A check of official records revealed that the university enrolled a total of about 20 Native Americans or American Indians, and that over 90 percent of the students were White, non-Hispanic-Caucasians. The percentage of respondents marking Black, African-American or Hispanic-Chicano matched the official records. We concluded that some White Caucasian respondents had been unfamiliar with the term "Native American" for "American Indian." Apparently, they had mistakenly marked it instead of "White, Caucasian." Since we expected about 7 Native Americans in the sample, we recoded the "Native American" responses as "White, Caucasian." This meant that we reclassified Native Americans in the sample as Caucasian. At this point, we were ready to analyze the data.

_____

the variable or scores are along the horizontal axis. A polygon appears when the dots are connected.

Measures of Central Tendency

Researchers often want to summarize the information about one variable into a single number.

They use three measures of central tendency, or measures of the center of the frequency distribution: mean, median, and mode, which are often called *averages* (a less precise and less clear way of saying the same thing).

The *mode* is the easiest to use and can be used with nominal, ordinal, interval, or ratio data. It is

FIGURE 12.1   Examples of Univariate Statistics

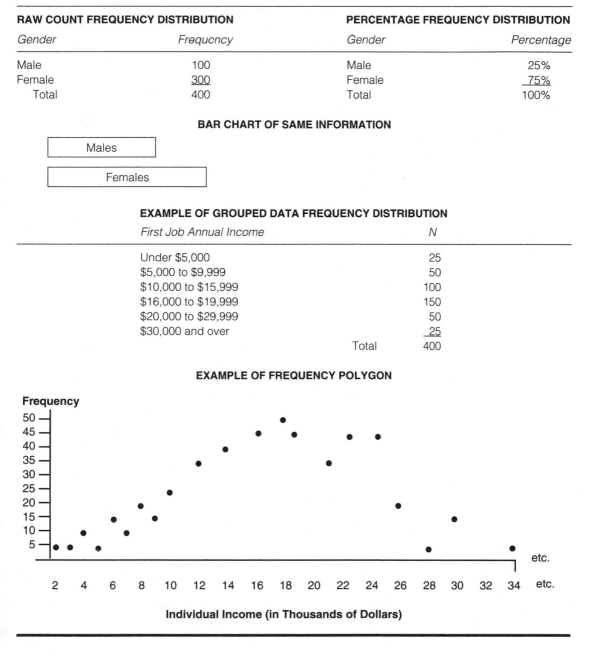

RAW COUNT FREQUENCY DISTRIBUTION		PERCENTAGE FREQUENCY DISTRIBUTION	
Gender	*Frequency*	*Gender*	*Percentage*
Male	100	Male	25%
Female	300	Female	75%
Total	400	Total	100%

BAR CHART OF SAME INFORMATION

Males

Females

EXAMPLE OF GROUPED DATA FREQUENCY DISTRIBUTION

First Job Annual Income	*N*
Under $5,000	25
$5,000 to $9,999	50
$10,000 to $15,999	100
$16,000 to $19,999	150
$20,000 to $29,999	50
$30,000 and over	25
Total	400

EXAMPLE OF FREQUENCY POLYGON

Individual Income (in Thousands of Dollars)

simply the most common or frequently occurring number. For example, the mode of the following list is 5: 6 5 7 10 9 5 3 5. A distribution can have more than one mode. For example, the mode of this list is both 5 and 7: 5 6 1 2 5 7 4 7. If the list

gets long, it is easy to spot the mode in a frequency distribution—just look for the most frequent score. There will always be at least one case with a score that is equal to the mode.

The *median* is the middle point. It is also the

50th percentile, or the point at which half the cases are above it and half below it. It can be used with ordinal-, interval- or ratio-level data (but not nominal level). You can "eyeball" the mode, but computing a median requires a little more work. The easiest way is first to organize the scores from highest to lowest, then count to the middle. If there is an odd number of scores, it is simple. Seven people are waiting for a bus; their ages are: 12 17 20 27 30 55 80. The median age is 27. Note that the median does not change easily. If the 55-year-old and the 80-year-old both got on one bus, and the remaining people were joined by two 31-year-olds, the median remains unchanged. If there is an even number of scores, things are a bit more complicated. For example, six people at a bus stop have the following ages: 17 20 26 30 50 70. The median is somewhere between 26 and 30. Compute the median by adding the two middle scores together and dividing by 2, or 26 + 30 = 56/2 = 28. The median age is 28, even though no person is 28 years old. Note that there is no mode in the list of six ages because each person has a different age.

The *mean*, also called the arithmetic average, is the most widely used measure of central tendency. It can be used *only* with interval- or ratio-level data.[3] Compute the mean by adding up all scores, then divide by the number of scores. For example, the mean age in the previous example is: 17 + 20 + 26 + 30 + 50 + 70 = 213; 213/6 = 35.5. No one in the list is 35.5 years old, and the mean does not equal the median.

The mean is strongly affected by changes in extreme values (very large or very small). For example, the 50- and 70-year-old left and were replaced with two 31-year-olds. The distribution now looks like this: 17, 20, 26, 30, 31, 31. The median is unchanged 28. The mean is: 17 + 20 + 26 + 30 + 31 + 31 = 155; 155/6 = 25.8. Thus, the mean dropped a great deal when a few extreme values were removed.

If the frequency distribution forms a "normal" or bell-shaped curve, the three measures of central tendency equal each other. If the distribution is a *skewed distribution* (i.e., more cases are in the upper or lower scores), then the three will

not be equal. If most cases have lower scores with a few extreme high scores, the mean will be the highest, the median in the middle, and the mode the lowest. If most cases have higher scores with a few extreme low scores, the mean will be the lowest, the median in the middle, and the mode the highest. In general, the median is best for skewed distributions, although the mean is used in most other statistics (See Figure 12.2).

Measures of Variation

Measures of central tendency are a one-number summary of a distribution; however, they give only its *center*. Another characteristic of a distribution is its spread, dispersion, or variability around the center. Two distributions can have identical measures of central tendency but differ in their spread about the center. For example, seven people are at a bus stop in front of a bar. Their ages are: 25 26 27 30 33 34 35. Both the median and the mean are 30. At a bus stop in front of an ice cream store, seven people have the identical median and mean, but their ages are: 5 10 20 30 40 50 55. The ages of the group in front of the ice cream store are spread more from the center, or the distribution has more variability.

Variability has important social implications. For example, in city X, the median and mean family income is $25,600 per year, and it has zero variation. Zero variation means that every family has an income of exactly $25,600. City Y has the same median and mean family income, but 95 percent of its families have incomes of $8,000 per year and 5 percent have incomes of $300,000 per year. City X has perfect income equality, whereas there is great inequality in city Y. A researcher who does not know the variability of income in the two cities misses very important information.

Researchers measure variation in three ways: range, percentile, and standard deviation. *Range* is the simplest. It consists of the largest and smallest scores. For example, the range for the bus stop in front of the bar is from 25 to 35, or 35 – 25 = 10 years. If the 35-year-old got onto a bus and was replaced by a 60-year-old, the range would

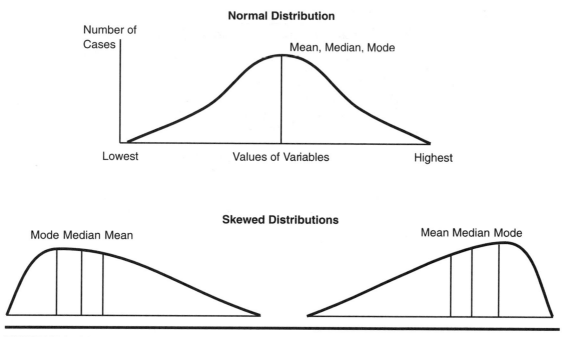

FIGURE 12.2 Measures of Central Tendency

change to $60 - 25 = 45$ years. Range has limitations. For example, here are two groups of six with a range of 35 years: 30 30 30 30 30 65, and 20 45 46 48 50 55.

Percentiles tell the score at a specific place within the distribution. One percentile you already learned is the median, the 50th percentile. Sometimes the 25th and 75th percentiles or the 10th and 90th percentiles are used to describe a distribution. For example, the 25th percentile is the score at which 25 percent of the distribution have either that score or a lower one. The computation of a percentile follows the same logic as the median. If I have 100 people and want to find the 25th percentile. I rank the scores and count up from the bottom until I reach number 25. If the total is not 100, I simply adjust the distribution to a percentage basis.

Standard deviation is the most difficult to compute measure of dispersion; it is also the most comprehensive and widely used. The range and percentile are for ordinal-, interval-, and ratio-level data, but the standard deviation requires an interval or ratio level of measurement. It is based on the mean and gives an "average distance" between all scores and the mean. People rarely compute the standard deviation by hand for more than a handful of cases because computers and calculators can do it in seconds.

Look at the calculation of the standard deviation in Table 12.2. If you add up the absolute difference between each score and the mean (i.e., subtract each score from the mean), you get zero. This is because the mean is equally distant from all scores. Also notice that the scores that differ the most from the mean have the largest effect on the sum of squares and on the standard deviation.

The standard deviation is of limited usefulness by itself. It is used for comparison purposes. For example, the standard deviation for the schooling of parents of children in class A is 3.317 years; for class B, it is 0.812; and for class C, it is 6.239. The standard deviation tells a researcher that the parents of children in class B are very similar, whereas those for class C are very different.

TABLE 12.2 The Standard Deviation

STEPS IN COMPUTING THE STANDARD DEVIATION

1. Compute the mean.
2. Subtract the mean from each score.
3. Square the resulting difference for each score.
4. Total up the squared differences to get the sum of squares.
5. Divide the sum of squares by the number of cases to get the variance.
6. Take the square root of the variance, which is the standard deviation.

EXAMPLE OF COMPUTING THE STANDARD DEVIATION

[8 respondents, variable = years of schooling]

Score	Score – Mean	Squared (Score – Mean)
15	15 – 12.5 = 2.5	6.25
12	12 – 12.5 = –0.5	.25
12	12 – 12.5 = –0.5	.25
10	10 – 12.5 = –2.5	6.25
16	16 – 12.5 = 3.5	12.25
18	18 – 12.5 = 5.5	30.25
8	8 – 12.5 = 4.5	20.25
9	9 – 12.5 = –3.5	12.25

Mean = 15 + 12 + 12 + 10 + 16 + 18 + 8 + 9 = 100, 100/8 = 12.5
Sum of squares = 6.25 + .25 + .25 + 6.25 + 12.25 + 30.25 + 20.25 + 12.25 = 88
Variance = Sum of squares/Number of cases = 88/8 = 11
Standard deviation = Square root of variance = $\sqrt{11}$ = 3.317 years.
Here is the standard deviation in the form of a formula with symbols.

Symbols:
X = SCORE of case   Σ = Sigma (Greek letter) for sum, add
                                        together
$\bar{X}$ = MEAN   N = Number of cases
Formula:[a]

$$\text{Standard deviation} = \sqrt{\frac{\sum (X - \bar{X})^2}{N}}$$

[a] There is a slight difference in the formula depending on whether one is using data for the population or a sample to estimate the population parameter.

In fact, in class B, the schooling of an "average" parent is less than a year above or below than the mean for all parents, so the parents are very homogeneous. In class C, however, the "average" parent is more than six years above or below the mean, so the parents are very heterogeneous.

The standard deviation and the mean are used to create z-scores. *Z-scores* let a researcher compare two or more distributions or groups. The z-score, also called a standardized score, expresses points or scores on a frequency distribution in terms of a number of standard deviations from the mean. Scores are in terms of their relative position within a distribution, not as absolute values.

For example, Katy, a sales manager in firm A, earns $50,000 per year, whereas Mike in firm

B earns $38,000 per year. Despite the absolute income differences between them, the managers are paid equally relative to others in the same firm. Katy is paid more than two-thirds of other employees in her firm, and Mike is also paid more than two-thirds of the employees in his firm.

Here is another example of how to use *z*-scores. Hans and Heidi are twin brother and sister, but Hans is shorter than Heidi. Compared to other girls her age, Heidi is at the mean height; she has a *z*-score of zero. Likewise, Hans is at the mean height among boys his age. Thus, within each comparison group, the twins are at the same *z*-score, so they have the same relative height.

Z-scores are easy to calculate from the mean and standard deviation (see Box 12.2). For example, an employer interviews students from Kings College and Queens College. She learns that the

colleges are similar and that both grade on a 4.0 scale. Yet, the mean grade-point average at Kings College is 2.62 with a standard deviation of .50, whereas the mean grade-point average at Queens College is 3.24 with a standard deviation of .40. The employer suspects that grades at Queens College are inflated. Suzette from Kings College has a grade-point average of 3.62, while Jorge from Queens College has a grade-point average of 3.64. Both students took the same courses. The employer wants to adjust the grades for the grading practices of the two colleges (i.e., create standardized scores). She calculates *z*-scores by subtracting each student's score from the mean, then dividing by the standard deviation. For example, Suzette's *z*-score is 3.62 − 2.62 = 1.00/.50 = 2, whereas Jorge's *z*-score is 3.64 − 3.24. = .40/.40 = 1. Thus, the employer

---

Box 12.2 _____

Calculating Z-Scores

Personally, I don't like the formula for z-scores, which is:

Z score = (Score − Mean)/Standard Deviation
or in symbols

$$z = \frac{X - \bar{X}}{\delta}$$

where: X = score, $\bar{X}$ = mean, δ = standard deviation

I usually rely on a simple conceptual diagram that does the same thing and that shows what z-scores really do. Consider data on the ages of schoolchildren with a mean of 7 years and a standard deviation of 2 years. How do I compute the z-score of 5-year-old, Miguel, or what if I know that Yashohda's z-score is a + 2 and I need to know her age in years? First, I draw a little chart from −3 to +3 with zero in the middle. I will put the mean value at zero, because a z-score of zero is the mean and z-scores measure distance above or below it. I stop at 3 because virtually all cases fall within 3 standard deviations of the mean in most situations. The chart looks like this:

```
 |____|____|____|____|____|____|
 -3   -2   -1    0   +1   +2   +3
```

Now, I label the values of the mean and add or subtract standard deviations from it. One standard deviation above the mean (+1) when the mean is 7 and standard deviation is 2 years is just 7 + 2, or 9 years. For a −2 z-score, I put 3 years. This is because it is 2 standard deviations, of 2 years each (or 4 years), lower than the Mean of 7. My diagram now looks like this:

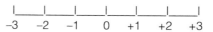

```
 1    3   5   7    9    11    13  age in years
 |____|___|___|____|____|____|
 -3   -2  -1   0   +1   +2   +3
```

It is easy to see that Miguel, who is 5 years old, has a z-score of −1, whereas Yashohda's z-score of +2 corresponds to 11 years old. I can read from z-score to age, or age to z-score. For fractions, such as a z-score of −1.5, I just apply the same fraction to age to get 4 years. Likewise, an age of 12 is a z-score of +2.5.

learns that Suzette is two standard deviations above the mean in her college, whereas Jorge is only one standard deviation above the mean for his college. Although Suzette's absolute grade-point average is lower than Jorge's, relative to the students in each of their colleges Suzette's grades are much higher than Jorge's.

RESULTS WITH TWO VARIABLES

A Bivariate Relationship

Univariate statistics describe a single variable in isolation. *Bivariate statistics* are much more valuable. They let a researcher consider two variables together and describe the relationship between variables. Even simple hypotheses require two variables.

Bivariate statistical analysis tells us about a *statistical relationship* between variables—that is, things that appear together. For example, a relationship exists between water pollution in a stream and the fact that people who drink the water get sick. It is a statistical relationship between two variables: pollution in the water and the health of the people who drink it.

Statistical relationships are based on two ideas, covariation and independence. *Covariation* means that things go together or are associated. To covary means to vary together; cases with certain values on one variable are likely to have certain values on the other one. For example, people with higher values on the income variable are likely to have higher values on the life expectancy variable. Likewise, those with lower incomes have lower life expectancy. This is usually stated in a shorthand way by saying that income and life expectancy are related to each other, or covary. We could also say that knowing one's income tells us one's probable life expectancy, or that life expectancy depends on income.

Independence is the opposite of covariation. It means there is no association or no relationship between variables. If two variables are independent, cases with certain values on one variable do not have any particular value on the other variable. For example, Rita wants to know whether

number of siblings is related to life expectancy. If the variables are independent, then people with many brothers and sisters have the same life expectancy as those who are only children. In other words, knowing how many brothers or sisters someone has tells Rita nothing about the person's life expectancy.

Most researchers state hypotheses in terms of a causal relationship or expected covariation; if they use the null hypothesis, the hypothesis is that there is independence. It is used in formal hypothesis testing and is frequently found in inferential statistics (to be discussed).

Three techniques help researchers decide whether a relationship exists between two variables: (1) a scattergram, or a graph or plot of the relationship; (2) cross-tabulation, or a percentaged table; (3) measures of association, or statistical measures that express the amount of covariation by a single number (e.g., correlation coefficient). Also see Box 12.3 on graphing data.

Seeing the Relationship: The Scattergram

What Is a Scattergram (or Scatterplot)?   A *scattergram* is a graph on which a researcher plots each case or observation, where each axis represents the value of one variable. It is used for variables measured at the interval or ratio level, rarely for ordinal variables, and never if either variable is nominal. There is no fixed rule for which variable (independent or dependent) to place on the horizontal or vertical axis, but usually the independent variable (symbolized by the letter X) goes on the horizontal axis and the dependent variable (symbolized by Y) on the vertical axis. The lowest value for each should be the lower left corner and the highest value should be at the top or to the right.

How to Construct a Scattergram.   Begin with the range of the two variables. Draw an axis with the values of each variable marked and write numbers on each axis (graph paper is helpful). Next, label each axis with the variable name and put a title at the top.

You are now ready for the data. For each case, find the value of each variable and mark the

Box 12.3 _____

Graphing Accurately

The pattern in Graph A shows drastic change. A steep drop in 1980 is followed by rapid recovery and instability. The pattern in Graph B is much more constant. The decline from 1979 to 1980 is smooth, and the other years are almost level. Both graphs are for identical data, the U.S. business failure rate from 1975 to 1992. The X axis (bottom) for years is the same. The scale of the Y axis is 60 to 160 in Graph A and 0 to 400 in Graph B. The pattern in graph A only looks more dramatic because of the Y axis scale. When reading graphs, be careful to check the scale. Some people purposely choose a scale to minimize or dramatize a pattern in the data.

Graph A

Graph B

graph at a place corresponding to the two values. For example, a researcher makes a scattergram of years of schooling by number of children. He or she looks at the first case to see years of schooling (e.g., 12) and at the number of children (e.g., 3). Then he or she goes to the place on the graph where 12 for the "schooling" variable and 3 for the "number of children" variable intersect and puts a dot for the case.

The scattergram in Figure 12.3 is a plot of data for 33 women. It shows a *negative relationship* between the years of education the woman completed and the number of children she gave birth to.

The scattergram is complete after all the cases have been plotted, which can take some time if there are many cases. Also, some types of computer software can plot a scattergram after the data are in the computer.

What Can You Learn from the Scattergram?   A researcher can see three aspects of a bivariate relationship in a scattergram: form, direction, and precision.

Form.   Relationships can take three forms: independence, linear, and curvilinear. *Independence* or no relationship is the easiest to see. It looks like a random scatter with no pattern, or a straight line that is exactly parallel to the horizontal or vertical axis. A *linear relationship* means that a straight line can be visualized in the middle of a maze of cases running from one corner to another. A *curvilinear relationship* means that the center of a maze of cases would form a U curve, right side up or upside down, or an S curve.

Direction.   Linear relationships can have a positive or negative direction. The plot of a *positive* relationship looks like a diagonal line from the lower left to the upper right. Higher values on *X* tend to go with higher values on *Y*, and vice versa. The income and life expectancy example described a positive linear relationship.

A *negative* relationship looks like a line from the upper left to the lower right. It means that higher values on one variable go with lower

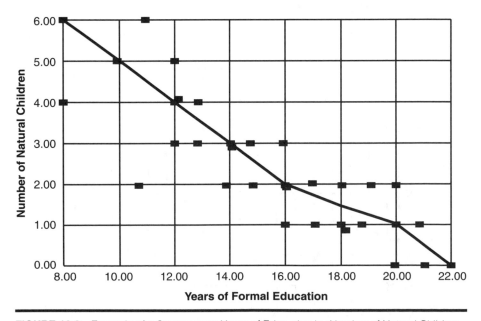

FIGURE 12.3   Example of a Scattergram: Years of Education by Number of Natural Children for 33 Women

values on the other. For example, people with more education are less likely to have been arrested. If we look at a scattergram of data on a group of males where years of schooling (X axis) are plotted by number of arrests (Y axis), we see that most cases (or men) with many arrests are in the lower right, because most of them completed few years of school. Most cases with few arrests are in the upper left because most have had more schooling. The imaginary line for the relationship can have a shallow or a steep slope. More advanced statistics provide precise numerical measures of the line's slope.

Precision. Bivariate relationships differ in their degree of precision. *Precision* is the amount of spread in the points on the graph. A high level of precision occurs when the points hug the line that summarizes the relationship. A low level occurs when the points are widely spread around the line. Researchers can "eyeball" a highly precise relationship. They can also use advanced statistics to measure the precision of a relationship in a way that is analogous to the standard deviation for univariate statistics.

Bivariate Tables

What Is a Bivariate Table? The bivariate percentaged table is widely used. It presents the same information as a scattergram in a more condensed form. The data can be measured at any level of measurement, although interval and ratio data must be grouped if there are many different values. The table is based on *cross-tabulation*; that is, the cases are organized in the table on the basis of two variables at the same time. Bivariate tables usually contain percentages.

Constructing Percentaged Tables. It is easy to construct a percentaged table, but there are ways to make it look professional. We will first review the steps for constructing a table by hand. The same principles apply if a computer makes the table. We begin with the raw data, which can be

organized into a format for computers. They might look like data from an imaginary survey in Box 12.4.

The next step is to create a *compound frequency distribution (CFD)*. This is similar to the frequency distribution, except that it is for each combination of the values of two variables. For example, a researcher wants to see the relationship between age and attitude. Age is a ratio measure, so it is grouped to treat the ratio-level variable as if it were ordinal. Ratio- or interval-level data are converted to the ordinal level for percentaged tables. Otherwise, there could be 50 categories for a variable and a table that was impossible to read.

The CFD has every combination of categories. Age has four categories and Attitude three, so there are $3 \times 4 = 12$ rows. The steps to create a CFD are as follows:

1. Figure all possible combinations of variable categories.
2. Make a mark next to the combination category into which each case falls.
3. Add up the marks for the number of cases in a combination category.

If there is no missing information problem, add up the numbers of categories (e.g., all the "Agree"s, or all the "61 and Older"s). In the example, missing data are an issue. The four "Agree" categories in the CFD add up to 37 (20 + 10 + 4 + 3), not 38, as in the univariate frequency distribution, because one of the 38 cases has missing information for age.

The CFD is an intermediate step that makes table construction easier. Computer programs give you the completed table right away.

The next step is to set up the parts of a table (see Table 12.3) by labeling the rows and columns. The independent variable usually is placed in the columns, but this convention is not always followed. Next, each number from the CFD is placed in a cell in the table that corresponds to the combination of variable categories. For example, the CFD shows that 20 of the under-30-year-olds agree (top number), and so does Table 12.3 (upper left cell).

Box 12.4 _____

Raw Data and Frequency Distributions

EXAMPLE OF RAW DATA

Case	Age	Gender	Schooling	Attitude	Political Party, etc. . . .
01	21	F	14	1	Democrat
02	36	M	8	1	Republican
03	77	F	12	2	Republican
04	41	F	20	2	Independent
05	29	M	22	3	Democratic Socialist
06	45	F	12	3	Democrat
07	19	M	13	2	Missing Information
08	64	M	12	3	Democrat
09	53	F	10	3	Democrat
10	44	M	21	1	Conservative
etc.					

(Attitude scoring, 1 = Agree, 2 = No Opinion, 3 = Disagree)

TWO FREQUENCY DISTRIBUTIONS:
AGE AND ATTITUDE TOWARD CHANGING THE DRINKING AGE

Age Group	Number of Cases	Attitude	Number of Cases
Under 30	26		
30–45	30	Agree	38
46–60	35	No Opinion	26
61 and older	15	Disagree	40
Missing	3	Missing	5
Total	109	Total	109

COMPOUND FREQUENCY DISTRIBUTION:
AGE GROUP AND ATTITUDE TOWARD CHANGING THE DRINKING AGE

Age	Attitude	Number of Cases
Under 30	Agree	20
Under 30	No Opinion	3
Under 30	Disagree	3
30–45	Agree	10
30–45	No Opinion	10
30–45	Disagree	5
46–60	Agree	4
46–60	No Opinion	10
46–60	Disagree	21
61 and older	Agree	3
61 and older	No Opinion	2
61 and older	Disagree	10
	Subtotal	101
Missing on either variable		8
Total		109

TABLE 12.3 Age Group by Attitude about Changing the Drinking Age, Raw Count Table (a)

[RAW COUNT TABLE]

Age Group (2)

Attitude (b)	Under 30	30–45	46–60	61 and Older	Total (c)
Agree	20	10	4	3	37
No opinion	3 (d)	10	10	2	25
Disagree	3	5	21	10	39
Total (c)	26	25	35	15	101

Missing cases (f) = 8.　　　　　　　　　　　　　　　　　　　　(e)

THE PARTS OF A TABLE

(a) Give each table a *title*, which names variables and provides background information.

(b) Label the row and column variable and give a name to each of the variable categories.

(c) Include the totals of the columns and rows. These are called the *marginals*. They equal the univariate frequency distribution for the variable.

(d) The numbers with the labeled variable categories and the totals are called the *body of a table*.

(e) Each number or place that corresponds to the intersection of a category for each variable is a *cell of a table*.

(f) If there is missing information (cases in which a respondent refused to answer, ended interview, said "don't know," etc.), report the number of missing cases near the table to account for all original cases.

Table 12.3 is a raw count or frequency table. Its cells contain a count of the cases. It is easy to make, but interpreting a raw count table is difficult because the rows or columns can have different totals, and what is of real interest is the relative size of cells compared to others.

Researchers convert raw count tables into percentaged tables to see bivariate relationships. There are three ways to percentage a table: by row, by column, and for the total. The first two are often used and show relationships.

Is it best to percentage by row or column? Either can be appropriate. Let us first review the mechanics of percentaging a table. When calculating column percentages, compute the percentage each cell is of the column total. This includes the total column or marginal for the column variable. For example, the first column total is 26 (there are 26 people under age 30), and the first cell of that column is 20 (there are 20 people under age 30 who agree). The percentage is 20/26 = 0.769 or 76.9 percent. Or, for the first number in the marginal, 37/101 = 0.366 = 36.6 percent (see

Table 12.4). Except for rounding, the total should equal 100 percent.

Computing row percentages is similar. Compute the percentage of each cell as a percentage of the row total. For example, using the same cell with 20 in it, we now want to know what percentage it is of the row total of 37, or 20/37 = 0.541 = 54.1 percent. Percentaging by row or column gives different percentages for a cell unless the marginals are the same.

The row and column percentages let a researcher address different questions. The row percentage table answers the question, Among those who hold an attitude, what percentage come from each age group? It says of respondents who agree, 54.1 percent are in the under-30 age group. The column percentage table addresses the question, Among those in each age group, what percentage hold different attitudes? It says that among those who are under 30, 76.9 percent agree. From the row percentages, a researcher learns that a little over half of those who agree are under 30 years old, whereas from column per-

TABLE 12.4   Age Group by Attitude about Changing the Drinking Age

COLUMN-PERCENTAGED TABLE

Age Group

Attitude	Under 30	30–45	46–60	61 and Older	Total
Agree	76.9%	40%	11.4%	20%	36.6%
No opinion	11.5	40	28.6	13.3	24.8
Disagree	11.5	20	60	66.7	38.6
Total	99.9	100	100	100	100
(N)	(26)*	(25) *	(35)*	(15)*	(101)*

Missing cases = 8.

ROW-PERCENTAGED TABLE

Age Group

Attitude	Under 30	30–45	46–60	61 and Older	Total	*(N)*
Agree	54.1%	27	10.8	8.1	100	(37)*
No opinion	12%	40	40	8	100	(25)*
Disagree	7.7%	12.8	53.8	25.6	99.9	(39)*
Total	25.7	24.8	34.7	14.9	100.1	(101)*

Missing cases = 8.

*For percentaged tables, provide the number of cases or *N* on which percentages are computed in parentheses near the total of 100%. This makes it possible to go back and forth from a percentaged table to a raw count table and vice versa.

centages, the researcher learns that among the under-30 people, over three-quarters agree. One way of percentaging tells about people who have specific attitudes; the other tells about people in specific age groups.

A researcher's hypothesis may imply looking at row percentages or the column percentages. When beginning, calculate percentages each way and practice interpreting, or figuring out, what each says. For example, my hypothesis is that age affects attitude, so column percentages are most helpful. However, if my interest was in describing the age makeup of groups of people with different attitudes, then row percentages are appropriate. As Zeisel (1985:34) noted, whenever one factor in a cross-tabulation can be considered the cause of the other, percentage will be most illuminating if they are computed in the direction of the causal factor.

Reading a Percentaged Table.   Once you understand how a table is made, reading it and figuring out what it says are much easier. To read a table, first look at the title, the variable labels, and any sources of background information. Next, look at the direction in which percentages have been computed—in rows or columns. Notice that the percentaged tables in Table 12.4 have the same title. This is because the same variables are used. It would have helped to note how the data were percentaged in the title, but this is rarely done. Sometimes, researchers present abbreviated tables and omit the 100 percent total or the marginals, which adds to the confusion. It is best to include all the parts of a table and clear labels.

Researchers read percentaged tables to make comparisons. Comparisons are made in the opposite direction from that in which percentages are computed. A rule of thumb is to compare across rows if the table is percentaged down (i.e., by column) and to compare up and down in columns if the table is percentaged across (i.e., by row).

For example, in row-percentaged Table 12.4, compare columns or age groups. Most of those who agree are in the youngest group, with the proportion declining as age increases. Most no-opinion people are in the middle-age groups, whereas those who disagree are found among older age groups, especially the 46-to-60 group. When reading column-percentaged Table 12.4, compare across rows. For example, a majority of the youngest group agree, and they are the only group in which most people agree. Only 11.5 percent disagree, compared to a majority in the two oldest groups.

It takes practice to see a relationship in a percentaged table. If there is no relationship in a table, the cell percentages look approximately equal across rows or columns. A linear relationship looks like larger percentages in the diagonal cells. If there is a curvilinear relationship, the largest percentages form a pattern across cells. For example, the largest cells might be the upper right, the bottom middle, and the upper left. It is easiest to see a relationship in a moderate-sized table (9 to 16 cells) where most cells have some cases (at least five cases are recommended) and the relationship is strong and precise.

Principles of reading a scattergram can help you see a relationship in a percentaged table. Imagine a scattergram that has been divided into 12 equal-sized sections. The cases in each section correspond to the number of cases in the cells of a table that is superimposed onto the scattergram. The table is a condensed form of the scattergram. The bivariate relationship line in a scattergram corresponds to the diagonal cells in a percentaged table. Thus, a simple way to see strong relationships is to circle the largest percentage in each row (for row-percentaged tables) or column (for column-percentaged tables) and see if a line appears.

The circle-the-largest-cell rule works—with one important caveat. The categories in the percentages table *must* be ordinal or interval and in

the same order as in a scattergram. In scattergrams the lowest variable categories begin at the bottom left. If the categories in a table are not ordered the same way, the rule does not work.

For example, Table 12.5a looks like a positive relationship and Table 12.5b like a negative relationship. Both use the same data and are percentaged by row. The actual relationship is negative. Look closely—Table 12.5b has age categories ordered as in a scattergram. When in doubt, return to the basic difference between positive and negative relationships. A positive relationship means that as one variable increases, so does the other. A negative relationship means that as one variable increases, the other decreases.

Bivariate Tables without Percentages. Researchers condense information in another kind of bivariate table with a measure of central tendency (usually the mean) instead of percentages. It is used when one variable is nominal or ordinal and another is measured at the interval or ratio level. The mean (or a similar measure) of the interval or ratio variable is presented for each category of the

TABLE 12.5a Age by Schooling

| Age | YEARS OF SCHOOLING | | | | |
	0–11	*12*	*13–14*	*16+*	*Total*
Under 30	5%	25	30	40	100
30–45	15	25	40	20	100
46–60	35	45	12	8	100
61 ı	45	35	15	5	100

TABLE 12.5b Age by Schooling

| Age | YEARS OF SCHOOLING | | | | |
	0–11	*12*	*13–14*	*16+*	*Total*
61 +	45%	35	15	5	100
46–60	35	45	12	8	100
30–45	15	25	40	20	100
Under 30	5	25	30	40	100

nominal or ordinal variable. Such tables are not constructed from the CFD. Instead, all cases are divided into the ordinal or nominal variable categories; then the mean is calculated for the cases in each variable category from the raw data.

Table 12.6 shows the mean age of people in each of the attitude categories. The results suggest that the mean age of those who disagree is much higher than for those who agree or have no opinion.

Measures of Association

A measure of association is a single number that expresses the strength, and often the direction, of a relationship. It condenses information about a bivariate relationship into a single number.

There are many measures of association. The correct one depends on the level of measurement. Many measures are called by letters of the Greek alphabet. Lambda, gamma, tau, chi (squared), and rho are commonly used measures. The emphasis here is on interpreting the measures, not on their calculation. In order to understand each measure, you will need to complete a beginning statistics course. See. Box 12.5 on the correlation.

Most of the elementary measures discussed here follow a *proportionate reduction in error (PRE)* logic. The logic asks: How much does knowledge of one variable reduce the errors that are made when guessing the values of the other variable? Independence means that knowledge of one variable does not reduce the chance of errors on the other variable. Measures of association equal zero if the variables are independent.

If there is a strong association or relationship, then few errors are made predicting a second variable on the basis of knowledge of the first, or the proportion of errors reduced is large. A large number of correct guesses suggests that the measure of association is a nonzero number if an association exists between the variables. Table 12.7 describes five commonly used bivariate measures of association. Notice that most range from −1 to +1, with negative numbers indicating a negative relationship and positive numbers a positive relationship. A measure of 1.0 means a 100 percent reduction in errors, or perfect prediction.

MORE THAN TWO VARIABLES

Statistical Control

Showing an association or relationship between two variables is not sufficient to say that an independent variable *causes* a dependent variable. In addition to temporal order and association, a researcher must eliminate alternative explanations—explanations that can make the hypothesized relationship spurious. Experimental researchers do this by choosing a research design that physically controls potential alternative explanations for results (i.e., that threaten internal validity).

In nonexperimental research, a researcher controls for alternative explanations with statistics. He or she measures possible alternative explanations with *control variables*, then examines the control variables with multivariate tables and statistics that help him or her decide whether a bivariate relationship is spurious. They also show the relative size of the effect of multiple independent variables on a dependent variable.

A researcher controls for alternative explanations in multivariate (more than two variables) analysis by introducing a third (or sometimes a fourth or fifth) variable. For example, a bivariate table shows that taller teenagers like baseball more than shorter ones do. But the bivariate relationship between height and attitude toward baseball may be spurious because teenage males are taller than females, and males tend to like baseball more than

TABLE 12.6 Attitude about Changing the Drinking Age by Mean Age of Respondent

DRINKING AGE ATTITUDE	MEAN AGE	(N)
Agree	26.2	(37)
No opinion	44.5	(25)
Disagree	61.9	(39)

Missing cases = 8.

Box 12.5 _____

Correlation

The formula for a correlation coefficient (rho) looks awesome to most people. Calculating it by hand, especially if the data have multiple digits, can be a very long and arduous task. Nowadays, we use computers to do it; they are extremely fast and accurate. The problem with relying on computers to do the work is that a researcher may not understand what the coefficient means. Here is a short, simplified example to show how it is done.

The purpose of a correlation coefficient is to us how much two variables "go together" or covary. Ideally, the variables have a ratio level of measurement (some use variables at the interval level). To calculate the coefficient, we first convert each score on a variable into its z-score. This "standardizes" the variable based on its mean and standard deviation. Next, we multiply the z-scores for each case together. This tells us how much the variables for a case vary together—cases with high z-scores on both variables get much bigger, while those low on both are much smaller. Finally, we divide the sum of the multiplied z-scores by the number of cases. It yields a type of "average" covariation that has been standardized. In short, a correlation coefficient is the product of z-scores added together, then divided by the number of cases. It is always between +1.0 and −1.0 and summarizes scattergram information about a relationship into a single number.

Let us look at the correlation between the age and price for five small bottles of red wine. First, anyone who is brave or lacks math-symbol phobia can look at one of the frequently used formulas for a correlation coefficient:

$$(\Sigma\, [z\text{-score}_1][z\text{-score}_2])/N$$

where: Σ = sum, $z\text{-score}_1$ = z-score for 1st variable (see Box 12.2), $z\text{-score}_2$ = z-score for 2nd variable, N = number of cases

Here is how to calculate a correlation coefficient without directly using the formula.

WINE	AGE	PRICE	(DIFFERENCE) Age	Price	SQUARED DIFF. Age	Price	Z-SCORES Age	Price	Z-SCORE Product
A	2	$10	−2	−5	4	25	−1.43	−.70	1.0
B	3	$ 5	−1	−10	1	100	−.71	−1.41	1.0
C	5	$20	+1	+5	1	25	.71	+.70	.50
D	6	$25	+2	+10	4	100	+1.43	+1.41	2.0
E	4	$15	0	0	0	0	0	0	0
Total	20	$75			10	250			4.50

Mean: Age = 4; Price = $15
Variance: Age = 10/5 = 2; Price = 250/5 = 50.
Stnd. Dev.: Age = square root of 2 = 1.4; Price = square root of 50 = 7.1
Correlation: 4.50/5 = .90

STEP 1: Calculate the mean and standard deviation for each variable. (For the standard deviation, first subtract each score from its mean, next square the difference, now sum squared differences, then divide the sum by the number of cases for the variance. Then take the square root of the variance.)
STEP 2: Convert each score for the variables into their z-scores. (Just subtract each score from its mean and divide by its standard deviation.)
STEP 3: Multiply the z-scores together for each case.
STEP 4: Sum the products of z-scores, then divide by the number of cases.

TABLE 12.7   Five Measures of Association

Lambda is used for nominal-level data. It is based on a reduction in errors based on the mode and ranges between 0 (independence) and 1.0 (perfect prediction or the strongest possible relationship).

Gamma is used for ordinal-level data. It is based on comparing pairs of variable categories and seeing whether a case has the same rank on each. Gamma ranges from – 1.0 to + 1.0, with 0 meaning no association.

Tau is also used for ordinal-level data. It is based on a different approach than gamma and takes care of a few problems that can occur with gamma. Actually, there are several statistics named tau (it is a popular Greek letter), and the one here is Kendall's tau. Kendall's tau ranges from – 1.0 to + 1.0, with 0 meaning no association.

Rho is also called Pearson's product moment correlation coefficient (named after the famous statistician Karl Pearson and based on a product moment statistical procedure). It is the most commonly used measure of correlation, the correlation statistic people mean if they use the term *correlation* without identifying it further. It can be used only for data measured at the interval or ratio level. Rho is used for the mean and standard deviation of the variables and tells how far cases are from a relationship (or regression) line in a scatterplot. Rho ranges from – 1.0 to + 1.0, with 0 meaning no association. If the value of rho is squared, sometimes called *R*-squared, it has a unique proportion reduction in error meaning. *R*-squared tells how the percentage in one variable (e.g., the dependent) is accounted for, or explained by, the other variable (e.g., the independent). Rho measures linear relationships only. It cannot measure nonlinear or curvilinear relationships. For example, a rho of zero can indicate either no relationship or a curvilinear relationship (see Box 12.5).

Chi-squared has two different uses. It can be used as a measure of association in descriptive statistics like the others listed here, or in inferential statistics. Inferential statistics are briefly described next. As a measure of association, chi-squared can be used for nominal and ordinal data. It has an upper limit of infinity and a lower limit of zero, meaning no association (see Box 12.8).

SUMMARY OF MEASURES OF ASSOCIATION

Measure	Greek Symbol	Type of Data	High Association	Independence
Lambda	λ	Nominal	1.0	0
Gamma	γ	Ordinal	+1.0, – 1.0	0
Tau (Kendall's)	τ	Ordinal	+1.0, – 1.0	0
Rho	ρ	Interval, ratio	+1.0, – 1.0	0
Chi-square	χ^2	Nominal, ordinal	Infinity	0

females. To test whether the relationship is actually due to sex, a researcher must *control for* gender; in other words, effects of sex are statistically *removed*. Once this is done, a researcher can see whether the bivariate relationship between height and attitude toward baseball remains.

A researcher controls for a third variable by seeing whether the bivariate relationship persists within categories of the control variable. For example, a researcher controls for sex, and the relationship between height and baseball attitude persists. This means that tall males and tall females both like baseball more than short males and short females do. In other words, the control variable has no effect. When this is so, the bivariate relationship is not spurious.

If the bivariate relationship weakens or disappears after the control variable is considered, it means that tall males are no more likely than short males to like baseball, and tall females are no more likely to like baseball than short females. It indicates that the initial bivariate relationship is spurious and suggests that the third variable, sex, and not height, is the true cause of differences in attitudes toward baseball.

Statistical control is a key idea in advanced statistical techniques. A measure of association like the correlation coefficient only suggests a relationship. Until a researcher considers control variables, the bivariate relationship could be spurious. Researchers are cautious in interpreting bivariate relationships until they have considered control variables.

After they introduce control variables, researchers talk about the *net effect* of an independent variable—the effect of the independent variable "net of," or in spite of, the control variable. There are two ways to introduce control variables: trivariate percentaged tables and multiple regression analysis. Each will be briefly discussed next.

The Elaboration Model of Percentaged Tables

Constructing Trivariate Tables. In order to meet all the conditions needed for causality, researchers want to "control for" or see whether or not an alternative explanation explains away a causal relationship. If an alternative explanation explains a relationship, then the bivariate relationship is spurious. Alternative explanations are operationalized as third variables, which are called *control variables* because they control for alternative explanation.

One way to take such third variables into consideration and see whether they influence the bivariate relationship is to statistically introduce control variables using trivariate or three-variable tables. Trivariate tables differ slightly from bivariate tables; they consist of multiple bivariate tables.

A trivariate table has a bivariate table of the independent and dependent variable for each category of the control variable. These new tables are called *partials*. The number of partials depends on the number of categories in the control variable. Partial tables look like bivariate tables, but they use a subset of the cases. Only cases with a specific value on the control variable are in the partial. Thus, it is possible to break apart a bivariate table to form partials, or combine the partials to restore the initial bivariate table.

Trivariate tables have three limitations. First, they are difficult to interpret if a control variable has more than four categories. Second, control variables can be at any level of measurement, but interval or ratio control variables must be grouped (i.e., converted to an ordinal level), and how cases are grouped can affect the interpretation of effects. Finally, the total number of cases is a limiting factor because the cases are divided among cells in partials. The number of cells in the partials equals the number of cells in the bivariate relationship multiplied by the number of categories in the control variable. For example, a control variable has three categories, and a bivariate table has 12 cells, so the partials have $3 \times 12 = 36$ cells. An average of five cases per cell is recommended, so the researcher will need $5 \times 36 = 180$ cases at minimum.

Like bivariate table construction, a trivariate table begins with a compound frequency distribution (CFD), but it is a three-way instead of a two-way CFD. An example of a trivariate table with "gender" as a control variable for the bivariate table in Table 12.2 is shown in Table 12.8.

As with the bivariate tables, each combination in the CFD represents a cell in the final (here the partial) table. Each partial table has the variables in an initial bivariate table.

For three variables, three bivariate tables are logically possible. In the example, the combinations are: (1) gender by attitude, (2) age group by attitude, and (3) gender by age group. The partials are set up on the basis of the initial bivariate relationship. The independent variable in each is "age group" and the dependent variable is "attitude." "Gender" is the control variable. Thus, the trivariate table consists of a pair of partials, each showing the age/attitude relationship for a given gender.

A researcher's theory suggests the hypothesis in the initial bivariate relationship; it also tells him or her which variables provide alternative explanations, (i.e., the control variables). Thus,

TABLE 12.8   CFD and Tables for a Trivariate Analysis

COMPOUND FREQUENCY DISTRIBUTION FOR TRIVARIATE TABLE

	MALES				FEMALES	
Age	*Attitude*	*Number of Cases*		*Age*	*Attitude*	*Number of Cases*
Under 30	Agree	10		Under 30	Agree	10
Under 30	No Opinion	1		Under 30	No Opinion	2
Under 30	Disagree	2		Under 30	Disagree	1
30–45	Agree	5		30–45	Agree	5
30–45	No Opinion	5		30–45	No Opinion	5
30–45	Disagree	2		30–45	Disagree	3
46–60	Agree	2		46–60	Agree	2
46–60	No Opinion	5		46–60	No Opinion	5
46–60	Disagree	11		46–60	Disagree	10
61 and older	Agree	3		61 and older	Agree	0
61 and older	No Opinion	0		61 and older	No Opinion	2
61 and older	Disagree	5		61 and older	Disagree	5
	Subtotal	51			Subtotal	50
Missing on either variable		4		Missing on either variable		4
Number of males		55		Number of females		54

PARTIAL TABLE FOR MALES

AGE GROUP

Attitude	*Under 30*	*30–45*	*46–60*	*61 and Older*	*Total*
Agree	10	5	2	3	20
No Opinion	1	5	5	0	11
Disagree	2	2	11	5	20
Total	13	12	18	8	51

Missing cases = 4

PARTIAL TABLE FOR FEMALES

AGE GROUP

Attitude	*Under 30*	*30–45*	*46–60*	*61 and Older*	*Total*
Agree	10	5	2	0	17
No Opinion	2	5	5	2	14
Disagree	1	3	10	5	19
Total	13	13	17	7	50

Missing cases = 4

the choice of the control variable is based on theory.

As with bivariate tables, the CFD provides the raw count for cells (partials here). A researcher converts them into percentages in the same way as for a bivariate table (i.e., divide cells by the row or column total). For example, in the partial table for females, the upper left cell has a 10. The row percentage for that cell is 10/17 = 58 percent.

The *elaboration paradigm* is a system for reading percentaged trivariate tables.[4] It describes the pattern that emerges when a control variable is introduced. Five terms describe how the partial tables compare to the initial bivariate table, or how the original bivariate relationship changes after the control variable is considered (see Box 12.6). The examples of patterns presented here show strong cases. More advanced statistics are needed when the differences are not as obvious.

The *replication pattern* is the easiest to understand. It is when the partials replicate or reproduce the same relationship that existed in the bivariate table before considering the control variable. It means that the control variable has no effect.

The *specification pattern* is the next easiest pattern. It occurs when one partial replicates the initial bivariate relationship, but other partials do not. For example, you find a strong (negative) bivariate relationship between automobile accidents and college grades. You control for gender and discover that the relationship holds only for males (i.e., the strong negative relationship was in the partial for males, but not for females). This is specification because a researcher can specify the category of the control variable in which the initial relationship persists.

The control variable has a large impact in both the interpretation and explanation patterns. In both, the bivariate table shows a relationship that disappears in the partials. In other words, the relationship appears to be independence in the partials. The two patterns cannot be distinguished by looking at the tables alone. The difference between them depends on the location of the control variable in the causal order of variables. Theoretically, a control variable can be in one of two places, either between the original independent and dependent variables (i.e., the control variable is intervening), or before the original independent variable.

The *interpretation pattern* describes the situation in which the control variable intervenes between the original independent and dependent variables. For example, you examine a relationship between religious upbringing and abortion

attitude. Political ideology is a control variable. You reason that religious upbringing affects current political ideology and abortion attitude. You theorize that political ideology is logically prior to an attitude about a specific issue, like abortion. Thus, religious upbringing causes political ideology, which in turn has an impact on abortion attitude. The control variable is an intervening variable, which helps you interpret the meaning of the complete relationship.

The *explanation pattern* looks the same as interpretation. The difference is the temporal order of the control variable. In this pattern, a control variable comes before the independent variable in the initial bivariate relationship. For example, the original relationship is between religious upbringing and abortion attitude, but now gender is the control variable. Gender comes before religious upbringing because one's sex is fixed at birth. The explanation pattern changes how a researcher explains the results. It implies that the initial bivariate relationship is spurious (see the discussion of spuriousness in Chapter 6).

The *suppressor variable pattern* occurs when the bivariate tables suggest independence but a relationship appears in one or both of the partials. For example, religious upbringing and abortion attitude are independent in a bivariate table. Once the control variable "region of the country" is introduced, religious upbringing is associated with abortion attitude in the partial tables. The control variable is a suppressor variable because it suppressed the true relationship. The true relationship appears in the partials.

Multiple Regression Analysis

Multiple regression is a statistical technique whose calculation is beyond the level in this book. Although it is quickly computed by the appropriate statistics software, a background in statistics is needed to prevent making errors in its calculation and interpretation. It requires interval- or ratio-level data. It is discussed here for two reasons. First, it controls for many alternative explanations and variables simultaneously (it is rarely possible to use more than one control variable at a time

Box 12.6 _____

Summary of the Elaboration Paradigm

PATTERN NAME	PATTERN SEEN WHEN COMPARING PARTIALS TO THE ORIGINAL BIVARIATE TABLE
Replication	Same relationship in both partials as in bivariate table.
Specification	Bivariate relationship is only seen in one of the partial tables.
Interpretation	Bivariate relationship weakens greatly or disappears in the partial tables (control variable is intervening).
Explanation	Bivariate relationship weakens greatly or disappears in the partial tables (control variable is before independent variable).
Suppressor variable	No bivariate relationship, relationship appears in partial tables only.

EXAMPLES OF ELABORATION PATTERNS

Replication

	Bivariate Table					**Partials**		
					Control = Low		*Control = High*	
	Low	*High*			*Low*	*High*	*Low*	*High*
Low	85%	15%		Low	84%	16%	86%	14%
High	15%	85%		High	16%	84%	14%	86%

Interpretation or Explanation

	Bivariate Table					**Partials**		
					Control = Low		*Control = High*	
	Low	*High*			*Low*	*High*	*Low*	*High*
Low	85%	15%		Low	45%	55%	55%	45%
High	15%	85%		High	55%	45%	45%	55%

Specification

	Bivariate Table					**Partials**		
					Control = Low		*Control = High*	
	Low	*High*			*Low*	*High*	*Low*	*High*
Low	85%	85%		Low	95%	5%	50%	50%
High	15%	15%		High	5%	95%	50%	50%

Suppressor Variable

	Bivariate Table					**Partials**		
					Control = Low		*Control = High*	
	Low	*High*			*Low*	*High*	*Low*	*High*
Low	54%	46%		Low	84%	16%	14%	86%
High	46%	54%		High	16%	84%	86%	14%

using percentaged tables). Second, it is widely used in sociology, and you are likely to encounter it when reading research reports or articles.

Multiple regression results tell the reader two things. First, the results have a measure called R-squared (R^2), which tells how well a set of variables explains a dependent variable. *Explain* means reduced errors when predicting the dependent variable scores on the basis of information about the independent variables (see PRE measures above). A good model with several independent variables might account for, or explain, a large percentage of variation in a dependent variable. For example, an R^2 of .50 means that knowing the independent and control variables improves the accuracy of predicting the dependent variable by 50 percent, or half as many errors are made as would be made without knowing about the variables.

Second, the regression results measure the direction and size of the effect of each variable on a dependent variable. The effect is measured precisely and given a numerical value. For example, a researcher can see how five independent or control variables simultaneously affect a dependent variable, with all variables controlling for the effects of one another. This is especially valuable for testing theories that state that multiple independent variables cause one dependent variable (see Chapter 3 for examples of causal diagrams).

The effect on the dependent variable is measured by a standardized regression coefficient or the Greek letter beta (β). It is similar to a correlation coefficient. In fact, the beta coefficient for two variables equals the r correlation coefficient.

Researchers use the beta regression coefficient to determine whether control variables have an effect. For example, the bivariate correlation between X and Y is .75. Next, the researcher statistically considers four control variables. If the beta remains at .75, then the four control variables have no effect. However, if the beta for X and Y gets smaller (e.g., drops to .20), it indicates that the control variables have an effect.

Consider an example of regression analysis with age, income, education, and region as independent variables. The dependent variable is a score on a political ideology index. The multiple regression results show that income and religious attendance have large effects, education and region minor effects, and age no effect. All the independent variables together have a 38 percent accuracy in predicting a person's political ideology (see Box 12.7).[5] The example suggests that high income, frequent religious attendance, and a southern residence are positively associated with

---

Box 12.7 _____

Example of Multiple Regression Results

DEPENDENT VARIABLE IS POLITICAL IDEOLOGY INDEX
(HIGH SCORE MEANS VERY LIBERAL)

Independent Variable	*Standardized Regression Coefficients*
Region = South	−.19
Age	.01
Income	−.44
Years of education	.23
Religious attendance	−.39
$R^2 = .38$	

conservative opinions, whereas having more education is associated with liberal opinions. The impact of income is more than twice the size of the impact of living in a southern region.

INFERENTIAL STATISTICS

The Purpose of Inferential Statistics

The statistics discussed so far in this chapter are descriptive statistics. But researchers often want to do more than describe; they want to test hypotheses, know whether sample results hold true in a population, and decide whether differences in results (e.g., between the mean scores of two groups) are big enough to indicate that a relationship really exists. Inferential statistics use probability theory to test hypotheses formally, permit inferences from a sample to a population, and test whether descriptive results are likely to be due to random factors or to a real relationship.

This section explains the basic ideas of inferential statistics but does not deal with inferential statistics in any detail. This area is more complex than descriptive statistics and requires a background in statistics.

Inferential statistics rely on principles from probability sampling, where a researcher uses a random process (e.g., a random number table) to select cases from the entire population. Inferential statistics are a precise way to talk about how confident a researcher can be when inferring from the results in a sample to the population.

You have already encountered inferential statistics if you have read or heard about "statistical significance" or results "significant at the .05 level." Researchers use them to conduct various statistical tests (e.g., a *t*-test or an *F*-test). Statistical significance is also used in formal hypothesis testing, which is a precise way to decide whether to accept or to reject a null hypothesis.[6]

Statistical Significance

Statistical significance means that results are not likely to be due to chance factors. It indicates the probability of finding a relationship in the sample when there is none in the population. Because probability samples involve a random process, it is always possible that sample results will differ from a population parameter. A researcher wants to estimate the odds that sample results are due to a true population parameter or to chance factors of random sampling. Statistical significance uses probability theory and specific statistical tests to tell a researcher whether the results (e.g., an association, a difference between two means, a regression coefficient) are produced by random error in random sampling.

Statistical significance only tells what is likely. It cannot prove anything with absolute certainty. It states that particular outcomes are more or less probable. Statistical significance is *not* the same as practical, substantive, or theoretical significance. Results can be statistically significant but theoretically meaningless or trivial. For example, two variables can have a statistically significant association due to coincidence, with no logical connection between them (e.g., length of fingernails and ability to speak French).

Levels of Significance

Researchers usually express statistical significance in terms of levels (e.g., a test is statistically significant at a specific level) rather than giving the specific probability. The *level of statistical significance* (usually .05, .01, or .001) is a way of talking about the likelihood that results are due to chance factors—that is, that a relationship appears in the sample when there is none in the population. If a researcher says that results are significant at the .05 level, this means the following:

— Results like these are due to chance factors only 5 in 100 times.

— There is a 95 percent chance that the sample results are not due to chance factors alone, but reflect the population accurately.

— The odds of such results based on chance alone are .05, or 5 percent.

— One can be 95 percent confident that the results are due to a real relationship in the population, not chance factors.

These all say the same thing in different ways. This may sound like the discussion of sampling distributions and the central limit theorem in the chapter on sampling. It is not an accident. Both are based on probability theory, which researchers use to link sample data to a population. Probability theory lets us predict what happens in the long run over many events when a random process is used. In other words, it allows precise prediction over many situations in the long run, but not for a specific situation. Since we have one sample and we want to infer to the population, probability theory helps us estimate the odds that our particular sample represents the population. We cannot know for certain unless we have the whole population, but probability theory lets us state our confidence— how likely it is that the sample shows one thing while something else is true in the population. For example, a sample shows that college men and women differ in how many hours they study. Is the result due to an unusual sample, and there is really no difference in the population, or does it reflect a true difference between the sexes in the population? (See Box 12.8 on Chi-Square.)

Type I and Type II Errors

If the logic of statistical significance is based on stating whether or not chance factors produce results, why use the .05 level? It means a 5 percent chance that randomness could cause the results. Why not use a more certain standard—for example, a 1 in 1,000 probability of random chance? This gives a smaller chance that randomness versus a true relationship caused the results.

There are two answers to this way of thinking. The simple answer is that the scientific community has informally agreed to use .05 as a rule of thumb for most purposes. Being 95 percent confident of results is the accepted standard for explaining the social world.

A second, more complex answer involves a trade-off between making Type I and Type II errors. A researcher can make two kinds of logical errors. A *Type I error* occurs when the researcher says that a relationship exists when in fact none exists. It means falsely rejecting a null hypothesis.

A *Type II error* occurs when a researcher says that a relationship does not exist, when in fact it does. It means falsely accepting a null hypothesis (see Table 12.9). Of course, researchers want to avoid both errors. They want to say that there is a relationship in the data only when it does exist and that there is no relationship only when there really is none, but they face a dilemma: As the odds of making one type of error decline, the odds of making the opposite error increase.

The idea of Type I and Type II errors may seem difficult at first, but the same logical dilemma appears outside research settings. For example, a jury can err by deciding that an accused person is guilty when in fact he or she is innocent. Or the jury can err by deciding that a person is innocent when in fact he or she is guilty. The jury does not want to make either error. It does not want to jail the innocent or to free the guilty, but the jury must make a judgment using limited information. Likewise, a pharmaceutical company has to decide whether to sell a new drug. The company can err by stating that the drug has no side effects when, in fact, it has the side effect of causing blindness. Or it can err by holding back a drug because of fear of serious side effects when in fact there are none. The company does not want to make either error. If it makes the first error, the company will face lawsuits and injure people. The second error will prevent the company from selling a drug that may cure illness and produce profits.

Let us put the ideas of statistical significance and the two types of error together. An overly cautious researcher sets a high level of significance and is likely to make one kind of error. For example, the researcher might use the .0001 level. He or she attributes the results to chance unless they are so rare that they would occur by chance only 1 in 10,000 times. Such a high standard means that the researcher is most likely to err by saying results are due to chance when in fact they are not. He or she may falsely accept the null hypothesis when there is a causal relationship (a Type II error). By contrast, a risk-taking researcher sets a low level of significance, such as .10. His or her results indicate a relationship would occur by chance 1 in 10 times.

Box 12.8

Chi-Square

The Chi-square (χ^2) is used in two ways. This creates confusion. As a *descriptive statistic*, it tells us the strength of the association between two variables; as an *inferential statistic*, it tells us the probability that any association we find is likely to be due to chance factors. The Chi-square is a widely used and powerful way to look at variables measured at the ordinal level. It is a more precise way to tell whether there is an association in a bivariate percentaged table than by just "eye balling" it.

Logically, we first figure out "expected values" in a table. We do this based on information from the marginals alone. Recall that marginals are frequency distributions of each variable alone. An expected value can be thought of as our "best guess" without looking at the body of the table. Next, we look at the data to see how much differs from the "expected value." If it differs by a lot, then there may be an association between the variables. If the data in a table are identical or very close to the expected values, then the variables are not associated; they are independent. In other words, *independence* means "what is going on" in a table is what we would expect based on the marginals alone. Chi-square is zero if there is independence and gets bigger as the association gets stronger. If the data in the table greatly differ from the expected values, then we know something is "going on" beyond what we would expect from the marginals alone (i.e. an association between the variables). See the example of an association between height and grade.

Raw or Observed Data Table

STUDENT HEIGHT	GRADE IN RESEARCH METHODS			TOTAL
	C	B	A	
Tall	30	10	10	50
Medium	10	30	10	50
Short	30	20	50	100
Total	70	60	70	200

Expected Values Table

Expected value = (Column total × Row total)/Grand total. EXAMPLE (70 × 50)/200 = 17.5

STUDENT HEIGHT	GRADE IN RESEARCH METHODS			TOTAL
	C	B	A	
Tall	17.5	15	17.5	50
Medium	17.5	15	17.5	50
Short	35	30	35	100
Total	70	60	70	200

Difference Table

Difference = (Observed – Expected). EXAMPLE (30 – 17.5) = 12.5

STUDENT HEIGHT	GRADE IN RESEARCH METHODS			TOTAL
	C	B	A	
Tall	12.5	–5	–7.5	0
Medium	–7.5	15	–7.5	0
Short	–5	–10	15	0
Total	0	0	0	0

Chi-Square = Sum of each difference squared, then divided by the expected value of the cell. Example: 12.5 squared = 156.25, divided by 17.5 = 8.93.

Box 12.8   (continued) _____

Chi-Square = 1st row (8.93 + 1.67 + 3.21) +
                   2nd row (3.21 + 15 + 3.21) +
                   3rd row (.71 + 3.33 + 6.43) = 45.7

Since Chi-squared is not zero, the data are not independent; there is an association. The Chi-square coefficient cannot tell us the direction (e.g., negative) of the association. For inferential statistics, we need to use a Chi-square table or computer program to evaluate the association (i.e., to see how likely such a large a Chi-square is to occur by chance alone). Without going into all the details about the Chi-Square table, this association is rare; it occurs by chance less than 1 in 1,000 times. For a table with nine cells, a Chi-square of 45.7 is significant at the .001 level.

He or she is likely to err by saying that a causal relationship exists, when in fact random factors (e.g., random sampling error) actually cause the results. The researcher is likely to falsely reject the null hypothesis (Type I error). In sum, the .05 level is a compromise between Type I and Type II errors.

This section outlines the basics of inferential statistics. The statistical techniques are precise and rely on the relationship between sampling error, sample size, and central limit theorem. The power of inferential statistics is their ability to let a researcher state, with specific degrees of certainty, that specific sample results are likely to be true in a population. For example, a researcher conducts statistical tests and finds that a relationship is statistically significant at the .05 level. He or she can state that the sample results are probably not due to chance factors. Indeed, there is a 95 percent chance that a true relationship exists in the social world.

Tests for inferential statistics are useful but limited. The data must come from a random sample, and tests only take into account sampling errors. Nonsampling errors (e.g., a poor sampling frame or a poorly designed measure) are not considered. Do not be fooled into thinking that such tests offer easy, final answers.

CONCLUSION

You learned about organizing quantitative data to prepare them for analysis, and analyzing them (organizing data into charts or tables, or summarizing them with statistical measures). Researchers use statistical analysis to test hypotheses and answer research questions. You saw how data must first be coded and then analyzed using univariate or bivariate statistics. Bivariate relationships might be spurious, so control variables and multivariate analysis are often necessary. You also learned some basics about inferential statistics.

TABLE 12.9   Type I and Type II Errors

	TRUE SITUATION IN THE WORLD	
WHAT THE RESEARCHER SAYS	*No Relationship*	*Causal Relationship*
No relationship	No error	Type II error
Causal relationship	Type I error	No error

Beginning researchers sometimes feel they have done something wrong if their results do not support a hypothesis. *There is nothing wrong with rejecting a hypothesis.* The goal of scientific research is to produce knowledge that truly reflects the social world, not to defend pet ideas or hypotheses. Hypotheses are theoretical guesses based on limited knowledge; they need to be tested. Excellent-quality research can find that a hypothesis is wrong, and poor-quality research can support a hypothesis. Good research depends on high-quality methodology, not on supporting a specific hypothesis.

Good research means guarding against possible errors or obstacles to true inferences from data to the social world. Errors can enter into the research process and affect results at many places: research design, measurement, data collection, coding, calculating statistics and constructing tables, or interpreting results. Even if a researcher can design, measure, collect, code, and calculate without error, another step in the research process remains. It is to interpret the tables, charts, and statistics, and to answer the question: What does it all mean? The only way to assign meaning to facts, charts, tables, or statistics is to use theory.

Data, tables, or computer output cannot answer research questions. The facts do not speak for themselves. As a researcher, you must return to your theory (i.e., concepts, relationships among concepts, assumptions, theoretical definitions) and give the results meaning. Do not lock yourself into the ideas with which you began. There is room for creativity, and new ideas are generated by trying to figure out what results really say. It is important to be careful in designing and conducting research so that you can look at the results as a reflection of something in the social world and not worry about whether they are due to an error or an artifact of the research process itself.

Before we leave quantitative research, there is one last issue. Journalists, politicians, and others increasingly use statistical results to make a point or bolster an argument. This has not produced greater accuracy and information in public debate. More often, it has increased confusion and made it more important to know what statistics can and cannot do. The cliché that you can prove anything with statistics is false; however, people can and do *misuse* statistics. Through ignorance or conscious deceit, some people use statistics to manipulate others. The way to protect yourself from being misled by statistics is not to ignore them or hide from the numbers. Rather, it is to understand the research process and statistics, think about what you hear, and ask questions.

We turn next to qualitative research. The logic and purpose of qualitative research differ from those of the quantitative, positivist approach of the past chapters. It is less concerned with numbers, hypotheses, and causality and more concerned with words, norms and values, and meaning.

KEY TERMS _____

bar chart	covariation	interpretation pattern
bivariate statistics	cross-tabulation	level of statistical significance
body of a table	curvilinear relationship	linear relationship
cell of a table	data records	marginals
code sheets	descriptive statistics	mean
codebook	direct entry method	median
coding	elaboration paradigm	mode
coding procedure	explanation pattern	net effect
compound frequency	field	optical scan sheet
distribution	frequency distribution	partials
computer programs	frequency polygon	percentile
contingency cleaning	histogram	pie chart
control variable	independence	possible code cleaning

proportionate reduction in
   error (PRE)
range
replication pattern
scattergram

skewed distribution
specification pattern
standard deviation
statistical relationship
statistical significance

suppressor variable pattern
Type I error
Type II error
univariate statistics
z-score

REVIEW QUESTIONS

1. What is a codebook and how is it used in research?
2. How do researchers clean data and check their coding?
3. Describe how researchers used the IBM card in data analysis.
4. In what ways can a researcher display frequency distribution information?
5. Describe the differences between mean, median, and mode.
6. What three features of a relationship can be seen from a scattergram?
7. What is a compound frequency distribution and how is it used?
8. When can a researcher generalize from a scattergram to a percentaged table to find a relationship among variables?
9. Discuss the concept of control as it is used in trivariate analysis.
10. What does it mean to say "statistically significant at the .001 level," and what type of error is more likely: Type I or Type II?

NOTES

1. Some of the best practical advice on coding and handling quantitative data come from survey research. See discussions in Babbie (1995:366–372), Backstrom and Hursh-Cesar (1981:309–400), Fowler (1984:127–133), Sonquist and Dunkelberg (1977:210–215), and Warwick and Lininger (1975:234–291).

2. For discussions of many different ways to display quantitative data, see Fox (1992), Henry (1995), Tufte (1983, 1991), and Zeisel (1985:14–33).

3. There are other statistics to measure a special kind of mean for ordinal data and for other special situations, which are beyond the level of discussion in this book.

4. For a discussion of the elaboration paradigm and its history, see Babbie (1995:400–409) and Rosenberg (1968).

5. Beginning students and people outside the social sciences are sometimes surprised at the low (10 to 50 percent) predictive accuracy in multiple regression

results. There are three responses to this. First, a 10 to 50 percent reduction in errors is really not bad compared to purely random guessing. Second, positivist social science is still developing. Although the levels of accuracy may not be as high as those of the physical sciences, they are much higher than for any explanation of the social world possible 10 or 20 years ago. Finally, the theoretically important issue in most multiple regression models is less than the accuracy of overall prediction than the effects of specific variables. Most hypotheses involve the effects of specific independent variables on dependent variables.

6. In formal hypothesis testing, researchers test the *null hypothesis*. They usually want to reject the null because rejection of the null indirectly supports the alternative hypothesis to the null, the one they deduced from theory as a tentative explanation. The null hypothesis was discussed in Chapter 6.

RECOMMENDED READINGS

Achen, Christopher H. (1982). *Interpreting and using regression*. Beverly Hills, CA: Sage. Although

multiple regression is a relatively complex statistical technique, this small book contains few formulas or statistical tables. It discusses how to read and understand regression results and what one needs to know to use regression correctly in statistics computer programs.

Andrews, Frank M., et al. (1981). *A guide for selecting statistical techniques for analyzing social science data*. Ann Arbor: Institute for Social Research, University of Michigan. This 70-page pamphlet is full of decision trees to help a reader choose the appropriate statistical technique for data analysis. It is organized by questions about the number of variables, the level of measurement of variables, and what a researcher wants to know about the variable or relationship. Appendixes tell the reader where to find out about the techniques in statistics textbooks and which statistical software programs compute the techniques.

Bohrnstedt, George, and David Knoke. (1994). *Statistics for social data analysis,* 3rd ed. Itasca, IL: Peacock. This is one of my favorites among the dozens of statistics books for social researchers. It covers both descriptive and inferential statistics from the basics to the advanced. It is clearly written and the authors use real data and real theories in the examples. In it you will find discussed most of the statistics that are used in recent articles of the major scholarly journals.

Henry, Gary T. (1995). *Graphing data: Techniques for display and analysis*. Thousand Oaks, CA: Sage. This is an accessible, short introduction to graphing quantitative social science data. Unlike the very sophisticated books on graphing by Edward Tufte (1983, 1991), Henry is for beginners and has many practical tips. For example, Henry notes that certain charts (three-dimensional charts, stacked bar charts) are confusing or misleading.

Jaeger, Richard M. (1983). *Statistics as a spectator sport*. Beverly Hills, CA: Sage. As the title implies, this is a nontraditional introduction to social statistics, which focuses more on understanding than on calculating statistics. It discusses research concepts, measures of central tendency, inferential statistics, and multiple regression analysis.

Zeisel, Hans. (1985). *Say it with figures,* 6th ed. New York: Harper & Row. This standard has been used since 1947. It discusses solutions to important data analysis issues in nontechnical language. It clearly discusses ways to present data analysis in the form of tables and elementary statistics. For example, there are three chapters on using percentages.

CHAPTER 13

QUALITATIVE RESEARCH DESIGN

> *The very business of sociology is assumed to be one of interpretation, not one of discovering objective facts from some Procrustean bed of empirical reality or of adducing lawful generalization about the causal ordering of facts. . . . As a community of scholars our goal must always be to promote discourse about our interpretations, not to advance them simply as authoritative pronouncements. Too often, however, interpretative sociology has served as a masquerade for shoddier research and pious opinions.*
> —Robert Wuthnow, *Meaning and Moral Order*, p. 17

INTRODUCTION

Qualitative and quantitative styles of research differ in several ways, but in other ways they are complementary. The nature of the data itself, and what researchers take to be data is one source of difference. All social researchers systematically collect and analyze empirical evidence to understand and explain social life. When data are in the form of words, sentences, and paragraphs rather than numbers, researchers use different research strategies and data collection techniques. Qualitative researchers rarely use the tools of quantitative research about which you learned in previous chapters, such as variables, reliability, statistics, hypotheses, replication, and scales.

A second reason for differences in the two styles is the orientation of qualitative research. It adopts assumptions about social life, objectives for research, and ways to deal with data that are often at odds with a quantitative approach. Such differences can create confusion among students, researchers, and the readers of research reports. Those who judge qualitative research using quantitative standards are often disappointed. Nevertheless, most people enjoy reading reports of qualitative research. The reports often contain rich description, colorful detail, and unusual characters instead of a formal, neutral tone with statistics. They give the reader a feel for particular people and events in concrete social settings.

Some people falsely think that qualitative research is easier to do than quantitative research. They believe that a qualitative researcher simply wanders into an intriguing area of social life, keeps his or her eyes open, and generates an insightful, fascinating report. Although qualitative researchers do not have to know about statistics and rarely begin with a formal theory, the belief that qualitative research is easy is a myth. Simple dichotomies between better and worse or easier and harder research will not help you understand the differences between qualitative and quantitative research. The triumph of classic qualitative studies is due more to the dedication, hard work, sensitivity, and writing skill of the individual researchers than to anything intrinsic in the research approach itself.

Qualitative research contains several techniques (e.g., grounded theory, ethnography, life history, conversational analysis). Specific techniques are more appropriate for particular topics. Interestingly, female researchers are more likely than male researchers to use qualitative research.[1] This chapter does not give you specific rules of qualitative research, nor does it explore the types of qualitative research. Instead, we will look at elements shared with the qualitative style of research, consider how they differ from quantitative research, and examine characteristics of qualitative research design. Of course, many researchers combine elements from qualitative and quantitative methods in specific research projects.

THE QUALITATIVE ORIENTATION

In this section, you will learn some ways in which a qualitative research orientation differs from that of quantitative research—approaches to data, reliance on nonpositivist perspectives to science, the greater use of *logic in practice*, and the following of a more cyclical research path (also see Table 13.1).

Approaching Data

A qualitative research style involves more than looking at qualitative data. Positivists often try to convert the data into a quantitative form or analyze it using quantitative techniques. For positivists, qualitative data are mental states or conditions that cause measurable behavior. The issue is how to capture it with precise, reliable quantitative measurement. By contrast, qualitative researchers view qualitative data as intrinsically meaningful, not as deficient. For them, the central issues are not how to convert qualitative data into reliable, objective numbers; rather, "they concern such matters as the accessibility of other (sub)cultures, the relativity of actor's accounts of their social worlds, and the relation between sociological descriptions and actors' conceptions of their actions" (Halfpenny, 1979:803). The qualitative research style values qualitative data. Its entire orientation is organized around theorizing, collecting, and analyzing qualitative data. Qualitative researchers may have different concerns about data. For example, they may be concerned more with generating new concepts than with testing existing ones.

Some people believe that qualitative data are "soft," intangiable, and immaterial. Such data are so fuzzy and elusive that researchers cannot really capture them. This is not necessarily the case. Qualitative data are empirical. They involve documenting real events, recording what people say (with words, gestures, and tone), observing specific behaviors, studying written documents, or examining visual images. These are all concrete aspects of the world. For example, some qualitative researchers take and closely scrutinize photos or videotapes of people or social events (Ball and Smith, 1992; Harper, 1994). This evidence is just as "hard" and physical as that used by quantitative

TABLE 13.1   Differences between Qualitative and Quantitative Research

QUANTITATIVE	QUALITATIVE
— Test hypothesis that the researcher begins with.	— Capture and discover meaning once the researcher becomes immersed in the data.
— Concepts are in the form of distinct variables.	— Concepts are in the form of themes, motifs, generalizations, taxonomies.
— Measures are systematically created before data collection and are standardized.	— Measures are created in an ad hoc manner and are often specific to the individual setting or researcher.
— Data are in the form of numbers from precise measurement.	— Data are in the form of words from documents, observations, transcripts.
— Theory is largely causal and is deductive.	— Theory can be causal or noncausal and is often inductive.
— Procedures are standard, and replication is assumed.	— Research procedures are particular, and replication is very rare.
— Analysis proceeds by using statistics, tables, or charts and discussing how what they show relates to hypotheses.	— Analysis proceeds by extracting themes or generalizations from evidence and organizing data to present a coherent, consistent picture.

researchers to measure attitudes, social pressure, intelligence, and the like.

A Nonpositivist Perspective

Qualitative social research relies largely on the interpretive and critical approaches to social science. The two approaches differ from each other in important ways, but both are alternatives to positivism, which is the foundation of quantitative research. Quantitative research is contrary to most of the core assumptions and goals of interpretive social science (see Chapter 4). In contrast to interpretive researchers, critical researchers use quantitative techniques. When they do so, however, critical social researchers diverge from strict positivism. They apply theory in a different way, give the historical context a major role, critique social conditions, and reveal deep structures of social relations.

There is no one-to-one correspondence between research techniques and the approaches to social science. Nevertheless, historical-compara-

tive research is most compatible with a critical approach. Sometimes, it is also used by researchers who adopt the interpretive or the positivist approach. Field research is suited to the assumptions of an interpretive approach, but some critical researchers also use it.

The significance of the three approaches is evident in how a researcher sees data. A quantitative researcher assumes that he or she can conceptualize sociological concepts as variables, and that he or she can develop objective, precise measures with numbers that capture important features of the social world. By contrast, a qualitative researcher focuses on subjective meanings, definitions, metaphors, symbols, and descriptions of specific cases. He or she attempts to capture aspects of the social world (e.g., sights, odors, atmosphere) for which it is difficult to develop precise measures expressed as numbers.

We can see how the three approaches relate to research techniques by considering the contrast between the technocratic and transcendent perspectives to research.[2] The *technocratic per-*

spective fits better with positivism, and, although unknowingly, quantitative researchers more frequently fall into it. In it, the researcher is the expert, and research questions often originate with the sponsors of the research (i.e., those who supply funds). The goal of research is to discover and document lawlike generalizations oriented toward increasing efficiency. Thus, this is the perspective of a technician who serves bureaucratic needs.

By contrast, the *transcendent perspective* more closely fits the interpretive and critical approaches. In it, research questions originate with the standpoint of the people being studied, not that of outsiders. Its goal is to remove false beliefs held by those being studied and to treat people as creative, compassionate living beings, not as objects. It often raises questions about power or inequality and views social relations more as the outcome of willful actions than as laws of human nature. It tries to help people grow, take charge of their lives, and engage in social change—that is, to transcend current social conditions.

A Logic in Practice

According to Kaplan (1964:3–11), statements about how to do social research follow two logics: reconstructed logic and logic in practice. All research mixes both types, although the proportion of each type of logic varies. Statements about quantitative research are likely to be "reconstructed," whereas qualitative research arises more "in practice."

Reconstructed logic means that the logic of how to do research is highly organized and restated in an idealized, formal, and systematic form. It is reconstructed into logically consistent rules and terms. It is a cleansed model of how good research should proceed. This logic appears in textbooks and in published research reports. For example, the rules for conducting a simple random sample are very straightforward and follow a step-by-step procedure.

Logic in practice is the logic of how research is actually carried out. It is relatively messy, with more ambiguity, and is tied to specific cases and oriented toward the practical completion of a task. It has fewer set rules. The logic is based on judgment calls or norms shared among experienced researchers. It depends on an informal folk wisdom passed among researchers when they get together over lunch, coffee, or beer and discuss doing research.

Quantitative research is usually described as using reconstructed logic. This makes it easier to define and learn from books or formal instruction. Quantitative researchers describe the technical research procedures they use (e.g., a systematic random sample of 300 drawn from a telephone directory, Likert scaling). The procedures are shared, explicit methods.

Qualitative research uses more of a logic in practice. It relies on the informal wisdom that has developed from the experiences of researchers. Qualitative research reports may not discuss method (common for historical-comparative research) or may have a personal autobiographical account tailored to a particular study (common for field research). Few procedures or terms are standardized and there is a debate among qualitative researchers about whether they ever should be. Many qualitative researchers learned how to do research by reading many reports, by trial and error, and by working in an apprentice role with an experienced researcher. This does not mean that qualitative research is less valid, but it may be more difficult for someone learning about it for the first time to grasp.

A Nonlinear Path

Researchers follow a path when conducting research. The path is a metaphor for the sequence of things to do: what is finished first or where a researcher has been, and what comes next or where he or she is going. The path may be one that is well worn and marked with signposts where many other researchers have trod. Alternatively, it may be a new path into unknown territory where few others have gone, and without signs marking the direction forward.

In general, quantitative researchers follow a more linear path than do qualitative researchers.

A *linear research path* follows a fixed sequence of steps. It is like a staircase leading in one clear direction. It is a way of thinking and a way of looking at issues—the direct, narrow, straight path that is most common in western European and North American culture.

Qualitative research is more nonlinear and cyclical. Rather than moving in a straight line, a *cyclical research path* makes successive passes through steps, sometimes moving backward and sideways before moving on. It is more of a spiral, moving slowly upward but not directly. With each cycle or repetition, a researcher collects new data and gains new insights.

People who are used to the direct, linear approach may be impatient with a less direct cyclical path. From a strict linear perspective, a cyclical path looks inefficient and sloppy. But the diffuse cyclical approach is not merely disorganized, undefined chaos. It can be highly effective for creating a feeling for the whole, for grasping subtle shades of meaning, for pulling together divergent information, and for switching perspectives. It is not an excuse for doing poor-quality research, and it has its own discipline and rigor. It borrows devices from the humanities (e.g., metaphor, analogy, theme, motif, irony) and is oriented toward constructing meaning. A cyclical path is suited for tasks such as translating languages, where delicate shades of meaning, subtle connotations, or contextual distinctions can be important.

CHARACTERISTICS OF QUALITATIVE RESEARCH

In this section, we look at six characteristics of a qualitative style of research: importance of the context, the case study method, the researcher's integrity, grounded theory, process, and interpretations.

The Context Is Critical

Qualitative researchers emphasize the importance of social context for understanding the social world. They hold that the meaning of a social action or statement depends, in an important way,

on the context in which it appears. When a researcher removes an event, social action, answer to a question, or conversation from the social context in which it appears, or ignores the context, social meaning and significance are distorted.

Attention to social context means that a qualitative researcher notes what came before or what surrounds the focus of study. It also implies that the same events or behaviors can have different meanings in different cultures or historical eras. For example, instead of ignoring the context and counting votes across time or cultures, a qualitative researcher asks: What does voting mean in the context? He or she may treat the same behavior (e.g., voting for a presidential candidate) differently depending on the social context in which it occurs (see Box 13.1). Qualitative researchers place parts of social life into a larger whole. Otherwise, the meaning of the part may be lost. For example, it is hard to understand what a baseball glove is without knowing something about the game of baseball. The whole of the game—innings, bats, curve balls, hits—gives meaning to each part, and each part without the whole has little meaning.

The Value of the Case Study

A quantitative researcher usually gathers specific information on a great many cases (e.g., respondents, subjects). By contrast, a qualitative researcher may use a case study approach. He or she might gather a large amount of information on one or a few cases, go into greater depth, and get more details on the cases being examined. He or she gathers a range of information about a few selected cases.

The case study researcher also goes about data analysis differently. Whereas a quantitative researcher looks for patterns in the variables on many cases, a case study researcher faces an overwhelming amount of data but has been immersed in it. Immersion gives the researcher an intimate familiarity with people's lives and culture. He or she looks for patterns in the lives, actions, and words of people in the context of the complete case as a whole.

Box 13.1 _____

Example of the Importance of Context for Meaning

"Voting in a national election" has different meanings in different contexts.

1. A one-party dictatorship with unopposed candidates, where people are required by law to vote. The names of nonvoters are recorded by the police. Nonvoters are suspected of being antigovernment subversives. They face fines and possible job loss for not voting.
2. A country in the midst of violent conflict between rebels and those in power. Voting is dangerous because the armed soldiers on either side may shoot voters they suspect of opposing their side. The outcome of the vote will give power to one or the other group and dramatically restructure the society. Anyone over the age of 16 can vote.
3. A context where people choose between a dozen political parties of roughly equal power that represent very different values and policies. Each party has a sizable organization, with its own newspapers, social clubs, and neighborhood organizers. Election days are national holidays, when no one has to work. A person votes by showing up with an identification card at any of many local voting locations. Voting itself is by secret ballot, and everyone over age 18 can vote.
4. A context in which voting is conducted in public by white males over age 21 who have regular jobs. Family, friends, and neighbors see how one another vote. Political parties do not offer distinct policies; instead, they are tied to ethnic or reli-

gious groups and are part of a person's ethnic-religious identity. Ethnic and religious group identities are very strong. They affect where one lives, where one works, whom one marries, and the like. Voting follows massive parades and weeklong community events organized by ethnic and religious groups.

5. A context in which one political party is very powerful and is challenged by one or two very small, weak alternatives. The one party has held power for the past 60 years through corruption, bribery, and intimidation. It has the support of leaders throughout society (in religious organizations, educational institutions, business, unions, and the mass media). The jobs of anyone working in any government job (e.g., every police officer, post office clerk, school teacher, garbage collector, etc.) depend on the political party staying in power.
6. A context in which the choice is between two parties and there is little difference between them. People select candidates primarily on the basis of television advertising. Candidates pay for advertising with donations by wealthy people or powerful organizations. Voting is a vague civic obligation that few people take seriously. Elections are held on a workday. In order to vote, a person must meet many requirements and register to vote several weeks in advance. Recent immigrants and anyone arrested for a crime cannot vote.

For example, a quantitative researcher surveys 1,000 married couples. He or she discovers that women perform the household chore of washing dishes in 70 percent of cases in which the woman works outside the home, and in 90 percent when the woman is a full-time homemaker. A qualitative researcher conducts a case study. He or she observes all chores and daily activities of 10 married couples for six months. The qualitative researcher discovers that if the woman works outside the home, interpersonal tension over doing chores is greater, and the male is likely to

assist in small household chores but does not take full responsibility for traditional female tasks.

Researcher Integrity

A **Question of Trust.** Researchers who adopt a positivist, quantitative approach ask: How can qualitative research be objective or unbiased? There are many opportunities for a researcher's personal influence to affect qualitative research. A field researcher hangs around and observes a social group for an extended period. He or she gets to know the people being studied, and his or her presence in the setting can affect what occurs. A field researcher sees, hears, remembers, and records only some of what occurs, and puts only some of what is in his or her field notes into a final report. Likewise, a historical-comparative researcher sorts through and reads many sources. The evidence about the past is incomplete, and he or she selects some available material for emphasis. Replication is rare in qualitative research, and researchers usually work alone.

Researcher integrity is a real issue. In fact, Collins (1984:339) argued that an important reason for an increased reliance on quantitative methods, replication, and statistics in social research is a lack of trust: "We set stringent statistical criteria not because logically they are crucial for establishing the truth of a theory but *because our intellectual community is socially distrustful of the honesty of investigators*" (emphasis added).

All research involves placing some degree of trust in the researcher. Opportunities for the dishonest and unethical researcher exist in all research. Nevertheless, the degree of trust and the kinds of checks on researchers differ between quantitative and qualitative research. Readers of qualitative research usually place more trust in the researcher's integrity and interpretations. A quantitative researcher substitutes explicit descriptions of standard techniques and statistics for trust.

Checks. Qualitative researchers ensure that their research accurately reflects the evidence and have checks on their evidence.[3] For example, the field researcher listens to and records a student who says, "Professor Smith threw an eraser at Professor Jones." The field researcher treats this evidence carefully. To strengthen the claim, the researcher considers what other people say, looks for confirming evidence, and checks for internal consistency. The researcher asks whether the student has firsthand knowledge of the event and whether the student's feelings or self-interest would lead him to lie (e.g., the student might dislike Professor Smith for other reasons). Even if the student made a false statement, it is evidence

about the student's perspective. Similarly, the researcher examining historical evidence uses techniques for verifying the authenticity of sources (see Chapter 16).

Another check is the great volume of detailed written notes that qualitative researchers record. Researchers vary the amount of detail they record, but they may have hundreds or thousands of pages of notes. Besides a detailed verbatim description of the evidence, notes include references to the sources, commentaries by the researcher, and key terms to help organize the notes. They also include quotes, maps, diagrams, paraphrasing, and counts.

There are other ways to cross-check research. Although qualitative researchers usually work alone, others know about the evidence. For example, a field researcher studies people who are alive and in a specific setting. The subjects being observed can read the details of a study. Likewise, historical documents are cited and other researchers can check references and sources.

The most important way that a qualitative researcher creates trust in readers is the way he or she presents evidence. A qualitative researcher does not present all of his or her detailed notes in a report; rather, he or she spins a web of interlocking details, providing sufficient texture and detail so that the readers feel that they are there. A qualitative researcher's firsthand knowledge of events, people, and situations cuts two ways. It raises questions of bias, but it also provides a sense of immediacy, direct contact, and intimate knowledge.

Different Kinds of Bias. The debate over researcher integrity involves opposing assumptions about the proper role of a researcher. A positivist, quantitative approach says that the influence of an individual researcher is a bias. It contaminates objective facts and should be eliminated.

Qualitative researchers assume it is impossible to eliminate the effect of the researcher completely. Although a reliance on mechanical techniques and fixed standards may appear to eliminate the human factor, it introduces its own form of bias: the bias of mechanical techniques. Smith (1988:5) warned, "Without firsthand information about the research setting, it is difficult for quantitative researchers to develop adequate conceptual frameworks for their studies."

Recognizing the human factor does not mean that a qualitative researcher arbitrarily interjects personal opinions or selects evidence to support personal prejudices. Instead, a researcher's presence is always an explicit issue. A qualitative researcher takes advantage of personal insight, feelings, and perspective as a human being to understand the social life under study, but is aware of his or her values or assumptions. He or she takes measures to guard against the influence of prior beliefs or assumptions when doing research. Rather than hiding behind "objective" techniques, the qualitative researcher is forthright and makes his or her values explicit in a report. Qualitative researchers tell readers how they gathered data and how they see the evidence.

Grounded Theory

A quantitative researcher gathers data after he or she theorizes, develops hypotheses, and creates measures of variables. By contrast, a qualitative researcher begins with a research question and little else. Theory develops during the data collection process. This more inductive method means that theory is built from data or grounded in the data. Moreover, conceptualization and operationalization occur simultaneously with data collection and preliminary data analysis. Many researchers use *grounded theory*. It makes qualitative research flexible and lets data and theory interact (see Box 13.2). Qualitative researchers remain open to the unexpected, are willing to change the direction or focus of a research project, and may abandon their original research question in the middle of a project.

A qualitative researcher builds theory by making comparisons. For example, when a researcher observes an event (e.g., a police officer confronting a speeding motorist), he or she immediately ponders questions and looks for similarities and differences. When watching a police

Box 13.2 _____

What Is Grounded Theory?

Grounded theory is a widely used approach in qualitative research. It is not the only approach and it is not used by all qualitative researchers. Grounded theory is "a qualitative research method that uses a systematic set of procedures to develop an inductively derived theory about a phenomenon" (Strauss and Corbin, 1990, p. 24). The purpose of grounded theory is to build a theory that is faithful to the evidence. It is a method for discovering new theory. In it the researcher compares unlike phenomena with a view towards learning similarities. He or she sees micro-level events as the foundation for a more macro-level explanation. Grounded theory shares several goals with more positivist-oriented theory. It seeks theory that is comparable with the evidence, that is precise and rigorous, that is capable of replication and that is generalizable. A grounded theory approach pursues generalizations by making comparisons across social situations.

Qualitative researchers use alternatives to grounded theory. Some qualitative researchers offer an in-depth depiction that is true to an informant's worldview. They excavate a single social situation to elucidate the micro processes that sustain stable social interaction. The goal of other researchers is to provide a very exacting depiction of events or a setting. They analyze specific events or settings in order to gain insight into the larger dynamics of a society. Still other researchers apply an existing theory to analyze specific settings that they have placed in a macro-level historical context. They show connections among micro-level events and between micro-level situations and larger social forces for the purpose of reconstructing the theory and informing social action (see Burawoy 1991:271–287 and Hammersley 1992 for a summary of several alternatives).

_____

officer stop a speeder, a qualitative researcher asks: Does the police officer always radio in the car's license number before proceeding? After radioing the car's location, does the officer ask the motorist to get out of the car sometimes, but in others casually walk up to the car and talk to the seated driver? When data collection and theorizing are interspersed, theoretical questions arise that suggest future observations, so new data are tailored to answer theoretical questions that came from thinking about previous data.

Process and Sequence

The passage of time is an integral part of qualitative research. Qualitative researchers look at the sequence of events and pay attention to what happens first, second, third, and so on. Because qualitative researchers examine the same case or set of cases over time, they can see an issue evolve, a conflict emerge, or a social relationship develop. The researcher can detect process and causal relations.

In historical research, the passage of time may involve years or decades. In field research, the passage of time is shorter. Nevertheless, in both types of research, a researcher notes what is occurring at different points in time and recognizes that *when* something occurs is often important.

Interpretation

The word *interpretation* means the assignment of significance or coherent meaning. Reports of quantitative research usually include tables and charts with numbers. Quantitative research is expressed in numbers (e.g., percentages or statistical coefficients), and a researcher gives meaning to the numbers and tells how they relate to hypotheses.

In qualitative research, interpretation is different. Qualitative research reports rarely include tables with numbers. The only visual presentations of data may be maps, photographs, or diagrams showing how ideas are related. A researcher weaves the data into discussions of their significance. The data are in the form of words, including quotes or descriptions of particular events. Any numerical information is supplementary to the textual evidence.

A qualitative researcher interprets data by giving them meaning, translating them, or making

them understandable. However, the meaning he or she gives begins with the point of view of the people being studied. He or she interprets data by finding out how the people being studied see the world, how they define the situation, or what it means for them. As Geertz (1979:228) remarked, "The trick is to figure out what the devil they think they are up to."

Thus, the first step in qualitative interpretation, whether a researcher is examining historical documents or the text of spoken words or human behavior, is to learn about its meaning for the people being studied.[4] The people who created the social behavior have personal reasons or motives for their actions. This is first-order interpretation. A researcher's discovery and reconstruction of this *first-order interpretation* is a *second-order interpretation*, because the researcher comes in from the outside to discover what occurred. In a second-order interpretation, the researcher elicits an underlying coherence or sense of meaning in the data. Because meaning develops within a set of other meanings, not in a vacuum, a second-order interpretation places the human action being studied in the "stream of behavior" or events to which it is related—its context.

A researcher who adopts a strict interpretive approach may stop at a second-order interpretation—that is, once he or she understands the significance of the action for the people being studied. Many qualitative researchers go further to generalize or link the second-order interpretation to general theory. They move to a broader level of interpretation, or *third-order interpretation*, where a researcher assigns general theoretical significance.

COMPLEMENTARY EVIDENCE

Most social researchers adopt either qualitative or quantitative research expertise and are often opponents on issues. However, it is a mistake to take this antagonism too far. Instead of observing a strict either-or dichotomy, many social researchers try to combine quantitative and qualitative research. The logic of qualitative research does not forbid the use of numbers, statistics, and precise quantitative measurement; such quantitative data can be a source of information, which supplements or complements qualitative data. Sprague and Zimmerman (1989:82) remarked,

We do not have to reject quantitative methods to approve of qualitative methods. Posing one against the other is presenting a false choice, especially from the perspective of feminist and other sociologies of knowledge which recognize that each way of doing research is a construction and has its biases.

In Chapter 7, you encountered the concept of triangulation, combining different methodological techniques to overcome weaknesses in specific techniques. The quantitative researcher uses triangulation to get a better fix on the objective truth when testing hypotheses and to reduce method effects.

Qualitative researchers also advocate triangulation, but for different reasons.[5] First, it increases the sophisticated rigor of their data collection and analysis; that is, it makes their methods more public or open to scrutiny. Second, triangulation helps reveal the richness and diversity of social settings. Qualitative researchers do not assume there is a single view of reality, but believe that different methods reveal different perspectives. Finally, data on the same social event collected by different methods, different researchers, or at different times may not converge into one consistent picture. For quantitative researchers, such differences are so-called errors or biases, to be eliminated. Qualitative researchers anticipate such differences and treat them as a valuable source of information about social life. They are themselves an aspect of social life to be analyzed. Lever (1981:200) noted, "Variation in results yielded by different methods, far from being an unwanted source of error or bias, can be an additional source of data." For example, Lever discovered greater sex-role stereotyping in children's play activities using some methods than with others.

Qualitative data give quantitative researchers rich information about the social processes in specific settings. They may also give critical researchers the potential to break through assumptions implicit in quantitative approaches. For example, Marshall (1985) noted that qualitative research methods are less likely to fit into the assumptions of the dominant paradigm of educational administration. In the *dominant paradigm*, educational issues are defined as managerial problems caused by ignorance, lack of motivation by students or their parents, inadequate resources, or lack of motivation by professionals or bureaucrats. Neutral and technical quantitative methods would be used to gather data needed to resolve the problems as they have been defined by the dominant paradigm. But a qualitative researcher asks critical theoretical and political questions (e.g., Who benefits?). He or she places issues in a larger sociohistorical context, observes everyday processes close up, and understands the viewpoints of all involved in schooling, including those who oppose the administrative perspective.

Qualitative research, such as field research, can be combined with quantitative techniques, such as survey research (see Table 13.2). Such a combination helps the critical researcher engage in praxis. Critical researchers say that technically competent, neutral, and unbiased survey research is expensive. Only those with power and money can pay for it. Interviewers ask isolated respondents to respond individually to questions that have been framed from the perspective of others. Researchers then generalize the quantitative results to help elites understand "the people." Rarely are results used to help respondents understand their own situation, to raise consciousness, or to focus people's attention on issues—the goals of critical social science. Consistent with such goals, a critical researcher may combine survey with field research to create a mutual learning experience and help respondents reflect on their own situations.[6]

Short Departure to Look at Elite Studies

Most quantitative studies that are conducted on individuals (e.g., experiments, surveys and existing statistics) and most field research in anthropology, sociology, education, and so on, focus on

TABLE 13.2 What Sample Survey Research and Field Research Can Do for Each Other

FIELD RESEARCH FOR SURVEYS	SURVEYS FOR FIELD RESEARCH
▬ Provides familiarity with an issue so researchers can develop new hypotheses and theories.	▬ Provides a way to select sites that ensures that they are more representative of the population of possible research sites.
▬ Verifies survey findings that are unexpected or unusual.	▬ Corrects for the tendency to see parts of a setting as congruent.
▬ Helps when interpreting statistical results.	▬ Demonstrates that a single observation may be generalizable.
▬ Helps when developing a scale or index.	▬ Verifies field observations and interpretations.
▬ Permits the validation of a scale or index that has been developed.	▬ Casts new light on observations by seeing if they are consistent with survey responses.
▬ Illustrates particular types of individuals or situations revealed in survey data.	▬ Helps overcome the tendency of researchers to use a subset of people in the setting as informants.
▬ Clarifies ambiguous but significant responses by revealing the subjective meanings of respondents.	▬ Reveals systematic themes the researcher may have overlooked when qualitative data are formally coded and systematically examined.
▬ Suggests which of several indicators are most important in the context.	▬ Helps researchers control for alternative explanations by measuring additional variables.

Source: Adapted from Sieber (1973), Agar (1980), and Robert B. Smith (1987, 1988).

the average person or the poor and powerless. Social researchers are aware that they also need to study powerful elites if they are to understand society. Yet, "few social researchers study elites because elites are by their very nature difficult to penetrate. Elites establish barriers that set their members apart from the rest of society" (Hertz and Imber, 1993:3). Researchers have produced some valuable studies of elites and have developed special techniques to study elites. These techniques clarify more general concerns and illustrate how qualitative research designs are valuable and distinct from quantitative research, but also complement it.

Researchers cannot study elites—people in the positions of formal or informal power—with random samples because they are too rare and because they are unlikely to participate. Quantitative researchers have studied elites, including content analyses of elite speeches (Seider, 1974), background studies of elite

careers (Freitag, 1983), studies of elite networks decision making (Knoke, 1993), and panel studies of elite survey data (Murray, 1992). This information, combined with data on the degree of social or economic inequality, provides a partial picture. Qualitative research on elites shows how elites socialize in private clubs, such as G. William Domhoff's (1974) study of Bohemian Grove, or what they discuss informally, such as Susan Ostrander's (1984) study of upper-class women. The upper class, the corporate elites, or the very wealthy belong to a distinct subculture. Some seek publicity, but most avoid it and prefer a private life away from the public intrusion and fortune seekers. It is not easy to identify or locate elites, and studying them is not for the naive researcher.

Here are some differences between interviewing elites and nonelites. First, gaining access to elites is often very difficult and the gatekeepers are formidable. A researcher studying corporate elites may face security guards, secretaries, and others whose official job is to prevent access. Thomas (1993:83) reported, "It took me nearly two years of phone calls, screening meetings with executive assistants, and networking to interview to executives." Also, time pressures are great. Elites are very busy, or give that appearance. Researchers will have to schedule meetings and may have limited time. Techniques to improve access include informal settings (meals, waiting in airports, travel time) and a willingness to adjust to an elite schedule. Issues of access are more common in qualitative than quantitative research.

Second, social contacts and connections are essential for gaining access and establishing trust. A researcher's personal social background or pedigree is an important resource. If the researcher is not from a wealthy family or was not socialized under privileged conditions, he or she may need to cultivate appropriate sponsors with the so-called right connections. He or she will need an ability to display proper form. Elites will use who you know, who talked to you, and who introduced whom as signs of approval or endorsement. The researcher who lacks a good sponsor or prestigious credentials or affiliations will seldom be treated seriously even he or she gains access. Ostrander (1993) and Hunter (1993) have said that elites are very interested with whom the researcher has already talked. In many types of qualitative research, personal contacts and connections are integral to the research process.

Elites are often highly educated and knowledgeable. This has several implications. It means that the researcher is expected to have conducted extensive library and background work prior to direct contact. It also means that the elite member may be aware of social research techniques and read studies. This can increase cooperation or it can have the opposite effect. Elites may try to dominate or manipulate the research situation. Most elites are used to being in charge and having others defer to them. Most are adept at detecting subtle shifts in the flow events and skilled at controlling social situations. This may include where people sit, the direction of a conversation, and so on. Elite members may direct conversation away from what the researcher finds of interest and use up the time, while the researcher must be cautious not to create offense. The reseacher needs to gain sufficient control to accomplish his or her purpose. He or she needs refined social skills and diplomacy, and wants to get the elite member to let down his or her guard without creating tension or distress. The researcher can do this, but only with great delicacy and dexterity. Researchers may use their poise and discretion in a formal survey or when dealing with experimental subjects, but for some qualitative research, such skills are an essential research tool.

A related concern in elite studies is sensitivity to frontstage and backstage performances. Frontstage social settings are public, outward settings and situations in which people know others may be observing and therefore display specific social performances. Backstage social settings are private and intimate settings where people let their guard down and feel comfortable and trusting. When studying elites, frontstage events are often intentional and highly managed to create specific impressions. Thus, a researcher may be ushered into a large plush office, with a beautiful view, original art on the walls, sofas along the wall and a huge, clean desk. A elite member, highly experienced in dealing with others, may smile and give a researcher the official, public relations version of events. This "front" may not correspond to the backstage of private clubs, home, and other informal discussions of elite member. The researcher may not get beyond the official, visible role. In backstage situations and settings, the elite member may reveal his or her true prejudices or feelings and may expose personal values or beliefs. Access to backstage situations is often very difficult. It may require developing a long-term relationship with the elite member. In quantitative studies, researchers rarely penetrate beyond the frontstage, while many qualitative studies are designed to go beyond public, surface relations.

A next set of differences involves gaining trust and handling an elite's settings or interview situations. The researcher needs to master the appropriate language and demeanor. All subcultures share ways of acting and speaking. Such informal customs and folkways contain assumptions and understandings of key events or situations. Using the proper phrases and adhering to subtle social rituals will signal that a researcher shares the outlook and assumptions of the elite subculture. The researcher who uses improper phases or who behaves unsuitably may signal that he or she is not to be trusted. For example, elite subcultures are built on an assumption of material security and inclusion. Many elites can bridge the social distance between themselves in others by managing an outward appearance of composure, radiating self-confidence, and expressing social graces and manners. Some researchers find this demeanor intimidating and may feel that they are being subtly "put in their place," but in a warm, friendly, and open manner. Qualitative researchers often find that they need to create trust and reduce interpersonal social distance when gathering data.

A last issue is protecting the integrity of research process. A degree of secrecy, or seclusion for privacy, if not physical protection, is common in elite settings. A researcher must exercise discretion. He or she needs to be sensitive to elite concerns about public exposure or fears of an exposé. Elites may be suspicious and demand a review of a research report, or only reveal things off the record. In addition, they may have the knowledge to detect subtle violations of agreed-upon limits or hire experts to review research reports. In addition, if a researcher violates trust, elites have the resources to bring law suits. At the same time, a researcher wants to learn as much as possible and uphold principles of good, unimpeded research. Qualitative researchers often find that they must stimultaneously balance protecting the confidentiality of subjects and ensuring the honesty of the research process itself.

EXAMPLE STUDIES

Examples of four specific qualitative research studies show how researchers apply the principles of qualitative research in practice, how qualitative researchers do not always follow a strict interpretive approach, and how they combine a qualitative method with quantitative principles.

Examples of Field Research

Siu (1987) is a Chinese American who studied the Chinese laundryman using the "Chicago school" style of participant observation (discussed in Chapter 14). His father was a laundry worker, and Siu himself worked for a laundry supplier before beginning his fieldwork. Speaking the same dialect as the Chinese laundrymen, he was adopted as a "cousin" and worked in another part of the Chinese immigrant economy—a "chop suey" house. He interviewed and spent time socializing with Chinese laundry workers and owners in the Chicago area. During his 20-year study, he developed new concepts: that of the immigrant economy (an isolated economic and social community of immigrants who specialize in a few industries) and that of sojourners (immigrants who travel without intending to stay).

Siu's book contains little analysis, but it includes many long quotes from interviews and excerpts from letters. He describes the daily life in a laundry by recounting personal events, jokes, and stories. He places his study in a context of the history of Chinese immigration to the United States and provides maps showing the spread of Chinese laundry establishments in the Chicago area over a 50-year period. He provides graphs and tables documenting the number of Chinese immigrants, the sex ratio of Chinese people in the United States, and the number of gamblers in Chinese gambling houses in Chicago. His book also contains a map of inside a typical laundry, examples of laundry tickets, personal financial accounts of laundrymen, and monthly expenditure reports of a laundry. The reader gains an in-depth feeling for and insight into the inner lives of Chinese laundrymen.

Dannefer (1981) conducted field research on old-car buffs and blended this research with quantitative principles. He conceptualized interest in old cars as a type of leisure activity called an *expressive* association. Dannefer examined how people became involved in this activity and the ways they became involved. He conducted intensive, two-hour unstructured interviews with 40 active old-car enthusiasts/club members in New Jersey in 1976. In addition, he conducted structured interviews with a systematic random sample of 189 participants at a national gathering of old-car clubs.

Based on open-ended questions, Dannefer developed a typology of four pathways to becoming an old-car buff and then refined them because of the structured interviews. He illustrated each of the four types with quotes from his open-ended interviews and gave the percentage of respondents in each category based on the structured interviews.

To understand old-car buffs, Dannefer used sociologist Peter Berger's theory of *subjectivism.* It says that in modern society, people no longer have a strong traditional religious or cultural world view to structure how they experience the world, especially in the area of leisure. In place of a traditional world view, people internalize, or make subjective, heavily advertised symbols of mass consumer society (beer cans, cars, baseball cards) and create new forms of collective identity around them. These new forms of identity become a basis for social interaction and feelings of belonging to a group.

Examples of Historical-Comparative Study

Light and Bonacich (1988) studied Koreans in the Los Angeles area between 1965 and 1982. Their study traces how changes in the Korean society and economy led to an increase in Korean migration to the United States. For example, the authors show that Koreans in Korea earned between 7.5 and 27 percent of the typical American wage. The authors weave a large set of factors (e.g., role of the Korean government, changes in the Korean economy, and the history of U.S. military intervention in Korea) into a story of Korean migration.

The authors compare Koreans in Korea with those in the United States and compare Koreans with other ethnic groups in the United States. They ask: Why do a high percentage of Koreans become small-business owners in the United States, when few were small business owners in Korea? They explore how small businesses owned by immigrants fit into the larger U.S. economy and how Christianity, Korean ethnic culture, and social class shaped a unique social and economic subculture at a particular juncture of history.

Many types of data were used by the authors: survey research, existing statistics, field research, government documents, international reports, and historical records. Their book contains photographs of Korean business establishments and advertisements, maps showing the spread of Korean-owned business in the Los Angeles area over 20 years, and information on the number of Koreans who migrated. They recount stories of particular people and describe in detail the responses of the Korean community to violent attacks against Asians in the Los Angeles area. The authors present limited generalizations and argue that a combination of specific circumstances (e.g., the political system in Korea, U.S. intervention, economic dislocation, U.S. wealth, cultural traditions) contributed to the formation of a community of Korean small-business owners, which concentrated in the Los Angeles area during the 1960s and 1970s.

Lachmann (1989) examined the question, How did the modern, powerful, centralized nation-state (e.g., government institutions and political authority) develop from the weak, fragmented political institutions of the Middle Ages? He examined France and England during the sixteenth and seventeenth centuries because both had very weak states in 1500, but by 1700 both had created very strong states.

Three theories are outlined by the author of how the state developed in the sixteenth and seventeenth centuries. One says that peasant rebellions forced the nobility to reorganize political power into a powerful state. Another says that a rising capitalist class based on the newly developing market economy gained power. By playing off the new capitalists and the old nobility, leaders in government strengthened the state. Later, the power of the nobility weakened. A third theory says that governments and political authority are self-generating. Elites acquire more power and resources, which they invest in bureaucracies and armies to defend and hold onto their power.

Lachmann contrasted parts of each theory as issues or questions. Each theory suggests different major forces and sequences of events, or answers to the questions. The questions and issues guide his investigation into the evidence. For example, the theories suggest that different groups played a major role in opposing the creation of a stronger state. For evidence, he read dozens of books and articles by historians of British and French history, written in English and French, describing specific details about events in history and major groups involved in conflicts (e.g., civil wars). He placed the events and groups in the context of the social, economic, and political institutions in each society then.

The author found support for each of the three theories in France or England or both, but the evidence did not wholly support any of the three. Instead, Lachmann discovered new factors and offered a new interpretation of what happened. He found that three separate elites outside the state conflicted with each other. The alliances

they formed and the outcomes of their conflicts produced a strong centralized state as each elite attempted to protect its interests from its rivals.

CONCLUSION

Little of this chapter discussed specific ways to design research, although there was a lot of information about qualitative research. This was not an oversight. This chapter is a necessary background to practical design issues in qualitative research. More practical design issues are found in the next two chapters. As the discussion of logic in practice and a cyclical research path suggest, such issues are difficult to separate from doing the research itself.

This chapter focused on the differences between quantitative and qualitative research and the general characteristics of qualitative research. Its primary purpose has been to acquaint you with the point of view of qualitative research. It is important to make the transition from the mindset of quantitative research before examining specific ways to conduct qualitative research.

As stated before, the qualitative and quantitative distinction is often overdrawn and presented as a false, rigid dichotomy. It is nevertheless important to understand and appreciate the strengths of each on its own terms. It is too easy to apply the assumptions, standards, and orientation of a positivist, quantitative approach and find qualitative research wanting.

KEY TERMS

cyclical research path	logic in practice	technocratic perspective
first-order interpretation	reconstructed logic	third-order interpretation
grounded theory	second-order interpretation	transcendent perspective
linear research path		

REVIEW QUESTIONS

1. How do the three approaches to science provide a guide for researchers?

2. What are the implications of saying that qualitative research uses more of a logic in practice than a reconstructed logic?

3. What does it mean to say that qualitative research follows a nonlinear path? In what ways is a more cyclical path valuable?

4. Why is the context of social event important for qualitative researchers?

5. What are the characteristics of the case study and why can it yield important information?

6. Compare the ways quantitative and qualitative researchers deal with personal bias and the issue of trusting the researcher.

7. How do qualitative researchers use theory?

8. Explain how qualitative researchers approach the issue of interpreting data. Refer to first-, second-, and third-order interpretations.

9. What are the three reasons qualitative researchers advocate triangulation that differ from the main reason given by quantitative researchers?

10. Identify five things survey research can do for field research and vice versa.

NOTES

1. Ward and Grant (1985) and Grant, Ward, and Rong (1987) analyzed research in sociology journals and suggested that journals with a higher proportion of qualitative research articles addressed gender topics, but that studies of gender are not themselves more likely to be qualitative.

2. See Lofland and Lofland (1984:118–121).

3. For examples of checking, see Agar (1980) and Becker (1970c).

4. See Blee and Billings (1986), Ricoeur (1970), and Schneider (1987) on the interpretation of text in qualitative research.

5. For additional discussion of triangulation, see Denzin (1989:234–247).

6. See Carr-Hill (1984b) on praxis and introducing qualitative features into survey research.

RECOMMENDED READINGS

Berger, Peter L., and Thomas Luckmann. (1970). *The social construction of reality: A treatise in the sociology of knowledge*. New York: Doubleday. This is a classic work in sociology on what is called a constructionist view—that people define and socially construct meaning. It is recommended for anyone unfamiliar with the view or interested in better understanding the background of qualitative research, especially field research.

Carr, Edward Hallet. (1961). *What is history?* New York: Vintage. This book began as a set of lectures and has since become a classic on the historical method. It discusses major issues in qualitative historical research and qualitative research in general. This book is required reading for anyone planning a serious historical or historical-comparative study.

Marshall, Catherine, and Gretchen B. Rossman. (1989). *Designing qualitative research*. Beverly Hills, CA: Sage. This unusual book includes some of the nuts and bolts of developing a proposal for qualitative research. It is especially valuable for beginning field researchers and includes discussions of managing time and framing a research question. An unusual feature of the book is its use of numerous vignettes containing concrete examples.

FIELD RESEARCH

Field research is the study of people acting in the natural courses of their daily lives. The fieldworker ventures into the worlds of others in order to learn firsthand about how they live, how they talk and behave, and what captivates and distresses them. . . . It is also seen as a method of study whose practitioners try to understand the meanings that activities observed have for those engaging in them.
—Robert Emerson, *Contemporary Field Research*, p. 1

INTRODUCTION AND HISTORY OF FIELD RESEARCH

In this chapter, you will learn about field research, sometimes called ethnography or participant observation. Many students are excited by field research because it involves hanging out with some exotic group of people. There are no cold mathematics or complicated statistics, no abstract deductive hypotheses. Instead, there is direct, face-to-face social interaction in a natural setting.

Field research appeals to those who like people watching or a loose approach to doing research. In addition, field research reports can be fascinating accounts of unfamiliar social worlds: nude beaches, the homeless, professional gamblers, street gangs, police squads, emergency rooms, artists' colonies, and so on.

In field research, the individual researcher directly talks with and observes the people being studied. Through interaction over months or years, the researcher learns about them, their life histories, their hobbies and interests, and their habits, hopes, fears, and dreams. Meeting new people, developing friendships, and discovering new social worlds can be fun. It is also time consuming, emotionally draining, and sometimes physically dangerous.

Research Questions Appropriate for Field Research

When should you use field research? Field research is appropriate when the research question involves learning about, understanding, or describing a group of interacting people. It is usually best when the question is: How do people do Y in the social world? or What is the social world of X like? It can be used when other methods (e.g., survey, experiments) are not practical, as in studying street gangs. Douglas (1976:xii) stated that most of what social researchers really want to learn about can be studied only through the direct involvement of a researcher in the field.

Field researchers study people in a location or setting. It has been used to study entire communities. Beginning field researchers should start with a relatively small group (30 or fewer) who interact with each other on a regular basis in a relatively fixed setting (e.g., a street corner, church, barroom, beauty parlor, baseball field). Field research is also used to study amorphous social experiences that are not fixed in place, but where intensive interviewing and observation are the only way to gain access to the experience—for example, the feelings of a person who has been

mugged, or who is the widow of someone who committed suicide.[1]

In order to use consistent terminology, we can call the people who are studied in a field setting *members*. They are insiders or natives in the field and belong to a group, subculture, or social setting that the "outsider" field researcher wants to penetrate and learn about.

Field researchers have explored a wide variety of social settings, subcultures, and aspects of social life, as illustrated by the examples of settings and subcultures listed here: laundromats (Kenen, 1982), camera clubs (Schwartz, 1986), waiting rooms (Gross, 1986; Goodsell, 1983; Lofland, 1972), battered women's shelters (Wharton, 1987), social movements (Downey, 1986; Snow, Baker, Anderson, and Martin, 1986b), social welfare offices (G. Miller, 1983), television stations (Altheide, 1976), airplane passengers (Zurcher, 1979), and bars (Byrne, 1978; LeMasters, 1975). In addition, field researchers have studied larger settings such as small towns (Vidich and Bensman, 1968), retirement communities (Hochschild, 1978; Jacobs, 1974; Marshall, 1975), working-class communities (Kornblum, 1974), and urban ethnic neighborhoods (Whyte, 1955). Additional studies can be found in two scholarly journals that specialize in field research, *Journal of Contemporary Ethnography* (previously named *Urban Life*) and *Qualitative Sociology*.

Field research is valuable for examining the culture of children's social worlds. Researchers have studied Little League baseball (Fine, 1979, 1987), children's playgrounds (Lever, 1978), and school children (Corsaro, 1988; Eder, 1981, 1985; Maynard, 1985; Thorne and Luria, 1986). Many occupations have been studied by field researchers, including medical students (Becker, Geer, Hughes, and Strauss, 1961), cab drivers (Davis, 1959), cocktail waitresses (Hearn and Stoll, 1976; Spradley and Mann, 1975), dogcatchers (Palmer, 1978), police officers (Hunt, 1984; Pepinsky, 1980; Van Maanen, 1973; Waegel, 1984), door-to-door salespeople (Bogdan and Taylor, 1975:174–186), social workers (Johnson, 1975), jazz musicians (Sudnow, 1978), factory workers (Burawoy, 1979; Burawoy and Lukacs, 1985), milkmen (Bigus, 1972), airline attendants (Hochschild, 1983), and artists (Basirico, 1986; McCall, 1980; Sharon, 1979; Sinha, 1979).

Field researchers have contributed to medical sociology by examining intensive care units (Coombs and Goldman, 1973) and emergency rooms (Kurz, 1987), and important life events such as pregnancy/birth (Annandale, 1988; Danziger, 1979; Weitz and Sullivan, 1986), abortion (Ball, 1967), and death (Glaser and Strauss, 1968). Field research is especially valuable for studying deviant behavior. Field researchers studied nude beaches (Douglas and Rasmussen, 1977), gambling (Hayano, 1982; Lesiuer and Sheley 1987), big-time drug dealing (Adler, 1985; Adler and Adler, 1983), drug addicts (Faupel and Klockars, 1987), street gangs (Moore, Vigil, and Garcia, 1983), street people, tramps, or hoboes (Liebow, 1967; Polsky, 1967; Snow, Bochford, Worden, and Beuford, 1986a; Spradley, 1970), prostitutes (Bryan, 1965; Prus and Vassilakopoulos, 1979), hippie communes (Cavan, 1974), pornographic bookstores (Karp, 1973; Sudhold, 1973), the occult (Jorgensen and Jorgensen, 1982), and cults (Bromley and Shupe, 1979; Gordon, 1987; Lofland, 1966).

A Short History of Field Research

Early Beginnings.   Field research can be traced back to the reports of travelers to distant lands.[2] In the 1200s, European explorers and missionaries wrote descriptions of the strange cultures and peoples they encountered. Others read these descriptions to learn about foreign cultures. Later, in the nineteenth century, when European trade and empires rapidly expanded and there were more literate, educated travelers, the number of reports grew.

Academic field research began in the late nineteenth century with anthropology. The first anthropologists only read the reports of explorers, government officials, or missionaries but lacked direct contact with the people they studied. The reports focused on the exotic and were highly racist and ethnocentric. Travelers rarely spoke the local language and had to rely on interpreters. Not until the 1890s did European anthropologists begin to travel to far-away lands to learn about other cultures.

British social anthropologist Bronislaw Malinoski (1844–1942) was the first researcher to live with a group of people for a long period of time and write about collecting data. In the 1920s, he presented intensive field work as a new method and argued for separating direct observation and native statements from the observer's inferences. He said that social researchers should directly interact with and live among the native peoples and learn their customs, beliefs, and social processes.

Researchers also used field research to study their own society. The observations of the London poor by Charles Booth and Beatrice Webb in the 1890s began both survey research and field research outside of anthropology. Booth and Webb directly observed people in natural settings and used an inductive data-gathering approach. Participant observation may have originated in Germany in 1890. Paul Gohre worked and lived as a factory apprentice for three months and took detailed notes each night at home in order to study factory life. His published work influenced scholars in the universities, including the sociologist Max Weber.

Chicago School of Sociology.   Sociological field research in the United States began at the University of Chicago Department of Sociology in what is known as the Chicago school of sociology. The Chicago school's influence on field research had two phases. In the first phase, from the 1910s to 1930s, the school used a variety of methods based on the case study or life history approach, including direct observation, informal interviews, and reading documents or official records. Important influences came from Booker T. Washington, William James, and John Dewey. In 1916, Robert E. Park (1864–1944) drew up a research program for the social investigation of the city of Chicago. Influenced by his background as a newspaper reporter, he said that social researchers should leave the libraries and "get their hands dirty" by direct observations and conversations on street corners, in barrooms, and in luxury hotel lobbies. Early studies such as *The Hobo* (Anderson, 1923), *The Jack Roller* (Shaw, 1930), and *The Gang* (Thrasher, 1927) established early Chicago school sociology as the descriptive study of street life with little analysis.

Journalistic and anthropological models of research were combined in the first phase. The journalistic model has a researcher get behind fronts, use informants, look for conflict, and expose what is "really happening." In the anthropological model, a researcher attaches himself or herself to a small group for an extended period of time and reports on the members' views of the world.

In the second phase, from the 1940s to the 1960s, the Chicago school developed participant observation as a distinct technique. It applied an expanded anthropological model to groups and settings in the researcher's society. Three principles emerged:

1. Study people in their natural settings, or in situ.
2. Study people by directly interacting with them.
3. Gain an understanding of the social world and make theoretical statements about the members' perspective.

Over time, the method moved from strict description to theoretical analyses based on involvement by the researcher in the field.

After World War II, field research faced increased competition from survey and quantitative research. Field research declined as a proportion of all social research from World War II to the 1970s. In the 1970s and 1980s, however, several changes rejuvenated field research. First, field researchers borrowed ideas and techniques from cognitive psychology, cultural anthropology, folklore, and linguistics. Second, researchers reexamined the epistemological roots and philosophical assumptions of social science (see Chapter 4) that justified their method. Finally, field researchers became more self-conscious about their techniques and methods. They wrote about methodology and became more systematic about it as a research technique.

Today, field research has a distinct set of methodologies. Field researchers directly observe and interact with members in natural settings to get inside their perspective. They embrace an activist or social constructionist perspective on social life. They do not see people as a neutral medium through which social forces operate, nor do they see social meanings as something "out there" to observe. Instead. they hold that people create and define the social world through their interactions. Human experiences are filtered through a subjective sense of reality, which affects how people see and act on events. Thus, they replace the positivist emphasis on "objective facts" with a focus on the everyday, face-to-face social processes of negotiation, discussion, and bargaining to construct social meaning.

Field researchers see research as simultaneously a description of the social world and a part of it. As part of a socially created setting, a researcher's presence in the field cannot be just neutral data gathering.

Ethnography and Ethnomethodology. Two modern extensions of field research, ethnography and ethnomethodology, build on the social constructionist perspective. Each is redefining how field research is conducted. They are not yet the core of field research, so they are discussed only briefly here.

Ethnography comes from cultural anthropology.[3] *Ethno* means people or folk, and *graphy* refers to describing something. Thus *ethnography* means describing a culture and understanding another way of life from the native point of view. As Franke (1983:61) stated, "Culture, the object of our description, resides within the thinking of natives." Ethnography assumes that people make inferences—that is, go beyond what is explicitly seen or said to what is meant or implied. People display their culture (what people think, ponder, believe) through behavior (e.g., speech, actions) in specific social contexts. Displays of behavior do not give meaning; rather, meaning is inferred, or someone figures out meaning. Moving from what is heard or observed to what is actually meant is at the center of ethnography. For example, when a student is invited to a "kegger," the student infers that it is an informal party with other student-aged people at which beer will be served, based on his or her cultural knowledge. Cultural knowledge includes symbols, songs, sayings, facts, ways of behaving, and objects (e.g., telephones, newspapers). We learn the culture by watching television, listening to parents, observing others, and the like.

Cultural knowledge includes both explicit knowledge, what we know and talk about, and tacit knowledge, what we rarely acknowledge. For example, *explicit knowledge* includes the social event (e.g., a "kegger"). Most people can easily describe what happens at one. *Tacit knowledge* includes the unspoken cultural norm for the proper distance to stand from others. People are generally unaware that they use this norm. They feel unease or discomfort when the norm is violated, but it is difficult to pinpoint the source of discomfort. Ethnographers describe the explicit and tacit cultural knowledge that members use. Their detailed descriptions and careful analysis take what is described apart and put it back together.

Anthropologist Clifford Geertz stated that a critical part of ethnography is *thick description*,[4] a rich, detailed description of specifics (as opposed to summary, standardization, generalization, or variables). A thick description of a three-minute event may go on for pages. It captures the sense of what occurred and the drama of events, thereby permitting multiple interpretations. It places events in a context so that the reader of an ethnographic report can infer cultural meaning.

Ethnomethodology is a distinct approach developed in the 1960s, with its own unique terminology.[5] It combines theory, philosophy, and method. Some do not consider it a part of sociology. Mehan and Wood (1975:3, 5) argued that

> *ethnomethodology is not a body of findings. nor a method, nor a theory, nor a world view. I view ethnomethodology as a form of life. . . . Ethno-methodology is an attempt to display the reality of a level which exists beyond the sociological level. . . . It differs from sociology much as sociology differs from psychology.*

A simple definition of *ethnomethodology* is the study of commonsense knowledge. Ethnomethodologists study common sense by observing its creation and use in ongoing social interaction in natural settings. Ethnomethodology is a radical or extreme form of field research, based on phenomenological philosophy and a social constructionist approach. It involves the specialized, highly detailed analysis of micro-situations (e.g., transcripts of short conversations or videotapes of social interactions). Compared to Chicago school field research, it is more concerned about method and argues that research findings result as much from the method used as from the social life studied.

Ethnomethodology assumes that social meaning is fragile and fluid, not fixed, stable, or solid. Meaning is constantly being created and re-created in an ongoing process. For this reason, ethnomethodologists analyze language, including pauses and the context of speech. They assume that people "accomplish" commonsense understanding by using tacit social-cultural rules, and social interaction is a process of reality construction. People interpret everyday events by using cultural knowledge and clues from the social context. Ethnomethodologists examine how ordinary people in everyday settings apply tacit rules to make sense of social life (e.g., to know whether or not someone is joking).

Ethnomethodologists examine ordinary social interaction in great detail to identify the rules for constructing social reality and common sense, how these rules are applied, and how new rules are created. For example, they argue that standardized tests or survey interviews measure a person's ability to pick up implicit clues and apply common sense more than measuring objective facts.

Ethnomethodologists sometimes use *breaching* experiments to demonstrate the simple tacit rules that people rely on to create a sense of reality in everyday life (also see the discussion of breakdown later on). The researchers purposefully violate a tacit social norm. The breach usually creates a powerful social response, which verifies the rule's existence, shows the fragility of social reality, and demonstrates that such tacit rules are essential for the flow of ordinary life. For example, ethnomethodology's founder, Harold Garfinkel, sent students to stores where they were told to "mistake" customers for sales clerks. At first, the customers were confused and stammered explanations. But as the students persisted in the misinterpretation, the bewildered customers either reluctantly accepted the new definition of the situation and awkwardly filled the sales clerk role, or "blew up" and "lost their cool." The breach illustrated how the operation of social reality depended on tacit knowledge (e.g., distinguishing sales clerks from customers). Filmmakers use similar situations for comic effect when people from a different culture who do not share the same tacit rules or who are unaware of the unspoken rules of proper behavior are seen as humorous.[6]

THE LOGIC OF FIELD RESEARCH

What Is Field Research?

It is difficult to pin down a specific definition of *field research* because it is more of an orientation toward research than a fixed set of techniques to apply.[7] A field researcher uses various methods to obtain information. As Schatzman and Strauss (1973:14) said, "Field method is more like an umbrella of activity beneath which any technique may be used for gaining the desired knowledge, and for processes of thinking about this information." A *field researcher* is a "methodological pragmatist" (Schatzman and Strauss, 1973:7), a resourceful, talented individual who has ingenuity, and an ability to think on her feet while in the field.

Field research is based on naturalism, which is also used to study other phenomena (e.g., oceans, animals, plants). *Naturalism* involves observing ordinary events in natural settings, not in contrived, invented, or researcher-created settings. Research occurs in the field and outside the safe settings of an office, laboratory, or classroom. Reiss (1992) has said that a researcher's direct observation of events in natural settings is central to sociology's status as a science, and that this status is threatened if sociology turns from naturalism.

A field researcher examines social meanings and grasps multiple perspectives in natural social settings. He or she gets inside the meaning system of members and then goes back to an outside or research viewpoint. As Van Maanen (1982:139) noted, "Fieldwork means involvement and detachment, both loyalty and betrayal, both openness and secrecy, and most likely, love and hate." The researcher switches perspectives and sees the setting from multiple points of view simultaneously: "Researchers maintain membership in the culture in which they were reared while establishing membership in the groups which they are studying; they are socialized into another culture" (Burgess, 1982a:1).

Let us look at what practicing field researchers do (see Box 14.1). Research is usually conducted by a single individual, although small teams have been effective. A researcher is directly involved in and part of the social world studied, so his or her personal characteristics are relevant in research. Wax (1979:509) noted:

> *Informal and quantitative methods, the peculiarities of the individual tend to go unnoticed. Electronic data processing pays no heed to the age, gender, or ethnicity of the research director or programmer. But, in fieldwork, these basic aspects of personal identity become salient; they drastically affect the process of field research.*

The researcher's direct involvement in the field often has an emotional impact. Field research can be fun and exciting, but it can also disrupt one's personal life, physical security, or mental well-being. More than other types of social research, it reshapes friendships, family life, self-identity, or personal values:

> *The price of doing fieldwork is very high, not in dollars (field work is less expensive than most other kinds of research) but in physical and mental effort. It is very hard work. It is exhausting to live two lives simultaneously. (Bogdan and Taylor, 1975:vi)*

A field researcher does the following:

1. Observes ordinary events and everyday activities as they happen in natural settings, in addition to any unusual occurrences
2. Becomes directly involved with the people being studied and personally experiences the process of daily social life in the field setting
3. Acquires an insider's point of view while maintaining the analytic perspective or distance of an outsider
4. Uses a variety of techniques and social skills in a flexible manner as the situation demands
5. Produces data in the form of extensive written notes, as well as diagrams, maps, or pictures to provide very detailed descriptions
6. Sees events holistically (e.g., as a whole unit, not in pieces) and individually in their social context
7. Understands and develops empathy for members in a field setting, and does not just record "cold" objective facts
8. Notices both explicit (recognized, conscious, spoken) and tacit (less recognized, implicit, unspoken) aspects of culture
9. Observes ongoing social processes without upsetting, disrupting, or imposing an outside point of view
10. Copes with high levels of personal stress, uncertainty, ethical dilemmas, and ambiguity

ognize and seize opportunities, "play it by ear," and rapidly adjust to fluid social situations. Douglas (1976:14–16) argued that the techniques of field research share much in common with those of other types of investigative inquiry such as investigative journalism and detective work.

A field researcher does not begin with a set of methods to apply or explicit hypotheses to test. Rather, he or she chooses techniques on the basis of their value for providing information. In the beginning, the researcher expects little control over data and little focus. Once socialized to the setting, however, he or she focuses the inquiry and asserts control over the data.

Getting Organized in the Beginning. Human and personal factors can play a role in any research project, but they are crucial in field research. Field projects often begin with chance occurrences or a personal interest. Field researchers can begin with their own experiences, such as working at a job, having a hobby, or being a patient or an activist.[8]

Field researchers use the skills of careful looking and listening, short-term memory, and regular writing. Before entering the field, a new researcher practices observing the ordinary details of situations and writing them down. Attention to details and short-term memory can improve with practice. Likewise, keeping a daily diary or personal journal is good practice for writing field notes.

As with all social research, reading the scholarly literature helps the researcher learn concepts, potential pitfalls, data collection methods, and techniques for resolving conflicts. In addition, a field researcher finds diaries, novels, journalistic accounts, and autobiographies useful for gaining familiarity and preparing emotionally for the field.

Field research begins with a general topic, not specific hypotheses. A researcher does not get locked into any initial misconceptions. He or she needs to be well informed but open to discovering new ideas. Finding the right questions to ask about the field takes time.

A researcher first empties his or her mind of preconceptions and defocuses. There are two

Steps in a Field Research Project

Naturalism and direct involvement mean that field research is more flexible or less structured than quantitative research. This makes it essential for a researcher to be well organized and prepared for the field. It also means that the steps of a project are not entirely predetermined but serve as an approximate guide or road map (see Table 14.1).

Flexibility. Field researchers rarely follow fixed steps. In fact, flexibility is a key advantage of field research, which lets a researcher shift direction and follow leads. Good field researchers rec-

TABLE 14.1 Steps in Field Research

1. Prepare oneself, read the literature, and defocus.
2. Select a field site and gain access to it.
3. Enter the field and establish social relations with members.
4. Adopt a social role, learn the ropes, and get along with members.
5. Watch, listen, and collect quality data.
6. Begin to analyze data, generate and evaluate working hypotheses.
7. Focus on specific aspects of the setting and use theoretical sampling.
8. Conduct field interviews with member informants.
9. Disengage and physically leave the setting.
10. Complete the analyses and write the research report.

Note: There is no fixed percentage of time needed for each step. For a rough approximation, Junker (1960:12) suggested that, once in the field, the researcher should expect to spend approximately one-sixth of his or her time observing, one-third recording data, one-third of the time analyzing data, and one-sixth reporting results. Also see Denzin (1989:176) for eight steps of field research.

types of *defocusing*.[9] The first is casting a wide net in order to witness a broad range of situations, people, and settings—getting a feel for the overall setting before deciding what to include or exclude. The second type of defocusing means not focusing exclusively on the role of researcher. As Douglas (1976:122) noted, it is important to extend one's experience beyond a strictly professional role. The researcher should move outside his or her comfortable social niche to experience as much as possible in the field without betraying a primary commitment to being a researcher.

Another preparation for field research is self-knowledge. A field researcher needs to know himself or herself and reflect on personal experiences. He or she can expect anxiety, self-doubt, frustration, and uncertainty in the field. Especially in the beginning, the researcher may feel that he or she is collecting the wrong data and may suffer emotional turmoil, isolation, and confusion. He or she often feels doubly marginal: an outsider in the field setting and also distant from friends, family, and other researchers.[10] The relevance of a researcher's emotional make-up, personal biography, and cultural experiences makes it important to be aware of his or her personal commitments and inner conflicts (see the later section on stress).

Fieldwork can have a strong impact on a researcher's identity and outlook. Researchers

may be personally transformed by the field experience. Some adopt new values, interests, and moral commitments, or change their religion or political ideology.[11] Hayano remarked from his study on gambling,

> By this time I felt more comfortable sitting at a poker table than I did at faculty meetings and in my classes. Most of my social life focused on poker playing, and often, especially after a big win, I felt the desire to give up my job as a university professor in order to spend more time in the cardroom. (Hayano, 1982:148)

CHOOSING A SITE AND GAINING ACCESS

Although a field research project does not proceed by fixed steps, some common concerns arise in the early stages. These include selecting a site, gaining access to the site, entering the field, and developing rapport with members in the field.

Selecting a Site

Where to Observe. Field researchers talk about doing research on a setting, or *field site*, but this term is misleading. A site is the context in which events or activities occur, a socially defined territory with shifting boundaries. A social group may interact across several physical sites. For example, a college football team may interact on the playing field, in the locker room, in a dormitory, at a training camp, or at a local hangout. The team's field site includes all five locations.

The field site and research question are bound up together, but choosing a site is not the same as focusing on a *case* for study. A case is a social relationship or activity; it can extend beyond the boundaries of the site and have links to other social settings. A researcher selects a site, then identifies cases to examine within it—for example, how football team members relate to authority figures.

Selecting a field site is an important decision, and researchers take notes on the site selection processes. Three factors are relevant when choosing a field research site: richness of data, unfamiliarity, and suitability.[12] Some sites are more likely than others to provide rich data. Sites that present a web of social relations, a variety of activities, and diverse events over time provide richer, more interesting data. Beginning field researchers should choose an unfamiliar setting. It is easier to see cultural events and social relations in a new site. Bodgan and Taylor (1975: 28) noted, *"We would recommend that researchers choose settings in which the subjects are strangers and in which they have no particular professional knowledge or expertise"* (emphasis in original). When "casing" possible field sites, one must consider such practical issues as the researcher's time and skills, serious conflicts among people in the site, the researcher's personal characteristics and feelings, and access to parts of a site.

A researcher's ascriptive characteristics can limit access. For example, an African American researcher cannot hope to study the Ku Klux Klan or neo-Nazis, although some researchers have successfully crossed some ascriptive lines.[13] Sometimes "insider" and "outsider" teams can work together. For example, the outsider Douglas teamed up with a member insider, Flanagan, for a study of nude beaches (Douglas and Rasmussen, 1977), and a white (Rainwater)

collaborated with a black (Yancey) to study a black housing project (Yancey and Rainwater, 1970).

Physical access to a site can be an issue. Sites are on a continuum, with open and public areas (e.g., public restaurants, airport waiting areas) at one end and closed and private settings (e.g., private firms, clubs, activities in a person's home) at the other. A researcher may find that he or she is not welcome or not allowed on the site, or there are legal and political barriers to access. Laws and regulations in institutions (e.g., public schools, hospitals, prisons) restrict access. In addition, institutional review boards (see Chapter 17) may limit field research on ethical grounds.

Gatekeepers. A *gatekeeper* is someone with the formal or informal authority to control access to a site.[14] It can be the thug on the corner, an administrator of a hospital, or the owner of a business. Informal public areas (e.g., sidewalks, public waiting rooms) rarely have gatekeepers; formal organizations have authorities from whom permission must be obtained.

Field researchers expect to negotiate with gatekeepers and bargain for access. The gatekeepers may not appreciate the need for conceptual distance or ethical balance. The researcher must set nonnegotiable limits to protect research integrity. If there are many restrictions initially, a researcher can often reopen negotiations later, and gatekeepers may forget their initial demands as trust develops. It is ethically and politically astute to call on gatekeepers. Researchers do not expect them to listen to research concerns or care about the findings, except insofar as these findings might provide evidence for someone to criticize them.

Dealing with gatekeepers is a recurrent issue as a researcher enters new levels or areas. In addition, a gatekeeper can shape the direction of research:

Even the most friendly and co-operative gatekeepers or sponsors will shape the conduct and development of research. To one degree or another, the ethnographer will be channeled in line with existing networks of friendship and enmity, territory, and equivalent boundaries. (Hammersley and Atkison, 1983:73)

In some sites, gatekeeper approval creates a stigma that inhibits the cooperation of members. For example, prisoners may not be cooperative if they know that the prison warden gave approval to the researcher. As West (1980:35) remarked regarding juvenile delinquents, "I am convinced that such access routes almost always retard—or in some cases prevent—the establishment of rapport with delinquents."

Strategy for Entering

Entering a field site requires having a flexible strategy or plan of action, negotiating access and relations with members, and deciding how much to disclose about the research to field members or gatekeepers.

Planning.   Entering and gaining access to a field site is a process that depends on commonsense judgment and social skills. Field sites usually have different levels or areas, and entry is an issue for each. Entry is more analogous to peeling the layers of an onion than to opening a door. Moreover, bargains and promises of entry may not remain stable over time. A researcher needs fallback plans or may have to return later for renegotiation. Because the specific focus of research may not emerge until later in the research process or may change, it is best to avoid being locked into specifics by gatekeepers.

Entry and access can be visualized as an *access ladder* (see Figure 14.1). A researcher begins at the bottom rung, where access is easy and where he or she is an outsider looking for public information. The next rung requires increased access. Once close on-site observation begins, he or she becomes a passive observer, not questioning what members say. With time in the field, the researcher observes specific activities that are potentially sensitive or seeks clarification of what he or she sees or hears. Reaching this access rung is more difficult. Finally, the researcher may try to shape interaction so that it reveals specific information, or he or she may

want to see highly sensitive material. This highest rung of the access ladder is rarely attained and requires deep trust.[15]

Negotiation.   Social relations are negotiated and formed throughout the process of fieldwork.[16] Negotiation occurs with each new member until a stable relationship develops to gain access, develop trust, obtain information, and reduce hostile reactions. The researcher expects to negotiate and explain what he or she is doing over and over in the field (see the discussion of normalizing social research, to follow).

Deviant groups and elites often require special negotiations for gaining access. To gain access to deviant subcultures, field researchers have used contacts from the researcher's private life, gone to social welfare or law enforcement agencies where the deviants are processed, advertised for volunteers, offered a service (e.g., counseling) in exchange for access, or gone to a location where deviants hang out and joined a group. For example, Harper (1982) gained access by living in a skid-row mission without any money and befriending homeless men who knew

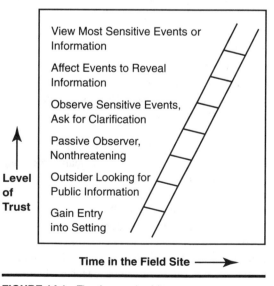

Time in the Field Site ⟶

FIGURE 14.1   The Access Ladder

street life. Bart (1987) argued that her background as a feminist activist and nonprofessional demeanor were essential for gaining access to an illegal feminist abortion clinic.[17]

Access to elites and professionals often depends on luck or personal ties (see Lofland and Lofland, 1995:12). Hoffman (1980) gained access to wealthy individuals on the boards of directors by using her family ties and including personal references in letters requesting interviews. Ostrander's (1984) access into a network of upper-class women depended on a chance meeting with a prominent upper-class woman through an academic colleague. Danziger (1979) gained access to physicians' activities because her father was a doctor. Johnson's (1975) access to a social work agency was aided by mentioning that someone in the agency was a friend of his wife.

Disclosure.   A researcher must decide how much to reveal about himself or herself and the research project. Disclosing one's personal life, hobbies, interests, and background can build trust and close relationships, but the researcher will also lose privacy, and he or she needs to ensure that the focus remains on events in the field.

A researcher also decides how much to disclose about the research project. Disclosure ranges on a continuum from fully covert research, in which no one in the field is aware that research is taking place, to the opposite end, where everyone knows the specifics of the research project. The degree and timing of disclosure depends on a researcher's judgment and particulars in the setting. Disclosure may unfold over time as the researcher feels more secure.

Researchers disclose the project to gatekeepers and others unless there is a good reason for not doing so, such as the presence of gatekeepers who would seriously limit or inhibit research for illegitimate reasons (e.g., to hide graft or corruption). Even in these cases, a researcher may disclose his or her identity as a researcher, but may pose as one who seems submissive, harmless, and interested in nonthreatening issues (see Acceptable Incompetent, page 359).

Entering the Field

After a field site is selected and access obtained, researchers must learn the ropes, develop rapport with members, adopt a role in the setting, and maintain social relations. Before confronting such issues the researcher should ask: How will I present myself? What does it mean for me to be a "measurement instrument"? How can I assume an "attitude of strangeness"?

Presentation of Self.   People explicitly and implicitly present themselves to others. We display who we are—the type of person we are or would like to be—through our physical appearance, what we say, and how we act. The presentation of self sends a symbolic message. It may be, "I'm a serious, hard-working student," "I'm a warm and caring person," "I'm a cool jock," or "I'm a rebel and party animal." Many selves are possible, and presentations of selves can differ depending on the occasion.

A field researcher is conscious of the presentation of self in the field. For example, how should he or she dress in the field? The best guide is to respect both oneself and those being studied. Do not overdress so as to offend or stand out, but copying the dress of those being studied is not always necessary. A professor who studies street people does not have to dress or act like one; dressing and acting informally is sufficient. Likewise, more formal dress and professional demeanor are required when studying corporate executives or top officials.[18]

A researcher must be aware that self-presentation will influence field relations to some degree. It is difficult to present a highly deceptive front or to present oneself in a way that deviates sharply from the person one is ordinarily.

Being herself and revealing her personal background as a Jewish woman helped Myerhoff (1989) gain access and develop rapport in a field site of elderly residents in a Jewish senior citizen home. At the same time, her understanding and awareness of her identity changed as a result of her field interactions. Stack (1989) began as an outsider, a white woman studying a low-income black industrial community. Eventually, she was accepted into a kinlike relationship with the women she studied. Assigned nickname "white Caroline" was a signal of acceptance and endearment. She performed many small favors, such as driving people to the hospital or welfare office, shopping, and visiting sick children. She achieved this by how she interacted with others—her openness and willingness to share personal feelings. Although he was a black man in a black bar, Anderson (1989) found social class to be a barrier. The setting was a corner bar and liquor store on the south side of Chicago in a poor African American neighborhood. Anderson developed a social relationship of trust and was "sponsored." This occurred when he befriended "Herman," a witty, easy-going person who was street smart and socially well connected in the setting. Anderson succeeded by "the low-key, non-assertive role I assumed . . . not to disrupt the consensual definition of the social order in this type of setting" (Anderson, 1989:19).

Researcher as Instrument. The researcher is the instrument for measuring field data. This has two implications. First, it puts pressure on the researcher to be alert and sensitive to what happens in the field and to be disciplined about recording data. Second, it has personal consequences. Fieldwork involves social relationships and personal feelings. Field researchers are flexible about what to include as data and admit their own subjective insights and feelings, or "experiential data."[19] Personal, subjective experiences are part of field data. They are valuable both in themselves and for interpreting events in the field. Instead of trying to be objective and eliminate personal reactions, field researchers treat their feelings toward field events as data. For example, Karp's (1973, 1980) personal feelings of tension in his study of pornographic bookstores were a critical part of the data. His personal discomfort in the field revealed some dynamics of the setting. "If we avoid writing about our reactions, we cannot examine them. We cannot achieve immersion without bringing our subjectivity into play" (Kleinman and Copp, 1993:19).

Field research can heighten a researcher's awareness of personal feelings. For example, a researcher may not be fully aware of personal feelings about nudity until he or she is in a nudist colony, or about personal possessions until he or she is in a setting where others "borrow" many items. The researcher's own surprise, indignation, or questioning then may become an opportunity for reflection and insight.[20]

An Attitude of Strangeness.   It is hard to recognize what we are very close to. The everyday world we inhabit is filled with thousands of details. If we paid attention to everything all the time, we would suffer from severe information overload. We manage by ignoring much of what is around us and by engaging in habitual thinking. Unfortunately, we fail to see the familiar as distinctive, and assume that others experience reality just as we do. We tend to treat our own way of living as natural or normal.

Field research in familiar surroundings is difficult because of a tendency to be blinded by the familiar. In fact, "intimate acquaintance with one's own culture can create as much blindness as insight" (McCracken, 1988:12). By studying other cultures, researchers encounter dramatically different assumptions about what is important and how things are done. This confrontation of cultures, or culture shock, has two benefits: It makes it easier to see cultural elements and it facilitates self-discovery. Researchers adopt the attitude of strangeness to gain these benefits. The *attitude of strangeness* means questioning and noticing ordinary details or looking at the ordinary through the eyes of a stranger. Strangeness helps a researcher overcome the boredom of observing ordinary details. It helps him or her see the ordinary in a new way, one that reveals aspects of the setting of which members are not consciously aware.

People rarely recognize customs they take for granted. For example, when someone gives us a gift, we say thank you and praise the gift. By contrast, gift-giving customs in many cultures include complaining that the gift is inadequate. The attitude of strangeness helps make the tacit culture visible—for example, that gift givers expect to hear "thank you" and "the gift is nice," and become upset otherwise. A field researcher adopts both a stranger's and an insider's point of view. The stranger sees events as specific social processes, whereas to an insider, they seem natural. Davis (1973) called this the Martian and the convert: The Martian sees everything as strange and questions assumptions, whereas the convert accepts everything and wants to become a believer. Researchers need both views, as well as the ability to switch back and forth.[21]

Strangeness also encourages a researcher to reconsider his or her own social world. Immersion in a different setting breaks old habits of thought and action. He or she finds reflection and introspection easier and more intense when encountering the unfamiliar, whether it is a different culture or a familiar culture seen through a stranger's eyes.

Building Rapport

A field researcher builds rapport by getting along with members in the field. He or she forges a friendly relationship, shares the same language, and laughs and cries with members. This is a step toward obtaining an understanding of members and moving beyond understanding to empathy—that is, seeing and feeling events from another's perspective.

It is not always easy to build rapport. The social world is not all in harmony, with warm, friendly people. A setting may contain fear, tension, and conflict. Members may be unpleasant, untrustworthy, or untruthful; they may do things that disturb or disgust a researcher. An experienced researcher is prepared for a range of events and relationships. He or she may find, however, that it is impossible to penetrate a setting or get really close to members. Settings where cooperation, sympathy, and collaboration are impossible require different techniques.[22] Also, the researcher accepts what he or she hears or sees at face value, but without being gullible. As Schatzman and Strauss (1973:69) remarked,

"The researcher believes 'everything' and 'nothing' simultaneously."

Charm and Trust. A field researcher needs social skills and personal charm to build rapport. Trust, friendly feelings, and being well liked facilitate communication and help him or her to understand the inner feelings of others. There is no magical way to do this. Showing a genuine concern for and interest in others, being honest, and sharing feelings are good strategies, but they are not foolproof. It depends on the specific setting and members.

Many factors affect trust and rapport—how a researcher presents, himself or herself; the role he or she chooses for the field; and the events that encourage, limit, or make it impossible to achieve trust. Trust is not gained once and for all. It is a developmental process built up over time through many social nuances (e.g., sharing of personal experiences, story telling, gestures, hints, facial expressions). It is constantly re-created and seems easier to lose once it has been built up than to gain in the first place.

Establishing trust is important, but it does not ensure that all information will be revealed. It may be limited to specific areas. For example, trust can be built up regarding financial matters but not to disclose intimate dating behavior. Trust may have to be created anew in each area of inquiry; it requires constant reaffirmation.

Freeze Outs. Some members may not be open and cooperative. *Freeze outs* are members who express an uncooperative attitude or an overt unwillingness to participate. Field researchers may never gain the cooperation of everyone, or a warm relationship may develop only after prolonged persistence.

Understanding. Rapport helps field researchers understand members, but understanding is a precondition for greater depth, not an end in itself. It slowly develops in the field as the researcher overcomes an initial bewilderment with a new or unusual language and system of social meaning. Once, he or she attains an understanding of the member's point of view, the next step is to learn how to think and act within a member's perspective. This is *empathy,* or adopting another's perspective. Empathy does not necessarily mean sympathy, agreement, or approval; it means feeling things as another does.[23]

Rapport helps create understanding and ultimately empathy, and the development of empathy facilitates greater rapport. The novel *To Kill a Mockingbird* notes the link between rapport and empathic understanding in the following passage:

> *"First of all," he said, "if you can learn a simple trick. Scout, you'll get along a lot better with all kinds of folks. You never really understand a person until you consider things from his point of view."*
>
> *"Sir?"*
>
> *"—until you climb into his skin and walk around in it." (Lee, 1960:34)*

RELATIONS IN THE FIELD

You play many social roles in daily life—daughter/son student, customer, sports fan—and maintain social relations with others. You choose some roles and others are structured for you. Few have a choice but to play the role of son or daughter. Some roles are formal (e.g., bank teller, police chief), others are informal (flirt, elder states person, buddy). You can switch roles, play multiple roles, and play a role in a particular way. Field researchers play roles in the field. In addition, they learn the ropes and maintain relations with members.

Roles in the Field

Preexisting versus Created Roles.   Sometimes, a researcher adopts an existing role. Some existing roles provide access to all areas of the site, the ability to observe and interact with all members, the freedom to move around, and a way to balance the requirements of researcher and member. At other times, a researcher creates a new role or modifies an existing one. For example, Fine (1987) created a role of the "adult

friend" and performed it with little adult authority when studying preadolescent boys. He was able to observe parts of their culture and behavior that were otherwise inaccessible to adults. The adoption of a field role takes time, and a researcher may adopt several different field roles over time.

Limits on the Role Chosen.   The field roles open to a researcher are affected by ascriptive factors and physical appearance. He or she can change some aspects of appearance, such as dress or hairstyle, but not ascriptive features such as age, race, gender, and attractiveness. Nevertheless, such factors can be important in gaining access and can restrict the available roles. For example, Gurney (1985) reported that being a female in a male-dominated setting required extra negotiations and "hassles." Nevertheless, her gender provided insights and created situations that would have been absent with a male researcher.

Since many roles are sex-typed, gender is an important consideration. Female researchers often have more difficulty when the setting is perceived as dangerous or seamy and where males are in control (e.g., police work, firefighting). They may be shunned or pushed into limiting gender stereotypes (e.g., "sweet kid," "mascot," "hard bitch"). Male researchers have more problems in routine and administrative sites where males are in control (e.g., courts, large offices). They may not be accepted in female-dominated territory. In sites where both males and females are involved, both sexes may be able to enter and gain acceptance.[24]

Level of Involvement.   Field roles can be arranged on a continuum by the degree of detachment or involvement a researcher has with members. At one extreme are roles of a detached outsider; at the other extreme are roles of an intimately involved insider. The range of field roles is described in three systems developed by Junker, Gans, and the Adlers (see Box 14.2). Junker's system is from the old Chicago school

Box 14.2 _____

Three Systems of Role Involvement by Field Researchers

Junker[a]

Complete observer

The researcher is behind a one-way mirror or in an "invisible role" (e.g., janitor) that permits undetected and unnoticed observation and eavesdropping.

Observer as participant

The researcher is a known, overt observer from the beginning, who has more limited or formal contact with members.

Participant as observer

The researcher and members are aware of the research role, but the researcher is an intimate friend who is a pseudomember.

Complete participant

The researcher acts as a member and shares the secret information of insiders because the researcher's identity is not known to members.

Gans[b]

Total researcher

The researcher has little personal involvement and is a passive observer, "on the sidelines," who does not influence events in the field.

Researcher participant

The researcher participates but is only partially involved or committed to a member's perspective.

Total participant

The researcher is completely emotionally involved while in the field, and becomes a detached researcher only after leaving.

The Adlers[c]

Peripheral membership

The researcher maintains distance between self and members; membership is limited by the researcher's beliefs, ascriptive characteristics, or discomfort with member activities.

Active membership

The researcher assumes a membership role and goes through the same induction as other members; participation in core activities produces high levels of trust and acceptance, but researchers retain a researcher identity and can periodically withdraw from the field.

Complete membership

The researcher converts and "goes native" but later becomes an ex-member researcher. By "surrendering" to membership and becoming an equal, fully committed member, the researcher experiences the same emotions as others. He or she needs to leave the field and undergo reorientation to return to being a researcher.

[a]See Junker (1960). Also see Denzin (1989), Gold (1969), Pearsail (1970), and Roy (1970).
[b]See Gans (1982).
[c]See Adler and Adler (1987).

and that by Gans is a simplification of Junker's system. The Adlers's system moves beyond the Chicago school to incorporate insights from ethnography and ethnomethodology.

A researcher's involvement depends on negotiations with members, specifics of the setting, the researcher's comfort, and the particular field role adopted. Many move from the outsider to the insider end of the continuum with time in the field.

Each level of involvement has advantages and disadvantages. Different field researchers advocate different levels of involvement. For example, the Adlers's complete member role is criticized by some for overinvolvement and loss of a researcher's perspective. Others argue that it is the only way to really understand a member's social world.

Roles at the outsider end of the continuum reduce the time needed for acceptance, make overrapport less an issue, and can sometimes help members open up. They facilitate detachment and protect the researcher's self-identity. A researcher feels marginal. Although there is less risk of "going native," he or she is also less likely to know an insider's experience and misinterpretation is more likely.

To really understand social meaning for those being studied, the field researcher must participate in the setting, as others do. Holy (1984: 29–30) observed,

> The researcher does not participate in the lives of subjects in order to observe them, but rather observes while participating fully in their lives ... through living with the people being studies. ... She comes to share the same meanings with them in the process of active particpation in their social life. ... Research means, in this sense, socialization to the culture being studied.

By contrast, roles at the insider end of the continuum facilitate empathy and sharing of a member's experience. The goal of fully experiencing the intimate social world of a member is achieved. Nevertheless, a lack of distance from, too much sympathy for, or overinvolvement with members is likely. A researcher's reports may be questioned, data gathering is difficult, there can be a dramatic impact on the researcher's self, and the distance needed for analysis may be hard to attain.[25]

Other Considerations.   Almost any role limits access to some parts of a field site. For example, the role of a bartender in a bar limits knowledge of intimate customer behavior or presence at customer gatherings in other locations. A field researcher takes care when choosing roles but recognizes that all roles involve trade-offs.

Most social settings contain cliques, informal groups, hierarchies, and rivalries. A role can help a researcher gain acceptance into or be excluded from a clique, be treated as a person in authority or as an underling, and be a friend or an enemy of some members. A researcher is aware that by adopting a role, he or she may be forming allies and enemies who can assist or limit research.

Learning the Ropes

As a researcher learns the ropes on the field site, he or she learns how to cope with personal stress, how to normalize the social research, and how to act like an "acceptable incompetent."

Stress.   Fieldwork can be highly rewarding, exciting, and fulfilling, but it also can be difficult:

> *Fieldwork must certainly rank with the more disagreeable activities that humanity has fashioned for itself. It is usually inconvenient, to say the least, sometimes physically uncomfortable, frequently embarrassing, and, to a degree, always tense. (Shaffir, Stebbins, and Turowetz, 1980:3)*

New researchers face embarrassment, experience discomfort, and are overwhelmed by the details in the field. For example, in her study of U.S. relocation camps for Japanese Americans during World War II, respected field researcher Rosalie Wax (1971) reported that she endured the discomfort of 120-degree Fahrenheit temperatures, filthy and dilapidated living conditions, dysentery, and mosquitoes. She felt isolated, she cried a lot, and she gained 30 pounds from compulsive eating. After months in the field, she thought she was a total failure; she was distrusted by members and got into fights with the camp administration.

Maintaining a "marginal" status is stressful; it is difficult to be an outsider who is not fully involved, especially when studying settings full of intense feelings (e.g., political campaigns, religious conversions). The loneliness and isolation of fieldwork may combine with the desire to develop rapport and empathy to cause overinvolvement. A researcher may "go native" and drop the professional researcher's role to become a full member of the group being studied. Or the researcher may feel guilt about learning intimate details as members drop their guard, and may come to overidentify with members.[26]

Some emotional stress is inevitable in field research. Instead of suppressing emotional responses, the field researcher is sensitive to emotional reactions. He or she copes in the field by keeping a personal diary, emotional journal, or written record of inner feelings, or by having sympathetic people outside the field site to in which to confide.[27]

Normalizing Social Research. A field researcher not only observes and investigates members in the field but is observed and investigated by members as well: "While the fieldworker is undertaking a study of others, others are undertaking a study of the fieldworker" (Van Maanen, 1982:110). As Wax (1979:363) argued, fieldwork is not performed by an isolated individual but is created by everyone in the field setting.

In overt field research, members are usually initially uncomfortable with the presence of a researcher. Most are unfamiliar with field research and fail to distinguish between sociologists, psychologists, counselors, and social workers. They may see the researcher as an outside critic or spy, or as a savior or all-knowing expert.

An overt field researcher must *normalize social research*—that is, help members redefine social research from something unknown and threatening to something normal and predictable. He or she can help members manage research by presenting his or her own biography, explaining field research a little at a time, appearing nonthreatening, or accepting minor deviance in the setting (e.g., minor violations of official rules).[28] For example, in a study of social workers, Johnson (1975:99–104) was accepted in the setting after the social workers realized that he accepted their minor deviance (e.g., leaving work early to go swimming) and said that he thought others did it also.

Another way to normalize research is to explain it in terms members understand. Sometimes, members' excitement about being written up in a book is useful, as Fine and Glassner (1979) and LeMasters (1975) found. In his study of a neighborhood tavern in Wisconsin, LeMasters became a regular over a five-year period, going to the bar several nights a week. He (1975:7) stated how he explained what he was doing to members:

> *I initially assumed the role of patron—just another person who liked to drink beer and shoot some pool. This finally became difficult because the amount of time I spent in the tavern began to raise questions. Some of the regular customers, I learned later, had decided I must be an undercover agent from the state liquor commission. . . . I adopted the following stance when queried about being in the tavern: that sociologists have to have some knowledge of various aspects of American society to be effective teachers, that I found The Oasis men and women to be helpful in understanding how blue-collar people feel about American society, and, further, that I became bored by constant association with white-collar people and that the tavern contacts were refreshing. All of the above statements were true.*

Acceptable Incompetent. A researcher is in the field to learn, not to be an expert. Depending on the setting, he or she appears to be a friendly but naive outsider. He or she is an acceptable incompetent who is interested in learning about the social life of the field. An *acceptable incompetent* is someone who is partially competent (skilled or knowledgeable) in the setting but who is accepted as a nonthreatening person who needs to be taught.[29] As Schatzman and Strauss (1973:25) noted, "The researcher should play down any expertise or profound knowledge he may have on the subject on which the hosts may claim to be expert; the researcher is and should act the learner, indicating no inclination to evaluate the host's activities."

A field researcher may know little about the setting or subculture at first. He or she may be seen as a fool who is hoodwinked or shortchanged, and may be the butt of jokes for his or her lack of adeptness in the setting. Even when the researcher is knowledgeable, he or she displays less than full information to draw out a member's knowledge. Of course, the researcher can overdo this and appear so ignorant that he or she is not taken seriously.

Maintaining Relations

Social Relations. With time, a field researcher develops and modifies social relationships. Members who are cool at first may warm up later. Or they may put on a front of initial friendliness, and their fears and suspicions surface only later. A researcher is in a delicate position. Early in a project, when not yet fully aware of everything about a field site, the researcher does not form close relationships because circumstances may change. Yet, if he or she does develop close friends, they can become allies who will defend the researcher's presence and help him or her gain access.

A field researcher monitors how his or her actions or appearance affects members. For example, a physically attractive researcher who interacts with members of the opposite sex may encounter crushes, flirting, and jealousy. He or she develops an awareness of these field relations and learns to manage them.[30]

In addition to developing social relationships, a field researcher must be able to break or withdraw from relationships as well. Ties with one member may have to be broken in order to forge ties with others or to explore other aspects of the setting. As with the end of any friendly relationship, the emotional pain of social withdrawal can affect both the researcher and the member. The researcher must balance social sensitivity and the research goals.

Small Favors. Exchange relationships develop in the field, in which small tokens or favors, including deference and respect, are exchanged.[31] A researcher may gain acceptance by helping out in small ways. Exchange helps when access to sensitive issues is limited. A researcher may offer small favors but not burden members by asking

for return favors. As the researcher and members share experiences and see each other again, members recall the favors and reciprocate by allowing access. For example, Fine (1987:242) learned a lot when he was providing small favors (e.g., driving the boys to the movies) as part of his "adult friend" role.

Conflicts in the Field. Fights, conflict, and disagreements can erupt in the field, or a researcher may study groups with opposing positions. In such situations, the researcher will feel pressure to take sides and will be tested to see if he or she can be trusted. In such occasions, a researcher usually stays on the neutral sidelines and walks a tightrope between opposing sides. This is because once he or she becomes aligned with one side, the researcher will cut off access to the other side.[32] In addition, he or she will see the situation from only one point of view. Nevertheless, some (e.g., Van Maanen, 1982:115) argue that true neutrality is illusory. As a researcher becomes involved with members and embroiled in webs of relationships and commitments, neutrality becomes almost impossible.

Appearing Interested. Field researchers maintain an *appearance of interest* in the field. An experienced researcher appears to be interested in and involved with field events by statements and behaviors (e.g., facial expression, going for coffee, organizing a party) even if he or she is not truly interested. This is because field relations may be disrupted if the researcher appears to be bored or distracted. Putting up such a temporary front of involvement is a common small deception in daily life and is part of being polite.[33]

Of course, selective inattention (i.e., not staring or appearing not to notice) is also part of acting polite. If a person makes a social mistake (e.g., accidentally uses an incorrect word, passes gas, etc.), the polite thing to do is to ignore it. Selective inattention is used in fieldwork as well. It gives an alert researcher an opportunity to learn by casually eavesdropping on conversations or observing events not meant to be public.

Social Breakdowns. A social breakdown occurs when two cultural traditions or social assumptions fail to mesh. *Breakdowns* highlight social meaning because hidden routine expectations and assumptions become explicit in a breakdown. They appear as misunderstandings or confusion over which of several implicit social rules to apply. For example, I go to a restaurant and sit down and wait for a server to appear. Twenty minutes later, having gotten no service, I become angry. I look around and notice that I have not seen any servers. I see customers enter from a doorway carrying their own food and realize my misunderstanding. My implicit expectation was that the restaurant had table service; in fact, it is one where patrons go to a counter, order, and pick up their own food. Once I recognize which rules to apply in the context, I can resolve the breakdown.

Breakdowns produce embarrassment because the mismatch of cultural meanings often causes a person to look foolish, ignorant, or uninformed. For example, you are invited to a party that begins at 8:00. You show up in your usual attire, old jeans and a wrinkled sweater, and arrive at your usual time for an 8:00 party—8:30. The door opens and you enter. Shocked, you see that everyone else is formally dressed and sitting at a formal dinner, which was served about 30 minutes ago. People stare at you, and you feel out of place. Your cultural expectation (this is an informal student party with loud music, dancing, beer, and informal dress) does not match the setting (this is a formal dinner party, where people expect to eat, engage in polite conversation, and act professional). The breakdown makes explicit the unspoken social rules that "everyone knows" or assumes.

Breakdowns can be unexpected or can be purposefully created to test working hypotheses. As with an ethnomethodologist's breaching experiments, a researcher may violate social rules to illustrate the existence of tacit rules and their importance. Researchers observe unplanned breakdowns, or they create breakdowns and watch reactions in order to pinpoint implicit social expectations.

OBSERVING AND COLLECTING DATA

This section looks at how to get good qualitative field data. Field data are what the researcher experiences and remembers, and what are recorded in field notes and become available for systematic analysis.

Watching and Listening

Observing. A great deal of what researchers do in the field is to pay attention, watch, and listen carefully. They use all the senses, noticing what is seen, heard, smelled, tasted, or touched. The researcher becomes an instrument that absorbs all sources of information.

A field researcher carefully scrutinizes the physical setting to capture its atmosphere. He or she asks: What is the color of the floor, walls, ceiling? How large is a room? Where are the windows and doors? How is the furniture arranged, and what is its condition (e.g., new or old and worn, dirty or clean)? What type of lighting is there? Are there signs, paintings, plants? What are the sounds or smells?

Why bother with such details? You may have noticed that stores and restaurants often plan lighting, colors, and piped-in music to create a certain atmosphere. Maybe you know that used-car sales people spray a new-car scent into cars. These subtle, unconscious signals influence human behavior.

Observing in field research is often detailed, tedious work. Silverman (1993:30) noted, "If you go to the cinema to see action [car chases, hold-ups, etc.], then it is unlikely that you will find it easy to be a good observer." Instead of the quick flash, motivation arises out of a deep curiosity about the details. Good field researchers are intrigued about details that reveal "what's going on here" through careful listening and watching. Field researchers believe that the core of social life is communicated through the mundane, trival, everyday minutia. This is what people often overlook, but field researchers need to learn how to notice.

In addition to physical surroundings, a field researcher observes people and their actions, noting each person's observable physical characteristics: age, sex, race, and stature. People socially interact differently depending on whether another person is 18, 40, or 70 years old; male or female; white or nonwhite; short and frail or tall, heavyset, and muscular. When noting such characteristics, the researcher is included. For example, an attitude of strangeness heightens sensitivity to a group's racial composition. A researcher who ignores the racial composition of a group of whites in a multiracial society because he or she too is white is being racially insensitive. Likewise, "Gender insensitivity occurs when the sex of participants in the research process is neglected" (Eichler, 1988:51).

The researcher records such details because something of significance *might* be revealed. It is better to err by including everything than to ignore potentially significant details. For example, "the tall, white muscular 19-year-old male sprinted into the brightly lit room just as the short, overweight black woman in her sixties eased into a battered chair" says much more than "one person entered, another sat down."

A field researcher notes aspects of physical appearance such as neatness, dress, and hairstyle because they express messages that can affect social interactions. People spend a great deal of time and money selecting clothes, styling and combing hair, grooming with makeup, shaving, ironing clothes, and using deodorant or perfumes. These are part of their presentation of self. Even people who do not groom, shave, or wear deodorant present themselves and send a symbolic message by their appearance. No one dresses or looks "normal." Such a statement suggests that a researcher is not seeing the social world through the eyes of a stranger or is insensitive to social signals.

What people do is also significant. A field researcher notices where people sit or stand, the pace at which they walk, and their nonverbal communication. People express social information, feelings, and attitudes through nonverbal communication, including gestures, facial expressions, and how one stands or sits (standing stiffly, sitting in a slouched position). People express

relationships by how they position themselves in a group and through eye contact. A researcher may read the social communication of people by noting that they are standing close together, looking relaxed, and making eye contact.

A field researcher also notices the context in which events occur: Who was present? Who just arrived or left the scene? Was the room hot and stuffy? Such details may help the researcher assign meaning and understand why an event occurred. If they are not noticed, the details are lost, as is a full understanding of the event.

Listening.   A field researcher listens carefully to phrases, accents, and incorrect grammar, listening both to *what* is said and *how* it is said or what was implied. For example, people often use phrases such as "you know" or "of course" or "et cetera." A field researcher knows the meaning behind such phrases. He or she can try to hear everything, but listening is difficult when many conversations occur at once or when eavesdropping. Luckily, significant events and themes usually recur.

Argot.   People who interact with each other over a time period develop shared symbols and terminology. They create new words or assign new meanings to ordinary words. New words develop out of specific events, assumptions, or relations. Knowing and using the language can signal membership in a distinct subculture. A field researcher learns the specialized language, or *argot*.[34]

> *Researchers must start with the premise that words and symbols used in their world may have different meaning in the world of their subjects. They must also be attuned to new words and words used in contexts other than those with which they are familiar. (Bogdan and Taylor, 1975:53; emphasis in original)*

A field researcher discovers how the argot fits into social relations or meanings. The argot gives a researcher clues to what is important to members and how they see the world. For example, Douglas (1976:125) discovered the term *vultching* in a study of nude beaches. It was a member's label for the practice of some males who sat around an attractive nude woman on the beach.

In their study of sales practices of a vacation condominium ownership firm, Katovich and Diamond (1986) conducted observations and informal interviews over six months when one researcher was employed and the other was a trainee. They analyzed the salesroom as a stage in which a series of events are presented to prospective buyers and discussed the argot used. For example, "drops" occurred when the finance manager enters and "drops" information during a discussion between the salesperson and potential buyers. The purpose of such staged events is to stimulate sales. Common revelations were: A major corporation that bought 20 units just decided it only needed 15, so 5 are suddenly available at a special price; a previous client was denied financing, so a property can be offered at a reduced price; or only a few charter members can qualify for a special deal.

A field researcher translates back and forth between the field argot and the outside world. James Spradley (1970:80) provided an example of argot when quoting an "urban nomad" he studied as saying, "If a man hasn't made the bucket, he isn't a tramp." This translates: A man is not considered a true member of the subculture (i.e., a tramp) until he has been arrested for public drunkenness and spent the night in the city or county jail (i.e., "made the bucket"). After a researcher has been in the field for some time, he or she may feel comfortable using the argot, but it is unwise to use the argot too soon and risk looking foolish.

Taking Notes

Most field research data are in the form of field notes. Good notes are the bricks and mortar of field research (Fetterman, 1989). Full field notes can contain maps, diagrams, photographs, interviews, tape recordings, videotapes, memos, objects from the field, notes jotted in the field, and detailed notes written away from the field.

A field researcher expects to fill many notebooks or file cabinets, or the equivalent in computer memory. He or she spends more time writing notes than being in the field. Some researchers produce 40 single-spaced pages of notes for three hours of observation. With practice, even a new field researcher can produce several pages of notes for each hour in the field.

Writing notes is often boring, tedious work that requires self-discipline. The notes contain extensive descriptive detail drawn from memory. A researcher makes it a daily habit or compulsion to write notes immediately after leaving the field. The notes must be neat and organized because the researcher will return to them over and over again. Once written, the notes are private and valuable. A researcher treats them with care and protects confidentiality. Members have the right to remain anonymous, and researchers often use *pseudonyms* (false names) in notes. Field notes may be of interest to hostile parties, blackmailers, or legal officials, so some researchers write field notes in code.

A researcher's state of mind, level of attention, and conditions in the field affect note taking. He or she will usually begin with relatively short one- to three-hour periods in the field before writing notes. Johnson (1975:187) remarked,

> *The quantity and quality of the observational records vary with the field worker's feelings of restedness or exhaustion, reactions to particular events, relations with others, consumption of alcoholic beverages, the number of discrete observations, and so forth.*

Types of Field Notes. Field researchers take notes in many ways.[35] The recommendations here (also see Box 14.3) are suggestions. Full field notes have several types or levels. Five levels will be described. It is usually best to keep all the notes for an observation period together and to distinguish types of notes by separate pages. Some researchers include inferences with direct observations if they are set off by a visible device such as brackets or colored ink. The quantity of notes varies across types. For example, six hours

Box 14.3 _____

Recommendations for Taking Field Notes

1. Record notes as soon as possible after each period in the field, and do not talk with others until observations are recorded.
2. Begin the record of each field visit with a new page, with the date and time noted.
3. Use jotted notes only as a temporary memory aid, with key words or terms, or the first and last things said.
4. Use wide margins to make it easy to add to notes at any time. Go back and add to the notes if you remember something later.
5. Plan to type notes and keep each level of notes separate so it will be easy to go back to them later.
6. Record events in the order in which they occurred, and note how long they last (e.g., a 15-minute wait, a one-hour ride).
7. Make notes as concrete, complete, and comprehensible as possible.
8. Use frequent paragraphs and quotation marks. Exact recall of phrases is best, with double quotes; use single quotes for paraphrasing.
9. Record small talk or routines that do not appear to be significant at the time; they may become important later.
10. "Let your feelings flow" and write quickly without worrying about spelling or "wild ideas." Assume that no one else will see the notes, but use pseudonyms.
11. Never substitute tape recordings completely for field notes.
12. Include diagrams or maps of the setting, and outline your own movements and those of others during the period of observation.
13. Include the researcher's own words and behavior in the notes. Also record emotional feelings and private thoughts in a separate section.
14. Avoid evaluative summarizing words. Instead of "The sink looked disgusting," say, "The sink was rust-stained and looked as if it had not been cleaned in a long time. Pieces of food and dirty dishes looked as if they had been piled in it for several days."
15. Reread notes periodically and record ideas generated by the rereading.
16. Always make one or more backup copies, keep them in a locked location, and store the copies in different places in case of fire.

---

in the field might result in 1 page of jotted notes, 40 pages of direct observation, 5 pages of researcher inference, and 2 pages total for methodological, theoretical, and personal notes.

Jotted Notes. It is nearly impossible to take good notes in the field. Even a known observer in a public setting looks strange when furiously writing. More important, when looking down and writing, the researcher cannot see and hear what is happening. The attention given to note writing is taken from field observation where it belongs. The specific setting determines whether any notes in the field can be taken. The researcher may be able to write, and members may expect it, or he or she may have to be secretive (e.g., go to the restroom).

Jotted notes are written in the field. They are short, temporary memory triggers such as words,

phrases, or drawings taken inconspicuously, often scribbled on any convenient item (e.g., napkin, matchbook). They are incorporated into direct observation notes but are never substituted for them.

Direct Observation Notes. The basic source of field data are notes a researcher writes immediately after leaving the field, which he or she can add to later. The notes should be ordered chronologically with the date, time, and place on each entry. They serve as a detailed description of what the researcher heard and saw in concrete, specific terms. To the extent possible, they are an exact recording of the particular words, phrases, or actions.

A researcher's memory improves with practice. A new researcher can soon remember exact phrases from the field. Verbatim statements should be written with double quote marks to distinguish them from paraphrases. Dialogue accessories (nonverbal communication, props, tone, speed, volume, gestures) should be recorded as well. A researcher records what was actually said and does not clean it up; notes include ungrammatical speech, slang, and misstatements (e.g., write, "Uh, I'm goin' home Sal," not "I am going home, Sally").

A researcher puts concrete details in notes, not summaries. For example, instead of, "We talked about sports," he or she writes, "Anthony argued with Sam and Jason. He said that the Cubs would win next week because they traded for a new shortstop, Chiappetta. He also said that the team was better than the Mets, who he thought had inferior infielders. He cited last week's game where the Cubs won against Boston by 8 to 3." A researcher notes who was present, what happened, where it occurred, when, and under what circumstances. New researchers may not take notes because "nothing important happened." An experienced researcher knows that events when "nothing happened" can reveal a lot. For example, members may express feelings and organize experience into folk categories even in trivial conversations.

Researcher Inference Notes. A field researcher listens to members in order to "climb into their skin" or "walk in their shoes."[36] This involves a three-step process. The researcher listens without applying analytical categories; he or she compares what is heard to what was heard at other times and to what others say; then the researcher applies his or her own interpretation to infer or figure out what it means. In ordinary interaction, we do all three steps simultaneously and jump quickly to our own inferences. A field researcher learns to look and listen without inferring or imposing an interpretation. His or her observations without inferences go into *direct observation notes.*

A researcher records inferences in a separate section that is keyed to direct observations. People never see social relationships, emotions, or meaning. They see specific physical actions and hear words; then they use background cultural knowledge, clues from the context, and what

is done or said to assign social meaning. For example, one does not see *love* or *anger*; one sees and hears specific actions (red face, loud voice, wild gestures, obscenities) and draw inferences from them (the person is angry).

People constantly infer social meaning on the basis of what they see and hear, but not always correctly. For example, my niece visited me and accompanied me to a store to buy a kite. The clerk at the cash register smiled and asked her whether she and her "Daddy" (looking at me) were going to fly the kite that day. The clerk observed our interaction, then inferred a father/daughter, not an uncle/niece relationship. She saw and heard a male adult and a female child, but she inferred the social meaning incorrectly.

A researcher keeps inferred meaning separate from direct observation because the meaning of actions is not always self-evident. Sometimes, people try to deceive others. For example, an unrelated couple register at a motel as Mr. and Mrs. Smith. More frequently, social behavior is ambiguous or multiple meanings are possible. For example, I see a white male and female, both in their late twenties, get out of a car and enter a restaurant together. They sit at a table, order a meal, and talk with serious expressions in hushed tones, sometimes leaning forward to hear each other. As they get up to leave, the woman, who has a sad facial expression and appears ready to cry, is briefly hugged by the male. They then leave together. Did I witness a couple breaking up, two friends discussing a third, two people trying to decide what to do because they have discovered that their spouses are having an affair with each other, or a brother and sister whose father just died? The *separation of inference* allows multiple meanings to arise upon rereading direct observation notes. If a researcher records inferred meaning without separation, he or she loses other possible meanings.

Analytic Notes. Researchers make many decisions about how to proceed while in the field. Some acts are planned (e.g., to conduct an interview, to observe a particular activity) and others attempted. Field researchers keep methodological ideas in analytic notes to record their plans, tactics, ethical and procedural decisions, and self-critiques of tactics.

Theory emerges in field research during data collection and is clarified when a researcher reviews field notes. Analytic notes have a running account of a researcher's attempts to give meaning to field events. He or she thinks out loud in the notes by suggesting links between ideas, creating hypotheses, proposing conjectures, and developing new concepts.

Analytic memos are part of the theoretical notes. They are systematic digressions into theory, where a researcher elaborates on ideas in depth, expands on ideas while still in the field, and modifies or develops more complex theory by rereading and thinking about the memos.

Personal Notes. As discussed earlier, personal feelings and emotional reactions become part of the data and color what a researcher sees or hears in the field. A researcher keeps a section of notes that is like a personal diary. He or she records personal life events and feelings in it ("I'm tense today, I wonder if it's because of the fight I had yesterday with . . ."; "I've got a headache on this gloomy, overcast day").

Personal notes serve three functions: They provide an outlet for a researcher and a way to cope with stress; they are a source of data about personal reactions; they give him or her a way to evaluate direct observation or inference notes when the notes are later reread. For example, if the researcher was in a good mood during observations, it might color what he or she observed (see Figure 14.2).

Maps and Diagrams. Field researchers often make maps and draw diagrams or pictures of the features of a field site.[37] This serves two purposes: It helps a researcher organize events in the field and it helps convey a field site to others. For example, a researcher observing a bar with 15 stools may draw and number 15 circles to simplify recording (e.g., "Yosuke came in and sat on stool 12, Phoebe was already on stool 10"). Field researchers find three types of maps helpful: spatial, social, and temporal. The first helps orient the data; the latter two are preliminary forms of data analysis. A *spatial map* locates people, equipment, and the like in terms of geographical physical space to show where activities occur (Figure 14.3A). A *social map* shows the number or variety of people and the arrangements among them of power, influence, friendship, and/or division of labor (Figure 14.3B). A *temporal map* shows the ebb and flow

Direct Observation	Inference	Analytic	Personal Journal
Sunday, October 4. Kay's Kafe 3:00 pm. Large white male in mid 40's, overweight, enters. He wears worn brown suit. He is alone; sits at booth #2. Kay comes by asks, "What'll it be?" Man says, "Coffee, black for now." She leaves and he lights cigarette and reads menu. 3:15 pm. Kay turns on radio.	Kay seems friendly today, humming. She becomes solemn and watchful. I think she puts on the radio when nervous.	Women are afraid of men who come in alone since the robbery.	It is raining. I am feeling comfortable with Kay but am bored today.

FIGURE 14.2 Types of Field Notes

A Spatial Map

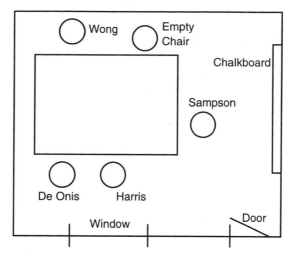

B Social Map

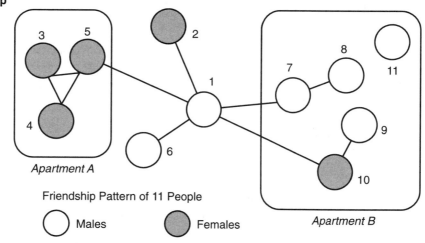

Friendship Pattern of 11 People

○ Males   ● Females

Apartment A

Apartment B

C Temporal Map

Day of Week, Buzz's Bar

	Mon	Tue	Wed	Thr	Fri	Sat
Open 10:00	Old Drunks	Old Drunks	Old Drunks	Old Drunks	Skip Work or Leave Early	Going to Fish
5:00	Football Watchers	Neighbors and Bridge Players	Softball Team (All-Male Night)	Young Crowd	Loud Music, Mixed Crowd	Loners and No Dates
Close 1:00						

FIGURE 14.3 Types of Maps Used in Field Research

of people, goods, services, and communications, or schedules (Figure 14.3C).

Machine Recordings to Supplement Memory. Tape recorders and videotapes can be helpful supplements in field research. They never substitute for field notes or a researcher's presence in the field. They cannot be introduced into all field sites, and can be used only after a researcher develops rapport. Recorders and videotapes provide a close approximation to what occurred and a permanent record that others can review. They help a researcher recall events and observe what does not happen, or nonresponses, which are easy to miss. Nevertheless, these items create disruption and an increased awareness of surveillance. Researchers who rely on them must address associated problems (e.g., ensure that batteries are fresh and there are enough blank tapes). Also, relistening to or viewing tapes can be time consuming. For example, it may take over 50 hours to listen to 50 hours recorded in the field. Transcriptions of tape are expensive and not always accurate; they do not always convey subtle contextual meanings or mumbled words.[38]

Interview Notes. If a researcher conducts field interviews (to be discussed), he or she keeps the interview notes separate.[39] In addition to recording questions and answers, he or she creates a *face sheet.* This is a page at the beginning of the notes with information such as the date, place of interview, characteristics of interviewee, content of the interview, and so on. It helps the interviewer when rereading and making sense of the notes.

Data Quality

The Meaning of Quality. What does the term *high-quality data* mean in field research, and what does a researcher do to get such data?[40] For a quantitative researcher, high-quality data are reliable and valid; they give precise, consistent measures of the same "objective" truth for all researchers. An interpretive approach suggests a different kind of data quality. Instead of assuming one single, objective truth, field researchers hold

that members subjectively interpret experiences within a social context. What a member takes to be true results from social interaction and interpretation. Thus, high-quality field data capture such processes and provide an understanding of the member's viewpoint.

A field researcher does not eliminate subjective views to get quality data; rather, quality data include his or her subjective responses and experiences. Quality field data are detailed descriptions from the researcher's immersion and authentic experiences in the social world of members.[41]

Reliability in Field Research. The reliability of field data addresses the question: Are researcher observations about a member or field event internally and externally consistent? *Internal consistency* refers to whether the data are plausible given all that is known about a person or event, eliminating common forms of human deception. In other words, do the pieces fit together into a coherent picture? For example, are a member's actions consistent over time and in different social contexts?

External consistency is achieved by verifying or cross-checking observations with other, divergent sources of data. In other words, does it all fit into the overall context? For example, can others verify what a researcher observed about a person? Does other evidence confirm the researcher's observations?

Reliability in field research also includes what is not said or done, but is expected or anticipated. Such omissions or null data can be significant but are difficult to detect. For example, when observing a cashier end her shift, a researcher notices that the money in a drawer is not counted. He or she may notice the omission only if other cashiers always count money at the end of the shift.

Reliability in field research depends on a researcher's insight, awareness, suspicions, and questions. He or she looks at members and events from different angles (legal, economic, political, personal) and mentally asks questions: Where does the money come from for that? What do those people do all day?

Field researchers depend on what members tell them. This makes the credibility of members and their statements part of reliability. To check member credibility, a researcher asks: Does the person have a reason to lie? Is she in a position to know that? What are the person's values and how might that shape what she says? Is he just saying that to please me? Is there anything that might limit his spontaneity?

Field researchers take subjectivity and context into account as they evaluate credibility. They know that a person's statements or actions are affected by subjective perceptions. Statements are made from a particular point of view and colored by an individual's experiences. Instead of evaluating each statement to see if it is true, a field researcher finds statements useful in themselves. Even inaccurate statements and actions can be revealing from a researcher's perspective.

As mentioned before, actions and statements are shaped by the context in which they appear. What is said in one setting may differ in other contexts. For example, when asked "Do you dance?" a member may say no in a public setting full of excellent dancers, but yes in a semiprivate setting with few good dancers and different music. It is not that the member is lying but that the answer is shaped by the context.

Other obstacles to reliability include behaviors that can mislead a researcher: misinformation, evasions, lies, and fronts.[42] *Misinformation* is an unintended falsehood caused by the uncertainty and complexity of life. For example, nurses in a hospital state something as "official hospital policy" when, in fact, there is no such written policy.

Evasions are intentional acts of avoiding or not revealing information. Common evasions include not answering questions, answering a different question than was asked, switching topics, or answering in a purposefully vague and ambiguous manner. For example, a salesman appears uncomfortable when the topic of using call girls to get customers comes up at a dinner party. He says, "Yes, a lot of people use them." But later, alone, after careful questioning, the salesman is drawn out and reveals that he himself uses the practice.

Lies are untruths intended to mislead or to give a false view. For example, a gang member gives the researcher a false name and address, or a church minister gives an inflated membership figure in order to look more successful. Douglas (1976:73) noted, "In all other research settings I've known about in any detail, lying was common, both among members and to researchers, especially about the things that were really important to the members."

Fronts are shared and learned lies and deceptions. They can include the use of physical props and collaborators. For example, a bar is really a place to make illegal bets. The bar appears legitimate and sells drinks, but its true business is revealed only by careful investigation. A common example is that of Santa Claus—a "front" put on for small children.

Validity in Field Research. Validity in field research is the confidence placed in a researcher's analysis and data as accurately representing the social world in the field. Replicability is not a criterion because field research is virtually impossible to replicate. Essential aspects of the field change: The social events and context change, the members are different, the individual researcher differs, and so on. There are four kinds of validity or tests of research accuracy: ecological validity, natural history, member validation, and competent insider performance.

Ecological validity is the degree to which the social world described by a researcher matches the world of members. It asks: Is the natural setting described relatively undisturbed by the researcher's presence or procedures? A project has ecological validity if events would have occurred without a researcher's presence.

Natural history is a detailed description of how the project was conducted. It is a full and candid disclosure of a researcher's actions, assumptions, and procedures for others to evaluate. A project is valid in terms of natural history if outsiders see and accept the field site and the researcher's actions.

Member validation occurs when a researcher takes field results back to members, who judge their adequacy. A project is member valid if members recognize and understand the researcher's description as reflecting their intimate social world. Member validation has limitations because conflicting perspectives in a setting produce disagreement with researcher's observations, and members may object when results do not portray their group in a favorable light. In addition, members may not recognize the description because it is not from their perspective or does not fit with their purposes.[43]

Competent insider performance is the ability of a nonmember to interact effectively as a member or pass as one. This includes the ability to tell and understand insider jokes. A valid field project gives enough of a flavor of the social life in the field, and sufficient detail so that an outsider can act as a member. Its limitation is that it is not possible to know the social rules for every situation. Also, an outsider might be able to pass simply because members are being polite and do not want to point out social mistakes.[44]

Focusing and Sampling

Focusing. The field researcher first gets a general picture, then focuses on a few specific problems or issues (see Figure 14.4).[45] A researcher decides on specific research questions and develops hypotheses only after being in the field and experiencing it firsthand. At first, everything seems relevant; later, however, selective attention focuses on specific questions and themes.

Sampling. Field research sampling differs from survey research sampling, although sometimes both use snowball sampling (see Chapter 9).[46] A field researcher samples by taking a smaller, selective set of observations from all possible observations. It is called *theoretical sampling* because it is guided by the researcher's developing theory. Field researchers sample times, situations, types of events, locations, types of people, or contexts of interest.

For example, a researcher samples time by observing a setting at different times. He or she observes at all times of the day, on every day of the week, and in all seasons to get a full sense of how the field site stays the same or changes. It is often best to overlap when sampling (e.g., to have sampling times from 7:00 A.M. to 9:00 A.M., from 8:00 A.M. to 10:00 A.M., from 9:00 A.M. to 11:00 A.M., etc.).

A researcher samples locations because one location may give depth, but a narrow perspective. Sitting or standing in different locations helps the researcher get a sense of the whole site. For example, the peer-to-peer behavior of school teachers usually occurs in a faculty lounge, but it also occurs at a local bar when teachers gather or in a classroom temporarily used for a teacher meeting. In addition, researchers trace the paths of members to various field locations.

Field researchers sample people by focusing their attention or interaction on different kinds of people (old-timers and newcomers, old and young, males and females, leaders and followers). As a researcher identifies types of people, or people with opposing outlooks, he or she tries to interact with and learn about all types.

For example, a researcher samples three kinds of field events: routine, special, and unanticipated. Routine events (e.g., opening up a store for business) happen every day and should not be considered unimportant simply because they are routine. Special events (e.g., annual office party) are announced and planned in advance. They focus member attention and reveal aspects of social life not otherwise visible. Unanticipated events are those that just happen to occur while a researcher is present (e.g., unsupervised workers when the man-

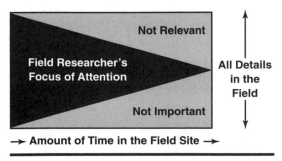

FIGURE 14.4 Focusing in Field Research

ager gets sick and cannot oversee workers at a store for a day). In this case, the researcher sees something unusual, unplanned, or rare by chance.

THE FIELD RESEARCH INTERVIEW

So far, you have learned how field researchers observe and take notes. They also interview members, but field interviews differ from survey research interviews. This section introduces the field interview.

The Field Interview

Field researchers use unstructured, nondirective, in-depth interviews, which differ from formal survey research interviews in many ways (see Table 14.2).[47] The field interview involves asking questions, listening, expressing interest, and recording what was said.

The field interview is a joint production of a researcher and a member. Members are active participants whose insights, feelings, and cooperation are essential parts of a discussion process that reveals subjective meanings. "The interviewer's presence and form of involvement—how she or he listens, attends, encourages, interrupts, digresses, initiates topics, and terminates responses—is integral to the respondent's account" (Mishler, 1986:82).

Field research interviews go by many names: unstructured, depth, ethnographic, open ended, informal, and long. Generally, they involve one or more people being present, occur in the field, are

TABLE 14.2 Field Research Interviews versus Survey Interviews

TYPICAL SURVEY INTERVIEW	TYPICAL FIELD INTERVIEW
1. It has a clear beginning and end.	1. The beginning and end are not clear. The interview can be picked up later.
2. The same standard questions are asked of all respondents in the same sequence.	2. The questions and the order in which they are asked are tailored to specific people and situations.
3. The interviewer appears neutral at all times.	3. The interviewer shows interest in responses, encourages elaboration.
4. The interviewer asks questions, and the respondent answers.	4. It is like a friendly conversational exchange, but with more interviewer questions.
5. It is almost always with one respondent alone.	5. It can occur in group setting or with others in area, but varies.
6. It has a professional tone and businesslike focus; diversions are ignored.	6. It is interspersed with jokes, asides, stories, diversions, and anecdotes, which are recorded.
7. Closed-ended questions are common, with rare probes.	7. Open-ended questions are common, and probes are frequent.
8. The interviewer alone controls the pace and direction of interview.	8. The interviewer and member jointly control the pace and direction of the interview.
9. The social context in which the interview occurs is ignored and assumed to make little difference.	9. The social context of the interview is noted and seen as important for interpreting the meaning of responses.
10. The interviewer attempts to mold the communication pattern into a standard framework.	10. The interviewer adjusts to the member's norms and language usage.

Source: Adapted from Briggs (1986), Denzin (1989), Douglas (1985), Mishier (1986), Spradley (1979a).

informal and nondirective (i.e., the respondent may take the interview in various directions) (see Fontana and Frey, 1994).

A field interview involves a mutual sharing of experiences. A researcher might share his or her background to build trust and encourage the informant to open up, but does not force answers or use leading questions. She or he encourages and guides a process of mutual discovery.

In field interviews, members express themselves in the forms in which they normally speak, think, and organize reality. A researcher retains members' jokes and narrative stories in their natural form and does not repackage them into a standardized format. The focus is on the member's perspective and experiences. In order to stay close to the member's experience, the researcher asks questions in terms of concrete examples or situations—for example, "Could you tell me things that led up to your quitting in June?" instead of "Why did you quit your job?"

Field interviews occur in a series over time. A researcher begins by building rapport and steering conversation away from evaluative or highly sensitive topics. He or she avoids probing inner feelings until intimacy is established, and even then, the researcher expects apprehension. After several meetings, he or she may be able to probe more deeply into sensitive issues and seek clarification of less sensitive issues. In later interviews, he or she may return to topics and check past answers by restating them in a nonjudgmental tone and asking for verification—for example. "The last time we talked, you said that you started taking things from the store after they reduced your pay. Is that right?"

The field interview is a "speech event," closer to a friendly conversation than the stimulus/response model found in a survey research interview (see Chapter 10). You are familiar with a friendly conversation, which has its own informal rules and the following elements: (1) a greeting ("Hi, it's good to see you again"); (2) the absence of an explicit goal or purpose (we don't say, "Let's now discuss what we did last weekend"); (3) avoidance of repetition (we don't say, "Could you clarify what you said about . . ."); (4) ques-

tion asking ("Did you see the race yesterday?"); (5) expressions of interest ("Really? I wish I could have been there!"); (6) expressions of ignorance ("No, I missed it. What happened?"); (7) turn taking, so the encounter is balanced (one person does not always ask questions and the other only answer); (8) abbreviations ("I missed the Derby, but I'm going to the Indy," not "I missed the Kentucky Derby horse race but I will go to the Indianapolis 500 automotive race"); (9) a pause or brief silence when neither person talks is acceptable; (10) a closing (we don't say, "Let's end this conversation"; instead, we give a verbal indicator before physically leaving—"I've got to get back to work now. See ya tomorrow.").

The field interview differs from a friendly conversation. It has an explicit purpose—to learn about the informant and setting. A researcher includes explanations or requests that diverge from friendly conversations. For example, he or she may say, "I'll like to ask you about. . . ," or "Could you look at this and see if I've written it down right?" The field interview is less balanced. A higher proportion of questions come from the researcher, who expresses more ignorance and interest. Also, it includes repetition, and a researcher asks the member to elaborate on unclear abbreviations.[48]

Field research interviewers watch for markers. A *marker* in a field interview is "a passing reference made by a respondent to an important event or feeling state" (Weiss, 1994:77). For example, during an interview with a 45-year-old physician, the interviewee mentions casually, while describing having difficulty in a high school class, "It was about that time that my sister was seriously injured in a car accident." Maybe the person never said anything about the sister or the accident before. By dropping it in, the respondent is indicating it was an important event at the time. A researcher should pick up on a marker and later may ask, "Earlier, you mentioned that your sister was seriously injured in a car accident. Could you tell me more about that?" Most importantly, the interviewer listens. He or she does not interrupt frequently, repeatedly finish the respondent's sentences, offer associations (e.g., "Oh, that is just like X"), insist on finishing asking a question that the respondent has begun to answer, fight for control over the interview process, or stay with a line of thought and ignore new leads (see Weiss, 1994:78).

Life History

Life history or a biographical interview is a special type of field interviewing. It overlaps with oral history (see Chapter 15).[49] There are multiple purposes for stories of the past and these may shape the forms of interview (see Smith, 1994). In a life history interview, researchers interview and gather documentary material about a particular individual's life, usually someone who is old. "The concept of *life story* is used to designate the retrospective information itself without the corroborative evidence often implied by the term *life history*" (Tagg, 1985:163). Researchers ask open-ended questions to capture how the person understands his or her own past. Exact accuracy in the story is less critical than the story itself. Researcher recognize that the person may reconstruct or add present interpretations to the past; the person may "rewrite" his or her story. The main purpose is to get at how the respondent sees/remembers the past, not just some kind of objective truth.

Researchers sometimes use a life story grid in which they ask the person what happened at various dates and in several areas of life. A grid may consist of categories such as migration, occupation, education, or family events for each of a dozen ages in the person's life. Researchers often supplement the interview information with artifacts (e.g., old photos) and may present them during the interview to stimulate discussion or recollection. "Life writing as an empirical exercise feeds on data: letters, documents, interviews" (Smith, 1994:290). McCraken (1988:20) gave an example of how objects aided the interview by helping him understand how the person being interviewed saw things. When interviewing a 75-year-old woman in her living room, McCraken initially thought the room just contained a lot of cluttered physical objects. After having the woman explain the meaning of each item, it was clear that she saw each as a memorial or a memento. The room was a museum to key events in her life. Only after the author looked at the objects in this new way did he begin to see the furniture and objects not a inanimate things but as objects that radiated meaning.

Sometimes, researchers find an existing archive with a person; other times, they must search out the documents and create an archive. Locating such documentary data can be a tremendous task, followed by that of carefully reviewing, cataloging, and organizing the information. The interview and documentary data together form the basis of the life story.

Types of Questions in Field Interviews

Field researchers ask three types of questions in a field interview: descriptive, structural, and contrast questions. All are asked concurrently, but each type is more frequent at a different stage in the research process (see Figure 14.5). During the early stage, a researcher primarily asks descriptive questions. He or she gradually adds structural questions until, in the middle stage after analysis has begun, they make up a majority of the questions. Contrast questions appear in the middle of a field research study and increase until, by the end, they are asked more than any other type.[50]

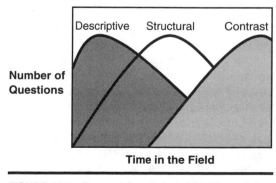

FIGURE 14.5 Types of Questions in Field Research

A researcher asks a *descriptive question* to explore the setting and learn about members. Descriptive questions can be about time and space—for example, "Where is the bathroom?" "When does the delivery truck arrive?" "What happened Monday night?" They can also be about people and activities: "Who is sitting by the window?" "What is your uncle like?" "What happens during the initiation ceremony?" They can be about objects: "When do you use a saber saw?" "Which tools do you carry with you on an emergency water leak job?" Questions asking for examples or experiences are descriptive questions—for example, "Could you give me an example of a great date?" "What were your experiences as a postal clerk?" Descriptive questions may ask about hypothetical situations: "If a student opened her book during the exam, how would you deal with it?" Another type of descriptive question asks members about the argot of the setting: "What do you call a deputy sheriff?" (The answer is: a "county mounty.")

A researcher uses *structural questions* after spending time in the field and starting to analyze data, especially with a domain analysis (to be discussed in Chapter 16). It begins after a researcher organizes specific field events, situations, and conversations into conceptual categories. For example, a researcher's observations of a highway truck-stop restaurant revealed that the employees informally classify customers who patronize the truck stop. In a preliminary analysis, he or she creates a conceptual category of kinds of customers and has members verify the categories with structural questions.

One way to pose a structural question is to ask the members whether a category includes elements in addition to those already identified by a researcher—for example, "Are there any types of customers other than regulars, greasers, pit stoppers, and long haulers?" In addition, a researcher asks for confirmation: "Is a greaser a type of customer that you serve?" "Would you call a customer who . . . a greaser?" "Would a pit stopper ever eat a three-course dinner?"

The *contrast question* builds on the analysis that has been verified by structural questions.

Questions focus on similarities or differences between elements in categories or between categories as the researcher asks members to verify similarities and differences: "You seem to have a number of different kinds of customers come in here. I've heard you call some customers 'regulars' and others 'pit stoppers.' How are a regular and a pit stopper alike?" or "Is the difference between a long hauler and a greaser that the greaser doesn't tip?" or "Two types of customers just stop to use the restroom—entire families and a lone male. Do you call both pit stoppers?"

Informants

An informant or key actor in field research is a member with whom a field researcher develops a relationship and who tells about, or informs on, the field.[51] Who makes a good informant? The ideal informant has four characteristics:

1. A member who is totally familiar with the culture and is in position to witness significant events makes a good informant. He or she lives and breathes the culture and engages in routines in the setting without thinking about them. The individual has years of intimate experience in the culture; he or she not a novice.

2. A member who is currently involved in the field makes a good informant. Ex-members who have reflected on the field may provide useful insights, but the longer they have been away from direct involvement, the more likely it is that they have reconstructed their recollections.

3. A member who can spend time with the researcher makes a better informant. Interviewing may take many hours, and some members are simply not available for extensive interviewing.

4. Nonanalytic members make better informants. A nonanalytic informant is familiar with and uses native folk theory or pragmatic common sense. This is in contrast to the analytic member, who preanalyzes the setting, using categories from the media or education. Even members educated in the social sciences can learn to

respond in a nonanalytic manner, but only if they set aside their education and use the member perspective.

A field researcher may interview several types of informants. Contrasting types of informants who provide useful perspectives include rookies and old-timers, people in the center of events and those on the fringes of activity, people who recently changed status (e.g., through promotion) and those who are static, frustrated or needy people and happy or secure people, the leader in charge and the subordinate who follows. A field researcher expects mixed messages when he or she interviews a range of informants.

Interview Context

Field researchers recognize that a conversation in a private office may not occur in a crowded lunchroom.[52] Often, interviews take place in the member's home environment so that he or she is comfortable. This is not always best. If a member is preoccupied or there is no privacy, a researcher will move to another setting (e.g., restaurant, university office).

The interview's meaning is shaped by its Gestalt or whole interaction of a researcher and a member in a specific context. For example, a researcher notes nonverbal forms of communication (e.g., shrugs, gestures) that add meaning.

> The investigator should note important facts that will not appear on the record of the interview itself, be it a tape recording or a video recording or a set of notes. Detailed notes on the setting, the participants, time of day, ongoing social or ritual events, and so forth should be complemented by the researcher's perceptions of the interaction. (Briggs, 1986:104)

LEAVING THE FIELD

Work in the field can last for a few weeks to a dozen years.[53] In either case, at some point work in the field ends. Some researchers (e.g., Schatzman and Strauss) suggest that the end comes naturally when theory building ceases or

reaches a closure; others (e.g., Bogdan and Taylor) feel that fieldwork could go on without end and that a firm decision to cut off relations is needed.

Experienced field researchers anticipate a process of disengaging and exiting the field. Depending on the intensity of involvement and the length of time in the field, the process can be disruptive or emotionally painful for both the researcher and the members. A researcher may experience the emotional pain of breaking intimate friendships when leaving the field. He or she may feel guilty and depressed immediately before and after leaving. He or she may find it difficult to let go because of personal and emotional entanglements. If the involvement in the field was intense and long, and the field site differed from his or her native culture, the researcher may need months of adjustment before feeling at home with his or her original cultural surroundings.

Once a researcher decides to leave—because the project reaches a natural end and little new is being learned, or because external factors force it to end (e.g., end of a job, gatekeepers order the researcher out)—he or she chooses a method of exiting. The researcher can leave by a quick exit (simply not return one day) or slowly withdraw, reducing his or her involvement over weeks. He or she also needs to decide how to tell members and how much advance warning to give.

The exit process depends on the specific field setting and the relationships developed. In general, a researcher lets members know a short period ahead of time. He or she fulfills any bargains or commitments that were built up and leaves with a clean slate. Sometimes, a ritual or ceremony, such as a going-away party or shaking hands with everyone, helps signal the break for members. Maintaining friendships with members is also possible and is preferred by feminist researchers.

A field researcher is aware that leaving affects members. Some members may feel hurt or rejected because a close social relationship is ending. They may react by trying to pull a researcher back into the field and make him or her more of a member, or they may become angry and resentful. They may grow cool and distant because of an awareness that the researcher is really an outsider. In any case, fieldwork is not finished until the process of disengagement and exiting is complete.

ETHICAL DILEMMAS OF FIELD RESEARCH

The direct personal involvement of a field researcher in the social lives of other people raises many ethical dilemmas. The dilemmas arise when a researcher is alone in the field and has little time to make a moral decision. Although he or she may be aware of general ethical issues before entering the field, they arise unexpectedly in the course of observing and interacting in the field. We will look at five ethical issues in field research: deception, confidentiality, involvement with deviants, the powerful, and publishing reports.[54]

Deception

Deception arises in several ways in field research: The research may be covert; or may assume a false role, name, or identity; or may mislead members in some way. The most hotly debated of the ethical issues arising from deception is that of covert versus overt field research.[55] Some support it (Douglas, 1976; Johnson, 1975) and see it as necessary for entering into and gaining a full knowledge of many areas of social life. Others oppose it (Erikson, 1970) and argue that it undermines a trust between researchers and society. Although its moral status is questionable, there are some field sites or activities that can only be studied covertly.

Covert research is never preferable and never easier than overt research because of the difficulties of maintaining a front and the constant fear of getting caught. As Lofland and Lofland (1995:35) noted, "As in all other ethical dilemmas of naturalistic research, we believe that the ethically sensitive, thoughtful and knowledgeable investigator is the best judge of whether covert research is justified."

Confidentiality

A researcher learns intimate knowledge from the field that is given in confidence. He or she has a moral obligation to uphold the confidentiality of data. This includes keeping information confidential from others in the field and disguising members' names in field notes.

Involvement with Deviants

Researchers who conduct field research on deviants who engage in illegal behavior face additional dilemmas. They know of and are sometimes involved in illegal activity. Fetterman (1989) called this *guilty knowledge*. Such knowledge is of interest not only to law enforcement officials, but also to other deviants. The researcher faces a dilemma of building trust and rapport with the deviants, yet not becoming so involved as to violate his or her basic personal moral standards. Usually, the researcher makes an explicit arrangement with the deviant members. West (1980:38) remarked,

> *I indicated my desire not to participate actively in the relatively risk-prone crimes with victims (e.g., theft, assault) explaining how such behavior was not worth the risk to me or was personally repugnant: I turned down invitations for "cuts in jobs." Although the few occasions when I was accidentally present at the commission of such victim crimes presented invaluable data, my wishes were generally respected and my obvious discomfort resulted in subjects warning me on subsequent occasions.*

The Powerful

Field researchers tend to study those without power in society (e.g., street people, the poor, children, lower level workers in bureaucracies). Powerful elites can block access and have effective gatekeepers. Researchers are criticized for ignoring the powerful, and they are also criticized by the powerful for being biased toward the less powerful. Becker (1970c) explained this by the *hierarchy of credibility*, which says that those who study deviants or low-level subordinates in an organization are viewed as biased, whereas those with authority are assumed to be credible. In groups with hierarchies or organizations, most people assume that those at or near the top have the right to define the way things are going to be, that they have a broader view and are in a position to do something. Thus, "the sociologist who favors officialdom will be spared the accusation of bias" (Becker, 1970c:20). When field researchers become immersed in the world of the less powerful and understand that point of view, they are expressing a rarely heard perspective. They may be accused of bias because they give a voice to parts of society that are not otherwise heard.

Publishing Field Reports

The intimate knowledge that a researcher obtains and reports creates a dilemma between the right of privacy and the right to know. A researcher does not publicize member secrets, violate privacy, or harm reputations. Yet, if he or she cannot publish anything that might offend or harm someone, some of what the researcher learned will remain hidden, and it may be difficult for others to believe general statements if critical details are omitted.

Some researchers suggest asking members to look at a report to verify its accuracy and to approve of their portrayal in print. For marginal groups (e.g., addicts, prostitutes, the mentally ill), this may not be possible, but researchers still have to respect member privacy. On the other hand, censorship or self-censorship can be a danger. A compromise position is that truthful but unflattering material may be published only if it is essential to the researchers' larger arguments.[56]

CONCLUSION

In this chapter, you learned about field research and the field research process (choosing a site and gaining access, relations in the field, observing and collecting data, and the field interview). Field researchers begin data analysis and theorizing during the data collection phase. The emphasis in this chapter has been on what field research involves, its origins, its use, and the overall process.

You can now appreciate implications of saying that in field research, the researcher is directly involved with those being studied and is immersed in a natural setting. Doing field research usually has a greater impact on the researcher's emotions, personal life, and sense of self than doing other types of research. Field research is difficult to conduct. Social researchers use it as a way to study parts of the social world that otherwise could not be studied.

Field research is strongest when a researcher wants to study a small group of people interacting in the present. It is valuable for micro-level or small-group face-to-face interaction. It is less effective when the concern is macro-level processes and social structures. It is nearly useless for events that occurred in the distant past or processes that stretch across decades. Historical-comparative research, discussed in the next chapter, is better suited to investigating these types of concerns.

KEY TERMS

acceptable incompetent	case	ethnography
access ladder	competent insider performance	ethnomethodology
analytic memos	contrast question	external consistency
appearance of interest	defocusing	face sheet
argot	descriptive question	field site
attitude of strangeness	direct observation notes	freeze outs
breakdown	ecological validity	fronts

gatekeeper	marker	pseudonyms
go native	member validation	separation of inference
guilty knowledge	natural history	structural question
hierarchy of credibility	naturalism	theoretical sampling
jotted notes	normalize social research	thick description

REVIEW QUESTIONS

1. What were the two major phases in the development of the Chicago school, and what are the journalistic and anthropological models?

2. List 5 of the 10 things the "methodological pragmatist" field researcher does.

3. Why is it important for a field researcher to read the literature before beginning fieldwork? How does this relate to defocusing?

4. Identify the characteristics of a field site that make it a good one for a beginning field researcher.

5. How does the "presentation of self" affect a field researcher's work?

6. What is the attitude of strangeness, and why is it important?

7. What are relevant considerations when choosing roles in the field, and how can the degree of researcher involvement vary?

8. Identify three ways to ensure quality field research data.

9. Compare differences between a field research and a survey research interview, and between a field interview and a friendly conversation.

10. What are the different types or levels of field notes, and what purpose does each serve?

NOTES

1. See Lofland and Lofland (1995:6;18–19).

2. History of field research: Adler and Adler (1987:8–35), Burgess (1982a), Douglas (1976:39–54), Holy (1984), and Wax (1971:21–41). For additional discussion of the Chicago School, see Blumer (1984) and Faris (1967).

3. Ethnography is described in Agar (1986), Franke (1983), Hammersley and Atkinson (1983), Sanday (1983), and Spradley (1979a:3–12; 1979b:3–16).

4. See Geertz (1973, 1979) on "thick description." Also see Denzin (1989:159–160) for additional discussion.

5. For more on ethnomethodology, see Cicourel (1964), Denzin (1970), Leiter (1980), Mehan and Wood (1975), and Turner (1974). Also see Emerson (1981:357–359) and Lester and Hadden (1980) on the relationship between field research and ethnomethodology. Garfinkel (1974a) discussed the origins of the term *ethnomethodology*.

6. The misunderstandings of people resulting from the disjuncture of different cultures is a common theme. Examples in film include *The Gods Must Be Crazy, Crocodile Dundee*, and *Coming to America*. The disjuncture of class cultures is also a common theme. The most famous example is George Bernard Shaw's play *Pygmalion*, which was later made into the musical *My Fair Lady*. A more recent example is the film *Educating Rita*.

7. For a general discussion of field research and naturalism, see Adler and Adler (1994), Georges and Jones (1980), Holy (1984), and Pearsall (1970). For discussions of contrasting types of field research, see Clammer (1984), Gonor (1977), Holstein and Gubrium (1994), Morse (1994), Schwandt (1994), and Strauss and Corbin (1994).

8. See Georges and Jones (1980:21–42) and Lofland and Lofland (1995:11–15).

9. Johnson (1975:65–66) has discussed defocusing.

10. See Lofland (1976:13–23) and Shaffir et al. (1980:18–20) on feeling marginal.

11. See Adler and Adler (1987:67–78).

12. See Hammersley and Atkinson (1983:42–45) and Lofland and Lofland (1995:16–30).

13. Jewish researchers have studied Christians (Kleinman, 1980), whites have studied blacks (Liebow, 1967), and adult researchers have become intimate with youngsters (Fine, 1987; Fine and Glassner, 1979; Thorne and Luria, 1986). Also see Eichler (1988), Hunt (1984), and Wax (1979) on the role of race, sex, and age in field research.

14. For more on gatekeepers and access, see Beck (1970:11–29), Bogdan and Taylor (1975:30–32), and Wax (1971:367).

15. Adapted from Gray (1980:311). See also Hicks (1984) and Schatzman and Strauss (1973:58–63).

16. Negotiation in the field is discussed in Gans (1982), John Johnson (1975:58–59, 76–77), and Schatzman and Strauss (1973:22–23).

17. Entering and gaining access to field sites with deviant groups is discussed in Becker (1970a:31–38), Lofland and Lofland (1995:31–41), and West (1980). Elite access is discussed by Hoffman (1980) and Spencer (1982). Also see Hammersley and Atkinson (1983:54–76).

18. For more on roles in field settings, see also Barnes (1970:241–244), Emerson (1981:364), Hammersley and Atkinson (1983:88–104), Warren and Rasmussen (1977), and Wax (1979). On dress, see Bogdan and Taylor (1975:45) and Douglas (1973).

19. See Strauss (1987:10–11).

20. See Georges and Jones (1980:105–133) and John Johnson (1975:159). Clarke (1975) noted that it is not necessarily "subjectivism" to recognize this in field research.

21. See Gurevitch (1988), Hammersley and Atkinson (1983), and Schatzman and Strauss (1973:53) on "strangeness" in field research.

22. See Douglas (1976), Emerson (1981:367–368), and John Johnson (1975:124–129) on the question of whether the researcher should always be patient, polite, and considerate.

23. See Wax (1971:13) for a discussion of understanding in field research.

24. For discussions of ascribed status (and, in particular, gender) in field research, see Adler and Adler (1987), Ardener (1984), Ayella (1993), Denzin (1989: 116–118), Douglas (1976), Easterday et al. (1982), Edwards (1993), Lofland and Lofland (1995:23), and Van Maanen (1982).

25. Roy (1970) argued for the "Ernie Pyle" role based on his study of union organizing in the southern United States. In this role, named after a World War II battle journalist, the researcher "goes with the troops" as a type of participant as observer. Trice (1970) discussed the advantages of an outsider role. Schwartz and Schwartz (1969) gave a valuable discussion of roles in participant observation and the effects of various roles.

26. See Gans (1982), Goward (1984b), and Van Maanen (1983b:282–286).

27. See Douglas (1976:216) and Corsino (1987).

28. For discussion of "normalizing," see Gans (1982:57–59), Georges and Jones (1980: 43–164), Hammersley and Atkinson (1983:70–76), Harkess and Warren (1993), J. Johnson (1975), and Wax (1971). Mann (1970) discussed how to teach members about a researcher's role.

29. The acceptable incompetent or learner role is discussed in Bogdan and Taylor (1975:46), Douglas (1976), Hammersley and Atkinson (1983:92–94), and Lofland and Lofland (1995:56).

30. See Warren and Rasmussen (1977) for a discussion of cross-sex tension.

31. Also see Adler and Adler (1987:40–42), Bogdan and Taylor (1975:35–37), Douglas (1976), and Gray (1980:321).

32. See Bogdan and Taylor (1975:50–51), Lofland and Lofland (1995:57–58), Shupe and Bromley (1980), and Wax (1971).

33. See J. Johnson (1975:105–108) for discussion.

34. See Becker and Geer (1970), Spradley (1979a, 1979b), and Schatzman and Strauss (1973) on argot.

35. For more on ways to record and organize field data, see Bogdan and Taylor (1975:60–73), Hammersley and Atkinson (1983:144–173), and Kirk and Miller (1986:49–59).

36. See Schatzman and Strauss (1973:69) on inference.

37. See Denzin (1989:87), Lofland and Lofland (1995:197–201), Stimson (1986), and Schatzman and Strauss (1973:34–36) for discussions of maps in field research.

38. See Albrecht (1985), Bogdan and Taylor (1975:109), Denzin (1989:210–233), and Jackson (1987) for more on taping in field research.

39. See Burgess (1982b), Lofland and Lofland (1995:89–98), and Spradley (1979a, 1979b) on notes for field interviews.

40. For additional discussion of data quality, see Becker (1970b), Dean and Whyte (1969), Douglas (1976:7), Kirk and Miller (1986), and McCall (1969).

41. Douglas (1976:115) argued that it is easier to "lie" with "hard numbers" than with detailed observations of

natural settings, especially if the field data were collected with others and have extensive quotes presented in context.

42. Adapted from Douglas (1976:56–104).

43. See Bloor (1983) and Douglas (1976:126).

44. For more on validity in field research, see Briggs (1986:24), Bogdan and Taylor (1975), Douglas (1976), Sanjek (1990), and Emerson (1981:361–363).

45. See Lofland (1976) and Lofland and Lofland (1995:99–116) for an especially valuable discussion of focusing. Spradley (1979b:100–111) also provides helpful discussion.

46. See Denzin (1989:71–73, 86–92), Glaser and Strauss (1967), Hammersley and Atkinson (1983: 45–53), Honigmann (1982), and Weiss (1994:25–29) on sampling in field research.

47. Discussion of field interviewing can be found in Banaka (1971), Bogdan and Taylor (1975:95–124), Briggs (1986), Burgess (1982c), Denzin (1989: 103–120), Douglas (1985), Lofland and Lofland (1995: 78–88), Spradley (1979a), and Whyte (1982).

48. For more on comparisons with conversations, see Briggs (1986:11), Spradley (1979a:56–68), and Weiss (1994:8).

49. See Denzin (1989:182–209), Nash and McCurdy (1989), Smith (1994), and Tagg (1985) on biographical or life history interviews.

50. The types of questions are adapted from Spradley (1979a, 1979b).

51. Field research informants are discussed in Dean, Eichhorn, and Dean (1969), Kemp and Ellen (1984), Schatzman and Strauss (1973), Spradley (1979a: 46–54), and Whyte (1982).

52. Interview contexts are discussed in Hammersley and Atkinson (1983:112–126) and in Schatzman and Strauss (1973:83–87). Briggs (1986) argued that nontraditional populations and females communicate better in unstructured interviews than with standardized forms of expression.

53. Altheide (1980), Bogdan and Taylor (1975: 75–76), Lofland and Lofland (1995:61), Maines et al. (1980), and Roadburg (1980) discuss leaving the field.

54. Ethical issues are discussed further in the last chapter. Also see Lofland and Lofland (1995:26, 63, 75, 168–177), Miles and Huberman (1994:288–297), and Punch (1986).

55. Covert, sensitive study is discussed in Ayella (1993), Edwards (1993), and Mitchell (1993).

56. See Barnes (1970), Becker (1969), Fichter and Kolb (1970), Goward (1984a), Lofland and Lofland (1995:204–230), Miles and Huberman (1994:298 –307), and Wolcott (1994) on publishing field research results.

RECOMMENDED READINGS

Denzin, Norman K., and Yvonna S. Lincoln (Eds.). (1994). *Handbook of qualitative research.* Thousand Oaks, CA: Sage. This is a comprehensive, up-to-date collection of essays on qualitative research, with special attention to various forms of field research. It is not a "how-to" book like Lofland and Lofland (1995) or Spradley (1979), but social researchers are seriously interested in understanding field research should study this overview of the major issues in modern qualitative research.

Emerson, Robert M. (1983). *Contemporary field research: A collection of readings.* Boston: Little, Brown. There are many books of essays and articles on field research. This one is especially helpful because it includes a variety of approaches to modern field research. It includes essays on the theory or assumptions behind field research as well as discussions of the practical problems in the field.

Lofland, John, and Lyn H. Lofland. (1995). *Analyzing social settings: A guide to qualitative observation and analysis.* 3rd ed. Belmont, CA: Wadsworth. The Loflands are well-respected field researchers. This is a brief introduction to conducting field research for the beginner. The book is short, clearly written, and assumes very little prior knowledge of field research. It includes many practical suggestions for doing field research.

Spradley, James P. (1979). *Participant observation.* New York: Holt, Rinehart and Winston. Spradley was a cultural anthropologist who crossed the fuzzy border between sociological field research and traditional anthropology. This book outlines one approach for conducting participant observation research for the beginner. The book is unusual in that it provides a very systematic, step-by-step, structured method for doing field research.

CHAPTER 15

HISTORICAL-COMPARATIVE RESEARCH

Sociological explanation is necessarily historical. Historical sociology is thus not some special kind of sociology; rather, it is the essence of the discipline.
—Philip Abrams, *Historical Sociology*, p. 2

Thinking without comparisons is unthinkable. And, in the absence of comparisons, so is all scientific thought and all scientific research. No one should be surprised that comparisons, implicit and explicit, pervade the work of social scientists and have done from the beginning.
—Guy Swanson, "Frameworks for Comparative Research," p. 145

INTRODUCTION

The classic social thinkers in the nineteenth century, such as Emile Durkheim, Karl Marx, Max

Weber, who founded the social sciences, used a historical and comparative method. This method is used extensively in a few areas of sociology (e.g., social change, political sociology, social

381

movements, social stratification) and has been applied in many others as well (e.g., religion, criminology, sex roles, race relations, family). Although much social research focuses on current social life in one country, historical and/or comparative studies have become more common in recent years. In his article "Is 1980s Sociology in the Doldrums?" Randall Collins (1986:1346) remarked, "There is no doubt that the last few decades have been the Golden Age of historical and comparative sociology."

Historical-comparative social research is a collection of techniques and approaches. Some blend into traditional history, others extend quantitative social research. The primary focus of this chapter is on the distinct type of social research that puts historical time and/or cross-cultural variation at the center of research—that is, which treats what is studied as part of the flow of history and situated in a cultural context.

A Short History of Historical-Comparative Research

The nineteenth-century founders of sociology conducted historical-comparative (H-C) research. The early H-C works were a blend of sociology, history, political science, and economics.

Beginning in the period prior to World War I, historical-comparative research declined as the social sciences separated. Comparative research was increasingly conducted by anthropologists and historical research by historians. Positivism shaped the thinking of most sociologists, while others turned toward field research. Sociologists conducted little historical-comparative research between World War I and the 1950s. There were a few important exceptions, however. Marc Bloch, George Homans and Robert Merton, and Karl Polanyi all produced H-C works that had widespread influence in this period.[1]

Scholarly interest in comparative research increased after World War II with improved international communication, the breakup of colonial empires, and a world leadership role for the United States. A few studies of significance that applied a structural functional approach appeared

during the 1950s; they included Robert Bellah's *Tokugawa Religion* (1957) and Neil Smelser's *Social Change in the Industrial Revolution* (1959). Reinhard Bendix's *Work and Authority in Industry* (1956), a unique four-nation comparison of historical change, also appeared in this period.

Several factors stimulated a return to H-C research in the 1960s. First, some historians (e.g., Lee Benson, Robert W. Fogel, Richard Jensen, Stephen Thernstrom) borrowed quantitative techniques from the social sciences, increasing the interchange between history and the social sciences. Statistical studies of mobility, railroad expansion, and voting showed historians the power of quantitative data and gave quantitative researchers new questions to address with their techniques. Second, survey techniques were exported from the United States and used to study different nations as in Almond and Verba's *The Civil Culture* (1963). Many new methodological issues and questions arose from attempts to use quantitative techniques for cross-national generalizations.

Third, the works of historical-comparative sociologists such as Max Weber and Karl Marx were translated and made available in English for the first time. "The translation of Weber probably did more to influence the writing of history in the 1960s than any other single influence from the social sciences" (Stone, 1987:13). Fourth, important book-length studies appeared that represented new ways to do H-C research and made important theoretical advances. Three such works include Charles Tilly's *The Vendee* (1964), Barrington Moore Jr.'s *The Social Origins of Dictatorship and Democracy* (1966), and E. P. Thompson's *The Making of the English Working Class* (1963). Tilly's study of France in the 1790s combined quantitative logic and new historical data. Moore's study of England, India, Japan, Germany, the United States, and the USSR traced how combinations of events and coalitions of social groups caused some nations to develop democratic and others nondemocratic governments. Thompson's study on England prior to 1840 showed new ways to study class consciousness and classes by examining the lives, words, and actions of ordinary people. "The inspiration for a good deal of the new social history came from E. P. Thompson's (1963) *The Making of the English Working Class*. Surely, no work in European history ever so profoundly and so rapidly influenced American historians" (Novick, 1988:440).

Interest in historical-comparative research grew in the 1970s as several books became models of how to do H-C research.[2] Three factors appear to have caused the expansion. First, researchers criticized both structural functionalism, with its static view of society, and economic determinism in orthodox Marxism. They constructed new theories that were sensitive to historical and cultural contexts and sought methods for the new theories. Second, as a result of dramatic political conflict in several Western nations, researchers became interested in fundamental questions about the nature of society and social change like those asked by the founders of the discipline. Historical-comparative research was appropriate for these questions (e.g., What are the basic processes of industrialism? What causes revolutionary politics? How does mass consciousness change? How are basic social structures transformed?). Third, many researchers saw limitations in an exclusive reliance on a strict positivist approach and felt that quantitative techniques alone were inadequate.

After expansion in the 1970s, H-C grew into a vital force during the 1980s. In 1983, a section of historical-comparative sociology was formed in the American Sociological Association (ASA). In his presidential address to the ASA, Melvin Kohn (1987) said that cross-national research was experiencing a revival after being nearly abandoned in the 1930s. More recently, Hunt (1989:1) remarked, "Historical sociology has become one of the most important subfields of sociology, and perhaps the fastest growing." Articles using some form of historical-comparative research appeared in leading scholarly journals. For example, about 40 percent of the articles published in the most prestigious U.S. sociology journals after 1990 were historical or comparative in some sense. This is a large increase over the previous period

(1985–1989) when it was about 28 percent.[3] By contrast, the percentage of historical or comparative articles in the journals between 1976 and 1978 was about 18 percent.[4]

Research Questions Appropriate for Historical-Comparative Research

Historical-comparative research is a powerful method for addressing big questions: How did major societal change take place? What fundamental features are common to most societies? Why did current social arrangements take a certain form in some societies but not in others? For example, historical-comparative researchers have addressed the questions of what caused societal revolutions in China, France, and Russia (Skocpol, 1979); how major social institutions, like medicine, have developed and changed over two centuries (Starr, 1982); how basic social relationships, like feelings about the value of children, change (Zelizer, 1985); why public policy toward treatment of the elderly developed in one way instead of another in the United States (Quadagno, 1988); whether race is declining in significance compared to social class as the major division in the United States (Wilson, 1978); why South Africa developed a system of greater racial separation as the United States moved toward greater racial integration (Fredrickson, 1981); and what caused the failure of a mass political movement in the United States that advocated greater equality and democracy (McNall, 1988).

Historical-comparative research is suited for questions such as which combinations of social factors produce a specific outcome (e.g., civil war). It is also appropriate for comparing entire social systems to see what is common across societies and what is unique, and to study long-term societal change. An H-C researcher may apply a theory to specific cases to illustrate its usefulness. He or she brings out or reveals the connections between divergent social factors or groups. And, he or she compares the same social processes and concepts in different cultural or historical contexts. For example, if France has highly centralized power and high political dissatisfaction, whereas the United States is low on both centralized power and political dissatisfaction, a researcher can begin to build a causal account relating centralized power and dissatisfaction. Changes within a country over time in centralization of power and dissatisfaction can verify causal links.[5]

Researchers also use the H-C method to reinterpret data or challenge old explanations. By asking different questions, finding new evidence, or assembling evidence in a different way, the H-C researcher raises questions about old explanations and finds support for new ones by interpreting the data in its cultural-historical context.

Historical-comparative research can strengthen conceptualization and theory building. By looking at historical events or diverse cultural contexts, a researcher can generate new concepts and broaden his or her perspectives. Concepts are less likely to be restricted to a single historical time or to a single culture; they can be grounded in the experiences of people living in specific cultural and historical contexts.[6]

A difficulty in reading H-C studies and macro-level theories based on H-C research is that one needs a knowledge of the past or other cultures to fully understand them (see Tuchman, 1994:307–308). Often, well-read scholars with an extensive knowledge of conditions in other times or other nations developed the macro-level theories. Readers who are familiar with only their own cultures or contemporary times will find it difficult to understand the H-C studies or classical theorists. For example, it is difficult to understand Karl Marx's "The Communist Manifesto" without a good knowledge of the conditions of feudal Europe and the world in which Marx was writing. In that time and place, serfs lived under severe oppression. Feudal society included caste-based dress codes in cities and a system of peonage that forced serfs to give a large percent of their product to landlords. The one and only Church had extensive landholdings, and tight familial ties existed among the aristocracy, landlords, and Church. Modern readers might ask, Why did the serfs not flee if conditions were so bad? The answer requires an understanding of the conditions at the time. The serfs realized that they had

little chance to survive in European forests living on roots, berries, and hunting. Also, no one would aid a fleeing serf refugee because the traditional societies did not embrace strangers, but feared them. If one wants to understand many classical theorists, "one must appreciate what they took for granted as characteristic of their time and their interpretations of the past" (Tuchman, 1994:310).

THE LOGIC OF HISTORICAL-COMPARATIVE RESEARCH

Confusion over terms reigns in H-C research. Researchers call what they do historical, comparative, or historical-comparative, but mean different things. The key question is: Is there a distinct historical-comparative method and logic, or is there just social research that happens to examine social life in the past or in several societies? "There has been a long dispute in society as to whether 'comparative' studies should be distinguished as a special category of research" (Nowak, 1989:37).

The Logic of Historical-Comparative Research and Quantitative Research

Quantitative versus Historical Comparative Research.   A source of the confusion is that some researchers use a positivist, quantitative approach to study historical or comparative issues. Others rely on the qualitative, interpretative, or critical approaches. According to Ragin and Zaret (1983), a Durkheimian (or positivist) and Weberian (or interpretative) approach to H-C research use different logics. Ragin (1987:2) argued. "The most distinctive aspect of comparative social science is the wide gulf between qualitative and quantitative work."[7]

Positivist researchers reject the idea that there is a distinct H-C method. They measure variables, test hypotheses, analyze quantitative data, and replicate research to discover generalizable laws that hold across time and societies. They see no fundamental difference between quantitative social research and historical-comparative research. They apply quantitative research techniques, with some minor adjustments, to study the past or other cultures.

This confusion is summarized by Øyen (1990, p. 7):

> The vocabulary for distinguishing between different kinds of comparative research is redundant and not very precise. Concepts such as cross-country, cross-national, cross-societal, cross-systemic, cross-institutional, as well as trans-national, trans-societal, trans-cultural, and comparisons on the macro-level, are used both as synonymous with comparative research in general and as denoting specific kinds of comparisons.

Most social research examines social life in the present in a single nation—that of the researcher. We can organize all possible H-C research along three dimensions. First, does the researcher focus on what occurs in one nation or a small set of nations, or does the researcher attempt to study many nations? Second, how does the researcher involve time or history: Does he or she focus on a single time period in the past, examine events across many years, or study the present or a recent time period? Finally, is the researcher's analysis based primarily on quantitative or qualitative data? If we cross-classify the three dimensions, we get a typology of 18 logi-

cally possible kinds of H-C research (see Table 15.1). No wonder there is so much confusion over what constitutes H-C research.

The H-C research currently being conducted does not fall evenly across all possible kinds. A large majority of social research fits into 11 kinds. Most research is in cells 1, 4, 5, 7, 8, 10, 11, 13, 14, 15, and 16. This includes all of the single-nation column. Researchers who examine small sets of nations over long time periods tend to use qualitative data. Those looking at the present tend to use quantitative data. This includes research on many nations. There are relatively few qualitative studies of many nations, with the exception of research by Immanuel Wallerstein and researchers who follow his world-system approach.

Here are brief summaries of studies in the 11 most common types of research.

Type 1: Single Nation, Past Time, Quantitative Data. Brown and Warner (1992) studied the relationship between immigrant populations and police behavior in large U.S. cities in 1900. Their quantitative data analysis included variables such as number of police, arrest rates and percentage foreign-born. The study by Sutton (1991) on the growth of asylums (discussed in Chapter 1) is also this type of H-C research.

TABLE 15.1 Logically Possible Kinds of Historical-Comparative Research

TIME DIMENSION AND KIND OF DATA	COMPARATIVE DIMENSION		
	Single Nation*	Few Nations	Many Nations
One time in past			
Quantatitive	1	2	3
Qualitative	4	5	6
Across time			
Quantitative	7	8	9
Qualitative	10	11	12
Present			
Quantitative	13	14	15
Qualitative	16	17	18

*Nation different than researcher's and audience of results for present time.

Type 4: Single Nation, Past Time, Qualitative Data. Beisel's (1990) qualitative study of campaigns against vice in three U.S. cities in the late 1880s is a good illustration of this type of H-C research. Blee's (1991) study of Women of the Klan (see Box 15.1) is also this type of H-C research.

Type 5: Few Nations, Past Time, Qualitative Data. Barkey (1991) studied the conditions under which peasants revolted in France and the Ottoman Empire in the seventeenth century using qualitative data. The study by Lachmann (1989) on elites in Europe (summarized in Chapter 13) is also an example of this type of H-C research.

Type 7: Single Nation, Across Time, Quantitative Data. Tolnay and Beck (1992) studied the migration of African Americans from the U.S.

South between 1910 and 1930. Their quantitative analysis looked at factors causing migration in different time periods. Their study on lynching, cited in Chapter 3 (Beck and Tolnay, 1990), is another example of this type of H-C research.

Type 8: Few Nations, Across Time, Quantitative. Brinton, Lee, and Parish (1995) examined the changing role of women in Korea and Taiwan (discussed in Chapter 11). The study covered two nations for the 20-year period 1970–1990. They analyzed many quantitative measures of education and labor supply by age and sex.

✗ *Type 10: Single Nation, Across Time, Qualitative Data.* Prechel (1990) examined the relationship between the U.S. steel industry and government

---

Box 15.1 _____

Women of the Klan

In *Women of the Klan,* Kathleen Blee (1991) noted that, prior to her research, no one had studied the estimated 500,000 women in the largest racist, right-wing movement in the United States. She suggested that this may have been due to an assumption that women were apolitical and passive. Her six years of research into the unknown members of a secret society over 60 years ago shows the ingenuity needed in historical-sociological research.

Blee focused on the state of Indiana, where as many as 32 percent of white Protestant women were members of the Klan at its peak in the 1920s. In addition to reviewing published studies on the Klan, her documentary investigation included newspapers, pamphlets, and unpublished reports. She conducted library research on primary and secondary materials at over half a dozen college, government, and historical libraries. The historical photographs, sketches, and maps in the book give readers a feel for the topic.

Finding information was difficult. Blee did not have access to membership lists. She identified Klan women by piecing together a few surviving rosters, locating newspaper obituaries that identified women as Klan members, scrutinizing public notices or anti-Klan documents for the names of Klan women, and interviewing surviving women of the Klan.

To locate survivors 60 years after the Klan was active, Blee had to be persistent and ingenious. She mailed a notice about her research to every local newspaper, church bulletin, advertising supplement, historical society, and public library in Indiana. She obtained 3 written recollections, 3 unrecorded interviews, and 15 recorded interviews. Most of her informants were over age 80. They recalled the Klan as an important part of their lives. Blee verified parts of their memories through newspaper and other documentary evidence.

Membership in the Klan remains controversial. In the interviews, Blee did not reveal her opinions about the Klan. Although she was tested, Blee remained neutral and did not denounce the Klan. She stated, "My own background in Indiana (where I lived from primary school through college) and white skin led informants to assume—lacking spoken evidence to the contrary—that I shared their worldview" (p. 5). She did not find Klan women brutal, ignorant, and full of hatred. Blee got an unexpected response to a question on why the women had joined the Klan. Most were puzzled by the question. To them it needed no explanation—it was just "a way of growing up" and "to get together and enjoy."

policy over a 50-year period, primarily using qualitative data.

Type 11: Few Nations, Across Time, Qualitative Data. Stephens's (1989) study of the transition to democracy and the breakdown of democracy in western Europe between 1870 and 1939 looks at 13 European nations, but Stephens focused on seven.

Type 13: Single Nation, Present Time, Quantitative Data. A study of Arabs and Oriental Jews in the education system of Israel by Shavit (1990) uses quantitative data in one nation. The hypothesis he tests is based on a general theory of minorities in education that was previously tested in the United States and Northern Ireland.

Type 14: Few Nations, Present Time, Quantitative Data. Wright and Cho (1992) examined friendship patterns across different social classes in the United States, Canada, Sweden, and Norway. Their quantitative analysis was based on survey data.

Type 15: Many Nations, Present Time, Quantitative Data. Wimberly (1990) studied 63 Third World nations to see how dependence on foreign aid and investment by multinational corporations affected infant mortality. His quantitative data come from the two most recent decades.

Type 16: Single Nation, Present Time, Qualitative Data. Broadbent (1989) conducted a study of the relationship between local government, business, and national government in shaping policies of economic growth in Japan. His study was based on qualitative data obtained from field research, open-ended interviews, and documentary research.

An Illustrative Debate. A debate between Burawoy (1977) and Treiman (1977) illustrates disagreements over historical-comparative research. Treiman conducted a series of quantitative cross-national studies on prestige rankings of occupations and social mobility from a positivist approach. Burawoy conducted participant observation studies of factory work in several coun-

tries, and qualitative historical research on migrant labor in South Africa and California using a critical social science approach.

Burawoy attacked Treiman's research on social mobility comparing the United States and Britain and cross-national quantitative research generally. He said that standard quantitative measures (e.g., survey questions) require a basic similarity across units of analysis. If a researcher uses quantitative techniques (e.g., random sampling, standard measures, and statistical analysis) across fundamentally different social realities or cultures, he or she creates false precision and distorted results. Burawoy said that it is impossible to draw conclusions without referring to the specific social-historical context of a society. He argued that the historically specific nature of education systems, cultural traditions, values about work, and the like in each society must be integral to an explanation. Finally, he rejected imposing a deductive theoretical framework with implicit values. Instead, he said that power relations and societal change had to be critically examined for a meaningful explanation. Burawoy (1977:1040) concluded, "Most of what is interesting, and also sociologically important, about Britain and the United States escapes the bland homogenizing of linear statistics and standardized scales."

Treiman defended his research by restating the principles of positivist social science. He argued that researchers must move from case study research and toward research in which the society is the unit of analysis. He believed that the goal of comparative research was to discover what is true for all societies, what varies regularly across societies, and what is unique to particular societies. He (1977:1044) said, "The advantage of standardized measurement is obvious—only by using such a procedure can one compare results for different units, in this case societies." Treiman felt that the answer to Burawoy's concerns was more, not less, positivist research—more precise measurement of more variables and more data for a large number of societies. He suggested that positivist research would eventually simplify the complexity of social life across societies into law-like generalizations.

In this debate, Burawoy and Treiman "talked past each other." Each took a different approach to social science (critical versus positivist) and used different fundamental assumptions and goals for doing H-C research.

The Logic of Historical-Comparative Research and Interpretive Research

A distinct, qualitative historical-comparative type of social research differs from the positivist approach. It also differs from an extreme interpretive approach, which some field researchers, cultural anthropologists, and historians advocate.

H-C researchers who use case studies and qualitative data may depart from positivist principles. Their research is an intensive examination of a limited number of cases in which social meaning and context are critical. An example of how positivist researchers view such an approach is illustrated by Stanley Lieberson's (1991) criticism of the wave of H-C research that uses a small number of comparative cases. Adopting a positivist approach to social science, Lieberson finds the H-C research inadequate. He does not believe that it can find a probabilistic causal effect of an independent variable on a dependent variable, which he assumes to be the proper model for social science. He claims that the comparative methods many H-C researchers adopt "frequently lead to erroneous conclusions."

Like interpretive field research, H-C research focuses on culture, tries to see through the eyes of those being studied, reconstructs the lives of the people studied, and examines particular individuals or groups.

An extreme interpretive position goes beyond a desire to see the world through the eyes of others. It says that an empathic understanding of the people being studied is the primary goal of social research. It takes a strict ideographic, descriptive approach and avoids causal statements, systematic concepts, or theoretical models. An extreme interpretive approach assumes that each social setting is unique and that comparisons are impossible. It recreates specific subjective experiences and describes particulars. As

Lawrence Stone (1987:31) noted, traditional history "deals with a particular problem and a particular set of actors at a particular time and a particular place." Hans Gadamer (1979:116) suggested this position when he said:

> *Historical consciousness is interested in knowing, not how men, people, or states develop in general, but, quite on the contrary, how* this *man,* this *people, or* this *state became what it is: how each of these particulars could come to pass and end up specifically* there. *(emphasis in original)*

A distinct H-C approach borrows from ethnography and cultural anthropology, and some varieties of H-C are close to "thick description" in their attempt to recreate the reality of another time or place. Yet, borrowing from the strengths of ethnography does not require adopting the extreme interpretive approach.[8]

A Distinct Historical-Comparative Approach

The distinct historical-comparative research method avoids the excesses of the positivist and interpretive approaches. It combines a sensitivity to specific historical or cultural contexts with theoretical generalization. Historical-comparative researchers may use quantitative data to supplement qualitative data and analysis. The logic and goals of H-C research are closer to those of field research than to those of traditional positivist approaches. The following discussion describes six similarities between H-C research and field research, and six more unique features of historical-comparative research (see Table 15.2).

Similarities to Field Research. First, both H-C research and field research recognize that the researcher's point of view is an unavoidable part of research. Both types of research involve interpretation, which introduces the interpreter's location in time, place, and world view. Historical-comparative research does not try to produce a single, unequivocal set of objective facts. Rather, it is a confrontation of old with new or of different world views. It recognizes that a researcher's reading of

TABLE 15.2 Summary of a Comparison of Approaches to Research: The Qualitative versus Quantitative Distinction

Topic	Both Field and H-C	Quantitative
Researcher's perspective	Include as an intergral part of the research process	Remove from research process
Approach to data	Immersed in many details to acquire understanding	Precisely operationalize variables
Theory and data	Grounded theory, dialogue between data and concepts	Deductive theory versus empirical data
Present findings	Translate a meaning system	Test hypotheses
Action/structure	People construct meaning but within structures	Social forces shape behavior
Laws/generalization	Limited generalizations that depend on context	Discover universal, context-free laws

FEATURES OF DISTINCT H-C RESEARCH APPROACH

Topic	Historical Comparative Researcher's Approach
Evidence	Reconstructs from fragments and incomplete evidence
Distortion	Guards against using own awareness of factors outside the social or historical context
Human role	Includes the consciousness of people in a context and uses their motives as causal factors
Causes	Sees cause as contingent on conditions, beneath the surface, and due to a combination of elements
Micro/macro	Compares whole cases and links the micro to macro levels or layers of social reality
Cross-contexts	Moves between concrete specifics in a context and across contexts for more abstract comparisons

historical or comparative evidence is influenced by an awareness of the past and by living in the present. "Our present-day consciousness of history is fundamentally different from the manner in which the past appeared to any foregoing people" (Gadamer, 1979: 109–110).

Second, both field and H-C research examine a great diversity of data. In both, the researcher becomes immersed in data to gain an empathic understanding of events and people. Both capture subjective feelings and note how everyday, ordinary activities signify important social meaning.

The researcher inquires, selects, and focuses on specific aspects of social life from the vast array of events, actions, symbols, and words. An H-C researcher organizes data and focuses attention on the basis of evolving concepts. He or she examines rituals and symbols that dramatize culture (e.g., parade, clothing, placement of objects) and investigates the motives, reasons, and justifications for behaviors. For example, Burrage and Corry (1981) used records of the official order of appearance of guilds at major public events (parades, pageants, feasts, royal visits) as a way to measure changes in occupation status in London between the fourteenth and seventeenth centuries.[9]

Third, both field and H-C researchers often use *grounded theory*. Theory usually emerges during the process of data collection. Both examine the data without beginning with fixed hypotheses. Instead, they develop and modify concepts and theory through a dialogue with the data, then apply theory to reorganize the evidence. Zaret (1978:118) remarked, "Historically grounded theory means that concepts emerge from the analytic problem of history: ordering the past into structures, conjunctures and events. History and theory can thus be simultaneously constructed." Thus, data collection and theory building interact. Thompson (1978:39) called this "a dialogue between concept and evidence, a dialogue conducted by successive hypotheses, on the one hand, and empirical research on the other."[10]

Next, both field and H-C research involve a type of translation. The researcher's meaning system usually differs from that of the people he or she studies, but he or she tries to penetrate and understand their point of view. Once the life, language, and perspective of the people being studied have been mastered, the researcher "translates" it for others who read his or her report.

Fifth, both field and H-C researchers focus on action, process, and sequence and see time and process as essential. Both say that people construct a sense of social reality through actions that occur over time. Both are sensitive to an ever-present tension between agency, the fluid-social action and changing social reality, and structure, the fixed regularities and patterns that shape social actions and perceptions. Both see social reality simultaneously as something created and changed by people and as imposing a restriction on human choice.[11]

Sixth, generalization and theory are limited in field and H-C research. Historical and cross-cultural knowledge is incomplete and provisional, based on selective facts and limited questions. Neither deduces propositions or tests hypotheses in order to uncover fixed laws. Likewise, replication is unrealistic because each researcher has a unique perspective and assembles a unique body of evidence. Instead, researchers offer plausible accounts and limited generalizations.

Unique Features of Historical-Comparative Research.

Despite its many similarities to field research, some important differences distinguish H-C research. As the title to David Lowenthal's *The Past Is a Foreign Country* (1985) suggests, research on the past and on an alien culture share much in common with each other, and what they share distinguishes them from other approaches.

First, the evidence for H-C research is usually limited and indirect. Direct observation or involvement by a researcher is often impossible. An H-C researcher reconstructs what occurred from the evidence, but he or she cannot have absolute confidence in his reconstruction. Historical evidence in particular depends on the survival of data from the past, usually in the form of documents (e.g., letters and newspapers). The researcher is limited to what has not been destroyed and what leaves a trace, record, or other evidence behind.

Historical-comparative researchers interpret the evidence. Different people looking at the same evidence often ascribe different meanings to it, so a researcher must reflect on evidence. An understanding of it based on a first glance is rarely possible. The researcher also becomes immersed in and absorbs details about a context. For example, a researcher examining the family in the past or a distant country needs to be aware of the full social context (e.g., the nature of work, forms of communication, transportation technology). He or looks at maps and gets a feel for the laws in effect, the condition of medical care, and common social practices. For example, the meaning of "a visit by a family member" is affected by conditions such as roads of dirt and mud, the inability to call ahead of time, and the lives of people who work on a farm with animals that need constant watching.

Another feature is that a researcher's reconstruction of the past or another culture is easily distorted. Compared to the people being studied, a historical-comparative researcher is usually more aware of events occurring prior to the time studied, events occurring in places other than the location studied, and events that occurred after the period studied. This awareness gives the researcher a greater sense of coherence than was experienced by those living in the past or in an isolated social setting. "In short, historical explanation surpasses any understanding while events are still occurring. The past we reconstruct is more coherent than the past when it happened" (Lowenthal, 1985:234). A researcher's broader awareness can create the illusion that things happened because they had to, or that they fit together neatly.

A researcher cannot easily see through the eyes of those being studied. Knowledge of the present and changes over time can distort how events people, laws, or even physical objects are perceived. For example, the old buildings that survive into the present are more permanent and solid than those that did not survive. Moreover, a surviving building looks different in 1996 than it did in 1796 because of the context in which it appears. When the 1796 building was newly built and standing among similar buildings, the people living at the time saw it differently than people do in the 1990s. They experienced various building styles differently, and the building did not appear as something preserved in an old style in the context of newer buildings from the subsequent two hundred years.

H-C researchers recognize the capacity of people to learn, make decisions, and act on what they learn to modify the course of events. When conscious people are involved, lawlike generalizations that hold across societies are limited.[12] For example, if a group of people are aware of or gain consciousness of their own past history and avoid the mistakes of the past, they may act consciously to alter the course of events. Of course, people will not necessarily learn or act on what they have learned, and if they do act they will not necessarily be successful. Nevertheless, people's capacity to learn introduces indeterminacy into historical-comparative explanations.

An H-C researcher wants to find out whether various courses of action were viewed as plausible by the people involved. Thus, the world view and knowledge of those people is a conditioning factor, shaping what the people being studied saw as possible or impossible ways to achieve goals. The researcher asks whether people were conscious of certain things. For example, if an army

knew an enemy attack was coming and so decided to cross a river in the middle of the night, the action "crossing the river" would have a different meaning than in the situation where the army did not know the enemy was approaching.

H-C research takes an approach to causality that is more contingent than determinist. An H-C researcher often uses combinational explanations. They are analogous to a chemical reaction in which several ingredients (chemicals, oxygen) are added together under specified conditions (temperature, pressure) to produce an outcome (explosion). This differs from a linear causal explanation. The logic is more "A, B, and C appeared together in time and place, then D resulted" than "A caused B, and B caused C, and C caused D." Ragin (1987:13) summarized,

Most comparativists, especially those who are qualitatively oriented, are interested in specific historical sequences or outcomes and their causes across a set of similar cases. Historical outcomes often require complex, combinational explanations, and such explanations are very difficult to prove in a manner consistent with the norms of mainstream quantitative social science.

For example, sociologist Max Weber used a fundamentally multicausal approach in his H-C research. His explanations gave cultural factors equal weight to economic, demographic, or social structural factors. His approach employed a combination of causal factors through the ideal type, which was neither a deductive formal theory to test, nor an inductive, problem-specific theory (see Kalberg, 1994).

H-C research focuses on whole cases and on comparisons of complex wholes versus separate variables across cases. A researcher approaches the whole as if it has multiple layers. He or she grasps surface appearances as well as reveals the general, hidden structures, unseen mechanisms, or causal processes.

A historical-comparative researcher integrates the micro (small-scale, face-to-face interaction) and macro (large-scale social structures) levels. Instead of describing micro-level or macro-level processes alone, the researcher describes both levels or layers of reality and links them to each other.[13] For example, an H-C researcher examines the details of individual biographies by reading diaries or letters to get a feel for the individuals: the food they ate, their recreational pursuits, clothing, sicknesses, relations with friends. He or she links this micro-level view of individuals to macro-level processes: increased immigration, mechanization of production, proletarianization, tightened labor markets, and the like.

A sixth feature of H-C research is its ability to shift between a specific context and a general comparison. A researcher examines several specific contexts, notes similarities and differences, then generalizes. He or she then looks again at the specific contexts using the generalizations.

Comparative researchers compare across cultural-geographic units (e.g., urban areas, nations, societies).[14] Historical researchers investigate past contexts, usually in one culture (e.g., periods, epochs, ages, eras), for sequence and comparison.[15] Of course, a researcher can combine both to investigate multiple cultural contexts in one or more historical contexts. Yet, each period or society has its unique causal processes, meaning systems, and social relations, which may lack equivalent elements across the units. This produces a creative tension between the concrete specifics in a context and the abstract ideas a researcher uses to make links across contexts.

The use of transcultural concepts in comparative analysis is analogous to the use of transhistorical ones in historical research.[16] In comparative research, a researcher translates the specifics of a context into a common, theoretical language. In historical research, theoretical concepts are applied across time. "The comparative investigator can thus be regarded as fighting a continuous struggle between the 'culture-boundness' of system-specific categories and the 'contentlessness' of system-inclusive categories" (Smelser, 1976:178).

The Annales School. Discussions of H-C research frequently refer to the *Annales school*,[17] a research method associated with a group of French historians (e.g., Marc Bloch, Fernand Braudel, Lucien Febvre, Emmanuel Le Roy Ladurie), and named after the scholarly journal *Annales: Économies, Sociétés, Civilisations*, founded in 1929. The school's orientation can be summarized by four interrelated characteristics used by some H-C researchers.

One characteristic is the school's synthetic, totalizing, holistic, or interdisciplinary approach. Annales researchers combine geography, ecology, economics, and demography with cultural factors to give a total picture of the past. They blend together the diverse conditions of material life and collective beliefs or culture into a comprehensive reconstruction of the past civilization.

A second characteristic is illustrated by a French term of the school, the *mentalities* of an era. This term is not directly translatable into English. It means a distinctive world view, perspective, or set of assumptions about life—the way that thinking was organized, or the overall pattern of conscious and unconscious cognition, belief, and values that prevailed in an era. Thus, researchers try to discover the overall arrangement of thought in a historical period that shaped subjective experience about fundamental aspects of reality: the nature of time, the relationship of humans to the physical environment, how truth is created, and the like.

The Annales approach mixes concrete historical specificity and abstract theory. Theory takes the form of models or deep underlying structures, which are causal or organizing principles that account for everyday events: "There is the geographical, economic, and social current which examines the long-run structural processes and continuities underlying observable events of history. This current is broadly synonymous with the Annales School of historians" (Lloyd, 1986:241). Annales historians look for both the deep-running currents that shape the surface events and the individual actions that are examined by traditional historians.

A last characteristic is an interest in long-term structures or patterns. In contrast to traditional historians who focus on particular individuals or events over short time spans, from several years to a few decades, Annales historians examine long-term changes, over periods of a century or more, in the fundamental way that social life is organized. To describe the long time span they study, they use the term *longue durée*. It means a long duration or a historical era in geographic space (e.g., feudalism in western Europe, or the fifteenth to eighteenth centuries in the Mediterranean region). To do this, a researcher must adopt a unique orientation toward history. As Fernand Braudel (1980:33) noted, "For the historian, accepting the *longue durée* entails a readiness to change his style, his attitudes. a whole reversal in his thinking, a whole new way of conceiving of social affairs."

The Annales school has influenced H-C research in several ways. It challenges the prevailing focus on short time spans and puts events in a broader context. It also reinforces the building of theory about underlying structures and emphasizes a sensitivity to the different subjective consciousness of the past. Finally, it encourages a holistic integration of diverse types of historical data.

STEPS IN A HISTORICAL-COMPARATIVE RESEARCH PROJECT

Earlier, you saw how H-C research compares with other types of social research. In this section, we turn to the process of doing H-C research. Conducting historical-comparative research does not involve a rigid set of steps and, with only a few exceptions, it does not use complex or specialized techniques.

Conceptualizing the Object of Inquiry

An H-C researcher begins by becoming familiar with the setting and conceptualizes what is being studied. He or she may start with a loose model or set of preliminary concepts and apply them to a specific setting. The provisional concepts contain implicit assumptions or organizing categories that he or she uses to see the world, "package" observations, and search through evidence.

If a researcher is not already familiar with the historical era or comparative settings, he or she conducts an orientation reading (reading several general works). This will help the researcher grasp the specific setting, assemble organizing concepts, subdivide the main issue, and develop lists of questions to ask.[18] Concepts and evidence interact to stimulate research. For example, Skocpol (1979) began her study of revolution with puzzles in macro-sociological theory and the histories of specific revolutions. The lack of fit between histories of revolutions and existing theories stimulated her research.

It is impossible to begin serious research without a framework of assumptions, concepts, and theory. Whether or not a researcher is conscious and explicit about it, he or she organizes specific details into analytic categories. Researchers find it best to recognize this process explicitly and avoid the *Baconian fallacy*. Named for Francis Bacon, it is assuming that a researcher operates without preconceived questions, hypotheses, ideas, assumptions, theories, paradigms, postulates, prejudices, or presumptions of any kind.

Locating Evidence

Next, a researcher locates and gathers evidence through extensive bibliographic work. A researcher uses many indexes, catalogs, and reference works that list what libraries contain. For comparative research, this means focusing on specific nations or units and on particular kinds of evidence within each. The researcher frequently spends weeks searching for sources in libraries, travels to several different specialized research libraries, and reads dozens (if not hundreds) of books and articles. Comparative research often involves learning one or more foreign languages.

As the researcher masters the literature and takes numerous detailed notes, he or she completes many specific tasks: creating a bibliography list (on cards or computer) with complete citations, taking notes that are neither too skimpy nor too extensive (i.e., more than one sentence but less than dozens of pages of quotes), leaving margins on note cards for adding themes later on, taking all notes in the same format (e.g., on cards, paper, etc.), and developing a file on themes or working hypotheses.

A researcher adjusts initial concepts, questions, or focus on the basis of what he or she discovers in the evidence. New issues and questions arise as he or she reads and considers a range of research reports at different levels of analysis (e.g., general context and detailed narratives on specific topics) and multiple studies on a topic, crossing topic boundaries. For example, Quadagno's (1988) study of old-age and welfare programs started with an interest in the history of U.S. programs for the aged. She began with government records on programs for the elderly. Soon, she discovered the importance of southern political pressure, so she spent months learning about southern U.S. history. As the issue unfolded, she examined the literature on social programs. Then, as her inquiry expanded, she read theoretical and empirical discussions showing connections to other social welfare programs. They suggested a comparison with extensive western European programs. In western Europe, organized labor is represented by the social democratic parties, which shaped most social programs in those countries. Therefore, Quadagno's research turned to U.S. labor history. The records of labor officials and labor history led her to examine the actions of employers and the power of the private sector. She stated, (1988:x), "I moved back and forth between theory and archival materials, with each new set of empirical observations guiding my generalizations about factors shaping welfare policy."

Evaluating Quality of Evidence

As an H-C researcher gathers evidence, he or she asks two questions. First, how relevant is the evidence to emerging research questions and evolving concepts? Second, how accurate and strong is the evidence?

The question of relevance is a difficult one. As Tilly (1981:13) remarked, "All documents are not equally valuable in reconstructing the past." As the focus of research shifts, evidence that was not relevant can become relevant. Likewise, some evidence may stimulate new avenues of inquiry and a search for additional confirming evidence.

Concerns about the accuracy of evidence will be discussed. An H-C researcher reads evidence for three things: the implicit conceptual framework, particular details, and empirical generalizations—factual statements on which there is agreement. He or she evaluates alternative interpretations of evidence and looks for "silences," or cases where the evidence fails to address an event, topic, or issue. For example, when examining a group of leading male merchants, a researcher may find documents that ignore their wives and many servants.

Researchers try to avoid possible fallacies in the evidence. Fischer (1970) provided an extensive list of such fallacies. For example, the fallacy of *pseudoproof* is a failure to place something into its full context. The evidence might state that there was a 50 percent increase in income taxes, but its impact is not meaningful outside of a context. The researcher must ask: Did other taxes decline? Did income increase? Did the tax increase apply to all income? Was everyone affected equally? Another fallacy to avoid with historical evidence is *anachronism*, when an event appears to have occurred before or after the time it actually did. A researcher should be precise about the sequence of events and note discrepancies in dating events in evidence.

Organizing Evidence

As a researcher gathers evidence and locates new sources, he or she begins to organize the data. Obviously, it is unwise to take notes madly and let them pile up haphazardly. A researcher usually begins a preliminary analysis by noting low-level generalizations or themes. For example, in a study of revolution, a researcher develops a theme: The rich peasants supported the old regime. He or she can record this theme in his or her notes and later assign it significance.

As a researcher organizes evidence, he or she uses theoretical insights to stimulate new ways to organize data and for new questions to ask of evidence. For example, Staples (1987) used

Burawoy's concept of *factory regime* in a case study of work relations in a British family hardware firm from 1791 to 1891. After examining the evidence, he discovered two regimes—patriarchy, which evolved into another, paternalism, and he extended the original concept.

The interaction of data and theory means that a researcher goes beyond a surface examination of the evidence to develop new concepts by critically evaluating the evidence based on theory. Keat and Urry (1975:113) suggested this process: "Any process of concept formation which is based on the way society presents itself will be inadequate, misleading and ideological." For example, a researcher reads a mass of evidence about a protest movement. The preliminary analysis organizes the evidence into a theme: People who are active in protest interact with each other and develop shared cultural meanings. He or she examines theories of culture and movements, then formulates a new concept: "oppositional movement subculture." The researcher then uses this concept to reexamine the evidence.

Synthesizing

The next step is the process of synthesizing evidence. The researcher refines concepts and moves toward a general explanatory model after most of the evidence is in. Old themes or concepts are discussed or revised, and new ones are created. Concrete events are used to give meaning to concepts. The researcher looks for patterns across time or units, and draws out similarities and differences with analogies. He or she organizes divergent events into sequences and groups them together to create a larger picture. Plausible explanations are then developed that subsume both concepts and evidence as he or she organizes the evidence into a coherent whole. The researcher then reads and rereads notes and sorts and resorts them into piles or files on the basis of organizing schemes. He or she looks for and writes down the links or connections he or she sees while looking at the evidence in different ways.

Synthesis links specific evidence with an abstract model of underlying relations or causal mechanisms. Researchers often develop models by using metaphors. For example, mass frustration leading to a revolution is "like an emotional roller coaster drop" in which things seem to be getting better, and then there is a sudden letdown after expectations have risen very fast. The models are sensitizing devices.

A researcher often looks for new evidence to verify specific links that appear only after an explanatory model is developed. He or she evaluates how well the model approximates the evidence and adjusts it accordingly. He or she goes back and forth from the abstract to the concrete. At each stage, the researcher asks: If this model is true, would it produce the whole of the evidence I found?

The major task for the historical-comparative researcher is organizing and giving new meaning to evidence. Skocpol (1979:xiv) argued,

> *The comparative historian's task—and potential distinctive scholarly contribution—lies not in revealing new data about particular aspects of the large time periods and distinctive places surveyed, but rather in establishing the interest and prima facie validity of an overall argument about causal regularities across various historical cases.*

H-C researchers also identify critical indicators and supporting evidence for themes or explanations. A *critical indicator* is unambiguous evidence, which is usually sufficient for inferring a specific theoretical relationship. Researchers seek these indicators for key parts of an explanatory model. Indicators critically confirm a theoretical inference and occur when many details suggest a clear interpretation. For example, a critical indicator of hostility between two nations is a formal declaration of war. A critical indicator of the rising political power of a social group is the formation of formal organizations with a large membership identified with the group and advocating its position. *Supporting evidence* is evidence for less central parts of a model. It can be evidence that builds the overall background or context, evidence that is less abundant or weaker, and evidence for which a clear and unambiguous theoretical interpretation is lacking.

Writing a Report

The last step is to combine evidence, concepts, and synthesis into a research report. (The report is discussed in detail in Appendix C.) The way in which the report is written is key in H-C research. Assembling evidence, arguments, and conclusions into a report is always a crucial step; but more than in quantitative approaches, the careful crafting of evidence and explanation makes or breaks H-C research. A researcher distills mountains of evidence into exposition and prepares extensive footnotes. She or he weaves together evidence and arguments to communicate a coherent, convincing picture to readers.

DATA AND EVIDENCE IN HISTORICAL CONTEXT

Types of Historical Evidence

First, some terms need clarification. *History* has several meanings: It means the events of the past (e.g., it is *history* that the French withdrew troops from Vietnam), a record of the past (e.g., a *history* of French involvement in Vietnam), and a discipline that studies the past (e.g., a department of *history*).[19] *Historiography* is the method of doing historical research or of gathering and analyzing historical evidence. Historical sociology is a part of historical-comparative research. It

> *is an approach to historical data, a style of historiography, that seeks to explain and understand the past in terms of sociological models and theories. . . . Alternatively, historical data may be used to illustrate and test the validity of sociological concepts, principles and theories. (Mariampolski and Hughes, 1978:104–105)*

Researchers draw on four types of historical evidence or data: primary sources, secondary sources, running records, and recollections.[20] Traditional historians rely heavily on primary sources. H-C researchers often use secondary sources or the different data types in combination. For example, Quadagno (1984) examined the U.S. Social Security Act to evaluate theories of political power. Of the 47 sources she cited for evidence, 23 were primary sources (letters, memos, official reports, newspaper or magazine articles of the period), 3 were recollections (memoirs or oral histories), and 21 were secondary sources (books by historians and other researchers). A study by Griffin, Wallace, and Rubin (1986) on an antiunion movement before 1930 combined primary sources (employer statements) and secondary sources (the historical context) with an analysis of running records (government data on economic conditions).

Primary Sources. The letters, diaries, newspapers, movies, novels, articles of clothing, photographs, and so forth of those who lived in the past and have survived to the present are *primary sources*. They are found in archives (a place where documents are stored), in private collections, in family closets, or in museums (see Box 15.2). Today's documents and objects (our letters, television programs, commercials, clothing, automobiles) will be primary sources for future historians. An example of a classic primary source is a bundle of yellowed letters written by a husband away at war to his wife and found in an attic by a researcher. Aminzade (1984) used primary sources when he studied patterns of protest in three French cities in the mid-1800s. He examined handwritten documents in French government archives produced by police spies, court officials, and others.

Published and unpublished written documents are the most important type of primary source. Researchers find them in their original form or preserved in microfiche or on film. They are often the only surviving record of the words, thoughts, and feelings of people in the past. Written documents are helpful for studying societies and historical periods with writing and literate people. A frequent criticism of written sources is that they were largely written by elites or those in official organizations; thus, the views of the illiterate, the poor, or those outside official social institutions may be overlooked. For example, it was illegal for slaves in the United States to read or write, and thus written sources on the

Box 15.2 _____

Using Archival Data

The archive is the main source for primary historical materials. Archives are accumulations of documentary materials (papers, photos, letters) in private collections, museums, libraries, or formal archives.

LOCATION AND ACCESS

Finding whether a collection exists on a topic, organization, or individual can be a long, frustrating task of many letters, phone calls, and referrals. If the material on a person or topic does exist, it may be scattered in multiple locations. Gaining access may depend on an appeal to a family member's kindness for private collections or traveling to distant libraries and verifying one's reason for examining many dusty boxes of old letters. Also, the researcher may discover limited hours (e.g., an archive is open only four days a week from 10 A.M. to 5 P.M., but the researcher needs to inspect the material for 40 hours).

SORTING AND ORGANIZATION

Archive material may be unsorted or organized in a variety of ways. The organization may reflect criteria that are unrelated to the researcher's interests. For example, letters and papers may be in chronological order, but the researcher is interested only in letters to four professional colleagues over three decades, not daily bills, family correspondence, and so on.

TECHNOLOGY AND CONTROL

Archival materials may be in their original form, on microforms, or, more rarely, in an electronic form.

Researchers may only be allowed to take notes, not make copies, or they may be allowed only to see select parts of the whole collection. Researchers become frustrated with the limitations of having to read dusty papers in one specific room and being allowed only to take notes by pencil for the few hours a day the archive is open to the public.

TRACKING AND TRACING

One of the most difficult tasks in archival research is tracing common events or persons through the materials. Even if all material is in one location, the same event or relationship may appear in several places in many forms. Researchers sort through mounds of paper to find bits of evidence here and there.

DRUDGERY, LUCK, AND SERENDIPITY

Archival research is often painstaking slow. Spending many hours pouring over partially legible documents can be very tedious. Also, researchers will often discover holes in collections, gaps in a series of papers, or destroyed documents. Yet, careful reading and inspection of previously untouched material can yield startling new connections or ideas. The researcher may discover unexpected evidence that opens new lines of inquiry (see Elder et al., 1993 and Hill, 1993).

---

experience of slavery have been indirect or difficult to find.

The written word on paper was the main medium of communication prior to the widespread use of telecommunications, computers, and video technology to record events and ideas. In fact, the spread of forms of communication that do not leave a permanent physical record (e.g., telephone conversations, computer records, and television or radio broadcasts), and which have largely replaced letters, written ledgers, and newspapers, may make the work of future historians more difficult.

Secondary Sources. Primary sources have realism and authenticity, but the practical limitation of time can restrict research on many primary sources to a narrow time frame or location. To get a broader picture, many H-C researchers use *secondary sources*, the writings of specialist historians who have spent years studying primary sources. For example, Lachmann's (1989) study of elites in France and England in the 1600s was based entirely on secondary sources: historians' books and articles in French and English, most published between 1955 and 1988 (see Chapter 13 for a discussion of the study).

Running Records.   *Running records* consist of files or existing statistical documents maintained by organizations. An example of a running record is a file in a country church that contains a record of every marriage and every death from 1910 to the present. Roy (1983) used running records when he studied the boards of directors of major U.S. corporations between 1886 and 1905. His evidence came from 150 primary documents, official reports and statistics, and annual business reference books, some of which are still being published.

Recollections.   The words or writings of individuals about their past lives or experiences based on memory are *recollections*. These can be in the form of memoirs, autobiographies, or interviews. Because memory is imperfect, recollections are often distorted in ways that primary sources are not. For example, Blee (1991) interviewed a woman in her late eighties about being in the Klu Klux Klan (see Box 15.1).

In gathering *oral history*, a type of recollection, a researcher conducts unstructured interviews with people about their lives or events in the past. This approach is especially valuable for nonelite groups or the illiterate. The oral history technique began in the 1930s and now has a professional association and scholarly journal devoted to it. Erikson (1978) used it in combination with other data for a study of a community devastated by a flood. Terkel (1970) used it to get an eyewitness perspective on everyday life during the Great Depression of the 1930s, and Wigginton (1972) used it in the famous *Foxfire* series.[21]

(Also see the dicussions of life history interviews in Chapter 14.)

Research with Secondary Sources

Uses and Limitations.   Social researchers often use secondary sources, the books and articles written by specialist historians, as evidence of past conditions.[22] As Skocpol (1984:382) remarked, the use of such materials is not systematized, and "comparative historical sociologists have not so far worked out clear, consensual rules and procedures for the valid use of secondary sources as evidence." Secondary sources have limitations and need to be used with caution.

The limitations of secondary historical evidence include problems of inaccurate historical accounts and a lack of studies in areas of interest. Such sources cannot be used to test hypotheses. Post facto (after-the-fact) explanations cannot meet positivist criteria of falsifiability, because few statistical controls can be used and replication is impossible.[23] Yet, historical research by others plays an important role in developing general explanations, among its other uses. For example, such research substantiates the emergence and evolution of tendencies over time.[24]

Potential Problems.   The many volumes of secondary sources present a maze of details and interpretations for an H-C researcher. He or she must transform the mass of specialized descriptive studies into an intelligible picture. This picture needs to be consistent with and reflective of the richness of the evidence. It also must bridge the many specific time periods or locales. The researcher faces potential problems with secondary sources.

One problem is in reading the works of historians.[25] Historians do not present theory-free, objective "facts." They implicitly frame raw data, categorize information, and shape evidence using concepts. The historian's concepts are a mixture drawn from journalism, the language of historical actors, ideologies, philosophy, everyday language in the present, and social science. Most lack a rigorous definition, are vague, are applied inconsistently, and are not mutually exclusive nor exhaustive. For example, a historian describes a group of people in a nineteenth-century town as upper class. But he never explicitly defines the term and fails to link it to a theory of social classes. The term helps him organize the primary evidence, but it makes the H-C researcher's job difficult. The methodological problem is that the historian's implicit theories constrain the evidence. A social researcher tries to find evidence for explanations that may be contrary to ones implicitly used by historians in secondary sources by reading through a disorderly set of concepts to reach the evidence.

A second problem is that the historian's selection procedure is not transparent. Historians select some information from all possible evidence. As Carr (1961:138) noted, "History therefore is a process of selection in terms of historical significance . . . from the infinite oceans of facts the historian selects those which are significant for his purpose." Yet, the H-C researcher does not know how this was done. Without knowing the selection process, a historical-comparative researcher must rely on the historian's judgments, which can contain biases.[26] For example, a historian reads 10,000 pages of newspapers, letters, and diaries, then boils down this information into summaries and selected quotes in a 100-page book. An H-C researcher does not know whether information that the historian left out is relevant for his or her purposes.

The typical historian's research practice also introduces an individualist bias. A heavy reliance on primary sources and surviving artifacts combines with an atheoretical orientation to produce a narrow focus on the actions of specific people. This particularistic, micro-level view directs a reader's attention away from integrating themes or patterns. Despite the typical historian's aversion to theory or models, this emphasis on the documented activities of specific individuals is itself a type of theoretical orientation.[27]

A third problem is in the organization of the evidence. Historians organize evidence as they write works of history. They often write *narrative history* (see Box 15.3). This compounds problems of undefined concepts and the selection of evidence. Jones (1976) argued that historians reconstruct events from the residues of the past and assign significance to some of these events.

In the historical narrative, the writer organizes material chronologically around a single coherent "story." The logic is that of a sequence of unfolding action. Thus, each part of the story is connected to each other part by its place in the time order of events. Together, all the parts form a unity or whole. Conjuncture and contingency are key elements of the narrative form—that is, if X (or X plus Z) occurred, then Y would occur, and if X (or X plus Z) had not occurred, something else would have followed. The contingency creates a logical interdependency between an earlier and later events.

With its temporal logic, the narrative organization differs from how sociologists create explanations. It differs from quantitative explanation in which the researcher identifies statistical patterns to infer causes. It also differs from most qualitative data analysis (see Chapter 16) in which researchers compare a model to specific cases (ideal-type analysis or illustrative method), compare similarities and differences in a collection of cases (analytic comparison), or abstract from a set of cases to theoretical statements (successive approximation).

A major difficulty of the narrative is that the organizing tool—time order or position in a sequence of events—does not alone denote theoretical or historical causality. In other words, the narrative meets only one of the three criteria for establishing causality (see Chapter 3)—that of temporal order. Moreover, narrative writing obscures any underlying causal models or processes. This occurs when a historian includes events in the narrative that have no causal significance. He or she adds them to enrich the background or context, to add color. Likewise, he or she presents events that have no immediate causal impact, but that may have a causal effect later in the process. In other words, narratives may include events with a delayed causal impact or that are temporarily "on hold."

Box 15.3 _____

The Narrative in History

Many historians write in the traditional narrative form, which can be a secondary source for the H-C researcher.

CHARACTERISTICS OF THE NARRATIVE
1. It tells a story or tale, with a plot and subplots, watersheds, and climaxes.
2. It follows a chronological order and sequence of events.
3. It focuses on specific individuals, not on structures or abstract ideas.
4. It is primarily particular and descriptive, not analytic and general.
5. It presents events as unique, unpredictable, and contingent.

STRENGTHS OF THE NARRATIVE FORM
1. It is colorful, interesting, and entertaining to read.
2. It gives an overall feel for life in a different era, so that readers get the sense that they were there.
3. It communicates the way people in the past subjectively experienced reality and helps readers identify emotionally with people in the past.
4. It surrounds individuals and specific events with a mix of many aspects of social reality.

WEAKNESSES OF THE NARRATIVE FORM
1. It hides causal theories and concepts or leaves them implicit.
2. It uses rhetoric, ordinary language, and commonsense logic to persuade, and therefore is subject to logical fallacies of semantic distortion and various rhetorical devices.
3. It tends to ignore the normal or ordinary for the unique, dramatic, extraordinary, or unusual.
4. It rarely builds on previous knowledge and does little to create general knowledge.
5. It tends to be overly individualistic, overstating the role of particular people and their ability to shape events voluntarily.

Also, few narrative historians explicitly state how combination or interaction effects operate. For example, the historian discusses three conditions for an event. Yet, rarely do readers know whether all three conditions must operate together to have a causal impact, but no two conditions alone, or no single condition alone, creates the same impact.[28]

The narrative organization creates difficulties for the researcher using secondary sources and creates conflicting findings. H-C researchers must read though weak concepts, unknown selection criteria, and unclear casual logic. Beneath the narrative may reside the historian's social theory, but it remains implicit and hidden. Burke (1980:35) noted, "Traditional historians often deny having anything to do with models, but in practice many of them use models. . . . Using models in this way without being aware of their logical status has sometimes landed historians in needless difficulties."

A last problem is that a historian is influenced by historiographic schools, personal beliefs, social theories, and current events at the time the research is conducted.

Historians writing in the 1990s examine primary materials differently from how those writing in the 1920s did. In addition, there are various schools of historiography (e.g., diplomatic, demographic, ecological, psychological, Marxist, intellectual) that have their own rules for seeking evidence and asking questions. Carr (1961:54) warned, "Before you study history, study the historian. . . . Before you study the historian, study his historical and social environment."

Research with Primary Sources

The historian is the major issue when a researcher uses secondary sources. When using primary sources, the key issue is that only a fraction of everything written or used in the past has survived into the present. Moreover, what survived is a nonrandom sample of what once existed. Lowenthal (1985:191–192) observed, "The surviving residues of past thoughts and things represent a tiny fraction of previous generations' contemporary fabric."

Historical-comparative researchers attempt to read primary sources with the eyes and assumptions of a contemporary who lived in the past. This means "bracketing," or holding back knowledge of subsequent events and modern values.

> *If you do not read the primary sources with an open mind and an intention to get inside the minds of the writings and look at things the way they saw them, you are wasting your time. (Cantor and Schneider, 1967:46)*

For example, when reading a source produced by a slave holder, moralizing against slavery or faulting the author for not seeing its evil is not worthwhile. The H-C researcher holds back moral judgments and becomes a moral relativist while reading primary sources. He or she must "think and believe like his subjects, discover how they performed in their own eyes" (Shafer, 1980:165).

Another problem is that locating primary documents is a time-consuming task. A researcher must search through specialized indexes and travel to archives or specialized libraries. Primary sources are often located in a dusty, out-of-the-way room full of stacked cardboard boxes containing masses of fading documents. These may be incomplete, unorganized, and in various stages of decay. Once the documents or other primary sources are located, the researcher evaluates them by subjecting them to external and internal criticism (see Figure 15.1).

External criticism means evaluating the authenticity of a document itself to be certain that it is not a fake or a forgery. Criticism involves asking: Was the document created when it is claimed to have been, in the place where it was supposed to be, and by the person who claims to be its author? Why was the document produced to begin with, and how did it survive?

Once the document passes as being authentic, a researcher uses *internal criticism*, an examination of the document's contents to establish credibility. A researcher evaluates whether what is recorded was based on what the author directly witnessed or is secondhand information. This requires examining both the literal meaning of

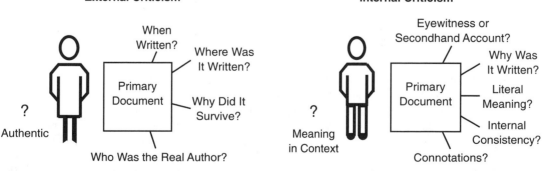

FIGURE 15.1 Internal and External Criticism

what is recorded and the subtle connotations or intentions. The researcher notes other events, sources, or people mentioned in the document and asks whether they can be verified. He examines implicit assumptions or value positions are also examined and the relevant conditions under which the document was produced is noted (e.g., during wartime or under a totalitarian regime). He or she also considers language usage at the time and the context of statements within the document to distill a meaning.

Many types of distortions can appear in primary documents. One is *bowdlerization* (Shafer, 1980:163)—a deliberate distortion designed to protect moral standards or furnish a particular image. For example, a photograph is taken of the front of a building. Trash and beer cans are scattered all around this building, and the paint is faded. The photograph, however, is taken of the one part of the building that has little trash and is framed so that the trash does not show; darkroom techniques make the faded paint look new. Another example is the practice of including famous people who did not actually attend a party in newspaper society column reports of the parties of well-to-do people.[29]

In addition to primary and secondary sources, historical researchers use what Topolski (1976) called *nonsource-based knowledge*. This is knowledge available to a researcher about the past that does not originate in a specific primary document or secondary source. It can be based on logical reasoning. For example, persons A and B are a married couple in a monogamous society that values sexual fidelity. When B has an affair. A is likely to become jealous. It is also knowledge of previous significant events that shape the context of what is studied. For example, a researcher studying France in the late 1920s is aware that a large proportion of French males in the 18- to 40-year-old age group were killed a few years earlier in World War I. Current knowledge, too, can help in understanding past events. For example, a researcher knows that the Black Plague was a disease spread by fleas carried by rats and due to poor sanitary conditions, but people in the past were unaware of the cause of this disease.

COMPARATIVE RESEARCH

Types of Comparative Research

A Comparative Method.   Problems in other types of research are magnified in a comparative study.[30] Holt and Turner (1970:6) said, "In principle, there is no difference between comparative cross-cultural research and research conducted in a single society. The differences lie, rather, in the magnitude of certain types of problems." Comparative research is more of a perspective or orientation than a separate research technique. In this section, we consider its strengths.

A comparative perspective exposes weaknesses in research design and helps a researcher improve the quality of research. The focus of comparative research is on similarities and differences between units, and "comparison is central to the very acts of knowing and perceiving" (Warwick and Osherson, 1973:7).

Comparative research helps a researcher identify aspects of social life that are general across units (e.g., cultures), as opposed to being limited to one unit alone. All researchers want to generalize to some degree. Positivist researchers are interested in discovering general laws or patterns of social behavior that hold across societies. But most positivist research is not comparative. Ragin (1994:107) observed,

> Comparative researchers examine patterns of similarities and differences across cases and try to come to terms with their diversity.... Quantitative researchers also examine differences among cases, but with a different emphasis, the goal is to explain the covariation of one variable with another, usually across many cases.... The quantitative researcher typically has only broad familiarity with the cases.

The comparative orientation improves measurement and conceptualization. Concepts developed by researchers who conduct research across several social units or settings are less likely to apply only to a specific culture or setting. It is difficult for a researcher to detect hidden biases, assumptions, and values until he or she applies a concept in different cultures or settings. Different social settings provide a wider range of events or behavior, and the range in one culture is usually narrower than for human behavior in general. Thus, research in a single culture or setting focuses on a restricted range of possible social activity. For example, two researchers, Hsi-Ping and Abdul, examine the relationship between the age at which a child is weaned and the onset of emotional problems. Hsi-Ping looks only at U.S. data, which show a range from 5 to 15 months at weaning, and indicate that emotional problems increase steadily as age of weaning increases. She concludes that late weaning causes emotional problems. Abdul looks at data from 10 cultures and discovers a range from 5 to 36 months at weaning. He finds that the rate of emotional problems rises with age of weaning until 18 months; it then peaks and falls to a lower level. Abdul arrives at more accurate conclusions: Emotional problems are likely for weaning between the ages of 6 and 24 months, but weaning either earlier or later reduces the chances of emotional problems. Hsi-Ping reached false conclusions about the relationship because of the narrow range of weaning age in the United States.

Comparative research can eliminate or offer alternative explanations for causal relationships. For example, Weil (1985) looked at the relationship between years of schooling and intolerance. Past research found such a relationship in the United States, and most researchers thought that education generally broadened perspectives and increased tolerance. Weil, who looked for the relationship in other nations (1985:470), concluded that the relationship "is weaker, nonexistent, or sometimes even reverse in nonliberal democracies or countries that did not have liberal-democratic regime forms in earlier decades, compared to countries which have been liberal democratic for some time." In other words, the existence of a certain type of government is a necessary condition for the relationship. Education does not have a universal effect of increasing tolerance; rather, education socializes people to their country's official values. Where the official values are for tolerance, education increases tolerance; elsewhere, it does not have that effect.

The way comparative research raises new questions and stimulates theory building is a major strength. For example, Kohn (1987) reported on a comparative study of Japan, Poland, and the United States in which a consistent pattern was discovered across all three: The higher a person's social class, the more likely he or she was to be intellectually flexible and psychologically self-directed. However, the study also found discrepancies. In the United States, higher social class is associated with lower stress; in Poland, it is associated with higher stress; and in Japan, there is no difference in stress levels. The discrepancy stimulated researchers to seek explanations for the relationship and to develop new research questions.

Comparative research also has limitations. It is more difficult, more costly, and more time consuming than research that is not comparative. The types of data that can be collected and problems with equivalence (to be discussed) are also frequent problems.

Another limitation is the number of cases. Comparative researchers can rarely use random sampling. Sufficient information is not available for all of the approximately 150 nations in the world. It is unavailable for a nonrandom subset (poor countries, nondemocratic countries). In addition, can a researcher treat all nations as equal units when some have over a billion people and others only 100,000? The small number of cases creates a tendency for researchers to particularize and see each case as unique, limiting generalization. For example, a researcher examines five cases (e.g., countries), but the units differ from each other in 20 ways. It is difficult to test theory or determine relationships when there are more different characteristics than units.

A third limitation is that comparative researchers can apply, not test, theory, and can make only limited generalizations. Despite the ability to use combinational theory and to consider cases as wholes in H-C research, rigorous theory testing or experimental research is rarely possible. For example, a researcher interested in the effects of economic recessions cannot cause one group of countries to have a recession while others do not. Instead, the researcher waits until a recession occurs and then looks at other characteristics of the country or unit.

Four Types.   Kohn (1987) has discussed four types of comparative research. The first two fit into a distinct H-C approach; the third is an extension of a positivist approach; and the last is a unique approach.[31]

The primary focus of *case study comparative research* is to compare particular societies or cultural units, not to make broad generalizations. Examples of questions addressed by this type are as follows: How do Canada and the United States differ? How did people experience old age in East and West Germany? In what ways are the educational systems of the United States and Russia alike and different? A researcher intensively examines a limited number of cases, where the "case" is a culturally defined group. By examining in depth a small number of cases, usually less than half a dozen, there is relatively little need to be concerned about the equivalence of units. This method is helpful for identifying factors that are constant or that vary among a few cases (Ragin, 1987:49–50).

A researcher uses *cultural-context research* to study cases that are surrogates for types of societies or units. For example, Burawoy and Lukacs's (1985) comparative study of machine shops in the United States and Hungary looked at shops in the two nations, not to compare the United States and Hungary, but to compare similar work settings in advanced capitalist and state socialist contexts. The United States and Hungary represented types of societies. Likewise, Skocpol's (1979) comparison of revolution in France, Russia, and China treated each nation as a backdrop for examining a common social process.

In the third type of comparative research, the nation is the unit of analysis. In *cross-national research*, researchers measure variables across many nations. Nations are not mentioned by name, but a researcher measures variation across nations, converting unique features of nations into variables. For statistical analysis, the cross-

national researcher needs information on at least 50 nations. Although there are nearly 150 independent nation-states, data are rarely available for more than 50 nations.

Transnational research is a type of comparative research in which a researcher uses a multination unit (e.g., a region of the globe such as the Third World) and focuses on the relations among blocs of nations as units. He or she does not see nations as isolated entities but as parts of an international system. Wallerstein's (1974) research on the long-term development of a "world system" since the 1400s illustrates this type of research. His writings spawned a new school of thought, world system theory, which has stimulated additional H-C research.

The Units Being Compared

Culture versus Nation.   For convenience, comparative researchers often use the nation-state as their unit of analysis. The nation-state is the major unit used in thinking about the divisions of people across the globe today. Although it is a dominant unit in current times, it is neither an inevitable nor a permanent one; in fact, it has been around for only about 300 years.

The nation-state is a socially and politically defined unit. In it, one government has sovereignty (i.e., military control and political authority) over populated territory. Economic relations (e.g., currency, trade), transportation routes, and communication systems are integrated within territorial boundaries. The people of the territory usually share a common language and customs, and there is usually a common educational system, legal system, and set of political symbols (e.g., flag, national anthem). The government claims to represent the interests of all people in the territory under its control.

The nation-state is not the only unit for comparative research. It is frequently a surrogate for culture, which is more difficult to define as a concrete, observable unit. *Culture* refers to a common identity among people based on shared social relations, beliefs, and technology. Cultural differences in language, custom, traditions, and norms often follow national lines. In fact, sharing a common culture is a major factor causing the formation of distinct nation-states.

The boundaries of a nation-state may not match those of a culture. In some situations, a single culture is divided into several nations; in other cases, a nation-state contains more than one culture. Over the past centuries, boundaries between cultures and distinct vibrant cultures have been destroyed, rearranged, or diffused as territory around the world was carved into colonies or nation-states by wars and conquest. For example, European empires imposed arbitrary boundaries over several cultural groups in nations that were once colonies.[32] Likewise, new immigrants or ethnic minorities are not always assimilated into the dominant culture in a nation. For example, one region of a nation may have people with a distinct ethnic background, language, customs, religion, social institutions, and identity (e.g., the province of Quebec in Canada). Such intranational cultures can create regional conflict, since ethnic and cultural identities are the basis for nationalism.[33]

The nation-state is not always the best unit for comparative research. A researcher should ask: What is the relevant comparative unit for my research question—the nation, the culture, a small region, or a subculture? For example, a research question is: Are income level and divorce related (i.e., are higher income people less likely to divorce?)? A group of people with a distinct culture, language, and religion live in one region of a nation. Among them, income and divorce are not related; elsewhere in the nation, however, where a different culture prevails, income and divorce are related. If a researcher uses the nation-state as his or her unit, the findings could be ambiguous and the explanation weak. Instead of assuming that each nation-state has a common culture, a researcher may find that a unit smaller than the nation-state is more appropriate.

Nevertheless, boundaries between cultures or subcultures are difficult to operationalize. Cultures are hard to define, are constantly evolving, and have boundaries that blend into each other. Except for cases of border disputes, boundaries between nations are less ambiguous, but

they, too, change over time. There is no easy answer. The issue of the appropriate unit to use remains a serious one.

Galton's Problem. The issue of the units of comparison is related to a problem named after Sir Francis Galton, who raised an issue at the Royal Anthropological Institute in 1889 regarding a paper by E. B. Taylor. When researchers compare units or their characteristics, they want the units to be distinct and separate from each other. If the units are not really different but are actually the subparts of a larger unit, then researchers will find spurious relationships. For example, the units are the states and provinces in Canada, France, and the United States; a researcher discovers a strong association between speaking English and having the dollar as currency, or speaking French and using the franc as currency. Obviously, the association exists because the units of analysis (i.e., states or provinces) are actually subparts of larger units (i.e., nations). The features of the units are due to their being parts of larger units and not to any relationship among the features. Social geographers also encounter this because many social and cultural features diffuse across geographic space.

Galton's problem is an important issue in comparative research because cultures rarely have fixed boundaries.[34] It is hard to say where one culture ends and another begins, whether one culture is distinct from another, or whether the features of one culture have diffused to another over time. Galton's problem occurs when the relationship between two variables in two different units is actually due to a common origin, and they are not truly distinct units (see Figure 15.2).

Galton's problem originated with regard to comparisons across cultures, but it applies to historical comparisons also. It arises when a researcher asks whether units are really the same or different in different historical periods. For example, is the Cuba of 1875 the same country as the Cuba of 1975? Do 100 years since the end of Spanish colonialism, the rise of U.S. influence, independence, dictatorship, and a communist revolution fundamentally change the unit?

Data in Cross-Cultural Research

Comparative Field Research.   Comparative researchers use field research and participant observation in cultures other than their own. Anthropologists are specially trained and prepared for this type of research. The exchange of methods between anthropological and field research suggests that there are small differences between field research in one's own society and in another culture. Field research in a different culture is usually more difficult and places more requirements on the researcher.

Existing Sources of Qualitative Data.   Comparative researchers can use secondary sources. For

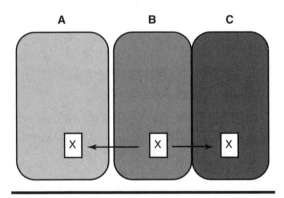

A	B	C

| X | X | X |

FIGURE 15.2   Galton's Problem. *Galton's problem* occurs when a researcher observes the same social relationship (represented by X) in different settings or societies (represented as A, B, and C) and falsely concludes that the social relationship arose independently in these different places. The researcher may believe he or she has discovered a relationship in three separate cases. But the actual reason for the occurrence of the social relation may be a shared or common origin that has diffused from one setting to others. This is a problem because the researcher who finds a relationship (e.g., a marriage pattern) in distinct settings or units of analysis (e.g., societies) may believe it arose independently in different units. This belief suggests that the relationship is a human universal. The researcher may be unaware that in fact it exists because people have shared the relationship across units.

example, a researcher who conducts a comparative study of the Brazilian, Canadian, and Japanese educational systems can read studies by researchers from many countries, including Brazil, Canada, and Japan, which describe the education systems in the three nations.

There may have been 5,000 different cultures throughout human history; about 1,000 of them have been studied by social researchers. A valuable source of ethnographic data on different cultures is the *Human Relations Area Files (HRAF)* and the related *Ethnographic Atlas*.[35] The HRAF is a collection of field research reports that anthropologist George Murdock began to gather and organize in 1938. It brings together information from ethnographic studies on various cultures, most of which are primitive or small tribal groupings. Extensive information on nearly 300 cultures has been organized by social characteristics or practices (e.g., infant feeding, suicide, childbirth). A study on a particular culture is divided up, and its information on a characteristic is grouped with that from other studies. This makes it easy to compare many cultures on the same characteristic. For example, a researcher interested in inheritance can learn that of 159 different cultures in which it has been studied, 119 have a patrilineal form (father to son), 27 matrilineal (mother to daughter), and 13 mixed inheritance.

Researchers can use the HRAF to study relationships among several characteristics of different cultures. For example, to find out whether sexual assault against women, or rape, is associated with patriarchy (i.e., the holding of power and authority by males), a researcher can examine the presence of sexual assault and the strength of patriarchy in many cultures to determine whether the two are associated.

There are limitations to using the HRAF, however. First, the quality of the original research reports varies. The quality of original information depends on the initial researcher's length of time in the field, familiarity with the language, and prior experience, as well as on the explicitness of the research report. In addition, the range of behavior observed by the initial researcher and the depth of inquiry can vary. For example, a researcher may say that in culture X the children are not punished, when in fact children are punished, but in private, and it is the public punishment of children that is taboo. In addition, the categorization of characteristics in the HRAF can be crude. For example, the importance of sorcery in a culture could be coded on a scale from highly important to not very important. Another limitation involves the cultures that have been studied. Western researchers have made contact with and conducted field research on a limited number of cultures prior to these cultures' contact with the outside world. The cultures studied are not a representative sample of all the human cultures that existed. In addition, Galton's problem (discussed earlier) can be an issue.

Cross-National Survey Research. Survey research was discussed in a previous chapter. This section examines issues that arise when a researcher uses the survey technique in other cultures.[36] The problems or limitations of a cross-cultural survey are not different in principle from those of a survey within one culture. Nevertheless, they are usually so much greater in magnitude and severity that a researcher must carefully consider whether the survey is the best method in a setting.

A cardinal precondition for survey research in a different culture is that the researcher must possess an in-depth knowledge of its norms, practices, and customs. Without such an in-depth knowledge, it is easy to make serious errors in procedure and interpretation. Knowing another language is not enough. A researcher needs to be multicultural and thoroughly know the culture in addition to being familiar with the survey method. Substantial advance knowledge about the other culture is needed prior to entering it or planning the survey. Close cooperation with the native people of the other culture is also essential.

A researcher's choice of the cultures or nations to include in a cross-cultural survey should be made on both substantive (e.g., theoretical, research question) and practical grounds. Each step of survey research (question wording,

data collection, sampling, interviewing, etc.) must be tailored to the culture in which it is conducted. One critical issue is how the people from the other culture experience the survey. In some cultures, the survey and interviewing itself may be a strange, frightening experience, analogous to a police interrogation.

Sampling for a survey is also affected by the cultural context. Comparative survey researchers must consider whether accurate sampling frames are available, the quality of mail or telephone service, and transportation to remote rural areas. They need to be aware of such factors as how often people move, the types of dwellings in which people live, the number of people in a dwelling, the telephone coverage, or typical rates of refusal. Researchers must tailor the sampling unit to the culture and consider how basic units, such as the family, are defined in that culture. Special samples or methods for locating people for a sample may be required. For example, in his survey in India, Elder (1973) reported that he undersampled people living in servant quarters located behind middle- and upper-income homes.

Questionnaire writing problems in the researcher's own culture are greatly magnified when studying a different culture. A researcher needs to be especially sensitive to question wording, questionnaire length, introductions, and topics included. He or she must be aware of local norms and of the topics that can and cannot be addressed by survey research. For example, open discussions of political issues can be life threatening in some societies; elsewhere, discussions of religion or sexuality are taboo. In addition to these cultural issues, translation and language equivalency pose problems (see the later discussion of equivalence). Techniques such as back translation (to be discussed) and the use of bilingual people are helpful, but there may be situations in which it is impossible to ask a question of interest in a different language.

Interviewing requires special attention in cross-cultural situations. Selection and training of interviewers depends on the education, norms, and etiquette of the other culture. The interview situation raises issues such as norms of privacy, ways to gain trust, beliefs about confidentiality, and differences in dialect. For example, in some cultures, an interviewer must spend a day in informal discussion before achieving the rapport needed for a short formal interview.

Comparative researchers need to be aware of a version of social desirability bias—the *courtesy bias*. It occurs when strong cultural norms cause respondents to hide anything unpleasant or give answers that the respondent thinks that the interviewer wants. Respondents may seriously understate or overstate some characteristics (e.g., income, accomplishments, education) because of cultural norms. In addition, the manner in which answers are given (e.g., tone of voice, situation) may change their meaning (see Box 15.4).

Access can be a serious issue in cultures where cultural norms limit openness or protect privacy. In addition, the researcher's origin from another country or culture may be a significant barrier in itself. Specific problems involve knowing what agencies and individuals to contact, the appropriate procedures for making contacts (e.g., a formal letter of introduction), how to maintain goodwill (e.g., gift giving), and the effects of such arrangements on the quality and comparability of research. In some cultures, bribery, family connections, or the approval of local political authorities

are required for access to sampling frames, certain sections of a town, or specific respondents. In addition, a researcher may have to take special precautions to protect the confidentiality and integrity of data once they have been collected.

Existing Sources of Quantitative Data. Quantitative data for many variables are available for different nations (see also Chapter 11). For example, the study on schooling and tolerance by Weil (1985) (cited earlier) used survey data from several nations. In addition, large collections of quantitative data have been assembled. They gather information on many variables from other sources (e.g., newspaper articles, official government statistics, United Nations reports).

One source, the *World Handbook of Political and Social Indicators* (Taylor and Jodice, 1983), has dozens of indicators for 156 countries for 35 years. Indicators include such variables as the literacy rate, the number of medical doctors, the degree of urbanization, and the number of protest demonstrations. There are many notes on how data were gathered and classified because of the complexity of using data from different countries.

There are significant limitations on existing cross-national data, many of which are shared by other existing statistics. The theoretical definition of variables and the reliability of data collection

---

Box 15.4

Cross-Cultural Answers to Survey Questions

The meaning of a statement or answer to a question often depends on the customs of a culture, the social situation, and the manner in which the answer is spoken. The manner of answering can reverse the different meanings of the same answer based on the manner in which the answer was spoken.

	ANSWER TO QUESTION	
Manner in Which Answer Spoken	*Yes*	*No*
Polite	No	Yes
Emphatic	Yes	No

Source: Adapted from Hymes (1970:329).

can vary dramatically across nations. Missing information is a frequent limitation. Intentional misinformation in the official data from some governments can be a problem. Another limitation involves the nations on which data is collected. For example, during a 35-year period, new nations come into existence and others change their names or change their borders.

The existing data are available in major national data archives in a form that computers can read, and researchers can conduct secondary analysis on international existing statistics data. For example, Peacock, Hoover, and Killian (1988) conducted secondary analysis on economic inequality using existing statistical data on 53 nations between 1950 and 1980. They divided all nations in three groups according to world system theory and found that inequality increased between the groups. It declined within nations in one group (core), but increased within the nations of the other two groups.

Western Cultural Bias

Most social research is conducted by people who live, work, or have been educated in any one of a handful of societies in which advanced Western culture is dominant. This creates a danger of a Western cultural bias and ethnocentrism. As Myrdal (1973:89) concluded, "a Western approach must be regarded as a biased approach."

Each culture has its own assumptions, modes of thought, orientation toward time, and fundamental values about human life. All these influence thinking and social relations. If social researchers were totally free of culture or had a unique professional culture apart from any specific culture, then cultural bias would not be an issue. But this is unrealistic. It is too easy for researchers to believe that their assumptions, concepts, findings, and values—which are colored by Western culture—apply universally to all people in the world.

Much social research has some cultural bias. Although this is not desirable, it does not mean that social science research is false or impossible to conduct. It means that researchers need to be aware of such a bias and constantly combat it. They can do this in two ways: by becoming aware of how their own culture influences thinking and by becoming familiar with a diverse range of cultures.

A comparative approach encourages researchers to ask questions that challenge their own cultural tradition.[37] In addition, a comparative perspective stimulates researchers to look beyond surface appearances. They may just be symptoms of deeper beliefs, values, and relationships. By becoming multicultural, a researcher gains a better awareness of problems in doing social research and of Western bias, and can produce improved social research as a result. Also see Box 15.5 on feminist research.

An issue related to Western bias is the very strong influence of the United States on the field of sociology and related disciplines. This has given rise to national sociologies for specific cultures or nations. Social researchers from non-U.S. cultures question how U.S. culture has shaped research methods, social theories, implicit value assumptions, and social problems or issues in the field of sociology. They developed sociologies that are partially nation specific. This has a direct bearing on claims for creating cross-cultural, universal knowledge. Hiller (1979:132) observed,

> *To the extend that the rules of scientific logic and procedures are globally similar, sociology retains its claims to universality. To the extent that the aim of sociology is to build a stronger comparative framework, the discipline is universal as well. However, to the extent that social life is too diverse and society-specific to be explained with universialistic theory, sociology benefits from the existence of national sociologies.*

EQUIVALENCE IN HISTORICAL-COMPARATIVE RESEARCH

The Importance of Equivalence

Equivalence is a critical issue in all research.[38] It is the issue of making comparisons across divergent contexts, or whether a researcher, living in a

Box 15.5 _____

Feminist Comparative Research

Feminist comparative researchers examine gender inequality and the common experiences of women across cultures. Intensive, qualitative case studies are most common. Ideally, the researchers are sensitive to specific cultural contexts, and their results affect policy. Feminist researchers question the male-dominated assumptions and data on women in other cultures. For example, they question research on economic development and social change. They argue that it often ignores the sexual division of labor in another culture. As a result, it encourages policies that may intensify the subordination of women.

Feminist comparative research can be controversial. Some criticize Western feminist researchers for being ethnocentric and having a Western cultural bias. They charge that feminists project their own experiences, usually that of the white middle class in a Western society, onto different cultures. Others charge that feminists assume the universal subordination of women in all cultures without first looking at the actual conditions in particular societies.

Cultural relativism is the opposite of ethnocentricism and imposing one's own values. Simple cultural relativism says that one should judge a social practice only in the context of the society in which it is found—that is, first understand it on its own terms. Feminist research, by contrast, rests on a value position—in favor of advancing human dignity and gender equity. Thus, feminist values can clash with cultural relativism when feminist researchers study a culture in which sexual domination and gender inequality are deep-rooted, long-standing practices. Feminists who study the practice of sexual slavery feel outrage. Neutrality and a nonjudgmental stance contradict their fundamental approaches to social research. Merely to place horrible conditions in their cultural context may separate and isolate a shared experience of women's degradation. Reinharz (1992, p. 123) remarked, "The challenge for feminist scholars, then, is to engage in research that avoids ethnocentricism and cultural relativism and builds cross-cultural solidarity."

---

specific time period and culture, correctly reads, understands, or conceptualizes data about people from a different historical era or culture. Without equivalence, a researcher cannot use the same concepts or measures in different cultures or historical periods, and this makes comparison difficult, if not impossible. It is similar to the problems that arise with measurement validity in quantitative research.

The equivalence issue varies on a continuum. At one extreme, a researcher discovers something that is totally foreign to his or her experience (e.g., infant children were treated harshly by their parents and frequently killed) or that is unique to a particular time or culture. At the opposite extreme, there are subtle differences, which are easily overlooked but could affect comparisons. For example, Elder (1973:127) noted this problem when translating the term *friend* across three European languages:

Take friend in English, Freund in German, and amigo in Spanish. Technically, they translate identically. Yet the German Freund refers to a few deep, personal associates; the English friend refers to a somewhat less intense and wider range of acquaintances; and the Spanish amigo refers to a very wide range of persons, some of whom might have been met only that day. Thus, the question, "How many friends do you have?" is asking something different in all three languages.

Types of Equivalence

The equivalence issue has implications for historical-comparative research. A researcher might misunderstand or misinterpret events in a different era or culture. Assuming that the interpretation is correct, a researcher may find it difficult to conceptualize and organize the events to make comparisons across times or places. If he or she fully grasps another culture, a researcher may still find it difficult to communicate with others from his or her own time and culture. The equivalence issue can be divided into four subtypes: lexicon equivalence, contextual equivalence, conceptual equivalence, and measurement equivalence.

Lexicon Equivalence. *Lexicon equivalence* is the correct translation of words and phrases, or finding a word that means the same thing as another word. This is clearest between two languages. Comparative researchers often use a technique called *back translation* to achieve lexicon equivalence.[39] In back translation, a phrase or question is translated from one language to another and then back again. For example, a phrase in English is translated into Korean and then independently translated from Korean back into English. A researcher then compares the first and second English versions. For example, in a study to compare knowledge of international issues by U.S. and Japanese college students, the researchers developed a questionnaire in English. They next had a team of Japanese college faculty translate the questionnaire into Japanese. Some changes were made in the questionnaire. When they used back translation, they discovered "30 translating errors, including some major ones" (Cogan et al., 1988: 285).

Back translation does not help when words for a concept do not exist in a different language (e.g., there is no word for *trust* in Hindi, for *loyalty* in Turkish, for *good quarrel* in Thai). Thus, translation may require complex explanations, or a researcher may not be able to use certain concepts.

Lexicon equivalence can also be significant in historical research because the meaning of words changes over time, even in the same language. The greater the distance in time, the greater the chance that an expression will have a different meaning or connotation. For example, today the word *weed* refers to unwanted plants or to marijuana, but in Shakespeare's era, the word meant clothing.

A sensitivity to subtle changes in language use can be crucial when a researcher tries to understand the perspective of other people. For example, Sewell (1980) found that differences in how peo-

ple living about a century and a half ago used certain terms helped him to understand changes in their consciousness and social experiences. However, Jones (1983:24) noted, "Harnessing elementary insights derived from theories of language to problems of substantive historical interpretation is in . . . an extremely primitive state."

Contextual Equivalence. *Contextual equivalence* is the correct application of terms or concepts in different social or historical contexts. It is an attempt to achieve equivalence within specific contexts. For example, in cultures with different dominant religions, a religious leader (e.g., priest, minister, rabbi) can have different roles, training, and authority. In some contexts, priests are full-time male professionals who are wealthy, highly esteemed, well-educated community leaders and also wield political power. In other contexts, a priest is anyone who rises above others in a congregation on a temporary basis but is without power or standing in the community. Priests in such a context may be less well educated, have low incomes, and be viewed as foolish but harmless people. A researcher who asks about "priests" without noticing the context could make serious errors in interpretations.

Context also applies across historical eras. For example, *attending college* has a different meaning today than in a historical context in which only the richest one percent of the population attended college, most colleges had fewer than 500 students, all were private all-male institutions that did not require a high school diploma for entry, and a college curriculum consisted of classical languages and moral training. Attending college 100 years ago was not the same as it is today; the historical context has altered the meaning of attending college.

Conceptual Equivalence. The ability to use the same concept across divergent cultures or historical eras is *conceptual equivalence*. Researchers live within specific cultures and historical eras. Their concepts are based on their experiences and knowledge from their own culture and era. Researchers may try to stretch their concepts by learning about other cultures or eras, but their views of other cultures or eras are colored by their current life situations. This creates a persistent tension and raises the question: Can a researcher create concepts that are simultaneously true reflections of life experiences in different cultures or eras and that also make sense to him or her?

The issue of a researcher's concept is a special case of a larger issue, because concepts can be incompatible across different time periods or cultures. Is it possible to create concepts that are true, accurate, and valid representations of social life in two or more cultural or historical settings that are very different? For example, Thompson (1967) argued that the subjective experience of time and its measurement were radically different in the preindustrial period. The concept of punctuality or of the workday had a very different meaning or did not exist at all. The researcher interested in comparing work in the late twentieth and the early sixteenth centuries is comparing apples and oranges. For example, Hazelrigg (1973) discussed measuring class consciousness in different societies. Although the word *class* exists in many societies, the system of classes (i.e., the role of income, wealth, job, education, status, relation to means of production), the number of classes, the connotations of being in a particular class, and class categories or boundaries differ across societies, making the study of social class across societies difficult.

Conceptual equivalence also applies to the study of different historical eras. For example, measuring income is very different in a historical era with a largely noncash society in which most people grow their own food, make their own furniture and clothing, or barter goods. Where money is rarely used, it makes no sense to measure income by number of dollars earned. Counting hogs, acres of land, pairs of shoes, servants, horse carriages, and the like may be more appropriate. Likewise, poor people today may have finished eight years of school; may own a black-and-white television; may live in a small, run-down house; and may own a rusted, battered, 15-year-old automobile. Being poor in a past era

may have meant sleeping in barns with animals, begging on the streets, being near starvation, never attending school, and owning only the clothing on one's back. Yet, despite the material differences, in terms of the specific societies and the concept of poverty, the poor of today and yesterday may be equivalent.

Measurement Equivalence. *Measurement equivalence* means measuring the same concept in different settings. If a researcher develops a concept appropriate to different contexts, the question remains: Are different measures necessary in different contexts for the same concept? Armer (1973:52) defined this idea as follows: "Conceptual equivalence with respect to measurement refers to whether the instruments used in separate societies in fact measure the same concept, regardless of whether the manifest content and procedures are identical or not." He argued that it may be necessary to use different indicators in different contexts. A researcher might measure a concept using an attitude survey in one culture but field research in another. The issue then becomes: Can a researcher compare results based on different indicators?

The measurement equivalence issue suggests that an H-C researcher must examine many sources of partial evidence in order to measure or identify a theoretical construct. When evidence exists in fragmentary forms, he or she must examine extensive quantities of indirect evidence in order to identify constructs. Noting this type of process in his study of early nineteenth-century French works, Sewell (1980:9) remarked,

> The ideas we were pursuing were stated partially and in fragments, written down in the heat of the action, often by an unknown person or by groups of persons, and are available only in the most heterogeneous forms—in manifestations, records of debates at meetings, posts, satirical prints, statutes of associations, pamphlets, and so on. In such situations the coherence of the thought lies not in particular texts ... but in the entire ideological discourse constituted by a large number of individually fragmentary and incomplete statements, gestures, images and actions.

ETHICS

Ethical problems are less intense in H-C research than in other types of social research because a researcher is less likely to have direct contact with the people being studied. Historical-comparative research shares the ethical concerns found in other nonreactive research techniques.

The use of primary historical sources occasionally raises special ethical issues. First, it is difficult to replicate research based on primary material. The researcher's selection criteria for use of evidence and external criticism of documents places a burden on the integrity of the individual researcher. Novick (1988:220) suggested,

> The historian has seen, at first hand, a great mass of evidence, often unpublished. The historian develops an interpretation of this evidence based on years of immersion in the material—together, of course, with the perception apparatus and assumptions he or she brings to it. Historians employ devices, the footnote being the most obvious example, to attain for their work something approaching "replicability," but the resemblance is not all that close.

Errors in documentation or the failure to document primary sources sufficiently may create an accusation of fraud against historians, especially from opposing historiographic schools.[40]

Second, the right to protect one's privacy may interfere with the right to gather evidence. A person's descendants may want to destroy or hide private papers or evidence of scandalous behavior. Even major political figures (e.g., presidents) want to hide embarrassing official documents.

Comparative researchers must be sensitive to cultural and political issues of cross-cultural interaction. They need to learn what is considered offensive within a culture. Sensitivity means showing respect for the traditions, customs, and meaning of privacy in a host country. For example, it may be taboo for a man to interview a married woman without her husband present.

In general, a researcher who visits another culture wants to establish good relations with the host country's government. He or she will not take data out of the country without giving something (e.g.,

results) in return. The military or political interests of the researcher's home nation or the researcher's personal values may conflict with official policy in the host nation. A researcher may be suspected of being a spy or may be under pressure from his or her home country to gather covert information.

Sometimes, the researcher's presence or findings may cause diplomatic problems. For example, a researcher who examines abortion practices in a country, then declares that official government policy is to force many women to have abortions, can expect serious controversy. Likewise, a researcher who is sympathetic to the cause of groups who oppose the government may be imprisoned or asked to leave the country. Social researchers who conduct research in another country should be aware of such issues and the potential consequences of their actions. (Also see the discussion of Project Camelot in Chapter 17 on ethics.)

CONCLUSION

In this chapter, you have learned methodological principles for organizing an inquiry into historical and comparative materials. The historical-comparative (H-C) approach has gained renewed attention in recent decades. It is appropriate when asking big questions about macro-level change, or for understanding social processes that operate across time or are universal across several societies. Historical-comparative research can be carried out in several ways, but a distinct qualitative H-C approach is similar to that of field research in important respects.

Historical-comparative research involves a different orientation toward research more than it means applying a specialized set of techniques. Some specialized techniques are used, such as the external criticism of primary documents. Nevertheless, the most vital feature of H-C research is how a researcher approaches a question, probes data, and moves toward explanations.

Historical-comparative research is more difficult to conduct than research that is neither historical nor comparative, but the difficulties are due to issues that are present to a lesser degree in other types of social research. For example, issues of equivalence exist to some degree in all social research. In H-C research, however, the problems cannot be treated as secondary concerns. They are at the forefront of how research is conducted and determine whether a research question can be answered.

We have examined qualitative data collection and research in the past two chapters. Both included some discussion of data analysis because data analysis occurs simultaneously with data collection. In the next chapter, we look more closely at the issue of qualitative data analysis and theoretical explanations.

KEY TERMS

anachronism
Annales school
back translation
Baconian fallacy
bowdlerization
case study comparative
  research
conceptual equivalence
contextual equivalence
courtesy bias
critical indicator

cross-national research
cultural-context research
external criticism
Galton's problem
grounded theory
historiography
Human Relations Area Files
  (HRAF)
internal criticism
lexicon equivalence
longue durée

measurement equivalence
mentalities
narrative history
nonsource-based knowledge
oral history
primary sources
recollections
running records
secondary sources
transnational research

REVIEW QUESTIONS

1. What are some of the unique features of historical-comparative research?

2. What are the similarities between field research and H-C research?

3. What is the Annales school, and what are three characteristics or terms in its orientation toward studying the past?

4. What is the difference between a critical indicator and supporting evidence?

5. What questions are asked by a researcher using external criticism?

6. What are the limitations of using secondary sources?

7. What was Galton's problem and why is it important in comparative research?

8. What strengths or advantages are there to using a comparative method in social research?

9. In what ways is cross-national survey research different from survey research within one's own culture?

10. What is the importance of equivalence in H-C research, and what are the four types of equivalence?

NOTES

1. The early works include the following: Marc Bloch, *Feudal society*, transl. L. A. Manyon (Chicago: University of Chicago Press, 1961; original 1939–1940); George Homans, *English villagers of the* *thirteenth century* (Cambridge, MA: Harvard University Press, 1941); Robert K. Merton, *Science, technology and society in seventeenth century England* (New York: Harper & Row, 1970; originally published

in 1938); Karl Polanyi, *The great transformation,* revised ed. (Boston: Beacon, 1957; originally published in 1957).

2. Some influential works of this period include Anderson (1974a, 1974b), Hector (1975), Paige (1975), Skocpol (1979), Tilly, Tilly, and Tilly (1975), and Wallerstein (1974).

3. Of 193 articles published in the *American Sociological Review (ASR)* between 1989 and 1991, 82 were broadly historical or comparative. Of 101 articles in the *American Journal of Sociology (AJS)* in the same time period, 32 were historical or comparative. They represent 114 of 294 articles, or 38.8 percent of articles. Between 1986 and 1988, approximately 174 articles appeared in the *ASR* and 105 in the *AJS*. Of all *ASR* articles 46 (26.4 percent) and of all *AJS* articles, 31 (29.5 percent) were either historical or comparative. In the period 1976 to 1978, H-C articles were 34 of the 165 appearing in the *ASR* (20.6 perent) and 18 of 126 in the *AJS* (14.3 percent).

4. Additional information on the history of historical-comparative research can be found in Johnson (1982), Kohn (1987, especially footnote 1), Lipset (1968), Novick (1988), Roy (1984), Skocpol (1984), Smith (1991), Warwick and Osherson (1973), and Zaret (1978).

5. For a discussion of differences between generalizations and analysis across temporal units and cultural units, see Firebaugh (1980) and Smelser (1976).

6. See McDaniel (1978), Przeworski and Teune (1970), and Stinchcombe (1978) for additional discussion.

7. Brown (1978), Johnson (1982), Lloyd (1986), and McLennan (1981:66–71) provided discussions of the relationship between positivist and nonpositivist approaches to historical-comparative research, and the turn toward a realist philosophy of science. See Murphey (1973) with regard to historical research. For comparative research, articles by Hymes (1970) and Mehan (1973) show the implications when nonpositivist approaches are taken seriously.

8. For more on borrowing from anthropology, see Biersack (1989), Desan (1989), Johnson (1982), Sewell (1980), Stone (1987), and Walters (1980).

9. See also Desan (1989), Griswold (1983), and Ryan (1989) for discussions of ritual and cultural symbolism.

10. Also see Carr (1961:35, 69), McDaniel (1978), Novick (1988:604), and Ragin (1987:164–166) on the dialogue metaphor for the relationship between theory and evidence in historical-comparative research.

11. For additional discussion, see Sewell (1987).

12. See Roth and Schluchter (1979:205).

13. For an additional discussion of the penetration of surface events, see Bloch (1953:13), Lloyd (1986), McLennan (1981:42–44), and Sewell (1987).

14. See Naroll (1968) for a discussion of difficulties in creating distinctions. Also see Whiting (1968). Sociologists often use the term *society* without realizing the theoretical-classificatory processes involved.

15. See the discussion on periodization in the next chapter.

16. Transhistorical concepts are discussed by others, such as Bendix (1963), Przeworski and Teune (1970), and Smelser (1976).

17. For more on the Annales school, see Braudel (1980), Darnton (1978), Hunt (1989), Lloyd (1986), and McLennan (1981).

18. Orientation reading is discussed in Shafer (1980:46–48).

19. Shafer (1980:2) discussed this in greater depth.

20. See Lowenthal (1985:187).

21. For additional information on oral history, see Dunaway and Baum (1984), Sitton, Mehaffy, and Davis (1983), and Thompson (1978). Also see Prucha (1987:78–80) for a guide to major collections of oral histories in the United States.

22. Bendix (1978:16) distinguished between the *judgments* of historians and the *selections* of sociologists. Sociologists are seen as restricted to selecting illustrative materials, deferring to expert historians who, despite their different purposes, possess far greater knowledge of specific historical materials.

23. Merton (1957:93–94) discussed the limitation of post-facto interpretations.

24. For a discussion of law versus tendency in historical social theory, see Applebaum (1978b) and McLennan (1981:75). Murphey (1973:86) provided a useful discussion of the issues.

25. The word *read*, as used here, means to bring a theoretical framework and analytic purpose to the text. Specific details and the historian's interpretations are read "through" (i.e., passed, but not without notice) in order to discover patterns of relations in underlying structures. See Sumner (1979) for discussion. This relates to the objectivity question in historiography, which is a current debate. See Novick (1988) and Winkler (1989).

26. Bonnell (1980:161), Finley (1977:132), and Goldthorpe (1977:189–190) discussed how historians use concepts. Selection in this context is discussed by Abrams (1982:194) and Ben-Yehuda (1983).

27. For introductions to how historians see their method, see Barzun and Graff (1970), Braudel (1980),

Cantor and Schneider (1967), Novick (1988), or Shafer (1980). Most focus on the assembly of historical details that are documented in artifacts, including those of collective biography. This focuses attention on specific historical actors, their actions and motives, so it takes on an individualistic-voluntaristic slant, and studies become ideographic accounts of micro behavior. See also Block (1977), Laslett (1980), and MacIver (1968).

28. The narrative is discussed in Abbott (1992), Gallie (1963), Griffin (1993), McLennan (1981:76–87), Reed (1989), Richardson (1990), Runciman (1980), and Stone (1987:74–96).

29. For more on the use and evaluation of primary sources, see Barzun and Graff (1970:63–128). Cantor and Schneider (1967:22–91), Dibble (1963), Mariampolski and Hughes (1978), Milligan (1979), Platt (1981), Shafer (1980:127–170), and Topolski (1976). Bloch's (1953:79–137) general discussion of the nature of historical criticism is still valuable today.

30. For more on the strengths and limitations of comparative research, see Anderson (1973), Holt and Turner (1970), Kohn (1987), Ragin (1987), Smelser (1976), Vallier (1971a, 1971b), Walton (1973), and Whiting (1968).

31. Similar classifications are provided in Bollen at al. (1993), Chase-Dunn (1989:309–333), and Ragin (1994). Also see Ragin (1989) for a critique of Kohn's typology.

32. For example, Eric Wolf's (1982) study of the cultures or civilizations around the world between 1400 and 1900 illustrates the existence of many separate cultures and civilizations prior to European colonization and the rise of nation-states.

33. For examples, see Hector (1975) and See (1986).

34. See Elder (1973) and Whiting (1968) on Galton's problem.

35. For more on the *Human Relations Area File* and the *Ethnographic Atlas*, see Murdock (1967, 1971) and Whiting (1968).

36. For more on comparative survey research, see Burton and White (1987), Elder (1973), Frey (1970), Verba (1971), Warwick and Lininger (1975), and Williamson et al. (1982:315–319). For an additional discussion of access issues, see Armer (1973:59) and Form (1973).

37. See Frey (1971), Grimshaw (1973), and McDaniel (1978).

38. For additional discussions of equivalence, see Anderson (1973), Armer (1973), Frey (1970), Holt and Turner (1970), Przeworski and Teune (1970, 1973), and Warwick and Osherson (1973).

39. For more on back translation, see Anderson (1973), Grimshaw (1973), and Hymes (1970).

40. See Novick (1988:612–622) for an extensive discussion of the David Abraham case.

RECOMMENDED READINGS

Griswold, Wendy. (1994). *Cultures and societies in a changing world.* Thousand Oaks, CA: Pine Forge Press. This short book builds on a series of essays and articles on historical and comparative issues by the author. The central idea in the book is cultural meaning. The reader is treated to a fascinating discussion on the creation, production, and distribution of cultural meanings, artifacts, or practices across time and nations.

Kohn, Melvin L. (Ed.). 1989. *Cross-national research in sociology.* Newbury Park, CA: Sage. This collection of essays provides a discussion of some general issues in comparative research and the contribution of Max Weber. It also provides a set of different kinds of research that are classified as cross-national by the author.

Skocpol, Theda (Ed.). (1984). *Vision and method in historical sociology.* New York: Cambridge University Press. This collection of essays discusses the works of nine major H-C researchers. The essays examine the lives, research, and thinking of those who shaped twentieth-century H-C research. In addition, the editor provides an informative essay on historical sociology and a useful annotated bibliography on the methods of H-C research.

Smelser, Neil. (1976). *Comparative methods in the social sciences.* Englewood Cliffs, NJ: Prentice-Hall. Smelser surveys issues in comparative research and examines the works of Alexis de Tocqueville, Emile Durkheim, and Max Weber to distill their comparative method. He argues that the basic logic of comparative research differs little from that of quantitative research, but that it has special problems because of the small number of cases involved.

Smith, Dennis. (1991). *The rise of historical sociology.* Philadelphia: Temple University Press. Smith provides a comprehensive summary and analysis of the rapid growth of historical and comparative research during the past 50 years. He also discusses central issues in the 1990s, including whether H-C is a distinct kind of social research.

Tilly, Charles. (1981). *As sociology meets history.* New York: Academic Press. These essays give us a sense of how this major H-C researcher approaches his work. It has three major themes: that historians and sociologists talk past one another, that serious historical work can be rigorous and quantitative, and that a solid grounding in historical evidence is required for any discussion of macro-level social change.

Yow, Valerie Raleigh. (1994). *Recording oral history: A practical guide for social scientists.* Thousand Oaks, CA: Sage. The central contribution of this book is expressed in the subtitle. It is a practical, "how-to" guide. The reader learns how to conduct an oral history interview and is given many examples. Included in an appendix are the standards of the Oral History Association.

CHAPTER 16

ANALYZING QUALITATIVE DATA

> *Much of the best work in sociology has been carried out using qualitative methods without statistical tests. This has been true of research areas ranging from organization and community studies to microstudies of face to face interaction and macrostudies of the world system. Nor should such work be regarded as weak or initial "exploratory" approaches to those topics.*
> —Randall Collins, "Statistics versus Words," p. 340

INTRODUCTION

Qualitative data are in the form of text, written words, phrases, or symbols describing or representing people, actions, and events in social life. Except for the occasional content analysis study, qualitative researchers rarely use statistical analysis. This does not mean that qualitative data analysis is based on speculation or on vague impressions. It can be systematic and logically rigorous, although in a different way from quantitative or statistical analysis.

In the past, few qualitative researchers explained how they analyzed data. In fact, a common criticism of qualitative research was that data analysis was not made explicit or open to inspection. Qualitative data analysis has moved to a more explicit and systematic step-by-step approach.[1] Nevertheless, no single qualitative data analysis approach is widely accepted. In this chapter, you will learn about a few qualitative analysis techniques. Some of the approaches are used more often in historical-comparative research and some more in field research.

QUANTITATIVE AND QUALITATIVE ANALYSIS

Qualitative and quantitative forms of data analysis have similarities and differences.

Similarities

First, the form of analysis for both types of data in both styles of research involves inference. Researchers infer from the empirical details of social life. To infer means to pass a judgment, to use reasoning, and to reach a conclusion based on evidence. In both forms of data analysis, the researcher carefully examines empirical information to reach a conclusion. The conclusion is reached by reasoning and simplifies the complexity in the data. There is some abstraction or distance from the data, but this varies by the style of research. Both forms of data analysis anchor statements about the social world in a inquiry that has adequacy (i.e., it is faithful to the data). "In qualitative research, *adequacy* refers to the amount of data collected, rather than to the number of subjects as in quantitative research. Adequacey is attained when sufficient data has been collected that saturation occurs" (Morse, 1994:230, emphasis in original).

A second similarity is that both forms of analysis involve a public method or process. Researchers systematically record or gather data and in so doing make accessible to others what they did. Both types of researchers collect large amounts of data. They describe the data and document how they collected and examined it. The degree to which the method is standardized and visible may vary, but all researchers reveal their study design in some way. "Research designs in qualitative research are not always made explicit, but they are at least implicit in every piece of research" (King, Keohane, and Verba, 1994:118).

Next, comparison is a central process to all data analysis, qualitative or quantitative. All social researchers compare features of the evidence they have gathered internally or with related evidence. Researchers identify multiple process, causes, properties, or mechanisms within the evidence. They then look for patterns—similarities and differences, aspects that are alike and unlike.

> [Qualitative] researchers examine patterns of similarities and differences across cases and try to come to terms with their diversity. . . . Quantitative researchers also examine differences among cases, but with a different emphasis, the goal is to explain the covariation of one variable with another, usually across many cases. . . . The quantitative researcher typically has only broad familiarity with the cases. (Ragin, 1994:107)

Fourth, in both qualitative and quantitative forms of data analysis, researchers strive to avoid errors, false conclusions, and misleading inferences. Researchers are also alert for possible fallacies or illusions. They sort through various explanations, discussions, and descriptions, and evaluate merits of rivals, seeking the more authentic, valid, true, or worthy among them.

Differences

Qualitative data analysis differs from quantitative analysis in four ways. First, quantitative researchers choose from a specialized, standardized set of data analysis techniques. Hypothesis testing and statistical methods vary little across different social research projects or across the natural and social sciences. Quantitative analysis is highly developed and builds on applied mathematics. By contrast, qualitative data analysis is less standardized. The wide variety in possible approaches to qualitative research is matched by the many approaches to data analysis. Qualitative research is often inductive. Researchers rarely know the specifics of data analysis when they begin a project. Schatzman and Strauss (1973:108) remarked, "Qualitative analysts do not often enjoy the operational advantages of their quantitative cousins in being able to predict their own analytic processes; consequently, they cannot refine and order their raw data by operations built initially into the design of research."

A second difference is that quantitative researchers do not begin data analysis until they have collected all of the data and condensed them into numbers. They then manipulate the numbers in order to see patterns or relationships. Qualitative researchers can look for patterns or relationships, but they begin analysis early in a research project, while they are still collecting data. The results of early data analysis guide subsequent data collection. Thus, analysis is less a distinct final stage of research than a dimension of research that stretches across all stages.

Another difference is the relation to social theory. Quantitative researchers manipulate numbers that represent empirical facts in order to test an abstract hypothesis with variable constructs. By contrast, qualitative researchers create new concepts and theory by blending together empirical evidence and abstract concepts. Instead of testing a hypothesis, a qualitative analyst may illustrate or color in evidence showing that a theory, generalization, or interpretation is plausible.

The fourth difference is the degree of abstraction or distance from the details of social life. In all data analysis, a researcher places raw data into categories that he or she manipulates in order to identify patterns and arrive at generalizations. In quantitative analysis, this process is clothed in statistics, hypotheses, and variables. Quantitative researchers use the symbolic language of statistical relationships between variables to discuss causal relations. They assume that social life can be measured by using numbers. When they manipulate the numbers according to the laws of statistics, the numbers reveal features of social life.

Qualitative analysis is less abstract than statistical analysis and closer to raw data. Qualitative analysis does not draw on a large, well-established body of formal knowledge from mathematics and statistics. The data are in the form of words, which are relatively imprecise, diffuse, and context-based, and can have more than one meaning.

Words are not only more fundamental intellectually; one may also say that they are necessarily superior to mathematics in the social structure of the discipline. For words are a mode of expression with greater open-endedness, more capacity for connecting various realms of argument and experience, and more capacity for reaching intellectual audiences. (Collins, 1984:353)

Explanations and Qualitative Data

Qualitative explanations take many forms. A qualitative researcher does not have to choose between a rigid ideographic/nomothetic dichotomy—that is, between describing specifics and verifying universal laws. Instead, a researcher develops explanations or generalizations that are close to concrete data and contexts but are more than simple descriptions. He or she usually uses a lower level, less abstract theory, which is grounded in concrete details. He or she may build new theory to create a realistic picture of social life and stimulate understanding more than to test a causal hypotheses. Explanations tend to be rich in detail, sensitive to context, and capable of showing the complex processes or sequences of social life. The explanations may be causal, but this is not always the case. The researcher's goal is to organize a large quantity of specific details into a coherent picture, model, or set of interlocked concepts.

A qualitative researcher rarely tries to document universal laws; rather, he or she divides explanations into two categories: highly unlikely and plausible. The researcher is satisfied by building a case or supplying supportive evidence. He or she may eliminate some theoretical explanations from consideration while increasing the plausibility of others because only a few explanations will be consistent with a pattern in the data. Qualitative analysis can eliminate an explanation by showing that a wide array of evidence contradicts it. The data might support more than one explanation, but *all* explanations will not be consistent with it. In addition to eliminating less plausible explanations, qualitative data analysis helps to verify a sequence of events or the steps of a process. This temporal ordering is the basis of finding associations among variables, and it is useful in supporting causal arguments.

The form of analysis and theorizing in qualitative research sometimes makes it difficult to see generalizations. Some qualitative researchers are almost entirely descriptive and avoid theoretical analysis. In general, it is best to make theories and concepts explicit. Without an analytic interpretation or theory provided by the researcher, the readers of qualitative research may use their own everyday, taken-for-granted ideas. Their commonsense framework is likely to contain implicit assumptions, biases, ethnocentrism, and ill-defined concepts from dominant cultural values.[2]

CONCEPT FORMATION

In this section, you will learn about themes or concepts, coding qualitative data, and analytic memo writing. Qualitative researchers sometimes use variables, but more often they use general ideas, themes, or concepts as analytic tools for making generalizations. Qualitative analysis often uses nonvariable concepts or simple nominal-level variables.

Conceptualization in Qualitative Research

Quantitative researchers conceptualize variables and refine concepts as part of the process of measuring variables that comes before data collection or analysis. By contrast, qualitative researchers form new concepts or refine concepts that are grounded in the data. Concept formation is an integral part of data analysis and begins during data collection. Thus, conceptualization is one way that a qualitative researcher organizes and makes sense of data.

A qualitative researcher analyzes data by organizing it into categories on the basis of themes, concepts, or similar features. He or she develops new concepts, formulates conceptual definitions, and examines the relationships among concepts. Eventually, he or she links concepts to each other in terms of a sequence, as oppositional sets (X is the opposite of Y), or as sets of similar categories that he or she interweaves into theoretical statements. Qualitative researchers conceptualize or form concepts as they read through and ask critical questions of data (e.g., field notes, historical documents, secondary sources). The questions can come from the abstract vocabulary of a discipline such as sociology—for example: Is this a case of class conflict? Was role conflict present in that situation? Is this a social movement? Questions can also be logical—for example: What was the sequence of events? How does the way it happened here compare to over there? Are these the same or different, general or specific cases?[3] Researchers often conceptualize as they code qualitative data.

In qualitative research, ideas and evidence are mutually interdependent. This applies particularly to case study analysis. Cases are not given preestablished empirical units or theoretical categories apart from data; they are defined by data and theory. By analyzing a situation, the researcher organizes data and applies ideas simultaneously to create or specify a case. Making or creating a case, called *casing*, brings the data and theory together. Determining what to treat as a case resolves a tension or strain between what the researcher observes and his or her ideas about it. "Casing viewed as a methodological step, can occur at any phase of the research process, but occurs especially at the beginning of the project and at the end" (Ragin, 1992b:218).

Coding Qualitative Data

A quantitative researcher codes after all the data have been collected. He or she arranges measures of variables, which are in the form of numbers, into a machine-readable form for statistical analysis.

Coding data has a different meaning and role in qualitative research. A researcher organizes the raw data into conceptual categories and creates themes or concepts, which he or she then uses to analyze data. Instead of a simple clerical task, qualitative coding is an integral part of data analysis. It is guided by the research question and leads to new questions. It frees a researcher from entanglement in the details of the raw data and encourages higher level thinking about them. It also moves him or her toward theory and generalizations.

> Codes are tags or labels for assigning units of meaning to the descriptive or inferential information complied during a study. Codes usually are attached to "chunks" of varying size—words, phases, sentences or whole paragraphs, connected or unconnected to a specific setting. (Miles and Huberman, 1994:56)

Coding is two simultaneous activities: mechanical data reduction and analytic categorization of data. The researcher imposes order on the data. "Contrasted with the weeks and weeks in which she will be engaged in mechanical processing, the truly analytic moments will occur during bursts of insight or pattern recognition" (Wolcott, 1994:24). Coding data is the hard work of reducing mountains of raw data into manageable piles. In addition to making a large mass of data manageable, coding makes allows a researcher to quickly retrieve relevant parts of it. Between the moments of thrill and inspiration, a great deal of coding qualitative data, or filework, can be wearisome and tedious. Plath (1990:375) remarked, it has "all the dramatic tension of watching paint dry."

> The task of shifting through much material can become daunting. For weeks, even months, you may have nothing to show as proof of effort expended. . . . Filework is the outward manifestation of an inward pledge that most of us make to continue striving to understand a particular people. (Plath, 1990:374)

Strauss (1987) defined three kinds of qualitative data coding, which are described next. The researcher reviews the data on three occasions, using a different coding each time, and codes the same raw data in three passes. Strauss (1987:55) warned, "Coding is the most difficult operation for inexperienced researchers to understand and to master." Others suggest similar types of coding (see Lofland and Lofland, 1995:192–193, Miles and Huberman, 1994:57–71, and Sanjek, 1990:388–392).

Open Coding.   *Open coding* is performed during a first pass through recently collected data. The researcher locates themes and assigns initial codes or labels in a first attempt to condense the mass of data into categories. He or she slowly reads field notes, historical sources, or other data, looking for critical terms, key events, or themes, which are then noted. Next, he or she writes a preliminary concept or label at the edge of a note card or computer record and highlights it with brightly colored ink or in some similar way. The researcher is open to creating new themes and to changing these initial codes in subsequent analysis. A theoretical framework helps if it is used in a flexible manner.

Open coding brings themes to the surface from deep inside the data. The themes are at a low level of abstraction and come from the researcher's initial research question, concepts in the literature, terms used by members in the social setting, or new thoughts stimulated by immersion in the data. As Schatzman and Strauss (1973:121) warn, it is important for researchers to see abstract concepts in concrete data and to move back and forth between abstract concepts and specific details.

> Novices occasionally, if not characteristically, bog down in their attempts to utilize substantive levers [i.e., concepts of a discipline] because they view them as real forms. Experienced researchers and scholars more often see through these abstract devices to the ordinary, empirical realities they represent; they are thereby capable of considerable conceptual mobility. Thus, we urge the novice in analysis to convert relatively inert abstractions into stories—even with plots.

An example of this is found in LeMasters's (1975) field research study of a working-class tavern when he found that marriage came up in many conversations. If he open coded field notes, he might have coded a block of field notes with the theme *marriage*. Following is an example of hypothetical field notes that can be open coded with the theme *marriage*:

> I wore a tie to the bar on Thursday because I had been at a late meeting. Sam noticed it immediately and said. "Damn it, Doc. I wore one of them things

once—when I got married—and look what happened to me! By God, the undertaker will have to put the next one on "I ordered a beer, then asked him, "Why did you get married?" He replied, "What the hell you goin' to do? You just can't go on shacking up with girls all your life—I did plenty of that when I was single" with a smile and wink. He paused to order another beer and light a cigarette, then continued, "A man, sooner or later, likes to have a home of his own, and some kids, and to have that you have to get married. There's no way out of it—they got you hooked." I said, "Helen [his wife] seems like a nice person." He returned, "Oh, hell, she's not a bad kid, but she's a goddamn woman and they get under my skin. They piss me off. If you go to a party, just when you start having fun, the wife says 'let's go home.'" (Adapted from LeMasters, 1975: 36–37)

Historical-comparative researchers also use open coding. For example, a researcher studying the Knights of Labor, an American nineteenth-century movement for economic and political reform, reads a secondary source about the activities of a local branch of the movement in a specific town. When reading and taking notes, the researcher notices that the Prohibition party was important in local elections and that temperance was debated by members of the local branch. The researcher's primary interest is in the internal structure, ideology, and growth of the Knights movement. Temperance is a new and unexpected category. The researcher codes the notes with the label "temperance" and includes it as a possible theme.

Although some researchers (e.g., Miles and Huberman, 1994:58) suggest that a researcher begins coding with a list of concepts, researchers generate most coding themes while reading data notes. Regardless of whether he or she begins with a list of themes, a researcher makes a list of themes *after* open coding. Such a list serves three purposes:

1. It helps the researcher see the emerging themes at a glance.
2. It stimulates the researcher to find themes in future open coding.
3. The researcher uses the list to build a universe of all themes in the study, which he or she reorganizes, sorts, combines, discards, or extends in further analysis.

Qualitative researchers vary in how completely and in how much detail they code. Some code every line or every few words; others code paragraphs and argue that much of the data are not coded and are dross or left over. The degree of detail in coding depends on the research question, the "richness" of the data, and the researcher's purposes.

Open-ended coding extends to analytic notes or memos that a researcher writes to himself or herself while collecting data. Researchers should write memos on their codes (see the later discussion of analytic memo writing).

Axial Coding.   This is a second pass through data. During open coding, a researcher focuses on the data themselves and assigns code labels for themes. There is no concern about making connections among themes or elaborating the concepts that the themes represent. By contrast, in *axial coding*, the researcher begins with an organized set of initial codes or preliminary concepts. In this second pass, he or she focuses on the initial coded themes more than on the data. Additional codes or new ideas may emerge during this pass, and the researcher notes them; but his or her primary task is to review and examine initial codes. He or she moves toward organizing ideas or themes and identifies the axis of key concepts in analysis.

Miles and Huberman (1994:62) have warned, "Whether codes are created and revised early or late is basically less important than whether they have some conceptual and structural order. Codes should relate to one another in coherent, study-important ways; they should be part of a governing structure."

During axial coding, a researcher asks about causes and consequences, conditions and interactions, strategies and processes, and looks for categories or concepts that cluster together. He or she asks questions such as: Can I divide existing concepts into subdimensions or subcategories? Can I combine several closely related concepts into one more general one? Can I organize categories into a sequence (i.e., A, then B, then C), or by their physical location (i.e., where they occur), or their relationship to a major topic of interest? For example, a field researcher studying working-class life divides the general issue of marriage into subparts (e.g., engagement, weddings). He or she marks all notes involving parts of marriage and then relates marriage to themes of sexuality, division of labor in household tasks, views on children, and so on. When the theme reappears in different places, the researcher makes comparisons so he or she can see new themes (e.g., men and women have different attitudes toward marriage).

In the example of historical research on the Knights of Labor, a researcher looks for themes related to temperance. He or she looks for discussions of saloons, drinking or drunkenness, and relations between the movement and political parties that support or oppose temperance. Themes that cluster around temperance could also include drinking as a form of recreation, drinking as part of ethnic culture, and differences between men and women regarding drinking.

Axial coding stimulates thinking about linkages between concepts or themes, and it raises new questions. It can suggest dropping some themes or examining others in more depth. In addition, it reinforces the connections between evidence and concepts. As a researcher consolidates codes and locates evidences, he or she finds evidence in many places for core themes and builds a dense web of support in the qualitative data for them. This is analogous to the idea of multiple indicators described with regard to reliability and measuring variables. The connection between a theme and data is strengthened by multiple instances of empirical evidence.[4]

Selective Coding.   By the time a researcher is ready for this last pass through the data, he or she has identified the major themes of the research project. *Selective coding* involves scanning data and previous codes. Researchers look selectively for cases that illustrate themes and make comparisons and contrasts after most or all data collection is complete. They begin after they have well-developed concepts and have started to organize their overall analysis around several core general-

izations or ideas. For example, a researcher studying working-class life in a tavern decides to make gender relations a major theme. In selective coding, the researcher goes through his or her field notes, looking for differences in how men and women talk about dating, engagements, weddings, divorce, extramarital affairs, or husband/wife relations. He or she then compares male and female attitudes on each part of the theme of marriage.

Likewise, the researcher studying the Knights of Labor decides to make the movement's failure to form alliances with other political groups a major theme. The researcher goes through his or her notes looking for compromise and conflict between the Knights and other political parties, including temperance groups and the Prohibition party. The array of concepts and themes that are related to temperance in axial coding helps him or her discover how the temperance issue facilitated or inhibited alliances.

During selective coding, major themes or concepts ultimately guide the researcher's search. He or she reorganizes specific themes identified in earlier coding and elaborates more than one major theme. For example, in the working-class tavern study, the researcher examines opinions on marriage to understand both the theme of gender relations and the theme of different stages of the life cycle. He or she does this because marriage can be looked at both ways. Likewise, in the Knights of Labor study, the researcher can use temperance to understand the major theme of failed alliances and also to understand another theme, sources of division within the movement that were based on ethnic or religious differences among members.

Analytic Memo Writing

Qualitative researchers are always writing notes. Their data are recorded in notes, they write comments on their method or research strategy in notes, and so on. They are compulsive note-takers, keep their notes organized in files, and often have many files with different kinds of notes: a file on methodological issues (e.g., locations of sources or ethical issues), a file of maps or diagrams, a file on possible overall outlines of a final report or chapter, a file on specific people or events.

The *analytic memo* is a special type of note.[5] It is a memo or discussion of thoughts and ideas about the coding process that a researcher writes to himself or herself. Each coded theme or concept forms the basis of a separate memo, and the memo contains a discussion of the concept or theme. The rough theoretical notes form the beginning of analytic memos.

The analytic memo forges a link between the concrete data or raw evidence and more abstract, theoretical thinking (see Figure 16.1). It contains a researcher's reflections on and thinking about the data and coding. The researcher adds to the memo and uses it as he or she passes through the data with each type of coding. The memos form the basis for analyzing data in the research report. In fact, rewritten sections from good-quality analytic memos can become sections of the final report.

The technology involved in writing analytic memos is simple: pen and paper, a few note-books, a stack of file folders, and photocopies of notes. Some researchers use computers, but it is not necessary (see Appendix D). There are many ways to write analytic memos; each researcher develops his or her own style or method. Some concrete suggestions based on the experience of other researchers are provided in Box 16.1. Some researchers make multiple copies of notes, then cut them and place parts of a copy into an analytic memo file. This works well if the physical files are large and analytic memos are kept distinct within the file (e.g., on different-colored paper or placed at the beginning). Other researchers list within the analytic memo file locations in the data notes where a theme appears. Then it is easy to move between the analytic memo and the data. Because data notes contain highlighted or marked themes, it is easy to find specific sections in the data. An intermediate strategy is to keep a running list of locations where a major theme appears in the data, but also include copies of a few key sections of the notes for easy reference.[6]

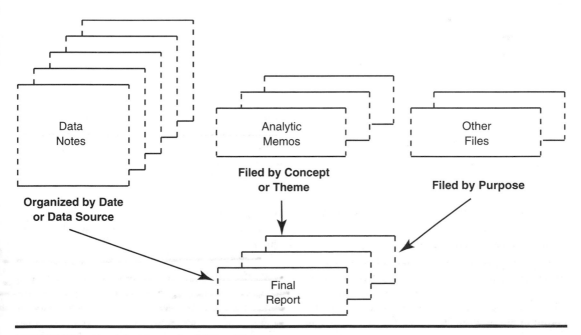

FIGURE 16.1   Analytic Memos and Other Files

Box 16.1 _____

Suggestions for Analytic Memo Writing

1. Start to write memos shortly after you begin data collection, and continue memo writing until just before the final research report is completed.
2. Put the date on memo entries so that you can see progress and the development of thinking. This will be helpful when rereading long, complicated memos, since you will periodically modify memos as research progresses and add to them.
3. Interrupt coding or data recording to write a memo. Do not wait and let a creative spark or new insight fade away—write it down.
4. Periodically read memos and compare memos on similar codes to see whether they can be combined, or whether differences between codes can be made clearer.
5. Keep a separate file for memos on each concept or theme. All memo writing on that theme or concept is kept together in one file, folder, or notebook. Label it with the name of the concept or theme so it can be located easily. It is important to be able to sort or reorganize memos physically as analysis progresses, so you should be able to sort the memos in some way.
6. Keep analytic memos and data notes separate because they have different purposes. The data are evidence. The analytic memos have a con-

ceptual, theory-building intent. They do not report data, but comment on how data are tied together or how a cluster of data is an instance of a general theme or concept.
7. Refer to other concepts within an analytic memo. When writing a memo, think of similarities to, differences between, or causal relationships to other concepts. Note these in the analytic memo to facilitate later integration, synthesis, and analysis.
8. If two ideas arise at once, put each in a separate memo. Try to keep each distinct theme or concept in a separate memo and file.
9. If nothing new can be added to a memo and you have reached a point of saturation in getting any further data on a theme or concept, indicate that in the memo.
10. Keep a list of codes or labels for the memos that will let you look down the list and see all the memos. When you periodically sort and regroup memos, reorganize this list of memo labels to correspond to the sorting.

Source: Adapted from Miles and Huberman (1994:72–76), Lofland and Lofland (1995:193–194), and Strauss (1987:127–129). Also see Lester and Hadden (1980).

As a researcher reviews and modifies analytic memos, he or she discusses ideas with colleagues and returns to the literature with a focus on new issues. Analytic memos may help to generate potential hypotheses, which can be added and dropped as needed, and to develop new themes or coding systems.

METHODS OF QUALITATIVE DATA ANALYSIS

The coding and memo-writing techniques discussed in the previous section are generic and can be used in most types of analyses. There are also more specific methods of qualitative data analysis. In this section, you will learn about five such methods selected from the all possible methods: successive approximation, the illustrative method, analytic comparison, domain analysis, and ideal types. Qualitative researchers sometimes combine the methods or use them with quantitative analysis.

In general, _data analysis_ means a search for patterns in data—recurrent behaviors, objects, or a body of knowledge. Once a pattern is identified, it is interpreted in terms of a social theory or the setting in which it occurred. The qualitative researcher moves from the description of a historical event or social setting to a more general interpretation of its meaning.

A potential source of confusion is the multiple forms that data take in various stages of qualitative research. For example, field research data are raw sense data that a researcher experiences, recorded data in field notes, and selected or processed data that appear in a final report (see Figure 16.2). Data analysis involves examining, sorting, categorizing, evaluating, comparing, synthesizing, and contemplating the coded data as well as reviewing the raw and recorded data.

Successive Approximation

This method involves repeated iterations or cycling through steps, moving toward a final analysis. Over time, or after several iterations, a researcher moves from vague ideas and concrete details in the data toward a comprehensive analysis with generalizations. This is similar to three kinds of coding discussed earlier.

A researcher begins with research questions and a framework of assumptions and concepts. He or she then probes into the data, asking questions of the evidence to see how well the concepts fit the evidence and reveal features of the data. He or she also creates new concepts by abstracting from the evidence and adjusts concepts to fit the evidence better. The researcher then collects additional evidence to address unresolved issues that appeared in the first stage, and repeats the process. At each stage, the evidence and the theory shape each other. This is called *successive approximation* because the modified concepts and the model approximate the full evidence and are modified over and over to become successively more accurate.

Each pass through the evidence is provisional or incomplete. The concepts are abstract, but they

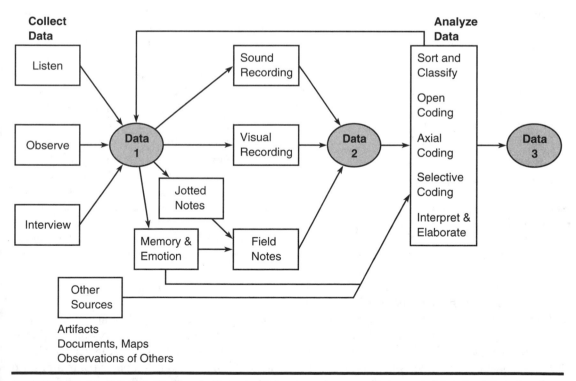

FIGURE 16.2 Data in Field Research (Data 1 = Raw sense data, experiences of researcher; Data 2 = Recorded data, physical record of experiences; Data 3 = Selected, processed data in a final report)
Source: Adapted from Ellen (1984a: 214).

are rooted in the concrete evidence and reflect the context. As the analysis moves toward generalizations that are subject to conditions and contingencies, the researcher refines generalizations and linkages to reflect the evidence better.[7] For example, a historical-comparative researcher believes that historical reality is not even or linear; rather, it has discontinuous stages or steps. He or she may divide 100 years of history into periods by breaking continuous time into discrete units or periods and define the periods theoretically. Theory helps him or her identify what is significant and what is common within periods or between different periods. As Carr (1961:76) remarked, "The division of history into periods is not a fact, but a necessary hypothesis." The breaks between periods are artificial; they are not natural in history, but they are not arbitrary.

The researcher cannot determine the number and size of periods and the breaks between them until after the evidence has been examined. He or she may begin with a general idea of how many periods to create and what distinguishes them, but will adjust the number and size of the periods and the location of the breaks after reviewing the evidence. He or she then reexamines the evidence with added data, readjusts the periodization, and so forth. After several cycles, he or she approximates a set of periods in 100 years on the basis of successively theorizing and looking at evidence.

The Illustrative Method

Another method of analysis uses empirical evidence to illustrate or anchor a theory. With the *illustrative method*, a researcher applies theory to a concrete historical situation or social setting, or organizes data on the basis of prior theory. Preexisting theory provides the *empty boxes*. The researcher sees whether evidence can be gathered to fill them.[8] The evidence in the boxes confirms or rejects the theory, which he or she treats as a useful device for interpreting the social world. The theory can be in the form of a general model, an analogy, or a sequence of steps.[9]

There are two variations of the illustrative method. One is to show that the theoretical model illuminates or clarifies a specific case or single situation. A second is the parallel demonstration of a model in which a researcher juxtaposes multiple cases (i.e., units or time periods) to show that the theory can be applied in multiple cases. In other cases, the researcher illustrates theory with specific material from multiple cases. An example of parallel demonstration is found in Paige's (1975) study of rural class conflict. Paige first developed an elaborate model of conditions that cause class conflict, and then provided evidence to illustrate it from Peru, Angola, and Vietnam. This demonstrated the applicability of the model in several cases.

Analytic Comparison

The British philosopher and social thinker, John Stuart Mill (1806–1873), developed logical methods for making comparisons that are still used today. His *method of agreement* and *method of difference* form the basis of *analytic comparison* in qualitative data analysis.[10] Aspects of this logic are also used when making comparisons in experimental research. This differs from the illustrative method in that a researcher does not begin with an overall model consisting of empty boxes to fill with details. Instead, he or she develops ideas about regularities or patterned relations from preexisting theories or induction. The researcher then focuses on a few regularities and makes contrasts with alternative explanations, then looks for regularities that are not limited to a specific setting (time, place, group). He or she is not seeking universal laws, only regularities within a social context. For example, the researcher looks for a pattern within all late twentieth-century American urban public schools, not a causal law that applies to all educational organizations or all bureaucracies.

Method of Agreement. The method of agreement focuses a researcher's attention on what is common across cases. The researcher establishes that cases have a common outcome, then tries to locate a common cause, although other features of the cases may differ. The method proceeds by a process of elimination. He or she eliminates features as possible causes if they are not shared across cases that have a common outcome. For example, a researcher looks at four cases, all of them either small social groups or entire societies. All four share two common features, but they also differ in many respects. He or she looks for one or more common causes to explain the common outcome in all cases. At the same time, alternative possibilities are eliminated and a few primary causal factors are identified. The researcher can argue that, despite the differences, the critical similarities exist.

Method of Difference. Researchers can use the method of difference alone or in conjunction with the method of agreement. The method of difference is usually stronger and is a "double application" of the method of agreement. A researcher first locates cases that are similar in many respects but differ in a few crucial ways. He or she pinpoints features whereby a set of cases are similar with regard to an outcome and causal features, and another set whereby they differ on outcomes and causal features. The method of difference reinforces information from positive cases (e.g., cases that have common causal features and outcomes) with negative cases (e.g., cases lacking the outcome and causal features). Thus, a researcher looks for cases that have many of the causal features of positive cases but lack a few key features and have a different outcome.

An Example. The method of agreement and method of difference are difficult to grasp in the abstract. Ragin (1987) provided a system for using the methods of agreement and difference. Look at Box 16.2 for an example of each method. In the method of agreement chart, note that *a* and *b* are common in all four cases and are crucial similarities despite the many differences (*c–q*). Suppose cases 1 through 4 represent four nations and the letters represent features of the nations. Thus, *a* is a democratic form of government, *b* is a social structure with several equally strong social classes, *c* is a weak army, *d* is a large professional army, *e* is a large drafted army, *f* is a large "free" public education system, and so on. Using the

method of agreement, a researcher interested in explaining outcome *a* (a democratic government) notes the regularity of *b* (several equally strong social classes) across all four cases where a democratic form of government developed. He or she hypothesizes that *b* is a critical causal factor for the development of *a*.

Now consider the second half of Box 16.2, the method of difference. Note that cases 1 and 2 are similar on five features. They differ from either case 5 or case 6 or both on all other features except *f*. A researcher who wants to explain conditions causing *a* (democratic form of government) without cases 5 or 6 may have difficulty. He or she could not separate out how important *b*, *c*, *o*, or *f* is for the form of government. Using the method of difference and including cases like cases 4 and 5, he or she notes that *x* (a dictatorship form of government) develops despite the presence of some characteristics common to democratic governments. Thus, the researcher concludes that some features such as *c* (a weak army), *o* (a single national language), and *f* (free public education system) probably are not critical to *a*. Again, it appears that *b* is the key causal feature, in that it is a crucial difference between the set of cases 1 and 2 and the set of cases 5 and 6.

Domain Analysis

The ethnographer James Spradley (1979a, 1979b) developed *domain analysis*, an innovative and comprehensive approach for analyzing qualitative data. A key part of his system, which is an organized structure for qualitative data analysis, is described here.

Spradley defined the basic unit in a cultural setting as a *domain,* an organizing idea or concept. His system is built on analyzing domains. Domains are later combined into taxonomies and broader themes to provide an overall interpretation of a cultural scene or social setting. Domains have three parts: a cover term or phrase, a semantic relationship, and included terms. The cover term is simply the domain's name. Included terms are the subtypes or parts of the domain. A semantic relationship tells how the included terms fit

Box 16.2

Example of Method of Agreement and Method of Difference

METHOD OF AGREEMENT

Case 1	Case 2	Case 3	Case 4
a	a	a	a
b	b	b	b
c	c	d	e
f	f	g	h
i	j	k	k
l	m	l	n
o	o	p	q

METHOD OF DIFFERENCE

Case 1	Case 2	Case 5	Case 6
a	a	x	x
b	b	z	q
c	c	d	c
f	f	f	f
i	j	k	k
l	m	l	n
o	o	o	q

Key: Each letter represents a characteristic of a society.

a = Society has a democratic form of government.
b = Society has a structure with several equally strong social classes.
c = Society has a weak army.
d = Society has a large professional army.
e = Society has a large drafted army.
f = Society has a large "free" and open public education system.
g = Society has a small private education system.
h = Society has a tiny, elite-only public education system.
i = Society has a single national religion.
j = Society has two equally strong religions.
k = Society has several weak religions.
l = Society has a tropical climate.
m = Society has an arctic climate.
n = Society has a temperate climate.
o = Society has a single national language.
p = Society has two equally strong languages.
q = Society has one major language and several lesser ones.
x = Society has a dictatorship form of government.

logically within the domain. For example, in the domain of a witness in a judicial setting, the cover term is "witness." Two subtypes or included terms are "defense witness" and "expert witness." The semantic relationship is "is a kind of." Thus, an expert witness and a defense witness are kinds of witnesses. Other semantic relationships are listed in Table 16.1.

TABLE 16.1   Forms of Relationships in Domains

SEMANTIC RELATIONSHIP	EXAMPLE OF USE
is a kind of	A bus *is a kind of* motor vehicle [kinds of vehicles].
is a part of/is a place in	A tire *is a part of* a car [parts of cars].
is a way to	Cheating *is a way to* get high grades in school [ways students get high grades].
is used for	A train *is used for* transporting goods [ways to transport goods].
is a reason for	High unemployment *is a reason for* public unrest [reasons for public unrest].
is a stage of	The charge *is a stage of* a battle [stages of battle].
is a result of/is a cause of	A coal power plant *is a cause of* acid rain [causes of acid rain].
is a place for	A town square *is a place for* a mob to gather [places where mobs gather].
is a characteristic of	Wearing spiked, colored hair *is a characteristic of* punks [characteristics of punks].

Spradley's system was developed by analyzing the argot of members in ethnographic field research, but it can be extended to other qualitative research. For example, Zelizer (1985) studied the changing social value of children by examining documents on attitudes and behaviors toward a child's death in the late nineteenth century. She could have used a domain analysis in which "attitude toward child's death" was a domain, and the statements of various attitudes she discovered in documents were included terms. The attitudes could be organized by the semantic relationship "is a kind of."

Spradley identified three types of domains: folk domains, mixed domains, and analytic domains. *Folk domains* contain terms from the argot of the members in a social setting. To use them, a researcher pays close attention to language and usage. The domain uses the relationship among terms from a subculture's argot or in the language of historical actors to identify cultural meaning:

Mixed domains contain folk terms, but the researcher adds his or her own concepts. For example, kinds of runners are named by the terminology of runners (e.g.. long-distance runner, track people), but a researcher observes other types of people for whom no term exists in the argot. He or she gives them labels (e.g., infrequent visitors, newcomers, amateurs).

Analytic domains contain terms from the researcher and social theory. They are most helpful when the meanings in a setting are tacit, implicit, or unrecognized by participants. The researcher infers meaningful categories and identifies patterns from observations and artifacts, then assigns terms to them.

Domains are constructed from data notes and are embedded in the notes. A researcher reads his or her notes looking for common semantic relationships (e.g., is a kind of place, is a kind of person, is a kind of feeling) in order to find them. He or she proceeds by identifying a list of cover terms. In the examples, a witness in a judicial setting or an attitude toward a child's death are cover terms for the domain. Once he or she has a list of cover terms, the researcher next organizes the information from the notes as included terms. He or she prepares a worksheet for each domain relationship. The worksheet contains the cover term, the list of included terms, and the semantic relationship. An example worksheet is shown in Box 16.3.

Next, the researcher locates examples of the domain relationship from his or her notes. The

Box 16.3 _____

Example of Domain Analysis Worksheet

1. Semantic relationship: <u>Strict inclusion</u>
2. Form: <u>X (is a kind of) Y</u>
3. Example: <u>An oak (is a kind of) tree</u>

INCLUDED TERMS	SEMANTIC RELATIONSHIP	COVER TERM
<u>laundromat</u> <u>hotel lobby</u> <u>motor box</u> <u>orchard</u>	is a kind of ——————▶	<u>flop</u>
<u>flophouse</u> <u>under bridge</u> <u>box car</u> <u>alley</u> <u>public toilet</u> <u>steam grate</u>		

Structural questions: <u>Would you call an alley a flop?</u>

INCLUDED TERMS	SEMANTIC RELATIONSHIP	COVER TERM
<u>trusty</u> <u>ranger</u> <u>bull cook</u> <u>mopper</u>	is a kind of ——————▶	<u>jail inmate</u>
<u>head trusty</u> <u>lockup</u> <u>bullet man</u> <u>sweeper</u> <u>lawn man</u> <u>inmate's barber</u>		

Structural questions: <u>Would you call a trusty a type of jail inmate?</u>

analysis proceeds until all relevant domains have been identified. He or she then organizes the domains by comparing their differences and similarities. Finally, the researcher reorganizes domains into typologies or taxonomies and reexamines the domains to create new, broader domains that include other domains as included terms.

Spradley's domain analysis formalizes six steps common to most forms of qualitative data analysis. A researcher (1) rereads data notes full of details, (2) mentally repackages details into organizing ideas, (3) constructs new ideas from notes on the subjective meanings or from the researcher's organizing ideas, (4) looks for relationships among ideas and puts them into sets on the basis of logical similarity, (5) organizes them into larger groups by comparing and contrasting

the sets of ideas, and (6) reorganizes and links the groups together with broader integrating themes. The process builds up from specifics in the notes to an overall set of logical relationships.

Ideal Types

Max Weber's *ideal type* is used by many qualitative researchers. Ideal types are models or mental abstractions of social relations or processes. They are pure standards against which the data or "reality" can be compared. An ideal type is a device used for comparison, because no reality ever fits an ideal type. For example, a researcher develops a mental model of the ideal democracy or an ideal college beer party. These abstractions, with lists of characteristics, do not describe any specific democracy or beer party; nevertheless, they are useful when applied to many specific cases to see how well each case measures up to the ideal. This stage can be used with the illustrative method described earlier.

Weber's method of ideal types also complements Mills's method of agreement. Recall that with the method of agreement, a researcher's attention is focused on what is common across cases, and he or she looks for common causes in cases with a common outcome. By itself, the method of agreement implies a comparison against actual cases. This comparison of cases could also be made against an idealized model. A researcher could develop an ideal type of a social process or relationship, then compare specific cases to it.

Qualitative researchers have used ideal types in two ways: to contrast the impact of contexts and as analogy.

Contrast Contexts.   Researchers who adopt a strongly interpretive approach may use ideal types to interpret data in a way that is sensitive to the context and cultural meanings of members. They do not test hypotheses or create a generalizable theory, but use the ideal type to bring out the specifics of each case and to emphasize the impact of the unique context.[11]

Researchers making contrasts between contexts often choose cases with dramatic contrasts or distinctive features. For example, in *Work and Authority in Industry*, Reinhard Bendix compared management relations in very different contexts, Czarist Russia and industrializing England.

When comparing contexts, researchers do not use the ideal type to illustrate a theory in different cases or to discover regularities. Instead, they accentuate the specific and the unique. Other methods of analysis focus on the general and ignore peculiarities. By contrast, a researcher who uses ideal types can show how unique features shape the operation of general processes. As Skocpol and Somers (1980:178) explained,

> Above all, contrasts are drawn between or among individual cases. Usually such contrasts are developed with the aid of references to broad themes or orienting questions or ideal type concepts. Themes and questions may serve as frameworks for pointing out differences among cases. Ideal types may be used as sensitized devices—benchmarks against which to establish the particular features of each case.

Thus, one use of the ideal type is to show how specific circumstances, cultural meanings, and the perspectives of specific individuals are central for understanding a social setting or process. The ideal type becomes a foil against which unique contextual features can be more easily seen.

Analogies.   Ideal types are used as analogies to organize qualitative data. An analogy is a statement that two objects, processes, or events are similar to each other. Researchers use them to communicate ideas and to facilitate logical comparisons. Analogies transmit information about patterns in data by referring to something that is already known or an experience familiar to the reader. Analogies can describe relationships buried deep within many details and are a shorthand method for seeing patterns in a maze of specific events. They make it easier to compare social processes across different cases or settings.[12] For example, a researcher says that a room went silent after person X spoke and "a chill like a cold gust of air" spread through it. This does not mean that the room temperature dropped or that a breeze was felt, but it succinctly expresses a rapid change in emotional tone. Likewise, a researcher reports that gender relations in society Y were such that women were "viewed like property and treated like slaves." This does not mean that the legal and social relations between genders were identical to those of slave owner and slave. It implies that an ideal type of a slave-and-master relationship would show major similarities to the evidence on relations between men and women if applied to society Y.

As analogies an ideal type serves as a <u>heuristic device (i.e., a device that helps one learn or see)</u>. It can represent something that is unknown and is especially valuable when researchers attempt to make sense of or explain data by referring to a deep structure or an underlying mechanism.[13] Ideal types do not provide a definitive test of an explanation. Rather, they guide the conceptual reconstruction of the mass of details into a systematic format.

Other Techniques

Qualitative researchers use many other analysis techniques. Here, we briefly look at four of the many other techniques to illustrate the variety (see Miles and Huberman [1994] for an extensive list). Some also stimulate researchers to gather data in new ways.

Network Analysis.   The idea of social networks was discussed in Chapter 3 with network theory and in Chapter 9 with snowball sampling. Qualitative researchers often "map" the connections among a set of people, organizations, events, or places. Using sociograms and similar mapping techniques, they can discover, analyze, and display sets of relations. For example, in a company, Harry gives Sue orders, Sue and Sam consult and help one another. Sam gets materials from Sandra. Sandra socializes with Mary. Researchers find that networks help them see and understand the structure of complex social relations.[14]

Time Allocation Analysis.   Time is an important resource. Researchers examine the way people or organizations spend or invest time to reveal implicit rules of conduct or priorities. Researchers document the duration or amount of time devoted to various activities. Often, people are unaware of or do not explicitly acknowledge the importance of an activity on which they spent time. For example, a researcher notices that certain people are required to wait before seeing a person, while others do not wait. The researcher may analyze the amount of time, who waits, what they do while waiting, and whether they feel waiting is just. Or the researcher documents that a people say that a certain celebration in a corporation is not important. Yet, everyone attends and spends two hours at the event. The collective allocation of two

hours during a busy week for the celebration signals its latent or implicit importance in the culture of the corporation.[15]

Flowchart and Time Sequence.   In addition to the amount of time devoted to various activities, researchers analyze the order of events or decisions. Historical researchers have traditionally focused on documenting the sequence of events, but comparative and field researchers also look at flow or sequence. In addition to when events occur, researchers use the idea of a decision tree or flowchart to outline the order of decisions, to understand how one event or decision is related to others. For example, an activity as simple as making a cake can be outlined (see Figure 16.3). The idea of mapping out steps, decisions, or events and looking at their interrelationship has been applied to many settings. For example, Brown and Canter (1985) developed a detailed flowchart for house-buying behavior. They divided it into 50 steps, with a time line and many actors (e.g., involved buyer, financial official, surveyor, buyer's attorney, advertising firm/realtor, seller, seller's attorney).[16]

Multiple Sorting Procedure.   Multiple sorting is a technique similar to domain analysis that a researcher can use in field research or oral history. Its purpose is to discover how people categorize their experiences or classify items into systems of similar or different. Multiple sorting procedure has been adopted by cognitive anthropologists and psychologists. It can be used to collect, verify, or analyze data. Here is how it works. The researcher gives those being studied a list of terms, photos, places, names of people, and so on, and asks them to organize the lists into categories or piles. The subjects or members use categories of their own devising. Once sorted, the researcher asks about the criteria used. The subjects are then given the items again and asked to sort them in other ways they may think of them. There is a similarity to Thurstone scaling in that people sort items, but here, the number of piles and type of items differ. More significantly, the purpose of the sorting is not to create a uniform scale but to

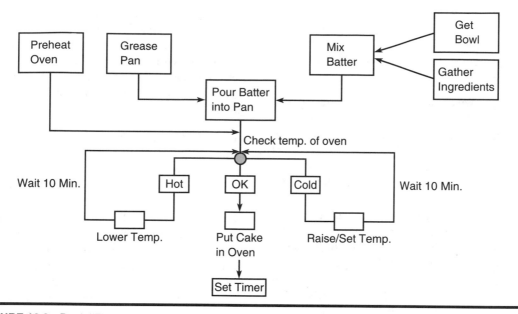

FIGURE 16.3   Partial Flowchart of Cake Making

discover the variety of ways people understand the world. For example (see Canter et al., 1985:90), a gambler sorts a list of eight gambling establishments five times. Each sort had three to four categories. One of the sorts organized them based on "class of casino" (high to low). Other sorts were based on "frills," "size of stake," "make me money," and "personal preference." By examining the sorts, the researcher sees how others organize their worlds.[17]

WHAT'S MISSING, OR THE IMPORTANCE OF NEGATIVE EVIDENCE

You have seen some of the ways that qualitative researchers analyze data. The emphasis has been on finding patterns, analyzing events, and using models to present what is found in the data. In this section, we look at how things that are *not* in the data can be important for analysis.

Negative Evidence

It may seem strange to look for things that did not happen, but the nonappearance of something can reveal a great deal and provide valuable insights.

Many researchers emphasize positive data and ignore what is not explicitly in the data, but being alert to absences is also important. For example, a field researcher notices that certain types of people are not present in a setting (e.g., older people, males) or that expected activities do not occur (e.g., no one is smoking cigarettes in a bar). The historical-comparative researcher asks why some things are not in the evidence (e.g., no reports of child abuse) or why social conditions are ignored (e.g., the U.S. has a high infant death rate for an industrial society but it is not a major public issue).

When rereading notes and coding data, it is easy to forget about things that do not appear, and it is hard to learn how to think about things that are not evident in the data but are important. One technique is to conduct a mind experiment. For example, how might things be different today if the South had won the American Civil War? Another technique is to consider nonevents when analyzing data. For example, why did the person not pick up the five-dollar bill lying on the floor when no one was looking? Comparison also helps. For example, many lower-class youths are arrested for a particular crime. Does this mean that middle-class youths do not engage in it? If not, why not?

Lewis and Lewis (1980) provided seven kinds of *negative evidence* to consider.

Events Do Not Occur. Some events are expected to occur on the basis of past experience, but do not. For example, research on the Progressive Era of U.S. history found that large corporations did not veto moderate labor reform legislation. Such a veto was expected after they had showed hostility toward labor for years. Instead, they actually encouraged the reform because it would quiet growing labor unrest and have little direct impact on them.

Likewise, nondecisions may occur when powerful groups do not have to participate directly in events because of their powerful positions which shape which issues arise. For example, a city has terrible air pollution, but there is no public action on the problem. This may be because "everyone" implicitly recognizes the power of polluting industry over jobs, tax revenue, and the community's economy. The power of the polluting industry is such that it does not have to oppose local regulations over pollution, because no such regulations are ever proposed.

Population Not Aware of Events. Some activities or events are not noticed by people in a setting or by researchers writing secondary documents. For example, at one time the fact that employers considered a highly educated woman only for clerical jobs was not noticed as an issue. Until societal awareness of sexism and gender equality grew, few saw this practice as limiting the opportunities of women. Another example is that country-western song writers deny writing with a formula. Despite their lack of awareness, a formula is apparent through a content analysis of lyrics.[18] The fact that members or participants in a setting are unaware of an issue does not mean that a researcher should ignore it or fail to look for its influence.

Population Wants to Hide Events. People may misrepresent events to protect themselves or others. For example, elites often refuse to discuss unethical behavior and may have documents destroyed or held from public access for a long period. Likewise, for many years, cases of incest went unreported in part because they violated such a serious taboo that incest was simply hushed up.

Overlook Commonplace Events. Everyday, routine events set expectations and create a taken-for-granted attitude. For example, television programs appear so often in conversations that they are rarely noticed. Because most people have a television set and watch TV regularly, only someone who rarely watches television or who is a careful analyst may notice the topic. Or a researcher observes a historical period in which cigarette smoking is common. He or she may become aware only if he or she is a nonsmoker or lives in a period when smoking has become a public health issue.

Effects of Researcher's Preconceived Notions. Researchers must take care not to let their prior theoretical framework or preconceived notions blind them to contrary events in a social setting. Strong prior notions of where to look and what data are relevant may inhibit a researcher from noticing other relevant or disconfirming evidence. For example, a researcher expects violent conflict between drug addicts and their children and notices it immediately, but fails to see that they also attempt to form a loving relationship.[19]

Unconscious Nonreporting. Some events appear to be insignificant and not worthy of being reported in the mind of a researcher. Yet, if detailed observations are recorded, a critical rereading of notes looking for negative cases may reveal overlooked events. For example, at first a researcher does not consider company picnics to be important. However, after rereading data notes and careful consideration, he or she realizes that they play an important symbolic role in building a sense of community.

Conscious Nonreporting. Researchers may omit aspects of the setting or events to protect individuals or relations in the setting. For example, a researcher discovers an extramarital affair involving a prominent person but wishes to protect the person's good name and image. A more serious problem is a breach of ethics. This occurs when a researcher fails to present evidence that does not support his or her argument or interpretation of data. Researchers should present evidence that both supports and fails to confirm an interpretation. Readers can then weigh both types of evidence and judge the support for the researcher's interpretation.

Limitation by Omission

Qualitative researchers need to be sensitive to distinctions of race, sex, and age, and to other major social divisions. For example, a white field or historical-comparative researcher who includes only whites in a study of a multiracial society needs to recognize that his or her analysis is limited and some perspectives are excluded. Had the researcher included all perspectives, his or her interpretations might have been different. When engaged in data analysis, a researcher needs to ask: What points of view are not being considered? What do events look like from the standpoint of all parts of society?

Likewise, gender has been recognized as a salient social category in most social situations. For example, it was not uncommon for historical works in the past to study "leaders," all of whom were males, and then make statements about social life in general. The same event (e.g., marriage, leisure, work) may have very different meanings and implications for each sex. Eichler (1988:160) warned: "Gender insensitivity in data interpretation takes two basic forms: ignoring sex as a socially significant variable, and ignoring a relevant sex-differentiated social context." This does not imply that single-sex or single-race studies are not valuable. Rather, when researchers interpret data, they need to be aware of alternative perspectives and not let the limits of the specific social group to which they belong, or which they studied, blind them to a broader view.

DIAGRAMS AND OTHER TOOLS

Quantitative researchers use computers to analyze data statistically. The data are often presented in the form of charts, diagrams, tables, and graphs. These researchers have been quick to adopt new information-processing technology and to employ a wide array of graphs or diagrams to present data analysis.

By contrast, qualitative researchers rely on notes, memos, and files and on technology from the nineteenth century. In the past decade, however, qualitative researchers have begun to incorporate diagrams and pictorial representations of their analysis and to use computers for data analysis (see Appendix D).

Diagrams and Qualitative Data

Qualitative researchers have moved toward presenting summaries of their data analysis in the form of diagrams and charts. They have many ways to present data analysis. Diagrams and charts help them organize ideas and systematically investigate relations in the data, as well as communicate results to readers. Researchers first use spatial or temporal maps (see Chapter 14), typology (see Chapter 3), or sociograms (see Chapter 9). For example, in his study of Little League baseball, Fine (1987) used sociograms to present the social relations among players. Likewise, Spradley's (1979a, 1979b) domain analysis makes extensive use of taxonomies.

Quantitative researchers have developed many graphs, tables, charts, and pictorial devices to present information. Qualitative researchers are beginning to do the same. Miles and Huberman (1994) advanced the visual presentation of qualitative data. They argued that data display is a critical part of qualitative analysis. In addition to taxonomies, maps, and lists, they suggested the use of flowcharts, organizational charts, causal diagrams, and various lists and grids to illustrate analysis (see Figure 16.4). An example of a diagram to assist qualitative analysis is found in Broadbent's (1989a, 1989b) study of Japanese environmental politics. He created a set of 24 small boxes

FIGURE 16.4   Example of the Use of Diagrams in Qualitative Analysis

EXAMPLE 1

Person	Worked Before College	Part-Time Job in College	Pregnant Now	Had Own Car
John	Yes	Yes	N/A	No
Mary	Yes	DK	No	Yes
Martin	No	Yes	N/A	Yes
Yoshi	Yes	No	Yes	Yes

DK = don't know, N/A = not applicable.

EXAMPLE 2

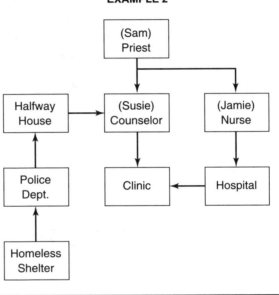

in a table to analyze and present his results. Six different political groups (e.g., political party, union, business interests, the legislature) are named across the top, and four levels or arenas of political conflict (national, prefectural, town, neighborhood) are listed up and down the side of the table to form the 24 boxes. Thus, each box represents the actions of a political group at a particular level or in one arena of politics. Broadbent drew arrows between the boxes to indicate a sequence of coalition formation, political conflict, or attempts at political influence among the groups at the different levels based on specific events and political actions.

Outcroppings

Many qualitative researchers operate on an assumption that the empirical evidence they gather is related to both their theoretical ideas and structures beneath observable reality. The relationship, modeled in Figure 16.5 suggests that a reseacher's data from the observable, surface reality are only samples of what happens on the visible, surface level. The researcher uses the data to generate and evaluate theories and generalizations. At the same time, he assumes that beneath the outer surface of reality lie deeper social structures or relationships.

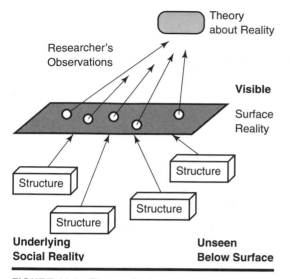

FIGURE 16.5 Theory, Surface Reality, and Underlying Structures

The surface reality that we see only partially reflects what goes on unseen, beneath the surface. Events on the surface are *outcroppings*, to use a term from geology (see Fetterman, 1989:68). In geology, an outcropping is the part of bedrock that is exposed on the surface for people to see. It is the outward manifestation of central, solid features of the land. Geologists study outcroppings to get clues about what lies beneath the surface.

There are many things we cannot directly observe in the social world. We cannot observe a deep loving relationship between two people. We can see its outward manifestation in a kiss, specific deeds of affection, and acts of kindness. Likewise, we cannot directly observe a social structure such as social class. We can see its outward signs in differences in how people act, their career assumptions, their material possessions,

and so forth. Sometimes, we are misled by outward observation. Researchers use qualitative data analysis to examine and organize the observable data so that their ideas and theories about the social world reflect not only the surface level of reality but, more important, the deeper structures and forces that may lie unseen beneath the surface.

CONCLUSION

In this chapter, you have learned how researchers analyze qualitative data. In many respects, qualitative data are more difficult to deal with than data in the form of numbers. Numbers have mathematical properties that let a researcher use statistical procedures. Qualitative analysis requires more effort by an individual researcher to read and reread data notes, reflect on what is read, and make comparisons based on logic and judgment.

Most forms of qualitative data analysis involve coding and writing analytic memos. Both are labor-intensive efforts by the researcher to read over data carefully and think about them seriously. In addition, you learned about methods that researchers have used for the analysis of qualitative data. They are a sample of the many methods of qualitative data analysis. You also learned about the importance of thinking about negative evidence and events that are not present in the data.

This chapter ends the section of the book on research design, data collection, and data analysis. Social research also involves preparing reports on a research project and dealing with ethical issues. These considerations are also part of the process of social research and are discussed in Chapter 17 and in Appendix C.

KEY TERMS

analytic comparison	empty boxes	mixed domains
analytic domain	folk domain	negative evidence
analytic memo	ideal type	open coding
axial coding	illustrative method	outcropping
domain	method of agreement	selective coding
domain analysis	method of difference	successive approximation

REVIEW QUESTIONS

1. Identify four differences between quantitative and qualitative data analysis.
2. How does the process of conceptualization differ in qualitative and quantitative research?
3. How does data coding differ in quantitative and qualitative research, and what are the three kinds of coding used by a qualitative researcher?
4. What is the purpose of analytic memo writing in qualitative data analysis?
5. Describe *successive approximation*.
6. What are the *empty boxes* in the illustrative method and how are they used?
7. What is the difference between the method of agreement and the method of difference? Can a researcher use both together? Explain why or why not.
8. What are the parts of a domain and how are they used in domain analysis?
9. How are ideal types used to contrast contexts?
10. Why is it important to look for "negative evidence," or things that do not appear in the data, for a full analysis?

NOTES

1. See Miles and Huberman (1994) and Ragin (1987). These should not be confused with statistical techniques for "qualitative" data (see Haberman, 1978). These are sophisticated statistical techniques (e.g., logit, log linear) for quantitative variables where the data are at the nominal or ordinal level. They are better labeled as techniques for categorical data.
2. Sprague and Zimmerman (1989) discuss the importance of an explicit theory.
3. See Hammersley and Atkinson (1983:174–206) for a discussion of questions.
4. See also Horan (1987) and Strauss (1987:25) for multiple indicator measurement models with qualitative data.
5. For more on memoing, see Lester and Hadden (1980), Lofland and Lofland (1995:193–197), Miles and Huberman (1994:72–77), and Strauss (1987:107–129).
6. Also see Barzun and Graff (1970:255–274), Bogdan and Taylor (1975), Lofland and Lofland (1984:131–140), Shafer (1980:171–200), Spradley (1979a, 1979b), and Schatzman and Strauss (1973:104–120) on notes and codes.
7. For more on successive approximation and a debate over it, see Applebaum (1978a), McQuaire (1978, 1979), Thompson (1978), Wardell (1979), and Young (1980).
8. For a discussion of empty boxes, see Bonnell (1980) and Smelser (1976).

9. For discussions of the illustrative method, see Bonnell (1980) and Skocpol (1984). Bogdan and Taylor (1975:79) describe a similar method.
10. For a discussion of methods of difference and agreement, see Ragin (1987:36–42), Skocpol and Somers (1980), Skocpol (1984), and Stinchcombe (1978:25–29).
11. See Skocpol (1984) and Skocpol and Somers (1980).
12. For a discussion of analogies and models, see Barry (1975), Glucksmann (1974), Harré (1972), Hesse (1970), and Kaplan (1964).
13. For discussions of the importance of analogies in social theory, see Lloyd (1986:127–132) and Stinchcombe (1978).
14. See Sanjek (1978) and Werner and Schoepfle (1986a).
15. See Gross (1984) and Miles and Huberman (1994:85, 119–126).
16. See Bernstein (1988:324–334), Lofland and Lofland (1995:199–200), and Werner and Schoepfle (1986a:130–146).
17. See Canter et al. (1985) and Werner and Schoepfle (1986a:180–181).
18. See Blee and Billings (1986) for a discussion of analyzing "silences" and unnoticed features in ethnographic or historical text.
19. See Becker and Geer (1982) for a discussion of negative cases and preconceived notions.

RECOMMENDED READINGS

Miles, Matthew B., and A. Michael Huberman. (1994). *Qualitative data analysis*, 2nd ed. Thousand Oaks, CA: Sage. This unusual book is full of diagrams, lists, and charts. The authors present a collection of ways to analyze qualitative field research data. They move from field observation, to coding notes, to organizing codes into generalizations, and finally to presenting generalizations in the form of diagrams.

Ragin, Charles C. (1987). *The comparative method: Moving beyond qualitative and quantitative strategies*. Berkeley: University of California Press. Ragin presents an innovative method for the analysis of qualitative data, using Boolean algebra. His method is based on a systematic investigation of logical relationships. It gives researchers a way to analyze a small number of cases in which several conditions are measured as present or absent in each case. He applies the method to several major works in historical-comparative research to show its utility. The method helps researchers find instances where the combination of several conditions produces a specific outcome.

Stinchcombe, Arthur L. (1978). *Theoretical methods in social history*. New York: Academic Press. In this short book, Stinchcombe examines major works by Reinhard Bendix, Alexis de Tocqueville, Neil Smelser, and Leon Trotsky to discover how they used theory in the analysis of historical phenomena. He argues for a method of qualitative historical analysis that forms concepts from specific details then uses analogies to organize descriptions of historical events into causal explanations.

Strauss, Anselm. (1987). *Qualitative analysis for social scientists*. New York: Cambridge University Press. Strauss provides an approach for the analysis of qualitative data based on a grounded theory model from field research. Although parts of this book are somewhat sophisticated, it is a step-by-step guide for qualitative data analysis, from gaining access to writing up a report. Strauss gives extensive examples of field notes, which he then analyzes.

CHAPTER 17

ETHICAL AND POLITICAL ISSUES IN SOCIAL RESEARCH

But since we do not as yet live in a period free from mundane troubles and beyond history, our problem is not how to deal with a kind of knowledge which shall be "truth in itself," but rather how man deals with his problems of knowing, bound as he is in his knowledge by his position in time and society.

—Karl Mannheim, *Ideology and Utopia*, p. 188

INTRODUCTION

How would you react if a person unexpectedly collapsed in front of you, perhaps with blood dripping from his mouth? Would you become upset? Is it ethical for researchers secretly to stage such behavior for people riding in a subway car, just to see how they react? Should you protect research subjects from the risk of being arrested simply because they were in a study? For example, in a field research study on a gang, you learn that the gang plans to rob a liquor store. What do you do—call the police, leave when the illegal behavior is discussed, tell gang members of the dilemma, destroy all your notes, or go to jail for refusing to cooperate with the police? Should you compromise the standards of good research in order to keep a job? For example, you get a job doing research for a government agency. Your preliminary results show that the agency is wasteful and disorganized. Your supervisor tells you to destroy these results and rig the study by using a biased sample and questionnaire. What do you do—go along to keep your job, or blow the whistle and cause controversy?

In this chapter, you will learn about the ethics and politics of social research. This final chapter touches all of the topics covered previously. It involves serious issues that you will probably continue to think about after finishing this book.

The researcher faces many ethical dilemmas and must decide how to act. Codes of ethics and other researchers provide guidance, but ethical conduct ultimately depends on the individual researcher. The researcher has a moral and professional obligation to be ethical, even when research subjects are unaware of or unconcerned about ethics. Indeed, many subjects are less concerned about protecting their privacy and other rights than are researchers.[1]

The ethical issues are the concerns, dilemmas, and conflicts that arise over the proper way to conduct research. Ethics define what is or is not legitimate to do, or what "moral" research procedure involves. There are few ethical absolutes. Most issues involve trade-offs between competing values and depend on the specific situation.

Although there are few fixed rules, there are agreed-upon principles. These principles may conflict in practice. Many ethical issues involve a balance between two values: the pursuit of scientific knowledge and the rights of those being studied or of others in society. Potential benefits such as advancing our understanding of social life, improving decision making, or helping research participants must be weighed against potential costs such as a loss of dignity, self-esteem, privacy, or democratic freedoms.

The standards for ethical research are stricter than those in many other areas of society (e.g., collection agencies, police departments, advertisers). Professional social research requires both knowledge of proper research techniques (e.g., sampling) and sensitivity to ethical concerns in research. This is not easy. As Reynolds (1979:7) observed, "The types of dilemmas now being confronted by social scientists have received attention for centuries by those concerned with general problems in moral, legal, and political philosophy."

ETHICAL CONCERNS AND THE INDIVIDUAL RESEARCHER

The Individual Researcher

Ethics begins and ends with you, the researcher. A researcher's personal moral code is the strongest defense against unethical behavior. Before, during, and after conducting a study, a researcher has opportunities to, and *should*, reflect on research actions and consult his or her conscience. Ethical research depends on the integrity of the individual researcher and his or her values. "If values are to be taken seriously, they cannot be expressed and laid aside but must instead be guides to actions for the sociologist. They determine who will be investigated, for what purpose and in whose service" (Sagarin, 1973:63).

Why Be Ethical?

Given that most people who conduct social research are genuinely concerned about others, why would a researcher act in an ethically irresponsible manner? Outside of the rare disturbed individual, most unethical behavior results from pressures on researchers to take ethical shortcuts. Researchers face pressures to build a career, publish, advance knowledge, gain prestige, impress family and friends, hold on to a job, and so forth. Ethical research takes longer to complete, costs more money, is more complicated, and is more likely to be terminated before completion. Moreover, written ethical standards are in the form of vague principles. There are many places where it is possible to act unethically, and the odds of getting caught are small.

There are few rewards available for ethical research. The unethical researcher, if caught, faces public humiliation, a ruined career, and possible legal action, but the ethical researcher wins no praise. Ethical behavior arises from a sensitivity to ethical concerns that researchers internalize during their professional training, from a professional role, and from personal contact with other researchers. Moreover, the norms of the scientific community reinforce ethical behavior with an emphasis on honesty and openness. Researchers who are oriented toward their professional role, who are committed to the scientific ethos, and who interact regularly with other researchers are likely to act ethically.

Scientific Misconduct. The research community and government agencies that fund research oppose unethical behavior called scientific misconduct, which includes research fraud and plagiarism. *Scientific misconduct* occurs when a researcher falsifies or distorts the data or the methods of data collection, or plagiarizes the work of others. It also includes significant departures from the generally accepted practices of the scientific community for doing or reporting on research. Research institutes and universities have policies and procedures to detect misconduct, report it to the scientific community and funding agencies, and penalize researchers who engage in it (e.g., through a pay cut or loss of job).[2]

Research fraud occurs when a researcher fakes or invents data that were not really collected, or falsely reports how research was conducted. Though rare, it is treated very seriously. The most famous case of fraud was the scandal of Sir Cyril Burt, the father of British educational psychology. Burt died in 1971 as an esteemed researcher who was famous for his studies with twins that showed a genetic basis of intelligence. In 1976, it was discovered that he had falsified data and the names of coauthors. Unfortunately, the scientific community had been misled for nearly 30 years.

Plagiarism is fraud that occurs when a researcher steals the ideas or writings of another or uses them without citing the source. A special type of plagiarism is stealing the work of another researcher, an assistant, or a student, and misrepresenting it as one's own. These are serious breaches of ethical standards, but they do sometimes occur.[3]

Unethical but Legal. Behavior may be unethical but not break the law. The distinction between legal and ethical behavior is illustrated in a plagiarism case. The American Sociological Association documented that a 1988 book without footnotes by a dean from Eastern New Mexico University contained large sections of a 1978 dissertation written by a sociology professor at Tufts University. The copying was not *illegal*; it did not violate copyright law because the sociologist's dissertation did not have a copyright filed with the U.S. government. Nevertheless, it was clearly *unethical* according to standards of professional behavior (see Figure 17.1 for relations between legal and moral actions).[4]

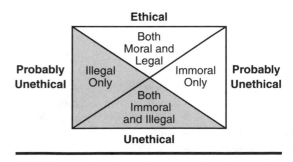

FIGURE 17.1 Typology of Legal and Moral Actions in Research

Power

The relationship between the researcher and subjects or employee-assistants involves power and trust. The experimenter, survey director, or research investigator has power relative to subjects or assistants. The power is legitimated by credentials, expertise, training, and the role of science in modern society. Some ethical issues involve an abuse of power and trust.

The researcher's authority to conduct research, granted by professional communities and the larger society, is accompanied by a responsibility to guide, protect, and oversee the interests of the people being studied. For example, a physician was discovered to have conducted experimental gynecological surgery on 33 women without their permission. The women had trusted the doctor, but he had abused the trust that the women, the professional community, and society placed in him.[5]

The researcher seeking ethical guidance is not alone. He or she can turn to a number of resources: professional colleagues, ethical advisory committees, institutional review boards or human subjects committees at a college or institution, codes of ethics from professional associations, and writings on ethics in research.

ETHICAL ISSUES INVOLVING RESEARCH SUBJECTS

Have you ever been a subject in a research study? If so, how were you treated? More attention is focused on the possible negative effects of research on those being studied than any other ethical issue, beginning with concerns about biomedical research. Ethical research requires balancing the value of advancing knowledge against the value of noninterference in the lives of others. Giving research subjects absolute rights of noninterference could make empirical research impossible, but giving researchers absolute rights of inquiry could nullify subjects' basic human rights. The moral question becomes: When, if ever, are researchers justified in risking physical harm or injury to those being studied, causing them great embarrassment, or frightening them?

The law and codes of ethics recognize some clear prohibitions: Never cause unnecessary or irreversible harm to subjects; secure prior voluntary consent when possible; and never unnecessarily humiliate, degrade, or release harmful information about specific individuals that was collected for research purposes. These are minimal standards and are subject to interpretation (e.g., what does *unnecessary* mean in a specific situation?).

Origins of Human Subject Protection

Concern over the treatment of research subjects arose after the revelation of gross violations of basic human rights in the name of science. The most notorious violations were "medical experiments" conducted on Jews and others in Nazi Germany. In these experiments, terrible tortures were committed. For example, people were placed in freezing water to see how long it took them to die, people were purposely starved to death, and limbs were severed from children and transplanted onto others.[6]

Such human rights violations do not occur only in Germany, nor did they happen only long ago. A symbol of unethical research is the Tuskegee Syphilis Study, also known as *Bad Blood*. Until the 1970s, when a newspaper report caused a scandal to erupt, the U.S. Public Health Service sponsored a study in which poor, uneducated black men in Alabama suffered and died of untreated syphilis, while researchers studied the severe physical disabilities that appear in advanced stages of the disease. The study began in 1929, before penicillin was available to treat the disease, but it continued long after treatment was available. Despite their unethical treatment of the subjects, the researchers were able to publish their results for 40 years.[7]

Unfortunately, the Bad Blood scandal was not unique. During the 1960s, live cancer cells were injected into ill patients without consent. The U.S. military gave LSD to unsuspecting individuals, a few of whom became mentally ill from the experience, and exposed soldiers to nuclear radiation, later resulting in high cancer rates. These examples are clear violations of ethical standards: The subjects suffered permanent physical harm and they did not give prior voluntary consent to participate in the study.[8]

Physical Harm, Psychological Abuse, Stress, or Legal Jeopardy

Social research can harm a research subject in several ways: physical harm, psychological harm, legal harm, and harm to a person's career or income. Physical harm is rare, even in biomedical research, where the intervention is much greater; 3 to 5 percent of studies involved any subject who suffered any harm. Different types of harm are more likely in different types of research (e.g., in experiments versus field research). Researchers need to be aware of all types of harm and minimize them at all times.[9]

Physical Harm.   A straightforward ethical principle is that researchers should not cause physical harm. An ethical researcher anticipates risks before beginning research, including basic safety concerns (safe buildings, furniture, and equipment). He or she screens out high-risk subjects (those with heart conditions, mental breakdown, or seizures) if stress is involved and anticipates the danger of injury or physical attacks on research subjects or assistants. The researcher accepts moral and legal responsibility for injury due to participation in research and terminates a project immediately if he or she can no longer guarantee the physical safety of the people involved (see the Zimbardo study in Box 17.1).

Psychological Abuse, Stress, or Loss of Self-Esteem.   The risk of physical harm is rare in social research, but social researchers may place people in stressful, embarrassing, anxiety-producing, or unpleasant situations. Researchers learn about how people respond in real-life, highly anxiety-producing situations by placing subjects in realistic situations of psychological discomfort or stress. Is it unethical to cause discomfort? The ethics of the famous Milgram obedience study are still debated (see Box 17.1). Some say that the precautions taken and the knowledge gained outweighed the stress and potential psychological

harm that subjects experienced. Others believe that the extreme stress and the risk of permanent harm were too great.

Social researchers have created high levels of anxiety or discomfort: exposing subjects to gruesome photos; falsely telling male students that they have strongly feminine personality traits; falsely telling students that they have failed; creating a situation of high fear (e.g., smoke entering a room in which the door is locked); asking subjects to harm others; placing people in a situation where they face social pressure to deny their convictions; having subjects lie, cheat, or steal.[10] Researchers who study helping behavior often place subjects in emergency situations to see whether the subjects will lend assistance. For example, Piliavin, Rodin, and Piliavin (1969) studied helping behavior in subways by faking someone's collapse onto the floor. In the field experiment, the riders in the subway car were unaware of the experiment and did not volunteer to participate in it.

A sensitive researcher is also aware of possible harm to a subject's self-esteem. For example, Walster (1965) wanted to see whether changes in feelings of female self-worth affect romantic liking. In her experiment, undergraduate women were given personality tests followed by phony feedback. Some subjects were told that they lacked imagination and creativity. Next, a handsome male graduate student who pretended to be another subject struck up a conversation with the women. The graduate student acted very interested in one woman and asked her out for a dinner date. The researcher wanted to measure the woman's romantic attraction to the male. After the experiment, the subject was told of the hoax; there was no date and the man was not interested in her. Although the subjects were debriefed, they suffered a loss of self-esteem and possible psychological harm.[11]

Only experienced researchers who take precautions before inducing anxiety, or discomfort should consider conducting experiments that induce significant stress or anxiety. They should consult with others who have conducted similar studies and mental health professionals when planning the study, screen out high-risk populations

Box 17.1 _____

Three Cases of Ethical Controversy

Stanley Milgram's *obedience study* (Milgram, 1963, 1965, 1974) attempted to discover how the horrors of the Holocaust under the Nazis could have occurred by examining the strength of social pressure to obey authority. After signing "informed consent forms," subjects were assigned, in rigged random selection, to be a "teacher" while a confederate was the "pupil." The teacher was to test the pupil's memory of word lists and increase the electric shock level if the pupil made mistakes. The pupil was located in a nearby room, so the teacher could hear but not see the pupil. The shock apparatus was clearly labeled with increasing voltage. As the pupil made mistakes and the teacher turned switches, she or he also made noises as if in severe pain. The researcher was present and made comments such as "You must go on" to the teacher. Milgram reported, "Subjects were observed to sweat, tremble, stutter, bite their lips, groan and dig their fingernails into their flesh. These were characteristic rather than exceptional responses to the experiment" (Milgram, 1963:375). The percentage of subjects who would shock to dangerous levels was dramatically higher than expected. Ethical concerns arose over the use of deception and the extreme emotional stress experienced by subjects.

In Laud Humphreys's (Humphreys, 1975) *tearoom trade study* (a study of male homosexual encounters in public restrooms), about 100 men were observed engaging in sexual acts as Humphreys pretended to be a "watchqueen" (a voyeur and lookout). Subjects were followed to their cars, and their license numbers were secretly recorded. Names and addresses were obtained from police registers when Humphreys posed as a market researcher. A year later, in disguise,

Humphreys used a deceptive story about a health survey to interview the subjects in their homes. Humphreys was careful to keep names in safety deposit boxes, and identifiers with subject names were burned. He significantly advanced knowledge of homosexuals who frequent "tearooms" and overturned previous false beliefs about them. There has been controversy over the study: The subjects never consented; deception was used; and the names could have been used to blackmail subjects, to end marriages, or to initiate criminal prosecution.

In the *Zimbardo prison experiment* (Zimbardo, 1972, 1973; Zimbardo et al., 1973, 1974), male students were divided into two role-playing groups: guards and prisoners. Before the experiment, volunteer students were given personality tests, and only those in the "normal" range were chosen. Volunteers signed up for two weeks, and prisoners were told that they would be under surveillance and would have some civil rights suspended, but that no physical abuse was allowed. In a simulated prison in the basement of a Stanford University building, prisoners were deindividualized (dressed in standard uniforms and called only by their numbers) and guards were militarized (with uniforms, nightsticks, and reflective sunglasses). Guards were told to maintain a reasonable degree of order and served 8-hour shifts, while prisoners were locked up 24 hours per day. Unexpectedly, the volunteers became too caught up in their roles. Prisoners became passive and disorganized, while guards became aggressive, arbitrary, and dehumanizing. By the sixth day, Zimbardo called off the experiment for ethical reasons. The risk of permanent psychological harm, and even physical harm, was too great.

_____

(e.g., those with emotional problems or a weak heart), and arrange for emergency interventions or termination of the research if dangerous situations arise. Researchers should always get informed consent (to be discussed) before the research and debrief subjects immediately afterward.

Researchers should never create *unnecessary* stress, beyond the minimal amount needed to create the desired effect, or stress that has no direct,

legitimate research purpose. Knowing the minimal amount comes with experience. It is better to begin with too little stress, risking finding no effect, than to create too much. If the level of stress could have long-term effects, the researcher should follow up and offer free psychological counseling.

Research that creates stress and anxiety also carries the danger that experimenters will develop a callous or manipulative attitude toward others. Researchers report guilt and regrets after conducting experiments that caused psychological harm to subjects. Experiments that place subjects in anxiety-producing situations may produce discomfort for the ethical researcher.

Legal Harm.   A researcher is responsible for protecting subjects from increased risk of arrest. If participation in research increases the risk of arrest, subjects will distrust researchers and be unwilling to participate in future research. Researchers may be able to secure clearance from law enforcement authorities before conducting certain types of research. For example, the U.S. Department of Justice provides written waivers for researchers studying criminal behavior.

Potential legal harm is one criticism of the study in Humphreys (see Box 17.1). In the New Jersey Negative Income Tax Experiment, those participating in the experiment received income supplements, but no explicit provision was made for monitoring whether they also received welfare checks. A local prosecuting attorney requested data on participants to identify "welfare cheats." In other words, subjects were at legal risk because they had participated in the experiment. Eventually, the conflict was resolved, but it illustrates that researchers should be aware of potential legal problems.

A related ethical issue arises when a researcher learns of illegal activity when collecting data. A researcher must weigh the value of protecting the researcher subject relationship and the benefits to future researchers against potential harm to innocent people. A researcher bears the cost of his or her judgment. For example, in his field research on police, Van Maanen (1982:114–115) reported seeing police beat people and witnessing illegal acts and irregular procedures, but said, "On and following these troublesome incidents . . . I followed police custom: I kept my mouth shut."

Field researchers often face difficult ethical decisions. For example, when studying a mental institution, Taylor (1987) discovered the mistreatment and abuse of inmates by the staff. He had

two choices: Abandon the study and call for an investigation, or keep quiet and continue with the study for several months, publicize the findings afterwards, and then advocate an end to abuse. After weighing the situation, he followed the latter course and is now an activist for the rights of mental institution inmates.

A similar ethical dilemma is illustrated by the case of a New York restaurant fire that was complicated by the issue of confidentiality. A sociology graduate student was conducting a participant observation study of waiters. During the research project, the field site, a restaurant, burned down, and arson was suspected. Local legal authorities requested the field notes and wanted to interrogate the researcher about activity in the restaurant. The researcher faced a dilemma: He could cooperate with the investigation and violate the trust, confidentiality, and integrity of ethical research; or he could uphold confidentiality and protect his subjects, but face contempt of court and obstruction of justice penalties, including fines and jail. He wanted to behave ethically but stay out of jail. After years of legal battles, the situation was resolved with limited cooperation by the researcher and a judicial ruling upholding the confidentiality of field notes. Nevertheless, the issue took years to resolve, and the researcher bore substantial financial and personal costs.[12]

Observing illegal behavior may be central to a research project. A researcher who covertly observes and records illegal behavior, then supplies information to law enforcement authorities, violates ethical standards regarding research subjects and undermines future research. Yet, a researcher who fails to report illegal behavior indirectly permits criminal behavior and could be charged as an accessory to a crime. Is the researcher a professional seeking knowledge or a free-lance undercover informant?

Other Harm to Subjects.   Research subjects may face other types of harm. For example, a survey interview may create anxiety and discomfort among subjects who are asked to recall unpleasant events. The ethical researcher is sensitive to any harm to subjects, considers possible precautions, and weighs potential harm against potential benefits. Another risk of harm to subjects is that of a negative effect on their careers or incomes. For example, a researcher conducts a survey of employees and concludes that the supervisor's performance is poor. As a consequence, the supervisor loses her job. Or a researcher studies welfare recipients. As a consequence, the recipients lose their health insurance and their quality of life declines. What is the researcher's responsibility? The ethical researcher considers the consequences of research for the lives of those being studied. But there is no fixed answer to such questions. A researcher must evaluate each case, weigh potential harm against potential benefits, and bear the responsibility for the decision.

Deception

Has anyone ever told you a half-truth or lie to get you to do something? How did you feel about it? Social researchers follow the ethical *principle of voluntary consent*: Never force anyone to participate in research, and do not lie unless it is required for legitimate research reasons. The people who participate in social research should, under most conditions, explicitly agree to participate. The right of a person not to participate becomes a critical issue whenever the researcher uses deception, disguises the research, or uses covert research methods.[13]

Social researchers sometimes deceive or lie to subjects in field and experimental research. A researcher might misrepresent his or her actions or true intentions for legitimate methodological reasons: If subjects knew the true purpose, they would modify their behavior, making it impossible to learn of their real behavior, or access to a research site might be impossible if he or she told the truth. Deception is never preferable if the researcher could accomplish the same thing without deception. Experimental researchers often deceive subjects to prevent them from learning the true hypothesis and to reduce reactive effects. Deception is acceptable only if there is a specific methodological purpose for it, and even then, it should be used only to the minimal degree necessary. A researcher who uses deception should obtain informed consent, never misrepresent risks, and always debrief subjects afterwards. He or she can describe the basic procedures involved and conceal only specific information about hypotheses being tested.

Covert observation may be required in some field research settings to gain entry and access. If a covert stance is not essential, a researcher should never use it. If he or she does not know whether covert access is necessary, then a strategy of gradual disclosure may be best. It is better to err in the direction of disclosing one's true identity and purpose. In some situations, such as the study of cults, small extremist political sects, illegal or deviant behavior, or behavior in a large public area, it may be impossible to conduct research if a researcher discloses her true purpose. Researchers have studied satanic cults, UFO cults, and homosexual contacts in public restrooms with covert observation. Covert research remains controversial, and some researchers feel that all covert research is unethical.[14] The code of ethics of the American Anthropological Association condemns it as "impractical and undesirable." Even those who accept covert research as ethical in some situations argue that it should be used only when overt observation is impossible. In addition, if possible, the researcher should inform subjects of the observation afterwards and give them an opportunity to express concerns.

Deception and covert research may increase mistrust and cynicism, and diminish public respect for social research. Misrepresentation in field research is analogous to being an undercover agent or informer in nondemocratic societies. Deception can increase distrust by people who are frequently studied. In one case, the frequent use of deception reduced helping behavior. When a student was shot at the University of Washington in Seattle in 1973, students crossing the campus made no attempt to assist. Later, it was discovered that many of the bystanders did not help because they thought that the shooting was staged as part of an experiment.[15]

Informed Consent

A fundamental ethical principle of social research is: Never coerce anyone into participating; participation *must* be voluntary. It is not enough to get permission from subjects; they need to know what they are being asked to participate in so that they can make an informed decision. Subjects can become aware of their rights and what they are getting involved in when they read and sign a statement giving *informed consent*, a written agreement to participate given by subjects after they learn something about the research procedure.

The U.S. federal government does not require informed consent in all research involving human subjects. Nevertheless, researchers should get written consent unless there are good reasons for not obtaining it (e.g., covert field research, use of secondary data) as judged by an institutional review board (IRB) (see the later discussion of IRBs).

Informed consent statements provide specific information (see Box 17.2).[16] A general statement about the kinds of procedures or questions

---

Box 17.2 _____

Informed Consent Statements Contain:

1. A brief description of the purpose and procedure of the research, including the expected duration of the study
2. A statement of any risks or discomfort associated with participation
3. A guarantee of anonymity and the confidentiality of records
4. The identification of the researcher and of where to receive information about subjects' rights or questions about the study
5. A statement that participation is completely voluntary and can be terminated at any time without penalty
6. A statement of alternative procedures that may be used
7. A statement of any benefits or compensation provided to subjects and the number of subjects involved
8. An offer to provide a summary of findings

---

involved and the uses of the data are sufficient for informed consent. In a study by Singer (1978), one random group of survey respondents received a detailed informed consent statement and another did not. No significant differences were discovered. If anything, people who refused to sign such a statement were more likely to guess or answer "no response" to questions.

In their meta-analysis of the literature on giving assurances of confidentiality (see Chapter 5 on meta-analysis), Singer, Von Thurn, and Miller (1995) found that assuring confidentiality modestly improved responses when researchers asked about highly sensitive topics. In other situations, extensive assurances of confidentiality failed to affect how or whether subjects responded.

Full disclosure with the researcher's identification helps protect subjects against fraudulent research, as well as protects legitimate researchers. Informed consent lessens the chance that a con artist in the guise of a researcher will defraud or abuse subjects, and it reduces the likelihood of the bogus use of a researcher's identity to market products or obtain information for personal advantage.

Signed informed consent statements are optional for most survey, field, and secondary data research, but are often mandated for experimental research. They are impossible to obtain in documentary research and in most telephone interview studies. The general rule is: The greater the risk of potential harm to subjects, the greater the need for a written consent statement. In sum, there are many reasons to get informed consent and few reasons not to get it.

Special Populations and New Inequalities

Special Populations and Coercion. Some populations or groups of subjects are not capable of giving true voluntary informed consent. They may lack the necessary competency or may be indirectly coerced. Students, prison inmates, employees, military personnel, the homeless, welfare recipients, children, or the mentally retarded may agree to participate in research. Yet, they may not be fully capable of making a decision, or may agree to participate only because some desired good—such as higher grades, early parole, promotions, or additional services—requires an agreement to participate.

It is unethical to involve "incompetent" people (e.g., children, the mentally retarded) in research unless two conditions are met: A legal guardian grants written permission, and the researcher follows all ethical principles against harm to subjects. For example, a researcher wants to conduct a survey of smoking and drug/alcohol use among high school students. If it is conducted on school property, school officials must give permission, and written parental permission is needed for any subject who is a legal minor. It is best to ask permission, from each student as well.

It is unethical to coerce people to participate, including offering them special benefits that they cannot otherwise attain. For example, it is unethical for a commanding officer to order a soldier to participate in a study, for a professor to require a student to be a research subject in order to pass a course, or for an employer to expect an employee to complete a survey as a condition of continued employment. It is unethical even if someone other than the researcher (e.g., an employer) coerced people (e.g., employees) to participate in research.

Whether or not coercion to participate is involved can be a complex issue, and a researcher must evaluate the issue in each case. For example, a convicted criminal is given the alternative of imprisonment or participation in an experimental rehabilitation program. The convicted criminal may not believe in the benefits of the program, but the researcher may believe that it will help the criminal. This is a case of coercion, but the researcher must judge whether the benefits to the subject and to society outweigh the ethical prohibition on coercion.

Teachers sometimes require students in social science courses to participate as subjects in research projects. This is a special case of coercion. Three arguments have been made in favor of requiring participation: (1) it would be difficult and prohibitively expensive to get subjects otherwise; (2) the knowledge created from research with students serving as subjects will benefit future students and society; (3) students will learn more about research by experiencing it directly in a realistic research setting. Of the three arguments, only the third justifies limited coercion. Limited coercion is acceptable only as long as it has a clear educational objective, the students are given a choice of research experience, and other ethical principles are upheld.[17]

Creating New Inequalities. Another type of harm occurs when one group of subjects is denied some service or benefit as a result of participation in a research project. This may be unavoidable for good research design. For example, a researcher has a new treatment for subjects with a terrible disease, such as acquired immune deficiency syndrome (AIDS). In order to determine the effects of the new treatment, some subjects receive it while others are given a placebo. The design will show whether or not the drug is effective, but subjects in the control group who receive the placebo may die. Of course, those receiving the drug may also die until more is known about whether it is effective. Is it ethical to deny subjects who have been randomly assigned to the control group the potentially life-saving treatment? What if a clear, definitive test of whether the drug is effective requires a control group that receives a placebo?

A researcher can reduce new inequality among subjects in three ways. First, subjects who do not receive the "new, improved" treatment continue to receive the best previously acceptable treatment. In other words, the control group is not denied all assistance, but they receive the best treatment available prior to the new one being tested. This ensures that subjects in the control group will not suffer in absolute terms, even if they temporarily fall behind in relative terms. Second, researchers can use *crossover designs*, whereby the control group for the first phase of the experiment becomes the experimental group in the second phase, and vice versa. Finally, the researcher carefully and continuously monitors results. If it appears early in the experiment that the new treatment is highly effective, the new treatment should be offered to control group subjects. Also, in high-risk experiments with medical treatments or possible physical harm, researchers may use animal or other surrogates for humans.

Privacy, Anonymity, and Confidentiality

How would you feel if private details about your personal life were shared with the public without your knowledge? Because social researchers transgress the privacy of subjects in order to study social behavior, they must take precautions to protect subjects' privacy.

Privacy.   Survey researchers invade a person's privacy when they probe into beliefs, backgrounds, and behaviors in a way that reveals intimate private details. Experimental researchers sometimes use two-way mirrors or hidden microphones to "spy" on subjects. Even if subjects are told they are being studied, they are unaware of what the experimenter is looking for. Field researchers may observe very private aspects of another's behavior or eavesdrop on conversations. In field experimentation and ethnographic field research, privacy may be violated without advance warning. When Humphreys served as a "watchqueen" in a public restroom where homosexual contacts took place, he observed very private behavior without informing subjects. When Piliavin and colleagues (1969) had people collapse on subways to study helping behavior, those in the subway car had the privacy of their ride violated. People have been studied in public places (e.g., in waiting rooms, walking down the street, in classrooms), but some "public" places are more private than others (consider, for example, the use of periscopes to observe people who thought they were alone in a public toilet stall).[18]

Eavesdropping on conversations and observing people in quasi-private areas raises ethical concerns. The ethical researcher violates privacy only to the minimum degree necessary and only for legitimate research purposes. In addition, he or she protects the information on research subjects from public disclosure.

In a few situations, privacy is protected by law. One case of the invasion of privacy led to the passage of a federal law. In the *Wichita Jury Study* of 1954, University of Chicago Law School researchers recorded jury discussions to examine group processes in jury deliberations. Although the findings were significant and great precautions were taken, a congressional investigation followed and a law was passed in 1956 to prohibit the "bugging" of any grand or petit jury for any purpose, even with the jurors' consent.[19]

Anonymity.   Researchers protect privacy by not disclosing a subject's identity after information is gathered. This takes two forms, both of which require separating an individual's identity from his or her responses: anonymity and confidentiality. *Anonymity* means that subjects remain anonymous or nameless. For example, a field researcher provides a social picture of a particular individual, but gives a fictitious name and location, and alters some characteristics. The subject's identity is protected, and the individual is unknown or anonymous. Survey and experimental researchers discard the names or addresses of subjects as soon as possible and refer to subjects by a code number only, to protect anonymity. If a researcher using a mail survey includes a code on the questionnaire to determine which respondents failed to respond, the respondent's anonymity is not being fully protected. In panel studies, where the same individuals are traced over time, anonymity is not possible. Likewise, historical researchers use specific names in historical or documentary research. They may do so if the original information was from public sources; if the sources were not publicly available, a researcher must obtain written permission from the owner of the documents to use specific names.

It is difficult to protect subject anonymity. In one study about a fictitious town, "Springdale," in *Small Town in Mass Society* (Vidich and Bensman, 1968), it was easy to identify the town and specific individuals in it. Town residents became upset about how the researchers portrayed them and staged a parade mocking the researchers. As in the famous Middletown study of Muncie, Indiana, people often recognize the towns studied in community research. Yet, if a researcher protects the identities of individuals with fictitious information, the gap between what was studied and what is reported to others raises questions about what was found and what was made up. A researcher may breach a promise of anonymity unknowingly in small samples. For example, you conduct a survey of 100 college students and ask many questions on a questionnaire including age, sex, religion, and home town. The sample contains one 22-year-old Jewish male born in Stratford, Ontario. With this information, you could find out who the specific individual is and how he answered very personal questions, even though his name was not directly recorded on the questionnaire.

Confidentiality.   Even if anonymity is not possible, researchers should protect confidentiality. Anonymity protects the identity of specific individuals from being known. *Confidentiality* means that information may have names attached to it, but the researcher holds it in confidence or keeps it secret from the public. The information is not released in a way that permits linking specific individuals to specific responses and is publicly presented only in an aggregate form (e.g., percentages, means, etc.).

A researcher may provide anonymity without confidentiality, or vice versa, although they usually go together. Anonymity without confidentiality means that all the details about a specific individual are made public, but the individual's name is withheld. Confidentiality without anonymity means that information is not made public, but a researcher privately links individual names to specific responses.

Attempts to protect the identity of subjects from public disclosure has resulted in elaborate procedures: eliciting anonymous responses, using a third-party list custodian who holds the key to coded lists, or using the random-response technique. Past abuses suggest that such measures may be necessary. For example, Diener and Crandall (1978:70) reported that during the 1950s, the U.S. State Department and the FBI requested research records on individuals who had been involved in the famous Kinsey sex

study. The Kinsey Sex Institute refused to comply with the government. They threatened to destroy all records rather than release any. Eventually, the government agencies backed down. The moral duty and ethical code of the researchers obligated them to destroy the records rather than give them to government officials. As Nelkin (1982b:705) remarked, "The right of researchers to protect their subjects is especially vulnerable when it conflicts with political or policy goals."

Confidentiality may protect subjects from physical harm. For example, I met a researcher who studied the inner workings of the secret police in a nondemocratic society. Had he released the names of informants, they would have faced certain death or imprisonment. To protect the subjects, he wrote all notes in code and kept all records secretly locked away. Although he resided in the United States, he was physically threatened by the foreign government and discovered attempts to burglarize his office. In other situations, other principles may take precedence over protecting confidentiality. For example, when studying patients in a mental hospital, a researcher discovers that a patient is preparing to kill an attendant. The researcher must weigh the benefit of confidentiality against the potential harm to the attendant.

Social researchers often pay high personal costs for being ethical. Although he was never accused or convicted of breaking any law and he closely followed the ethical principles outlined by the American Sociological Association, Rik Scarce, a doctoral sociology student at Washington State University spent 16 weeks in a Spokane Jail for contempt of court. He was jailed because he refused to testify before a grand jury and break the confidentiality of social research data. Scarce had been studying radical animal liberation groups and already published one book on the subject. He had interviewed a research subject who was suspected of leading a group that broke into animal facilities and caused $150,000 damage. Two judges refused to acknowledge the confidentiality of social research data.[20]

In 1989, the U.S. government established a way to protect confidentiality. A researcher can apply for a *certificate of confidentiality*, issued by the U.S. National Institute of Health, by submitting a research proposal. The certificate guarantees the confidentiality of data on subjects from federal, state, or local government criminal or civil legal action. The research data are protected whether or not federal government funds were used to support the project. Unfortunately, the certificate protects the data on subjects, but it does not protect the researcher from legal action.

A special concern with anonymity and confidentiality arises when a researcher studies "captive" populations (e.g., students, prisoners, employees, patients, soldiers). Gatekeepers, or those in positions of authority, may restrict access unless they receive information on subjects.[21] For example, a researcher studies drug use and sexual activity among high school students. School authorities agree to cooperate under two conditions: (1) students need parental permission to participate and (2) school officials get the names of all drug users and sexually active students in order to assist the students with counseling and inform the students' parents. An ethical researcher will refuse to continue rather than meet the second condition.

ETHICS AND THE SCIENTIFIC COMMUNITY

Physicians, attorneys, counselors, and other professionals have a *code of ethics* and peer review boards or licensing regulations. The codes formalize professional standards and provide guidance when questions arise in practice.[22] Social researchers do not provide a service for a fee, receive limited ethical training, and are rarely licensed. They incorporate ethical concerns into research because it is morally and socially responsible, and to protect social research from charges of insensitivity or abusing people.

Professional social science associations have codes of ethics. The codes state proper and improper behavior and represent a consensus of professionals on ethics. All researchers may not agree on all ethical issues, and ethical rules are subject to interpretation, but researchers are expected to uphold ethical standards as part of their membership in a professional community.

Codes of research ethics can be traced to the *Nuremberg code*, which was adopted during the Nuremberg Military Tribunal on Nazi war crimes held by the Allied Powers immediately after World War II. The code, developed as a response to the cruelty of concentration camp experiments, outlines ethical principles and rights of human subjects. These include:

- The principle of voluntary consent
- Avoidance of unnecessary physical and mental suffering
- Avoidance of any experiment where death or disabling injury is likely
- Termination of research if its continuation is likely to cause injury, disability, or death
- The principle that experiments should be conducted by highly qualified people using the highest levels of skill and care
- The principle that the results should be for the good of society and unattainable by any other method

The principles in the Nuremberg code dealt with the treatment of human subjects and focused on medical experimentation, but they became the basis for the ethical codes in social research. Similar codes of human rights, such as the 1948 Universal Declaration of Human Rights by the United Nations and the 1964 Declaration of Helsinki, also have implications for social researchers.[23] Table 17.1 lists some of the basic principles of ethical social research.

Professional social science associations (e.g., the American Psychological Association, American Anthropological Association, American Political Science Association, and American Sociological Association) adopted codes of ethics beginning in the 1960s or 1970s. A copy of the codes of ethics for the American Association for Public Opinion Research and the American Sociological Association are provided in Appendix A. These codes are similar, and some principles in them go beyond those in the Nuremberg code.

Professional social science associations have committees that review codes of ethics and hear about possible violations, but there is no strict enforcement of the codes. The penalty for a minor

TABLE 17.1   Basic Principles of Ethical Social Research

- Ethical responsibility rests with the individual researcher.
- Do not exploit subjects or students for personal gain.
- Some form of informed consent is highly recommended or required.
- Honor all guarantees of privacy, confidentiality, and anonymity.
- Do not coerce or humiliate subjects.
- Use deception only if needed, and always accompany it with debriefing.
- Use the research method that is appropriate to a topic.
- Detect and remove undesirable consequences to research subjects.
- Anticipate repercussions of the research or publication of results.
- Identify the sponsor who funded the research.
- Cooperate with host nations when doing comparative research.
- Release the details of the study design with the results.
- Make interpretations of results consistent with the data.
- Use high methodological standards and strive for accuracy.
- Do not conduct secret research.

violation rarely goes beyond a letter. If laws have not been violated, the main penalty is the negative publicity surrounding a well-documented and serious ethical violation. The publicity may result in the loss of employment, a refusal to publish research findings in scholarly journals, and a prohibition from receiving funding for research—in other words, banishment from the community of professional researchers.

Codes of ethics do more than codify thinking among researchers and provide guidance; they also help universities and other institutions defend ethical research against abuses from external political interests. For example, after interviewing 24 staff members and conducting observations, a researcher in 1994 documented that the staff at the Milwaukee Public Defenders Office were seriously overworked and could not effectively provide legal defense for poor people. Learning of the findings, top officials at the office contacted the university and demanded to know who on their staff had talked to the researcher, with implications that there might be reprisals against the staff members. The university administration defended the researcher and refused to release the information, citing widely accepted codes that protect human research subjects.[24]

Among the codes of ethics, Greenwald (1992: 585–586) remarked, "Sociology stands out among the learned professions as critical of the authority of established insitutions such as government or large business firms" and in its provision to "explicity state the shortcoming of methodologies and the openeness of findings to varying interpretations."

ETHICS AND THE SPONSORS OF RESEARCH

Special Considerations

You might find a job where you do research for a sponsor—an employer, a government agency, or a private firm that contracts with a researcher to conduct research. Special ethical problems arise when a sponsor pays for research, especially applied research. Researchers may be asked to compromise ethical or professional research standards as a condition for receiving a contract or for continued employment. Researchers need to set ethical boundaries beyond which they will refuse sponsor demands. When confronted with an illegitimate demand from a sponsor, a researcher has three basic choices: loyalty to an organization or larger group, exiting from the situation, or voicing opposition.[25] These present themselves as caving in to the sponsor, quitting, or becoming a whistleblower. The researcher must choose his or her own course of action, but it is best to consider ethical issues early in a relationship with a sponsor and to express concerns up front.

Whistle-blowing can be strenuous and risky. Three parties are involved: the researcher who sees ethical wrongdoing, an external agency or the media, and supervisors in an employing organization. The researcher must be convinced that the breach of ethics is serious and approved of in the organization. After exhausting internal avenues to resolve the issue, he or she turns to outsiders. The outsiders may or may not be interested in the problem or able to help. Outsiders often have their own priorities (making an organization look bad, sensationalizing the problem)— ones that differ from the researcher's main concern (ending unethical behavior). Supervisors or managers may try to discredit or punish anyone who exposes problems and acts disloyal. As Frechette-Schrader (1994:78) noted, "An act of whistle blowing is a special kind of organizational disobedience or, rather, obedience to a higher principle than loyalty to an employer." Under the best of conditions, the issue may take a long time to resolve and create great emotional strain. By acting moral, a whistle-blower needs to be prepared to make many sacrifices—losing a job or promotions, lowered pay or undesirable transfer, being abandoned by friends at work, or incurring legal costs. There is no guarantee that doing the right thing will change the unethical behavior or protect the researcher from retaliation.

Applied social researchers in sponsored research settings need to think seriously about their professional roles. They may want to maintain some independence from an employer and affirm their membership in a community of dedicated professionals. Many find a defense against sponsor pressures by participating in professional organizations (e.g., the Evaluation Research Society), maintaining regular contacts with researchers outside the sponsoring organization, and staying current with the best research practices. The researcher least likely to uphold ethical standards in a sponsored setting is someone who is isolated and professionally insecure. Whatever the situation, unethical behavior is never justified by the argument that "If I didn't do it, someone else would have."

Arriving at Particular Findings

What should you do if a sponsor tells you, directly or indirectly, what results you should come up with? An ethical researcher refuses to participate if he or she must arrive at specific results as a precondition for doing research. All research should be conducted without restrictions on the findings that the research yields. For example, a survey organization obtained a contract to conduct research for a shopping mall association. The association was engaged in a court battle with a political group that wanted to demonstrate at a mall. An interviewer in the survey organization objected to many survey questions that he believed were invalid and slanted to favor the shopping mall association. After he contacted a newspaper and exposed the biased questions, the interviewer was fired. Several years later, however, in a "whistle-blower" lawsuit, the interviewer was awarded more than $60,000 for back pay, mental anguish, and punitive damages against the survey organization.[26]

Another example of pressure to arrive at particular findings developed in the area of educational testing. Standardized tests to measure achievement by U.S. school children have come under criticism. For example, children in about 90 percent of school districts in the United States score "above average" on such tests. This was called the *Lake Wobegon effect* after the mythical town of Lake Wobegon, where, according to radio show host Garrison Keillor, "all the children are above average." This unusual finding came about for several reasons. The main reason was that the researchers compared current students to standards based on tests taken by students many years ago. The researchers faced strong pressure from teachers, school principals, superintendents, and school boards for results that would allow them to report to parents and voters that their school district was "above average."[27]

Limits on How to Conduct Studies

Can a sponsor limit research by defining what can be studied or by limiting the techniques used, either directly or indirectly (by limiting funding)?

Sponsors can legitimately set conditions on research techniques used (e.g., survey versus experiment) and limit costs for research. However, the researcher must follow generally accepted research methods. Researchers should give a realistic appraisal of what can be accomplished for a given level of funding.

The issue of limits is common in *contract research*, when a firm or government agency asks for work on a particular research project. For example, the U.S. Department of Labor wants to learn about the employment histories and spending patterns of people in three large cities. It issues a request for proposals describing such a project. Any technically qualified company, researcher, or research institute can submit a proposal outlining the research it will conduct and how much it will charge. The agency will award the contract to the proposal that promises to do the research for the lowest cost.

A trade-off may develop between quality and cost in contract research. Abt (1979), the president of a major private social research firm, Abt Associates, argued that it is difficult to get a contract by bidding what the research actually costs. Once the research begins, a researcher may need to redesign the project, or costs may be higher. The contract procedure makes midstream changes difficult. A researcher may find that he or she is forced by the contract to use research procedures or methods that are less than ideal. The researcher then confronts a dilemma: Complete the contract and do low-quality research, or fail to fulfill the contract and lose money and future jobs.

A researcher should refuse to continue if he or she cannot uphold generally accepted standards of research. If a sponsor wants biased samples or leading questions, the ethical researcher refuses to cooperate. If legitimate research shows the sponsor's pet idea or project to be a bad course of action, a researcher may anticipate the end of employment or pressure to violate professional research standards. In the long run, the sponsor, the researcher, the scientific community, and the larger society are harmed by the violation of sound research practice. The researcher has to decide whether he or she is a "hired hand" who

gives the sponsors whatever they want, even if it is ethically wrong, or a professional who is obligated to teach, guide, or even oppose sponsors in the service of higher moral principles.[28]

A researcher should ask: Why would sponsors want the social research conducted if they are not interested in using the findings or in the truth? The answer is that such sponsors see social research only as a cover they can use to legitimate a decision or practice that they could not otherwise carry out. They abuse the researcher's status as a professional to advance their own narrow goals. They are being deceitful and trying to "cash in" on the reputation of social research for honesty and integrity. When it occurs, an ethical researcher has a moral responsibility to expose and stop the abuse.

Suppressing Findings

What happens if you conduct research and the findings make the sponsor look bad or the sponsor does not want to release the results? This is not an uncommon situation for applied researchers. For example, a sociologist conducted a study for the Wisconsin Lottery Commission on the effects of state government-sponsored gambling. After she completed the report, but before the report was released to the public, the commission asked her to remove sections that outlined many negative social effects of gambling and to eliminate her recommendations to create social services to help compulsive gamblers. The researcher was in a difficult position. Which ethical value took precedence: covering up for the sponsor that had paid for the research, or revealing the truth for all to see but then suffering the consequences?[29] Governments are not the only organizations that attempt to suppress research findings. A Roman Catholic priest who surveyed American bishops on their dissatisfaction with official church policy was ordered by his superiors to suppress findings and destroy the questionnaires. Instead, he resigned after 24 years in the priesthood and made his results public.[30] Researchers pay high personal and economic costs for being ethical.

It is not uncommon for government agencies to suppress scientifically based information that contradicts official policy or embarrasses high officials. Retaliation against social researchers employed by government agencies who make the information public also occurs. For example, a social researcher employed by the U.S. Census Bureau who studied death caused by the 1991 Gulf War against Iraq reported that government officials suppressed findings for political reasons. The researcher, whom the agency attempted to fire, reported that findings of high death rates were delayed and underestimated by the U.S. government's main agency for social statistics. Before information could be released, it had to go through an office headed by a political appointee. She charged that the political appointee was more interested in protecting the administration's foreign policy than in releasing relevant scientific findings to the public. In another example, the U.S. Defense Department ordered studies destroyed that showed 10 percent of the U.S. military to be gay or lesbian destroyed and no support for the banning of gays from the military.[31]

In sponsored research, a researcher can negotiate conditions for releasing findings *prior to beginning* the study and sign a contract to that effect. It may be unwise to conduct the study without such a guarantee, although competing researchers who have fewer ethical scruples may do so. Alternatively, a researcher can accept the sponsor's criticism and hostility and release the findings over the sponsor's objections. Most researchers prefer the first choice, since the second one may scare away future sponsors.

In addition to control over social research or a supression of findings by sponsors or government officials, social researchers sometimes self-censor or delay the release of findings. They do this to protect the identity of informants, to maintain access to a research site, to hold on to their jobs, or to protect the personal safety of themselves or of family members (Adler and Adler, 1993). This is a less disturbing type of censorship because it is not imposed by an outside power. It is done by someone who is close to the research and who is knowledgable about possible conse-

quences. Researchers shoulder the ultimate responsibility for their research. Often, they can draw on many different resources but they face many competing pressures as well (see Figure 17.2).

Concealing the True Sponsor

Is it ethical to keep the identity of a sponsor secret? For example, an abortion clinic would like to fund a study on the attitudes of religious groups opposed to abortion. The researcher must balance the ethical value of making the sponsor's identity public to subjects and releasing results against the sponsor's desire for confidentiality and the likelihood of reduced cooperation from subjects. If the results are published, there is a clear overriding ethical mandate to reveal the true sponsor. There is less agreement on the ethical issue of revealing the true sponsor to subjects. Presser, Blair, and Triplett (1992) found that the answers given by respondents may depend on the sponsor of a survey. If a respondent believes a survey is conducted by a newspaper that has taken a strong position on an issue, the respondent is less likely to contradict the newspaper's public stand on the issue. This is less of a problem if the respondent believes the survey sponsor is a neutral academic organization.

EFFECTS OF THE LARGER SOCIETY OR GOVERNMENT

The preceding sections focused on harm to subjects, codes of ethics, and dealing with sponsors. A related issue is how powerful groups in society or the government shape research. In an extreme case, 40 percent of German scientists were dismissed from their jobs for political reasons when the Nazis "purified" universities and research centers in 1937.[32] Another example is the purge of hundreds of professors and researchers in the United States who did not publicly swear to anticommunism and collaborate with the McCarthy investigations of the 1950s. At that time, people who objected to mandatory loyalty oaths, supported racial integration, or advocated the teach-

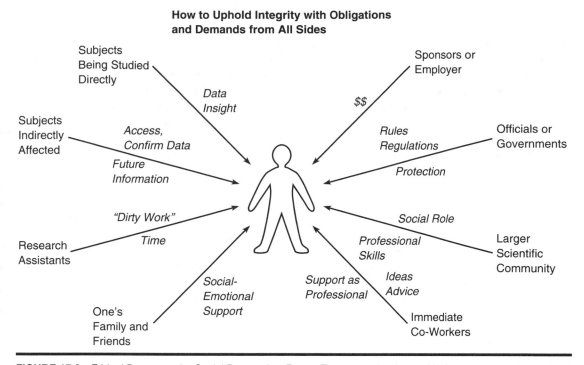

How to Uphold Integrity with Obligations and Demands from All Sides

FIGURE 17.2   Ethical Pressures the Social Researcher Faces. The researcher is provided with resources, but each entails responsibilities.

ing of sex education were suspected of subversion and threatened with dismissal. For example, at the University of California alone, 25 professors were fired for refusing to sign loyalty oaths.[33]

Governments can limit, constrain, or direct social research, both through legislation and by the allocation of research funds. The question is: What is the proper relationship between government or other powerful institutions and social research? What is the balance between the value of a government's overseeing science for society versus the value of free and autonomous research without political interference?

Mandated Protections of Subjects

The U.S. federal government has regulations and laws to protect research subjects and their rights. The legal restraint is found in rules and regulations issued by the U.S. Department of Health and Human Services Office for the Protection from

Research Risks. Although this is only one federal agency, most researchers and other government agencies look to it for guidance. Current U.S. government regulations have evolved from Public Health Service policies adopted in 1966 and expanded in 1971. The National Research Act (1974) established the National Commission for the Protection of Human Subjects in Biomedical and Behavioral Research, which significantly expanded regulations, and required informed consent in most social research. The responsibility for safeguarding ethical standards was assigned to research institutes and universities. The Department of Health and Human Services issued regulations in 1981, which are still in force. Regulations on scientific misconduct and protection of data confidentiality were expanded in 1989.

Federal regulations follow a biomedical model and protect subjects from physical harm. Other rules require *institutional review boards (IRBs)* at all research institutes, colleges, and universities to review all use of human subjects. The IRB is staffed by researchers and community members. Similar committees oversee the use of animals in research. The IRB oversees, monitors, and reviews the impact of all research procedures on human subjects and applies ethical guidelines. The IRB reviews research procedures at the preliminary stage when first proposed. Educational tests, "normal educational practice," most surveys, most observation of public behavior, and studies of existing data in which individuals cannot be identified are exempt from the IRB.[34]

Limits on What Can Be Studied

Governments or powerful groups in society may try to restrict free scientific inquiry. In nondemocratic societies, control over or the censorship of social research is the rule, not the exception. This is particularly the case with politically sensitive topics, including public opinion surveys. Thus, in China, eastern Europe, South Africa, Taiwan, and other places, social researchers have been suspect, limited to "safe" topics, or forced to support official government policy.[35] In a number of countries (e.g., Greece, Chile), the study of sociology itself was banned as subversive after a military coup.

There are few restrictions on research in the United States. Most officials recognize that an open and autonomous social scientific community is the best path to unbiased, valid knowledge. The peer review process promotes autonomous research because proposals for funds to conduct research submitted to a government agency are reviewed by researcher peers who evaluate the proposal on its scientific merit. Although the federal government funds most basic research, research itself is decentralized and conducted at many colleges, universities, and research centers across the nation.

Two Limitations: Gatekeepers and Defining Indicators. Two limitations on research involve gatekeepers who control access to data or subjects and the types of data collected in official statistics. As mentioned before, gatekeepers may limit what is studied. For example, a researcher wants to study the socialization of military officers at West Point: top military officials control access to the academy. Likewise, gatekeepers control access to corporate employees, patients in hospitals, school children, and the like. Requests may be denied on the basis of noninterference, privacy, or possible disruption. Gatekeepers often want to protect themselves or the structure of power in their organization from criticism or embarrassment. In addition to an outright denial of access, the gatekeepers may limit access only to subjects or areas with which they feel confident.

Another limitation involves official or existing statistics that are collected by governments or other large organizations. As mentioned in Chapter 11, the conceptualization of variables. whether information is collected, and how accurately information is collected affect the research. How phenomena (e.g., unemployment, income, educational success) are defined in official statistics and whether such data are collected may be affected by political pressures, which can limit what a researcher is able to study using such statistics.[36]

Limits Due to the Influence of Politicians. Unfortunately, some people outside the scientific community attack social research because it disagrees with their social or political values. A politician or journalist may hear about a research project in a controversial area or may misinterpret the project, then use the occasion to attract publicity. For example, Professor Harris Rubin at the University of Southern Illinois intended to investigate the effects of THC (the active agent in marijuana) on sexual arousal. Almost no scientific evidence existed, only contradictory myths. He very carefully followed all procedures and clearances, and the research project was funded by the National Institute of Mental Health in 1975. A conservative congressman learned of the research topic from nearby newspapers and introduced an amendment in Congress to prohibit further funding. In addition, all funds for the project were to be repaid to the federal government. Despite arguments by scientists that politicians should not interfere with legitimate research, funding was cut. Politicians are afraid to support social research if an opposing candidate could make a case to voters that the government appeared to be paying for students to "get stoned and watch porno films."[37]

Senator William Proxmire's "Golden Fleece" awards have gone to social research projects whose scientific significance was not appreciated by the senator. Studies of human attraction and affection, and of stress and tension were singled out for public ridicule as a "waste of taxpayer money." In one case, a Michigan primate researcher who was attacked by the senator subsequently lost his position and funding. In a legal case that ended up in the U.S. Supreme Court, the Court ruled that the senator's statements attacking individuals on the floor of the U.S. Senate were protected, but if he mailed out newsletters and made attacks outside the Senate, he could be sued for libel or slander.[38] Another example of political pressure occurred in 1989, when funding for a major national survey on sexual behavior to combat the AIDS epidemic was blocked in Congress by members who did not believe that it was proper for researchers to inquire into human sexual behavior.[39]

A research project on teenage sex conducted by the National Institutes of Health was canceled in late 1991 after action by the U.S. Senate. Social researchers took this action as a serious-threat. The study was to survey 24,000 teens about their social activities, family life, and sexual behavior, in order to provide background for understanding AIDS and other sexually transmitted diseases. Many researchers said they did not want to speak out on the issue for fear that they would become the target of political groups. Some who spoke out said that the ability of a small minority with an extreme political ideology to kill important research was "a scandalous act" and "frightening." One sociology researcher noted that the project was not canceled because of questions about its scientific quality or importance; rather, it was an ideologically based decision that "we don't need to know this."[40]

Public attacks on social research, even noncontroversial but misunderstood research, hurts all researchers. Politicians may "kill" research that the scientific community recognizes as legiti-

mate, or they may promote pet projects that have little scientific value. Researchers who apply for government funds sometimes restate their project in terms that do not attract attention. The public ridicule of unsuspecting researchers or the denial of research funds also encourages self-censorship and fosters a negative public opinion about social research.

In May 1992, members of the U.S. Congress identified 31 specific research projects to be funded by the National Science Foundation (NSF) as a waste of taxpayer money. The projects singled out to be cut included "Monogamy and Aggression," "A Systematic Study of Senate Elections," and "American Perceptions of Justice." Although the proposals had undergone a rigorous review on scientific merit, several politicians decided to overrule the judgment of the scientific community. The politicians had not studied the research proposals and lacked a background in the social or natural sciences. The politicians also criticized the NSF for supporting basic social research. After extensive lobbying by the research community, specific research projects were no longer targeted, but still Congress cut the research budget of the NSF by the amount allocated for these research projects.[41]

Adverse publicity that could destroy a researcher's career may keep researchers from investigating sensitive topics. Yet, scientific knowledge is especially important precisely because the topics are sensitive ones. Without scientifically based knowledge, fear, prejudice, and ideology dominate public policy and popular opinion. Fear of adverse publicity could encourage researchers to use jargon or hide the true purpose of research behind complex statistics or technical language. By making the theories and techniques of social sciences appear to be more like those of the "safe" natural sciences, a researcher may avert political attacks. Yet, this creates an additional burden for the researchers and makes research less accessible to students or the general public.

National Security and Limits on Social Research. Military secrecy and national security became major issues during World War I and

World War II. Most of the concern was with technology to create weapons, but social researchers have been limited in their study of foreign nations, issues of military interest, and research into government itself. U.S. security agencies such as the National Security Administration and the Central Intelligence Agency (CIA) have influenced social and natural science research into the Cold War period of the 1950s.

One government research project in the 1960s created a great controversy. The U.S. Army funded *Project Camelot*, which involved respected social researchers who went to Chile to study political insurgency and mobilization. Several aspects of the project created controversy. First, the project's goal was to find out how to prevent peasants and disadvantaged groups in Third World countries from taking independent political action to oppose a dictator. Such counterinsurgency research is usually conducted by the Central Intelligence Agency. The researchers were accused of using their skills and knowledge to advance military interests against disadvantaged Third World people. Second, some researchers were unaware of the source of funds. Third, the people and the government of Chile were not informed about the project. Once they discovered it, they asked that it end and that all researchers leave.[42]

By the late 1960s and 1970s, freedom to conduct research expanded, restrictions on researchers were relaxed, and the government classified fewer documents. The U.S. Congress passed the *Freedom of Information Act (FOIA)* in 1966 and strengthened it in 1974. The law opened many government documents to scholars and members of the public if they file requests with government agencies. The trend toward greater openness of information and freedom of research was reversed in the 1980s. The U.S. government limited the publication of information, expanded the range of classified documents, and made less information publicly available in the name of national security and budget cutting. This has restrained academic inquiry, scientific progress, and democratic decision making.[43]

In the 1980s, the definition of national security was broadened, the system for classifying government documents was expanded, and new limits were imposed on research into "sensitive areas," even if no government agency or funds are involved. It became easier to classify information and classify documents that were already in the public domain. In addition, under the Export Control Act (1979 and 1985), military and security officials could restrict researchers from outside the U.S. from attending scholarly meetings or visiting U.S. classrooms, libraries, and research centers.[44]

In the past, CIA undercover agents have posed as social researchers to get information in foreign nations. Until 1986, the CIA had a blanket rule barring researchers from disclosing CIA sponsorship of their research. At that time, the rule was loosened to cover only cases where the CIA believed such disclosure "would prove damaging to the United States." For example, a Harvard professor had a contract with the CIA not to reveal that the agency paid for the research for a scholarly book on U.S. foreign policy.[45]

Cross-national research involves unique ethical issues. The research community condemns the use of undercover agents in the guise of researchers and the practice of hiding the source of funding for research. Researchers want to make funding sources known and provide results to subjects, to host nations in cross-national research, and to other scientists. Researchers have developed ethical guidelines for conduct in other nations, which specify cooperation with host officials, the protection of subjects, and leaving information in the host nation. Nevertheless, a researcher may find interference from his or her own government, or the researcher's respect for the basic human rights of the people being studied in a nondemocratic society may lead him or her to hide information from the host government involved.[46]

Funding as an Influence on the Direction of Research

Large-scale social research can be expensive. The sums for social research are tiny compared to those spent by large corporations on research or to federal funding for natural science or military research. The funds affect the type of social research that is conducted. In the United States, most social research funding comes from the federal government, with university and private foundation funding more limited in amount, scope, and number. Thus, for large projects, researchers are forced to go to the federal government for funding.

This was not always the case. Prior to World War II in the United States, a few private foundations set up by wealthy families (Carnegie, Ford, Rockefeller, Sage) funded most sociological research. The foundations sought information about the serious social problems that appeared with early industrialism. They also wanted to discourage links between radicals and social researchers and protect established social institutions. After a number of years, "The production of social science research thus becomes regularized or routinized, and its connection with sponsoring organizations becomes obscured from the public's view" (Seybold, 1987:197). Private funds redirected social research efforts away from its early focus that was applied, action oriented, critical, neighborhood centered, and involved participation by subjects and toward a focus that was detached, professional, positivist, and academic. After World War II, government research funding expanded. Private foundations maintained a role setting research priorities through the 1960s, when federal government funds surpassed private funds.[47] Government research funds grew, but funding for the social sciences and sociology remained tiny. In the United States, research funding for sociology has been less than 1 percent of federal funding for basic research (D'Antoino, 1992: 123).

In the United States, social research funding is available from several federal agencies, including the National Science Foundation, Department of Defense, Agriculture Department, Commerce Department, Department of Housing and Urban Development, Department of Education, National Endowment for the Humanities, Small Business Administration, Department of Justice, Department of Labor, and the many institutes under the De-

partment of Health and Human Services. The federal government itself employs researchers to monitor advances in knowledge and conduct research. Most social research is conducted at colleges and universities or independent research institutes.

The *National Science Foundation (NSF)*, created in 1950, is the main source of basic research funding in the United States. The *National Institutes of Health (NIH)* within the Department of Health and Human Services is also important in certain topic areas and sets most regulations protecting research subjects. Almost all other federal agencies fund only applied research. The decision to allocate specific amounts of funds to various agencies for social research and the applied/basic split varies from year to year and is determined largely by political processes. Although the scientific review committees within the NSF and NIH evaluate the scientific merit of submitted proposals, political officials decide the total amount of funds available, and whether funds must be used for applied or basic research. Useem (1976a:159) noted,

> Since federal research policies are oriented around producing policy-relevant quantitative research, the result of responsiveness to these policies is that academic research is more oriented toward topics and techniques useful to government agencies than would be the case in the absence of federal funding. Both substantive and methodological priorities in academic social research are significantly affected by government priorities.

Social researchers and others can lobby for funds or programs, but the Congress and the executive branch set priorities. Thus, conflicts between the political parties or ideological interests affect the amount of research funding available and how it can be spent.

Political values are relevant when money is allocated for research on certain questions and priorities. For example, politicians decide that money is allocated for applied research to demonstrate how "burdensome" the costs of regulation are for large corporations, but none is available to investigate the benefits of regulation for consumers. They increase funds to study crime committed by drug addicts, but eliminate funds to study crime by corporate executives. They make available new funds for research on how to promote entrepreneurship, while cutting back funds to study the human consequences of social program cutbacks.[48]

Funds for basic research can be allocated in ways that promote specific theoretical or value perspectives. For example, funds may be allocated to study how individual attributes correlate with undesirable social behaviors, while no funding exists for investigating structural and community factors. By focusing on some research questions and limiting alternatives, political groups try to shape the research that is conducted and what is scientifically known.

Many issues that social researchers address bear directly on social beliefs, values, and policies. Political groups set priorities for research on these issues that are distinct from those of the scientific community. As Useem noted (1976b:625), "These priorities are unlikely to be identical to with the discipline's own priorities." This has both positive and negative effects. It ensures that the concerns of politicians or vocal public groups are addressed and that social problems that politically influential groups define as important get researched. If scientific research does not support a popular public myth (e.g., that capital punishment has a deterrent effect or that women who have abortions suffer psychological harm), funds are repeatedly allocated to try to discover evidence that will confirm popular beliefs, while scientifically central issues go unfunded.

The scientific community has some freedom to define what should be researched, but problems affecting less politically vocal groups or issues for which there is no lobby receive limited research funding. This imbalance of funding creates an imbalance in knowledge across issues. Eventually, there is substantial knowledge on the issues of interest to powerful political groups, while their opponents are weakened by a lack of knowledge.

During the 1970s, U.S. federal funding for social research failed to keep pace with inflation. Funding for social science research in the National

Science Foundation declined 24 percent between 1976 and 1980 in constant dollars. Significant conflict arose in the United States over federal funding for social science research in the early 1980s. Despite an outcry, funding dropped another 17 percent between 1980 and 1983. Social research became a source of controversy. Political leaders thought that too many research results supported the policies of their political opponents. Applied research was also reduced. In response, the professional associations of several social science disciplines joined together to form a lobbying organization: the *Consortium of Social Science Associations (COSSA)*. COSSA was able to reduce the size of some cuts.[49]

After dramatic shifts that followed the ebb and flow of conflicts between White House and Congress, by the start of the 1990s, fewer inflation-adjusted federal dollars went to sociological research than had been available 20 years earlier (D'Antonio, 1992: 122). Incredible as it may seem, the funding for social research may be unchanged for 70 years. Funds from the private Social Science Research Council in the late 1920s, once adjusted for inflation and the size of academic profession, were probably greater than funding for social science research from the National Science Foundation at the start of the 1990s.[50]

Another issue is the use of political criteria when appointing researchers to review boards for applied research in the departments of Education and Agriculture. Executive branch officials who believed that social researchers disapproved of their political goals and values have screened researchers on their political beliefs. Before the 1980s, scientific merit, irrespective of political ideology, had been the only criterion used. Federal government officials also tried to modify funded research. For example, in 1984 a Department of Housing and Urban Development (HUD) research contract with Harvard University was dropped by researchers because HUD insisted that politically appointed officials be allowed to make "corrections" to data, findings, or methodology prior to publication.[51] In 1991, a U.S. federal court ruled that federal government agencies cannot legally require researchers to get prior approval from government officials before publishing findings from research. A judge ruled that such a requirement would amount to censorship and would infringe on academic freedom.[52]

The scientific community views such political interference with alarm. Many political officials cannot distinguish between a researcher who produces legitimate scientific results that do not support a politician's ideological beliefs and a political opponent with different values.

Social researchers admit that some research is trivial or without practical value. Yet, they prefer the autonomy of science and free inquiry. The tiny proportion of trivial research that is funded under the present system is a small price to pay for free inquiry. It is far superior to the censorship and imposition of research priorities by government.

Some social researchers, especially historical researchers or those who rely on existing statistics, depend on the government less for funding than to supply information or documents. The Paperwork Reduction Act of 1980 created an Office of Information and Regulatory Affairs to determine whether or not it was necessary to collect information and maintain records. The act resulted in fewer publications of findings from government-sponsored research. In addition, the implementation of the law had been "used on occasion to restrict information not supportive of executive branch policy goals" (Shattuck and Spence, 1988:47). For example, in the health field, research projects with an environmental focus that indirectly criticized business or government policy were more likely to be rejected for publication under "paperwork reduction" justification than those with a traditional disease focus that indirectly blamed the victim.

In the name of cost cutting, federal agencies stopped collecting information, removed information from public circulation, and shifted information collection to profit-making private businesses. The number of outlets of the U.S. government publishing offices were cut and prices were raised. For example a 67-page pamphlet titled "Infant Care," which was distributed free to mothers by public health programs, now

costs \$4.75.[53] Bureaucratic decisions not to collect information can have policy implications. For example, 40 percent of the nonmoney items were eliminated from national educational statistics in the early 1980s. Information on the gender mix of teachers or administrators, which had been added in 1974 to detect sex discrimination, was eliminated from statistical reporting. Thus, budget decisions not to collect certain information makes it more difficult to show sex discrimination.[54]

Data collected by the government have been sold at low bulk rates to private business. The private businesses are then the only source of these data and charge high prices to researchers. For example, information that was once free to the public from a government agency became available only through a private company that charges a \$1,495 annual subscription fee. As Starr and Corson (1987:447) remarked,

> The privatizing of statistical information poses some specific problems for the future of the social sciences and intellectual life. Without the capacity to make use of the new information resources in private hands, the universities and other nonprofit research centers may be left as intellectual backwaters.

In sum, there is still substantial free inquiry and independent social research. Nevertheless, there have been politically motivated attempts to limit what social researchers can study as well.

THE DISSEMINATION AND USE OF RESEARCH FINDINGS

What do you do with your research findings? Positivist researchers recognize two areas where values legitimately come into play. First, researchers can select a topic area or research question. Although there are "frontier" areas of inquiry in topic areas, researchers can choose a research question on the basis of personal preference.[55] Second, once research is completed, a researchers' values shape where they disseminate their findings. They are expected to report findings to the scientific community, and funding agencies require a report, but beyond these requirements, it is up to the researcher.

Why researchers conduct research and what they do with findings is linked to how they see the entire social research enterprise and their role in society as intellectuals.[56] The issue has been debated among leading social thinkers for over 50 years in such works as Howard Becker's (1967) "Whose Side Are We On?," Robert Lynd's (1939) *Knowledge for What?*, Alfred McClung Lee's (1978) *Sociology for Whom?*, and C. Wright Mills's (1959) *The Sociological Imagination.*

Models of Relevance

What happens when the research completed involves an ethical-political concern that Rule (1978a, 1978b) has called *models of relevance*? Rule reviewed the positions that social researchers took toward their research and its use and argued that the positions can be collapsed into five basic types (see Table 17.2).

The models of relevance are ideal types of

TABLE 17.2 Models of Relevance

1. *No net effects:* Social science findings produce no greater social good. Several famous social scientists who argue this are William Graham Sumner, Vilfredo Pareto, Herbert Spencer, Edward Banfield, and James Q. Wilson. These conservative social scientists see the products of research as capable of being used for anyone's self-interest and believe that, in the long run, as much harm as good has come from the greater knowledge social science yields.

2. *Direct and positive effects:* Social science knowledge results in an improvement for all. Liberal social scientists, such as Robert Merton, who adopt this stance see knowledge about social relations leading to a more rational world. Research results on social problems help us understand the social world much better, enabling us to know how we can modify it toward some greater good. For example, Lindblom and Cohen (1979) urged a redirection of social science toward what they see as social problem solving.

3. *Special constituency, the proletariat:* Social science should be used to advance the interests and position of the working class. This is the Marxist model of the appropriate use of social research. According to it, all social science falls into three categories: the trivial, that which helps the bourgeoisie, and that which aids the proletariat. Consistent with a critical science approach, research findings should be used to advocate and defend the interests of the working class and assist workers by exposing and combating exploitation, oppression, injustice, and repression.

4. *Special constituency, the uncoopted:* Social science should be used to aid any disadvantaged or underprivileged group in society. This model, associated with Karl Mannheim or C. Wright Mills, is more general than the Marxian position. It sees many social groups as lacking power in society (women, consumers, racial minorities, gays, the poor) and argues that these groups are oppressed by the powerful in society who have access to education, wealth, and knowledge. The social researcher should defend those who lack a voice in society and who are manipulated by those in power. The powerful can use or purchase social science research for their own ends. Because they have a unique role in society and are in a position to learn about all areas of society, social researchers have an obligation to help the weak and share knowledge with them.

5. *Special constituency, the government:* Social science's proper role is to aid the decision makers of society, especially public officials. This model has been expressed by Senator Daniel Patrick Moynihan and in official NSF policy reports, and is common in nondemocratic societies. It is similar to the second model (benefits only), but adds the assumption that government is in the best position to make use of social research findings and is fully committed to eradicating social problems. It is also similar to the first (no net effects) model but implies "selling" or providing findings to the highest bidder within the limits of national loyalty. It assumes that the government operates in the best interests of everyone, and that researchers have a patriotic duty to give what they learn to those with political power.

the positions social scientists take. Is the researcher a technician, who produces valid, reliable information about how society works, to be used by others? Or does the researcher belong to an independent community of professionals who have a say in what research questions are asked and how results are used? On a continuum, one extreme is the amoral researcher who lacks any concern or control over research or its use. He or she supplies the knowledge that others request and nothing more. This was the stance many scientists in Nazi Germany used to justify collaboration with Nazi practices later classified as "crimes against humanity." He or she "just follows orders" and "just does the job" but asks "no questions." At the other extreme are researchers who have total control over research and its use.

The approaches to social science discussed in Chapter 4 are associated with different models of relevance, as are different political views.[57] Positivists tend to follow the "direct and positive effects" or "special constituency, the government" model. The interpretive researcher follows the "no net effects" or the "uncoopted" model. Critical social scientists follow the "special constituency, the proletariat" or "special constituency, the uncoopted" models.

The models are ideal types. Specific researchers or research projects cross between models. For example, Whyte (1986) described research on employee ownership as crossing between three constituencies (the proletariat, the uncoopted, and the government) and as having direct and positive effects.

Since Rule developed models of relevance, a new politicized model has appeared with the growth of nongovernment, private "think tanks" in the United States. This sixth model is *special constituency, wealthy individuals, and corporations.* It says social research can reflect a researcher's personal political values and advance the political goals of wealthy groups who seek to maintain or expand their power. The think tanks are research and publicity organizations funded by wealthy individuals, corporations, and political groups. For example, the Manhattan Institute, Cato Institute, Heritage Foundation, and American Enterprise

Institute grew dramatically from the early 1980s to the 1990s. They seek to advance a political viewpoint and use social research or quasi-research among other means. Think tanks pay researchers and others, they sponsor research reports, and they draw public attention to results that support their political viewpoint.

Think tank studies vary greatly in quality, lack peer review, and are short on solid evidence but long on suggestions. The audience for this research is not the scientific community, and the goal is not to generally advance knowledge. Rather, think tank researchers conduct policy-oriented studies with an ideological viewpoint in an attempt to shape public thinking and influence political debate. Many receive significant media publicity, fame, and fortune, although their research may be inferior and lacks scientific peer review. At the same time, more traditional social scientists who operate with meager funds, but who lack connections to the mass media, find that their more rigorous, careful studies of the same public issues get overlooked. The public and policy officials are often overwhelmed by the greater publicity of think tank research results.

After Findings Are Published

The norm of the scientific community is to make findings public. Once findings are part of the public domain, the researcher loses control over them. This means that others can use the findings for their own purposes. Although the researcher may have chosen a topic based on his or her values, once the findings are published, others can use them to advance opposing values.

For example, a researcher wants to increase the political rights of a Native American tribe. He or she studies the tribe's social practices, including social barriers to their achieving greater power in the community. Once the findings are published, members of the tribe can use the results to break down barriers. Yet, opponents can use the same findings about the Native Americans to restrict the power of the tribe and to reinforce the barriers.

A few researchers try to retain control over research findings by keeping their findings secret.

At best, this is a short-term solution and has several drawbacks. First, other researchers can conduct similar studies and discover the same results. Second, others cannot benefit from the knowledge. Third, the findings are not evaluated, replicated, and legitimized by the scientific community. A better solution is to make the findings public, but also make special efforts to supply specific others with the findings.

Subject Information as Private Property

If you freely give information about yourself for research purposes, do you lose all rights to it? Can it be used against you? People who participate in research have knowledge about them taken away and analyzed by others. The information can then be used for a number of purposes, including actions against the subject's interests. Is it ethical to use or exploit results from research for profit, or for use by others against the subjects' interests?

An information industry exists in which information about people is collected, bought, sold, analyzed, and exchanged by large organizations on a regular basis. Information about buying habits, personal taste, spending patterns, credit ratings, voting patterns, and the like is used by many private and public organizations. Information is a form of private property. Like other "intellectual" property (copyrights, software, patents) and unlike most physical property, information continues to have value or relevance for its original owner after it is exchanged.

Most people do not consider information about themselves to be their property; they freely give it away, like a gift. They give a researcher their time and information for little or no compensation. Yet, concerns about privacy and the collection of more information makes it reasonable to see personal information as private property. If it is private property, a subject's right to keep, sell, or give it away becomes clear. The ethical issue is strongest where the information is used against subjects or used in ways they would disapprove of if they were fully informed.

This issue is relevant for the information collected by private businesses. For example, I have filled out many forms giving information on my financial situation, my health history, my marital status, my living habits, and the like. This information is used by others and exchanged or sold among organizations; it can be used to grant or deny me a loan, refuse or grant me health insurance, permit or disallow me to rent an apartment, refuse or permit me to take a job, and target or exclude me from sales promotions and special discounts. I no longer control the information or its use. It is used to affect me directly and is someone else's private property. For example, a group of committed nonsmokers is studied to learn about their habits and psychological profiles. A market research firm obtains the information and is hired by a tobacco company to design a campaign to promote smoking among nonsmokers. Had the nonsmokers been fully informed about the use of their responses, they might have chosen not to participate. A researcher can increase fairness by giving subjects a copy of the findings and describing the sponsor and the uses to which the information will be put in an informed consent statement. Informed consent forms could have a stipulation: If the information is later sold in the marketplace, the original owners get a share of the price.

The issue of who controls data on research subjects is relevant to the approaches to social science outlined in Chapter 4. In positivism and natural science, the description and understanding of the physical world have become the province of specialized experts. The experts control information removed from the average person, and use it outside democratic control to create miracle drugs, convenience items, fortunes for individuals or firms, or nightmarish weapons. Positivism implies the collection and use of information by experts separate from research subjects and the ordinary citizen. The two alternatives to positivism, each in its own way, argue for the involvement and participation of those who are studied in the research process and in the use of research data and findings.[58]

Findings Influence Future Behavior

Did you ever do something differently than before because of research findings you read? If so, you are not alone. Sometimes the dissemination of findings affect social behavior. One example is the effect of political poll results. Public opinion polls affect the political preferences of voters; that is, parts of the population change their views to correspond to what opinion polls say they have found.[59] Starr (1987:54) remarked, "Official statistics count even if the methods are faulty and the data incorrect. . . . If official statistics affect social perception and cognition, so they also powerfully affect social norms."

Other social research findings can affect behavior. In fact, the widespread dissemination of research findings may affect behavior in a way that negates or alters the original findings. For example, a study finds that professionals are likely to put a great deal of stress on the academic achievement of their children. This creates highly anxious, unhappy children. If professionals read the findings, they may alter their child-rearing behavior. Then another study, years later, might find that professionals are not likely to rear their children to achieve in academic areas any more than other groups do.

Researchers have several responses to research findings that affect social behavior.

1. They ruin predictability and regularity of human social behavior, undermining replication.

2. Only trivial behaviors are changed, so this is an issue only to researchers working in very narrow applied areas.

3. Human behavior can change because there are few unalterable laws of human behavior, and people will use knowledge in the public domain to change their lives.

In any case, social research has not uncovered the full complexity of human relations and behavior. Even if it did, and such knowledge were fully and accurately disseminated to the entire population, social researchers would still have to study which human behaviors change and how.

Academic Freedom

Most students have heard about academic freedom, but few understand it. *Academic freedom* is the existence of an open and largely unrestricted atmosphere for the free exchange of ideas and information. In open democratic societies, many people value intellectual freedom and believe in providing scholars with freedom from interference. This idea is based on the belief that fundamental democratic institutions, the advance of unbiased knowledge, and freedom of expression require a free flow of ideas and information.

Academic freedom is related to the autonomy of research, and it is necessary for high-quality social research. New ideas for research topics, the interpretation of findings, the development of theories or hypotheses, and the open discussion of ideas require academic freedom.

Academic freedom in colleges, universities, and research institutes provides a context for the free discussion and open exchange of ideas that scientific research requires. For knowledge to advance, researchers, professors, and students need a setting where they feel free to advance or debate diverse, and sometimes unpopular, opinions or positions—a setting where people are not afraid to explore a full range of ideas in open discussion, in classrooms, in public talks, or in publications.

The importance of academic freedom is demonstrated by the paucity of social research in places where it is nonexistent. The major threat to academic freedom comes from social or political groups that want to restrict discussion or impose a point of view. Restrictions on academic freedom limit the growth of knowledge about society and undermine the integrity of the research process.

Academic freedom was a significant issue in the late nineteenth and early twentieth centuries, when the social sciences were institutionalized in universities. In the early years, professors frequently lost their jobs because political officials or economic elites disliked the views expressed in their classrooms or publications. Famous scholars in the early period of American social science, like Thorsten Veblen, were forced out of several colleges because of what they said in the classroom or ideas they wrote about. The development of tenure, the idea that faculty could not be fired after a long probationary period without a very good reason, advanced academic freedom, but did not guarantee complete academic freedom. Many professors and researchers have been fired for advocating unpopular ideas.[60]

Academic freedom is threatened not only when a researcher fears losing his or her job but also when he or she is intimidated by a possible lawsuit for presenting findings. For example, a study of corporate crime was delayed and the results changed after the threat of a lawsuit by managers who had been interviewed in the study; the publication of a study of a boarding school was stopped due to a possible lawsuit after school officials wanted to change what they had said in interviews and make other changes in the book because they disagreed with the researcher's finding; and an article was changed after a researcher threatened a lawsuit over the exposure conflicts that occurred during a study conducted by a team of researchers in a book on how research actually occurs.[61]

The American Association of University Professors (AAUP) maintains a "censure" list of colleges where violations of academic freedom have been documented. Most professional associations also have academic freedom committees, which also censure colleges that violate standards of academic freedom. The censure lists contain over a dozen colleges, but their only influence is to embarrass the college.

Political attacks on social science are not new. They illustrate the conflict between the independent pursuit of knowledge and the views of political groups who want to impose their beliefs. These attacks raise the question: How autonomous should social science be from the values in the larger culture? The findings of social research frequently conflict with social beliefs based on nonscientific knowledge systems such as religion or political ideology. Galileo faced this issue about 400 years ago, before natural science was accepted. His astronomical findings, based on free-thinking science, contradicted official Church doctrine. Galileo was forced to recant his findings publicly, under the threat of torture. Silencing him slowed the advance of knowledge for a generation. The challenges of evolutionary theory also illustrate how scientific knowledge and popular beliefs conflict with one another.

Academic freedom is integral to good research. Scientific research involves more than knowing technical information (e.g., how to draw a random sample); it requires a spirit of free and open discussion, criticism on the basis of scientific merit irrespective of values, and inquiry into all areas of social life. These values are threatened when academic freedom is restricted.

OBJECTIVITY AND VALUE FREEDOM

You have probably heard the terms *value free, objective*, and *unbiased*. Some argue that social science must be as objective and unbiased as the natural sciences; others maintain that value-free, objective social science is impossible. This debate cannot be resolved here, but you should understand the definitions and terminology used. The easiest way to clear up confusion is to recognize that each term has at least two alternative definitions. Sometimes, two different terms share the same definitions (see Box 17.3).

The positivist approach holds that science is value free, unbiased, and objective. It collapses the definitions together. Value neutrality is guaranteed by logical-deductive, formal theory and a complete separation of facts from value-based concepts. The scientific community is free of prejudice and governed by free and open discussion. With complete value freedom and objectivity, science reveals the one and only, unified, unambiguous truth.

Max Weber, Alvin Gouldner, and Karl Mannheim are three major nonpositivist social thinkers who discussed the role of the social scientist in society. Weber (1949) argued that the fact value separation is not clear in the social sciences. He suggested that value-laden theories define social facts or socially meaningful action. Thus, social theories necessarily contain value-based concepts, because all concepts about the social world are created by members of specific cultures. The cultural content of social concepts cannot be purged, and socially meaningful action makes sense only in a cultural context. For example, when social researchers study racial groups, they are not interested in the biological differences between races. Race is a social concept; it is studied because the members of a culture attach social meaning to racial appearance.

Box 17.3 _____

Objective, Value-Free, and Unbiased

1. *Objective:*
   a. Opposite of subjective, external or observable, factual, precise, quantitative
   b. Logical, created by an explicit rational procedure, absence of personal or arbitrary decisions, follows specific preestablished rules
2. *Value Free:*
   a. Absence of any metaphysical values or assumptions; devoid of a priori philosophical elments, amoral
   b. Lack of influence from personal prejudice or cultural values, devoid of personal opinion, no room for unsupported views, neutral
3. *Unbiased:*
   a. Nonrandom error eliminated, absence of systematic error, technically correct
   b. Lack of influence from personal prejudice or cultural values, devoid of personal opinion, no room for unsupported views, neutral

---

Race would be meaningless if people did not attach such a social meaning to observable racial differences.

Other social researchers have built on Weber's ideas. For example, Moore (1973) asked whether majority-group (e.g., Anglo, white) researchers, as "outsiders," can accurately study racial minorities, since their questions, assumptions, and interests come from a dominant, nonminority perspective. Are the culture, values, and belief system of the dominant white culture appropriate for asking important questions and really understanding the subculture of racial minorities? Similar concerns have been raised regarding gender.[62] Being from a different culture may not preclude researching a group, but it calls for extra care and sensitivity from a researcher.

Weber (1949) also argued that social scientists cannot avoid taking stands on social issues they study. Researchers *must* be unbiased (i.e., neutral and devoid of personal opinion and unsupported views) when applying accepted research techniques and focus on the means or mechanisms of how the social world works, not on ends, values, or normative goals. A researcher's values must be separate from the findings, and he should advocate positions on specific issues only when speaking as a private citizen.

Gouldner (1976) attacked the notion of value-free, objective social science. He argued that the notion of value freedom was used in the past to disguise specific value positions. In fact, value freedom is itself a value—a value in favor of "value free." Gouldner said that complete value freedom was impossible and that scientists and other professionals use the term to hide their own values. He recommended making values explicit. A researcher can be motivated to do research by a desire to do more than dispassionately study the world. He can be motivated by a strong moral desire to effect change, which need not invalidate good research practice.

Mannheim (1936) also questioned the ideas of *value neutrality* and objectivity. He saw the intellectuals of a society, especially those involved in social research, as occupying a unique social role. A person's social location in society shapes his or her ideas and viewpoints. Yet, social researchers are separate from others and are less shaped by their social position because they try to learn the viewpoints of other people and empathize with all parts of society. Social researchers and intellectuals are not beholden to powerful elites, and they are also less subject to shifts in popular opinion, fads, and crazes. They can and should adopt a *relational position*—a position apart from any other specific social group, yet in touch with all groups. They should be detached or marginal in society, yet have connections with all parts of society, even parts that are often overlooked or hidden.

CONCLUSION

I want to end this chapter by urging you, as a consumer of social research or a new social researcher, to be self-aware. Be aware of the place of the thinking researcher in modern society and of the societal context of social research itself. Social researchers, and sociologists in particular, bring a unique perspective to the larger society. Social researchers have a responsibility and role as intellectuals in society. They need an awareness of how the social sciences acquired their current place in society. It is easier to understand many ethical and political issues if they are seen in the context of the historical development of the social sciences.

In Chapter 1, we discussed the distinctive contribution of science to modern society and how social research is a source of knowledge about the social world. The perspectives and techniques of social research can be powerful tools for understanding the world. Nevertheless, with that power comes responsibility—a responsibility to yourself, a responsibility to your sponsors, a responsibility to the community of researchers, and a responsibility to the larger society. These responsibilities can and do come into conflict with each other at times.

Ultimately, you personally must decide to conduct research in an ethical manner, to uphold and defend the principles of the social science approach you adopt, and to demand ethical conduct by others. The truthfulness of knowledge produced by social research and its use or misuse depends on individual researchers like you, reflecting on their actions and on how social research fits into society.

KEY TERMS

academic freedom
anonymity
"Bad Blood"
certificate of confidentiality
code of ethics
confidentiality
Consortium of Social Science
    Associations (COSSA)
contract research
crossover design

informed consent
institutional review board
    (IRB)
Milgram's obedience study
models of relevance
National Institutes of Health
    (NIH)
National Science Foundation
    (NSF)
Nuremberg code

plagiarism
principle of voluntary consent
Project Camelot
relational position
research fraud
scientific misconduct
tearoom trade study
value neutrality
Wichita Jury Study
Zimbardo prison experiment

REVIEW QUESTIONS

1. What is the primary defense against unethical conduct in research?
2. How do deception and coercion to participate in research conflict with the principle of voluntary consent?
3. Explain the ethical issues in the Milgram, Humphreys, and Zimbardo examples.
4. What is informed consent, and how does it protect research subjects?
5. What is the difference between anonymity and confidentiality?
6. What are the origins of codes of ethics in social research?
7. In what ways might a sponsor attempt to influence a researcher illegitimately, and what can the researcher do about it?

8. In what ways can political groups or politicians affect social research?

9. What would happen if research subjects treated information about themselves as their private property?

10. What is the relationship between academic freedom and research ethics?

NOTES

1. See Reynolds (1979:56–57) and Sieber (1993).

2. Research fraud is discussed by Broad and Wade (1982), Diener and Crandall (1978:154–158), and Weinstein (1979). Also see Hearnshaw (1979) and Wade (1976) on Cyril Burt. Kusserow (1989) and the September 1, 1989, issue of the National Institutes of Health weekly *Guide* summarize some recent scientific misconduct issues.

3. See "Noted Harvard Psychiatrist Resigns Post after Faculty Group Finds He Plagiarized," *Chronicle of Higher Education*, December 7, 1988.

4. See Blum (1989) and D'Antonio (1989) on this case of plagiarism.

5. See "Doctor Is Accused of 'Immoral' Tests," *New York times*, December 9, 1988. For a more general discussion of power and trust, see Reynolds (1979:32).

6. Lifton (1986) provides an account of Nazi medical experimentation.

7. See Jones (1981) on the Bad Blood case.

8. Diener and Crandall (1978:128) discuss these examples.

9. See Warwick (1982) on types of harm to research subjects. See Reynolds (1979:62–68) on rates of harm in biomedical research. Kelman (1982) discusses different types of harms from different types of research.

10. College counselors report that anxiety and low self-esteem over dating are major problems among college women (Diener and Crandall, 1978:21–22). Also see Kidder and Judd (1986:481–484).

11. See Dooley (1984:330) and Kidder and Judd (1986:477–484).

12. See Hallowell (1985) and "Threat to Confidentiality of Fieldnotes." *ASA Footnotes*, Volume 12, October 1984. p. 6.

13. For more on the general issue of the right not to be researched, see Barnes (1979), Boruch (1982), Moore (1973), and Sagarin (1973).

14. The debate over covert research is discussed in Denzin and Erikson (1982), Homan (1980), and Sieber (1982). Also see the section on ethics in Chapter 14.

15. See Diener and Crandall (1978:87) and Warwick (1982:112).

16. Informed consent requirements and regulations are discussed in detail in Maloney (1984). Also see Capron (1982) and Diener and Crandall (1978:64–66).

17. See Diener and Crandall (1978:173–177) and Kidder and Judd (1986:469).

18. See Boruch (1982), Caplan (1982), Katz (1972), and Vaughan (1967) on privacy.

19. For more on the Wichita Jury Study, see Dooley (1984:338–339), Gray (1982), Robertson (1982), Tropp (1982:391), and Vaughan (1967).

20. See Monaghan (1993a, 1993b, 1993c).

21. For more on gatekeepers, see Broadhead and Rist (1976).

22. See Freidson (1986) on professionals.

23. See Beecher (1970:227–228) and Reynolds (1979:28–31, 428–441).

24. See "UW Protects Dissertation Sources," *Capital Times*, December 19, 1994, page 4.

25. See Hirschman (1970) on loyalty, exit, or voice. Also see Rubin (1983:24–40) on ethical issues in applied research.

26. Additional discussion can be found in Schmeling and Miller (1988).

27. See Fiske (1989), Koretz (1988), and Weiss and Gruber (1987) on educational statistics.

28. See Staggenborg (1988) on "hired hand" research.

29. See "State Sought, Got Author's Changes in Lottery Report," *Capital Times*, July 28, 1989, p. 21.

30. See Chambers (1986).

31. See Dale W. Nelson (Associated Press), "Analyst: War Death Counts Falsified," *Wisconsin State Journal*, April 14, 1992, p. 3A, and "Ex-Official Says Pentagon Dumped Findings on Gays," *Capital Times*, April 1, 1993.

32. See Greenberg (1967:71).

33. For more on the decade of the 1950s and its effect on social researchers. see Caute (1978:403–430), Goldstein (1978:360–369), and Schrecker (1986).

34. IRBs are discussed in Maloney (1984) and Chadwick, Bahr, and Albrecht (1984:20).

35. For recent changes in Soviet social science research, see Keller (1988, 1989) and Swafford (1987). Also see "Soviet Sociologist Calls Attention

for Her Science," American Sociological Association *Footnotes*, April 1987, p. 2.

36. In addition to the discussion in Chapter 9, see Block and Burns (1986) and Starr (1987).

37. See Bermant (1982:138). Nelkin (1982a) provides a general discussion of "forbidden" topics in social science research.

38. For more on the Proxmire award, see Cordes (1988).

39. "Sex Survey Is Dealt a Setback," *New York Times*, July 26, 1989, page. 7.

40. See Stephen Burd, "Scientists Fear Rise of Intrusion in Work Supported by NIH," in *Chronicle of Higher Education*, October 2, 1991, p. Alff.

41. See "NIH FY 1991 Budget Rescinded by $3.1 Million, Congress Objects to 31 Research Projects Funded by NSF," *The Blue Sheet* (F-D-C Reports, Inc.), May 27, 1992, p. 3.

42. Project Camelot is described in Horowitz (1965).

43. See Dickson (1984), Nelkin (1982b), and Shattuck and Spence (1988:2).

44. See Shattuck and Spence (1988) and Josephson (1988). Also see "Librarians Charge Plan Would Cut Flow of Data," *New York Times*, February 21, 1989.

45. For more on the CIA and social researchers, see Shattuck and Spence (1988:39–40) and Stephenson (1978).

46. For sensitive situations involving cross-national research, see Fuller (1988) and Van den Berge (1967).

47. For discussion, see Bannister (1987), Blumer (1991b), D'Antonio (1992), Hyman (1991), Ross (1991), and Seybold (1987).

48. For more on the effects of politics and funding cuts on social research in the 1980s, see Cummings (1984), Himmelstein and Zald (1984), McCarthy (1984), and Zuiches (1984). For more general discussion of the effect of funding on research, see Galliher and McCartney (1973) and Dickson (1984).

49. See Dynes (1984) on COSSA.

50. The SSRC spent $20 million for the social sciences in 1924–1928 (Gieger, 1986:152) compared to $136 million allocated in 1989 by the NSF for the social sciences (D'Antonio, 1992). In the late 1920s, the number of academic social scientists was about one-tenth and a dollar purchased over six times more. The number of social science doctorates—including psychology, teaching, or conducting basic research—in 1986 was about 129,000 (Science and Engineering Personnel: A National Overview, Document NSF 90-310). The size of the higher educational faculty in all academic fields in 1930 was under 83,000 (Historical Statistics of the United States, 1970, Table H696). The $20 million over four years in the 1920s, or $5 million per year, would be equivalent to roughly $300 million in 1990. The median family income before taxes in 1929 was $2,335 (Historical Statistics, Table G308).

51. See Shattuck and Spence (1988:35–37).

52. Stephen Burd, "U.S. Cannot Require Preview of Research, Federal Judge Rules." *Chronicle of Higher Education*, October 9, 1991, p. Alff.

53. See Starr and Corson (1987:435).

54. See Weiss and Gruber (1987:369).

55. For more discussion on how researchers select research questions or problems, see Gieryn (1978) and Zuckerman (1978).

56. See Brym (1980) on role of intellectuals in society.

57. See Rule (1978a:67–139).

58. See Gustavsen (1986).

59. Marsh (1984), Noelle-Neumann (1974, 1984) and Price (1989) discuss the effects of research results on subsequent public behavior and opinion.

60. Bartiz (1960), Schrecker (1986), Schwendinger and Schwendinger (1974), and Silva and Slaughter (1980) discuss the history of social researchers in society.

61. See Punch (1986:18–19, 49–69).

62. Committees on the Status of Women in Sociology (1986).

RECOMMENDED READINGS

Alonso, William, and Paul Starr (Eds.). (1987). *The politics of numbers*. New York: Russell Sage. This book contains essays on how quantitative data collected by governments are influenced by political and cultural factors. Many different types of official or existing statistics are discussed, and the primary theme of the essays is that politics often has an effect on statistics that are used by researchers and policy makers.

Barnes, J. A. (1979). *Who should know what? Social science, privacy and ethics*. New York: Cambridge University Press. Barnes addresses the question of whether people should participate in research studies and of what happens to the information they provide. He raises important questions about the power of social researchers and their relationship to those whom they study.

Committees on the Status of Women in Sociology. (1986). *The treatment of gender in research.* Washington, DC: American Sociological Association. This pamphlet discusses the place of gender in social research. It describes how to include gender sensitivity in the areas of research assumptions, research design, operationalization of concepts, and data analysis. It includes some examples of the type of sex-biased research that was common in the recent past.

Kimmel, Allen J. (1988). *Ethics and values in applied social research.* Newbury Park, CA: Sage. Kimmel provides a good introduction to ethical issues in research. He is very strong at showing how applied research often raises complex issues with sponsors and others. He also covers basic principles of ethical social research and describes how ethical concerns may conflict with methodological demands.

Rule, James. (1978). *Insight and social betterment.* New York: Oxford University Press. Rule raises important issues about the use of social research and the dissemination of findings. He describes alternative ways in which social researchers have defined their social role and discusses the implications of such definitions.

Sieber, Joan E. (1992). *Planning ethically responsible research: A guide for students and internal review boards.* Thousand Oaks, CA: Sage. This is an excellent introduction to the ethical issues of social research and the operation of IRBs. It can also serve as a "how-to" manual for new researchers or members of an IRB.

CODES OF ETHICS

American Association for Public Opinion Research
American Sociological Association

ARTICLE IX
THE CODE

The code of AAPOR shall be entitled and provide as follows:

Code of Professional Ethics and Practices

We, the members of the American Association for Public Opinion Research, subscribe to the principles expressed in the following code. Our goals are to support sound and ethical practice in the conduct of public opinion research and in the use of such research for policy and decision-making in the public and private sectors, as well as to improve public understanding of opinion research methods and the proper use of opinion research results.

We pledge ourselves to maintain high standards of scientific competence and integrity in conducting, analyzing, and reporting our work and in our relations with survey respondents, with our clients, with those who eventually use the research for decision-making purposes, and with the general public. We further pledge ourselves to reject all tasks or assignments that would require activities inconsistent with the principles of this code.

THE CODE

I. *Principles of Professional Practice in the Conduct of Our Work*
  A. We shall exercise due care in developing research designs and survey instruments, and in collecting, processing, and analyzing data, taking all reasonable steps to assure the reliability and validity of results.

   1. We shall recommend and employ only those tools and methods of analysis which, in our professional judgment, are well suited to the research problem at hand.
   2. We shall not select research tools and methods of analysis because of their capacity to yield misleading conclusions.
   3. We shall not knowingly make interpretations of research results, nor shall we tacitly permit interpretations that are inconsistent with the data available.
   4. We shall not knowingly imply that interpretations should be accorded greater confidence than the data actually warrant.
  B. We shall describe our methods and findings accurately and in appropriate detail in all research reports, adhering to the standards for minimal disclosure specified in Section III, below.
  C. If any of our work becomes the subject of a formal investigation of an alleged violation of this Code, undertaken with the approval of the AAPOR Executive Council, we shall provide additional information on the survey in such detail that a fellow survey practitioner would be able to conduct a professional evaluation of the survey.

II. *Principles of Professional Responsibility in Our Dealings With People*
  A. The Public:
   1. If we become aware of the appearance in public of serious distortions of our research, we shall publicly disclose what is required to correct these distortions, including, as appropriate, a statement to the public media, legislative body, regulatory agency, or other appropriate group, in or

before which the distorted findings were presented.

B. Clients or Sponsors:

1. When undertaking work for a private client, we shall hold confidential all proprietary information obtained about the client and about the conduct and findings of the research undertaken for the client, except when the dissemination of the information is expressly authorized by the client, or when disclosure becomes necessary under terms of Section I-C or II-A of this Code.

2. We shall be mindful of the limitations of our techniques and capabilities and shall accept only those research assignments which we can reasonably expect to accomplish within these limitations.

C. The Profession:

1. We recognize our responsibility to contribute to the science of public opinion research and to disseminate as freely as possible the ideas and findings which emerge from our research.

2. We shall not cite our membership in the Association as evidence of professional competence, since the association does not so certify any persons or organizations.

D. The Respondent:

1. We shall strive to avoid the use of practices or methods that may harm, humiliate, or seriously mislead survey respondents.

2. Unless the respondent waives confidentiality for specified uses, we shall hold as privileged and confidential all information that might identify a respondent with his or her responses. We shall also not disclose or use the names of respondents for nonresearch purposes unless the respondents grant us permission to do so.

III. *Standards for Minimal Disclosure*
Good professional practice imposes the obligation upon all public opinion researchers to include, in any report of research results, or to make available when that report is released, certain essential information about how the research was conducted. At a minimum, the following items should be disclosed:

1. Who sponsored the survey, and who conducted it.

2. The exact wording of questions asked, including the text of any preceding instruction or explanation to the interviewer or respondent that might reasonably be expected to affect the response.

3. A definition of the population under study, and a description of the sampling frame used to identify this population.

4. A description of the sample selection procedure, giving a clear indication of the method by which the respondents were selected by the researcher, or whether the respondents were entirely self-selected.

5. Size of sample and, if applicable, completion rates and information on eligibility criteria and screening procedures.

6. A discussion of the precision of the findings, including, if appropriate, estimates of sampling error, and a description of any weighting or estimating procedures used.

7. Which results are based on parts of the sample, rather than on the total sample.

8. Method, location, and dates of data collection.

CODE OF ETHICS: AMERICAN SOCIOLOGICAL ASSOCIATION PREAMBLE

Sociologists recognize that the discovery, creation, and accumulation of knowledge and the practice of sociology are social processes involving ethical considerations and behavior at every stage. Careful attention to the ethical dimensions of sociological practice and scholarship contributes to the broader project of finding ways to maximize the beneficial effects that sociology may bring to humankind and to minimize the harm that might be a consequence of sociological work. The strength of the Code, its binding force, rests ultimately on the continuing active discussion, reflection, and use by members of the profession.

Sociologists subscribe to the general tenets of science and scholarship. Sociologists are especially sensitive to the potential for harm to individuals, groups, organizations, communities and societies that may arise out of the incompetent or unscrupulous use of sociological work and knowledge.

Sociology shares with other disciplines the commitment to the free and open access of knowledge and service, and to the public disclosure of findings. Sociologists are committed to the pursuit of accurate and precise knowledge and to self-regulation through peer review and appraisal, without personal and methodological prejudice and without ideological malice. Because sociology necessarily entails study of individuals, groups, organizations and societies, these principles may occasionally conflict with more general ethical concerns for the rights of clients and respondents to privacy and for the treatment of clients and respondents with due regard for their integrity, dignity, and autonomy. This potential conflict provides one of the reasons for a Code of Ethics.

The styles of sociological work are diverse and changing. So also are the contexts within which sociologists find employment. These diversities of procedures and context have led to ambiguities concerning appropriate professional behavior. The ambiguities provide another reason for this Code.

Finally, this Code also attempts to meet the expressed needs of sociologists who have asked for guidance in how best to proceed in a variety of situations involving relations with respondents, students, colleagues, employers, clients and public authorities.

This Code establishes feasible requirements for ethical behavior. These requirements cover many—but not all—of the potential sources of ethical conflict that may arise in research, teaching and practice. Most represent *prima facie* obligations that may admit of exceptions but which should generally stand as principles for guiding conduct. The Code states the Associations's consensus about ethical behavior upon which the Committee on Professional Ethics will base its judgments when it must decide whether individual members of the Association have acted unethically in specific instances. More than this, however, the Code is meant to sensitize all sociologists to the ethical issues that may arise in their work, and to encourage sociologists to educate themselves and their colleagues to behave ethically.

To fulfill these purposes, we, the members of the American Sociological Association, affirm and support the following Code of Ethics. Members accept responsibility for cooperating with the duly constituted committees of the American Sociological Association by responding to inquiries promptly and completely. Persons who bring complaints in good faith under this Code should not be penalized by members of the Association for exercising this right.

I. THE PRACTICE OF SOCIOLOGY

    A. Objectivity and Integrity.

        Sociologists should strive to maintain objectivity and integrity in the conduct of sociological research and practice.

1. Sociologists should adhere to the highest possible technical standards in their research, teaching and practice.

2. Since individual sociologists vary in their research modes, skills, and experience, sociologists should always set forth ex ante the limits of their knowledge and the disciplinary and personal limitations that affect whether or not a research project can be successfully completed and condition the validity of findings.

3. In practice or other situations in which sociologists are requested to render a professional judgment, they should accurately and fairly represent their areas and degrees of expertise.

4. In presenting their work, sociologists are obligated to report their findings fully and should not misrepresent the findings of their research. When work is presented, they are obligated to report their findings fully and without omission of significant data. To the best of their ability, sociologists should also disclose details of their theories, methods and research designs that might bear upon interpretations of research findings.

5. Sociologists must report fully all sources of financial support in their publications and must not have any special relations to any sponsor.

6. Sociologists should not make any guarantees to respondents, individuals, groups or organizations—unless there is full intention and ability to honor such commitments. All such guarantees, once made, must be honored.

7. Consistent with the spirit of full disclosure of method and analysis, sociologists should cooperate in efforts to make raw data and pertinent documentation collected and prepared at public expense available to other social scientists, at reasonable costs, after they have completed their own analyses, except in cases where confidentiality, the client's rights to proprietary information and privacy or the claims of a fieldworker to the privacy of personal notes necessarily would be violated. The timeliness of this cooperation is especially critical.

8. Sociologists should provide adequate information and citations concerning scales and other measures used in their research.

9. Sociologists must not accept grants, contracts or research assignments that appear likely to require violation of the principles enunciated in this Code, and should dissociate themselves from research when they discover a violation and are unable to achieve its correction.

10. When financial support for a project has been accepted, sociologists must make every reasonable effort to complete the proposed work on schedule, including reports to the funding source.

11. When several sociologists, including students, are involved in joint projects, there should be mutually accepted explicit agreements at the outset with respect to division of work, compensation, access to data, rights of authorship, and other rights and responsibilities. Such agreements may need to be modified as the project evolves and such modifications must be agreed upon jointly.

12. Sociologists should take particular care to state all significant qualifications on the findings and interpretations of their research.

13. Sociologists have the obligation to disseminate research findings, except those likely to cause harm to clients, collaborators and participants, or those which are proprietary under a formal or informal agreement.

14. In their roles as practitioners, researchers, teachers, and administrators, sociologists have an important social responsibility because their recommendations, decision, and actions may alter the lives of others. They should be aware of the situations and pressures that might lead to the misuse of their influence and authority. In these various roles, sociologists should also recognize that professional problems and conflicts may interfere with professional effectiveness. Sociologists should take steps to insure that these conflicts do not produce deleterious results for clients, research participants, colleagues, students and employees.

B. Disclosure and Respect for the Rights of Research Populations.

Disparities in wealth, power, and social status between the sociologist and respondents and clients may reflect and create problems of equity in research collaboration. Conflict of interest for the sociologist may occur in research and practice. Also to follow the precepts of the scientific method—such as those requiring full disclosure—may entail adverse consequences or personal risks for individuals and groups. Finally, irresponsible actions by a single researcher or research team can eliminate or reduce future access to a category of respondents by the entire profession and its allied fields.

1. Sociologists should not misuse their positions as professional social scientists for fraudulent purposes or as a pretext for gathering intelligence for any organization or government. Sociologists should not mislead respondents involved in a research project as to the purpose for which that research is being conducted.

2. Subjects of research are entitled to rights of biographical anonymity.

3. Information about subjects obtained from records that are opened to public scrutiny cannot be protected by guarantees of privacy or confidentiality.

4. The process of conducting sociological research must not expose respondents to substantial risk of personal harm. Informed consent must be obtained when the risks of research are great er than the risks of everyday life. Where modest risk or harm is anticipated, informed consent must be obtained.

5. Sociologists should take culturally appropriate steps to secure informed consent and to avoid invasions of privacy. Special actions may be necessary where the individuals studied are illiterate, have very low social status, or are unfamiliar with social research.

6. To the extent possible in a given study sociologists should anticipate potential threats to confidentiality. Such means as the removal of identifiers, the use of

randomized responses and other statistical solutions to problems of privacy should be used where appropriate.

7. Confidential information provided by research participants must be treated as such by sociologists, even when this information enjoys no legal protection or privilege and legal force is applied. The obligation to respect confidentiality also applies to members of research organizations (interviewers, coders, clerical staff, etc.) who have access to the information. It is the responsibility of administrators and chief investigators to instruct staff members on this point and to make every effort to insure that access to confidential information is restricted.

8. While generally adhering to the norm of acknowledging the contributions of all collaborators, sociologists should be sensitive to harm that may arise from disclosure and respect a collaborator's wish or need for anonymity. Full disclosure may be made later if circumstances permit.

9. Study design and information gathering techniques should conform to regulations protecting the rights of human subject, irrespective of source of funding, as outlined by the American Association of University Professors (AAUP) in "Regulations Governing Research on Human Subjects: Academic Freedom and the Institutional Review Board," *Academe*, December 1981: 358–370.

10. Sociologists should comply with appropriate federal and institutional requirements pertaining to the conduct of research. These requirements might include but are not necessarily limited to failure to obtain proper review and approval for research that involves human subjects and failure to follow recommendations made by responsible committees concerning research subjects, materials, and procedures.

II. PUBLICATIONS AND REVIEW PROCESS

A. Questions of Authorship and Acknowledgment.

1. Sociologists must acknowledge all persons who contribute to their research and to their copyrighted publications. Claims and ordering of authorship and acknowledgments must accurately reflect the contributions of all main participants in the research and writing process, including students, except in those cases where such ordering or acknowledgment is determined by an official protocol.

2. Data and material taken verbatim from another person's published or unpublished written work must be explicitly identified and referenced to its author. Citations to ideas developed in the written work of others, even if not quoted verbatim, should not be knowingly omitted.

B. Authors, Editors and Referees Have Interdependent Professional Responsibilities in the Publication Process.

1. Editors should continually review the fair application of standards without personal or ideological malice.

2. Journal editors must provide prompt decisions to authors of submitted manuscripts. They must monitor the work of associate editors and other referees so that delays are few and reviews are conscientious.

3. An editor's commitment to publish an essay must be binding on the journal. Once accepted for publication, a manuscript should be published expeditiously.

4. Editors receiving reviews of manuscripts from persons who have previously reviewed those manuscripts for another journal should ordinarily seek additional reviews.

5. Submission of a manuscript to a professional journal clearly grants that journal first claim to publish. Except where journal policies explicitly allow multiple submissions, a paper submitted to one English language journal may not be submitted to another journal published in English until after an official decision has been received for the first journal. Of course, the article can be withdrawn from all consideration to publish at any time.

C. Participation in Review Processes.

Sociologists are frequently asked to provide evaluations of manuscripts, research proposals, or other work of professional colleagues. In such work, sociologists should hold themselves to high standards of performance in several specific ways:

1. Sociologists should decline requests for reviews of work of others where strong conflicts of interest are involved, such as may occur when a person is asked to review work by teachers, friends, or colleagues for whom he or she feels an overriding sense of personal obligation, completion, or enmity, or when such request cannot be fulfilled on time.
2. Materials sent for review should be read in their entirety and considered carefully and confidentially. Evaluations should be justified with explicit reasons.
3. Sociologists who are asked to review manuscripts and books they have previously reviewed should make this fact known to the editor requesting review.

III. TEACHING AND SUPERVISION

The routine conduct of faculty responsibilities is treated at length in the faculty codes and AAUP rules accepted as governing procedures by the various institutions of higher learning. Sociologists in teaching roles should be familiar with the content of the codes in force at their institutions and should perform their responsibilities within such guidelines. Sociologists who supervise teaching assistants should take steps to insure that they adhere to these principles.

A. Sociologists are obligated to protect the rights of students to fair treatment.
1. Sociologists should provide students with a fair and honest statement of the scope and perspective of their courses, clear expectations for student performance, and fair, timely, and easily accessible evaluations of their work.
2. Departments of Sociology must provide graduate students with explicit policies and criteria about conditions for admission into the graduate program, financial assistance employment, funding, evaluation and possible dismissal.
3. Sociology departments should help students in their efforts to locate professional employment in academic and practice settings.
4. Sociology departments should work to insure the equal and fair treatment of all students, by adhering both in spirit and content to established affirmative action guidelines, laws, and policies.

5. Sociologists must refrain from disclosure of personal information concerning students where such information is not directly relevant to issues of professional competence.
B. Sociologists must refrain from exploiting students.
1. Sociologists must not coerce or deceive students into serving as research subjects.
2. Sociologists must not represent the work of students as their own.
3. Sociologists have an explicit responsibility to acknowledge the contributions of students and to act on their behalf in setting forth agreements regarding authorship and other recognition.
C. Sociologists must not coerce personal or sexual favors or economics or professional advantages from any person, including respondents, clients, patients, students, research assistants, clerical staff or colleagues.
D. Sociologists must not permit personal animosities or intellectual differences vis-à-vis colleagues to foreclose student access to those colleagues.

IV. ETHICAL OBLIGATIONS OF EMPLOYERS, EMPLOYEES, AND SPONSORS

No sociologists should discriminate in hiring, firing, promotions, salary, treatment, or any other conditions of employment or career development on the basis of sex, sexual preference, age, race, religion, national origin, handicap, or political orientation. Sociologists should adhere to fair employment practices in hiring, promotion, benefits, and review processes. The guidelines outlined below highlight some, but not all, ethical obligations in employment practices. Clear specification of the requirements covering practices of fair and equal treatment are stated in the guidelines of the equal employment opportunity commission and the AAUP. Employers, employees, and sponsors should abide by these guidelines and consult them when a more complete description of fair employment practices is needed.

A. Employment Practices and Adherence to Guidelines.
1. When acting as employers, sociologists should specify the requirements for hiring, promotion, and tenure and communicate these requirements thoroughly to employees and prospective employees. Voting on tenure and promotion should be based solely on professional criteria.

2. When acting as employers, sociologists should make every effort to ensure equal opportunity and fair treatment to all persons at all levels of employment.

3. When acting as employers, sociologists have the responsibility to be informed of fair employment codes, to help to create an atmosphere upholding fair employment practices, and to attempt to change any existing unfair practices within the organization or university.

4. All employees, including part-time employees, at all levels of employment, should be afforded the protection of due process through clear grievance procedures. It is the obligation of sociologists when acting as employers, to communicate these procedures and to protect the rights of employees who initiate complaints. They should also communicate standards of employment, and provide benefits, and compensation.

B. Responsibility of Employees.

1. When seeking employment sociologists should provide prospective employers with accurate information on their relevant professional qualifications and experiences.

2. Sociologists accepting employment in academic and practice settings should become aware of possible constraints on research and publication in those settings and should negotiate clear understandings about such conditions accompanying their research and scholarly activity. In satisfying their obligations to employers, sociologists in such settings must make every effort to adhere to the professional obligations contained in this Code.

3. When planning to resign a post, sociologists should provide their employers with adequate notice of intention to leave.

C. Sponsor's Participation in Employment Processes.

1. In helping to secure employment for students and trainees, sociologists should make every attempt to avoid conflicts of interest. When a conflict of interest does arise, full disclosure of potential biases should be made to job seekers.

APPENDIX B

A TABLE OF RANDOM NUMBERS

TABLE OF RANDOMLY SELECTED FIVE-DIGIT NUMBERS

10819	85717	64540	95692	44985	88504	50298	20830	67124	20557
28459	13687	50699	62110	49307	84465	66518	08290	96957	45050
19105	52686	51336	53101	81842	20323	71091	78598	60969	74898
35376	72734	13951	27528	36140	42195	25942	70835	45825	49277
93818	84972	66048	83361	56465	65449	87748	95405	98712	97183
35859	82675	87301	71211	78007	99316	25591	63995	40577	78894
66241	89679	04843	96407	01970	06913	19259	72929	82868	50457
44222	37633	85262	65308	03252	36770	51640	18333	33971	49352
54966	75662	80544	48943	87983	62759	55698	41068	35558	60870
43351	15285	38157	45261	50114	35934	05950	11735	51769	07389
11208	80818	78325	14807	19325	41500	01263	09211	56005	44250
71379	53517	15553	04774	63452	50294	06332	69926	20592	06305
63162	41154	78345	23645	74235	72054	84152	27889	76881	58652
17457	68490	19878	04981	83667	00053	12003	84614	14842	29462
28042	42748	55801	94527	21926	07901	89855	21070	80320	91153
32240	24201	24202	45025	07664	11503	97375	83178	26731	45568
87288	22996	67529	38344	29757	74161	16834	40238	48789	99995
39052	23696	42858	85695	50783	51790	80882	97015	81331	76819
71528	74553	32294	86652	15224	07119	45327	69072	64572	07658
76921	04502	78240	89519	02621	40829	88841	66178	01266	10906
45889	22839	77794	94068	85709	96902	19646	40614	03169	45434
10486	79308	75231	33615	42194	49397	91324	79553	66976	83861
42051	14719	80056	74811	58453	04526	90724	36151	09168	04291
47919	11314	80282	09297	02824	59530	31237	26311	62168	46591
19634	40589	28985	40577	33213	52852	17556	85342	66881	18944
10265	45549	38771	38740	48104	63990	73234	19398	33740	97345
74975	33526	36190	25201	19239	06254	02198	99109	01005	20983
37677	76778	15736	57675	81153	59651	69262	89250	75156	59164
18774	15979	26466	80236	65400	24272	02088	09307	33426	11230
93728	14965	85141	27821	53791	38728	66369	29415	55330	99228
34212	15590	41336	23614	26153	19466	44176	80885	00015	40077
81984	54478	45226	97338	14064	45768	13538	49093	05691	69720
72755	15743	00552	89374	85400	37392	26598	71917	64275	16125
13162	57044	75982	15819	23385	40860	51585	44542	39656	91139
64686	62224	34124	79171	73909	26196	54057	63264	72089	06658
00157	64594	03178	75774	32315	34443	37224	85593	55251	42666
84194	83591	82152	24311	22414	43244	81542	31491	42075	17275
05776	60399	65218	89299	20273	30071	53077	18853	56652	63896
33365	18314	81074	49433	10884	75467	56085	14731	98085	60895
67928	38976	38480	59980	23156	72335	33489	59420	67819	51874

64394	45154	81851	54228	73095	97217	16908	90242	92869	17311
73000	20948	57065	70195	87563	41590	85047	71743	94916	50534
63555	03388	96638	16591	13641	73342	59131	63144	63587	62084
84005	02035	08182	16395	44928	08897	44750	71378	67522	20180
42593	35102	14577	38102	60403	04540	53992	27069	69574	76682
49519	49517	88147	83375	87045	57466	91259	06680	45586	36257
42149	01579	83056	19423	28165	25620	68035	17919	09120	59078
66192	98427	10152	96970	89990	34604	49632	46533	63362	43151
16124	88620	87074	37851	77131	73855	03740	10306	63858	04349
35492	47334	57189	26465	70078	14477	00881	00929	86907	73764
54503	40155	94734	20689	32475	62851	13216	21419	95502	36783
88063	53451	15642	67345	06935	70644	68570	79176	31975	83082
83689	14426	40357	34906	56282	96104	83796	57663	88627	17521
40393	72810	00681	15351	28858	72086	99090	39741	17914	27385
76648	61322	06817	64674	50317	52373	78223	84222	14021	43432
42091	27088	37686	88033	68007	71009	24018	49568	64351	94130
78925	41509	14319	92389	85492	40880	01487	85509	48316	62618
61915	98081	87996	53798	51485	38912	85858	43392	64678	44458
29504	66960	42645	54547	20615	77035	79942	33972	46112	78290
90170	97643	46284	34591	42692	72933	66166	98389	37460	14545
96439	06806	76714	80084	57685	37447	44901	64699	89142	64657
98365	28725	84376	50634	79289	31106	71351	10533	57545	27399
74794	91013	89791	54236	02369	35317	31103	82481	52256	94510
37499	85907	16293	17673	13373	06599	50138	19860	46716	36928
77530	25960	33671	54383	25144	82627	99266	75134	96539	47242
67990	35106	05214	82928	39824	11128	31390	76293	52809	54881
07355	29187	09357	94498	69697	92515	89812	90794	44738	46806
40716	05787	68975	38937	44033	50064	25582	09428	10220	42455
97748	64395	13937	60406	99182	92720	80805	26242	81943	40341
83682	18775	60095	78600	03994	30313	21418	58563	47258	75582
73506	30672	18213	37887	26698	87700	75784	86878	74004	88636
36274	02333	43132	93725	87912	90341	74601	77001	30717	60002
73508	00852	94044	98474	12621	91655	55258	85551	76122	68052
06488	12362	60020	66902	90734	73689	22382	40896	09028	72925
20201	31560	98885	32275	46818	76114	07959	65639	33267	98595
49947	13114	06773	06454	95070	26564	08974	11640	76202	86105
79928	50600	06586	72129	37233	02564	83265	32579	21234	83535
76360	86412	36240	20210	17692	80482	67007	15474	23198	74250
54601	84643	66759	57661	16434	61708	93185	75957	61056	90678
23441	63863	95238	59665	55789	26180	12566	58645	15125	76707
47093	90509	48767	09874	23363	84954	09789	30178	28804	93294
93603	11580	94163	85561	71328	88735	69859	84563	25579	52858
68812	15299	99296	45906	37303	49507	70680	74412	96425	38134
69023	84343	36736	52659	90751	20115	89920	44995	17109	96613
76913	03158	83461	27842	03903	34683	89761	80564	45806	88009
99426	99643	00749	79376	44910	27490	59668	93907	73112	46365
59429	08121	06954	28120	17606	22482	91924	00401	16459	15570
38121	05358	01205	00662	73934	97834	56917	64058	05148	87599
97781	32170	99914	75565	79802	38905	17167	08196	46043	72094
79068	21760	78832	93795	67798	54968	87328	46494	74338	89805
46601	04015	00484	39366	56233	22622	90706	02327	60807	39009

(continued)

64821	72859	83471	60448	49159	38242	84473	05512	20200	91109
49216	15978	76313	82040	79322	53190	99705	86694	39000	59173
85909	77399	56836	38084	24480	16180	58023	20122	78348	36906
72284	62418	84313	85377	00039	90894	72976	19553	22917	58585
20210	90083	06608	43380	76224	87362	81200	91427	34115	36488
63659	42186	61396	94269	58196	42997	96272	02004	63365	75665
60022	62412	97267	13525	36794	68402	10902	87223	95682	18000
32399	18357	80684	50976	28717	95782	31227	99800	62642	33563
88488	73641	06447	51771	17572	68734	75964	54434	21852	80662
87642	39726	67296	75473	82899	06689	09402	18953	07418	89659
89586	59644	02486	95252	57771	97979	44761	10361	99589	57982
72544	38997	64243	04873	97006	55074	63062	06692	69940	94364
50807	84525	33191	49539	51414	87457	36296	68915	78902	60245
59490	00996	40795	05159	14215	72282	99887	93436	73440	57270
38626	50552	71131	69450	00534	26851	63155	61856	31104	52773
51982	59414	61762	30549	38914	30613	48661	47104	84319	71299
37747	69944	81040	53066	72265	63828	33559	21167	44864	91959
35752	01162	55189	98224	83276	35108	65759	47387	78381	53662
39473	21252	53693	49359	00691	82273	87378	90967	06356	77705
55572	52235	46693	87891	13626	50676	16806	23052	49743	44683
86396	26942	31794	03215	14813	07506	40853	79461	69114	32357
33555	56824	39948	35309	27279	78587	02790	98720	57920	30931
23433	11441	30625	68538	85671	78168	60754	37067	99579	76294
08339	60862	33225	85288	47812	89681	04184	87755	59664	46025
12952	73728	73346	54435	12067	18137	24559	99949	29504	82736
31065	41220	40348	71545	27046	95290	38752	13456	16147	20025
38062	29620	11459	24800	99422	31514	42673	62254	50236	52802
22365	00954	49547	16844	04006	09907	87626	60601	21891	14980
86779	89664	29030	91894	73718	73392	65469	79340	90014	00229
43233	48154	74284	65921	63641	00481	08578	22188	38029	68894
74503	33076	28357	23271	05919	12247	65814	51837	17689	67065
80697	09861	44996	94438	79742	44904	43997	30676	47959	91749
66890	59837	08731	62577	45661	40331	20461	40292	58324	50957
65029	71853	28424	48445	86207	05328	12631	18104	56863	84071
03322	46034	72527	42011	69919	00090	04986	06121	81888	04985
37951	98690	60776	79282	17148	79300	67391	53561	46702	99623
36747	35157	67719	81282	86592	21054	10617	10464	79204	16241
49340	44927	10914	17275	58227	91974	75268	28733	43893	17837
92271	64437	96956	18631	88405	96753	81024	21948	63478	73161
92299	36704	68944	92681	77662	54685	48356	21081	76717	47337
48344	93928	34136	47466	72646	18566	96759	31149	74706	37745
61726	51613	52816	33027	24383	07647	95883	28605	62283	18197
54433	70788	83880	31335	21145	16946	98191	37417	11780	41066
58541	72719	59340	60681	11593	06237	94809	58680	87392	55946
61516	65817	41065	83854	15993	83786	78324	06439	17050	62552
29215	08513	25460	52439	15219	69991	59623	35029	02632	33829
50164	57477	50446	22847	43803	56626	88506	88224	84080	29224
46923	73217	29155	22288	27172	09824	49339	80134	53208	89901
39385	54156	74135	82779	58336	79663	26502	78853	95172	24059
75334	79987	15894	18571	81773	50842	49946	04147	92224	41201
41285	32053	40984	90635	22067	11948	11443	99064	14675	16826

27423	31830	04828	05954	38820	94218	32586	04261	80975	47008
35906	67533	20585	21162	75252	73296	37607	92368	10867	69657
08554	70414	77644	99739	27390	80574	80240	19485	45190	36046
70966	52860	29353	41888	80187	97313	32440	08527	47081	17205
34154	79907	00949	54009	49291	48157	17375	13343	44727	36956
86436	46594	80734	80081	02314	42041	67591	78793	15440	21127
06339	10486	48944	44373	78872	90269	36662	40163	95780	06374
17715	18488	29772	86669	12401	86000	78660	00923	77884	44633
39611	02846	95861	49731	95395	26893	13314	07928	77911	53123
87271	46990	77790	79885	68909	54505	83646	78409	72846	28686
11996	29733	05629	93964	14193	83846	99389	50959	31927	79226
46940	09460	89582	17701	60658	71768	45426	93490	35636	70854
03412	41860	78660	76735	61981	37962	16512	87707	27622	17311
25077	14423	76933	16748	00741	62390	43843	80842	10219	54622
36495	82476	90894	71327	38924	07373	84495	31424	21285	08333
58500	55613	12395	00199	57097	24914	01779	02403	93251	44807
75248	35900	97246	15383	43870	60826	54130	63156	50504	52135
92175	62718	99616	61643	26886	14107	90719	47074	91737	97462
32463	69375	39095	36324	78594	57722	23596	36217	96947	44887
03693	77597	35029	70206	04705	91187	18602	86022	87337	23965
06721	33386	12162	55884	10420	30100	28445	77620	05067	10724
98591	40854	94023	57651	02409	76108	19790	48544	26777	42597
82535	71772	85767	76266	29140	47778	73492	53870	45014	08608
20105	25926	56710	14862	44589	57022	17734	38841	92896	40737
01749	78458	35863	82790	02427	87027	40106	94542	70051	68439
66826	49905	97602	26543	32418	22873	58878	34287	98272	00311
19242	91018	31082	73167	82661	20369	22976	86145	11196	51282
07788	16036	93946	83038	33324	79508	15514	84539	76833	02366
10238	51425	12133	60556	66023	78920	45286	79512	93581	56294
70278	45813	02647	70584	58543	31479	69235	12031	72235	67157
68633	59965	98891	65043	20653	78122	38989	65198	18659	79978
45164	32766	09525	49788	28780	54551	09208	91609	28711	97751
44701	18094	65320	24871	03285	61221	76401	81827	52742	90754
51254	38946	10820	30486	43737	91703	54377	04192	24354	21605
84819	68816	08575	93437	41898	71419	69327	00712	64283	82111
18122	52721	39067	33039	57890	71647	29730	09964	42192	59661
74518	17688	24087	59431	94219	31903	31093	95252	78310	29618
29507	76366	37600	35446	66362	17595	37560	14716	94629	39897
17615	22514	51864	04371	67231	61647	94074	24199	35525	69556
10735	07934	13585	35967	14790	78730	59122	01989	95596	05732
27515	94008	99354	12854	19839	02870	09161	52671	74303	58650
87240	67750	02552	56223	09496	21435	43859	17700	55974	93075
30474	21865	41837	44887	38330	51929	92959	72672	65078	33986
81033	89276	51464	63498	12766	55494	86208	16462	55022	56727
03550	49560	71142	85413	90974	88062	52135	84299	37041	88678
91516	90902	16387	47167	06377	86048	97771	53715	57709	61076
60915	35579	76264	72403	02744	52525	70804	28840	15504	80628
20281	63058	68322	36364	88444	68667	48877	28781	98458	05481

THE RESEARCH REPORT AND PROPOSALS

> But that's our business: to arrange ideas in so rational an order that
> another person can make sense of them. We have to deal with that
> problem on two levels. We have to arrange the ideas in a theory or
> narrative, to describe causes and conditions that lead to the effects that
> we want to explain, and do it in an order that is logically and empirically
> correct. . . . Finally, we want our prose to make the order we have
> constructed clear. We don't want imperfection in our prose to interfere
> with our readers' understanding. These two jobs converge and cannot be
> separated.
>
> —Howard Becker, *Writing for Social Scientists*, p. 133

INTRODUCTION

Why Write the Report?

After a researcher completes a project or a significant phase of a large project, it is time to communicate the findings to others through a research report. You can learn a lot about writing a research report by reading many reports and taking a course in scientific and technical writing.

This appendix summarizes the principles of writing a report, describes various types of reports, and discusses preparing a proposal for research.

A *research report* is a written document (or oral presentation based on a written document) that communicates the methods and findings of a research project to others. The research report is more than a summary of findings; it is a record of the research process. A researcher cannot wait until the research is done to think about the report;

he or she must think ahead to the report and keep careful records while conducting research. In addition to findings, the report includes the reasons for initiating the project, a description of the project's steps, a presentation of data, and a discussion of how the data relate to the research question or topic.

There are almost as many reasons for writing a report as there are for doing research. The basic reason for writing a report is to tell others what you, the researcher, did, and what you discovered. In other words, the research report is a way of disseminating knowledge. As you saw in Chapter 1, the research report plays a significant role in binding together the scientific community. Other reasons for writing a report are to fulfill a class or job assignment, to meet an obligation to an organization that paid for the research, to persuade a professional group about specific aspects of a problem, or to tell the general public about findings. Communicating with the general public is rarely the primary method for communication of scientific results; it is usually a second stage of dissemination.

Your Audience

Professional writers say: Always know whom you are writing for. This is because communication is more effective when it is tailored to a specific audience. You should write a research report differently depending on whether the primary audience is an instructor, other students, professional social scientists, practitioners, or the general public. It goes without saying that the writing should be clear, accurate, and well organized.

Instructors assign a report for different reasons and may place requirements on how it is written. In general, instructors want to see writing and an organization that reflect clear, logical thinking. Student reports should demonstrate a solid grasp of substantive and methodological concepts. A good way to do this is to use technical terms explicitly *when appropriate*; they should not be used excessively or incorrectly.

When writing for other students, it is best to define technical terms and label each part of the report. The discussion should proceed in a logical, step-by-step manner with many specific examples. Use straightforward language to explain how and why you conducted the various steps of the research project. One strategy is to begin with the research question, then structure the report as an answer.

Scholars do not need definitions of technical terms or explanations of why standard procedures (e.g., random sampling) were used. They are interested in how the research is linked to abstract theory or previous findings in the literature. They want a condensed, detailed description of research design. They pay close attention to how variables are measured and the methods of data collection. Scholars like a compact, tightly written, but extensive section on data analysis, with a meticulous discussion of results.

Practitioners prefer a short summary of how the study was conducted and results presented in a few simple charts and graphs. They like to see an outline of alternative paths of action implied by results with a discussion of the practical outcomes of pursuing each path. Practitioners must be cautioned not to overgeneralize from the results of one study. It is best to place the details of research design and a complete discussion of results in an appendix.

If you write for the general public, use simple language, provide concrete examples, and focus on the practical implications of findings for social problems. Do not include details of research design or of results when writing for the general public, and be careful not to make unsupported claims when writing for the public. Informing the public, however, is an important service, which can help nonspecialists make better judgments about public issues.

Style and Tone

Research reports are written in a narrow range of styles and have a distinct tone. Their purpose is to communicate clearly the research method and findings.

Style refers to the types of words chosen by the writer and the length and form of sentences or paragraphs used. *Tone* is the writer's attitude or relation toward the subject matter. For example, an informal, conversational style (e.g., colloquial words, idioms, clichés, incomplete sentences) with a personal tone (e.g., these are my feelings) is appropriate for writing a letter to a close friend, but not for research reports. Research reports have a formal and succinct (saying a lot in few words) style. The tone expresses distance from the subject matter; it is professional and serious. Field researchers sometimes use an informal style and a personal tone, but this is the exception. Avoid moralizing and flowery language. The goal is to inform, not to advocate a position or to entertain.

A research report should be objective, accurate, and clear. Check and recheck details (e.g., page references in citations) and fully disclose how you conducted the research project. If readers detect carelessness or omissions in writing, they may question the research itself. The details of a research project can be complex, and such complexity means that confusion is always a danger. It makes clear writing essential. Clear writing can be achieved by thinking and rethinking the research problem and design, explicitly defining terms and labeling tables, writing with short declarative sentences, and limiting conclusions to what is supported by the evidence.

THE WRITING PROCESS

Organizing Thoughts

Writing is not something that happens magically or simply flows out of a person when he or she puts pen to paper (or fingers to keyboard) although many people have such an illusion. Rather, it is hard work, involving a sequence of steps and separate activities that result in a final product. Writing a research report is not radically different from other types of writing. Although some steps differ and the level of complexity may be greater, most of what a good writer does when writing a long letter, a poem, a set of instructions, or a short story applies to writing a research report.

First, a writer needs something to write about. The "something" in the research report includes the topic, research question, design and measures, data collection techniques, results, and implications. With so many parts to write about, organization is essential. The most basic tool for organizing writing is the outline. Outlines help a writer ensure that all ideas are included and that the relationship between them is clear. Outlines are made up of topics (words or phrases) or sentences. Most of us are familiar with the basic form of an outline (see Table C.1).

Outlines can help the writer, but they can also become a barrier if they are used improperly. An outline is simply a tool or mechanism to help the writer organize ideas. It helps the writer do three things: (1) put ideas in a sequence (e.g., what will be said first, second, third); (2) group related ideas together (e.g., these are similar to each other, but differ from those); and (3) separate the more general, or higher level, ideas from more specific ideas, and the specific ideas from very specific details.

Some students feel that they need a complete outline before writing, and that once an outline is prepared, deviations from it are impossible. Few writers begin with a complete outline. The initial outline is necessarily sketchy because until you write everything down, it is impossible to put all ideas in a sequence, group them together, or separate the general from the specific. For most writers, new ideas develop or become clearer in the process of writing itself.

A beginning outline may differ from the final outline by more than degree of completeness. The process of writing may not only reveal or clarify ideas for the writer, but also stimulate the creation of new categories of ideas, new connections between ideas, a different sequence, or new relations between the general and the specific. In addition, the process of writing may involve reanalysis or a reexamination of the literature or findings. This does not mean beginning all over again. Rather, it means keeping an open mind to new insights and being candid, not defensive, about the research project.

Back to the Library

Few researchers finish their review and reading of the relevant literature before completing a research project. You, the researcher, should be familiar with the literature before beginning a project, but you will usually need to return to the literature after completing data collection and analysis, for several reasons. First, time has passed between the beginning and the end of a research project, and new studies may have been published. Second, after completing a research project, you will know better what is or is not central to the study. You may have new questions in mind when rereading the most critical studies in the literature. Finally, when writing the report, you may find that your notes are not complete enough or that you missed a detail in the citation of a reference source. The visit to the library after data collection is less extensive and more selective or focused than that conducted at the beginning of research.

When writing a research report, researchers frequently discard some of the notes and sources that were gathered prior to completing the research project. This does not mean that the initial library work and literature review were a waste of time and effort. You should expect that some of the notes (e.g., 25 percent) taken before completing the project will become irrelevant as the project gains focus. Do not include notes or references in a report that are no longer relevant, because they distract from the flow of ideas and reduce clarity.

Returning to the library to verify and expand references will allow you to focus and elaborate ideas. It also helps you avoid plagiarism. *Plagiarism* is taking and passing off the ideas or writings of another as one's own. It is stealing another writer's words or ideas and treating them as if they were your own. Plagiarism is a serious form of cheating, and many universities expel students caught engaging in it. If a professional ever plagiarizes in a scholarly journal, it is treated as a very serious offense.[1] Take careful notes and identify the exact source of phrases or ideas to avoid unintentional plagiarism. Cite the sources of both directly quoted words and paraphrased ideas. For direct quotes, include the location of the quote with page numbers in the citation.

Using another's written words and failing to give credit is definitely wrong, but paraphrasing is less clear. *Paraphrasing* is not using another's exact words; it is restating another's ideas in your

TABLE C.1 Form of Outline

I. First major topic	One of the most important
A. Subtopic of topic I	Second level of importance
1. Subtopic of A	Third level of importance
a. Subtopic of 1	Fourth level of importance
b. Subtopic of 1	"
(1) Subtopic of b	Fifth level of importance
(2) Subtopic of a	
(a) Subtopic of (2)	Sixth level of importance
(b) Subtopic of (2)	"
i. Subtopic of (b)	Seventh level of importance
ii. Subtopic of (b)	"
2. Subtopic of A	Third level of importance
B. Subtopic of topic I	Second level of importance
II. Second major topic	One of the most important

own words, usually condensing at the same time. Researchers regularly paraphrase, and good paraphrasing requires a solid understanding of what is being paraphrased. It means more than replacing another's words with synonyms; paraphrasing is borrowing an idea, boiling it down to its essence, and giving credit to the source.[2]

The Writing Process

Writing is a process. The way to learn to write is by writing.[3] It takes time and effort, and it improves with practice. There is no single correct way to write, but some methods are associated with good writing. The writing process has three steps. Beginning writers jump to the second step and end there, which results in poor-quality writing.

1. *Prewriting:* Prepare to write by arranging notes on the literature, making lists of ideas, outlining, completing bibliographic citations, and organizing comments on data analysis.
2. *Composing:* Get your ideas onto paper as a first draft by freewriting, drawing up the bib-

liography and footnotes, preparing data for presentation, and forming an introduction and conclusion.
3. *Rewriting:* Evaluate and polish the report by improving coherence, proofreading for mechanical errors, checking citations, and reviewing voice and usage.

Many people find that getting started is difficult. Prewriting means that a writer begins with a file folder full of notes, outlines, and lists. You must think about the form of the report and audience. Thinking time is important. It often occurs in spurts over a period of time before the bulk of composing begins.

Some people become afflicted with a strange ailment when they sit down to compose writing. It is known as *writer's block*—a temporary inability to write. It comes when the mind goes blank, the fingers freeze, and panic sets in. Writers from beginners through experts occasionally experience it. If you experience it, calm down and work on overcoming it (see Table C.2).

Numerous writers begin to compose by *freewriting*, a process of sitting down and writing

TABLE C.2 Suggestions for Ending Writer's Block

1. *Begin early.* Do not procrastinate or wait until the last minute. This not only gives you time to come back to the task but it also reduces the tension because you have time to write a poor-quality first draft that can be improved upon. Shafer (1980:205) chided, "Writing is hard work, and the excuses authors find for postponing it are legendary." Set yourself a deadline for a first draft that is at least a week before the final deadline, and keep it!

2. *Take a break, then return.* I sometimes find that if I take a walk, get a snack, read a newspaper, and come back to the task a half hour later, the block is gone. Small diversions, if they remain small and short term, can help on occasion.

3. *Begin in the middle.* You do not have to begin at the beginning. Begin in the middle and just start writing, even if does not seem to be directly

relevant. It may be easier to get to your topic once the writing/thinking process is moving.

4. *Engage in personal magic rituals.* Some people have unusual habits or rituals that they engage in before writing (e.g., washing dishes, clearing a desk, sharpening pencils). These can serve as mental triggers to help you get started. Do what gets you started writing.

5. *Break it into small parts.* Do not feel that you have to sit down and complete the writing task as a whole. Begin with pieces that come easily to you and stitch together the pieces later.

6. *Do not expect perfection.* Write a draft, which means that you can throw away, revise, and change what you wrote. It is always easier to revise a rough draft than to create perfect writing the first time.

down everything you can as quickly as it enters into your mind. Freewriting establishes a link between a rapid flow of ideas in the mind and writing. When you freewrite, you do not stop to reread what you wrote, you do not ponder the best word, you do not worry about correct grammar, spelling, or punctuation. You just put ideas on paper as quickly as possible to get and keep the creative juices or ideas flowing. You can later clean up what you wrote.

Writing and thinking are so intertwined that it is impossible to know where one ends and the other begins. This means that if you plan to sit and stare at the wall, the computer output, the sky, or whatever until all thoughts become totally clear before beginning, you will rarely get anything written. All that you need to begin is the spark of an idea. The thinking process can be ignited during the writing itself.

Rewriting

Perhaps one in a million writers is a creative genius who can produce a first draft that communicates with astounding accuracy and clarity. For the rest of us mortals, writing means that rewriting—and rewriting again—is necessary. For example, Ernest Hemingway is reported to have rewritten the end of *Farewell to Arms* 39 times.[4] It is not unusual for a professional researcher to rewrite a report a dozen times. Do not become discouraged. If anything, the idea of rewriting reduces the pressure; it means you can start writing soon and get out a rough draft that you can polish later. You should plan to rewrite a draft at least three or four times. A draft is a complete report, from beginning to end, not a few rough notes or an outline.

Rewriting helps a writer express himself or herself with a greater clarity, smoothness, precision and economy of words. When rewriting, the focus is on clear communication, not pompous or complicated language. As Leggett, Mead, and Charvat (1965:330) stated, "Never be ashamed to express a simple idea in simple language. Remember that the use of

complicated language is not in itself a sign of intelligence."

Rewriting means reading what you have written slowly and, if necessary, out loud to see whether it sounds right. It is a good idea to share your writing with others. Professional writers always have others read and criticize their writing. New writers soon learn that friendly, constructive criticism is very valuable. Sharing your writing with others may be difficult at first. It means exposing your written thoughts and encouraging criticism. Yet, the purpose of the criticism is to clarify writing, and the critic is doing you a favor.

Rewriting involves two related processes: revising and editing. *Revising* is the process of inserting new ideas, adding supporting evidence, deleting or changing ideas, moving sentences around to clarify meaning, or strengthening transitions and links between ideas. *Editing* is the process of cleaning up and tightening the more mechanical aspects of writing, such as spelling, grammar, usage, verb tense, sentence length, and paragraph organization. When you rewrite, go over a draft and revise it brutally to improve it. This is easier if some time passes between a draft and rewriting. Phrases that seemed satisfactory in a draft may look fuzzy or poorly connected after a week or two (see Table C.3).

Even if you have not acquired typing skills or access to a word processor, it is a good idea to type, or print out if you use a word processor, at least one draft before the final draft. This is because it is easier to see errors and organization problems in a clean, typed draft. Feel free to cut and paste, cross out words, or move phrases on the typed copy.

Good typing skills and an ability to use a word processor are extremely valuable when writing reports and other documents. Serious researchers and other professionals find that the time they invest into building typing skills and learning to use a word processor pays huge dividends later. Word processors make editing much easier, and most have a feature for checking spelling and offering synonyms. In addition, there are programs that check grammar. You cannot rely on the computer

TABLE C.3 Suggestions for Rewriting

1. *Mechanics:* Check grammar, spelling, punctuation, verb agreement, verb tense, and verb/subject separation with each rewrite. Remember that each time new text is added, new errors can creep in. Mistakes are not only distracting but they also weaken the confidence readers place in the ideas you express.

2. *Usage:* Reexamine terms, especially key terms, when rewriting to see whether you are using the exact word that expresses your intended meaning. Do not use technical terms or long words unnecessarily. Use the plain word that best expresses meaning. Get a thesaurus and use it. A *thesaurus* is an essential reference tool, like a dictionary, that contains words of similar meaning and can help you locate the exact word for a meaning you want to express. Precise thinking and expression requires precise language. Do not say *average* if you use the *mean*. Do not say *mankind* or *policeman* when you intend *people* or *police officer*. Do not use *principal* for *principle*.

3. *Voice:* Writers of research reports often make the mistake of using the passive instead of the active voice. It may appear more authoritative, but passive voice obscures the actor or subject of action. For example, the passive, "The relationship between grade in school and more definite career plans was confirmed by the data" is better stated as the active, "The data confirm the relationship between grade in school and more definite career plans." The passive, "Respondent attitude toward abortion was recorded by an interviewer" reads easier in the active voice: "An interviewer recorded respondent attitude towards abortion." Also avoid unnecessary qualifying language, such as "seems to" or "appears to."

4. *Coherence:* Sequence, steps, and transitions should be logically tight. Try reading the entire report one paragraph at a time. Does the paragraph contain a unified idea? A topic sentence? Is there a transition between paragraphs within the report?

5. *Repetition:* Remove repeated ideas, wordiness, and unnecessary phrases. Ideas are best stated once, forcefully, instead of repeatedly in an unclear way. When revising, eliminate deadwood (words that add nothing) and circumlocution (the use of several words when one more precise word will do). Directness is preferable to wordiness. The wordy phrase, "To summarize the above, it is our conclusion in light of the data that X has a positive effect of considerable magnitude on the occurrence of Y, notwithstanding the fact that Y occurs only on rare occasions," is better stated, "In sum, we conclude that X has a large positive effect on Y, but Y occurs infrequently." As Selvin and Wilson (1984) warned, verbose and excessive words or qualifiers make it difficult to understand what is written.

6. *Structure:* Research reports should have a transparent organization. Move sections around as necessary to fit the organization better, and use headings and subheadings. A reader should be able to follow the logical structure of a report.

7. *Abstraction:* A good research report mixes abstract ideas and concrete examples. A long string of abstractions without the specifics is difficult to read. Likewise, a mass of specific concrete details without periodic generalization also loses readers.

8. *Metaphors:* Many writers use metaphors to express ideas. Phases like "the cutting edge," "the bottom line," or "penetrating to the heart" are used to express ideas by borrowing images from other contexts. Metaphors can be an effective method of communication, but they need to be used sparingly and with care. A few well-chosen, consistently used, fresh metaphors can communicate ideas quickly and effectively; however, the excessive use of metaphors, especially overused metaphors (like "bottom line"), is a sloppy, unimaginative method of expression.

---

program to do all the work, but it makes writing easier. The speed and ease that a word processor offers is so dramatic that few people who become skilled at using one ever go back to writing by hand or typing. This textbook was written on a word processor. It would have taken at least twice as long to complete if I had used a typewriter instead.

One last suggestion: Rewrite the introduction and title after completing a draft so that they accurately reflect what is said.[5] Titles should be short and descriptive. They should communicate the topic and the major variables to readers. They can describe the type of research (e.g., "An experiment on . . ." but should not have unnecessary words or phrases (e.g., "An investigation into the . . .").

THE QUANTITATIVE RESEARCH REPORT

The principles of good writing apply to all reports, but the parts of a report differ depending on whether the research is quantitative or qualitative. Before writing any report, read reports on the same kind of research for models.

We begin with the quantitative research report. The sections of the report roughly follow the sequence of steps of a research project.[6]

Abstract or Executive Summary

Quantitative research reports usually begin with a short summary called an abstract. The size of an abstract varies; it can be as few as 50 words (this paragraph has 90 words) or as long as a full page. Most scholarly journal articles have abstracts that are printed on the first page of the article, or all abstracts for articles in an issue appear together on a separate page. The abstract has information on the topic, the research problem, the basic findings, and any unusual research design or data collection features.

Reports of applied research that are written for practitioners have a longer summary called the *executive summary*. It contains more detail than an article abstract and includes the implications of research and major recommendations made in the report. Although it is longer than an abstract, an executive summary rarely exceeds four or five pages.

Abstracts and executive summaries serve several functions: For the less interested reader, they tell what is in a report; for readers looking for specific information, they help the reader determine whether the full report contains important information. Readers use the abstract or summary to screen information and decide whether the entire report should be read. It prepares serious readers who intend to read the full report by giving them a quick mental picture of the report which makes reading the report easier and faster.

Presenting the Problem

The first section of the report defines the research problem. It can be placed in one or more sections with titles such as "Introduction," "Problem Definition," "Literature Review," "Hypotheses," or "Background Assumptions." Although the subheadings vary, the contents include a statement of the research problem and a rationale for what is being examined. Here, you explain the significance of and provide a background to the research question.

You can explain the significance of the research by showing how different solutions to the problem lead to different applications or theoretical conclusions. Introductory sections frequently include a context literature review and link the problem to theory. Introductory sections also define key concepts and present conceptual hypotheses that are tested in the study.

Describing Methods

The next section of the report describes how you designed the study and collected the data. It goes by several names (e.g., methods, research design, data) and may be subdivided into other parts (e.g., measures, sampling, manipulations). It is the most important section for evaluating the methodology of the project because it gives the reader details on how you conducted the study. The section answers several questions for the reader:

1. What type of study (e.g., experiment, survey) was conducted?

2. Exactly how were data collected (e.g., study design, type of survey, time and location of data collection, experimental design used)?
3. How were variables measured? Are the measures reliable and valid?
4. What is the sample? How many subjects or respondents are involved in the study? How were they selected?
5. How were ethical issues and specific concerns of the design dealt with?

Results and Tables

After describing how data were collected, methods of sampling, and measurement, you then present the data. This section presents—it does not discuss, analyze, or interpret the data. Researchers sometimes combine the "Results" section with the next section, called "Discussion" or "Findings."

You have choices in how to present the data.[7] When analyzing the data, look at dozens of univariate, bivariate, and multivariate tables and statistics to get a feel for the data. This does not mean that you place every statistic or table in a final report. Rather, you select the minimum number of charts or tables that fully inform the reader and rarely present the raw data itself. You provide data analysis techniques that summarize the data and permit tests of hypotheses (e.g., frequency distributions, tables with means and standard deviations, correlations, other statistics).

As a researcher, you want to give a complete picture of the data without overwhelming the reader. You do not provide data in excessive detail, nor do you present irrelevant data. Disclose the data so that readers can make their own interpretations, even if they contradict yours. You may place detailed summary statistics in appendixes or remind readers that they can write for the raw data.

Discussion

In the discussion section, talk about what you see in the data and give the reader a concise, unambiguous interpretation of its meaning. The discussion is not a selective emphasis or partisan interpretation; rather, it is a candid discussion of what is in the results section. The discussion section is separated from the results so that a reader can examine the data and arrive at different interpretations. Grosof and Sardy (1985:386) warned, "The arrangement of your presentation should reflect a strict separation between data (the record of your observations) and their summary and analysis on one hand, and your interpretations, conclusion, and comment on the other."

Beginning researchers often find it difficult to organize a discussion section. One approach is to organize the discussion according to hypotheses because you need to discuss how the data relate to each hypothesis. In addition, discuss unanticipated findings, possible alternative explanations of results, and weaknesses or limitations.

Drawing Conclusions

Researchers restate the research question and summarize findings in the conclusion. Its purpose is to summarize the report, and it is sometimes titled "Summary." Here, you should point to directions for future research so others can build on the findings.

The only sections after the conclusion are the references and appendixes. The reference section contains only sources that were referred to in the text or notes of the report. Appendixes, if used, usually contain additional information on methods of data collection (e.g., questionnaire wording) or results (e.g., descriptive statistics). The footnotes or endnotes in quantitative research reports expand or elaborate on information in the text. Researchers use them sparingly to provide secondary information that clarifies the text but might distract from the flow of the reading. Publications require various formats for citations to sources, but they are usually in the form of authors' names in parentheses instead of in notes.

THE QUALITATIVE RESEARCH REPORT

Compared to quantitative research, it is more difficult to write a report on qualitative social research. It has fewer rules and less structure. Nevertheless, the purpose is the same: to clearly communicate the research process and the data collected through the process. As Bogdan and Taylor (1975:142) remarked, "A report, article, or monograph based on qualitative research is not, or should not be, an individual's off-the cuff view of a situation. Rather, it should be a descriptive and analytic presentation of data that have been laboriously and systematically collected and interpreted."

Quantitative research reports present hypotheses and evidence in a logically tight and condensed style. By contrast, qualitative research reports tend to be longer, and book-length reports are common. Qualitative research requires greater length for five reasons.

1. The data in a qualitative report are more difficult to condense. Data are in the form of words, pictures, or sentences and include many quotes and examples. If there are charts, diagrams, and tables, they are to supplement, not to replace, the qualitative data.

2. Qualitative researchers may want to create a subjective sense of empathy and understanding among readers in addition to presenting factual evidence and analytic interpretations. Detailed descriptions of specific settings and situations help readers better understand or get a feel for settings. Researchers attempt to transport the reader into the subjective world view and meaning system of a social setting.

3. Qualitative researchers use less standardized techniques of gathering data, creating analytic categories, and organizing evidence. The techniques applied may be particular to individual researchers or unique settings. Thus, researchers explain what they did and why, because it has not been done before.

4. Exploring new settings or constructing new theory is a common goal in qualitative research. The development of new concepts and examination of relationships among them adds to the length of reports. In addition, theory flows out of evidence, and detailed descriptions demonstrate how the researcher created interpretations from evidence.

5. Qualitative researchers may use more varied and literary writing styles, which increases length. They have greater freedom to employ literary devices to tell a story or recount a tale when translating a meaning system for the reader.

Field Research

Field research reports rarely follow a fixed format with standard sections, and theoretical generalizations and data are not separated into distinct sections.[8] Generalizations are intertwined with the evidence, which takes the form of detailed description with frequent quotes.

Researchers balance the presentation of data and analysis. They want to avoid an excessive separation of data from analysis, called the *error of segregation*. This occurs when researchers separate data from analysis so much that readers cannot see the connection.[9]

The tone of field research reports also differs from those on quantitative research. It is less objective and formal, and more personal. Field research reports may be written in the first person (i.e., using the pronoun *I*) because you were directly involved in the setting, interacted with the people studied, and were the measurement "instrument." The decisions or indecisions, feelings, reactions, and personal experiences of the researcher are parts of the field research process.

Field research reports often face more skepticism than quantitative reports do. This makes it essential for you to assess an audience's demands for evidence and establish credibility. The key is to provide readers with enough evidence so that they believe the recounted events and accept your interpretations as plausible. A degree of selective observation is accepted in field research, so the critical issue is whether other observers could reach the same conclusion if they examined the same data.[10] Schatzman and Strauss (1973:133) stressed the issue of establishing credibility, "An essential prerequisite to establishing credibility with any audience is the researcher's conviction that what he is saying or writing is so. And this conviction rests upon necessary and credible procedures performed, as well as upon the sense of certainty that the observer did in fact see what he says he saw."

As a field researcher, you face a data reduction dilemma when presenting evidence. Most evidence or data are in the form of an enormous volume of field notes, but you cannot directly share observations or recorded conversations with the readers. For example, in their study of medical students, *Boys in White*, Becker and Geer had about 5,000 pages of single-spaced field notes. Field researchers can only include 5 to 10 percent of their field notes in a report as quotes. The remaining 90 to 95 percent is not wasted; there is just no room for it. Thus, writers select quotes and indirectly convey the rest of the data to readers. In quantitative research, you condense numerical data with statistics, tables, and charts.

There is no fixed organization for a field research report, although a literature review often appears near the beginning. There are many acceptable organizational forms. Lofland (1976) suggests the following:

1. Introduction
   a. Most general aspects of situation
   b. Main contours of the general situation
   c. How materials were collected
   d. Details about the setting
   e. How the report is organized
2. The situation
   a. Analytic categories
   b. Contrast between situation and other situations
   c. Development of situation over time
3. Strategies
4. Summary and implications

Devices for organizing evidence and analysis also vary a great deal.[11] For example, writers can organize the report in terms of a *natural history*, an unfolding of events as you discovered them, or as a *chronology*, following the developmental cycle or career of an aspect of the setting or people in it. Another possibility is to organize the report as a *zoom lens*, beginning broadly and then focusing increasingly narrowly on a specific topic. Statements can move from universal statements about all cultures, to general statements about a specific cultures, to statements about specific cultural scene, to specific statements about an aspect of culture, to specific statements about specific incidents.[12]

Field researchers also organize reports by themes. A writer chooses between using abstract analytic themes and using themes from the categories used by the people who were studied. The latter is sometimes preferred because it is crucial to give readers a vivid description of the setting and to display knowledge of the language, concepts, categories, and beliefs of those being written about.[13]

Field researchers discuss the methods used in the report, but its location and form vary. One technique, especially common when a natural history organization is used, is to interweave a description of the setting, the means of gaining access, your role as the researcher, and the subject/researcher relationship into the discussion of evidence and analysis. This is intensified if the writer adopts what John Van Maanen (1988:73) called a "confessional" style of writing. When you use a chronological, zoom lens, or theme-based organization, the data collection method may be discussed near the beginning or the end. In book-length reports, methodological issues are usually discussed in a separate appendix.

Field research reports can contain transcriptions of tape recordings, maps, photographs, or charts illustrating analytic categories. They supplement the discussion and are placed near the discussion they complement. Qualitative field research is sometimes reported in creative formats that differ from the usual written text with examples from field notes. Douglas Harper's (1982) book contains many photographs with text. The photographs give a visual inventory of the settings described in the text and present the meanings of settings in the terms of those being studied. For example, field research articles have appeared in the form of all photographs (Jackson, 1978) or as a script for a play (Becker et al., 1989). A documentary film on a setting is another form of data presentation.[14]

Another issue in field research reports is that of *negative cases*. A negative case is evidence from field notes and observations that contradicts your interpretation. It can take two forms: members of a setting who have not yet been fully socialized into the meaning system being studied, or individuals who operate on the margins and use an alternative meaning system.[15] Although they do not contradict your primary investigation, negative cases reveal the complexity of the setting and your integrity as a researcher.

Your direct, personal involvement in the intimate details of a social setting heightens ethical concerns. Ethical concerns are discussed with methodological issues or as a separate topic. Researchers write their reports in a manner that protects the privacy of those being studied and helps prevent the publication of a report from harming those who were studied.[16] Field researchers usually change the names of members and exact locations in field reports. When writing a field research report, you must decide how much to disclose about the field setting and about yourself. Personal involvement in field research sometimes leads researchers to include a short autobiography as part of a report. For example, in the appendix to *Street Corner Society* the author, William Foote Whyte, gave a detailed account of the occupations of his father and grandfather, his hobbies and interests, the jobs he held, how he ended up going to graduate school, and how his research was affected by his getting married.

Historical-Comparative Research

There is no single way to write a report on historical-comparative research. Most frequently, researchers "tell a story" or describe details in general analytic categories. The writing usually goes beyond description and includes limited generalizations and abstract concepts.

Historical-comparative researchers rarely describe their methods in great detail. Explicit sections of the report or an appendix that describes the methods used are unusual. Occasionally, a book-length report contains a bibliographic essay that discusses major sources used. More often, numerous detailed footnotes or endnotes describe the sources and evidence. For example, a 20-page report on quantitative or field research typically has 5 to 10 notes, whereas a historical-comparative research report of equal length may have 40 notes. Likewise, it is not unusual to find that notes (printed in small type) constitute one-fifth of the pages in a book-length historical-comparative report.

Historical-comparative reports can contain photographs, maps, diagrams, charts, or tables of statistics. These are placed throughout the report and appear in the section that discusses evidence that relates to them. The charts, tables, and so forth in historical-comparative research reports supplement a discussion or give the reader a better feel for the places and people being described. They are used in conjunction with frequent quotes as one among several types of evidence. Historical-comparative reports rarely summarize data to test specific hypotheses as quantitative research does. Instead, the writer builds a web of meaning or descriptive detail and organizes the evidence itself to convey interpretations and generalizations.

There are two basic modes of organizing historical-comparative research reports: by topic and chronologically. Most writers mix the two types. For example, information is organized chronologically within topics, or organized by topic within chronological periods. Occasionally other forms of organization are used— by place, by individual person, or by major events. If the report is truly comparative, the writer has additional options, such as making comparisons within topics. Table C.4 provides a sample of some techniques used by historical comparative researchers to organize evidence and analysis.[17]

Some historical-comparative researchers mimic the quantitative research report and use

1. *Sequence:* Historical-comparative researchers are sensitive to the temporal order of events and place a series of events in order to describe a process. For example, a researcher studying the passage of a law or the evolution of a social norm may break the process into a set of sequential steps.

2. *Comparison:* Comparing similarities and differences lies at the heart of comparative historical research. Make comparisons explicit and identify both similarities and differences. For example, a researcher comparing the family in two historical periods or countries begins by listing shared and nonshared traits of the family in each setting.

3. *Contingency:* Researchers often discover that one event, action, or situation depends on or is conditioned by others. Outlining the linkages of how one event was contingent on others is critical. For example, a researcher examining the rise of local newspapers notes that it depended on the spread of literacy,

4. *Origins and consequences:* Historical-comparative researchers trace the origins of an event, action, organization, or social relationship back in time, or follow its consequences into subsequent time periods. For example, a researcher explaining the end of slavery traces its origins to many movements, speeches, laws, and actions in the preceding fifty years.

5. *Sensitivity to incompatible meaning:* Meanings change over time and vary across cultures. Historical-comparative researchers ask themselves whether a word or social category had the same meaning in the past as in the present or whether a word in one culture has a direct translation in another culture. For example, a college degree had a different meaning in a historical era when it was extremely expensive and less than 1 percent of the 18- to 22-year-old population received a degree compared to the twentieth century, when college is relatively accessible.

6. *Limited generalization:* Overgeneralization is always a potential problem in historical-comparative research. Few researchers seek rigid, fixed laws in historical, comparative explanation. They qualify statements or avoid strict determination. For example, instead of a blanket statement that the destruction of the native cultures in areas settled by European whites was the inevitable consequence of advanced technological culture, a researcher may list the specific factors that combined to explain the destruction in particular social-historical settings.

7. *Association:* The concept of association is used in all forms of social research. As in other areas, historical comparative researchers identify factors that appear together in time and place. For example, a researcher examining a city's nineteenth-century crime rate asks whether years of greater migration into the city are associated with higher crime rates and whether those arrested tended to be recent immigrants.

8. *Part and whole:* It is important to place events in their context. Writers of historical comparative research sketch linkages between parts of a process, organization, or event and the larger context in which it is found. For example, a researcher studying a particular political ritual in an eighteenth-century setting describes how the ritual fit within the eighteenth-century political system.

9. *Analogy:* Analogies can be useful. The overuse of analogy or the use of an inappropriate analogy is dangerous. For example, a researcher examined feelings about divorce in country X describes them as "like feelings about death" in country Y. This analogy requires a description of "feelings about death" in country Y.

10. *Synthesis:* Historical-comparative researchers often synthesize many specific events and details into a comprehensive whole. Synthesis results from weaving together many smaller generalizations and interpretations into coherent main themes. For example, a researcher studying the French Revolution synthesizes specific generalizations about changes in social structure, international pressures, agricultural dislocation, shifting popular beliefs and problems with government finances into a compact, coherent explanation. Researchers using the narrative form summarize the argument in an introduction or conclusion. It is a motif or theme embedded within the description. Thus, theoretical generalizations are intertwined with the evidence and appear to flow inductively out of the detailed evidence.

quantitative research techniques. They extend quantitative research rather than adopting the logic of a distinct historical comparative research method. Their reports follow the model of a quantitative research report. By contrast, many historical-comparative researchers apply the model of narrative history, which is more consistent with the logic of qualitative social research. Stone (1987:74) described narrative history:

> *Narrative is taken to mean the organization of material in a chronologically sequential order, and the focusing of the content into a single coherent story, albeit with subplots. Two essential ways in which narrative history differs from structural history is that its arrangement is descriptive rather than analytical and that its central focus is on man not circumstances. It therefore deals with the particular and specific rather than the collective and statistical.*

THE RESEARCH PROPOSAL

What Is the Proposal?

A research *proposal* is a document that presents a plan for a project to reviewers for evaluation. It can be a supervised project submitted to instructors as part of an educational degree (e.g., a master's thesis or Ph.D. dissertation) or it can be a research project proposed to a funding agency. Its purpose is to convince reviewers that you, the researcher, are capable of successfully conducting the proposed research project. Reviewers have more confidence that a planned project will be successfully completed if the proposal is well written and organized, and if you demonstrate careful planning.

The proposal is similar to a research report, but it is written before the research project begins. A proposal describes the research problem and its importance, and gives a detailed account of the methods that will be used and why they are appropriate.

The proposal for quantitative research has most of the parts of a research report: a title, an abstract, a problem statement, a literature review, a methods or design section, and a bibliography. It lacks results, discussion, and conclusion sections. The proposal has a plan for data collection and analysis (e.g., types of statistics). It frequently includes a schedule of the steps to be undertaken and an estimate of the time required for each step.

Proposals for qualitative research are more difficult to write because the research process itself is less structured and preplanned. You prepare a problem statement, literature review, and bibliography. You may demonstrate an ability to complete a proposed qualitative project in two ways. First, the proposal is well written, with an extensive discussion of the literature, significance of the problem and sources. This shows reviewers that you are familiar with qualitative research and the appropriateness of the method for studying the problem. Second, the proposal describes a qualitative pilot study you have conducted. This demonstrates your motivation, familiarity with research techniques, and ability to complete a report about unstructured research.

Proposals to Fund Research

The purpose of a research grant is to provide the resources needed to help you complete a worthy project. You should evaluate why funds are needed before writing a proposal for funding. Researchers whose primary goal is to use funding for personal benefit or prestige, to escape from other activities, or to build an "empire" are less successful. The strategies of proposal writing and getting grants has become an industry called *grantsmanship*.

There are many sources of funding for research proposals. Colleges, private foundations, and government agencies have programs to award grants to researchers. Funds may be used to purchase equipment, to pay your salary or that of others, for research supplies, for travel to collect data, or for help with the publication of results. The degree of competition for a grant varies a great deal, depending on the source. Some sources fund more than 3 out of 4 proposals they receive, others fund fewer than 1 in 20.

There are many sources of funding for social research, but there may be no source willing to fund a specific project. You will need to investigate funding sources and ask questions: What types of projects are funded—applied versus basic research, specific topics, or specific research techniques? What are the deadlines? What kind (e.g., length, degree of detail) of proposal is necessary? How large are most grants? What aspects (e.g., equipment, personnel, travel) of a project are or are not funded? There are many sources of information on funding sources. Librarians or officials who are responsible for research grants at a college are good resource people. For example, private foundations are listed in an annual publication, the *Foundation Directory*. The *Guide to Federal Funding for Social Scientists* lists sources in the U.S. government. In the United States, there are many newsletters on funding sources and two national computerized data bases (SPIN and IRIS), which subscribers can search for funding sources. Some agencies periodically issue *Requests for Proposals (RFPs)* that ask for proposals to conduct research on a specific issue. You will need to learn about funding sources, because it is essential to send your proposal to an appropriate source in order to be successful.[18]

You will need to show a track record of past success in the proposal, especially if you are going to be in charge of the project. The researcher in charge of a research project is the *principal investigator (PI)* or project director. Proposals usually include a curriculum vitae or academic resumé, letters of support from other researchers, and a record of past research. Reviewers feel safer investing funds in a project headed by someone who already has research experience than in a novice. You can build a track record with small research projects or by assisting an experienced researcher before seeking funding as a principal investigator.

The reviewers who evaluate a proposal judge whether the proposal project is appropriate to the funding source's goals. Most funding sources have guidelines stating the kinds of projects they fund. For example, programs that fund basic research have the advancement of knowledge as a goal. Programs to fund applied research often have improvements in the delivery of services as a goal. Instructions will ask you to state project objectives and procedures. In addition, they will specify page length, number of copies, deadlines, and the like. Follow all instructions exactly. Why would reviewers give thousands of dollars to a researcher to carry out a complicated research project if he or she cannot even follow instructions on the page length of a proposal?

Proposals should be neat and professional looking. The instructions usually ask for a detailed plan for the use of time, services, and personnel. These should be clearly stated and realistic for the project. Excessively high or low estimates, unnecessary add-ons or omitted essentials will lower how reviewers evaluate a proposal. Creating a budget for a proposed project is complicated and usually requires technical assistance. For example, pay rates, fringe benefit rates, and so on that must be charged may not be easy to obtain. It is best to consult a grants officer at a college or an experienced proposal writer. In addition, endorsements or clearances of regulations are often necessary (e.g., IRB approval, see Chapter 17 on ethics). Proposals should also include specific plans for disseminating results (e.g., publications, presentations before professional groups) and a plan for evaluating whether the project met its objectives.

The proposal is a kind of contract between you and the funding source to complete the project. Funding agencies often require a final report including details on how funds were spent, the findings, and an evaluation of whether the project met its objectives. If you fail to spend funds properly, do not complete the project described in the proposal, or do not file a final report, you may find yourself barred from receiving future funding or may even face legal action. A serious misuse of funds may result in the banning of others at your institution from receiving future funding.

The process of reviewing proposals after they are submitted to a funding source takes anywhere from a few weeks to almost a year, depending on the funding source. In most cases, reviewers rank a large group of proposals, and only highly ranked proposals receive funding. A proposal often undergoes a blind peer review in which the reviewers are other researchers who know the proposer from the vitae in the proposal, but the proposer does not know the reviewers. Sometimes a proposal is reviewed by a group of nonspecialists or nonresearchers. Instructions on preparing a proposal will tell you whether to write for specialists in a field or for an educated general audience. A proposal may be evaluated by more than one group of reviewers. In general, proposals that ask for larger amounts of money receive closer review.

If a proposal is funded, you can celebrate, but only for a short time. Soon, you must begin the work of the project. If the proposal is rejected, which is more likely, do not despair. Most proposals are rejected the first or second time they are submitted. Many funding sources will provide you with written reviewer evaluations of the proposal. Always request them if they are provided. Sometimes, a courteous talk on the telephone with a person at the funding source will reveal the reasons for rejection. Often, you can strengthen and resubmit a proposal on the basis of the reviewer's comments. Most funding sources accept repeated resubmissions of revised proposals, and proposals that have been revised may be stronger in subsequent competitions.

In sum, a proposal for funds to support a research project is a plan for research and a type of contract. It competes with other proposals and is evaluated and ranked by reviewers. If a proposal has been submitted to an appropriate funding source and all instructions are followed, reviewers are more likely to rate it high when:

1. It addresses an important research question. It builds on prior knowledge and represents a substantial advance of knowledge for basic research. It documents a major social problem and holds promise for solutions for applied research.
2. It follows all instructions, is well written, and is easy to follow, with clearly stated objectives.
3. It completely describes research procedures that include high standards of research methodology, and it applies research techniques that are appropriate to the research question.
4. It includes specific plans for disseminating the results and evaluating whether the project has met its objectives.
5. The project is well designed and shows serious planning. It has realistic budgets and schedules.
6. You have the necessary experience or background to complete the project successfully.

CONCLUSION

In this appendix, you learned about writing the research report, different forms of the report, and proposals. Most people find that writing a research report is a difficult task. Yet, as with many difficult tasks that are well done, a genuine feeling of pride and sense of accomplishment develop when the task is completed. Writing is a learned skill that develops with practice.

You saw how the research report is an essential part of the research process. A research project is not finished until it is written as a research report. Writing the report requires time and skill. It also requires planning for it and thinking about it during earlier stages of research. Writing a proposal is similar to writing a research report and involves careful planning and investigation before doing research.

Writing the research report at the end of the research project can be exciting. It is exciting not only because it signals the end of the project and lets you tell others what you did and discovered, but also because the process of writing the report generates new ideas and insights. Often, ideas are unclear and relationships in the data are fuzzy until they are written, and rewritten, into a report. Thus, the report gives you an opportunity to clarify and strengthen your thinking.

KEY TERMS

abstract	paraphrasing	research report
composing	plagiarism	revising
editing	prewriting	rewriting
error of segregation	principal investigator (PI)	style
executive summary	proofreading	thesaurus
freewriting	proposal	tone
negative cases	RFP	writer's block

REVIEW QUESTIONS

1. Why should you write differently for different audiences?

2. What are some of the advantages and disadvantages of using outlines?

3. What can you do if you experience writer's block?

4. What is plagiarism and how can you avoid it?

5. What is the difference between editing and revising writing?

6. At least a partial statement of the findings of a study can appear in more than one section of a quantitative research report. In which section can findings appear?

7. Why are many qualitative research reports longer than those reporting quantitative research?

8. Why is it that field researchers cannot show all their data to readers in reports?

9. What organizational features are used in historical-comparative research reports?

10. Where are the methods used described for quantitative research reports, field research reports, and historical-comparative reports?

NOTES

1. See "Plagiarism Case Documented," in American Sociological Association *Footnotes*, 17(2) (February 1989), p. 2, or "Noted Harvard Psychiatrist Resigns Post after Faculty Group Finds He Plagiarized," in *Chronicle of Higher Education*, 35(15) (December 7, 1989), p. 1.

2. From the Sociology Writing Group (1991).

3. For suggestions on writing, see Donald et al. (1983) and Leggett et al. (1965).

4. From Sociology Writing Group (1991:40).

5. See Fine (1988) for this and other suggestions on writing.

6. See Mullins (1977:11–30) for a discussion of outlines and the organization of quantitative research reports. Also see Williams and Wolfe (1979:85–116) for good hints on how to organize ideas in a paper.

7. Grosof and Sardy (1985:386–389) provide suggestions on how to explain quantitative findings.

8. Lofland (1974) inductively discovered what he identifies as five major writing styles for reporting field research (generic, novel, elaborated, eventful, and interpenetrated) and discusses how they are evaluated.

9. The error of segregation is discussed in Lofland and Lofland (1984:146).
10. See Becker and Geer (1982:244) and Schatzman and Strauss (1973:130) for a discussion of this and related issues.
11. See Hammersley and Atkinson (1983) and Van Maanen (1988).
12. Discussed in Spradley (1970:162–167).
13. See Van Maanen (1988:13).
14. See Dabbs (1982) for a discussion of graphic and other visual forms of analyzing and presenting qualitative data.

15. See Becker and Geer (1982).
16. For a discussion of ethical concerns in writing field research reports, see Becker (1969), Punch (1986), and Wax (1971).
17. See Barzun and Graff (1970) and Shafer (1980) for excellent suggestions on writing about historical research.
18. For more on writing proposals to fund research projects, see Bauer (1984), Locke, Spirduso, and Silverman (1987), and Quarles (1986). A somewhat dated but useful short introduction to proposal writing is Krathwohl (1965).

RECOMMENDED READINGS

Becker, Howard S. (1986). *Writing for social scientists: How to start and finish your thesis, book or article.* Chicago: University of Chicago Press. This is a warm, cheerful book about writing. By recounting his own trials and errors with writing sociology for 35 years, Becker gives advice on all aspects of the very human activity of writing. All writers will benefit from his examples and discussions of such issues as how to get started and how to overcome writer's block. He demonstrates that writing is central to the process of doing social research.

Locke, Lawrence F., Spirduso, Warren Wyrick, and Stephen J. Silverman (1987). *Proposals that work: A guide for planning dissertations and grant proposals*, 2nd ed. Beverly Hills, CA: Sage. Proposals for funding for large projects differ somewhat from research reports. This book includes suggestions on how to plan a proposal, what to include in it, and examples of proposals. In addition to suggestions for writing a proposal, there are descriptions of how proposals are evaluated and the process of grant getting.

Mullins, Carolyn J. (1977). *A guide to writing and publishing in the social and behavioral sciences*. New York: Wiley. Here is a handbook on all aspects of writing and publishing in the social sciences. It includes a wealth of details on writing outlines for different types of research, how scholarly journals and other publication outlets operate, and the mechanics of preparing a manuscript for publication.

Sociology Writing Group, UCLA. (1991). *A guide to writing sociology papers*, 2nd ed. New York: St. Martin's Press. If you need an introductory book on writing an undergraduate sociology paper for a course, this is it. It includes suggestions for organizing time, writing notes, and using the library. It also has examples of student papers with comments noting strengths and weaknesses. The book discusses writing qualitative and quantitative research reports as well as literature review and theoretical analysis papers.

Van Maanen, John. (1988). *Tales of the field: On writing ethnography*. Chicago: University of Chicago Press. Van Maanen offers informal essays on how to write about ethnographic or field research. He also looks at the tension between an ethnographic approach to research and the rhetorical and literary devices available to the researcher to convey the meanings discovered in research.

COMPUTERS IN SOCIAL RESEARCH

> *The implementation of technical innovations implies not only changes in the social structure but in the culture of society. Social conduct is technically patterned. It takes place within the context of a configuration of technologies.*
> —Nico Stehr, *Knowledge Societies*, p. 71

INTRODUCTION

Computers have revolutionized the conduct of social research and have become an essential tool in many areas of social research. Today, most social researchers use computers as regularly as others operate telephones, televisions, or automobiles, and they do so for the same reason—to perform specific tasks more productively. Computers enable researchers to perform specialized tasks (e.g., organize data, calculate statistics, write reports) more quickly and efficiently.

Reading this appendix cannot teach you how to use computers. That requires hands-on assistance and instruction tailored to the specific computer system you will be using. Instead, this appendix will give you a general background on computers, present some basic terminology, and explain how computers are used in social research.

It outlines the broad contours and guides you to the relevant questions. The uses and types of computers are changing so quickly that more specific information would be out of date within a year or two.

A Short History

The ancestors of today's computer were mechanical devices developed in the 1800s to sort cards that had holes punched into them. Researchers punched holes in specific locations, and each hole represented information on a variable. The card-sorting machines organized information more quickly, reliably, and efficiently than previous paper-and-pencil methods. For example, in the 1890s, card-sorting machines reduced the time for the U.S. Census Bureau to count and process information from nine years to six weeks.[1]

During World War II and the Cold War years of the 1950s, huge amounts of money and human resources went into military research for the purpose of detecting and directing missiles and other weapons. Also, new and related technologies such as television and space exploration accelerated the advancement of electronics. By the 1960s, engineers redirected these new inventions and technology to build general application machines that could manipulate numerical information. Although they were crude and clumsy by modern standards, the early computers radically enlarged the capacity to manipulate data and changed thinking about information.

As late as the mid-1960s, the only use of computers in social research was for statistical data analysis. Researchers used newer card-sorting machines that were faster and more accurate than those of the 1800s. With the machines, the researchers analyzed survey and existing data using cross-tabulation techniques. The machines could sort and count many thin cardboard cards, called *IBM cards* after the largest maker of cards. The IBM card had 80 columns and 12 rows, or 960 spaces for information. Researchers punched holes exactly into one of the 960 spaces with a large, noisy *keypunch machine*. Thus, data were stored as holes in specific locations on cards. After punching the holes, a researcher used a card-sorting machine to sort large stacks of cards into piles based on the locations of holes.

When I first began to analyze research data statistically, I used such cards. My data from a study of 100 cases was a stack of cards about 10 inches (20.5 centimeters) tall. I made three sets of the cards and bound them with rubber bands. With age and wear from the sorting machine, the cards tore and warped, causing problems and constant frustration. It would take me 20 to 30 minutes to create a few raw-count cross-tabulation tables. I took the frequencies and raw-count tables and spent another hour using a calculator to compute percentages or measures of association. The calculators were as large and expensive as today's laptop computers. They could perform only the statistics that one can do with modern handheld calculators that cost less than a decent restaurant

meal. With today's computers, I can do the same thing in seconds.

By 1990s standards, the early computers were very large, outrageously expensive, and exceedingly slow. They cost over $1 million, were the size of a dozen large refrigerators, consumed huge quantities of electricity, had to be kept in special rooms under controlled temperature conditions, and were constantly watched by a team of highly trained technicians. Nevertheless, these large computers, called *mainframe computers*, were more accurate, handled more information, and could precisely perform complex calculations much faster than the card-sorting and calculating machines combined. Most significantly, they could "read" and follow complex instructions called *computer programs*. The programs or instructions told the machine to carry out a huge number of precise logical steps on large amounts of information.

Highly trained computer programmers wrote programs to carry out specific types of tasks (e.g., data sorting, statistics). Programs depend on an overall *operating system*. It is special software that comes with computers. The operating system allows the software programs to communicate with the hardware, and it controls the traffic of information to and from programs.

By the 1970s, mainframe computers were cheaper and much more powerful. Most colleges, libraries, government agencies, and large companies acquired them for statistical, accounting, and information storage purposes. Today, many still use mainframe computers for analyzing large amounts of data. Modern mainframe computers are much more powerful and can be used by many people at the same time through *time sharing*. This means that the computer is so powerful and fast that it can do thousands of different tasks for many people simultaneously. Researchers who use very complex statistics with dozens of variables and very large data sets (e.g., a million cases) still use mainframes, but many can now use smaller, microcomputers.

Advances in technology have turned the punched cards that I used when doing research in 1972 into museum artifacts. Today, researchers type data and instructions directly into the computer where they are electronically stored. They use computer terminals or microcomputers. A computer terminal is a simple typewriterlike device connected to a mainframe computer. It has a keyboard (keys like those on a typewriter) and a televisionlike screen. Computer terminals can do very little by themselves. They exist to communicate with mainframe computers that do the work for them.

The electronic apparatus (boxes, switches, machines, wires) of the computer is called *hardware*. This is to distinguish it from *software*, the electronic messages that computers read, including computer programs or instructions that computers follow. A researcher needs both hardware and software, and without the correct software, the hardware can do nothing.

The Microcomputer Revolution

In the late 1970s, a new type of computer was invented: the micro- or personal computer. Modern microcomputers are as powerful as mainframe computers of the 1960s, cost about 1/1,000 as much, are about 1/1,000 the size, and can be used in many locations by people with just a little training. Microcomputer technology is still rapidly changing. Each year, microcomputers are faster and capable of performing more complex tasks. Microcomputers have replaced mainframes for many chores, have made computer technology accessible to more people, and have stimulated new uses for computers. Often, many microcomputers are linked together in a *LAN* (local area network) or network of computers. In this situation, several microcomputers are linked by electronic cables to a powerful microcomputer or mainframe that allows them to share software or information within the network.

Microcomputers look like terminals, but they are self-contained units that do not need a mainframe computer to perform most tasks. They have three basic parts:

1. *Monitor*, also known as a *CRT (cathode ray tube)* or *VDT (video display terminal):* A televisionlike screen that displays information (words or pictures) communicated to or from a computer.

2. *Keyboard:* A typewriterlike keyboard with additional special keys, used to type information into the computer. Most computers in the 1990s also come with a *mouse.* It is a hand-sized device that rolls on a desk and controls a pointer within the computer. People who use computers (called *users*) can select options from a program using it.

3. *CPU (central processing unit):* The main box that holds the core computer parts. These include a box to manage electric power and parts that temporarily store electronic information (the memory), follow electronic instructions (the microprocessor), and a part to read and write electronic information on floppy diskettes (discussed later) called disk drives. The temporary memory or *RAM (random access memory)* can be thought of as "active thinking space." Its size can greatly affect the speed and performance of software.

Some microcomputers fuse the three parts together. Laptop or notebook computers are lightweight (4 to 7 pounds, about 2 to 3 kilograms) and about the size of a medium-sized book. Most use battery power, but need to be plugged into an electric outlet for extended use. Other types of microcomputers connect the main parts with heavy wires or cables. Additional microcomputer equipment may include a *hard disk* (expanded internal storage memory that persists when the computer is turned off), a *CD-ROM* (compact disk–read only memory) reader (to read words, music, numbers or pictures from a CD), a printer, a scanner, and a modem.

Printers can vary widely in speed and quality or sharpness of printing. Some use a dot-matrix technology of pins hitting an inked ribbon, others use an ink-jet technology where tiny drops of ink are sprayed onto paper, and some use laser-jet technology where tiny specks of a fine power called toner are melted onto the paper. More expensive, newer printers produce color as well as black and white images. A *scanner* is machine that electronically "reads" a photograph or text page, similar to a photocopy machine, and converts the image into an electronic signal that computer software recognizes. A *modem* sends and receives electronic messages over telephone wires and is connected to a telephone jack or outlet. It may be a separate small box connected to the CPU unit by wires or contained in the CPU. Modems help different computers communicate with one other.

Most microcomputers are built to one of two basic standards: IBM-compatible and Apple, named after the major microcomputer manufacturers. Two standards use different types of microprocessors and operating systems, sometimes called *platforms*. In addition, within each standard, there are multiple computer types with different capabilities that arose as technology changed. IBM-compatible types of computers vary by the version of the Intel™-brand or similar microprocessor used. You may have heard of a 486 or a Pentium™ chip. These are names of Intel™-brand microprocessors. Apple™ or MacIntosh™ types of machines are based on a different type of chip called Motorola,™ which also goes by numbers, such as 6300. Processors operate at different speeds. Today, 66 megahertz is a reasonable speed, but fast, high-end models operate at over 120 megahertz. Twelve years ago, a good microcomputer could operate at 12 megahertz!

The operating system in a MacIntosh™ computer has small pictures and offers choices that a user can select with the mouse. There are currently two main types of IBM-compatible operating systems: DOS™ and Windows.™ Windows™ operates a lot like the MacIntosh operating system. Most programs can work only on a specific a type of computer (MacIntosh™ or IBM-compatible) and operating system (e.g., Windows™, DOS™), and version of operating system (e.g., Windows 3.11,™ Windows 95™). Equipment or programs designed for one type of computer or operating system will rarely work properly on another.

Information enters a microcomputer in six ways.

1. It is built into the computer memory itself.
2. A user types in on the keyboard or selects it using a mouse.
3. It comes across a telephone or communication line and through a modem or hardware device called a network card used in a LAN.
4. It is stored on floppy disks or diskettes, which computers can read.
5. It is stored on CD-ROM disks or other disks for computers.
6. It is read into the computer from a scanner.

Computers organize the information into files. A file can contain text (words) for word processing, computer programs, graphics or pictures, music or sound, video segments, or numerical data. The sizes of files vary greatly. For example, a text file, or one with words, can range in size from one letter to thousands of pages long. Files that contain good-quality graphics, photographic materials, or video information are many times larger than text or numerical files.

Most users store information on a *floppy disk* or diskette, a medium on which electronic information is stored and read by a microcomputer. The diskettes are specially treated paper-thin plastic material enclosed in a protective cover with an opening. The most common floppy disk size is about one-eighth inch (0.5 centimeter) thick by three and one-half inches square (about 1.5 centimeters). Older diskettes were larger and flexible (hence the name *floppy*) but stored much less information. A user places the disk into the slot of a disk drive, so the computer can read and write onto the disk.

Floppy disks can store different amounts of information. They can often hold the equivalent of several hundred typed pages of information. For example, in writing this book, I put Chapters 1 through 10 on one disk and still had room to spare. Yet, a disk costs less than many ballpoint pens, and information on it is easy to copy, revise, or update. Although they are inexpensive and easy to use, diskettes wear out. Also, information on them is easily destroyed by invisible magnetic fields. Microcomputer users should always make backup copies of the files on a diskette onto other diskettes.

Most modern microcomputers have a hard drive or hard disk. They are similar to floppy disks, but they are built in to the computer. Hard drives vary in size, but most store 50 to 1,000 times more information than a diskette. Hard drives are essential for storing large software programs and large documents or data sets. Although they can wear out or fail and need to be backed up, they are safer than floppy disks. Hard drive capacity has grown dramatically. The hard drive in my current computer has 50 times more memory than one I used 10 years ago and is three times faster, but it is the same price.

Memory size is measured in megabytes (millions of bytes) or gigabytes (billions of bytes). A byte is a very tiny piece of electronic information. The computer converts tens of thousands of bytes into something humans might recognize (e.g., a word or picture). The size of most diskettes is 1.44 MB or megabytes, and the minimum size of RAM for a lot of software is 4 MB.

HOW COMPUTERS HELP
THE SOCIAL RESEARCHER

Most social researchers trained before the 1980s learned research tools based on paper, charts, or card files. Looking back from the late 1990s, it is as if the researchers trained 15 years ago had learned how to use horses and wagons or the telegraph rather than automobiles or telephones. Other technological advances (e.g., photocopiers, FAX machines, videorecorders) have affected social research, but microcomputers have had an enormous impact.

Today, social researchers use computers for five purposes: locating published literature, analyzing quantitative data, analyzing qualitative data, communicating with others and retrieving distant information, and writing research reports and organizing information. Each task requires a specific type of software.

Locating Literature

Researchers use computers to locate literature or previous studies in three ways. They use computers to see what is in a library. By the 1990s, many university and major public libraries had con-

verted their catalogs of holdings from cardboard cards in file drawers to electronic records. Libraries have many different systems, and often only more recent works are in the "on-line" catalog. In addition to a local library, researchers use the Internet (see Box D.1) to search the on-line catalogs of distant libraries.

Second, researchers search scholarly journal indexes or abstracts using computers. A researcher first converts his or her topic into a set of keywords, then uses a computer to search a database of journal article information on a local CD-ROM or at another location through the Internet. Many indexes or abstracts for scholarly journal articles are available by computer. (Chapter 5 discussed the indexes that are available by computers.) Some major ones include *Social Science Index, CARL* (Colorado Area Research Library), *Socio-File* (includes *Sociological Abstracts*), *Sociological Abstracts*, the *Social Science Citation Index*, and *PsychLit*.

A third use is discussed in more detail later in the section on communication. Researchers get "onto" the Internet and locate people or places that list specific bibliographies. A few scholarly journals are published electronically on the Internet and can be read only using a computer. These are still in the early stages of development.

Quantitative Data Analysis

Computers are a necessity for modern quantitative social research. Without the appropriate computer and software, a researcher cannot analyze the data from a large-scale research project or calculate complicated statistics in a reasonable amount of time. Although a researcher must invest time and effort into learning how to use computers, the investment can save enormous amounts of time and effort later. A trained researcher with the proper equipment can accomplish in a few hours what once took a year to do by hand.

Data formatting for modern computers can be traced to the earlier card technology. The IBM card had a location system of rows and columns.

Box D.1

The Internet

The Internet is not a single thing in one place. Rather, the Internet is a system or interconnected web of computers around the world. It is changing very rapidly. I cannot describe everything on the Internet; many large books attempt to do that. Plus, even if I tried, it would be out of date in six months. The Internet is changing, in a powerful way, how many people communicate and share information. During the past few years, the number of people using the Internet has been doubling every six months.

The Internet provides low-cost (often free), worldwide, fast communication among people with computers or between people with computers and information in the computers of organizations (e.g., universities, government agencies, businesses). There are special hardware and software requirements, but the Internet potentially can transmit elec-tronic versions of text material, up to entire books, as well as photos, music, video, and other information.

To get onto the Internet, a person needs an account in a computer that is connected to the Internet. Most college mainframe computers are connected, many business or government computers are connected, and individuals with modems can purchase a connection in some areas from private companies that provide access over telephone lines. In addition to a microcomputer, the person needs only a little knowledge about using computers. As more people learn to use computers, as computers become more powerful, and as the Internet expands to more people, it has the potential to accelerate significantly the exchange of various types of information around the globe.

Each row represented a number (e.g., 0–9) and cards had 80 columns. The codebook matched the locations to code categories for variables. Usually, each respondent or case in a study (the unit of analysis) was given one IBM card or was a separate record.[2] Researchers divided the 80 columns into data fields for each variable. For example, a researcher might assign columns 15–21 as the data field for the variable "family income." The field had 7 columns to permit seven digits (i.e., incomes from $0 to $9,999,999), with the number of digits needed for the highest value determining the size of a field. Each column of the field was assigned a digit 0 to 9. Modern computers still use data fields, but there is no longer a limit of 80 columns.

Social researchers use one of the dozens of statistical software packages (e.g., SPSS™, SAS™, Minitab™, or Microcase™) to organize quantitative data into charts, tables, and graphs and to perform statistical calculations. The so-called packages collect many statistical procedures into a large, coordinated software program. Today, all quantitative social researchers have learned how to use at least one statistical software package. *SPSS™* (*Statistical Package for the Social Sciences*) is one of the more popular ones. The packages are easier to learn than computer languages and are specifically designed for analyzing quantitative data. Before learning how to use such software, a researcher must know the fundamentals of organizing quantitative data and have some background in statistics.

Choosing a software package for statistics can get complicated, and there is a wide range of prices. Companies that sell statistical software packages for mainframes and microcomputers periodically develop new, updated versions. What a user does to accomplish a task may vary by version, and a user may not be able to transfer information back and forth from old and new versions. Also, many companies sell both large, full-featured and smaller, limited-feature forms of the same software.

All statistical packages can compute very basic statistics. They vary in ease of use, clarity of instructions, and format of output. They also vary a great deal in the features for modifying the data, presenting data as graphs, and the more advanced statistics that are calculated in the various software packages. Software packages differ in the maximum number of cases and variables they can process.

Some software packages use interactive processing, others use batch processing. Almost all used *batch* processing in the past. In a batch form, the user writes a set of instructions and links them to the data. Next, the user submits them to the computer for processing and waits to receive the output after all data and instructions have been processed. Increasingly, software is *interactive*. This means that a user provides the data and a few core instructions at the start. The user then submits short, one-step instructions, one by one, and immediately gets back the output for that step. The speed of calculation depends on the efficiency of the software, the number of cases and type of statistical calculation, and the capacity of the computer hardware (microprocessor speed, RAM memory, math coprocessor computer chip).

Qualitative Data Analysis

Researchers adopting a qualitative approach are also increasingly using computers for the analysis of nonnumerical data.[3] A researcher who enters notes into a word-processing document can search quickly for particular words and phrases or copy and duplicate sections of the notes using a computer. He or she can also enter codes on field notes in a word-processing document and later locate occurrences of the codes. With word processing, a researcher finds it easier to write analytic memos, add to them, divide them into parts, revise them, and move sections from one place to another. A researcher can also use software to keep track of files or documents, create categories within files, or show linkages among many different files.

During the last 10 years, the growth of specialized programs available for data analysis from a qualitative approach to research has been phenomenal. Weitzman and Miles (1995:4) noted, "Things have happened so fast that many qualitative researchers feel bewildered and uncertain." Next, I discuss the major categories of qualitative analysis of data outlined in Weitzman and Miles

(1995). I focus on the types of programs and the kinds of analysis they can perform, rather than discuss details of specific programs. New programs are created each year and new features are being added to existing programs all the time.

Text Retrieval. Some programs perform searches of text documents. What they do is similar to the searching function available in most word-processing software. The specialized text retrieval programs are faster and have the capability of finding close matches, slight misspellings, similar sounding words, or synonyms. For example, when a researcher looks for the keyword *boat,* the program might also tell whether any of the following appeared: ship, battleship, frigate, rowboat, schooner, vessel, yacht, steamer, ocean liner, tug, canoe, skiff, cutter, aircraft carrier, dinghy, scow, galley, ark, cruiser, destroyer, flagship, and submarine. In addition, some programs permit the combination of words or phases using logical terms *(and, or, not)* in what are called *Boolean searches.* For example, a researcher may search long documents for when the keywords *college student* and *drinking* and *smoking* occur within four sentences of one another, but only when the word *fraternity* is not present in the block of text. This Boolean search uses *and* to seek the intersection of *college student* with either of two behaviors that are connected by the logical term *or,* whereas the logical search word *not* excludes situations in which the term *fraternity* appears.

Most programs show the keyword or phrase and the surrounding text. The programs may also permit a researcher to write separate memos or add short notes to the text. Some programs count the keywords found and give their location. Most programs create a very specific index for the text, based only on the terms of interest to the researcher. Examples of such programs include Metamorph™ and ZyIndex™.

Textbase Managers.   The textbase managers are similar to text retrieval programs. The key difference is their ability to organize or sort information about search results. Many programs create subsets of text data that help a researcher make comparisons and contrasts. They allow researchers to sort notes by a key idea or to add factual information. For example, where the data are detailed notes on interviews, a researcher can add information on the date and length of the interview, gender of interviewee, location of interview, and so on. The researcher can then sort and organize each interview or part of the interview notes using a combination of key words and added information.

In addition, some programs have *Hypertext* capability. Hypertext is a way of linking terms to other information. It works such that clicking the mouse on one term causes a new screen (one that has related information) to appear. The researcher can identify keywords or topics and link them together in the text. For example, a field researcher wants to examine the person, Susan, and the topic of hair (including haircuts, hairstyles, hair coloring, and hats or hair covering). The researcher can use Hypertext to connect all places Susan's name appears to discussions of hair. By the mouse clicking on Susan's name, one block of text quickly jumps to another in the notes to see all places where Susan and the hair topic appear together.

Some textbase manager software creates cross-tabulation or scatterplot cross-classifications from information in text documents. For example, students keep journals on a course. They write their feelings about each day using one of four categories (boring, stimulating, challenging, creative). The students also describe the major activities of each day (e.g., group work, discussion, watch videotape, lecture, or demonstration). A researcher can cross-classify student feelings by activity. By adding other information (e.g., male or female), the researcher can see how students with different characteristics felt about various activities and examine whether the feelings changed with the topic being presented or time during the academic year. Two example programs are askSam™ and Folio VIEWS™.

Code-and-Retrieve Programs.
Researchers often assign codes or abstract terms to qualitative data (text field notes, interview records, and video or audiotape transcripts). Code and retrieve programs allow a researcher to attach codes to lines, sentences, paragraphs, or blocks of text. The programs may permit multiple codes for the same data. In addition to attaching codes, most programs also allow the researcher to organize the codes. For example, a program can help a researcher make outlines or "trees" of connections (e.g., trunks, branches, twigs) among the codes, and among the data to which the codes refer. The qualitative data are rearranged in the program based on the researcher's codes and the relations among codes that a researcher specifies. Two example programs are and Kwalitan™ and Ethnograph™.

Code-Based Theory Builders.
Qualitative researchers are often interested in the evaluation and generation of theory. Code-based theory builders require that a researcher first assign codes to the data. The programs provide ways for manipulating or drawing contrasts and comparisons among the codes. The relationships among the codes then become the basis for a researcher to test or generate theory.

The types of relations created among the codes may vary by program. A program may permit *if-then* type of logical relations or analytic comparison techniques (discussed in Chapter 17). For example, Corsaro and Heise (1990) described how they coded field research data on young children into separate events. They then examined the logical sequence and relations among the events to search for principles or a "grammar" of implicit rules. They looked for rules that guided the sequencing, combination, or disconnection among events. The program they used, ETHNO™, asks for logical connections among the events (e.g., time order, necessary precondition, cooccurrence), then the program shows the pattern among events.

In contrast to other qualitative programs, code-based theory builders have a powerful ability to manipulate codes to reveal patterns or show relations in data that are not immediately evident. It becomes easier for researchers to compare and classify categories of data. The program QCA™ (Qualitative Comparative Analysis) uses Boolean logic or algebra to help a researcher analyze the characteristics of several cases and apply the method of difference and method of agreement (see Chapter 17). It performs algebraic computations to identify common and unique characteristics among a set of cases. The algebra is not difficult but it can be time consuming and subject to human error without the program. NUD*IST™ is another program of this type.

Conceptual Network Builders. This category of programs helps a researcher build and test theory by presenting graphic displays or networks. The displays do more than diagram data, they help organize a researcher's concepts or thinking about the data. The programs use nodes, or key concepts, that the researcher identifies in data. They then show links or relationships among the nodes. Most programs give graphic presentations with boxes or circles and connected by lines with arrows. The output looks similar to a flowchart diagram, with a web or network of connections among concepts. For example, the data might be a family tree in which the relationships among several generations of family members are presented. Relations among family members (X is a sibling of Y, Z is married to Y, G is an offspring of X) can be used to discuss and analyze features of the network. Example programs include MetaDesign™ and SemNet™.

Communication and Data

E-Mail. Electronic communication across distances is one of the fastest growing uses of computers. This takes many forms, the most common being electronic mail, or e-mail. E-mail spread in the 1990s with computer networks on college campuses and in large companies, and with the creation of the Internet. E-mail can operate within a single organization (e.g., a university, government agency, or corporation) or between organizations. E-mail lets people send messages (e.g., memos, letters, data files, and sometimes pic-

tures) to one another almost instantly. The messages must be in an electronic format that computers can read, and both the sender and receiver must have e-mail addresses in a large computer.

An Internet e-mail address has several parts. The beginning is a personal name or identification number. This can be one word or a set of words or numbers separated by a period. It is followed by the @ symbol. Next comes a computer system name and an organization name separated by periods. The last part or parts may be the type of organization (e.g., EDU for educational, GOV for government, AC for academic, COM for commercial) or the organization type and country (e.g., JP for Japan, NZ for New Zealand).

For example, I am writing this while teaching for a year in Japan. My e-mail address here is NEUMANL@sal.tohoku.ac.jp. After a version of my name is the computer system name (sal) and the name of the organization (Tohoku University). It is followed by the type of organization (academic) and the country (Japan). Social researchers and those in government and private companies increasingly have e-mail addresses. For example, a message to Info @troweprice.com will get you information from the T. Rowe Price mutual fund company.

If the receiving person is not using e-mail at the time the message arrives, the e-mail system stores the message and lets the user know that a message is waiting. Similar to voice messages held in a telephone answering machine, computer e-mail holds written messages. Larger computers that are connected to the Internet operate all the time and have backup systems, so they can receive messages 24 hours a day, every day.

Many publishers and other organizations can be reached by Internet. For example, I wanted to locate a book that I had seen advertised several months ago. I could not recall the author's name or its exact title, but I remembered it was published by the University of Chicago Press. I used the Internet to locate the University of Chicago Press computer and selected their catalog. From the catalog I could find the book, along with its title, author, and other information on it. There was even a way I could get information on ordering a copy of the book. I did all this in five minutes from Japan at no cost.

The Internet can also connect you to others who are interested in a topic and sometimes to bibliographies or data sets that they have created. One way to locate information on the Internet is to use Gopher (discussed later); the other way is to join one of the hundreds, if not thousands, of Internet "discussion groups."

LISTSERV. A popular feature of the Internet is LISTSERV. It works when a user subscribes (at no cost) to a mailing list by sending an e-mail message. The list or discussion group is a topic of interest. For example, there is a list for teachers of research methods, one for people who like Italian cooking, one for science-fiction readers, one for people with an interest in qualitative social research methods, or one for users of a statistical software package (e.g., Minitab, SPSS). Subscribers receive announcements and e-mail messages from other subscribers and can ask questions or provide information. Because anyone with Internet access can join and submit messages, a LISTSERV can become a free for all. New Internet users are advised to read one of the many sets of rules about proper etiquette on the Internet that are "posted" on the Internet.

Searching GopherSpace with Veronica. The Gopher is a very popular tool for using the Internet. It is an electronic menu system first developed by the University of Minnesota. It does not provide fancy graphics or photos, but it is widely available, is easy to use, and requires only a low-level computer. The Gopher presents a list of choices, and a user indicates a choice.

There are several ways to get to Gopher. Often, it requires only typing the word *Gopher* on a Internet computer system. A common choice will be Gophers Around the World. Selecting this option (by moving an arrow symbol next to the option and hitting the return key) opens up a list of nations or world regions. Selecting a nation from the list in the same way opens up a list of places in the country. The places may be states in

the United States or organizations. For example, when looking for the book by the University of Chicago Press, I chose North America, then United States, then Illinois, then found University of Chicago Press. Once at the University of Chicago Press's Gopher, I selected Sociology titles and looked for the book. Note that I had to know a little geography and each Gopher list of options took me to a more specific level. Returning to the previous menu is easy. You just type the letter *U* (for up) or the left arrow ← key. To leave Gopher, just type the letter *Q* (for quit) and answer *Y* (for yes) when asked whether you really want to quit.

Veronica (or Very Easy Rodent Oriented Network Index of Computerized Archives) is a way to search all the Gopher menus on the Internet or GopherSpace. Gopher can take the user to a huge array of resources, but it can be very time consuming to find specific information. Veronica is an index and retrieval system that locates items throughout the Internet. A user reaches Veronica through a Gopher menu and can search for keywords in directories, or Gopher menus, or in all titles. Searching all titles can be slow.

The Web. The "web" (or World Wide Web) is a Hypertext-based Internet information retrevial system. Like Gopher, it allows a user to find information on the Internet, including Gophers. It uses Hypertext. This means that words or phrases in a document or text shown on the screen are connected to other screens of information. For example, in the middle of a sentence you read the word **Hypertext** and notice that it is in boldface. Clicking a mouse on the word will quickly connect to a new screen on Hypertext.

A more showy way to browse the web is with a system that has pictures or graphics. Some graphic "browers" are Mosaic™, Cello™, MacWeb™, and Netscape™. They permit a user, who has the right software and a very powerful computer, to search the Internet with a friendlier, easier "interface" or set of screens and instructions. As more powerful computers spread, these will probably replace Gophers.

Telnet and FTP. Telnet is a program that allows an Internet user to log onto, or connect to, large computers in remote locations. For example, I had accounts on mainframe computers in two different countries. Using Telnet, I could do most tasks on the remote computer in Japan that I could do on a computer in Wisconsin. The advantage was that I did not have to leave Japan.

Telnet requires the user to have permission to use an account in the remote computer, unless the remote computer is an *anonymous FTP server*. This means it permits public access or anonymous FTP. Such access is usually limited to viewing a directory of file names and copying files from a remote to a local computer.

FTP stands for *file transfer protocol*. It is software available on most computers that are connected to the Internet. It lets an Internet user transfer files to or from a remote computer to a local computer. The file may contain data, text, or graphic information. Its main advantage is a fast speed of transferring information across the Internet. Some Gopher menus offer it as a choice. Unless a researcher has a private account on such computers with a password and other information, he or she is limited to public or "anonymous FTP" accounts that can be entered temporarily as a guest.

Writing and Organizing

Writing, storing, and organizing information are an essential part of the research process. Most social researchers today use a word processor for their writing. The word processor is a type of software for computers (and a few low-end computers specially designed for writing purposes only). Word-processing software spread very rapidly during the 1980s as microcomputer hardware became more powerful.

In the past, researchers typed their reports using a typewriter or had a typist type it from a handwritten copy. The typewriter was invented in the late 1800s and spread to office settings in the early 1900s. Electric versions appeared in the 1930s and spread in the 1950s. By the 1960s, electronic versions that could store small amounts of text were developed. Today, word-processing software for microcomputers has replaced many typewriters.

To write reports, papers, and the like, a researcher needs word-processing software (e.g., Word Perfect™, Wordstar™, Microsoft Word™). Most word-processing software allows a user to delete, edit, and revise much easier. The user can move text to different locations, copy text for multiple uses, and format the text in many ways. Most software also provides spell-checking. Storage is also a major advantage of word processing. Once a user enters text, it can be stored indefinitely for later additions, revision, copying, or printing. The storage usually takes much less space than a paper version of the same text.

Despite the many advantages, there are a few drawbacks to word processing. First, one needs access to a microcomputer, software, and printer. Second, the user needs minimal typing skills and has to invest some time into learning the software. Some of the learning may not be transferable, because how one does the same task in different software might vary. Last, it is not always possible to convert material written with one word-processoring software into another without some complications.

CONCLUSION

This appendix has offered a brief introduction to computer terms and ways that social researchers use computers. The number and scope of computer uses has expanded greatly during the past decade. Thirty years ago, computers were only used by quantitative researchers to perform what now appear to be simple calculations. Today, all types of social researchers use computers, including the Internet, for many steps in the research process. Researchers use computers when doing literature reviews, when performing quantitative and qualitative data analysis, when communicating with others, and when writing a research report.

KEY TERMS

batch processing
Boolean searching
CD-ROM
computer program
CPU (central processing unit)
e-mail
floppy disk
FTP (file transfer protocol)
Gopher
hard drive

hardware
Hypertext
IBM cards
interactive processing
Internet
LAN (local area network)
LISTSERV
mainframe computer
modem
mouse

operating system
scanner
software
SPSS (Statistical Package for
 the Social Sciences)
Telnet
time sharing
user
Veronica
World Wide Web

REVIEW QUESTIONS

1. Name three advances in the history of computers that had a direct impact on social science research and describe the impact of each.

2. Describe e-mail and give two major ways that social researchers use it.

3. What three ways could you use computer technology to help you conduct a literature review more quickly or comprehensively than you could without computers?

4. Describe Gopher and give two examples of how one might use it when conducting a social research project.

5. How would you respond to someone who said. "I do not need to learn about computers because I only collect and examine qualitative data." Give at least two specific examples in your answer.

NOTES

1. For a discussion of computer use in social research, see Cozby (1984), Grosof and Sardy (1985:191–206), Heise (1981), Karweit and Meyers (1983), and Norusis (1986).

2. When the data for a case took more than one 80-column card, the researcher created multiple-card records. This required adding an identification number of the case and the card number as separate fields on each card to keep track of information for each case.

3. See Weitzman and Miles (1995) for a comprehensive review of 24 software programs for qualitative data analysis. Also see Fielding and Lee (1991) and Richards and Richards (1994).

RECOMMENDED READINGS

Butler, Mark. (1994). *How to use the Internet*. Emeryville, CA: Ziff-Davis. This is one of the dozens of recent books on using the Internet. It is one that I have used, but there is so much to choose from, it is largely a matter of personal preference.

Fielding, Nigel G., and Raymond M. Lee (eds.). (1991). *Using computers in qualitative research*. Newbury Park, CA: Sage. This early collection of essays describes the basic issues involved when social researchers use computers to examine broadly defined qualitative date.

Grafton, Carl, and Anne Permaloff (1993). Statistical Analysis and Data Graphics. *Advances in Social Science and Computers* 3:267–284. This essay is a short introduction on ways to use computers to display quantitative data in creative ways. It is an easy start for the beginner.

National Journal. (1995). *The federal Internet source*. 3rd ed. Washington, DC: National Journal. This is one of a subset of books on Internet resources. Many government agencies in the United States now make information available on the Internet.

Weitzman, Eben A., and Matthew B. Miles, (1995). *A software sourcebook: Computer programs for qualitative data analysis*. Thousand Oaks, CA: Sage. This is more of a catalog, handbook, or reference manual than text. It provides a detailed analysis of software that provides many new ways of organizing, thinking about, and looking at qualitative forms of data.

Wiggins, Richard W. (1995). *The Internet guide for everyone*. New York: McGraw Hill. See comments on the book by Mark Butler above.

BIBLIOGRAPHY

Abelson, Robert P., Elizabeth F. Loftus, and Anthony G. Greenwald. (1992). Attempts to improve the accuracy of self-reports of voting. In *Questions about questions: Inquiries into the cognitive bases of surveys*, edited by Judith M. Turner, pp. 138–153. New York: Russell Sage Foundation.

Abrams, Philip. (1982). *Historical sociology*. Ithaca, NY: Cornell University Press.

Abt, Charles. (1979). Government constraints on evaluation quality. In *Improving evaluation*, edited by L. Datta and R. Perloff. Beverly Hills, CA: Sage.

Achen, Christopher H. (1982). *Interpreting and using regression*. Beverly Hills, CA: Sage.

Adams, Gerald R., and Jay D. Schvaneveldt. (1985). *Understanding research methods*. New York: Longman.

Adler, Patricia A. (1985). *Wheeling and dealing*. New York: Columbia University Press.

Adler, Patricia A., and Peter Adler. (1983). Shifts and oscillations in deviant careers: The case of upper-level drug dealers and smugglers. *Social Problems*, 31:195–207.

Adler, Patricia A., and Peter Adler. (1987). *Membership roles in field research*. Beverly Hills, CA: Sage.

Adler, Patricia A., and Peter Adler. (1993). Ethical issues in self-censorship: Ethnographic research on sensitive topics. In *Research on Sensitive Topics*, edited by Claire Renzetti and Raymond Lee, pp. 249–266. Thousand Oaks, CA: Sage.

Adler, Patricia A., and Peter Adler. (1994). Observational techniques. In *Handbook of qualitative research*, edited by Norman Denzin and Yvonna Lincoln, pp. 377–392, Thousand Oaks, CA: Sage.

Adorno, Theodor W. (1976a). Sociology and empirical research. In *The positivist dispute in German sociology*, edited by Theodor Adorno et al., trans. Glyn Adey and David Frisby, pp. 68–86. New York: Harper and Row.

Adorno, Theodor W. (1976b). The logic of the social sciences. In *The positivist dispute in German sociology*, edited by Theodor Adorno et al., trans. Glyn Adey and David Frisby, pp. 87–104. New York: Harper and Row.

Agar, Michael. (1980). Getting better quality stuff: Methodological competition in an interdisciplinary niche. *Urban Life*. 9:34–50.

Agar, Michael. (1986). *Speaking of ethnography*. Beverly Hills, CA: Sage.

Agger, Ben. (1991). Critical theory, poststructuralism, postmodernism: Their sociological relevance. *Annual Review of Sociology*, 17:105–131.

Agnew, Neil McK., and Sandra W. Pyke. (1991). *The science game: An introduction to research in the social sciences*, 5th ed. Englewood Cliffs, NJ: Prentice-Hall.

Albrecht, Gary L. (1985). Videotape safaris: Entering the field with a camera. *Qualitative Sociology*, 8: 325–344.

Aldenderfer, Mark S., and Roger K. Blashfield. (1984). *Cluster analysis*. Beverly Hills, CA: Sage.

Allen, Michael Patrick. (1974). Construction of composite measures by the canonical-factor-regression method. In *Sociological methodology*, 1973–74, edited by H. L. Costner, pp. 51–78. San Francisco: Jossey-Bass.

Almond, Gabriel A., and Sidney Verba. (1963). *The civic culture*. Princeton, NJ: Princeton University Press.

Altheide, David L. (1976). *Creating reality*. Beverly Hills, CA: Sage.

Altheide, David L. (1980). Leaving the newsroom. In *Fieldwork experience*, edited by W. B. Shaffir, R. Stebbins, and A. Turowetz, pp. 301–310. New York: St. Martin's Press.

Alwin, Duane F. (1977). Making errors in surveys. *Sociological Methods and Research*, 6:131–150.

Alwin, Duane F. (1988). The general social survey: A national data resource for the social sciences. *PS: Political Science and Politics*, 21:90–94.

Alwin, Duane F., and David J. Jackson. (1980). Measurement models for response errors in surveys: Issues and applications. In *Sociological methodology, 1980*, edited by Samuel Leinhardt. San Francisco: Jossey-Bass.

Alwin, Duane F., and Jon A. Krosnick. (1985). The measurement of values in surveys: A comparison of ratings and rankings. *Public Opinion Quarterly*, 49:535–552.

Aminzade, Ronald. (1984). Capitalist industrialization and patterns of industrial protest: A comparative urban study of nineteenth century France. *American Sociological Review*, 49:437–453.

Anderson, Andy B., Alexander Basilevsky, and Derek P. J. Hum. (1983). Measurement: Theory and techniques. In *Handbook of survey research*, edited by Peter Rossi, James D. Wright, and Andy B. Anderson, pp. 231–287. New York: Academic Press.

Anderson, Barbara A., Brian D. Silver, and Paul R. Abramson. (1988). The effects of the race of interviewer on race-related attitudes of black respondents in SRC/CPS national election studies. *Public Opinion Quarterly*, 52:289–324.

Anderson, Elijah. (1989). Jelly's place. In *In the field*, edited by Carolyn Smith and William Kornblum, pp. 9–20, New York: Praeger.

Anderson, N. (1923). *The hobo*. Chicago: University of Chicago Press.

Anderson, Perry. (1974a). *Linkages of the absolutist state*. London: New Left Books.

Anderson, Perry. (1974b). *Passages from antiquity to feudalism*. London: New Left Books.

Anderson, R. Bruce W. (1973). On the comparability of meaningful stimuli in cross-cultural research. In *Comparative research methods*, edited by D. Warwick and S. Osherson, pp. 149–186. Englewood Cliffs, NJ: Prentice-Hall.

Andren, Gunnar. (1981). Reliability and content analysis. In *Advances in content analysis*, edited by Karl Erik Rosengren, pp. 43–67. Beverly Hills, CA: Sage.

Andrews, Frank M., Laura Klem, Terrence Davidson, Patrick O'Malley, and Willard Rodgers. (1981). *A guide for selecting statistical techniques for analyzing social science data*. Ann Arbor: Institute for Social Research, University of Michigan.

Annandale, Ellen C. (1988). How midwives accomplish natural birth: Managing risk and balancing expectations. *Social Problems*, 35:95–110.

Applebaum, Richard. (1978a). Marxist method: Structural constraints and social praxis. *American Sociologist*, 13:73–81.

Applebaum, Richard. (1978b). Marx's theory of the falling rate of profit.

American Sociological Review, 43: 67–80.

Aquilino, William S. (1993). Effects of spouse presence during the interview on survey response concerning marriage. *Public Opinion Quarterly*, 57:358–376.

Aquilino, William S., and Leonard Losciuto. (1990). Effects of interview mode on self-reported drug use. *Public Opinion Quarterly*, 54: 362–395.

Ardener, Shirley. (1984). Gender orientations in fieldwork. In *Ethnographic research: A guide to general conduct*, edited by R. F. Ellen, pp. 118–129. Orlando: Academic Press.

Ariès, E. (1977). Male-female interpersonal styles in all male, all female, and mixed groups. In *Beyond sex roles*, edited by Alice G. Sargent, pp. 292–299. Boulder, CO: West.

Armer, Michael. (1973). Methodological problems and possibilities in comparative research. In *Comparative social research*, edited by M. Armer and A. D. Grimshaw, pp. 49–79. New York: Wiley.

Armstrong, J. Scott, and Edward J. Lusk. (1987). Return postage in mail surveys: A meta-analysis. *Public Opinion Quarterly*, 51:233–248.

Aronson, Elliot, and J. Merrill Carlsmith. (1968). Experimentation in social psychology. In *The handbook of social psychology*, Vol. 2: *Research methods*, edited by Gardner Lindzey and Elliott Aronson, pp. 1–78. Reading, MA: Addison-Wesley.

Auriat, Nadia. (1993). My wife knows best: A comparison of event dating accuracy between the wife, the husband, the couple, and the Belgium population register. *Public Opinion Quarterly*, 57:165–190.

Auster, Carol J. (1985). Manual for socialization: Examples from Girl Scout handbooks, 1913–1984. *Qualitative Sociology*, 8:359–367.

Ayella, Marybeth. (1993). "They must be crazy:" Some of the difficulties in researching cults. In *Research on Sensitive Topics*, edited by Claire Renzetti and Raymond Lee, pp. 108–124. Thousand Oaks, CA: Sage.

Babbie, Earl. (1989). *The practice of social research*, 5th ed. Belmont, CA: Wadsworth.

Babbie, Earl R. (1990). *Survey research methods*, 2nd ed. Belmont, CA: Wadsworth.

Babbie, Earl. (1995). *The practice of social research*, 7th ed. Belmonth, CA: Wadsworth.

Backstrom, Charles H., and Gerald Hursh-Cesar. (1981). *Survey research*, 2nd ed. New York: Wiley.

Bailar, Barbara A., and C. Michael Lanphier. (1978). *Development of survey methods to access survey practices*. Washington, DC: American Statistical Association.

Bailey, Kenneth D. (1975). Cluster analysis. In *Sociological methodology, 1975*, edited by David R. Heise, pp. 59–128. San Francisco: Jossey-Bass.

Bailey, Kenneth D. (1983). Sociological classification and cluster analysis. *Quality and Quantity*, 17: 251–268.

Bailey, Kenneth D. (1984). A three-level measurement model. *Quality and Quantity*, 18:225–245.

Bailey, Kenneth D. (1986). Philosophical foundations of sociological measurement: Notes on the three-level model. *Quality and Quantity*, 20:327–337.

Bailey, Kenneth D. (1987). *Methods of social research*, 3rd ed. New York: Free Press.

Bailey, Kenneth D. (1988). Ethical dilemmas in social problems research: A theoretical framework. *American Sociologist*, 19:121–137.

Bailey, Kenneth D. (1992). Typologies. *Encyclopedia of Sociology*, Vol. 4, edited by Edgar and Marie Borgatta, pp. 2188–2194. New York: Macmillan.

Bakanic, Von, Clark McPhail, and Rita J. Simon. (1987). The manuscript review and decision-making process. *American Sociological Review*, 52: 631–642.

Bakanic, Von, Clark McPhail, and Rita Simon. (1989). Mixed messages: Referees' comments on the manuscripts they review. *Sociological Quarterly*, 30:639–654.

Ball, Donald. (1967). An abortion clinic ethnography. *Social Problems*, 14:293–301.

Ball, Michael, and Gregory W. H. Smith. (1992). *Analyzing visual data*. Thousand Oaks, CA: Sage.

Ball, Richard A., and G. David Curry. (1995). The logic of definition in criminology: Purposes and methods for defining "gangs." *Criminology*, 33:225–245.

Banaka, William H. (1971). *Training in depth interviewing*. New York: Harper & Row.

Bankston, William B., and Carol Y. Thompson. (1989). Carrying firearms for protection. *Sociological Inquiry*, 59:75–87.

Bannister, Robert C. (1987). *Sociology and scientism: The American quest for objectivity, 1880–1940*. Chapel Hill: University of North Carolina Press.

Bardack, Nadia R., and Francis T. McAndrew. (1985). The influence of physical attractiveness and manner of dress on success in a simulated personnel decision. *Journal of Social Psychology*, 125:777–778.

Barkey, Karen. (1991). Rebellious alliances: The state and peasant unrest in early seventeenth-century France and the Ottoman Empire. *American Sociological Review*, 56: 699–715.

Barlow, Melissa Hickman, David E. Barlow, and Theodore G. Chiricos. (1995). Economic conditions and ideologies of crime in the media: A content analysis of crime news. *Crime and Delinquency*, 41:3–19.

Barnes, Barry. (1974). *Scientific knowledge and sociological theory*. Boston: Routledge and Kegan Paul.

Barnes, J. A. (1970). Some ethical problems in modern fieldwork. In *Qualitative methodology*, edited by W. J. Filstead, pp. 235–251. Chicago: Markham.

Barnes, J. A. (1979). *Who should know what? Social science, privacy and ethnics*. New York: Cambridge University Press.

Barry, Brian. (1975). On analogy. *Political Studies*, 23:208–224.

Bart, Pauline. (1987). Seizing the means of reproduction: An illegal feminist abortion collective—How and why it worked. *Qualitative Sociology*, 10:339–357.

Bart, Pauline, and Linda Frankel. (1986). *The student sociologist's handbook*, 4th ed. New York: Random House.

Bartiz, Loren. (1960). *Servants of power: A history of the use of social science in American industry*. Middletown, CT: Wesleyan University Press.

Barzun, Jacques, and Henry F. Graff. (1970). *The modern researcher*, rev. ed. New York: Harcourt, Brace and World.

Basirico, Laurence A. (1986). The art and craft fair: An institution in an old art world. *Qualitative Sociology*, 9:339–353.

Bateson, Nicholas. (1984). *Data construction in social surveys*. Boston: George Allen and Unwin.

Bauer, David G. (1988). *The "how to" grants manual*, 2nd ed. New York: Macmillan.

Bauer, Raymond, ed. (1966). *Social indicators*. Cambridge: MIT Press.

Bausell, R. Barker. (1994). *Conducting meaningful experiments: Forty steps to becoming a scientist*. Thousand Oaks CA: Sage.

Bayless, David L. (1981). Twenty-two years of survey research at the Research Triangle: 1959–1980. In *Current topics in survey sampling*, edited by D. Krewski, R. Platek, and J. N. K. Rao, pp. 87–103. New York: Academic Press.

Beasley, David. (1988). *How to use a research library*. New York: Oxford University Press.

Beck, Bernard. (1970). Cooking welfare stew. In *Pathways to data*, edited by R. W. Habenstein, pp. 7–29. Chicago: Aldine.

Beck, E. M., and Stewart E. Tolnay. (1990). The killing fields of the Deep South: The market for cotton and the lynching of blacks, 1882–1930. *American Sociological Review*, 55: 526–539.

Becker, Howard. (1967). Whose side are we on? *Social Problems*, 14: 239–247.

Becker, Howard S. (1969). Problems in the publication of field studies. In *Issues in participant observation*, edited by G. McCall and J. L. Simmons, pp. 260–275. Reading, MA: Addison-Wesley.

Becker, Howard S. (1970). Problems of inference and proof in participant observation. In *Qualitative methodology: Firsthand involvement with the social world*, edited by William J. Filstead, pp. 189–201. Chicago: Markham.

Becker, Howard S. (1970a). Practitioners of vice and crime. In *Pathways to data*, edited by R. W. Habenstein, pp. 30–49. Chicago: Aldine.

Becker, Howard S. (1970b). Problems of inference and proof in participant observation. In *Qualitative methodology*, edited by W. J. Filstead, pp. 189–201. Chicago: Markham.

Becker, Howard S. (1970c). Whose side are we on? In *Qualitative methodology*, edited by W. J. Filstead, pp. 15–26. Chicago: Markham.

Becker, Howard S. (1986). *Writing for social scientists: How to start and finish your thesis, book or article*. Chicago: University of Chicago Press.

Becker, Howard S. (1993). How I learned what a crock was. *Journal of Contemporary Ethnography*, 22:28–35.

Becker, Howard S., and Blanche Geer. (1970). Participant observation and interviewing: A comparison. In *Qualitative methodology*, edited by W. J. Filstead, pp. 133–142. Chicago: Markham.

Becker, Howard S., and Blanche Geer. (1982). Participant observation: The analysis of qualitative field data. In *Field research: A sourcebook and field manual*, edited by Robert G. Burgess, pp. 239–250. Boston: George Allen and Unwin.

Becker, Howard S., Blanche Geer, Everett C. Hughes, and Anselm Strauss. (1961). *Boys in white: Student culture in medical school*. Chicago: University of Chicago Press.

Becker, Howard S., Michal M. McCall, and Lori V. Morris. (1989). Theatres and communities: Three scenes. *Social Problems*, 36:93–116.

Beecher, H. K. (1970). *Research and the individual: Human studies*. Boston: Little, Brown.

Beisel, Nicola. (1990). Class, culture, and campaigns against vice in three American Cities, 1872–1892. *American Sociological Review*, 55: 44–62.

Belenky, Mary Field, Blythe McVicker Clinchy, Nancy Rule Goldberger, and Jill Mattuck Tarule. (1986). *Women's ways of knowing: The development of self, voice and mind*. New York: Basic Books.

Bellah, Robert N. (1957). *Tokugawa religion*. Glencoe, IL: Free Press.

Ben-David, Joseph. (1971). *The scientist's role in society*. Englewood Cliffs, NJ: Prentice-Hall.

Ben-Yehuda, Nachman. (1983). History, selection and randomness—Towards an analysis of social historical explanations. *Quality and Quantity*, 17:347–367.

Bendix, Reinhard. (1956). *Work and authority in industry*, New York: Wiley.

Bendix, Reinhard. (1963). Concepts and generalizations in comparative sociological studies. *American Sociological Review*, 28:91–116.

Bendix, Reinhard. (1978). *Kings or people: Power and the mandate to rule*. Berkeley: University of California Press.

Benton, Ted. (1977). *Philosophical foundations of the three sociologies*. Boston: Routledge and Kegan Paul.

Berelson, B. (1952). *Content analysis in communication research*. Glencoe, IL: Free Press.

Berg, Bruce L. (1989). *Qualitative research methods*. Boston: Allyn and Bacon.

Berger, Peter. (1963). *An invitation to sociology: A humanistic perspective*. Garden City, NY: Anchor.

Berger, Peter, and Thomas Luckman. (1967). *The social construction of reality: A treatise in the sociology of knowledge*. Garden City, NY: Anchor.

Berk, Richard A. (1983). An introduction to sample selection bias in sociological data. *American Sociological Review*, 48:386–397.

Bermant, Gordon. (1982). Justifying social science research in terms of social benefit. In *Ethical Issues in Social Science Research*, edited by Tom L. Beauchamp, R. Faden, R. J. Wallace, and L. Walters, pp. 125–142. Baltimore: Johns Hopkins University Press.

Bernard, H. Russell. (1988). *Research methods in cultural anthropology*, Newbury Park: Sage.

Bernard, H. Russell, Peter Killworth, David Kronenfeld, and Lee Sailer. (1984). The problem of information accuracy: The validity of retrospective data. *Annual Review of Anthropology*, 13:495–517.

Bhaskar, Roy. (1975). *A realist theory of science*. Atlantic Highlands, NJ: Humanities.

Biersack, Aletta. (1989). Local knowledge, local history: Geertz and beyond. In *The new cultural history*, edited by L. Hunt, pp. 72–96. Berkeley: University of California Press.

Bigus, Odis. (1972). The milkman and his customer: A cultivated relationship. *Urban Life and Culture*, 1:131–165.

Billiet, Jacques, and Geert Loosveldt. (1988). Improvement of the quality of responses to faculty survey questions by interviewer training. *Public Opinion Quarterly*, 52:190–211.

Bishop, George F. (1987). Experiments with the middle response alternative in survey questions. *Public Opinion Quarterly*, 51:220–232.

Bishop, George F., Robert W. Oldendick, and Alfred J. Tuchfarber. (1983). Effects of filter questions in public opinion surveys. *Public Opinion Quarterly*, 47:528–546.

Bishop, George F., Robert W. Oldendick, and Alfred J. Tuchfarber. (1984). What must my interest in politics be if I just told you "I don't know?" *Public Opinion Quarterly*, 48:510–519.

Bishop, George F., Robert W. Oldendick, and Alfred J. Tuchfarber. (1985). The importance of replicating a failure to replicate: Order effects on abortion items. *Public Opinion Quarterly*, 49:105–114.

Bishop, George F., Alfred J. Tuchfarber, and Robert W. Oldendick. (1986). Opinions on fictitious issues: The pressure to answer survey questions. *Public Opinion Quarterly*, 50:240–251.

Blakie, Norman. (1993). *Approaches to social enquiry*. Cambridge MA: Polity.

Blalock, Hubert M., Jr. (1968). The measurement problem: A gap between the language of theory and research. In *Methodology in social research*, edited by Hubert Blalock and Ann Blalock, pp. 5–27. New York: McGraw-Hill.

Blalock, Hubert M., Jr. (1969). *Theory construction: From verbal to mathematical formulations*. Englewood Cliffs, NJ: Prentice-Hall.

Blalock, Hubert M., Jr. (1979a). Measurement and conceptualization problems: The major obstacle to integrating theory and research. *American Sociological Review*, 44:881–894.

Blalock, Hubert M., Jr. (1979b). *Social statistics*, 2nd ed. New York: McGraw-Hill.

Blalock, Hubert M., Jr. (1982). *Conceptualization and measurement in the social sciences*. Beverly Hills, CA: Sage.

Blalock, Hubert M., Jr., and Ann B. Blalock, eds. (1968). *Methodology in social research*. New York: McGraw Hill.

Blankenship, Albert B. (1977). *Professional telephone surveys*. New York: McGraw-Hill.

Blau, Judith R. (1978). Sociometric structure of a scientific discipline. *Research in Sociology of Knowledge, Sciences and Art*, 1:191–206.

Blee, Kathleen M. (1991). *Women of the Klan: Racism and gender in the 1920s*. Berkeley: University of California Press.

Blee, Kathleen M., and Dwight B. Billings. (1986). Reconstructing daily life in the past: An hermeneutical approach to ethnographic data. *Sociological Quarterly*, 27:443–462.

Bleicher, Josef. (1980). *Contemporary hermeneutics*. Boston: Routledge and Kegan Paul.

Bloch, Marc. (1953). *The historian's craft*, trans. Peter Putnam. New York: Vintage.

Block, Fred. (1977). Beyond corporate liberalism. *Social Problems*, 24:353–361.

Block, Fred, and Gene A. Burns. (1986). Productivity as a social problem: The uses and misuses of social indicators. *American Sociological Review*, 51:767–780.

Bloor, Michael J. (1983). Notes on member validation. In *Contemporary field research*, edited by R. M. Emerson, pp. 156–171. Boston: Little, Brown.

Blum, Debra E. (1989). A dean is charged with plagiarizing a dissertation for his book on Muzak. *Chronicle of Higher Education*, 35: A17.

Blume, Stuart S. (1974). *Toward a political sociology of science*. New York: Free Press.

Blumer, M. (1984). *The Chicago school of sociology*. Chicago: University of Chicago.

Blumer, Martin. (1991a). W. E. B. DuBois as a social investigator: *The Philadelphia Negro* 1989. In *The social survey in historical perspective, 1880–1940*, edited by M. Blumer, K. Bales, and K. Sklar, pp. 170–188. New York: Cambridge University Press.

Blumer, Martin. (1991b). The decline of the social survey movement and the rise of American empirical sociology. In *The social survey in histor-ical perspective, 1880–1940*, edited by M. Blumer, K. Bales, and K. Sklar, pp. 271–315. New York: Cambridge University Press.

Blumer, Martin. (1992). The growth of applied sociology after 1945: The prewar establishment of the postwar infrastructure. *Sociology and its publics: The forms and fates of disciplinary organization*, edited by Terence C. Halliday and Morris Janowitz, pp. 317–346. Chicago: University of Chicago.

Blumer, Martin, K. Bales, and K. Sklar. (1991). The social survey in historical perspective. In *The social survey in historical perspective, 1880–1940*, edited by M. Blumer, K. Bales, and K. Sklar, pp. 1–48. New York: Cambridge University Press.

Blumstein, Alfred. (1974). Seriousness weights in an index of crime. *American Sociological Review*, 39:854–864.

Bogardus, Emory S. (1959). *Social distance*. Yellow Springs, OH: Antioch Press.

Bogdan, Robert, and Steven J. Taylor. (1975). *Introduction to qualitative research methods: A phenomenological approach to the social sciences*. New York: Wiley.

Bohm, Robert M. (1990). Death penalty opinions: A classroom experience and public commitment. *Sociological Inquiry*, 60:285–297.

Bohrnstedt, George. (1992a). Reliability. *Encyclopedia of Sociology*, Vol. 3, edited by Edgar and Marie Borgatta, pp. 1626–1632. New York: Macmillan.

Bohrnstedt, George. (1992b). Validity. *Encyclopedia of Sociology*, Vol. 4, edited by Edgar and Marie Borgatta, pp. 2217–2222. New York: Macmillan.

Bohrnstedt, George W., and Edgar F. Borgatta, eds. (1981). *Social measurement: Current issues*. Beverly Hills, CA: Sage.

Bohrnstedt, George, and David Knoke. (1994). *Statistics for social data analysis*, 3rd ed. Itasca, IL: Peacock.

Bollen, Kenneth A., Barbara Entwisle, and Arthur S. Alderson. (1993). Macrocomparative research methods. *Annual Review of Sociology*, 19:321–351.

Bond, Charles F., Jr., and Evan L. Anderson. (1987). The reluctance to transmit bad news: Private discomfort or public display? *Journal of Experimental Social Psychology*, 23:176–187.

Bonnell, Victoria E. (1980). The uses of theory, concepts and comparison in historical sociology. *Comparative Studies in Society and History*, 22:156–173.

Borgatta, Edgar F., and George W.

Bohrnstedt. (1980). Level of measurement: Once over again. *Sociological Methods and Research*, 9:147–160.

Boruch, Robert F. (1982). Methods for revolving privacy problems in social research. In *Ethical issues in social science research*, edited by Tom L. Beauchamp, R. Faden, R. J. Wallace, and L. Walters, pp. 292–313. Baltimore: Johns Hopkins University Press.

Bottomore, Thomas. (1984). *The Frankfurt School*. New York: Travistock.

Bouchard, Thomas J., Jr. (1976). Unobtrusive measures: An inventory of uses. *Sociological Methods and Research*, 4:267–300.

Bradburn, Norman M. (1983). Response effects. In *Handbook of survey research*, edited by Peter Rossi, James Wright, and Andy Anderson, pp. 289–328. Orlando, FL: Academic.

Bradburn, Norman M., and Carrie Miles. (1979). Vague qualifiers. *Public Opinion Quarterly*, 43:92–101.

Bradburn, Norman M., and Seymour Sudman. (1980). *Improving interview method and questionnaire design*. San Francisco: Jossey-Bass.

Bradburn, Norman M., and Seymour Sudman. (1988). *Polls and surveys: Understanding what they tell us*. San Francisco: Jossey-Bass.

Brannigan, Augustine. (1992). Postmodernism. *Encyclopedia of Sociology*, Vol. 3, edited by Edgar and Marie Borgatta, pp. 1522–1525. New York: Macmillan.

Braudel, Fernand. (1980). *On history*, trans. Sarah Matthews. Chicago: University of Chicago Press.

Bredo, Eric, and Walter Feinberg, eds. (1982). *Knowledge and values in social and educational research*. Philadelphia: Temple University Press.

Brenner, Michael. (1985). Survey Interviewing. In *The research interview: Uses and approaches*, edited by Michael Brenner, Jennifer Brown, and David Canter, pp. 9–36. New York: Academic Press.

Brenner, Michael, Jennifer Brown, and David Canter, eds. (1985). *The research interview: Uses and approaches*. Orlando, FL: Academic Press.

Briggs, Charles L. (1986). *Learning how to ask: A sociolinguist appraisal of the role of the interview in social science research*. New York: Cambridge University Press.

Brinberg, David, and Joseph E. McGrath. (1982). A network of validity concepts. In *Forms of validity in research*, edited by David

Brinberg and Louise H. Kidder, pp. 5–21. San Francisco: Jossey-Bass.

Brinton, Mary C., Yean-Ju Lee, and William L. Parish. (1995). Married women's employment in rapidly industrializing societies: Examples from East Asia. *American Journal of Sociology*, 100: 1009–1130.

Britton, Dana M. (1990). Homophobia and homosociality: An analysis of boundary maintenance. *Sociological Quarterly*, 31:423–440.

Broad, W. J., and N. Wade. (1982). *Betrayers of the truth*. New York: Simon and Schuster.

Broadbent, Jeffrey. (1989a). Environmental politics in Japan: An integrated structural analysis. *Sociological Forum*, 4:179–202.

Broadbent, Jeffrey. (1989b). Strategies and structural contractions: Growth coalition politics in Japan. *American Sociological Review*, 54:707–721.

Broadhead, Robert, and Ray Rist. (1976). Gatekeepers and the social control of social research. *Social Problems*, 23:325–336.

Brodsky, Stanley L. and H. O'Neal Smitherman. (1983). *Handbook of scales for research in crime and delinquency*. New York: Plenum.

Brody, Charles J. (1986). Things are rarely black or white: Admitting gray into the converse model of attitude stability. *American Journal of Sociology*, 92:657–677.

Bromley, David G., and Anson D. Shupe, Jr. (1979). *Moonies in America: Culture, church and crusade*. Beverly Hills, CA: Sage.

Brown, Jennifer, and David Canter. (1985). The uses of explanation in the research interview. In *The research interview: Uses and approaches*, edited by Michael Brenner, Jennifer Brown, and David Canter, pp. 217–245. New York: Academic Press.

Brown, M. Craig, and Barbara Warner. (1992). Immigrants, urban politics, and policing in 1900. *American Sociological Review*, 57:293–305.

Brown, Richard Harvey. (1978). Symbolic realism and sociological thought. In *Structure, consciousness and history*, edited by R. H. Brown and S. M. Lyman, pp. 14–37. New York: Cambridge University Press.

Brown, Richard Harvey. (1989). *Social science as civic discourse: Essays on the invention, legitimation and uses of social theory*. Chicago: University of Chicago Press.

Brown, Steven R. (1980). *Political subjectivity: Applications of Q methodology in political science*. New Haven: Yale University Press.

Brown, Steven R. (1986). Q technique and method: Principles and procedures. In *New tools for social scientists: Advances and applications in research methods*, edited by William D. Berry and Michael S. Lewis-Beck, pp. 57–76. Beverly Hills, CA: Sage.

Bryan, James H. (1965). Apprenticeships in prostitution. *Social Problems*, 12:287–297.

Brym, Robert J. (1980). *Intellectuals and politics*. Boston: George Allen and Unwin.

Burawoy, Michael. (1977). Social structure, homogenization, and the process of status attainment in the United States and Great Britain. *American Journal of Sociology*, 82:1031–1042.

Burawoy, Michael. (1979). *Manufacturing consent*. Chicago: University of Chicago Press.

Burawoy, Michael. (1985). Karl Marx and the satanic mills: Factory politics under early capitalism in England, the United States, and Russia. *American Journal of Sociology*, 90:247–282.

Burawoy, Michael. (1989). Two methods in search of science: Skocpol versus Troksky. *Theory and Society*, 18:759–806.

Burawoy, Michael. (1990). Marxism as science: Historical challenges and theoretical growth. *American Sociological Review*, 55:775–793.

Burawoy, Michael. (1991). The extended case method. In *Ethnography unbound: Power and resistance in the modern metropolis*, edited by Michael Burawoy et al., pp. 271–287. Berkeley: University of California Press.

Burawoy, Michael, and Janos Lukacs. (1985). Mythologies of work: A comparison of firms in state socialism and advanced capitalism. *American Sociological Review*, 50:723–737.

Burgess, Robert G. (1982a). Approaches to field research. In *Field research*, edited by R. G. Burgess, pp. 1–11. Boston: George Allen and Unwin.

Burgess, Robert G. (1982b). Keeping field notes. In *Field research*, edited by R. G. Burgess, pp. 191–194. Boston: George Allen and Unwin.

Burgess, Robert G. (1982c). The unstructured interview as a conversation. In *Field research*, edited by R. G. Burgess, pp. 107–110. Boston: George Allen and Unwin.

Burke, Peter. (1980). *Sociology and history*. Boston: George Allen and Unwin.

Burke, Peter. (1992). *History and social theory*. Ithaca, NY: Cornell University Press.

Burnstein, Leigh, Howard E. Freeman, and Peter H. Rossi, eds. (1985). *Collecting evaluation data: Problems and solutions*. Beverly Hills, CA: Sage.

Burrage, Michael C., and David Corry. (1981). At sixes and sevens: Occupational status in the city of London from the 14th to the 17th century. *American Sociological Review*, 46:375–392.

Burton, Michael L., and Douglas R. White. (1987). Cross-cultural surveys today. *Annual Review of Anthropology* 16:143–160.

Byrne, Noel. (1978). Sociotemporal considerations of everyday life suggested by an empirical study of the bar milieu. *Urban Life*, 6:417–438.

Camic, Charles. (1980). The institutionalization of the role of scientist: England in the seventeenth century and ancient Greece. *Comparative Social Research*, 3:271–285.

Camic, Charles, and Yu Xie. (1994). The statistical turn in American social science: Columbia University, 1890–1915. *American Sociological Review*, 59: 773–805.

Campbell, Donald T., and D. W. Fiske. (1959). Convergent and discriminant validation by the multitrait-multimethod matrix. *Psychological Bulletin*, 56:81–105.

Campbell, Donald T., and Julian C. Stanley. (1963). *Experimental and quasi-experimental designs for research*. Chicago: Rand McNally.

Campbell, John P., Richard L. Daft, and Charles L. Hulin. (1982). *What to study: Generating and developing research questions*. Beverly Hills, CA: Sage.

Cancian, Francesca M., and Cathleen Armstead. (1992). Participatory research. *Encyclopedia of Sociology*, Vol. 3, edited by Edgar and Marie Borgatta, pp. 1427–1432. New York: Macmillan.

Cannell, Charles F., and Robert L. Kahn. (1968). Interviewing. In *Handbook of social psychology*, 2nd ed., Vol. 2, edited by Gardner Lindzey and Elliot Aronson, pp. 526–595. Reading, MA: Addison-Wesley.

Cannell, Charles F., Peter V. Miller, and Lois Oksenberg. (1981). Research on interviewing techniques. In *Sociological methodology, 1981*, edited by Samuel Leinhardt, pp. 389–436. San Francisco: Jossey-Bass.

Canter, David, Jennifer Brown, and Linda Goat. (1985). Multiple sorting procedure for studying conceptual systems. In *The Research Interview: Uses and Approaches*, edited by Michael Brenner, Jennifer Brown and David Canter, pp. 79–114. New York: Academic Press.

Cantor, Norman F., and Richard I.

Schneider. (1967). *How to study history.* New York: Thomas Y. Crowell.

Caplan, Arthur L. (1982). On privacy and confidentiality in social science research. In *Ethical issues in social science research*, edited by Tom L. Beauchamp, R. Faden, R. J. Wallace, and L. Walters, pp. 315–327. Baltimore: Johns Hopkins University Press.

Cappell, Charles L., and Thomas M. Guterbock. (1992). Visible colleges: The social and conceptual structure of sociology specialties. *American Sociological Review*, 57:266–273.

Capron, Alexander Morgan. (1982). Is consent always necessary in social science research? In *Ethical issues in social science research*, edited by Tom L. Beauchamp, R. Faden, R. J. Wallace, and L. Walters, pp. 215–231. Baltimore: Johns Hopkins University Press.

Carl, Jim. (1994). Parental choice as national policy in England and the United States. *Comparative Education Review*, 38:294–322.

Carley, Michael. (1981). *Social measurement and social indicators: Issues of policy and theory.* London: George Allen and Unwin.

Carmines E., and R. Zeller. (1979). *Reliability and validity assessment.* Beverly Hills, CA: Sage.

Carney, Thomas F. (1972). *Content analysis: A technique for systematic inference from communications.* Winnipeg: University of Manitoba Press.

Carr, Edward Hallett. (1961). *What is history?* New York: Vintage.

Carr-Hill, Roy A. (1984a). The political choice of social indicators. *Quality and Quantity*, 18: 173–191.

Carr-Hill, Roy A. (1984b). Radicalising survey methodology. *Quantity and Quality*, 18:275–292.

Caute, David. (1978). *The great fear.* New York: Touchstone.

Cavan, Sherri. (1974). Seeing social structure in a rural setting. *Urban Life*, 3:329–361.

Cerulo, Karen A. (1989). Sociopolitical control and the structure of national symbols: An empirical analysis of anthems. *Social Forces*, 68:76–99.

Chadwick, Bruce A., Howard M. Bahr, and Stan L. Albrecht. (1984). *Social science research methods.* Englewood Cliffs, NJ: Prentice-Hall.

Chafetz, Janet Saltzman. (1978). *A primer on the construction and testing of theories in sociology.* Itasca, IL: Peacock.

Chambers, Marcia. (1986). Jesuit priest standing by the survey that Vatican attempted to suppress. *New York Times*, October 22, 1986.

Channels, Noreen L. (1993). Anticipating media coverage: Method-

ological decisions regarding criminal justice research. In *Research on Sensitive Topics*, edited by Claire Renzetti and Raymond Lee, pp. 267–280. Thousand Oaks, CA: Sage.

Chase-Dunn, Christopher. (1989). *Global formation: Structures of the world economy.* Cambridge, MA: Blackwell.

Chebat, Jean-Charles, and Jacques Picard. (1988). Receivers' self-acceptance and the effectiveness of two-sided messages. *Journal of Social Psychology*, 128:353–362.

Chicago manual of style for authors, editors and copywriters, 13th ed., revised and expanded. (1982). Chicago: University of Chicago Press.

Church, Allan H. (1993). Estimating the effect of incentives on mail survey response rates: A meta analysis. *Public Opinion Quarterly*, 57:62–80.

Churchill, Gilbert A., Jr. (1983). *Marketing research: Methodological foundations*, 3rd ed. New York: Dryden.

Cicourel, Aaron. (1964). *Method and measurement in sociology.* Glencoe, IL: Free Press.

Cicourel, Aaron. (1973). *Cognitive sociology*, London: Macmillan.

Cicourel, Aaron. (1982). Interviews, surveys, and the problem of ecological validity. *American Sociologist*, 17:11–20.

Clammer, John. (1984). Approaches to ethnographic research. In *Ethnographic research: A guide to general conduct*, edited by R. F. Ellen, pp. 63–85. Orlando: Academic Press.

Clark, Herbert H., and Michael F. Schober. (1992). Asking questions and influencing answers. In *Questions about questions: Inquiries into the cognitive bases of surveys*, edited by Judith M. Turner, pp. 15–48. New York: Russell Sage Foundation.

Clarke, Michael. (1975). Survival in the field: Implications of personal experience in field work. *Theory and Society*, 2:95–123.

Clogg, Clifford C., and D. O. Sawyer. (1981). A comparison of alternative models for analyzing the scalability of response patterns. In *Sociological methodology 1981*, edited by S. Leinhardt, pp. 240–280. San Francisco: Jossey-Bass.

Clubb, Jerome M., E. Austin, C. Geda, and M. Traugott. (1985). Sharing research data in the social sciences. In *Sharing research data*, edited by Stephen E. Fineberg, M. Martin, and M. Straf, pp. 39–88. Washington, DC: National Academy Press.

Cogan, Johan, Judith Torney-Purta, and Douglas Anderson. (1988).

Knowledge and attitudes toward global issues: Students in Japan and the United States. *Comparative Education Review*, 32:283–297.

Cohen, Patricia Cline. (1982). *A calculating people: The spread of numeracy in early America.* Chicago: University of Chicago Press.

Cohen, Stephen R. (1991). The Pittsburg survey and the social survey movement: A sociological road not taken. In *The social survey in historical perspective, 1880–1940*, edited by M. Blumer, K. Bales, and K. Sklar, pp. 245–268, New York: Cambridge University Press.

Cole, Jonathan R., and Stephen Cole. (1973). *Social stratification in science.* Chicago: University of Chicago Press.

Cole, Stephen. (1978). Scientific reward systems: A comparative analysis. *Research in the Sociology of Knowledge, Science and Art*, 1:167–190.

Cole, Stephen. (1983). The hierarchy of the sciences? *American Journal of Sociology*, 89:111–139.

Cole, Stephen. (1994). Why sociology doesn't make progress like the natural sciences. *Sociological Forum*, 9:133–154.

Cole, Stephen, Jonathan Cole, and Gary A. Simon. (1981). Chance and consensus in peer review. *Science*, 214:881–885.

Collins, H. M. (1983). The sociology of scientific knowledge: Studies of contemporary science. *American Review of Sociology*, 9:265–285.

Collins, Randall. (1984). Statistics versus words. *Sociological Theory*, 2:329–362.

Collins, Randall. (1986). Is 1980s sociology in the doldrums? *American Journal of Sociology*, 91:1336–1355.

Collins, Randall. (1988). *Theoretical sociology.* New York: Harcourt Brace Jovanovich.

Collins, Randall. (1989). Sociology: Proscience or anti-science? *American Sociological Review*, 54:124–139.

Collins, Randall. (1994). Why the social sciences won't become high-consensus, rapid-discoversy science. *Sociological Forum*, 9:155–177.

Collins, Randall, and Sal Restivo. (1983). Development, diversity and conflict in the sociology of science. *Sociological Quarterly*, 24:185–200.

Comaroff, John, and Jean Comeroff. (1992). *Ethnography and the historical imagination.* Boulder, CO: Westview.

Committees on the Status of Women in Sociology. (1986). *The treatment of gender in research.* Washington,

DC: American Sociological Association.

Contrad, Peter, and Shulamit Reinharz. (1984). Computers and qualitative data: Editors' introductory essay. *Qualitative Sociology*, 7:3–15.

Converse, Jean M. (1984). Strong arguments and weak evidence: The open/closed questioning controversy of the 1940s. *Public Opinion Quarterly*, 48:267–282.

Converse, Jean M. (1987). *Survey research in the United States: Roots and emergence, 1890–1960*. Berkeley: University of California Press.

Converse, Jean M., and Stanley Presser. (1986). *Survey questions: Handcrafting the standardized questionnaire*, Beverly Hills, CA: Sage.

Converse, Jean M., and Howard Schuman. (1974). *Conversations at random: Survey research as interviewers see it*. New York: Wiley.

Cook, Judith A., and Mary Margaret Fonow. (1990). Knowledge and women's interests: Issues of epistemology and methodology in feminist sociological research. In *Feminist research methods*, edited by Joyce McCarl Nielsen, pp. 69–93. Boulder: Westview.

Cook, Thomas D., and Donald T. Campbell. (1979). *Quasi-experimentation: Design and analysis issues for field settings*. Chicago: Rand McNally.

Coombs, R. H., and L. J. Goldman. (1973). Maintenance and discontinuity of coping mechanisms in an intensive care unit. *Social Problems*, 20:342–355.

Cooper, Harris M. (1984). *The integrative research review: A systematic approach*. Beverly Hills, CA: Sage.

Cordes, Colleen. (1988). Legacy of "Golden Fleece" awards to survive Proxmire's retirement. *Chronicle of Higher Education*, December 14.

Corsaro, William A. (1988). Routines in the peer culture of American and Italian nursery school children. *Sociology of Education*, 61:1–14.

Corsaro, William A. (1992). Cross-cultural analysis. In *Encyclopedia of Sociology*, Vol. 1, edited by Edgar and Marie Borgatta, pp. 390–395, New York: Macmillan.

Corsaro, William A., and David Heise. (1990). Event structure models from ethnographic data. *Sociological Methodology*, 20:1–57.

Corsino, Louis. (1987). Fieldworkers blues: Emotional stress and research underinvolvement in fieldwork settings. *Social Science Journal*, 24:275–285.

Coser, Lewis. (1981). Uses of classical sociological theory. *The future of the sociological classics*, edited by Buford Rhea, pp. 170–182. Boston: George Allen and Unwin.

Costner, Herbert L. (1969). Theory, deduction and rules of correspondence. *American Journal of Sociology*, 75:245–263.

Costner, Herbert L. (1985). Theory, deduction and rules of correspondence. In *Causal models in the social sciences*, 2nd ed., edited by H. M. Blalock, Jr., pp. 229–250. New York: Aldine.

Cotter, Patrick R., Jeffrey Cohen, and Philip B. Coulter. (1982). Race of interviewer effects in telephone interviews. *Public Opinion Quarterly*, 46:278–286.

Couch, Carl J. (1987). Objectivity: A crutch and club for bureaucrats/subjectivity: A haven for lost souls. *Sociological Quarterly*, 28:105–118.

Cox, Stephen, and William Davidson. (1995). A meta-analysis of alternative education programs: *Crime and Delinquency*, 41:219–230.

Cozby, Paul C. (1984). *Using computers in the behavioral sciences*. Palo Alto, CA: Mayfield.

Craib, Ian. (1984). *Modern social theory: From Parsons to Habermas*. New York: St. Martins.

Crane, Diana. (1967). The gatekeepers of science: Some factors affecting the selection of articles for scientific journals. *American Sociologist*, 2: 195–201.

Crane, Diana. (1972). *Invisible colleges*. Chicago: University of Chicago Press.

Creswell, John W. (1994). *Research design: Qualitative and quantitative approaches*. Thousand Oaks, CA: Sage.

Croyle, Robert T., and Elizabeth Loftus. (1992). Improving episodic memory performance of survey respondents. In *Questions about questions: Inquiries into the cognitive bases of surveys*, edited by Judith M. Turner, pp. 95–101. New York: Russell Sage Foundation.

Cullen, Francis T., Bruce Link, and Craig Polanzi. (1982). The seriousness of crime revisited: Have attitudes toward white collar crime changed? *Criminology*, 20:83–102.

Cummings, Scott. (1984). The political economy of funding for social science research. *Sociological Inquiry*. 54:154–170.

Curran, Daniel J., and Sandra Cook. (1993). Doing research in post-Tiananmen China. In *Research on Sensitive Topics*, edited by Claire Renzetti and Raymond Lee, pp. 71–81. Thousand Oaks, CA: Sage.

Czaja, Ronald, Johnny Blair, and Jutta P. Sebestik. (1982). Respondent selection in a telephone survey: A comparison of three techniques. *Journal of Marketing Research*, 19:381–385.

D'Antonio, William V. (1989). Executive office report: Sociology on the move. *ASA Footnotes*, 17(August):2ff.

D'Antonio, William V. (1992). Recruiting sociologists in a time of changing opportunities. In *Sociology and its publics: The forms and fates of disciplinary organization*, edited by Terence Halliday and Morris Janowitz, pp. 99–136. Chicago: University of Chicago Press.

Dabbs, James M., Jr. (1982). Making things visible. In *Varieties of qualitative research*, edited by John Van Maanen, James M. Dabbs, Jr., and Robert R. Faulkner, pp. 31–64. Beverly Hills, CA: Sage.

Dale, Angela, S. Arber, and Michael Procter. (1988). *Doing secondary analysis*. Boston: Unwin Hyman.

Dannefer, Dale. (1981). Neither socialization nor recruitment: The avocational careers of old car enthusiasts. *Social Forces*, 60:395–413.

Danziger, Kurt. (1988). The question of identity: Who participated in psychological experiments? In *The rise of experimentation in American psychology*, edited by Jill G. Morawski, pp. 35–52. New Haven: Yale University Press.

Danziger, Sandra K. (1979). On doctor watching: Fieldwork in medical settings. *Urban Life*, 7:513–532.

Darnton, Robert. (1978). The history of mentalities. In *Structure, consciousness and history*, edited by R. H. Brown and S. M. Lyman, pp. 106–136. New York: Cambridge University Press.

Davis, Fred. (1959). The cabdriver and his fare: Facets of a fleeting relationship. *American Journal of Sociology*, 65:158–165.

Davis, Fred. (1973). The Martian and the convert: Ontological polarities in social research. *Urban Life*, 2: 333–343.

Davis, James A. (1985). *The logic of causal order*. Beverly Hills, CA: Sage.

Davis, James A., and Tom W. Smith. (1986). *General social surveys 1972–1986 cumulative codebook*. Chicago: National Opinion Research Center, University of Chicago.

Davis, James A., and Tom W. Smith. (1992). *The NORC General Social Survey: A user's guide*. Newbury Park, CA: Sage.

Dawes, R. M., and T. W. Smith. (1985). Attitude and opinion measurement. In *Handbook of social psychology*, 3rd ed., Vol. 1, edited by G. Lindzey and E. Aronson, pp. 509–566. New York: Random House.

Dean, John P., Robert L. Eichhorn, and Lois R. Dean. (1969). Fruitful informants for intensive interviewing. In *Issues in participant observation*, edited by G. McCall and J. L. Simmons, pp. 142–144. Reading, MA: Addison-Wesley.

Dean, John P., and William Foote Whyte. (1969). How do you know if the informant is telling the truth? In *Issues in participant observation*, edited by G. McCall and J. L. Simmons, pp. 105–115. Reading. MA: Addison-Wesley.

Deegan Mary Jo. (1988). *Jane Adams and the men of the Chicago School, 1892–1918*. New Brunswick: Transaction.

DeLamater, John, and Pat Mac-Corquodale. (1975). The effects of interview schedule variations on reported sexual behavior. *Sociological Methods and Research*, 4:215–236.

DeMaio, Theresa J. (1980). Refusals: Who, where and why? *Public Opinion Quarterly*, 44:223–233.

DeMaio, Teresa J. (1984). Social desirability and survey measurement: A review. In *Surveying Subjective Phenomena*, Vol. 2, edited by Charles Turner and Elizabeth Martin, pp. 257–282. New York: Russell Sage Foundation.

Denzin, Norman K. (1970). Symbolic interactionism and ethnomethodology. In *Understanding everyday life*, edited by Jack D. Douglas, pp. 261–286. Chicago: Aldine.

Denzin, Norman K. (1989). *The research act: A theoretical introduction to sociological methods*. 3rd. ed. Englewood Cliffs, NJ: Prentice-Hall.

Denzin, Norman K. and Kai Erikson. (1982). On the ethics of disguised observation: An exchange. In *Social research ethics*, edited by M. Blume. New York: Macmillan.

Denzin, Norman K, and Yvonna S. Lincoln, eds. (1994). Introduction: Entering the field of qualitative research. In *Handbook of qualitative research*, pp. 1–18. Thousand Oaks, CA: Sage.

Derksen, Linda, and John Gartrell. (1992). Scientific explanation. In *Encyclopedia of Sociology*, Vol. 4, edited by Edgar and Marie Borgatta, pp. 1711–1720. New York: Macmillan.

Desan, Susanne. (1989). Crowds, community and ritual in the work of E. P. Thompson and Natalie Davis. In *The new cultural history*, edited by L. Hunt, pp. 24–46. Berkeley: University of California Press.

Devault, Marjorie L. (1990). Talking and listening from women's standpoint: Feminist strategies for interviewing and analysis. *Social Problems*, 37:96–116.

deVaus, D. A. (1986). *Surveys in social research*. Boston: George Allen and Unwin.

Dexter, Lewis A. (1970). *Elite and specialized interviewing*. Evanston, IL: Northwestern University Press.

Diamond, Sigmund. (1988). Informed consent and survey research: The FBI and the University of Michigan Survey Research Center. In *Surveying social life: Papers in honor of Herbert H. Hyman*, edited by Hubert J. O'Gorman, pp. 72–99. Middletown, CT: Wesleyan University Press.

Dibble, Vernon K. (1963). Four types of inference from documents to events. *History and Theory*, 3:203–221.

Dickson, David. (1984). *The new politics of science*, Chicago: University of Chicago Press.

Diener, Edward, and Rick Crandall. (1978). *Ethics in social and behavioral research*. Chicago: University of Chicago Press.

Dijkstra, Wil, and Johannes van der Zouwen, eds. (1982). *Response behavior in the survey interview*. New York: Academic Press.

Dillman, Don A. (1978). *Mail and telephone surveys: The total design method*. New York: Wiley.

Dillman, Don A. (1983). Mail and other self-administered questionnaires. In *Handbook of survey research*, edited by Peter H. Rossi, James D. Wright, and Andy B. Anderson, pp. 359–377. Orlando, FL: Academic Press.

Dillman, Donald A. (1991). The design and administration of mail surveys. *Annual Review of Sociology*, 17:225–249.

Domhoff, G. William. (1974). *The Bohemian Grove and other retreats*. New York: Harper and Row.

Donald, Robert B. et al., (1983). *Writing clear paragraphs*, 2nd ed. Englewood Cliffs, NJ: Prentice-Hall.

Dooley, David. (1984). *Social research methods*. Englewood Cliffs, NJ: Prentice-Hall.

Douglas, Jack D. (1976). *Investigative social research*. Beverly Hills, CA: Sage.

Douglas, Jack D. (1985). *Creative interviewing*. Beverly Hills, CA: Sage.

Douglas, Jack D., and Paul K. Rasmussen. (1977). *The nude beach*. Beverly Hills, CA: Sage.

Downey, Gary L. (1986). Ideology and the Clamshell identity: Organizational dilemmas in the anti-nuclear power movement. *Social Problems*, 33:357–373.

Drass, Kriss. (1980). The analysis of qualitative data: A computer program. *Urban Life*, 9:332–353.

DuBois, W. E. Burghardt. (1899). *The Philadelphia Negro*. New York: Benjamin Bloom.

Dunaway, David K., and Willa K. Baum, eds. 1984. *Oral history*, Nashville, TN: Association for State and Local History.

Duncan, Otis Dudley. (1975). *Introduction to structural equation models*. New York: Academic Press.

Duncan, Otis Dudley. (1984). *Notes on social measurement: Historical and critical*. New York: Russell Sage Foundation.

Duncan, Otis Dudley, and Magnus Stenbeck. (1988). No opinion or not sure? *Public Opinion Quarterly*, 52:513–525.

Durkheim, Emile. (1938). *Rules of the sociological method*, trans. Sarah Solovay and John Mueller, edited by George E. G. Catlin. Chicago: University of Chicago Press.

Dynes, Russell R. (1984). The institutionalization of COSSA. *Sociological Inquiry*, 54:211–229.

Easterday, Lois, Diana Papademas, Laura Schorr, and Catherine Valentine. (1982). The making of a female researcher: Role problems in fieldwork. In *Field research*, edited by R. G. Burgess, pp. 62–67. Boston: George Allen and Unwin.

Eastrope, Gary. (1974). *History of social research methods*. London: Longman.

Eckberg, Douglas Lee, and Lester Hill, Jr. (1979). The paradigm concept and sociology. *American Sociological Review*, 44:937–947.

Eder, Donna. (1981). Ability grouping as a self-fulfilling prophecy: A microanalysis of teacher-student interaction. *Sociology of Education*, 54:151–162.

Eder, Donna. (1985). The cycle of popularity: Interpersonal relations among female adolescents. *Sociology of Education*, 58:154–165.

Edward, G. Franklin. (1974). E. Franklin Frazier. In *Black sociologists: Historical and contemporary perspectives*, Edited by James E. Blackwell and Morris Janowitz, pp. 85–117. Chicago: University of Chicago Press.

Edwards, Allen L. (1957). *Techniques of attitude scale construction*. New York: Appleton-Century-Crofts.

Edwards, Rosalind. (1993). An education in interviewing: Placing the researcher and research. In *Research on sensitive topics*, edited by Claire Renzetti and Raymond Lee, pp. 181–196. Thousand Oaks, CA: Sage.

Eichler, Margrit. (1988). *Nonsexist research methods: A practical guide*. Boston: George Allen and Unwin.

Elder, Glen H., Jr., Eliza Pavalko, and Elizabeth Clipp. (1993). *Working with archival data: Studying lives.* Thousand Oaks, CA: Sage.

Elder, Joseph W. (1973). Problems of crosscultural methodology: Instrumentation and interviewing in India. In *Comparative social research,* edited by M. Armer and A. D. Grimshaw, pp. 119–144. New York: Wiley.

Ellen, R. F., ed. (1984a). *Ethnographic research: A guide to general conduct.* Orlando: Academic Press.

Ellen, R. F. (1984b). Some other interactionist methods. In *Ethnographic research: A guide to general conduct,* Edited by R. F. Ellen, pp. 273–293. Orlando: Academic Press.

Emerson, Robert M. (1981). Observational field work, *Annual Review of Sociology,* 7:351–378.

Emerson, Robert M. (1983). Introduction. In *Contemporary field research,* edited by R. M. Emerson, pp. 1–16. Boston: Little, Brown.

Ennis, James G. (1992). The social organization of sociological knowledge: Modeling the intersection of specialties. *American Sociological Review,* 57:259–265.

Erikson, Kai T. (1970). A comment on disguised observation in sociology. In *Qualitative methodology,* edited by W. J. Filstead, pp. 252–260. Chicago: Markham.

Erikson, Kai T. (1978). *Everything in its path.* New York: Touchstone.

Evans, Peter, and John D. Stephens. (1989). Studying development since the sixties: The emergence of a new comparative political economy. *Theory and Society,* 17:713–746.

Evans, William A., Michael Krippendorf, Jae Yoon, Paulette Posluszny, and Sari Thomas. (1990). Science in the prestige and national tabloid press. *Social Science Quarterly,* 71:105–117.

Faris, R. E. L. (1967). *Chicago sociology, 1920–1932.* San Francisco: Chandler.

Faupel, Charles E., and Carl B. Klockars. (1987). Drugs-crime connections: Elaborations from the life history of hard-core heroin addicts. *Social Problems,* 34:54–68.

Fay, Brian. (1975). *Social theory and political practice.* London: George Allen and Unwin.

Fay, Brian. (1987). *Critical social science: Liberation and its limits.* Ithaca, NY: Cornell University Press.

Featherman, David L., and Richard C. Rockwell. (1992). Social science research council. *Encyclopedia of Sociology,* Vol. 4, edited by Edgar and Marie Borgatta, pp. 1942–1945. New York: Macmillan.

Ferriss, Abbott L. (1988). The uses of social indicators. *Social Forces,* 66:601–617.

Fetterman, David M. (1989). *Ethnography: Step by step.* Newbury Park, CA: Sage.

Fichter, Joseph H., and William L. Kolb. (1970). Ethical limitations on sociological reporting. In *Qualitative methodology,* edited by W. J. Filstead, pp. 261–270. Chicago: Markham.

Fielding, Nigel G., and Raymond M. Lee, eds. (1991). *Using computers in qualitative research.* Newbury Park, CA: Sage.

Fine, Gary Alan. (1979). Small groups and culture creation: The idioculture of Little League baseball teams. *American Sociological Review,* 44: 733–745.

Fine, Gary Alan. (1987). *With the boys: Little League baseball and preadolescent culture.* Chicago: University of Chicago Press.

Fine, Gary Alan. (1988). The ten commandments of writing. *The American Sociologist,* 19:152–157.

Fine, Gary Alan. (1990). Organizational time: The temporal experience of restaurant kitchens: *Social Forces,* 69:95–114.

Fine, Gary Alan. (1992). The culture of production: Aesthetic choices and constraints in culinary work. *American Journal of Sociology,* 97:1268–1294.

Fine, Gary Alan, and Barry Glassner. (1979). Participant observation with children: Promise and problems. *Urban Life,* 8:153–174.

Finkel, Steven E., Thomas M. Guterbock, and Marian J. Borg. (1991). Race-of-interviewer effects in a preelection poll: Viriginia 1989. *Public Opinion Quarterly,* 55: 313–330.

Finley, M. I. (1977). Progress in historiography. *Daedalus,* Summer, pp. 125–142.

Finsterbusch, Kurt, and Annabelle Bender Motz. (1980). *Social research for policy decisions.* Belmont, CA: Wadsworth.

Finsterbusch, Kurt, and C. P. Wolf. (1981). *Methodology of social impact assessment.* Stroudsburg, PA: Hutchinson Ross.

Firebaugh, Glenn. (1980). Cross-national versus historical regression models. *Comparative Social Research,* 3:333–344.

Firebaugh, Glenn, and Kevin Chen. (1995). Vote turnout of nineteenth amendment women: The enduring effect of disenfranchisement. *American Journal of Sociology* 100:972–996.

Fischer, Claude S. (1992). *America calling: A social history of the tele-phone to 1940.* Berkeley: University of California Press.

Fischer, David H. (1970). *Historians' fallacies: Towards a logic of historical thought.* New York: Harper & Row.

Fischer, Frank. (1985). Critical evaluation of public policy: A methodological case study. In *Critical theory and public life,* edited by John Forester, pp. 231–257. Cambridge, MA: MIT Press.

Fiske, Donald W. (1982). Convergent-discriminant validation in measurements and research strategies. In *Forms of validation in research,* edited by David Brinberg and Louise H. Kidder, pp. 72–92. San Francisco: Jossey-Bass.

Fiske, Edward B. (1989). The misleading concept of "average" on reading tests changes, and more students fall below it. *New York Times,* July 12.

Fitchen, Janet M. (1991). *Endangered spaces, enduring places: Change, identity and survival in rural America.* Boulder, CO: Westview.

Fletcher, Colin. (1974). *Beneath the surface: An account of three styles of sociological research.* Boston: Routledge and Kegan Paul.

Flora, Cornelia Butler. (1979). Changes in women's status in women's magazine fiction: Differences by social class. *Social Problems,* 26:558–569.

Foddy, William. (1993). *Constructing questions for interviews and questionnaires: Theory and practice in social research.* New York: Cambridge University Press.

Fontana, Andrea, and James H. Frey. (1994). Interviewing: The art of science. In *Handbook of qualitative research,* edited by Denzin and Lincoln, pp. 361–376. Thousand Oaks, CA: Sage.

Form, Willam H. (1973). Field problems in comparative research. In *Comparative social research,* edited by M. Armer and A. D. Grimshaw, pp. 83–117. New York: Wiley.

Fowler, Floyd J., Jr. (1984). *Survey research methods.* Beverly Hills, CA: Sage.

Fowler, Floyd J., Jr. (1992). How unclear terms can affect survey data. *Public Opinion Quarterly,* 56: 218–231.

Fox, James Alan, and Paul E. Tracy. (1986). *Randomized response: A method for sensitive surveys.* Beverly Hills, CA: Sage.

Fox, John. (1992). Statistical graphics. In *Encyclopedia of Sociology,* Vol. 4, edited by Edgar and Marie Borgatta, pp. 2054–2073. New York: Macmillan.

Fox, Richard, Melvin R. Crask, and Jonghoon Kim. (1988). Mail survey response rate: A meta-analysis of selected techniques for inducing response. *Public Opinion Quarterly*, 52:467–491.

Franke, Charles O. (1983). Ethnography. In *Contemporary field research*, edited by R. M. Emerson, pp. 60–67. Boston: Little, Brown.

Franke, Richard H., and James D. Kaul. (1978). The Hawthorne experiments: First statistical interpretation. *American Sociological Review*, 43:623–643.

Frankel, Martin. (1983). Sampling theory. In *Handbook of survey research*, edited by Peter H. Rossi, James D. Wright, and Andy B. Anderson, pp. 21–67. Orlando, FL: Academic Press.

Frazier, E. Franklin. (1957). *The black bourgeoisie*. Glencoe IL: Free Press.

Frechette-Schrader, Kristin. (1994). *Ethics of scientific research*, Lanham, MD: Rowland and Littlefield.

Fredrickson, George. (1981). *White supremacy*. New York: Oxford University Press.

Freeman, Howard. (1983). *Applied sociology*. San Francisco: Jossey-Bass.

Freeman, Howard E. (1992). Evaluation research. In *Encyclopedia of Sociology*, Vol. 2, edited by Edgar and Marie Borgatta, pp. 594–598. New York: Macmillan.

Freeman, Howard, and Peter H. Rossi. (1984). Fur-thering the applied side of sociology. *American Sociological Review*, 49:571–580.

Freeman, Howard, and Merrill J. Shanks, eds. (1983). The emergence of computer assisted survey research. *Sociological Methods and Research*, 23:115–230.

Freidson, Eliot. (1986). *Professional powers: A study of the institutionalization of formal knowledge*. Chicago: University of Chicago Press.

Freire, Paulo. (1970). *Pedagogy of the oppressed*, trans. Myra Bergman Ramos. New York: Seabury.

Freitag, Peter. (1983). The myth of corporate capture: Regulatory commissions in the United States. *Social Problems*, 30:480–491.

Frey, Frederick W. (1970). Cross-cultural survey research in political science. In *The methodology of comparative research*, edited by R. Holt and J. Turner, pp. 173–294. New York: Free Press.

Frey, James H. (1983). *Survey research by telephone*. Beverly Hills, CA: Sage.

Friedrichs, Robert W. (1970). *A sociology of sociology*. New York: Free Press.

Frost, Peter, and Ralph Stablein, eds. (1992). *Doing exemplary research*. Newbury Park, CA: Sage.

Fuchs, Stephan, and Jonathan H. Turner. (1986). What makes a science "mature"? Patterns of organizational control in scientific production. *Sociological Theory*, 4:143–150.

Fuller, Linda. (1988). Fieldwork in forbidden terrain: The U.S. state and the case of Cuba. *American Sociologist*, 19:99–120.

Gadamer, Hans-Georg. (1979). The problem of historical consciousness. In *Interpretative social science: A reader*, edited by Paul Rabinow and William Sullivan, pp. 103–160. Berkeley: University of California Press.

Galaskiewicz, Joseph. (1985). Professional networks and the institutionalization of a single mind set. *American Sociological Review*, 50:639–658.

Galaskiewicz, Joseph. (1987). The study of a business elite and corporate philanthropy in a United States metropolitan area. In *Research methods for elite studies*, edited by George Moyser and Margaret Wagstaffe, pp. 147–165. Boston: George Allen and Unwin.

Galaskiewicz, Joseph, and Stanley Wasserman. (1993). Social network analysis: Concepts, methodology and directions for the 1990s. *Sociological Methods and Research*, 22:3–22.

Gallie, W. B. (1963). The historical understanding. *History and Theory*, 3:149–202.

Galliher, John F., and James L. McCartney. (1973). The influence of funding agencies on juvenile delinquency research. *Social Problems*, 21:77–90.

Gamson, William A. (1992). *Talking politics*. Cambridge: Cambridge University Press.

Gans, Herbert J. (1982). The participant observer as a human being: Observations on the personal aspects of fieldwork. In *Field research*, edited by R. G. Burgess, pp. 53–61. Boston: George Allen and Unwin.

Garfinkel, Harold. (1967). *Studies in ethnomethodology*. Englewood Cliffs, NJ: Prentice-Hall.

Garfinkel, Harold. (1974a). The origins of the term "ethnomethodology." In *Ethnomethodology*, edited by Roy Turner, pp. 15–18. Middlesex: Penguin.

Garfinkel, Harold. (1974b). The rational properties of scientific and common sense activities. In *Positivism and sociology*, edited by Anthony Giddens, pp. 53–74. London: Heinemann.

Gaston, Jerry. (1978). *The reward system in British and American science*. New York: Wiley.

Geer, John G. (1988). What do open-ended questions measure? *Public Opinion Quarterly*, 52:365–371.

Geertz, Clifford. (1973). *The interpretation of cultures*. New York: Basic Books.

Geertz, Clifford. (1979). From the native's point of view: On the nature of anthropological understanding. In *Interpretative social science: A reader*, edited by Paul Rabinow and William Sullivan, pp. 225–242. Berkeley: University of California Press.

Geiger, Roger L. (1986). *To advance knowledge: The growth of America n research universities, 1900–1940*. New York: Oxford University Press.

Georges, Robert A., and Michael O. Jones. (1980). *People studying people*. Berkeley: University of California Press.

Gephart, Robert P., Jr. (1988). *Ethnostatistics: Qualitative foundations for quantitative research*. Newbury Park, CA: Sage.

Gibbs, Jack. (1989). Conceptualization of terrorism. *American Sociological Review*, 54:329–340.

Giddens, Anthony. (1976). *New rules of sociological method: Positivist critique of interpretative sociologies*. New York: Basic Books.

Giddens, Anthony. (1978). Positivism and its critics. In *A history of sociological analysis*, edited by Tom Bottomore and Robert Nisbet. New York: Basic Books.

Gieryn, Thomas F. (1978). Problem retention and problem change in science. In *The sociology of science*, edited by Jerry Gaston. San Francisco: Jossey-Bass.

Gilbert, Margaret. (1992). *On social facts*. Princeton, NJ: Princeton University Press.

Gillespie, Richard. (1988). The Hawthorne experiments and the politics of experimentation. In *The rise of experimentation in American psychology*, edited by Jill G. Morawski, pp. 114–137. New Haven: Yale University Press.

Gillespie, Richard. (1991). *Manufacturing knowledge: A history of the Hawthorne experiments*. New York: Cambridge University Press.

Gilljam, Mikael, and David Granberg. (1993). Should we take Don't Know for an answer? *Public Opinion Quarterly*, 57:348–357.

Glaser, Barney, and Anselm Strauss. (1967). *The discovery of grounded theory*. Chicago: Aldine.

Glaser, Barney, and Anselm Strauss. (1968). *A time for dying*. Chicago: Aldine.

Glasser, Gerald J., and Gale O. Metzger. (1972). Random digit dialing as a method of telephone Sampling.

Journal of Marketing Research, 9:59–64.

Glock, Charles Y. (1987). Reflections on doing survey research. In *Surveying social life: Papers in honor of Herbert H. Hyman,* edited by Hubert J. O'Gorman, pp. 31–59, Middletown, CT: Wesleyan University Press.

Glucksmann, Miriam. (1974). *Structuralist analysis in contemporary social thought: A comparison of the theories of Claude Levi-Strauss and Louis Althusser.* Boston: Routledge and Kegan Paul.

Gold, Raymond L. (1969). Roles in sociological field observation. In *Issues in participant observation,* edited by G. J. McCall and J. L. Simmons. pp. 30–38. Reading, MA: Addison-Wesley.

Goldstein, Robert Justin. (1978). *Political repression in modern America.* New York: Schenckman.

Goldthorpe, John. (1977). The relevance of history to sociology. In *Sociological research methods,* edited by M. Bulmer, pp. 178–191. London: Macmillan.

Gonor, George. (1977). "Situation" versus "frame": The "interactionist" and the "structuralist" analysis of everyday life. *American Sociological Review,* 42:854–867.

Goodsell, Charles B. (1983). Welfare waiting rooms. *Urban Life,* 12:464–477.

Gordon, David F. (1987). Getting close by staying distant: Fieldwork with proselytizing groups. *Qualitative Sociology,* 10:267–287.

Gordon, Randall A., T. A. Bindrim, M. L. McNicholas, and T. L. Walden. (1988). Perceptions of blue-collar and white-collar crime: The effect of defendant race on simulated juror decisions. *Journal of Social Psychology,* 128:191–197.

Gordon, Raymond. (1980). *Interviewing: Strategy, techniques and tactics,* 3rd ed. Homewood, IL: Dorsey Press.

Gordon, Raymond. (1992). *Basic interviewing skills.* Itasca, IL: Peacock.

Gorelick, Sherry. (1991). Contradictions of feminist methodology. *Gender and Society,* 5:459–477.

Gould, Roger V. (1991). Multiple networks and mobilization in the Paris Commune, 1871. *American Sociological Review,* 56:716–729.

Gouldner, Alvin. (1970). *The coming crisis of Western sociology.* New York: Basic Books.

Gouldner, Alvin W. (1976). The dark side of the dialectic: Toward a new objectivity. *Sociological Inquiry,* 46:3–16.

Goward, Nicola. (1984a). Publications on fieldwork experiences. In *Ethnographic research: A guide to general conduct,* edited by R. F. Ellen, pp. 88–100. Orlando: Academic Press.

Goward, Nicola. (1984b). Personal interaction and adjustment. In *Ethnographic research: A guide to general conduct,* edited by R. F. Ellen, pp. 100–118. Orlando: Academic Press.

Goyder, John C. (1982). Factors affecting response rates to mailed questionnaires. *American Sociological Review,* 47:550–554.

Graham, Sandra. (1992). Most of the subjects were white and middle class: Trends in published research on African Americans in selected APA journals, 1970–1989. *American Psychologist,* 47:629–639.

Granovetter, Mark. (1976). Network sampling: Some first steps. *American Journal of Sociology,* 81: 1287–1303.

Grant, Linda, Kathryn B. Ward, and Xue Lan Rong. (1987). Is there an association between gender and methods of sociological research? *American Sociological Review,* 52: 856–862.

Gray, Bradford H. (1982). The regulatory context of social and behavioral research. In *Ethical issues in social science research,* edited by Tom L. Beauchamp, R. Faden, R. J. Wallace, and L. Walters, pp. 329–354. Baltimore: Johns Hopkins University Press.

Gray, Paul S. (1980). Exchange and access in field work. *Urban Life,* 9: 309–331.

Greenwald, Howard P. (1992). Ethics in social research. In *Encyclopedia of sociology,* Vol. 2., edited by Edgar and Marie Borgatta, pp. 584–588. New York: Macmillan.

Griffin, Larry J. (1992). Comparative-historical analysis. In *Encyclopedia of sociology,* Vol. 1, edited by Edgar and Marie Borgatta, pp. 263–271. New York: Macmillan.

Griffin, Larry J. (1993). Narrative, event structure analysis and causal interpretation in historical sociology. *American Journal of Sociology,* 98:1094–1133.

Griffin, Larry J., Michael E. Wallace, and Beth A. Rubin. (1986). Capitalist resistance to the organization of labor before the New Deal: Why? How? Success? *American Sociological Review,* 51:147–167.

Grimshaw, Allen D. (1973). Comparative sociology. In *Comparative social research,* edited by M. Armer and A. Grimshaw, pp. 3–48. New York: Wiley.

Grinnell, Frederick. (1987). *The scientific attitude.* Boulder, CO: Westview.

Griswold, Wendy. (1983). The devil's techniques: Cultural legitimation and social change. *American Sociological Review,* 48:668–680.

Griswold, Wendy. (1987). A methodological framework for the sociology of culture. In *Sociological methodology,* 1987, edited by Clifford C. Clogg, pp. 1–35. San Francisco: Jossey-Bass.

Griswold, Wendy. (1994). *Cultures and societies in a changing world.* Thousand Oaks, CA: Pine Forge Press.

Grosof, Miriam Schapiro, and Hyman Sardy. (1985). *A research primer for the social and behavioral sciences.* Orlando, FL: Academic Press.

Gross, Daniel R. (1984). Time allocation: A tool for the study of cultural behavior. *Annual Review of Anthropology,* 13:519–558.

Gross, Edward. (1986). Waiting at Mayo. *Urban Life,* 15:139–164.

Groves, Robert M., Nancy H. Fultz, and Elizabeth Martin. (1992). Direct questioning about comprehension in a survey setting. In *Questions about questions: Inquiries into the cognitive bases of surveys,* edited by Judith M. Turner, pp. 49–61. New York: Russell Sage Foundation.

Groves, Robert M., and Robert L. Kahn. (1979). *Surveys by telephone: A national comparison with personal interviews.* New York: Academic Press.

Groves, Robert M., and Nancy Mathiowetz. (1984). Computer assisted telephone interviewing: Effects on interviewers and respondents. *Public Opinion Quarterly,* 48:356–369.

Guba, Egon G., and Yvonna S. Lincoln. (1994). Competing paradigms in qualitative research. In *Handbook of qualitative research,* edited by Norman K. Denzin and Yvonna S. Lincoln, pp. 105–117. Thousand Oaks, CA: Sage.

Gubrium, Jaber F., and James A. Holstein. (1992). Qualitative methods. In *Encyclopedia of sociology,* Vol. 3, edited by Edgar and Marie Borgatta, pp. 1577–1582. New York: Macmillan.

Gurevitch, Z. D. (1988). The other side of the dialogue: On making the other strange and the experience of otherness. *American Journal of Sociology,* 93:1179–1199.

Gurney, Joan Neff. (1985). Not one of the guys: The female researcher in a male-dominated setting. *Qualitative Sociology,* 8:42–62.

Gusfield, Joseph. (1976). The literary rhetoric of science: Comedy and pathos in drinking driver research.

American Sociological Review, 41: 16–34.

Gustavsen, Bjørn. (1986). Social research as participatory dialogue. In *The use and abuse of social science*, edited by Frank Heller, pp. 143–156. Beverly Hills, CA: Sage.

Gustin, Bernard H. (1973). Charisma, recognition and the motivation of scientists. *American Journal of Sociology*, 86:1119–1134.

Guttman, Louis. (1950). The basis for scalogram analysis. In *Measurement and prediction*, edited by S. A. Stouffer, L. Buttman, E. A. Suchman, P. F. Lazarfeld, S. A. Star, and J. A. Clausen, pp. 60–90. Princeton, NJ: Princeton University Press.

Guttman, Louis. (1970). A basis for scaling qualitative data. In *Attitude measurement*, edited by Gene Summers, pp. 174–186. Chicago: Rand McNally.

Guy, Rebecca F., Charles E. Edgley, Ibtihaj Arafat, and Donald E. Allan. (1987). *Social research methods: Puzzles and solutions*. Boston: Allyn and Bacon.

Haberman, Shelby J. (1978). *Analysis of qualitative data*. New York: Academic Press.

Habermas, Jurgen. (1971). *Knowledge and human interests*. Boston: Beacon.

Habermas, Jurgen. (1973). *Theory and practice*. Boston: Beacon.

Habermas, Jurgen. (1976). *Legitimation crisis*. Boston: Beacon.

Habermas, Jurgen. (1979). *Communication and the evolution of society*. Boston: Beacon.

Habermas, Jurgen. (1988). *On the logic of the social sciences*. Oxford: Polity.

Hagan, John. (1990). The gender stratification of income inequality among lawyers. *Social Forces*, 63:835–855.

Hage, Jerald. (1972). *Techniques and problems of theory construction in sociology*. New York: Wiley.

Hagstrom, Warren. (1965). *The scientific community*. New York: Basic Books.

Hakim, Catherine. (1987). *Research design: Strategies and choices in the design of social research*. Boston: Allen and Unwin.

Halfpenny, Peter. (1979). The analysis of qualitative data. *Sociological Review*, 27:799–823.

Halfpenny, Peter. (1982). *Positivism and sociology: Explaining social life*. London: George Allen and Unwin.

Hallin, Daniel C. (1985). The American news media: A critical theory perspective. In *Critical theory and public life*, edited by John Forester, pp.

121–146. Cambridge, MA: MIT Press.

Hallowell, Lyle. (1985). *Ethical and legal problems of research: Professional workshop*. Presentation at the American Sociological Association annual meeting, Washington, D.C., August 26.

Hammersley, Martyn. (1992). *What's wrong with ethnography? Methodological explorations*. New York: Routledge.

Hammersley, Martyn, and Paul Atkinson. (1983). *Ethnography: Principles in practice*. London: Tavistock.

Hannan, Michael T. (1985). Problems of aggregation. In *Causal models in the social sciences*, 2nd ed. edited by Hubert M. Blalock, Jr., pp. 403–439. Chicago: Aldine.

Harari, Herbert, Oren Harari, and Robert V. White. (1985). The reaction to rape by American bystanders. *Journal of Social Psychology*, 125:653–658.

Harding, Sandra. (1986). *The science question in feminism*. Ithaca, NY: Cornell University Press.

Hargens, Lowell L. (1991). Impressions and misimpressions about sociology journals. *Contemporary Sociology*, 20:343–349.

Hargens, Lowell L. (1988). Scholarly consensus and journal rejection rates. *American Sociological Review*, 53:139–151.

Harkens, Shirley, and Carol Warren. (1993). The social relations of intensive interviewing: Constellations of strangeness and science. *Sociological Methods and Research*, 21: 317–339.

Harper, Douglas. (1982). *Good company*. Chicago: University of Chicago Press.

Harper, Douglas. (1987). *Working knowledge*. Chicago: University of Chicago.

Harper, Douglas. (1994). On the authority of the image: Visual methods at the crossroads. In *Handbook of qualitative research*, edited by Norman Denzin and Yvonna Lincoln, pp. 403–412. Thousand Oaks, CA: Sage.

Harre, Rom. (1972). *The philosophies of science*. London: Oxford University Press.

Harre, R., and P. F. Secord. (1979). *The explanation of social behavior*. Totowa, NJ: Littlefield, Adams.

Harris, Benjamin. (1988). Key words: A history of debriefing in social psychology. In *The rise of experimentation in American psychology*, edited by Jill G. Morawski, pp. 188–212. New Haven: Yale University Press.

Harvey, Lee. (1990). *Critical social research*. London: Urwin Hyman.

Hastings, Philip K., and Dean R. Hodge. (1986). Religious and moral attitude trends among college students, 1948–84. *Social Forces*, 65:370–377.

Hauck, Matthew, and Michael Cox. (1974). Locating a sample by random digit dialing: Some hypotheses and a random sample. *Public Opinion Quarterly*, 38:253–260.

Hayano, David M. (1982). *Poker faces: The life and work of professional card players*. Berkeley: University of California Press.

Hazelrigg, Lawrence E. (1973). Aspects of the measurement of class consciousness. In *Comparative social research*, edited by M. Armer and A. D. Grimshaw, pp. 219–246. New York: Wiley.

Hearn, H. L., and P. Stoll. (1976). The continuance of commitment in low status occupations: The cocktail waitress. *Sociological Quarterly*, 16:105–114.

Hearnshaw, L. S. (1979). *Cyril Burt: Psychologist*. London: Holder and Stoughten.

Heberlein, Thomas A., and Robert Baumgartner. (1978). Factors affecting response rates to mailed questionnaires: A quantitative analysis of the published literature. *American Sociological Review*, 43:447–462.

Heberlein, Thomas A., and Robert Baumgartner. (1981). Is a questionnaire necessary in a second mailing? *Public Opinion Quarterly*, 45:102–107.

Hector, Michael. (1975). *Internal colonialism*. Berkeley: University of California Press.

Hegtvedt, Karen A. (1992). Replication. In *Encyclopedia of sociology*, Vol. 3, edited by Edgar and Marie Borgatta, pp. 1661–1663. New York: Macmillan.

Heise, David. (1965). Semantic differential profiles for 1,000 most frequent English words. *Psychological Monographs*, 70, No. 8.

Heise, David. (1970). The semantic differential and attitude research. In *Attitude measurement*, edited by Gene F. Summers, pp. 235–253. Chicago: Rand McNally.

Heise, David R. (1974). Some issues in sociological measurement. In *Sociological methodology, 1973–74*, edited by H. L. Costner, pp. 1–16. San Francisco: Jossey-Bass.

Heise, David, ed. (1981). *Microcomputers in social research*. Beverly Hills, CA: Sage.

Held, David. (1980). *Introduction to critical theory: Horkheimer to Habermas*. Berkeley: University of California Press.

Heller, Nelson B., and J. Thomas McEwen. (1973). Applications of crime seriousness information in police departments. *Journal of Criminal Justice*, 1:241–253.

Henry, Gary T. (1990). *Practical sampling*, Newbury Park, CA: Sage.

Henry, Gary T. (1995). *Graphing data: Techniques for display and analysis*. Thousand Oaks, CA: Sage.

Herting, Jerald R. (1985). Multiple indicator models using LISREL. In *Causal models in the social sciences*, 2nd ed., edited by Hubert M. Blalock, Jr., pp. 263–320. New York: Aldine.

Herting, Jerald R., and Herbert L. Costner. (1985). Re-specification in multiple indicator models. In *Causal models in the social sciences*, 2nd ed., edited by Hubert M. Blalock, Jr., pp. 321–394. Chicago: Aldine.

Herzberger, Sharon D. (1993). The cyclical pattern of child abuse: A study of research methodology. In *Research on sensitive topics*, edited by Claire Renzetti and Raymond Lee, pp. 33–51. Thousand Oaks, CA: Sage.

Herzog, A. Regula, and Jerald G. Bachman. (1981). Effects of questionnaire length on response quality. *Public Opinion Quarterly*, 45:549–559.

Hertz, Rosanna, and Jonathan B. Imber. (1993). Fieldwork in elite settings. *Journal of Contemporary Ethnography*, 22:3–6.

Hesse, Mary B. (1970). *Models and analogies in science*. Notre Dame, IN: Notre Dame Press.

Hicks, David. (1984). Getting into the field and establishing routines. In *Ethnographic research: A guide to general conduct*, edited by R. F. Ellen, pp. 192–199. Orlando: Academic Press.

Hill, Michael R. (1993). *Archival strategies and techniques*. Thousand Oaks, CA: Sage.

Hiller, Harry H. (1979). Universality of science and the question of national sociologies. *American Sociologist*, 14:124–135.

Himmelstein, Jerome L., and Mayer Zald. (1984). American conservatism and government funding of the social sciences and arts. *Sociological Inquiry*, 54:171–187.

Hindess, Barry. (1973). *The use of official statistics in sociology: A critique of positivism and ethnomethodology*. New York: Macmillan.

Hippler, Hans, J., and Norbert Schwartz. (1986). Not forbidding isn't allowing: The cognitive basis of the forbid-allow asymmetry. *Public Opinion Quarterly*, 50:87–96.

Hirschman, Albert O. (1970). *Exit, voice, and loyalty: Response to decline in firms, organizations and states*. Cambridge, MA: Harvard University Press.

Hochschild, Arlie. (1978). *The unexpected community: Portrait of an old age subculture*. Berkeley: University of California Press.

Hochschild, Arlie. (1983). *The managed heart*. Berkeley: University of California Press.

Hochschild, Jennifer L. (1981). *What's fair? American beliefs about distributive justice*. Cambridge, MA: Harvard University Press.

Hoffmann, Joan Eakin. (1980). Problems of access in the study of social elites and boards of directors. In *Fieldwork experience*, edited by W. B. Shaffir., R. A. Stebbins, and A. Turowetz, pp. 45–56. New York: St. Martin's Press.

Hoffman-Lange, Ursula. (1987). Surveying national elites in the Federal Republic of Germany. In *Research methods for elite studies*, edited by George Moyser and Margaret Wagstaffe, pp. 27–47. Boston: Allen and Unwin.

Hollander, Myles, and Frank Proschan. (1984). *The statistical exorcist: Dispelling statistics anxiety*. New York: Marcel Decker.

Hollis, Martin. (1977). *Models of man: Philosophical thoughts on social action*. New York: Cambridge University Press.

Holstein, James A., and Jaber F. Gubrium. (1994). Phenomenology, ethnomethodology and interpretative practice. In *Handbook of qualitative research*, edited by Norman Denzin and Yvonna Lincoln, pp. 262–272. Thousand Oaks: CA.

Holsti, Ole R. (1968). Content analysis. In *Handbook of social psychology*, 2nd ed., Vol. 2, edited by Gardner Lindzey and Elliot Aronson, pp. 596–692. Reading, MA: Addison-Wesley.

Holsti, Ole R. (1969). *Content analysis for the social sciences and humanities*. Reading, MA: Addison-Wesley.

Holt, Robert T., and John E. Turner. (1970). The methodology of comparative research. In *The methodology of comparative research*, edited by R. Holt and J. Turner, pp. 1–20. New York: Free Press.

Holub, Robert C. (1991). *Jürgen Habermas: Critic in the public sphere*. New York: Routledge.

Holy, Ladislav. (1984). Theory, methodology and the research process. In *Ethnographic research: A guide to general conduct*, edited by R. F. Ellen, pp. 13–34. Orlando: Academic Press.

Homan, Roger. (1980). The ethics of covert methods. *British Journal of Sociology*, 31:46–57.

Honigmann, John J. (1982). Sampling in ethnographic fieldwork. In *Field research*, edited by R. G. Burgess, pp. 79–90. Boston: Allen and Unwin.

Horan, Patrick. (1987). Theoretical models in social history research. *Social Science History*, 11:379–400.

Horn, Robert V. (1993). *Statistical indicators for the economic and social sciences*. Cambridge: Cambridge University Press.

Hornstein, Gail A. (1988). Quantifying psychological phenomena: Debates, dilemmas and implications. In *The rise of experimentation in American psychology*, edited by Jill G. Morawski, pp. 1–34. New Haven, CT: Yale University Press.

Horowitz, Irving Louis. (1965). The life and death of Project Camelot. *Transaction*, 3:3–7, 44–47.

House, Ernest R. (1980). *Evaluating with validity*. Beverly Hills, CA: Sage.

Hoy, David Couzens. (1994). *Critical theory*. Cambridge, MA: Blackwell.

Hubbard, Raymond, and Eldon Little. (1988). Promised contributions to charity and mail survey responses: Replication with extension. *Public Opinion Quarterly*, 52:223–230.

Huck, Schuyler W., and Howard M. Sandler. (1979). *Rival hypotheses: Alternative interpretations of data based conclusions*, New York: Harper & Row.

Humphreys, Laud. (1975). *Tearoom trade: Impersonal sex in public places*, enlarged ed. Chicago: Aldine.

Hunt, Jennifer. (1984). The development of rapport through the negotiation of gender in field work among police. *Human Organization*, 45:283–296.

Hunt, Lynn. (1989). Introduction. In *The new cultural history*, edited by Lynn Hunt, pp. 1–22. Berkeley: University of California Press.

Hunter, Albert. (1993). Local knowledge and local power: Notes on the ethnography of local community elites. *Journal of Contemporary Ethnography*, 22:36–58.

Hunter, James Davidson. (1991). *Culture wars: The struggle to define America*. New York: Basic Books.

Hunter, John E., Frank L. Schmidt, and Gregg B. Jackson. (1982). *Meta-analysis: Cumulating research findings across studies*. Beverly Hills, CA: Sage.

Hyman, Herbert H. (1975). *Interviewing in social research*. Chicago: University of Chicago Press.

Hyman, Herbert H. (1991). *Taking society's measure: A personal history of survey research*. New York: Russell Sage.

Hymes, Dell. (1970). Linguistic aspects of comparative political research. In

The methodology of comparative research, edited by Robert T. Holt and John E. Turner, pp. 295–341. New York: Free Press.

Hymes, Dell. (1983). *Essays in the history of linguistic anthropology*. Philadelphia: John Benjamins Publishers.

Inverarity, James M. (1976). Populism and lynching in Louisiana, 1889–1896: A test of Erikson's theory of the relationship between boundary crisis and repressive justice. *American Sociological Review*, 41:262–280.

Isaac, Larry W., and Larry J. Griffin. (1989). A historicism in time series analysis of historical process: Critique, redirection, and illustrations from U.S. labor history. *American Sociological Review*, 54:873–890.

Jackson, Bruce. (1978). Killing time: Life in the Arkansas penitentiary. *Qualitative Sociology*, 1:21–32.

Jackson, Bruce. (1987). *Fieldwork*. Urbana: University of Illinois Press.

Jackson, David J., and Edgar F. Borgatta, eds. (1981). *Factor analysis and measurement in sociological research*. Beverly Hills, CA: Sage.

Jacob, Herbert. (1984). *Using published data: Errors and remedies*. Beverly Hills, CA: Sage.

Jacobs, Jerry. (1974). *Fun City: An ethnographic study of a retirement community*. New York: Holt, Rinehart and Winston.

Jaeger, Richard M. (1983). *Statistics as a spectator sport*. Beverly Hills, CA: Sage.

Johnson, Bruce. (1982). Missionaries, tourists and traders. *Studies in Symbolic Interaction*, 4:115–150.

Johnson, David Richard, and James C. Creech. (1983). Ordinal measures in multiple indicator models: A simulation study of categorization error. *American Sociological Review*, 48:398–407.

Johnson, David W., and Roger T. Johnson. (1985). Relationships between black and white students in intergroup cooperation and competition. *Journal of Social Psychology*, 125:421–428.

Johnson, John M. (1975). *Doing field research*. New York: Free Press.

Johnson, P. Timonty, James G. Hougland, Jr., and Richard R. Clayton. (1989). Obtaining reports of sensitive behavior: A comparison of substance-use reports from telephone and face-to-face interviews. *Social Science Quarterly*, 70:173–183.

Johnson, Stephen D. (1985). Religion as a defense in a mock-jury trial.

Journal of Social Psychology, 125:213–220.

Jones, Gareth Stedman. (1976). From historical sociology to theoretical history. *British Journal of Sociology*, 27:295–305.

Jones, Gareth Stedman. (1983). *Languages of class*. New York: Cambridge University Press.

Jones, J. H. (1981). *Bad blood: The Tuskegee syphilis experiment*. New York: Free Press.

Jones, Wesley H. (1979). Generalizing mail survey inducement methods: Populations' interactions with anonymity and sponsorship. *Public Opinion Quarterly*, 43:102–111.

Jordan, Lawrence A., Alfred C. Marcus, and Leo G. Reeder. (1980). Response styles in telephone and household interviewing: A field experiment. *Public Opinion Quarterly*, 44:210–222.

Jorgensen, Danny L., and Lin Jorgensen. (1982). Social meanings of the occult. *Sociological Quarterly*, 23:373–389.

Josephson, Paul R. (1988). The FBI menaces academic freedom. *New York Times*, November 1, 1988.

Junker, Buford H. (1960). *Field work*. Chicago: University of Chicago Press.

Juster, F. Thomas, and Kenneth C. Land, eds. (1981). *Social accounting systems: Essays on the state of the art*. New York: Academic Press.

Kalberg, Stephen. (1994). *Max Weber's comparative-historical sociology*. Chicago: University of Chicago Press.

Kalmijn, Matthijus. (1991). Shifting boundaries: Trends in religious and educational homogamy. *American Sociological Review*, 56:786–801.

Kalton, Graham. (1983). *Introduction to survey sampling*. Beverly Hills, CA: Sage.

Kandel, Denise B. (1980). Drug and drinking behavior among youth. *Annual Review of Sociology*, 6:235–265.

Kane, Emily W., and Laura J. MacAulay. (1993). Interview gender and gender attitudes. *Public Opinion Quarterly*, 57:1–28.

Kaplan, Abraham. (1964). *The conduct of inquiry: Methodology for behavioral science*. New York: Harper & Row.

Karp, David A. (1973). Hiding in pornographic bookstores: A reconsideration of the nature of urban anonymity. *Urban Life*, 1:427–452.

Karp, David A. (1980). Observing behavior in public places: Problems and strategies. In *Fieldwork experience*, edited by W. B. Shaffir, R. A. Stebbins, and A. Turowetz, pp.

82–97. New York: St. Martin's Press.

Karweit, Nancy, and Edmund D. Meyers, Jr. (1983). Computers in survey research. In *Handbook of survey research*, edited by Peter H. Rossi, James D. Wright, and Andy B. Anderson, pp. 379–414. Orlando, FL: Academic Press.

Katovich, Michael A., and Ron L. Diamond. (1986). Selling time: Situated transactions in a noninstitutional setting. *Sociological Quarterly*, 27:253–271.

Katz, Jay. (1972). *Experimentation with human beings*. New York: Russell Sage Foundation.

Katzer, Jeffrey, Kenneth H. Cook, and Wayne W. Crouch. (1982). *Evaluating information: A guide for users of social science research*, 2nd ed. Reading, MA: Addison-Wesley.

Katzer, Jeffrey, Kenneth H. Cook, and Wayne W. Crouch. (1991). *Evaluating information: A guide for users of social science research*, 3rd ed. New York: McGraw Hill.

Keat, Russell. (1981). *The politics of social theory: Habermas, Freud and the critique of positivism*. Chicago: University of Chicago Press.

Keat, Russell, and John Urry. (1975). *Social theory as science*. London: Routledge and Kegan Paul.

Keeter, Scott. (1995). Estimating telephone noncoverage bias with a telephone survey. *Public Opinion Quarterly*, 59:196–217.

Keith, Verna M., and Cedric Herring. (1991). Skin tone and stratification in the black community. *American Journal of Sociology*, 97:760–778.

Keller, Bill. (1988). Ups and downs of conducting the poll. *New York Times*, May 27, 1988.

Keller, Bill. (1989). Prying where it counts: Into census. *New York Times*, January 19, 1989.

Keller, Evelyn Fox. (1983). *A feeling for the organism: The life and work of Barbara McClintock*. New York: W. H. Freeman.

Keller, Evelyn Fox. (1985). *Reflections on gender and science*. New Haven: Yale University Press.

Keller, Evelyn Fox. (1990). Gender and science. In *Feminist research methods*, edited by Joyce McCarl Nielsen, pp. 41–57. Boulder: Westview.

Kelman, Herbert. (1982). Ethical issues in different social science methods. In *Ethical issues in social science research*, edited by Tom Beauchamp, R. Faden, R. J. Wallace, and L. Walters, pp. 40–99. Baltimore: Johns Hopkins University Press.

Kemp, Jeremy, and R. F. Ellen. (1984). Informants. In *Ethnographic re-*

search: A guide to general conduct, edited by R. F. Ellen, pp. 224–236. Orlando: Academic Press.

Kenen, Regina. (1982). Soapsuds, space and sociability: A participant observation of a laundromat. *Urban Life*, 11:163–184.

Kent, Stephen A. (1992). Historical sociology. In *Encyclopedia of sociology*, Vol. 2, edited by Edgar and Marie Borgatta, pp. 837–843. New York: Macmillan.

Kercher, Kyle. (1992). Quasi-experimental research designs. In *Encyclopedia of sociology*, Vol. 3, edited by Edgar and Marie Borgatta, pp. 1595–1613. New York: Macmillan.

Kerlinger, Fred N. (1979). *Behavioral research: A conceptual approach*. New York: Holt, Rinehart and Winston.

Kidder, Louise H. (1982). Face validity from multiple perspectives. In *Forms of validity in research*, edited by David Brinberg and Louise H. Kidder, pp. 41–57. San Francisco: Jossey-Bass.

Kidder, Louise H., and Charles M. Judd. (1986). *Research methods in social relations*, 5th ed. New York: Holt, Rinehart and Winston.

Kiecolt, K. Jill, and Laura E. Nathan. (1985). *Secondary analysis of survey data*. Beverly Hills, CA: Sage.

Kim, Jae-On, and Charles W. Mueller. (1978). *Introduction to factor analysis: What it is and how to do it*. Beverly Hills, CA: Sage.

Kimmel, Allan J. (1988). *Ethics and values in applied social research*. Newbury Park, CA: Sage.

Kincheloe, Joe L., and Peter L. McLaren. (1994). Rethinking critical theory and qualitative research. In *Handbook of qualitative research*, edited by Norman Denzin and Yvonna Lincoln, pp. 138–157. Thousand Oaks, CA: Sage.

King, Gary, Robert O. Keohane, and Sidney Verba. (1994). *Designing social inquiry: Scientific inference in qualitative research*. Princeton, NJ: Princeton University Press.

Kirk, Jerome, and Marc L. Miller. (1986). *Reliability and validity in qualitative research*. Beverly Hills, CA: Sage.

Kish, L. (1965). *Survey sampling*. New York: Wiley.

Kleinman, Sherry. (1980). Learning the ropes as fieldwork analysis. In *Fieldwork experience*, edited by W. B. Shaffir, R. A. Stebbins, and A. Turowetz, pp. 171–183. New York: St. Martin's Press.

Kleinman, Sherryl, and Martha A. Copp. (1993). *Emotions and field work*. Thousand Oaks, CA: Sage.

Knapp, Peter. (1990). The revival of macrosociology: Methodological issues of discontiuity in comparative-historical theory. *Sociological Forum* 5:545–567.

Knoke, David. (1993). Networks of elite structure and decision-making. *Sociological Methods and Research*, 22:23–45.

Kohn, Melvin L. (1987). Cross-national research as an analytic strategy. *American Sociological Review*, 52:713–731.

Kohn, Melvin L., ed. (1989). *Cross-national research in sociology*. Newbury Park, CA: Sage.

Koretz, Daniel. (1988). Arriving in Lake Wobegon: Are standardized tests exaggerating achievement and distorting instruction? *American Educator*, 12, Summer, pp. 8–15.

Kornblum, William. (1974). *Blue collar community*. Chicago: University of Chicago Press.

Kraemer, Helena Chmura, and Sue Thiemann. (1987). *How many subjects? Statistical power analysis in research*. Newbury Park, CA: Sage.

Krathwohl, D. R. (1965). *How to prepare a research proposal*. Syracuse, NY: Syracuse University Bookstore.

Krippendorff, Klaus. (1980). *Content analysis: An introduction to its methodology*. Beverly Hills, CA: Sage.

Krosnick, Jon A., and Robert P. Abelson. (1992). The case for measuring attitude strength in surveys. In *Questions about questions: Inquiries into the cognitive bases of surveys*, edited by Judith M. Turner, pp. 177–203. New York: Russell Sage Foundation.

Krosnick, Jon A., and Duane F. Alwin. (1988). A test of the form-resistant correlation hypothesis: Ratings, rankings and the measurement of values. *Public Opinion Quarterly*, 52:526–538.

Krueger, Richard A. (1988). *Focus groups: A practical guide for applied research*. Beverly Hills, CA: Sage.

Kuhn, Thomas S. (1970). *The structure of scientific revolutions*, 2nd ed. Chicago: University of Chicago Press.

Kuhn, Thomas S. (1979). The relations between history and the history of science. In *Interpretive social science: A reader*, edited by Paul Rabinow and William Sullivan. Berkeley: University of California Press.

Kurz, Demie. (1987). Emergency department responses to battered women: Resistance to medicalization. *Social Problems*, 34:69–81.

Kusserow, Richard P. (1989). *Misconduct in scientific research*.

Report of the Inspector General of the U.S. Department of Health and Human Services, March 1989. Washington, DC: Department of Health and Human Services.

Kviz, Frederick J. (1984). Bias in a directory sample for mail survey of rural households. *Public Opinion Quarterly*, 48:801–806.

Labaw, Patricia J. (1980). *Advanced questionnaire design*. Cambridge, MA: Abt Books.

Lachmann, Richard. (1988). Graffiti as career and ideology. *American Journal of Sociology* 94:251–272.

Lachmann, Richard. (1989). Elite conflict and state formation in 16th and 17th century England and France. *American Sociological Review*, 54:141–162.

Lagemann, Ellen Condliffe. (1989). *The politics of knowledge: The Carnegie Corporation, philanthropy and public policy*. Chicago: University of Chicago.

Land, Kenneth. (1992). Social indicators. *Encyclopedia of sociology*, Vol. 4, edited by Edgar and Marie Borgatta, pp. 1844–1850. New York: Macmillan.

Lane, Michael. (1970). *Structuralism*. London: Jonathan Cape.

Lang, Eric. (1992). Hawthorne effect. *Encyclopedia of sociology*, Vol. 2., edited by Edgar and Marie Borgatta, pp. 793–794, New York: Macmillan, 793–794.

Laslett, Barbara. (1980). Beyond methodology. *American Sociological Review*, 45:214–228.

Laslett, Barbara. (1992). Gender in/and social history. *Social Science History* 16:177–196.

Laxer, Gordon. (1989). *Open for business: The roots of foreign ownership in Canada*. New York: Oxford University Press.

Layder, Derek. (1993). *New strategies in social research*. Cambridge MA: Polity.

Lazarsfeld, Paul F., and Jeffrey G. Reitz. (1975). *An introduction to applied sociology*. Amsterdam: Elsevier.

Lazere, Donald, ed. (1987). *American media and mass culture: Left perspectives*. Berkeley: University of California Press.

Lee, Alfred McClung. (1978). *Sociology for whom?* New York: Oxford University Press.

Lee, Harper. (1960). *To kill a mockingbird*. New York: Warner Books.

Leggett, Glenn, C. David Mean, and William Charvat. (1965). *Prentice-Hall handbook for writers*, 4th ed. Englewood Cliffs, NJ: Prentice-Hall.

Leiter, Kenneth. (1980). *A primer on ethnomethodology*. New York: Oxford University Press.

LeMasters, E. E. (1975). *Blue collar aristocrats*. Madison: University of Wisconsin Press.

Lemert, Charles. (1979). Science, religion and secularization. *Sociological Quarterly*, 20:445–461.

Lemert, Charles, ed. (1981). *French sociology: Rupture and renewal since 1968*. New York: Columbia University Press.

Lenski, Gerhard E. (1966). *Power and privilege*. New York: McGraw-Hill.

Lenzer, Gertrud, ed. (1975). *Auguste Comte and positivism: Essential writings*. New York: Harper & Row.

Lesiuer, Henry R., and Joseph F. Sheley. (1987). Illegal appended enterprises: Selling the lines. *Social Problems*, 34:249–260.

Lessler, Judith T. (1984). Measurement error in surveys. In *Surveying subjective phenomena*, Vol. 2, edited by Charles Turner and Elizabeth Martin, pp. 405–440. New York: Russell Sage Foundation.

Lester, Marilyn, and Stuart C. Hadden. (1980). Ethnomethodology and grounded theory methodology: An integration of perspective and method. *Urban Life*, 9:3–33.

Lever, Janet. (1978). Sex differences in the complexity of children's play and games. *American Sociological Review*, 43:471–483.

Lever, Janet. (1981). Multiple methods of data collection: A note on divergence. *Urban Life*, 10:199–213.

Levine, Joel H. (1993). *Exceptions are the rule: An inquiry into methods in the social sciences*. Boulder, CO: Westview.

Lewis, George H., and Jonathan F. Lewis. (1980). The dog in the nighttime: Negative evidence in social research. *British Journal of Sociology*, 31:544–558.

Lieberson, Stanley. (1985). *Making it count: The improvement of social research and theory*. Berkeley: University of California Press.

Lieberson, Stanley. (1991). Small N's and big conclusions: An examination of the reasoning of comparative studies based on a small number of cases. *Social Forces*, 70:101–320.

Liebetrau, Albert M. (1983). *Measures of association*. Beverly Hills, CA: Sage.

Liebman, Robert, John R. Sutton, and Robert Wuthnow. (1988). Exploring social sources of denominationalism: Schisms in American Protestant denominations, 1890–1980. *American Sociological Review*, 53:343–352.

Liebow, Elliot. (1967). *Talley's corner*. Boston: Little, Brown.

Lifton, Robert J. (1986). *Nazi doctors*. New York: Basic Books.

Light, Ivan, and Edna Bonacich.

(1988). *Immigrant entrepreneurs: Koreans in Los Angeles, 1965–1982*. Berkeley: University of California Press.

Light, Richard J., and David B. Pillemer. (1984). *Summing up: The science of reviewing research*. Cambridge, MA: Harvard University Press.

Likert, Rensis. (1970). A technique for the measurement of attitudes. In *Attitude measurement*, edited by Gene Summers, pp. 149–158. Chicago: Rand McNally.

Lindblom, Charles E., and David K. Cohen. (1979). *Usable knowledge: Social science and social problem solving*. New Haven, CT: Yale University Press.

Lindzey, Gardner, and Donn Byrne. (1968). Measurement of social choice and interpersonal attractiveness. In *The handbook of social psychology*, Vol. 2: Research methods, edited by Gardner Lindzey and Elliott Aronson, pp. 452–525. Reading, MA: Addison-Wesley.

Lipset, Seymour Martin. (1968). History and sociology: Some methodological considerations. In *Sociology and history: Methods*, edited by S. M. Lipset and R. Hofstadter, pp. 20–58. New York: Basic Books.

Little, Daniel. (1991). *Varieties of social explanation: An introduction to the philosophy of science*. Boulder, CO: Westview.

Lloyd, Christopher. (1986). *Explanation in social history*. New York: Basil Blackwell.

Locke, Lawrence F., Warren Wyrick Spirduso, and Stephen J. Silverman. (1987). *Proposals that work: A guide for planning dissertations and grant proposals*, 2nd ed. Beverly Hills, CA: Sage.

Loewenstein, Gaither. (1985). The new underclass: A contemporary sociological dilemma. *Sociological Quarterly*, 26:35–48.

Lofland, John. (1966). *Doomsday cult*. Englewood Cliffs, NJ: Prentice-Hall.

Lofland, John. (1974). Styles of reporting qualitative field research. *American Sociologist*, 9:101–111.

Lofland, John. (1976). *Doing social life: The qualitative study of human interaction in natural settings*. New York: Wiley.

Lofland, John, and Lyn H. Lofland. (1984). *Analyzing social settings*, 2nd ed. Belmont, CA: Wadsworth.

Lofland, John, and Lyn H. Lofland. (1995). *Analyzing social settings*, 3rd ed. Belmont, CA: Wadsworth.

Lofland, Lyn H. (1972). Self management in public settings: Parts I and II. *Urban Life*, 1:93–108, 217–231.

Loftus, Elizabeth, Mark Klinger, Kyle

Smith, and Judith Fiedler. (1990). A tale of two questions: Benefit of asking more than one question. *Public Opinion Quarterly*, 54:330–345.

Loftus, Elizabeth, Kyle D. Smith, Mark R. Klinger, and Judith Fiedler. (1992). Memory and mismemory of health events. In *Questions about questions: Inquiries into the cognitive bases of surveys*, edited by Judith M. Turner, pp. 102–137. New York: Russell Sage Foundation.

Long, J. Scott. (1976). Estimation and hypothesis testing in linear models containing measurement error: A review of Joreskog's model for the analysis of covariance structures. *Sociological Methods and Research*, 5:157–206.

Long, J. Scott. (1978). Productivity and academic positions in a scientific career. *American Sociological Review*, 43:889–908.

Longino, Helen E. (1990). *Science as social knowledge: Values and objectivity in scientific inquiry*. Princeton, NJ: Princeton University Press.

Lorr, Maurice. (1983). *Cluster analysis for social scientists: Techniques for analyzing and simplifying complex blocks of data*. San Francisco: Jossey-Bass.

Lovdal, Lynn T. (1989). Sex role messages in television commercials: An update. *Sex Roles*, 20:715–724.

Lovin-Smith, Lynn, and Charles Brody. (1989). Interruptions in group discussions: The effects of gender and group composition. *American Sociological Review*, 54:424–435.

Lowenthal, David. (1985). *The past is a foreign country*. New York: Cambridge University Press.

Lynd, Robert S. (1964). *Knowledge for what? The place of social science in American culture*. New York: Grove. (Originally published in 1939 by Princeton University Press.)

Luebke, Barbara F. (1989). Out of focus: Images of men and women in newspaper photographs. *Sex Roles*, 20:121–133.

MacFarlane, Alan. (1977). *Reconstructing historical communities*. New York: Cambridge University Press.

MacIver, A. M. (1968). Levels of explanation in history. In *Readings in the philosophy of the social sciences*, edited by M. Brodbeck, pp. 304–316. New York: Macmillan.

MacKeun, Michael B. (1984). Reality, the Press and Citizens Political Agendas. In *Surveying subjective phenomena*, Vol. 2, edited by Charles Turner and Elizabeth Martin, pp. 443–473. New York: Russell Sage Foundation.

Maier, Mark H. (1991). *The data game:*

Controversies in social science statistics. Armonk: M. E. Sharpe.

Maines, David R., William Shaffir, and Allan Turowetz. (1980). Leaving the field in ethnographic research. In *The fieldwork experience: Qualitative approaches to social research,* edited by William B. Shaffir, R. Stebbins, and A. Turowetz, pp. 261–280. New York: St. Martin's.

Makkai, Toni, and John Braithwaite. (1993). Praise, price and corporate compliance. *International Journal of the Sociology of Law,* 21:73–91.

Maloney, Dennis M. (1984). *Protection of human research subjects: A practical guide to federal laws and regulations.* New York: Plenum.

Mann, Floyd C. (1970). Human relations skills in social research. In *Qualitative methodology,* edited by W. J. Filstead. Chicago: Markham.

Mannheim, Karl. (1936). *Ideology and utopia.* New York: Harcourt, Brace and World.

Mariampolski, Hyman, and Dana C. Hughes. (1978). The use of personal documents in historical sociology. *The American Sociologist,* 13:104–113.

Markoff, John, Gilbert Shapiro, and Sasha R. Weitman. (1974). Toward the integration of content analysis and general methodology. In *Sociological methodology, 1974,* edited by David Heise, pp. 1–58. San Francisco: Jossey-Bass.

Marradi, Alberto. (1981). Factor analysis as an aid in the formation and refinement of empirically useful concepts. In *Factor analysis and measurement in social research: A multi-dimensional perspective,* edited by David Jackson and Edgar Borgatta, pp. 11–50. Beverly Hills, CA: Sage.

Marsh, Catherine. (1982). *The survey method: The contribution of surveys to sociological explanation.* Boston: George Allen and Unwin.

Marsh, Catherine. (1984). Do polls affect what people think? In *Surveying subjective phenomena,* Vol. 2, edited by Charles Turner and Elizabeth Martin, pp. 565–592. New York: Russell Sage Foundation.

Marshall, Catherine. (1985). Appropriate criteria of trustworthiness and goodness for qualitative research on educational organizations. *Quality and Quantity,* 19:353–373.

Marshall, Catherine, and Gretchen B. Rossman. (1989). *Designing qualitative research.* Beverly Hills, CA: Sage.

Marshall, Susan E. (1986). In defense of separate spheres: Class and politics in the antisuffrage movement. *Social Forces,* 65:327–351.

Marshall, Victor W. (1975). Socialization for impending death in a retirement village. *American Journal of Sociology,* 80:1124–1144.

Martin, Elizabeth. (1985). Surveys as social indicators: Problems of monitoring trends. In *Handbook of survey research,* edited by Peter Rossi, James Wright, and Andy Anderson, pp. 677–743. Orlando, FL: Academic.

Martin, Jay. (1973). *The dialectical imagination.* Boston: Little, Brown.

Martin, John L., and Laura Dean. (1993). Developing a community sample of gay men for an epidemiological study of AIDS. In *Research on sensitive topics,* edited by Claire Renzetti and Raymond Lee, pp. 82–100. Thousand Oaks, CA: Sage.

Marvell, Thomas R, and Carlisle E. Moody. (1995). The impact of enhanced prison terms for felonies committed with guns. *Criminology,* 33: 247–281.

Marx, Karl, and Friedrich Engels. (1947). *The German ideology, Parts I & III,* edited with introduction by R. Pascal. New York: International Publishers.

Masterman, Margaret. (1970). The nature of a paradigm. In *Criticism and the growth of knowledge,* edited by Imre Lakatos and Alan Musgrove, pp. 59–90. Cambridge: Cambridge University Press.

Mayer, Charles S., and Cindy Piper. (1982). A note on the importance of layout in self-administered questionnaires. *Journal of Marketing Research,* 19:390–391.

Mayhew, Bruce H. (1980). Structuralism versus individualism, Part I: Shadowboxing in the dark. *Social Forces,* 59:335–375.

Mayhew, Bruce H. (1981). Structuralism versus individualism, Part II: Ideological and other obfuscations. *Social Forces,* 59: 627–648.

Maynard, Douglas W. (1985). On the functions of conflict among children. *American Sociological Review,* 50:207–223.

McCabe, Donald L. (1992). The influence of situational ethics on cheating among college students. *Sociological Inquiry,* 62:365–374.

McCall, George. (1969). Quality control in participant observation. In *Issues in participant observation,* edited by George McCall and J. L. Simmons, pp. 128–141. Reading, MA: Addison-Wesley.

McCall, George. (1984). Systematic field observation. *Annual Review of Sociology,* 10:263–282.

McCall, Michal. (1980). Who and where are the artists? In *The fieldwork experience: Qualitative approaches to social research,* edited by William B. Shaffir, R. Stebbins, and A. Turowetz, pp. 145–158. New York: St. Martin's.

McCarthy, Thomas. (1978). *The critical theory of Jurgen Habermas.* Cambridge, MA: MIT Press.

McCartney, James L. (1984). Setting priorities for research: New politics for the social sciences. *Sociological Quarterly,* 25:437–455.

McConaghy, Maureen. (1975). Maximum possible error in Guttman scales. *Public Opinion Quarterly,* 39:343–357.

McCracken, Grant. (1988). *The long interview.* Thousand Oaks, CA: Sage.

McDaniel, Timothy. (1978). Meaning and comparative concepts. *Theory and Society,* 6:93–118.

McDiarmid, Garnet. (1971). *Teaching prejudice: A content analysis of social studies textbooks authorized for use in Ontario.* Ontario: Ontario Institute for Studies in Education.

McFarland, Sam G. (1981). Effects of question order on survey responses. *Public Opinion Quarterly,* 45: 208–215.

McGrath, Joseph, Joanne Martin, and Richard A. Kulka. (1982). *Judgment calls in research.* Beverly Hills, CA: Sage.

McIver, John P., and Edward G. Carmines. (1981). *Unidimensional scaling.* Beverly Hills, CA: Sage.

McKee, J. McClendon, and David J. O'Brien. (1988). Question order effects on the determinants of subjective well being. *Public Opinion Quarterly,* 52:351–364.

McKelvie, Stuart J., and Linda A. Schamer. (1988). Effects of night, passengers and sex on driver behavior at stop signs. *Journal of Social Psychology,* 128:658–690.

McKeown, Bruce. (1988). *Q methodology.* Thousand Oaks, CA: Sage.

McLennan, Gregor. (1981). *Marxism and the methodologies of history.* London: Verso.

McMurtry, John. (1978). *The structure of Marx's world view.* Princeton, NJ: Princeton University Press.

McNall, Scott G. (1988). *The road to rebellion.* Chicago: University of Chicago Press.

McQuaire, Donald. (1978). Marx and the method of successive approximations. *Sociological Quarterly,* 20:431–435.

McQuaire, Donald. (1979). Reply to Wardell. *Sociological Quarterly,* 20:431–435.

Meadows, A. J. (1974). *Communication in science.* Toronto: Butterworths.

Mehan, Hugh. (1973). Assessing children's language using abilities (with discussion). In *Comparative social research*, edited by M. Armer and A. Grimshaw, pp. 309–345. New York: Wiley.

Mehan, Hugh, and Houston Wood. (1975). *The reality of ethnomethodology*. New York: Wiley.

Melbin, Murray. (1978). Night as frontier. *American Sociological Review*, 43:3–22.

Mendenhall, William, Lyman Ott, and Richard L. Scheaffer. (1971). *Elementary survey sampling*. Belmont, CA: Duxbury Press.

Merton, Robert K. (1957). *Social theory and social structure*. New York: Free Press.

Merton, Robert K. (1967). *On theoretical sociology: Five essays, old and new*. New York: Free Press.

Merton, Robert K. (1970). *Science, technology and society in seventeenth century England*. New York: Harper & Row.

Merton, Robert K. (1973). *The sociology of science*. Chicago: University of Chicago Press.

Miles, Matthew B., and A. Michael Huberman. (1984). *Qualitative data analysis*. Beverly Hills, CA: Sage.

Miles, Matthew B., and A. Michael Huberman. (1994). *Qualitative data analysis*, 2nd ed. Thousand Oaks, CA: Sage.

Milgram, Stanley. (1963). Behavioral study of obedience. *Journal of Abnormal and Social Psychology*, 6:371–378.

Milgram, Stanley. (1965). Some conditions of obedience and disobedience to authority. *Human Relations*, 18:57–76.

Milgram, Stanley. (1974). *Obedience to authority*. New York: Harper & Row.

Miller, Delbert C. (1991). *Handbook of research design and social measurement*, 5th ed. Newbury Park, CA: Sage.

Miller, Gale. (1983). Holding clients accountable: The micro-politics of trouble in a work incentive program. *Social Problems*, 31:139–151.

Miller, Gale. (1992). Case studies. In *Encyclopedia of sociology*, Vol. 1, edited by Edgar and Marie Borgatta, pp. 167–172. New York: Macmillan.

Miller, Richard. (1987). *Fact and method: Explanation, confirmation and reality in the natural and social Sciences*. Princeton, NJ: Princeton University Press.

Miller, William L. (1983). *The survey method in the social and political sciences: Achievements, failures and prospects*. London: Frances Pinter.

Milligan, John D. (1979). The treatment of historical source. *History and Theory*, 18:177–196.

Mills, C. Wright. (1959). *The sociological imagination*. New York: Oxford University Press.

Mishler, Elliot G. (1986). *Research interviewing: Context and narrative*. Cambridge, MA: Harvard University Press.

Mitchell, J. Clyde. (1984). Case studies. In *Ethnographic research: A guide to general conduct*, edited by R. F. Ellen, pp. 237–241. Orlando, FL: Academic Press.

Mitchell, Mark, and Janina Jolley. (1988). *Research design explained*. New York: Holt, Rinehart and Winston.

Mitchell, Richard G., Jr. (1993). *Secrecy and fieldwork*. Thousand Oaks, CA: Sage.

Mitroff, Ian. (1974). Norms and counter-norms in a select group of the Apollo moon scientists: A case study of ambivalence of scientists. *American Sociology Review*, 39: 579–595.

Monoghan, Peter. (1993a). Facing jail, a sociologist raises question about a scholar's right to protect sources. *Chronicle of Higher Education*, April 7, 1993, p. A10.

Monoghan, Peter. (1993b). Sociologist is jailed for refusing to testify about research subject. *Chronicle of Higher Education*, May 26, 1993, p. A10.

Monaghan, Peter. (1993c). Sociologist jailed because he "wouldn't snitch" ponders the way research ought to be done. *Chronicle of Higher Education*, September 1, 1993, pp. A8–A9.

Mooney, Linda, and Robert B. Gramling. (1991). Asking threatening questions and situational framing: The effects of decomposing survey items. *Sociological Quarterly*, 32:277–288.

Moore, Barrington, Jr. (1966). *The social origins of dictatorship and democracy*. Boston: Beacon Press.

Moore, Joan. (1973). Social constraints on sociological knowledge: Academic and research concerning minorities. *Social Problems*, 21:65–77.

Moore, Joan, Diego Vigil, and Robert Garcia. (1983). Residence and territoriality in Chicago gangs. *Social Problems*. 31:182–194.

Morrow, Raymond Allan. (1994). *Critical theory and methodology*. Thousand Oaks, CA: Sage.

Morse, Janice M. (1994). Designing funded qualitative research. In *Handbook of qualitative research*. Edited by Norman K. Denzin and Yvonna S. Lincoln, pp. 220–235. Thousand Oaks, CA: Sage.

Moser, C. A., and G. Kalton. (1972). *Survey methods in social investigation*. New York: Basic Books.

Mostyn, Barbara. (1985). The content analysis of qualitative research data:

A dynamic approach. In *The research interview; Uses and approaches*, edited by Michael Brenner, Jennifer Brown, and David Canter, pp. 115–145, New York: Academic Press.

Mulkay, Michael. (1979). *Science and the sociology of knowledge*. London: George Allen and Unwin.

Mullins, Carolyn J. (1977). *A guide to writing and publishing in the social and behavioral sciences*. New York: Wiley.

Mullins, Nicholas C. (1971). *The art of theory: Construction and use*. New York: Harper & Row.

Mullins, Nicholas C. (1973). *Theory and theory groups in American sociology*. New York: Harper & Row.

Murdock, George P. (1967). Ethnographic atlas. *Ethnology*, 6: 109–236.

Murdock, George P. (1971). *Outline of cultural materials*, 4th ed. New Haven. CT: Human Relations Area Files.

Murphey, Murray G. (1973). *Our knowledge of the historical past*. Indianapolis: Bobbs-Merrill.

Murray, Shoon. (1992). Turning an elite cross-sectional survey into a panel study while protecting anonymity. *Journal of Conflict Resolution*, 36:586–595.

Myerhoff, Barbara. (1989). So what do you want from us here? In *In the field*, edited by Carolyn Smith and William Kornblum, pp. 83–90. New York: Praeger.

Myers, Gloria, and A. V. Margavio. (1983). The black bourgeoisie and reference group change: A content analysis of Ebony. *Qualitative sociology*, 6:291–307.

Myrdal, Gunnar. (1973). The beam in our eyes. In *Comparative research methods*, edited by D. Warwick and S. Osherson, pp. 89–99. Englewood Cliffs, NJ: Prentice-Hall.

Nadeau, Richard, Richard Miemi, and Jeffrey Levine. (1993). Innumeracy about minority population. *Public Opinion Quarterly*, 57:332–347.

Nafziger, E. Wayne. (1988). *Inequality in Africa: Political elites, proletariat, peasants and the poor*. New York: Cambridge University Press.

Nagin, Daniel S., David P. Farrington, and Terrie E. Moffitt. (1995). Life course trajectories of different types of offenders. *Criminology*, 33:111–139.

Namenwirth, J. Z. (1970). Prestige newspapers and assessment of elite opinions. *Journalism Quarterly*, 47:318–323.

Naroll, Raoul. (1968). Some thoughts on comparative method in cultural anthropology. In *Methodology in social research*, edited by H.

Blalock and A. Blalock, pp. 236–277. New York: McGraw-Hill.

Nash, Jeffrey E., and David W. McCurdy. (1989). Cultural knowledge and systems of knowing. *Sociological Inquiry*, 59:117–126.

Neapolitan, Jerry. (1988). The effects of different types of praise and criticism on performance. *Sociological Focus*, 21:223–232.

Nederhof, Anton J. (1986). Effects of research experiences of respondents. *Quality and Quantity*, 20:277–284.

Nelkin, Dorothy. (1982a). Forbidden research: Limits on inquiry in the social sciences. In *Ethical issues in social science research*, edited by Tom L. Beauchamp, R. Faden, R. J. Wallace, and L. Walters, pp. 163–174. Baltimore: Johns Hopkins University Press.

Nelkin, Dorothy. (1982b). Intellectual property: The control of scientific information. *Science*, 216 (May): 704–708.

Neuberg, Leland Gerson. (1988). Distorted transmission: A case study in the diffusion of "social scientific" research. *Theory and Society*, 17: 487–526.

Neuman, W. Lawrence. (1992). Gender, race and age differences in student definitions of sexual harassment. *Wisconsin Sociologist*, 29: 63–75.

Neuman, W. Russell, Marion R. Just, and Ann N. Crigler. (1992). *Common knowledge: News and the construction of political meaning*. Chicago: University of Chicago Press.

Noelle-Neumann, Elisabeth. (1974). Spiral of silence: A theory of public opinion. *Journal of Communication*, 24:43–51.

Noelle-Neumann, Elisabeth. (1984). *The spiral of silence: Public opinion our social skin*. Chicago: University of Chicago Press.

Norris, M. (1981). Problems in the analysis of soft data and some suggested solutions. *Sociology*, 15:337–351.

Norusis, Marija J. (1986). *The SPSS-X guide to data analysis*. Chicago: SPSS, Inc.

Novick, Peter. (1988). *That noble dream: The "objectivity question" and the American historical profession*. New York: Cambridge University Press.

Nowak, Stefan. (1989). Comparative studies and social theory. In *Cross-national research in sociology*, edited by Melvin Kohn, pp. 34–56. Newbury Park, CA: Sage.

Nowotny, Helga, and Hilary Rose, eds. (1979). *Counter-movements in the sciences*. Boston: D. Reidel.

Nunnally, Jum C. (1978). *Psychometric theory*. New York: McGraw-Hill.

O'Brien, Robert M. (1992). Levels of analysis. *Encyclopedia of sociology*, Vol. 3, edited by Edgar and Marie Borgatta, pp. 1107–1112. New York: Macmillan.

O'Donnell, John M. (1985). *The origins of behaviorism: American psychology, 1870–1920*. New York: New York University Press.

Oakley, Ann. (1981). Interviewing women: A contradiction in terms. In *Doing feminist research*, edited by Helen Roberts, pp. 30–61, London: Routledge.

Offe, Claus. (1981). The social sciences: Contract research or social movements? *Current Perspectives on Social Theory*, 2:31–37.

Oksenberg, Lois, Lerita Coleman, and Charles F. Cannell. (1986). Interviewers' voices and refusal rates in telephone surveys. *Public Opinion Quarterly*, 50:97–111.

Olsen, Marvin E., and Michael Micklin, eds. (1981). *Handbook of applied sociology*. New York: Praeger.

Olsen, Virginia. (1994). Feminism and models of qualitative research. In *Handbook of qualitative research*, edited by Norman Denzin and Yvonna Lincoln, pp. 158–174. Thousand Oaks, CA: Sage.

Orloff, Ann Shola. (1993). *The politics of pensions: A comparative analysis of Britain, Canada and the United States, 1880–1940*. Madison: University of Wisconsin Press.

Osgood, C. E., G. Suci, and H. Tannenbaum. (1957). *The measurement of meaning*. Urbana: University of Illinois Press.

Ostrander, Susan. (1984). *Women of the upper class*. Philadelphia: Temple University Press.

Ostrander, Susan. (1993). "Surely you're not in this just to be helpful": Access, rapport and interview in three studies of elites. *Journal of Contemporary Ethnography*, 22: 7–27.

Øyen, Else. (1990). The imperfection of comparisons. In *Comparative methodology: Theory and practice in international social research*, edited by Else Øyen, pp. 1–18. Newbury Park, CA: Sage.

Paige, Jeffrey M. (1975). *Agrarian revolution*. New York: Free Press.

Palmer, C. Eddie. (1978). Dog catchers: A descriptive study. *Qualitative Sociology*. 1:19–104.

Parcel, Toby L. (1992). Secondary data analysis and data archives. *Encyclopedia of sociology*, Vol. 4, edited by Edgar and Marie Borgatta, pp. 1720–1728. New York: Macmillan.

Peacock, Walter Gillis, Greg A. Hoover, and Charles D. Killian.

(1988). Divergence and convergence in international development. *American Sociological Review*, 53:838–852.

Pearsall, Marion. (1970). Participant observation as role and method in behavioral research. In *Qualitative methodology*, edited by W. J. Filstead, pp. 340–352. Chicago: Markham.

Pearson, Michael Ross, and Robyn M. Dawes. (1992). Personal recall and the limits of retrospective questions in surveys. In *Questions about questions: Inquiries into the cognitive bases of surveys*, edited by Judith M. Turner, pp. 65–94. New York: Russell Sage Foundation.

Pepinsky, Harold E. (1980). A sociologist on police control. In *Fieldwork experience*, edited by W. B. Shaffir, R. Stebbins, and A. Turowetz, pp. 223–234. New York. St. Martin's.

Peterson, Robert A. (1984). Asking the age question: A research note. *Public Opinion Quarterly*, 48:379–383.

Pfohl, Stephen. (1990). Welcome to the parasite cafe: Postmodernity as a social problem. *Social Problems*, 37:421–442.

Phillips, Bernard. (1985). *Sociological research methods: An introduction*. Homewood, IL: Dorsey.

Phillips, D. C. (1987). *Philosophy, science and social inquiry: Contemporary methodological controversies in social science and related applied fields of research*. New York: Pergamon.

Phillips, Derek. (1971). *Knowledge from what?* Chicago: Rand McNally.

Piliavin, Irving M., J. Rodin, and Jane A. Piliavin. (1969). Good samaritanism: An underground phenomenon? *Journal of Personality and Social Psychology*, 13:289–299.

Plath, David W. (1990). Field notes, filed notes and the conferring of note. In *Field notes: The makings of anthropology*, edited by Roger Sanjek, pp. 371–384. Ithaca, NY: Cornell University Press.

Platt, Jennifer. (1981). Evidence and proof in documentary research. *Sociological Review*, 29:31–66.

Poe, Gail S., et al. (1988). "Don't know" boxes in factual questions in a mail questionnaire: Effects on level and quality of response. *Public Opinion Quarterly*, 52:212–222.

Polsky, Ned. (1967). *Hustlers, beats and others*. Chicago: Aldine.

Pottick, Kathleen, and Paul Lerman. (1991). Maximizing survey response rates for hard-to-reach inner-city populations. *Social Science Quarterly*, 72:172–180.

Prechel, Harland. (1990). Steel and the state: industry politics and business policy formation, 1940–1989.

American Sociological Review, 55:648–668.

Presser, Stanley. (1984). Is inaccuracy on factual survey items item-specific or respondent-specific? *Public Opinion Quarterly*, 48:344–355.

Presser, Stanley. (1990). Measurement issues in the study of social change. *Social Forces*, 68:856–868.

Presser, Stanley, Johnny Blair, and Timothy Triplett. (1992). Survey sponsorship, response rates and response effects. *Social Science Quarterly*, 73: 699–702.

Prewitt, Kenneth. (1983). Management of survey organizations. In *Handbook of social research*, edited by P. Rossi, J. Wright, and A. Anderson, pp. 123–143. Orlando, FL: Academic Press.

Price, Vincent. (1989). Social identification and public opinion: Effects of communicating group conflict. *Public Opinion Quarterly*, 53: 197–224.

Prucha, Francis Paul. (1987). *Handbook for research in American history: A guide to bibliographies and other reference works*. Lincoln: University of Nebraska Press.

Prus, Robert C., and Steve Vassilakopoulos. (1979). Desk clerks and hookers. *Urban Life*, 8:52–71.

Przeworski, Adam, and Henry Teune. (1970). *The logic of comparative inquiry*. New York: Wiley.

Przeworski, Adam, and Henry Teune. (1973). Equivalence in cross-national research. In *Comparative research methods*, edited by D. Warwick and S. Osherson, pp. 119–137. Englewood Cliffs, NJ: Prentice-Hall.

Punch, Maurice. (1986). *The politics and ethics of fieldwork*. Beverly Hills, CA: Sage.

Pusey, Michael. (1987). *Jügen Habermas*. New York: Tavistock.

Pyke, Sandra W., and Neil McK. Agnew. (1991). *The science game*, 5th ed. Englewood Cliffs, NJ: Prentice-Hall.

Quadagno, Jill S. (1984). Welfare capitalism and the Social Security Act of 1935. *American Sociological Review*, 49:632–648.

Quadagno, Jill S. (1988). *The transformation of old age security*. Chicago: University of Chicago Press.

Quarles, Susan D., ed. (1986). *Guide to federal funding for social scientists*. New York: Russell Sage Foundation.

Rabinow, Paul, and William M. Sullivan. (1979). The interpretative turn: Emergence of an approach. In *Interpretative social science: A reader*, edited by Paul Rabinow and William Sullivan, pp. 1–24.

Berkeley: University of California Press.

Ragin, Charles C. (1987). *The comparative method*. Berkeley: University of California Press.

Ragin, Charles. (1989). New directions in comparative research. In *Cross-national research in sociology*, edited by Melvin Kohn, pp. 57–76. Newbury Park, CA: Sage.

Ragin, Charles C. (1992a). Introduction: Cases of "what is a case?" In *What is a case: Exploring the foundations of social inquiry*, edited by Charles Ragin and Howard Becker, pp. 1–18. New York: Cambridge University Press.

Ragin, Charles C. (1992b). Casing and the process of social inquiry. In *What is a case: Exploring the foundations of social inquiry*, edited by Charles Ragin and Howard Becker, pp. 217–226. New York Cambridge University Press.

Ragin, Charles C. (1994). *Constructing social research*. Thousand Oaks, CA: Pine Forge Press.

Ragin, Charles C., and David Zaret. (1983). Theory and method in comparative research. *Social Forces*, 61:731–754.

Rathje, W. L., and W. W. Hughes. (1976). The garbage project as nonreactive approach: Garbage in–garbage out. In *Perspective on attitude assessment: Surveys and their alternatives*, edited by H. W. Sinaiko and L. A. Broeding. Champaign, IL: Pendleton Publications.

Rathje, William, and Cullen Murphy. (1992). *Rubbish: The archaeology of garbage*. New York: Vintage.

Reason, Peter. (1994). Three approaches to participative inquiry. In *Handbook of qualitative research*, edited by Norman K. Denzin and Yvonne S. Lincoln, pp. 324–339. Thousand Oaks, CA: Sage.

Reese, Stephen, W. Danielson, P. Shoemaker, T. Chang, and H. Hsu. (1986). Ethnicity of interview effects among Mexican Americans and Anglos. *Public Opinion Quarterly*, 50:563–572.

Reinharz, Shulamit. (1979). *On becoming a social scientist*. San Francisco: Josey-Bass.

Reinharz, Shulamit. (1992). *Feminist methods in social research*. New York: Oxford University Press.

Reiss, Albert J., Jr. (1992). Training incapacities of sociologists. In *Sociology and its publics: The forms and fates of disciplinary organization*, edited by Terence C. Halliday and Morris Janowitz, pp. 297–315. Chicago: University of Chicago Press.

Reskin, Barbara. (1977). Scientific productivity and the reward structure of

science. *American Sociological Review*, 42:491–504.

Reynolds, Paul Davidson. (1971). *A primer in theory construction*. Indianapolis: Bobbs-Merrill.

Reynolds, Paul Davidson. (1979). *Ethical dilemmas and social science research*. San Francisco: Jossey-Bass.

Reynolds, Paul Davidson. (1982). *Ethics and social science research*. Englewood Cliffs, NJ: Prentice-Hall.

Richards, Thomas J., and Lyn Richards. (1994). Using computers in qualitative research. In *Handbook of qualitative research*, edited by Norman K. Denzin and Yvonne S. Lincoln, pp. 445–462. Thousand Oaks, CA: Sage.

Ricoeur, Paul. (1970). The model of the text: Meaningful action considered as a text. In *Interpretive social science: A reader*, edited by Paul Rabinow and William Sullivan, pp. 73–102. Berkeley: University of California Press.

Ritzer, George. (1975). *Sociology: A multi-paradigm science*. Boston: Allyn and Bacon.

Roadburg, Alan. (1980). Breaking relationships with field subjects: Some problems and suggestions. In *Fieldwork experience*, edited by W. B. Shaffir, R. Stebbins, and A. Turowetz, pp. 281–291. New York: St. Martin's.

Roberts, Carl W. (1989). Other than counting words: A linguistic approach to content analysis. *Social Forces*, 68:147–177.

Robertson, John A. (1982). The social scientist's right to research and the IRB system. In *Ethical issues in social science research*, edited by Tom L. Beauchamp, R. Faden, R. J. Wallace, and L. Walters, pp. 356–372. Baltimore: Johns Hopkins University Press.

Robinson, John P., Jerrold G. Rusk, and Kendra B. Head. (1972). *Measures of political attitudes*. Ann Arbor: Center for Political Studies, Institute for Social Research, University of Michigan.

Robinson, John P., and Philip R. Shaver. (1969). *Measures of social psychological attitudes*. Ann Arbor: Survey Research Center, Institute for Social Research, University of Michigan.

Roderick, Rick. (1986). *Habermas and the foundations of critical theory*. New York: St. Martin's.

Roethlisberger, F. J., and Dickenson, W. J. (1939). *Management and the worker*. Cambridge, MA: Harvard University Press.

Rose, Gerry. (1982). *Deciphering social research*. Beverly Hills, CA: Sage.

Rosen, Lawrence. (1995). The creation of the Uniform Crime Report: The role of social science. *Social Science History*, 19:215–238.

Rosenau, Pauline Marie. (1992). *Postmodernism and the social sciences*. Princeton, NJ: Princeton University Press.

Rosenberg, Morris. (1968). *The logic of survey analysis*. New York: Basic Books.

Rosenthal, Robert. (1984). *Meta-analytic procedures for social research*. Beverly Hills, CA: Sage.

Rosnow, Ralph L. (1981). *Paradigms in transition: The methodology of social inquiry*. New York: Oxford University Press.

Ross, Dorothy. (1991). *The origins of American social science*. New York: Cambridge University Press.

Rossi, Peter H., ed. (1982). *Standards for evaluation practice*. San Francisco: Jossey-Bass.

Rossi, Peter H., and Howard E. Freeman. (1985). *Evaluation: A systematic approach*, 3rd ed. Beverly Hills, CA: Sage.

Rossi, Peter H., James D. Wright, and Andy Anderson. (1983). Sample surveys: History, current practice and future prospects. In *Handbook of social research*, edited by P. Rossi, J. Wright, and A. Anderson, pp. 1–20. Orlando, FL: Academic Press.

Rossi, Peter H., James D. Wright, and Eleanor Weber-Burdin. (1982). *Natural hazards and public choice*. New York: Academic.

Rossi, Robert J., and Kevin J. Gilmartin. (1980). *The handbook of social indicators: Sources, characteristics and analysis*. New York: Garland STPM Press.

Roth, Guenther, and Wolfgang Schluchter. (1979). *Max Weber's vision of history: Ethics and methods*. Berkeley: University of California Press.

Roy, Donald. (1970). The study of southern labor union organizing campaigns. In *Pathways to data*, edited by R. W. Habenstein, pp. 216–244. Chicago: Aldine.

Roy, William G. (1983). The unfolding of the interlocking directorate structure of the United States. *American Sociological Review*, 48:248–257.

Roy, William G. (1984). Class conflict and social change in historical perspective. *Annual Review of Sociology*, 10:483–506.

Rubin, Herbert J. (1983). *Applied social research*. Columbus, OH: Charles E. Merrill.

Rueschemeyer, Dietrich, Evelyne Huber Stephens, and John D. Stephens. (1992). *Capitalist development and democracy*. Chicago: University of Chicago Press.

Rule, James. (1978a). *Insight and social betterment: A preface to applied social science*. New York: Oxford University Press.

Rule, James. (1978b). Models of relevance: The social effects of sociology. *American Journal of Sociology*, 84:78–98.

Runciman, W. G. (1980). Comparative sociology or narrative history. *European Journal of Sociology*, 21:162–178.

Runyon, Richard P., and Audry Haber. (1980). *Fundamentals of behavioral statistics*. Reading, MA: Addison-Wesley.

Ryan, Mary. (1989). The American parade. In *The new cultural history*, edited by L. Hunt, pp. 131–153. Berkeley: University of California Press.

Ryder, Norman B. (1992). Cohort analysis. In *Encyclopedia of sociology*, Vol. 1, edited by Edgar and Marie Borgatta, pp. 227–231. New York: Macmillan.

Sabia, Daniel R., Jr., and Jerald T. Wallulis. (1983). *Changing social science: Changing theory and other critical perspectives*. Albany: State University of New York at Albany.

Sagarin, Edward. (1973). The research setting and the right not to be researched. *Social Problems*, 21: 52–64.

Sanchez, Maria Elena. (1992). Effects of questionnaire design on the quality of survey data. *Public Opinion Quarterly*, 56:206–217.

Sanday, Peggy Reeves. (1983). The ethnographic paradigm(s). In *Qualitative methodology*, edited by John Van Maanen, pp. 19–36. Beverly Hills, CA: Sage.

Sanjek, Roger. (1978). A network method and its uses in urban anthropology. *Human Organization*, 37: 257–268.

Sanjeck, Roger. (1990). On ethnographic validity. In *Field notes: The makings of anthropology*, edited by Roger Sanjek, pp. 385–418. Ithaca, NY: Cornell University Press.

Saxe, Leonard, and Michelle Fine. (1981). *Social experiments: Methods for design and evaluation*. Beverly Hills, CA: Sage.

Sayer, Andrew. (1992). *Method in social science: A realist approach*, 2nd ed. New York: Routledge.

Schaffer, Nora Cate. (1980). Evaluating race-of-interviewer effects in a national survey. *Sociological Methods and Research*, 8:400–419.

Schatzman, Leonard, and Anselm L. Strauss. (1973). *Field research: Strategies for a natural sociology*. Englewood Cliffs, NJ: Prentice-Hall.

Scheibe, Karl E. (1988). Metamorphosis in the psychologist's advantage. In *The rise of experimentation in American psychology*, edited by Jill G. Morawski, pp. 53–71. New Haven, CT: Yale University Press.

Scheuch, Erwin K. (1990). The development of comparative research: Towards causal explanations. In *Comparative methodology*, edited by Else Øyen, pp. 19–37. Newbury Park, CA: Sage.

Schiffman, Josepha. (1991). Fight the power: Two groups mobilize for peace. In *Ethnography unbound: Power and resistance in the modern metropolis*, edited by Michael Burawoy et al., pp. 58–79. Berkeley: University of California Press.

Schmeling, Sharon L., and Mike Miller. (1988). Whistleblower wins suit against UW. *Capital Times* (Madison, Wisconsin), August 11.

Schneider, Mark A. (1987). Culture-as-text in the work of Clifford Geertz. *Theory and Society*, 16:809–883.

Schrager, Laura, and James Short. (1980). How serious a crime? Perceptions of organizational and common crimes. In *White collar crime*, edited by G. Geis and E. Stotland, pp. 14–31. Beverly Hills, CA: Sage.

Schrecker, Ellen. (1986). *No ivory tower: McCarthyism and the university*. New York: Oxford University Press.

Schuessler, Karl. (1982). *Measuring social life feelings*. San Francisco: Jossey-Bass.

Schuman, Howard, and Lawrence Bobo. (1988). Survey-based experiments on white racial attitudes towards racial integration. *American Journal of Sociology*, 94:273–299.

Schuman, Howard, and Jean M. Converse. (1971). Effects of black and white interviewers on black response in 1968. *Public Opinion Quarterly*, 65:44–68.

Schuman, Howard, and Otis Dudley Duncan. (1974). Questions about attitude survey questions. In *Sociological methodology, 1973–1974*, edited by Herbert L. Costner, pp. 232–251. San Francisco: Jossey-Bass.

Schuman, Howard, and Jacob Ludwig. (1983). The norm of even-handedness in surveys as in life. *American Sociological Review*, 48:112–120.

Schuman, Howard, and Stanley Presser. (1977). Question wording as an independent variable in survey analysis. *Sociological Methods and Research*, 6:151–170.

Schuman, Howard, and Stanley Presser. (1979). The open and closed question. *American Sociological Review*, 44:692–712.

Schuman, Howard, and Stanley Presser. (1981). *Questions and answers in attitude surveys: Experiments on question form, wording and content.* New York: Academic Press.

Schuman, Howard, and Cheryl Rieger. (1992). Historical analogies, generational effects and attitudes towards war. *American Sociological Review,* 57:315–326.

Schwandt, Thomas A. (1994). Constructivist, interpretivist approaches to human inquiry. In *Handbook of qualitative research,* edited by Norman Denzin and Yvonna Lincoln, pp. 118–137. Thousand Oaks, CA: Sage.

Schwartz, Dona. (1986). Camera clubs and fine art photography: The social construction of an elite code. *Urban Life,* 15:165–196.

Schwartz, Howard, and Jerry Jacobs. (1979). *Qualitative sociology: A method to the madness.* New York: Free Press.

Schwartz, Morris, and Charolotte Green Schwartz. (1969). Problems in field observation. In *Issues in participant observation,* edited by George J. McCall and J. L. Simmons, pp. 89–105. Reading, MA: Addison-Wesley.

Schwarz, Norbert, and Hans-J. Hippler. (1995). Subsequent questions may influence answers to preceding questions in mail surveys. *Public Opinion Quarterly,* 59:93–97.

Schwarz, Norbert, Bäurbel Knäuper, Hans-J. Hippler, Elizabeth Noelle-Neumann, and Leslie Clark. (1991). Rating scales: Numeric values may change the meaning of scale labels. *Public Opinion Quarterly,* 55: 570–582.

Schwendinger, H., and J. Schwendinger. (1974). *Sociologists of the chair.* New York: Basic Books.

Scott, William A. (1968). Attitude measurement. In *The handbook of social psychology,* Vol. 2: *Research methods,* edited by Gardner Lindzey and Elliott Aronson, pp. 204–273. Reading, MA: Addison-Wesley.

See, Katherine O'Sullivan. (1986). *First world nationalisms.* Chicago: University of Chicago Press.

Seeman, Melvin, and Carolyn S. Anderson. (1983). Alienation and alcohol: The role of work, mastery and community in drinking behavior. *American Sociological Review,* 48:60–77.

Seider, Maynard S. (1974). American big business ideology: A content analysis of executive speeches. *American Sociological Review,* 39:802–815.

Sellin, Thorsten, and Marvin E. Wolfgang. (1964). *The measurement of delinquency.* New York: Wiley.

Selvin, Hanan C., and Everett K. Wilson. (1984). On sharpening sociologists' prose. *Sociological Quarterly,* 25:205–223.

Sepstrup, P. (1981). Methodological developments in content analysis. In *Advances in content analysis,* edited by Karl E. Rosengren, pp. 133–158. Beverly Hills, CA: Sage.

Sewell, William H., Jr. (1980). *Work and revolution in France.* New York: Cambridge University Press.

Sewell, William H., Jr. (1987). Theory of action, dialectic, and history: Comment on Coleman. *American Journal of Sociology,* 93:166–171.

Seybold, Peter. (1987). The Ford Foundation and the transformation of political science. In *The structure of power in America,* edited by Michael Schwartz, pp. 185–198. New York: Holmes and Meier.

Shafer, Robert Jones. (1980). *A guide to historical method,* 3rd ed. Homewood, IL: Dorsey.

Shaffir, William B., Robert A. Stebbins, and Allan Turowetz. (1980). Introduction. In *Fieldwork experience,* edited by W. B. Shaffir, R. Stebbins, and A. Turowetz, pp. 3–22. New York: St. Martins.

Sharon, Batia. (1979). Artist-run galleries: A contemporary institutional change in the visual arts. *Qualitative Sociology,* 2:3–28.

Shattuck, John, and Muriel Morisey Spence. (1988). *Government information controls: Implications for scholarship, science and technology.* Washington. DC: Association of American Universities.

Shavit, Yossi. (1990). Segregation, tracking, and the educational attainment of minorities: Arabs and oriental Jews in Israel. *American Sociological Review,* 55:115–126.

Shaw, C. (1930). *The jack roller.* Chicago: University of Chicago Press.

Sheatsley, Paul B. (1983). Questionnaire construction and item writing. In *Handbook of social research,* edited by P. Rossi, J. Wright, and A. Anderson, pp. 195–230. Orlando, FL: Academic Press.

Shively, JoEllen. (1992). Cowboys and Indians: Perceptions of western films among American Indians and Anglos. *American Sociological Review,* 57:725–734.

Shupe, Anston D., Jr., and David G. Bromley. (1980). Walking a tightrope: Dilemmas of participation observation of groups in conflict. *Qualitative Sociology* 2:3–21.

Sieber, Joan. ed. (1982). *The ethics of social research: Fieldwork, regulation, and publication.* New York: Springer-Verlag.

Sieber, Joan E. (1992). *Planning ethically responsible research: A guide for students and internal review boards.* Thousand Oaks, CA: Sage.

Sieber, Joan E. (1993). The ethics and politics of sensitive research. In *Research on sensitive topics,* edited by Claire Renzetti and Raymond Lee, pp. 14–26. Thousand Oaks, CA: Sage.

Sieber, Sam D. (1973). The integration of fieldwork and survey methods. *American Journal of Sociology,* 78:1335–1359.

Sigelman, Lee. (1982). The uncooperative interviewee. *Quality and Quantity,* 16:345–353.

Silva, Edward T., and Sheila Slaughter. (1980). Prometheus bound: Limits of social science professionalization. *Theory and Society,* 9:781–819.

Silverman, David. (1972). Some neglected questions about social reality. In *New directions in sociological theory,* edited by Paul Filmer et al. Cambridge. MA: MIT Press.

Silverman, David. (1993). *Interpreting qualitative data.* Thousand Oaks, CA: Sage.

Singer, Benjamin D. (1989). The criterial crisis of the academic world. *Sociological Inquiry.* 59:127–143.

Singer, Eleanor. (1978). Informed consent: Consequences for response rate and response quality in social survey. *American Sociological Review.* 43: 144–162.

Singer, Eleanor. (1988). Surveys in the mass media. In *Surveying social life: Papers in honor of Herbert H. Hyman,* edited by Hubert J. O'Gorman, pp. 413–436. Middletown, CT: Wesleyan University Press.

Singer, Eleanor, and Martin R. Frankel. (1982). Informed consent procedures in telephone interviews. *American Sociological Review.* 47:416–426.

Singer, Eleanor, and Luane Kohnke-Aguirre. (1979). Interviewer expectation effects: A replication and extension. *Public Opinion Quarterly,* 43:245–260.

Singer, Eleanor, Dawn R. Von Thurn, and Ester R. Miller. (1995). Confidentiality assurances and response: A quantitative review of the experimental literature. *Public Opinion Quarterly,* 59:66–77.

Singleton, Royce, Jr., B. Straits, Margaret Straits, and Ronald McAllister. (1988). *Approaches to social research.* New York: Oxford University Press.

Sinha, Anita. (1979). Control in craft work: The case of production potters. *Qualitative Sociology.* 2:3–25.

Sitton, Thad, G. Mehaffy, and O. L. Davis, Jr. (1983). *Oral history.* Austin: University of Texas Press.

Siu, Paul C. P. (1987). *The Chinese laundryman: A study of social isolation,* edited by John Kuo Wei Tchen.

New York: New York University Press.

Skidmore, William. (1979). *Theoretical thinking in sociology*, 2nd ed. New York: Cambridge University Press.

Sklar, Kathryn Kish. (1991). Hull House maps and papers: Social science as women's work in the 1890s. In *The social survey in historical perspective, 1880–1940*, edited by M. Blumer, K. Bales, and K. Sklar, pp. 111–147. New York: Cambridge University Press.

Skocpol, Theda. (1979). *States and social revolutions*. New York: Cambridge University Press.

Skocpol, Theda. (1984). Emerging agendas and recurrent strategies in historical sociology. In *Vision and method in historical sociology*, edited by T. Skocpol, pp. 356–392. Cambridge: Cambridge University Press.

Skocpol, Theda. (1988). The "uppity generation" and the revitalization of macroscopic sociology: Reflections at mid-career of a woman from the sixties. *Theory and Society*, 17:627–644.

Skocpol, Theda, and Margaret Somers. (1980). The uses of comparative history in macrosocial inquiry. *Comparative Studies in Society and History*, 22:174–197.

Slater, Phil. (1977). *Origin and significance of the Frankfurt School*. Boston: Routledge and Kegan Paul.

Smart, Barry. (1976). *Sociology, phenomenology, and Marxian analysis: A critical discussion of the theory and practice of a science of society*. Boston: Routledge and Kegan Paul.

Smelser, Neil J. (1959). *Social change in the industrial revolution*. Chicago: University of Chicago Press.

Smelser, Neil J. (1976). *Comparative methods in the social sciences*. Englewood Cliffs, NJ: Prentice-Hall.

Smith, Christopher. (1995). Asian New York: The geography and politics of diversity. *International Migration Review*, 29:59–84.

Smith, Dennis. (1991). *The rise of historical sociology*. Philadelphia: Temple University Press.

Smith, Louis M. (1994). Biographical method. In *Handbook of qualitative research*, edited by Norman Denzin and Yvonna Lincoln, pp. 286–305. Thousand Oaks, CA: Sage.

Smith, Mary Lee, and Gene V. Glass. (1987). *Research and evaluation in education and the social sciences*. Englewood Cliffs, NJ: Prentice-Hall.

Smith, Robert B. (1987). Linking quality and quantity. Part I: Understanding and explanation. *Quantity and Quality*, 21:291–311.

Smith, Robert B. (1988). Linking quality and quantity, Part II: Surveys as formalizations. *Quantity and Quality*, 22:3–30.

Smith, Tom W. (1984). The subjectivity of ethnicity. In *Surveying subjective phenoemona*, Vol. 2, edited by Charles Turner and Elizabeth Martin, pp. 117–128. New York: Russell Sage Foundation.

Smith, Tom W. (1987). That which we call welfare by any other name would smell sweeter: An analysis of the impact of question wording on response patterns. *Public Opinion Quarterly*, 51:75–83.

Snow, David A., Susan G. Baker, Leon Anderson, and Michael Martin. (1986b). The myth of pervasive mental illness among the homeless. *Social Problems*, 33:407–423.

Snow, David A., E. Burke Bochford, Jr., Steven K. Worden, and Robert D. Benford. (1986a). Frame alignment process, micromobilization and movement participation. *American Sociological Review*, 51:464–481.

Sobal, Jeffery. (1984). The content of survey introductions and the provision of informed consent. *Public Opinion Quarterly*, 48:788–793.

Sociology Writing Group, UCLA. (1991). *A guide to writing sociology papers*, 2nd ed. New York: St. Martin's.

Sohn-Rethel, Alfred. (1978). *Intellectual and manual labor: A critique of epistemology*. New York: Macmillan.

Sonquist, J. A., and C. Dunkelberg. (1977). *Survey and opinion research: Procedures for processing and analysis*. Englewood Cliffs. NJ: Prentice-Hall.

South, Scott, and Kim Lloyd. (1995). Spousal alternatives and marital dissolution. *American Sociological Review*, 60:126–140.

Spector, Paul E. (1981). *Research designs*. Beverly Hills, CA: Sage.

Spector, Paul E. (1992). *Summated rating scale construction*. Newbury Park, CA: Sage.

Spencer, Gary. (1982). Methodological issues in the study of bureaucratic elites: A case study of West Point. In *Field research*, edited by R. G. Burgess, pp. 23–30. Boston: Allen and Unwin.

Spillers, Cindy S. (1982). An investigation of children's attitudes towards physically disabled peers. *Mid-American Review of Sociology*, 7:55–69.

Spradley, James P. (1970). *You owe yourself a drunk*. Boston: Little, Brown.

Spradley, James P. (1979a). *The ethnographic interview*. New York: Holt, Rinehart and Winston.

Spradley, James P. (1979b). *Participant observation*. New York: Holt, Rinehart and Winston.

Spradley, James P., and B. J. Mann. (1975). *The cocktail waitress*. New York: Wiley.

Sprague, Joey, and Mary K. Zimmerman. (1989). Quality and quantity: Reconstructing feminist methodology. *American Sociologist*, 20:71–86.

Stack, Carol. (1989). Doing research in the flats. In *In the field*, edited by Carolyn Smith and William Kornblum, pp. 21–26. New York: Praeger.

Stack, Steven. (1987). Celebrities and suicide: A taxonomy and analysis. 1948–1983. *American Sociological Review*, 52:401–412.

Stack, Steven. (1990). The effect of divorce on suicide in Denmark. 1951–1980. *Sociological Quarterly*, 31:359–370.

Staggenborg, Susan. (1988). "Hired hand research" revised. *American Sociologist*, 19:260–269.

Stake, Robert E. (1994). Case studies. In *Handbook of qualitative research*, edited by Norman Denzin and Yvonna Lincoln, pp. 236–247. Thousand Oaks, CA: Sage.

Staples, William G. (1987). Technology, control, and the social organization of work at a British hardware firm, 1791–1891. *American Journal of Sociology*, 93:62–88.

Starr, Paul. (1982). *The social transformation of American medicine*. New York: Basic Books.

Starr, Paul. (1987). The sociology of official statistics. In *The politics of numbers*, edited by William Alonso and Paul Starr, pp. 7–58. New York: Russell Sage Foundation.

Starr, Paul, and Ross Corson. (1987). Who will have the numbers? The rise of the statistical services industry and the politics of public data. In *The politics of numbers*, edited by William Alonso and Paul Starr, pp. 415–447. New York: Russell Sage Foundation.

Stech, Charlotte G. (1981). Trends in nonresponse rates, 1952–1979. *Public Opinion Quarterly*, 45:40–57.

Stempel, G., III. (1971). Visibility of blacks in news and news-picture magazines. *Journalism Quarterly*, 48:337–339.

Stephens, John. (1989). Democratic transition and breakdown in western Europe. 1870–1939: A test of the Moore thesis. *American Journal of Sociology*, 94:1019–1077.

Stephens, Mary Ann Parris, N. S. Cooper, and J. M. Kinney. (1985). The effects of effort on helping the physically disabled. *Journal of Social Psychology*, 125:495–503.

Stephenson, Richard M. (1978). The CIA and the professor: A personal account. *American Sociologist*, 13: 128–133.

Stern, Paul C. (1979). *Evaluating social science research*. New York: Oxford University Press.

Stewart, David W. (1984). *Secondary research: Information sources and methods*. Beverly Hills, CA: Sage.

Stewart, Donald E. (1983). *The television family*. Melborne: Institute of Family Studies.

Stimson, Gerry B. (1986). Place and space in sociological fieldwork. *The Sociological Review*. 34:641–656.

Stinchcombe, Arthur L. (1968). *Constructing social theories*. New York: Harcourt, Brace and World.

Stinchcombe, Arthur L. (1973a). Theoretical domains and measurement, Part 1. *Acta Sociologica*, 16:3–12.

Stinchcombe, Arthur L. (1978). *Theoretical methods in social history*. New York: Academic Press.

Stoeker, Randy. (1993). The federated frontstage structure and localized social movements: A case study of the Ceder-Riverside neighborhood movement. *Social Science Quarterly*, 74:169–184.

Stoianovich, Traian. (1976). *French historical method*. Ithaca, NY: Cornell University Press.

Stone, John. (1985). *Racial conflict in contemporary society*. Cambridge, MA: Harvard University Press.

Stone, Lawrence. (1987). *The past and present revisited*. Boston: Routledge and Kegan Paul.

Stone, Philip, et al. (1966). *The general inquirer: A computer approach to content analysis in the behavioral sciences*. Cambridge, MA: MIT Press.

Stone, Philip J., and Robert P. Weber. (1992). Content analysis. In *Encyclopedia of sociology*, Vol. 1, edited by Edgar and Marie Borgatta, pp. 290–295. New York: Macmillan.

Stoner, Norman W. (1966). *The social system of science*. New York: Holt, Rinehart and Winston.

Strauss, Anselm. (1987). *Qualitative analysis for social scientists*. New York: Cambridge University Press.

Strauss, Anselm, and Juliet Corbin. (1990). *Basics of qualitative research: Grounded theory procedures and techniques*. Newbury Park, CA: Sage.

Strauss, Anselm, and Juliet Corbin. (1994). Grounding theory methodology: An overview. In *Handbook of qualitative research*, edited by Norman Denzin and Yvonna Lincoln, pp. 273–285. Thousand Oaks, CA: Sage.

Suchman, Luch, and Brigitte Jordan. (1992). Validity and the collaborative construction of meaning in face-to-face surveys. In *Questions about questions: Inquiries into the cognitive bases of surveys*, edited by

Judith M. Turner, pp. 241–267. New York: Russell Sage Foundation.

Sudholm, Charles A. (1973). The pornographic arcade: Ethnographic notes on moral men in immoral places. *Urban Life*, 2:85–104.

Sudman, Seymour. (1976a). *Applied sampling*. New York: Academic Press.

Sudman, Seymour. (1976b). Sample surveys. *Annual Review of Sociology*, 2:107–120.

Sudman, Seymour. (1983). Applied sampling. In *Handbook of survey research*, edited by Peter H. Rossi, James D. Wright, and Andy B. Anderson. pp. 145–194. Orlando, FL: Academic Press.

Sudman, Seymour, and Norman M. Bradburn. (1983). *Asking questions: A practical guide to questionnaire design*. San Francisco: Jossey-Bass.

Sudman, Seymour, and Norman M. Bradburn. (1987). The organizational growth of public opinion research in the United States. *Public Opinion Quarterly*, 51:S67–S78.

Sudnow, David. (1978). *Ways of the hand: The organization of improvised conduct*. Cambridge, MA: Harvard University Press.

Sullivan, John L., and Stanley Feldman. (1979). *Multiple indicators: An introduction*. Beverly Hills, CA: Sage.

Suls, Jerry M., and Ralph L. Rosnow. (1988). Concerns about artifacts in psychological experiments. In *The rise of experimentation in American psychology*, edited by Jill G. Morawski, pp. 153–187. New Haven, CT: Yale University Press.

Sumner, Colin. (1979). *Reading ideologies*. New York: Academic.

Suppe, Frederick, ed. (1977). *The structure of scientific theories*, 2nd ed. Urbana: University of Illinois Press.

Survey Research Center, Institute for Social Research. (1976). *Interviewer's manual*, rev. ed. University of Michigan.

Sutton, John R. (1991). The political economy of madness: The expansion of the asylum in progressive America. *American Sociological Review*. 56: 665–678.

Swafford, Michael. (1987). Soviet, U.S. sociologists work together. *American Sociological Association Footnotes*. 15(November):9.

Swanson, Guy E. (1971). Frameworks for comparative research. In *Comparative methods in sociology*, edited by I. Vallier, pp. 141–203. Berkeley: University of California Press.

Swidler, Ann. (1986). Culture in action: Symbols and strategies. *American Sociological Review*, 51: 273–286.

Tagg, Stephen K. (1985). Life story in-

terviews and their interpretation. In *The research interview: Uses and approaches*, edited by Michael Brenner, Jennifer Brown, and David Canter, pp. 163–199. New York: Academic Press.

Tanur, Judith H., ed. (1992). *Questions about questions: Inquiries into the cognitive bases of surveys*. New York: Russell Sage Foundation.

Tanur, Judith M. (1983). Methods for large scale surveys and experiments. In *Sociological Methodology, 1983–1984*, edited by Samuel Leinhardt, pp. 1–71. San Francisco: Jossey-Bass.

Taylor, Charles. (1979). Interpretation and the sciences of man. In *Interpretative social science: A reader*, edited by Paul Rabinow and William Sullivan. pp. 25–72. Berkeley: University of California Press.

Taylor, Charles Lewis, ed. (1980). *Indicator systems for political, economic and social analysis*. Cambridge, MA: Oelgeschlager, Gunn and Hain.

Taylor, Charles L., and David Jodice. (1983). *World handbook of political and social indicators*, 3rd ed. New Haven, CT: Yale University Press.

Taylor, Marylee C. (1995). White backlash to workplace affirmative action: Peril or myth? *Social Forces*, 73: 1385–1414.

Taylor, Steven. (1987). Observing abuse: Professional ethics and personal morality in field research. *Qualitative Sociology*, 10:288–302.

Terkel, Studs. (1970). *Hard times*. New York: Pantheon.

Thomas, Robert J. (1993). Interviewing important people in big companies. *Journal of Contemporary Ethnography*, 22:80–96.

Thompson, E. P. (1963). *The making of the English working class*. New York: Vintage.

Thompson, E. P. (1967). Time, work-discipline, and industrial capitalism. *Past and Present*, 38:56–97.

Thompson, E. P. (1978). *The poverty of theory and other essays*. New York: Monthly Review Press.

Thompson, Paul. (1978). *The voice of the past: Oral history*. New York: Oxford University Press.

Thorne, Barrie, and Zella Luria. (1986). Sexuality and gender in children's daily world. *Social Problems*, 33: 176–190.

Thrasher, F. M. (1927). *The gang*. Chicago: University of Chicago Press.

Thurstone, L. L. (1970). Attitudes can be measured. In *Attitude measurement*, edited by Gene Summers, pp. 127–141. Chicago: Rand McNally.

Tickamyer, Ann R. (1981). Wealth and

power: A comparison of men and women in the property elite. *Social Forces*. 60:463–481.

Tilly, Charles. (1964). *The vendee*. Cambridge, MA: Harvard University Press.

Tilly, Charles. (1981). *As sociology meets history*. New York: Academic Press.

Tilly, Charles, Louise Tilly, and Richard Tilly. (1975). *The rebellious century, 1830–1930*. Cambridge, MA: Harvard University Press.

Tolnay, Stewart E., and E. M. Beck. (1992). Racial violence and black migration in the American South, 1910–1930. *American Sociological Review*, 57:103–117.

Topolski, Jerzy. (1976). *Methodology of history*, trans. Olgierd Wojtasiewicz. Boston: D. Reidel.

Toulmin, Stephen. (1953). *The philosophy of science: An introduction*. New York: Harper & Row.

Traugott, Michael W. (1987). The importance of persistence in respondent selection for preelection surveys. *Public Opinion Quarterly*, 51:48–57.

Treiman, Michael. (1977). Towards methods for a quantitative comparative sociology: A reply to Burawoy. *American Journal of Sociology*, 82:1042–1056.

Trice, H. M. (1970). The "outsider's" role in field study. In *Qualitative methodology*, edited by W. J. Filstead. pp. 77–82. Chicago: Markham.

Tropp, Richard A. (1982). A regulatory perspective on social science research. In *Ethical issues in social science research*, edited by Tom L. Beauchamp, R. Faden, R. J. Wallace, and L. Walters, pp. 391–415. Baltimore: Johns Hopkins University Press.

Tuchman, Gaye. (1994). Historical social science: Methodologies, methods and meanings. In *Handbook of qualitative research*, edited by Norman Denzin and Yvonna Lincoln, pp. 306–323. Thousand Oaks, CA: Sage.

Tucker, Clyde. (1983). Interviewer effects in telephone interviewing. *Public Opinion Quarterly*, 47:84–95.

Tufte, Edward. (1983). *The visual display of quantitative information*. Cheshire, CT: Graphics Press.

Tufte, Edward. (1991). *Envisioning information*, rev. ed. Cheshire, CT: Graphics Press.

Tuma, Nancy B., and Andrew Grimes. (1981). A comparison of models of role orientations of professionals in a research oriented university. *Administrative Science Quarterly*, 21:187–206.

Turner, Charles. (1984). Why do surveys disagree? Some preliminary hypotheses and some disagreeable examples. In *Surveying subjective phenomena*, Vol. 2, edited by Charles Turner and Elizabeth Martin, pp. 157–214. New York: Russell Sage Foundation.

Turner, Charles, and Elizabeth Martin, eds. (1984). *Surveying subjective phenomena*, Vol. 1. New York: Russell Sage Foundation.

Turner, Jonathan H. (1985). In defense of positivism. *Sociological Theory*, 3:24–30.

Turner, Jonathan H. (1992). Positivism. In *Encylopedia of sociology*, Vol. 3, edited by Edgar and Marie Borgatta, pp. 1509–1512. New York: Macmillan.

Turner, Roy. (1974). *Ethnomethodology*. Middlesex: Penguin.

Turner, Stephen P. (1980). *Sociological explanation as translation*. New York: Cambridge University Press.

Turner, Stephen P. (1991). The world of academic quantifiers: The Columbia University family and its connections. In *The social survey in historical perspective, 1880–1940*, edited by M. Blumer, K. Bales, and K. Sklar, pp. 269–290. New York: Cambridge University Press.

Turner, Stephen Park, and Jonathan H. Turner. (1990). *The impossible science: An institutional analysis of American sociology*. Newbury Park, CA: Sage.

Umberson, Debra, and Meichu D. Chen. (1994). Effects of a parent's death on adult children: Relationship salience and reaction to loss. *American Sociological Review*, 59:152–168.

Useem, Michael. (1976a). Government influence on the social science paradigm. *Sociological Quarterly*, 17:146–161.

Useem, Michael. (1976b). State production of social knowledge: Patterns of government financing of academic social research. *American Sociological Review*, 41:613–629.

Useem, Michael. (1984). *The inner circle: Large corporations and the rise of business political activity in the U.S. and the U.K.* New York: Oxford University Press.

Valentine-French, Suzanne, and H. Lorraine Radtke. (1989). Attributions of responsibility for an incident of sexual harassment in a university setting. *Sex Roles*, 21: 545–555.

Vallier, Ivan, ed. (1971a). *Comparative methods in sociology: Essays on trends and applications*. Berkeley: University of California Press.

Vallier, Ivan. (1971b). Empirical comparisons of social structure. In *Comparative methods in sociology*, edited by I. Vallier, pp. 203–263.

Berkeley: University of California Press.

Van den Berg, Harry, and Cees Van der Veer. (1985). Measuring ideological frames of references. *Quality and Quantity*, 19:105–118.

Van den Berge, Pierre L. (1967). Research in South Africa: The story of my experiences with tyranny. In *Ethics, politics and social research*, edited by Gideon Sjøberg. New York: Schenckman.

Van Maanen, John. (1973). Observations on the making of policemen. *Human Organization*, 32:407–418.

Van Maanen, John. (1982). Fieldwork on the beat. In *Varieties of qualitative research*, edited by John Van Maanen, James M. Dabbs, Jr., and Robert R. Faulkner, pp. 103–151. Beverly Hills, CA: Sage.

Van Maanen, John. (1983a). Epilogue: Qualitative methods reclaimed. In *Qualitative methodology*, edited by John Van Maanen, pp. 247–268. Beverly Hills, CA: Sage.

Van Maanen, John. (1983b). The moral fix: On the ethics of fieldwork. In *Contemporary field research*, edited by R. M. Emerson, pp. 269–287. Boston: Little, Brown.

Van Maanen, John. (1988). *Tales of the field: On writing ethnography*. Chicago: University of Chicago Press.

Vaughan, Diane. (1992). Theory elaboration: The heuristics of case analysis. In *What is a case? Exploring the foundations of social inquiry*, edited by Charles Ragin and Howard S. Becker, pp. 173–202. Cambridge: Cambridge University Press.

Vaughan, Ted R. (1967). Government intervention in social research: Political and ethical dimensions of the Wichita jury recordings. In *Ethics, politics and social research*, edited by Gideon Sjøberg. New York: Schenckman.

Veltmeyer, Henry. (1978). Marx's two methods of sociological analysis. *Sociological Inquiry*, 48:101–112.

Verba, Sidney. (1971). Cross-national survey research. In *Comparative methods in sociology*, edited by I. Vallier, pp. 309–356. Berkeley: University of California Press.

Verba, Sidney, and Gary R. Orren. (1985). *Equality in America: The view from the top*. Cambridge, MA: Harvard University Press.

Vidich, Arthur Joseph, and Joseph Bensman. (1968). *Small town in mass society*, rev. ed. Princeton, NJ: Princeton University Press.

Wade, Nicholas. (1976). IQ and heredity: Suspicion of fraud beclouds classic experiment. *Science*, 194: 916–919.

Waegel, William B. (1984). How police justify the use of deadly force. *Social Problems*, 32:133–143.

Waksberg, J. (1978). Sampling methods for random digit dialing. *Journal of the American Statistical Association*, 73:40–46.

Wallace, Walter. (1971). *The logic of science in sociology*. Chicago: Aldine.

Wallerstein, Immanuel. (1974). *The modern world system*. New York: Academic Press.

Walsh, David. (1972). Varieties of positivism. In *New directions in sociological theory*, edited by Paul Filmer et al. Cambridge, MA: MIT Press.

Walster, Elaine. (1965). The effect of self-esteem on romantic liking. *Journal of Experimental Social Psychology* 1:194–197.

Walters, Ronald G. (1980). Signs of the times. *Social Research* 47:537–556.

Walton, John. (1973). Standardized case comparison. In *Comparative social research*, edited by M. Armer and A. Grimshaw, pp. 173–191. New York: Wiley.

Walton, John. (1992a). *Western times and water wars: State, culture and rebellion in California*. Berkeley: University of California Press.

Walton, John. (1992b). Making the theoretical case. In *What is a case? Exploring the foundations of social inquiry*, edited by Charles Ragin and Howard S. Becker, pp. 121–138. Cambridge: Cambridge University Press.

Ward, Benjamin. (1972). *What's wrong with economics*. New York: Basic Books.

Ward, Kathryn B., and Linda Grant. (1985). The feminist critique and a decade of published research in sociology journals. *Sociological Quarterly*, 26:139–158.

Wardell, Mark L. (1979). Marx and his method: A commentary. *Sociological Quarterly*, 20:425–436.

Warner, R. Stephen. (1971). The methodology of Marx's comparative analysis of modes of production. In *Comparative methods in sociology*, edited by Ivan Vallier, pp. 49–74. Berkeley: University of California Press.

Warren, Carol A. B., and Paul K. Rasmussen. (1977). Sex and gender in field research. *Urban Life*, 6:349–369.

Warwick, Donald P. (1982). Types of harm in social science research. In *Ethical issues in social science research*, edited by Tom L. Beauchamp, R. Faden, R. J. Wallace, and L. Walters, pp. 101–123. Baltimore: Johns Hopkins University Press.

Warwick, Donald P., and Charles A. Lininger. (1975). *The sample survey: Theory and practice*. New York: McGraw-Hill.

Warwick, Donald P., and Samuel Osherson. (1973). Comparative analysis in the social sciences. In *Comparative research methods*, edited by D. Warwick and S. Osherson, pp. 3–11. Englewood Cliffs, NJ: Prentice-Hall.

Wax, Rosalie H. (1971). *Doing fieldwork: Warnings and advice*. Chicago: University of Chicago Press.

Wax, Rosalie H. (1979). Gender and age in fieldwork and fieldwork education: No good thing is done by any man alone. *Social Problems*, 26:509–522.

Webb, Eugene J., Donald T. Campbell, Richard D. Schwartz, Lee Sechrest, and Janet Belew Grove. (1981). *Nonreactive measures in the social sciences*, 2nd ed. Boston: Houghton Mifflin.

Weber, Max. (1949). *The methodology of the social sciences*, trans, and edited by Edward A. Shils and Henry A. Finch. New York: Free Press.

Weber, Max. (1974). Subjectivity and determinism. In *Positivism and sociology*, edited by Anthony Giddens, pp. 23–32. London: Heinemann.

Weber, Max. (1978). *Economy and society*, Vol. 1, edited by Guenther Roth and Claus Wittich, Berkeley: University of California Press.

Weber, Max. (1981). Some categories of interpretative sociology. *Sociological Quarterly*, 22:151–180.

Weber, Robert P. (1983). Measurement models for content analysis. *Quality and Quantity*, 17:127–149.

Weber, Robert P. (1984). Computer assisted content analysis: A short primer. *Qualitative Sociology*, 7:126–149.

Weber, Robert P. (1985). *Basic content analysis*. Beverly Hills, CA: Sage.

Weeks, M. F., and R. P. Moore. (1981). Ethnicity of interviewer effects on ethnic respondents. *Public Opinion Quarterly*, 45:245–249.

Weil, Frederick D. (1985). The variable effects of education on liberal attitudes. *American Sociological Review*, 50:458–474.

Weinstein, Deena. (1979). Fraud in science. *Social Science Quarterly*, 59:639–652.

Weiss, Carol H. (1972). *Evaluation research: Methods of assessing program effectiveness*. Englewood Cliffs, NJ: Prentice-Hall.

Weiss, Janet A., and Judith E. Gruber. (1987). The managed irrelevance of educational statistics. In *The politics of numbers*, edited by William Alonso and Paul Starr, pp. 363–391. New York: Russell Sage Foundation.

Weiss, Robert S. (1994). *Learning from strangers: The arts and method of qualitative interview studies*. New York: Free Press.

Weitz, Rose, and Deborah A. Sullivan. (1986). The politics of childbirth: The re-emergence of midwifery in Arizona. *Social Problems*, 33:163–175.

Weitzman, Eben, and Matthew Miles. (1995). *Computer programs for qualitative data analysis*. Thousand Oaks, CA: Sage.

Weitzman, Lenore, D. Eifler, E. Hokada, and C. Ross. (1972). Sex role socialization in picture books for preschool children. *American Journal of Sociology*, 77:1125–1150.

Wenger, G. Clare, ed. (1987). *The research relationship: Practice and politics in social policy research*. Boston: Allen and Unwin.

Wentworth, Ellen J. (1993). *Survey responses: An evaluation of their validity*. New York: Academic Press.

Werner, Oswald, and G. Mark Schoepfle. (1987a). *Systematic fieldwork, Vol. 1: Foundations of ethnography and interviewing*. Beverly Hills: Sage.

Werner, Oswald, and G. Mark Schoepfle. (1987b). *Systematic fieldwork, Vol. 2: Ethnographic analysis and data management*. Beverly Hills: Sage.

West, W. Gordon. (1980). Access to adolescent deviants and deviance. In *Fieldwork experience*, edited by W. B. Shaffir, R. A. Stebbins, and A. Turowetz, pp. 31–44. New York: St. Martin's.

Whalley, Peter. (1984). Deskilling engineers? The labor process, labor markets, and labor segmentation. *Social Problems*, 32:117–132.

Wharton, Carol S. (1987). Establishing shelters for battered women. *Qualitative Sociology*, 10:146–163.

Whiting, John W. M. (1968). Methods and problems in cross-cultural research. In *The handbook of social psychology*, 2nd ed., edited by G. Lindzey and E. Aronson, pp. 693–728. Reading, MA: Addison-Wesley.

Whyte, William Foote. (1955). *Street corner society: The social structure of an Italian slum*, 2nd ed. Chicago: University of Chicago Press.

Whyte, William Foote. (1982). Interviewing in field research. In *Field research*, edited by R. G. Burgess, pp. 111–122. Boston: George Allen and Unwin.

Whyte, William Foote. (1984).

Learning from the field: A guide from experience. Beverly Hills: Sage.

Whyte, William Foote. (1986). On the uses of social science research. *American Sociological Review,* 51: 555–563.

Whyte, William F. (1989). Advancing scientific knowledge through participatory action research. *Sociological Forum,* 4:367–385.

Wieder, D. Lawrence. (1977). Ethnomethodology and ethnosociology. *Mid-American Review of Sociology,* 2:1–18.

Wigginton, Eliot, ed. (1972). *Foxfire book.* New York: Doubleday.

Wilcox, Clyde, Lee Sigelman, and Elizabeth Cook. (1989). Some like it hot: Individual differences in responses to group feeling thermometers. *Public Opinion Quarterly,* 53:246–257.

Williams, Bill. (1978). *A sampler on sampling.* New York: Wiley.

Williams, Carol I., and Gary K. Wolfe. (1979). *Elements of research: A guide for writers.* Palo Alto, CA: Mayfield.

Williamson, John B., David Karp, John Dalphin, and Paul Gray. (1982). *The research craft: An introduction to social research methods.* Boston: Little, Brown.

Willimack, Diane K., Howard Schuman, Beth-Ellen Pennell, and James M. Lepkowski. (1995). Effects of prepaid non-monetary incentives on response rates and response quality in face-to-face survey. *Public Opinion Quarterly,* 59:78–92.

Willis, Paul. (1977). *Learning to labor: How working class kids get working class jobs.* New York: Columbia University Press.

Wilson, John. (1982). Realist philosophy as a foundation for Marx's social theory. *Current Perspectives in Social Theory,* 3:243–263.

Wilson, Julius W. (1978). *The declining significance of race.* Chicago: University of Chicago Press.

Wilson, Thomas P. (1970). Normative and interpretative paradigms in sociology. In *Understanding everyday life: Toward the reconstruction of sociological knowledge,* edited by Jack D. Douglas, pp. 57–79. New York: Aldine.

Wimberly, Dale W. (1990). Investment dependence and alternative explanations of third world mortality: A cross-national study. *American Sociological Review,* 55:75–91.

Winkler, Karen J. (1989). Dispute over validity of historical approaches pits traditionalists against advocates of new methods. *Chronicle of Higher Education,* January 11, pp. A4ff.

Winston, Chester. (1974). *Theory and measurement in sociology.* New York: Wiley.

Wolcott, Harry F. (1994). *Transforming qualitative data: Description, analysis and interpretation.* Thousand Oaks, CA: Sage.

Wolf, Eric R. (1982). *Europe and the people without history.* Berkeley: University of California Press.

Woodrum, Eric. (1984). "Mainstreaming" content analysis in social science: Methodological advantages, obstacles, and solutions. *Social Science Research,* 13:1–19.

Wright, Erik O. (1978). *Class, crisis and state.* London: New Left Books.

Wright, Erik O., and Donmoon Cho. (1992). The relative permeability of class boundaries to cross-class friendships: A comparative study of the United States, Canada, Sweden and Norway. *American Sociological Review,* 57:85–102.

Wright, James D., and Peter H. Rossi, eds. (1981). *Social science and natural hazards.* Cambridge. MA: Abt Books.

Wuthnow, Robert. (1979). The emergence of modern science and world system theory. *Theory and Society,* 8:215–243.

Wuthnow, Robert. (1987). *Meaning and moral order: Explorations in cultural analysis.* Berkeley: University of California Press.

Yammarino, Francis, Steven Skiner, and Terry Childers. (1991). Understanding mail survey response behavior: A meta-analysis. *Public Opinion Quarterly,* 55:613–640.

Yancey, William L., and Lee Rainwater. (1970). Problems in the ethnography of the urban underclasses. In *Pathways to data,* edited by R. W. Habenstein. pp. 245–269. Chicago: Aldine.

Yeo, Eileen James. (1991). The social survey in social perspective, 1830–1930. In *The social survey in historical perspective, 1880–1940,* edited by M. Blumer, K. Bales and K. Sklar, pp. 49–65. New York: Cambridge University Press.

Yin, Robert K. (1988). *Case study research,* rev. ed. Newbury Park, CA: Sage.

Young, T. R. (1980). Comment on the McQuaire-Wardell debate. *Sociological Quarterly,* 21:459–462.

Yow, Valerie Raleigh. (1994). *Recording oral history: A practical guide for social scientists.* Thousand Oaks, CA: Sage.

Yu, J., and H. Cooper. (1983). A quantitative review of research design effects on response rates to questionnaires. *Journal of Marketing Research,* 20:36–44.

Zaller, John, and Stanley Feldman. (1992). A simple theory of survey responses: Answering questions versus revealing preferences. *American Journal of Political Science,* 36: 579–616.

Zane, Anne, and Euthemia Matsoukas. (1979). Different settings, different results? A comparison of school and home responses. *Public Opinion Quarterly,* 43:550–557.

Zaret, David. (1978). Sociological theory and historical scholarship. *The American Sociologist,* 13:114–121.

Zeisel, Hans. (1985). *Say it with figures,* 6th ed. New York: Harper & Row.

Zelizer, Viviana A. (1985). *Pricing the priceless child.* New York: Basic Books.

Zeller, Richard, and Edward G. Carmines. (1980). *Measurement in the social sciences: The link between theory and data.* New York: Cambridge University Press.

Ziman, John. (1968). *Public knowledge: An essay concerning the social dimension of science.* New York: Cambridge University Press.

Ziman, John. (1976). *The force of knowledge: The scientific dimension of society.* New York: Cambridge University Press.

Zimbardo, Philip G. (1972). Pathology of imprisonment. *Society,* 9:4–6.

Zimbardo, Philip G. (1973). On the ethics of intervention in human psychological research. *Cognition,* 2:243–256.

Zimbardo, Philip G., et al. (1973). The mind is a formidable jailer: A pirandellian prison. *New York Times Magazine,* 122(April 8):38–60.

Zimbardo, Philip G., et al. (1974). The psychology of imprisonment: Privation, power and pathology. In *Doing unto others,* edited by Zick Rubin. Englewood Cliffs, NJ: Prentice-Hall.

Zuckerman, Harriet. (1972). Interviewing an ultra-elite. *Public Opinion Quarterly,* 36:159–175.

Zuckerman, Harriet. (1978). Theory choice and problem choice in science. In *Sociology of science,* edited by Jerry Gaston, pp. 65–95. San Francisco: Jossey-Bass.

Zuiches, James J. (1984). The organization and funding of social science in the NSF. *Sociological Inquiry,* 54: 188–210.

Zurcher, Louis A. (1979). The airline passenger: Protection of self in an encapsulated group. *Qualitative Sociology,* 1:77–99.

Name Index

SUBJECT INDEX

Is critical theory or critical social
science similar in assumptions to
participatory action research?

independent variable 107
dependent
intervening

nominal, ordinal, interval   147